Latin-American Studies in the Non-Western World and Eastern Europe

A bibliography on Latin America in the languages of Africa, Asia, the Middle East, and Eastern Europe, with transliterations and translations in English

by *oward*

Martin H. Sable
Associate Professor
University of Wisconsin-Milwaukee

The Scarecrow Press, Inc.
Metuchen, N.J.   1970

To the memory of

Norman Nathan, B. S. Pharm.

1934-1966

Beloved son of Mr. & Mrs. Max Nathan

TABLE OF CONTENTS

THE MIDDLE EAST

PART II

EASTERN EUROPE

Part I covers Africa, Asia and the Middle East,
and contains entry numbers 1 to 933.

Part II, containing entry numbers 934 to 2926, covers
the following nations of Eastern Europe: Bulgaria,
Czechoslavakia, Finland, Greece, Hungary, Poland,
Rumania and Yugoslavia.   Iceland is included in a
separate, final section.

PREFACE

The title of this book is LATIN AMERICAN STUDIES IN
THE NON-WESTERN WORLD AND EASTERN EUROPE:
A BIBLIOGRAPHY ON LATIN AMERICA IN THE LANGUAGES
OF ASIA, AFRICA, THE MIDDLE EAST AND EASTERN
EUROPE, WITH TITLES TRANSLITERATED AND TRANS-
LATED INTO ENGLISH. In order to avoid confusion and to
specify insofar as is possible the contents of the bibliography,
the title was thus purposely worded.

The potential user and purchaser will therefore understand
that this is not a bibliography of writings about the field of
Latin American Studies in the languages of the nations of the
non-western world, for example, but rather a listing, arranged
by nation, of books, pamphlets, conference proceedings,
government publications and periodical articles, published in
the languages of the non-western nations represented herein.
Efforts were expended to have the languages of all non-western
nations represented. In almost all instances, those nations in
the non-western world not herein represented have no published
output of materials on the Latin American nations. Libraries,
universities, and professional organizations world-wide were
contacted not once but several times, in order to achieve the
coverage presented herein. In any given nation from which a
positive reply was not forthcoming, the search was extended to
additional sources in that nation from which the required material
might be obtained.

i

Not all the material included herein was secured from abroad. The entries in Indonesian, Bulgarian, Chinese, Greek, Persian, Turkish as well as the bibliography for the Philippines and some Arabic & Japanese-language items were compiled from the sources available in the University Research Library and in the Oriental Library at UCLA. There follows a listing of the languages in which materials covering all types of topics, in all fields of knowledge, are to be found in the present work: Afrikaans (spoken in South Africa), Arabic, Bengali, Bulgarian, Chinese, Czech, Finnish, Greek, Hebrew, Hindi, Hungarian, Icelandic, Indonesian, Japanese, Persian, Korean, Malayalam, Marathi and Oriya (the last three languages mentioned being spoken in India), Polish, Rumanian, Serbo-Croat, Thai and Turkish.

Spoken by Boers in South Africa, the descendants of Dutch settlers, Afrikaans is native to that nation, hence was included as an African language. Icelandic is included as the "exception which proves the rule", for Iceland is indeed a nation of the western world, and its inclusion underscores the representation of materials in Bulgarian, Finnish, Greek, Hungarian, Polish, Rumanian and Serbo-Croat (spoken in Yugoslavia). These languages, spoken in their respective nations of Eastern and Southern Europe, strictly speaking are part and parcel of the western world. However, due to their relative rarity in the United States and in the western hemisphere in general, and especially with respect to their general neglect in terms of the study of Latin America in the western hemisphere, they have been included together with the nations of Asia, Africa and the Middle East. Therefore, if it is possible to include items from Iceland as an example of a "neglected" western nation (situated well within the "western world"), then it is all the more appropriate to have bibliographic representation for Bulgaria, Finland, Greece, Hungary, Poland, Rumania and Yugoslavia. Why is the Soviet Union not represented herein? The answer is to be found not only in the relatively great number of Russian speakers in the United States but also in the items listed in the following source which covers the Soviet Union in depth: Okinshevich, Leo A. Latin America in Soviet writings: a bibliography. Edited by Robert G. Carlton. 2v. Baltimore, published for the Library of Congress by The Johns Hopkins Press, 1966 (Hispanic Foundation Publications 1-2).

Government agencies, research centers, and any individual may scan the titles included for materials of interest to their respective activities. In so doing, one becomes conscious of a preponderant interest in certain topics, depending of course upon the given nation whose bibliographic output one peruses: Japanese interest in trade and economic development is pointed up in the section for Japan; the differences in topics and view-points between those items published in Taiwan and those issued on mainland China is at once manifest; the sympathy of South Korea to the United States position vis-a-vis Latin America and conversely, the outright hostility to the United States and concern for the security of Castro Cuba are obvious in periodical articles issued in Cairo, United Arab Republic. Nor are the political affiliations of most of the Balkan nations difficult to

iii

discern: for each of these countries, under the section on
Cuba, one notices a rash of publications issued since 1960.
It appears that both Poles and Japanese have preferred Brazil
to other Latin American countries, and there is a rich literature
of the experiences in Brazil of the emigrants of each nation.
An added characteristic of the section representing Poland
is the selection of nineteenth century books on Columbus and
the Discovery in general, as well as reminiscences of Poles
who served under Emperor Maximilian I in Mexico. Socio-
political-economic conditions characterize Yugoslavia's prime
interest in Latin America. Highly scholarly are the contributions of Finland, primarily in anthropology, geology and geography, but one is also impressed by many articles on the
forests of Latin America, and this is as it should be in view of
the rich experience of Finns in forestry. Senegal has manifested
interest in its similarities, based on population, with Brazil.
Incidentally, for further data on socio-political-economic contacts between Latin America and the Far East see Anita Bradley's
Trans-Pacific relations of Latin America (New York, 1942,
120p.).

In addition to its utilization by learned institutions and
official agencies, LATIN AMERICAN STUDIES IN THE NON—
WESTERN WORLD has been compiled as a service to scholars
world-wide who are concerned with the study of Latin America
and wish to know of the existence of materials in their own as
well as in allied disciplines published in languages with which
they may not be familiar. The future will undoubtedly bring
with it the benefits of rapid machine translation (as well as an

increased number of works translated by individuals), so that a record of available materials in languages unknown to Latin American specialists is in and of itself a service. Since the world is becoming more closely tied together (the results of research on this bibliography indicate that the preponderance of works representing the bulk of the nations of Asia, Africa and the Middle East was issued on an ever-increasing scale during the 1960's), and since the study of the languages of these areas is growing apace, it can reasonably be assumed that the knowledge and utilization of their respective languages will become commonplace, rather than a rare phenomenon.

It is hoped that the present work will enhance the research results of graduate students and mature scholars. It is certainly logical to assume that a United States graduate student utilizing materials written in ten or more languages, and representing the writings of Latin American specialists from, let us say, Bulgaria, China, Finland, Greece, Israel, Indonesia, Japan, Poland, Senegal and the United Arab Republic, would turn out a much more highly enriched research report or thesis than another student utilizing sources written only in English and Spanish, on his given topic, for the width of viewpoint is directly proportional to the spectrum. What is presented here, then, is in the nature of a plea for a bibliographic mechanism to make known internationally the existence of research materials, so that these may be made available to scholars and researchers world-wide, wherever they may be located, and on whatever topic they may be laboring. We are assuming that the research results will be of benefit to mankind:

if this be so, then it is in the interest of all nations to cooperate in so noble an undertaking.

The Library of Congress of the United States performs a magnanimous service in its world-wide lending activities. What is suggested here is a revival of the aims of the International Institute of Bibliography, established in Brussels, Belgium in 1895 by Paul Otlet and Henri LaFontaine, but this time on a regional basis, world-wide. Regional bibliographic centers might be set up in each major world region: Scandinavia, Western, Eastern and Southern Europe, the Soviet Union, East Asia, South Asia, the Middle East, East, West and South Africa, South, Central and North America. One important purpose of these centers would be the collection of materials in languages of secondary and even tertiary importance, insufficiently announced on the international level at present. Another advantage would be the presentation on a world scale of periodicals of significance in certain fields, which have thus far enjoyed only regional distribution. A possible side-advantage would be the awareness of "organizations in the field" of which the researcher would be apprised as a result of his contact with their conference proceedings. It could even be possible to dream that the hitherto often-disregarded pamphlet, as a transmitter of information, might "come into its own." This bibliography is presented, therefore, in the hope that it might be a harbinger of such an international bibliographic transmission program as is outlined above.

With regard to the arrangement of the work, there are four main divisions: Africa, Asia, Middle East and Eastern Europe,

with a separate and final section for Iceland. At the beginning
of many of the country-sections there are descriptions of the
status of the development of Latin American Studies in the
universities of the corresponding nations. In some instances
organizations concerned with Latin American Studies (and with
Latin America in general) are also listed. Within each of the
four divisions each item is arranged by: (1) nation in which the
given item was published; (2) Latin American nation to which
it refers; (3) by physical form (i. e. , whether books or periodical
articles); (4) alphabetically by author's last name. A specific
example will illustrate:

Division:	Asia
Nation in which item was published:	China
Latin American Nation Concerned:	Brazil
Physical Form:	I. Books
Author:	Lu, Hsi-Chou

Each item is numbered consecutively throughout the bibliography,
for purposes of speedy location through the indexes. In instances
where the author is represented by one or two letters (e. g. ,
M. K.), such instances indicate a pseudonym. In the case of
languages not using Roman script (Arabic, Bengali, Bulgarian,
Chinese, Persian, Greek, Hebrew, Hindi, Japanese, Korean,
Malayalam, Marathi, Oriya, Thai and Yiddish, the last-named
language being included together with Hebrew in the section for
Israel), the individual bibliographic entry is first presented in
the corresponding native script, followed by transliteration of
the entire entry, and finally by the English translation of the
title only. For languages which are written in Roman script,
each bibliographic item is presented in full, followed by the

English translation of the title only. In each section for books, titles are underlined: (1) in transliteration, for languages not utilizing Roman script; (2) in the initial presentation of the complete bibliographic item, in instances of languages written in Roman script; (3) in both instances, in the English translation, where there is a corporate author, as opposed to a personal author. In all sections for periodical articles, titles are set off by quotation marks.

In all instances the English translation of the title of each item is to be found directly under the title in the original language, and on the line immediately following the entire bibliographic entry.

The author index is arranged geographically by nation, and then alphabetically according to author in that nation. There are thus as many individual author indexes as there are nations represented, with the exceptions that (as opposed to nations per se) Africa and The Arab World each has its respective author index. Thus the user must turn to that nation (or to Africa or The Arab World) in the author index, to consult items of the nation (or region) of his interest. All books without authors have been entered by title, but only periodical articles having no author of more than four pages have been included in the author index. In such instances the books have been underlined and the periodical articles have been, as usual, set off between quotation marks.

The subject index has been arranged geographically by nation, as has the author index, and covers topics of interest in the nation and language in which the books concerning those topics were published. It is thus a general geographic language-subject index and is comprised of many small nation-indexes, as per the format of the author index.

Mention should here be made of those who collaborated on the various sections of the bibliography: Arabic, Mr. Panayotis G. Zaronis, Librarian at the American University, Cairo, U.A.R.; Bulgarian, Mr. D. Talev, graduate student in Slavic Languages, UCLA; Chinese (and some of the Japanese-language items), Mr. Che-Hwei Lin, Reference Librarian, Oriental Library, UCLA; Hebrew and Yiddish, Mrs. Rachel Meirav, formerly of the State Archives Library, Jerusalem, Israel; Hungarian, Mrs. Vera Deri (Chief of the Information Service), and Mrs. A. Bezenyi, Librarian, both of the University Library, Budapest, Hungary; Icelandic, Mr. Olafur F. Hjartar of the National Library of Iceland in Reykjavik; Japanese, Mr. Hajime Mizuno (Chief of the Library Division), and Miss Yukiko Hasegawa (who typed the entries), both of the Japan Economic Research Center in Tokyo; Polish, Miss Jolanta Bennett, student at the University of California, Berkeley; Thai, Miss Chureerat Paweenbampen of Thammasat University Library, Bangkok, Thailand; Turkish, Mr. Ronald Matz, graduate student in Near Eastern languages at UCLA. Mrs. Phyllis Solomon, Librarian of Rondebosch, South Africa, compiled all of the materials (including those in Afrikaans) for South Africa, and most of the balance of the African entries were contributed by my colleague, Professor René Durand, Director of the Afro-Ibero-American Center, University of Dakar, Dakar, Senegal. Collaborating institutions include the University Libraries of Prague,

Czechoslovakia, and Belgrade, Yugoslavia, the State Central Library, Bucharest, Rumania, and the National Library of India, in Calcutta.

My work included: originating and formulating the idea on which the project was based; seeking out sources abroad and on campus who would collaborate, and maintaing correspondence with them; establishing policy for inclusion of materials, and bibliographic style; editing all materials received for appropriateness, re-working and verifying entries bibliographically; checking translations into English for correctness and style; checking typists' copy against the original, compiling the prefatory material at the beginning of each country-section, and all additional matters incidental to the successful termination of the project. From materials at UCLA, I also compiled some entries in Czech, Rumanian and Serbo-Croat.

I wish to thank Miss Elvira Montes, who typed almost all of the manuscript, and typed and arranged the sequence of individual entries. Thanks also go to Mr. Robert Vago, a highly competent assistant, who compiled the Philippine bibliography and the subject index. Aides on the indexes, who also deserve a vote of thanks, include Bernadine Star and Louise Carroll. Diego Delgado a graduate student at UCLA from Mexico, translated this Preface into the excellent Spanish which follows. Mr. Luis Ortiz, another student from Mexico, was also of service.

Finally, it is essential that I express my thanks to my dad, Mr. Benjamin Sable, of Chestnut Hill, Massachusetts. It was at the age of five or six that I was first impressed by his overwhelming interest in faraway peoples and places. From my childhood I vividly recall his self-imposed rule to correctly pronounce place-names: when the capital of American Samoa was "in the news" and all were pronouncing it as spelled (Pago Pago), my dad made certain he said "Pango Pango".

It is apparent that my international interests, which finally focussed on Latin America, derive in good measure from my dad's example. It is equally apparent, then, that the germ of the idea for this book, embracing the nations of the non-Western world and Eastern Europe, is an indirect result. Therefore, it is with a great deal of filial pride and gratitude that I hereby acknowledge the significant contribution of my dad. Because of it, this book, which will serve scholars worldwide, is in existence today.

The efforts expended to make the present reference source available will have been compensated if long-range results serve to increase knowledge concerning Latin America, and bring closer together in a common understanding, the peoples of that area and those of the other regions of the world.

Martin H. Sable

PREFACIO

El título de este libro, traducido al español, sería ESTUDIOS
LATINOAMERICANOS EN EL MUNDO NO OCCIDENTAL Y EN
EUROPA DEL ESTE: UNA BIBLIOGRAFIA SOBRE AMERICA
LATINA EN LOS IDIOMAS QUE SE HABLAN EN ASIA, AFRICA,
MEDIO ORIENTE, Y EUROPA ORIENTAL, CON TITULOS
TRANSCRITOS Y TRADUCIDOS AL INGLES. El largo título fué
así confeccionado con el propósito de evitar confusiones y de es-
pecificar hasta donde fuera posible el contenido de la bibliografía.

Por lo tanto, el comprador y potencial usuario de esta obra
entenderá que ésta no es una bibliografía de escritos relacionados
al campo de Estudios Latinoamericanos en los idiomas de las
naciones del mundo no occidental, sino más bien una lista,
ordenada por países, de libros, folletos, actas de conferencias,
publicaciones gubernamentales, y artículos de revistas, publicados en los idiomas de los países no occidentales aquí repre-
sentados. Se desplegaron esfuerzos para incluir a todos los
idiomas de los países no occidentales. En la mayoría de los
casos, aquellas naciones no occidentales que no están aquí
incluídas no tienen producción de escritos sobre los países de la
América Latina. Se hizo contacto, no en una sino en varias
ocasiones, con bibliotecas, universidades, y organismos
mundiales de profesionistas para lograr el cubrimiento aquí
presentado. De aquellos países de los cuales no se recibía una
contestación afirmativa, la búsqueda se extendió a otras fuentes
en esos países en donde se podría obtener el material requerido.

No todo el material aquí presente se obtuvo del exterior.
Las fichas en indonesio, búlgaro, chino, griego, perso y turco,

así como la bibliografía de Filipinas y de algunas fichas en
árabe y japonés, fueron recopiladas en fuentes disponibles
en la University Research Library y en la Oriental Library de
la Universidad de California en Los Angeles. A continuación
se presenta una lista de los idiomas en los cuales materiales
que cubren todo tipo de tópicos, en todos los campos del saber,
se pueden encontrar en la presente obra: afrikaans (que se
habla en el Africa del Sur), árabe, bengalí, búlgaro, checo,
chino, finlandés, griego, hebreo, hindí, húngaro, indonesio,
islandés, japonés, perso, coreano, malayalam, maratí y oriya
(estos tres últimos se hablan en la India), polaco, rumano, serbocroata, tailandés, y turco.

El idioma afrikaans lo hablan los Bóer, del Africa del Sur,
los descendientes de los colonizadores holandeses; por lo tanto,
fué incluído como uno de los idiomas del Africa. El islandés
fué incluído como "la excepción que confirma la regla", pues
Islandia es sin duda alguna un país miembro del mundo occidental, y su presencia subraya la inclusión de material en búlgaro,
finlandés, griego, húngaro, polaco, rumano, y serbocroata (que
se habla en Yugoslavia). Estos idiomas oriundos de la Europa
Oriental y del Sur, estrictamente son uña y carne del mundo
occidental. Sin embargo, dada su relativa rareza en los
Estados Unidos y en el hemisferio occidental en general, y
especialmente dada su general negligencia del estudio de
América Latina en términos del hemisferio occidental, se les
incluyó junto con las naciones del Asia, Africa, y Medio Oriente.
Por consiguiente, si es posible incluir fichas de Islandia como
ejemplo de un "olvidado" país occidental (y bien situado dentro

del mundo occidental), por lo tanto es mucho más apropiado
tener una representación bibliográfica de Bulgaria, Finlandia,
Grecia, Hungría, Polonia, Rumania, y Yugoslavia.   Y entonces
por qué no está aquí representada la Unión Soviética? La res-
puesta se halla no sólo en el mayor número de personas en los
Estados Unidos que hablan ruso y en los libros rusos accesibles
que tratan de la América Latina, sino también en el hecho que
las fichas correspondientes se pueden encontrar en la siguiente
obra que ampliamente cubre a la Unión Soviética:

Okinshevich, Leo A. Latin America in Soviet writings: a
bibliography. Editada por Robert G. Carlton. 2 volúmenes,
Baltimore, publicada para la Biblioteca del Congreso por la Johns
Hopkins Press, 1966 (Publicaciones 1-2 de la Hispanic Foundation).

Las agencias gubernamentales, los centros de investigación,
o cualquier individuo puede escudriñar los títulos incluídos en
busca de materiales de interés a su actividad respectiva. Al
así hacerlo, se cobra conciencia de un interés preponderante en
ciertos tópicos, dependiendo por supuesto del país cuya producción bibliográfica uno lee con detenimiento: el interés del
japonés en el comercio y en el desarrollo económico sobresale
en la sección del Japón; las diferencias de tópicos y de puntos
de vista se manifiestan de inmediato entre los temas publicados
en Taiwan y aquellos publicados en la China territorial; la
simpatía de Corea del Sur hacia la posición de los Estados
Unidos frente a la América Latina contrasta con la abierta
hostilidad hacia los Estados Unidos así como el interés por la
seguridad de la Cuba de Castro que se manifiestan en los artículos de revistas publicados en el Cairo, República Arabe Unida.

Tampoco son difíciles de ocultar las filiaciones políticas de la mayor parte de los países balcánicos, pues para cada uno de estos países, bajo la sección de Cuba, nota uno la erupción de publicaciones a partir de 1960. Parece ser que tanto los polacos como los japoneses han preferido al Brasil de entre los otros países latinoamericanos, y existe una literatura rica en experiencias de los emigrantes de esos países al Brasil. Otra característica más de la sección que representa a Polonia es la selección de libros del siglo XIX sobre Colón y el descubrimiento de América en general, así como también los recuerdos de los polacos que sirvieron al emperador Maximiliano I en México. Las condiciones socio-político-económicas caracterizan el interés primordial en la América Latina de Yugoslavia. Altamente escolásticas son las contribuciones finlandesas, principalmente en antropología, geología, y geografía, aunque también se impresiona uno con los muchos artículos relativos a la silvicultura de la América Latina, y así debía de ser, en virtud de la larga experiencia de los finlandeses en cuestión de bosques. El Senegal tiene interés manifiesto en sus similitudes de población con Brasil. Para más informes sobre conexiones socio-economico-políticas entre Latinoamérica y el continente asiático, se dirige el lector a Bradley, Anita. Trans-Pacific relations of Latin America (New York, 1942, 120p.).

Además de su utilidad para las instituciones científicas y las agencias oficiales, esta obra se recopiló para beneficio de los estudiosos en el mundo entero que se interesan en la América Latina, y que desean conocer la existencia de materiales en

sus propias y asociadas disciplinas, publicados en idiomas con
los cuales no están familiarizados. No cabe duda que el porvenir
traerá consigo los beneficios de una rápida traducción mecánica
(así como también un mayor número de obras traducidas perso-
nalmente), de tal manera que el mero registro de materiales
disponibles en idiomas desconocidos a los especialistas de
Latinoamérica es en si y por si mismo servicial. Puesto que
el mundo se está uniendo más cada vez (en esta bibliografía se
muestra que el grueso de las obras de la mayor parte de los
países del Asia, Africa, y Medio Oriente, fueron publicadas en
escala ascendiente a partir de 1960), y como el estudio de los
idiomas de estas áreas está en aumento, se puede asumir con
certeza que en el futuro el conocimiento y el uso de esos idiomas
serán más comúnes y corrientes en vez de ser un fenómeno raro
como lo es en la actualidad.

Es de esperar que la presente obra acrecente las investigaciones de los estudiantes graduados y de los investigadores
maduros. Es lógico suponer que un estudiante graduado estadounidense que utilice materiales en diez o más idiomas repre-
sentando a los especialistas de Latino América de, digamos,
Bulgaria, China, Finlandia, Grecia, Israel, Indonesia, Japón,
Polonia, Senegal, y la República Arabe Unida, producirá una
tesis o un reporte de investigaciones mucho mejor que otro
estudiante que sólo utilice obras escritas sobre un tema dado
en sólo inglés y español, ya que la amplitud de visión es
directamente proporcional al espectro. Entonces, lo que aquí
se presenta es por naturaleza súplica que ruega por un meca-
nismo bibliográfico que haga conocer internacionalmente la

existencia de materiales de investigación, para que éstos se
pongan al alcance de los estudiosos e investigadores del mundo
entero, donde quiera que se encuentren, y sobre cualquier
tópico que laboren. Se asume que las investigaciones serán
en beneficio de la humanidad; si así fuere, es de interés de
todas las naciones cooperar en tan noble tarea.

    La Biblioteca del Congreso de los Estados Unidos desempeña
un magnánimo servicio con su préstamo de libros a todo el
mundo. Aquí se sugiere el renacimiento de las metas del
Instituto Internacional Bibliográfico establecido en Bruselas,
Bélgica, en 1895, por Paul Otlet y Henri LaFontaine, pero en
esta ocasión con bases regionales pero de alcance mundial.
Centros bibliográficos regionales pueden establecerse en cada
una de las principales regiones del mundo: Escandinavia,
Europa Occidental, Europa Oriental, Europa del Sur, Unión
Soviética, Asia Oriental, Asia del Sur, Medio Oriente, Africa
Oriental, Africa Occidental, Africa del Sur, América del Sur,
América Central, y América del Norte. Un importante propósito de estos centros sería recolectar materiales en idiomas
de segunda o aún de tercera importancia, que en la actualidad
no son suficientemente conocidos en el plano internacional.
Otra ventaja más sería la presentación a escala mundial de
revistas de importancia en algunos campos, que hasta ahora
sólo se distribuyen regionalmente. Una posible ventaja auxi-
liar sería el dar a conocer las "organizaciones de campo"
como resultado del contacto del investigador individual con
las actas de sus conferencias. Aún sería posible soñar que
el hasta la fecha despreciado folleto, gran transmisor de

información, llegue a su máxima expresión. Se presenta
esta bibliografía, por lo tanto, con el deseo que sea precursor
del tal programa de transmisión internacional bibliográfico
como anteriormente se apunta.

Con relación al arreglo interno de la obra, hay cuatro
divisiones principales: Africa, Asia, Medio Oriente, y Europa
Oriental, con una separada y final sección para Islandia. Al
principio de muchas de las secciónes-países hay descripciones del
estado de desarrollo de los Estudios Latinoamericanos en las
universidades de los correspondientes países. En algunos
casos, las organizaciones que tratan con los Estudios Latinoamericanos (y con América Latina en general) están también
anotadas. Dentro de cada una de las cuatro divisiones cada
tema está arreglado por: (1) país en el cual el tema dado fué
publicado; (2) países latinoamericanos a los cuales se refiere;
(3) por forma física (por ejemplo: ya sean libros o artículos de
revistas); (4) alfabéticamente por el apellido del autor. Se
ilustra con un ejemplo específico:

Division: ASIA
País en el cual se publicó el tema: China
País latinoamericano a que se refiere: Brasil
Forma física: I. Libros
Autor: Lu, Hsi-Chou

Cada asiento está numerado consecutivamente a través de
la bibliografía para una rápida localización en los índices. En
los casos en que el autor está con una o dos letras (ejemplo:
M. K.), tales casos indican un pseudónimo. En el caso de
idiomas que no utilizan escritura romana (árabe, bengalí,
búlgaro, chino, griego, hebreo, hindí, japonés, coreano,

malayalam, maratí, oriya, perso, tailandés, y yiddish (este
último está incluído junto al hebreo en la sección de Israel),
la ficha bibliográfica individual se presenta primero en la
correspondiente escritura original, seguida por una transcripción
de la ficha entera, y finalmente por la traducción en inglés
solamente del título. En cada sección para libros, los títulos
se subrayan: (1) en transcripción con los idiomas que no usan
escritura romana; (2) en la presentación inicial de la ficha
bibliográfica completa, en casos de idiomas con escritura
romana; (3) en ambos casos, en la traducción inglesa, cuando
existe un autor colectivo (organizacion o institución), en contraste de cuando hay autor personal. En todas las secciones de
artículos de revistas, los títulos están entre commillas. En
todos los casos la traducción inglesa del título de cada tema se
encuentra directamente bajo el título en el idioma original, y
en la línea que sigue inmediatamente la ficha bibliográfica
completa.

El índice de autores está arreglado geograficamente por
país, y después alfabéticamente de acuerdo al autor en esa
nación. Por lo tanto, hay tantos índices de autores como hay
países presentados, con la excepción (en contraste con los
países mismos) de Africa y Mundo Arabe, los cuales cuentan
con un sólo índice de autores respectivamente. Así el lector
debe buscar en el país (o en Africa o en Mundo Arabe) en el
índice de autores para consultar los temas de su interés en
ese país (o región). Todo libro sin autor ha sido inscrito con
su título, pero sólo los artículos de revistas que no tienen
autor, de más de cuatro páginas, han sido incluídos en el

índice de autores. En tales casos los libros han sido sub-
rayados mientras que los artículos de revistas, como de costumbre,
se han indicado entre comillas.

El índice de temas ha sido arreglado geograficamente por
país al igual que el índice de autores, y cubre tópicos del país
e idioma en que se publicaron los libros referentes a esos tópicos.
Es así un índice general geográfico-idioma-tema que se compone
de muchos pequeños índices de países, de formato igual al índice
de autores.

Se debe mencionar aquí a quienes colaboraron en las distintas
secciones de la bibliografía: árabe, Sr. Panayotis G. Zaronis,
bibliotecario de la American University del Cairo, República
Arabe Unida; búlgaro, Sr. D. Talev, estudiante graduado en
idiomas eslavos en la U. C. L. A. ; chino (y algunas fichas en
idioma japonés), Sr. Che-Hwei Lin, bibliotecario de consulta
en la Biblioteca Oriental de la U. C. L. A. ; finlandés, Srita.
Eila Junnila de la Biblioteca Universitaria en Helsinki, Finlandia;
griego, Sr. Nikos Antzoulatos, pasante en la U. C. L. A. ; hebreo
y yiddish, Sra. Rachel Meirav, antes de la Biblioteca de Archivos
de Jerusalén, Israel; húngaro, Sra. Vera Deri (Jefe del Servicio
de Información) y Sra. A. Bezenyi, bibliotecaria, ambas de la
Biblioteca Universitaria de Budapest, Hungría; islandés, Sr.
Olafur F. Hjartar de la Biblioteca Nacional de Islandia en
Reykjavik; japonés, Sr. Hajime Mizuno (Jefe de la División de
Bibliotecas) y Srita. Yukiko Hasegawa (quien escribió a máquina
las fichas) ambos de la Japan Economic Research Center de
Tokio; polaco, Srita. Jolanta Bennętt, estudiante de la Univer-
sity of California en Berkeley; tailandés, Srita. Chureerat

Paweenbampen de la Biblioteca de la Universidad Thammasat
en Bangkok, Tailandia; turco, Sr. Ronald Matz, estudiante
graduado en idiomas del Cercano Oriente en la U. C. L. A.
La Sra. Phyllis Solomon, Bibliotecaria de Rondebosch, Africa
del Sur, recopiló los materiales (incluyendo aquellos en afrikaans)
del Africa del Sur; la mayor parte del resto de fichas africanas
fueron contribución de mi colega, el profesor René Durand,
Director del Centro Afro-Ibero-Americano en la Universidad
de Dakar en Dakar, Senegal. Entre las instituciones colaboradoras
se incluyen a las Bibliotecas Universitarias de Praga, Checoslo-
vaquia, y de Belgrado, Yugoslavia, la Biblioteca Estatal Central
de Bucarest, Rumania, y la Biblioteca Nacional de India en
Calcuta.

Mi trabajo consistió en: originar y formular la idea sobre
la cual se basó el proyecto; búsqueda de fuentes en el extranjero
y de universidades que colaboraran, y mantenimiento de corres-
pondencia con ellas; establecer la política para la inclusión de
materiales, y el estilo bibliográfico; redactar todo asiento para
aptitud; checar las traducciones al inglés en corrección y
estilo bibliográfico; verificar las copias recibidas de las mecanó-
grafas contra los originales; recopilar el material introductario
de cada sección-país; y todos los otros asuntos concernientes al
feliz término del proyecto. Del material en la U. C. L. A. ,
también recopilé yo algunas fichas en checo, rumano, y serbocroata.

Deseo agradecer a la Srita. Elvira Montes el escribir a máquina casi todo el material incluído en la transcripción y en la traducción inglesa, así como el arreglo de los materiales. Las gracias también se extienden al Sr. Robert Vago, ayudante muy competente; recopiló el Sr. Vago la bibliografía filipina así como la mayor parte del índice de asuntos. Mecanógrafa bastante apta es la Srita. Bernardine Star. La Srita. Louise Carroll ayudó en la recopilación de los índices. El Arq. Diego W. Delgado, estudiante mexicano graduado en la U. C. L. A., tradujo a excelente español este Prefacio. El Sr. Luis Ortiz, estudiante de México en la U. C. L. A., también fué de utilidad como asistente.

Por fin, es indispensable expresar mis reconocimientos a mi padre, el senor Benjamín Sable, de Chestnut Hill, Massachusetts. A la edad de cinco o seis anos, me dí cuenta de su profundo interés en personas y lugares lejanos. De mi niñez me acuerdo graficamente su regla pronunciar correctamente los nombres de lugares: cuando se mencionaba la capital de Samoa Americana y mientras todo el mundo la pronunciaba tal como fue deletreada (Pago Pago), dijo mi papá correctamente "Pango Pango".

Es evidente que se remonta mi interés en asuntos latinoamericanos (y sobre todo, por Latinoamérica) por mayor parte del ejemplo de mi padre. Es patente también, que el origen de la idea de este libro, abarcando las naciones del mundo no Occidental y las de la Europa del Este, es consecuencia indirecta de su ejemplo. Por eso, es con mucho orgullo filial y con mucho agradecimiento que reconozco la sobresaliente contribución de mi papá. A causa de esa contribución este libro, destinado para servir las necesidades de estudiosos e investigadores en todas partes del mundo, existe actualmente.

Los esfuerzos realizados para hacer acesible la presente obra de referencia serán ampliamente recompensados si los resultados sirven para incrementar el conocimiento sobre la América Latina, y en un comun entendimiento, de acercar más a las gentes de esa área con las de otras regiones del mundo.

Martin H. Sable

AFRICA

Although there are literally hundreds of native languages
spoken in the continent of Africa (exclusive of the Arabic
spoken in North and East Africa), little has been published
in Africa in these languages, in comparison with the
output of books, pamphlets and articles issued there in the
languages of Europe.

Accordingly, the items listed herein, under the African
region, were originally published in French, Portuguese,
and English; English is also represented in the sections for
Nigeria, Tanzania and South Africa (the last also containing
materials in Afrikaans). For items in Arabic, please
refer to the Middle East division.

Only since the mid-1950's, concomitant with the declarations
of independence of many of the African nations, has the
awareness on the part of these nations of the possibility
of contacts with Latin America been made manifest. It
should be noted, as a result, that the bulk of the items
included bear publication dates subsequent to 1960. It
is in the nature of things, however, that we should antic-
ipate an expansion of the current Afro-Latin American
rapprochement, as indicated by the great interest of
the Republic of Senegal, West Africa in contacts with
Brazil, pointed up by the visits of the Senegalese President,
Leopold Sedar Senghor, to Brazil during the 1960's, and
in his official remarks. Both the African as well as
Latin American nations desire and require official and
non-governmental contacts, and these relationships,
whether political, economic or cultural, will not be
restricted to nations with predominantly Negro popula-
tions, such as Haiti and Brazil, which are already
being imitated by other Latin American nations in their
concern with African Studies.

It is suggested, therefore, that the future will unfold an enhanced interest in African Studies (on the part of Latin American educational institutions), and an expansion in African universities of the pioneering efforts of the University of Dakar, Senegal, which in the early 1960's established a Center for Afro-Ibero-American Studies. Its publications on Latin America are listed in this section. As of early 1968, the sole museum institution in Africa with interests in Latin America, in addition to the aforementioned Center, was the Ibero-American Section of the Dr. Joaquim de Carvalho Museum, located in Inhambane, Mozambique. During the period 1958-65 the Municipality of Nova Lisboa, Angola, issued the four-volume <u>Panorama das literaturas das Américas, de 1900 a actualidade,</u> compiled by the Director of the Museum, Dr. Joaquim de Montezuma de Carvalho. Aside from the University of Dakar, to the author's knowledge the only additional African university teaching courses on Brazil is the University of the Witwatersrand, located in Johannesburg, South Africa, which maintains the Ernest Oppenheimer Institute of Portuguese Studies.

Even a cursory perusal of the items in this section will indicate a preoccupation with the fields of literature and anthropology. It is anticipated that by the close of the twentieth century a similar compilation will disclose an interest which will include all of the social sciences as well as religion, philosophy, the arts, and some fields of applied science.

The English translation of the title of each bibliographic item is to be found directly under the title in the original language, and immediately following the entire bibliographic description.

———————

Aunque hay centenares de lenguas nativas que se hablan
en el continente de Africa (exclusivas del árabe hablado
en el Norte y el Este de Africa), poco ha sido publicado
en Africa en estos idiomas, en comparación con el número de libros, folletos y artículos de revistas redactados allí en las lenguas de Europa. Según, los asientos
descritos aquí, bajo la región africana, fueron publicados
originalmente en francés, portugués, e inglés; también
el inglés se representa en las secciones para Nigeria,
Tanzania y Sur-Africa (el último contiene fichas en
Afrikaans). Para items en árabe, sírvase consultar en
la división de Medio Oriente.

Desde los mediados de 1950, simultaneamente con las
declaraciones de independencia de muchas de las naciones
africanas, se conoce en la parte de estas naciones la
posibilidad de establecer contactos con Latinoamérica.
Se debe notar, como resultado, que la mayoría de las
fichas incluidas fueron publicadas después del año 1960.
Sin embargo, es natural que deberíamos esperar un
acercamiento aumentado entre los países africanos y
latinoamericanos, como se indica por el gran interés
de la República de Senegal, Africa Occidental, en sus
contactos con Brasil. El ·Presidente de Senegal, señor
Leopoldo Sedar Senghor, visitó Brasil durante el año
de 1963, y en sus conferencias oficiales habló sobre los
vínculos fuertes existentes entre Africa, Brasil, y las
naciones latinoamericanas en general. Las naciones
africanas y latinoamericanas desean y necesitan contactos
oficiales y no-gubernamentales, y estas conexiones
políticas, económicas o culturales, no estarán limitadas
a las naciones por poblaciones negras, tales como Haití
y Brasil, las cuales ya han sido imitadas por otros
países latinoamericanos en cuanto a su interés por Estudios
Africanos.

Se indica que en el porvenir habrá un gran interés por
Estudios Africanos por parte de las instituciones educacio-
nales latinoamericanas, y un aumento en las universidades
africanas de los esfuerzos pioneros de la Universidad de

Dakar, Senegal, la cual estableció a principios de los 1960
un Centro de Estudios Afro-Ibero-Americanos. Sus publicaciones sobre Latinoamérica se encuentran en esta sección.
La única institución de tipo museo en Africa con interés en
Latinoamérica es la Sección Iberoamericana del Museo
"Dr. Joaquim de Carvalho", situado en Inhambane, Mozambique. Durante el período 1958-65 la Municipalidad de Nova
Lisboa, Angola publicó los cuatro volúmenes Panorama das
literaturas das Américas, de 1900 a actualidade, recopilados
por el señor Director del Museo, Dr. Joaquim de Montezuma
de Carvalho.

Aparte de la Universidad de Dakar, la única universidad
africana que enseña cursos sobre Brasil es la Universidad
de Witwatersrand, situada en Johannesburg, Sur-Africa,
la cual mantiene el Instituto "Ernest Oppenheimer de Estudios
Portugueses. "

Si se leen las fichas en esta sección, inmediatamente se dará
cuenta del gran interés por los campos de literatura y antropología. Se predica que para fines del siglo XX habrán
muchas publicaciones africanas que traten no solamente
letras y antropología, sino también todas las ciencias
sociales, así como religión, filosofía, artes, y algunos
campos de ciencias aplicadas.

(La traducción inglesa del título de cada asiento se
encuentra directamente bajo el titulo de la lengua
original, seguida de la ficha entera).

I. Books

AFRICA

1 Rayner, P. R. Wafugaji. London, Evans Bros., 1952 (Chapter 5).
        (Breeders of Animals in Argentina is the Topic of Chapter 5)
- This English-language book has a Swahili title, which translates to "Animal Breeders."

ALGERIA

2 Bassières, L. Les Origines de l'Entente Cordiale. Un Episode de la Conquête des Îles d'Amérique par les Puissances Européennes (1625-1635). Algiers, Imprimerie la Typo-Litho, 1935, 64p.
        (The Origins of the "Entente Cordiale": an Episode in the Conquest of the Islands of America by the European Powers, 1625-1635)

NIGERIA

3 Verger, P. Bahia and the West African Trade, 1549-1851. Ibadan, Ibadan University Press, 1964, 39p.
-Slave Labor; Brazil, Bahia State

ANGOLA

4   Cascudo, L. da C. A Cosinha Africana no Brasil(In *Publicações de Museu de Angola*. Luanda, 1964, pp. 35-36)
        (African Cookery in Brazil)

5   Elia, A. d'. O Velho e o Cão. Sá da Bandeira, Angola, 1962,
    27p.
        (The Old Man and the Dog; Short Story)

6   Fernandes, L. Cançao dos Meus Tipoieiros; Poemas. Luanda,
    1961, 76p.
        (The Song of my Porters: Poems)

7   Mesquitela, L. Da Importançia dos Estudos Bantos para a
    Compreensão da Problemática Socio-Cultural Brasileira.
    Luanda, Instituto de Investigação Científica de Angola, 1963,
    16p.
        (The Importance of Bantu Studies in the
    Understanding of Socio-Cultural Problems in Brazil)

8   Nogueira, H. Nova Rota; Versos. Sá da Bandeira, Angola,
    Publicaçoes Imbondeiro, 1962, 126p.
        (New Road: Verses)

9   Panorama das Literaturas das Américas, de 1900 á Actualidade.
    Ed. by Joaquim de Montezuma de Carvalho. 1st ed. 4v.
    Nova Lisboa, Ed. do Municipio de Nova Lisboa, Angola,
    1958-65.
    (Panorama of the Literatures of the Americas, from 1900 to
    the Present)

I. Books

SENEGAL

10 Arboleda, J. R. Histoire et Anthropologie du Noir en
    Colombie. Dakar, Centre de Hautes Études Afro-Ibéro-
    Américaines de l'Université de Dakar, 1968, 32p.
            (The History and Anthropology of the
    Negro in Colombia)

11 Auteurs Africains, Antillais et Malgaches. Dakar, Centre
    Culturel Français, 1962, 30p.
    (Authors from Africa, the Antilles and the Malagasy Republic)

12 Chrysostome, P. Pour une Histoire des Sucreries Antillaises.
    Quelques Instructions de Colons (1690-1788). Dakar,
    Université de Dakar, 1964, 62p.
            (A History of Sugar Mills in the Antilles:
    Some Instructions of the Colonists, 1690-1788)

13 Debien, I. Plantations et Esclaves à St-Domingue. Publications
    de la Section D'Histoire, No. 3, Faculté des Lettres et Sciences
    Humaines de L'Université de Dakar. Dakar, 1962, 184p.
            (Plantations and Slaves in Santo Domingo)

14 Franco, J. L. Présence Africaine au Nouveau Monde. Dakar,
    Centre de Hautes Études Afro-Ibéro-Américaines de L'Université
    de Dakar, 1967, 30p.
            (The African Presence in the New World)

15 Garavito, J. Introduction á la Culture Colombienne. Dakar,
    Centre de Hantes Etudes Afro-Ibéro-Américaines de l'Uni-
    versité de Dakar, 1967, 189p.
            (Introduction to Colombian Civilization)

16   Lapointe, J.   Bibliographie de L'Espagnol D'Amérique.   Dakar, Centre de Hautes Études Afro-Ibéro-Américaines de l'Université de Dakar, 1968, 105p.

         (Bibliography on Latin America)

17   Sedar Senghor, L.   Latinité et Négritude: Discours Prononcés a L'Université de Bahia, le 21 Septembre, 1964.   Dakar, Centre de Hautes Études Afro-Ibéro-Américaines de l'Université de Dakar, 1966, 50p.

         (Latinity and Negritude: Speech Delivered at the University of Bahia, September 21, 1964)

18   Senghor, L. S.   Textes Complets des Discours, Allocutions et Toasts Prononcés par S. E. Léopold Sédar Senghor, Président de la République du Sénégal, Lors de son Voyage Officiel Aux Etats-Unis du Brésil.   Edité par le Comissariat a l'Information, a la Radiodiffusion et au Tourisme.   Dakar, 1964, 44p.

         (Complete Texts of the Speeches, Statements and Toasts of his Excellency Leopold Sedar Senghor, President of the Republic of Senegal, on his Official Trip to Brazil)

II. Periodical Articles

19 "Les Afro-Américains." Dakar, <u>Mémoires de l'Institut Français d'Afrique Noire</u>, I. F. A. N. (27), 1952, pp. 1-268. ("The Afro-Americans")

20 Debien, G. "Les Origines des Esclaves des Antilles." Dakar, <u>Bulletin de L'I. F. A. N.</u> (XIII: 3-4), Series B, 1961, pp. 363-387.
("The Origins of the Slaves of the Antilles")

21 Debien, G., & J. Houdaille. "Les Origines des Esclaves aux Antilles." Dakar, <u>Bulletin de L'I. F. A. N.</u> (XXVI: 1-2), Series B, 1964, pp. 166-211.
("The Origins of the Slaves of the Antilles")

22 Richard, R., & G. Debien. "Les Origines des Esclaves des Antilles." Dakar, <u>Bulletin de L'I. F. A. N.</u> (XXIV: 1-2), Series B, 1961, pp. 1-38.
("The Origins of the Slaves of the Antilles")

23 Verger, P. "Notes Sur le Culte des Orisa et des Voduns a Bahia, La Baie de Tous les Saints, Au Brésil et a L'Ancienne Côte des Esclaves en Afrique." Dakar, <u>Mémoires de l'Institut Francais d'Afrique Noire</u> I. F. A. N. (51), 1957, pp. 1-610.
("Notes on the Cult of the Orisa and of the Voduns in Bahia, All-Saints' Bay, in Brazil and on the Old Slave Coast in Africa")

SOUTH AFRICA

(Note: The languages of South Africa include English as well as Afrikaans, the language of the Boer population, based on Dutch. For this reason there are included in this section items in both languages).

(Nota: En el país de Sur-Africa se habla inglés así como Afrikaans, el lenguaje de la población bóer basado en holandés. Por esta razón incluimos en esta sección asientos en ambas lenguas).

I. Books

LATIN AMERICA

24 Van Heerden, E. Die Wolk Van Die Mooi Weer. Suid Amerikanse Reisjoernal. Cape Town, Human & Rousseau, 1964, 160p.
            (The People of the Good Weather: South American Travel Journal)
-A description of a motor trip through South America. All the large centres are described. Attention is paid to social customs.

ARGENTINA

25 Henning, P. H. 'n Boer in Argentinie. Cape Town, Nasionale Pers,
       1940, 286p.
                    (A South African Farmer in Argentina)
    -A description of the Boer colony in Chubut- the Boers had emigrated
    after the Boer War.

26 Jacobs, A. J. Argentina - Description & Travel. Reis Avonture
       op Land en See. Cape Town, Rustic Press, 1920, 303p.
                    (Argentina - Description & Travel; an Adventure
    Journey on Land and Sea)
    -In 1906 a party of South Africans left for Argentina in the ship
    Saxon. Descriptions of the journey, of arrival at Rio and of the
    difficulties encountered in settling in a new country are included.

27 Van Huysteen, D. P. 'n Besoek aan die Boere in Argentinie.
       Cape Town, Nasionale Pers [n. d.] 91p.
                    (A Visit to the Boers in Argentina)
    -A description of the life and the difficulties of the Boer community
    in Chubut. He describes how Afrikaans secondary schools were established.
    Included are reports of discussions held with the mother church in South
    Africa to repatriate the immigrants, eventually turned down by the church.

BOLIVIA

28 Griffith, Margaret. Tiquimani. Stellenbosch, Kosmo Publishers,
       1965, 164p.
    -An account of the Andean Expedition of 1963 that climbed the peak
    of Tiquimani in the Bolivian Andes, until then considered unclimbable.

BRAZIL

29   Du Plessis, I. D. <u>Rugby in Rio.</u> Cape Town, Nasionale Pers
         Bpk., 1941, 126p.
      -A rugby tour in South America - no date of tour given. Description
      of games, entertainment enjoyed and towns visited.

30   Glass, Fredrick C. <u>Die Skerp Swaard. (Kolportasie in Brasilea)</u>
         <u>Uit Die Engles Vertaal Deur Timo Kriel.</u> Cape Town, Citadel
      Press, 1949, 196p.
                              (The Sharp Sword: Canvassing in Brazil.
      Translated from the English by Timo Kriel)
      -The writer sailed for Brazil in 1892. Through a misunderstanding
      he was jailed - this gave him a feeling for prisoners. He joined an
      Evangelist mission, maintaining that Brazil needed the Protestant faith.

31   Marais, Ben J. <u>Colour-Unsolved Problem of the West.</u> Cape Town,
         Howard B. Timmins, [n. d.] 328p.
                              (Also Published in Afrikaans - Die Kleur-Krises en die
      Weste. Johannesburg, Goeie Hoop Uitgewers, 1952)
      -The author was awarded travel grants and among other institutions
      did work in the universities of Rio and São Paulo. Chapter VII & VIII
      deal with South America, mainly the Negro in Brazil and race
      relations in Brazil today. A short historical introduction to the
      chapters emphasizes class lines but not color line.

32   Serton, Petrus. <u>Suid Afrika en Brasilie: Sociaal - Geografiese</u>
         <u>Vergelyking.</u> Cape Town, Oxford University Press, 1960, 221p.
                              (South Africa and Brazil: Social - Geographical
      Comparison)
      -A social and geographical comparison; a background of politics and
      history. Comparisons of economics with reference to mining and
      farming. Comparisons of the press and other cultural aspects. He
      concludes that apartheid exists in Brazil, but is not legislated.

ECUADOR

33   Wittner, Margret. <u>Posbus Floreana: 'n Paradys op die Galàpagos
     Eilande,</u> (Uit Duits, Vertaal Deur J. J. Human) Cape Town, H. A.
    U. M., 1959, 179p.
                    (Postbox Floreana: A Paradise on the
    Galapagos Islands. From Dutch, Translated by J. J. Human)
    -An account, in the first person, of a husband, wife and friend who
    settle, from Holland, on the island. The couple raise a family there;
    a general account of life on the island is included.

II. Periodical Articles

LATIN AMERICA

34   Blunt, M. "Goods from South America." Johannesburg,
       Forum (7: 2), April 8, 1944, pp. 129-131.

35   David, Evan R. "A South African Student Looks at Latin
       America." Bloemfontein, Outspan (43: 1104), April 1948, p. 29.

36   De Jong, C. "Monetere Stabiliteit in Latyns-Amerika." Pretoria,
       T. Geestewet, September 1963, pp. 180-196.
                 ("Monetary Stability in Latin America")

37   Elwes, M. "Glimpses of South America." Pietermaritzburg,
       Farmer & home companion (37: 48), November 26, 1948, p. 15.

38   "Handelsmoontlikhede in Suid Amerika." Pretoria, Volkshandel
       (23: 3), May 1962, pp. 23-24.
       ("Business Opportunities in South America")

39   "Minerals in South America: Increasing Range of Production."
       Johannesburg, South African mining & engineering journal
       (58: 1), June 28, 1947, pp. 555-557.

40   "South Atlantic Discord (Freight Charged on South American
       Consignment." Cape Town, South African industry & trade
       (40: 2), February, 1944, pp. 25- 27.

ARGENTINA

41   "Argentine Crises." Cape Town, South African industry & trade
     (40: 1), January 1944, pp. 111-115.

42   "Argentine- South African Trade." Cape Town, South African
     industry & trade (40: 6), June 1944, pp. 91-93.

43   Brownrigg, R. "Industrially and in Other Respects Argentina
        is Going Ahead Rapidly.' Bloemfontein, Outspan (40: 1037),
     January 10, 1947, p. 21.

44   Brownrigg, R. "Buenos Aires and a Shipwreck off Brazil." Bloemfontein,
     Outspan (40: 1028), November 8, 1946, pp. 47-49.

45   Henning, A. "Die Eerste Afrikaner in Argentinie." Bloemfontein,
     Outspan , November 2, 1951, p. 23.
                 ("The First Afrikaner in Argentina")

46   "Peronism in Schools." Pretoria, Transvaal educational news
     (45: 3), March 1949, p. 11.

BOLIVIA

47   De Villiers, J. E. "Hoe Lyk Dit in Bolivie? " Johannesburg, Ruiter (1: 50), April 1948, pp. 4-5.
("What is Bolivia Like? ")

BRAZIL

48   "Brazil's Iron & Steel Development. " Johannesburg, South African mining & engineering journal (54: 2), January 29, 1944, p. 513.

49   Malzemoff, A. "United Nations Newest Sources of Iron - Brazil's Huge Itabira Deposits. " Johannesburg, Mining & industrial review (31), May 1943, p. 313.

ECUADOR

50   Green, R. "How the Mars Men Came to Quito. " Bloemfontein, Outspan (46: 1177), September 16, 1949, p. 21.

MEXICO

51 Beard, J. S. "Introduction of Trees from Mexico." Johannesburg, Journal of the Tree Society of Southern Africa (1), April-June, 1955, pp. 14-16.

52 "Economic Conditions During 1963 (Mexico)." Pretoria, Commerce & industry (23), October 1964, p. 160.

53 "Guide for South African Exporters to Mexico, Morocco, Mukalla, Muscat and Oman." Pretoria, Commerce & industry (21), July 1963, pp. 711-714.

54 "Iron Mountain or Cerro de Mercado: a Mexican Wonder." Johannesburg, Mining and industrial review (33), February 1945, p. 95.

55 "Mexico's Mineral Wealth." Johannesburg, South African mining & engineering journal (58: 2), September 20, 1947, pp. 59-61.

56 "Mexico's Rising Production." Johannesburg, South African citrus journal (355), July 1963, p. 21.

57 Pani, M. "Satellite City for Mexico." Cape Town, Architect & builder (9: 7), July 1959, pp. 54-60.

PERU

58   "Stimulating Mineral Development - Peru Establishes a Mining
      Bank." Johannesburg, South African mining & engineering
      journal (51: 2), November 9, 1940, p. 233.

TANZANIA

Documents Located in List A, Government Archives, Zanzibar

	Reference	Item	Description
59	RES. B. 52	Letters from British Guiana (1904)	Bound volume.
60	" S. 7	Report from 1887 on the Trade and Commerce of Rio de Janeiro (1888)	Printed pamphlet No. 265: file on Brazil
61	" S. 10	Report for 1887 on Trade of... South America (Geographical, also on Railroads and Agriculture (1888)	Printed pamphlet No. 314: file on South America
62	" S. 12	Report for 1887 on Agriculture of Pernambuco (1888)	Printed pamphlet No. 37: file on South America
63	" S. 14	Report for 1887 of Trade of El Salvador (1888)	Printed pamphlet No. 378: file on El Salvador
64	" S. 19	Report on Trade of El Salvador (1888)	Printed pamphlet No. 548: file on El Salvador
65	" G. 12	Correspondence Relative to Slave Trade, from Central Africa, Honduras, etc. (1887)	Bound volume – file on Slave Trade
66	" ARC. 101	Letter from Margaret McDonald to Syd. Hamoud bin Mohamed, from West Indies, dated November, 25, 1899.	

CHINA

On mainland China Spanish is taught in the Faculty of
Western Languages and Literatures, at Fu Tan University
in Shanghai, Peking University (where there also exist
Institutes of Latin American Studies, International Relations,
and Foreign Languages), and at Sun Yat Sen University, in
Canton. At Peking are located the China Institute for New
Political Science Research as well as a Foreign Trade
Institute. Peking is the educational center of China, for
there also is the seat of the Chinese Academy of Sciences.

On Taiwan Latin American literature is taught at Taiwan
Provincial Chung Hsing University, and the College of
Chinese Culture (Huakang, Yang Min Shan) offers a course
in Latin American history and geography. The Catholic
University (Fu Jen) teaches Spanish literature. There is
a China-Latin America Society in Taipei, the capital.

En el continente chino se enseña español en las Facultades
de Lenguas Occidentales de la Universidad Fu Tan (en
Shanghai) en la Universidad de Peking (donde existen
Institutos de Estudios Latinoamericanos, Relaciones Internacionales, e Idiomas Extranjeros), y en la Universidad
Sun Yat Sen, situada en la ciudad de Canton. En la ciudad
de Peking también hay un Instituto para Comercio Internacional así como el Instituto Chino para la Nueva Investigación
Política. Peking es el centro educativo de la nación, visto que
allá está situada la sede de la Academia China de Ciencias.

En la isla de Taiwan se enseña literatura latinoamericana en
la Universidad Provincial Chung Hsing de Taiwan, y el Colegio
de Cultura China (Huakang, Yang Min Shan) ofrece asignatura
en historia y geografía latinoamericanas. En la Universidad
Católica (Fu Dzen) se enseñan letras españolas. Hay una Sociedad
China-Latinoamérica en Taipei, la capital.

LATIN AMERICA

67　趙渢　　南美見聞　　上海
上海人民出版社　[1958]

Chao, Fêng. <u>Nan Mei Chien Wên</u>. Shanghai, Shang Hai
Jên Min Ch'u Pan Shê, 1958, 64p.
(Sightseeing in South America)

68　陳栄豪　　拉丁美洲古代美術　　上海
上海人民美術出版社

Ch'ên, Jung-hao. <u>La-ting-Mei-Chou Ku Tai Mei Shu</u>.
Shanghai, Shang Hai Jên Min Mei Shu Ch'u Pan Shê, 1963,
75 + 4pp.

(Ancient Art of Latin America)

陳宗経　　拉丁美洲之経済　　台北
69　中華文化出版事業委員会

Ch'ên, Tsung-Ching. <u>La-ting-Mei-Chou Chih Ching Chi</u>.
Taipei, Chung Hua Wên Hua Ch'u Pan Shih Yeh Wei Yüan Hui,
1956, 3+4+108+33pp.

(Latin American Economy)

屈武圻　　中南米風光　　香港
70　章記公司

Ch'ü, Wu-ch'i. <u>Chung Nan Mei Fêng Kuang</u>. Hong Kong,
Chang Chi Kung Ssü, 1962, 101p.
(Scenery of Central and South America)

71　易敏子　　拉丁美洲国家　　台北
中華文化出版事業委員会

I, Min-tzu. <u>La-ting Mei-Chou Kuo Chia</u>. Taipei, Chung Hua
Wên Hua Ch'u Pan Shih Yeh Wei Yüan Hui, 1955, 224+6pp.
(Latin American Countries)

72　易敏子編　　拉丁美洲国家　　台北
中華文化出版事業委員会

I, Min Tzu, ed. <u>La-Ting-Mei-Chou Kuo Chia</u>. Taipei, Chinese
Cultural Publication Committee, 1955.
(Latin America)

任強　　哥倫布發現新大陸　　上海
73　上海人民出版社

Jên, Ch'iang. <u>Ko-lun-pu fa Hsien Hsin ta lu.</u> Shanghai, Shang
Hai Jên Min Ch'u pan Shê, 1956, 18p.
(Columbus's Discovery of the New World)

74　刘光华　　美国侵略拉丁美洲简史　　北京
世界知識出版社

Liu, Kuang-hua. <u>Mei-kuo Ch'in Lüeh La- Ting-Mei-Chou-Chien
Shih.</u> Peking, Shih Chieh Chih Shih Ch'u Pan Shê, 1957, 204p.
(A Brief History of U.S. Invasions of Latin
America)

要到了　　時候就　　北京,
75　人民文学出版社

Paim, Alina. <u>Shih Hou Chiu Yao Tao Liao.</u> Peking, Jên Min Wen
Hsüeh Ch'u Pan She, 1959, 386p.
(Time Will Soon Come)

76

Shih Chieh Chih Shih Ch'u Pan Shê. <u>Ying Yung Tou Chêng
Chung ti La-Ting-Mei-Chou Ko Kuo Kung Ch'an Tang.</u> Peking,
Shih Chieh Chih Shih Ch'u Pan Shê, 1959, 201p.
(Bravely- Struggling
Communist Parties of Various Latin American Countries)

在覺醒中的拉丁美洲　　北京,
77　通俗讀物出版社

Ting, Wên. <u>Tsai Chüeh Hsing Chung ti La-Ting-Mei-Chou.</u>
Peking, T'ung Su Tu Wu Ch'u Pan Shê, 1956, 26p.
(Awakening Countries in Latin America)

78 王戈情　　南美河旅行記　　上海
新文芸出版

Wang, Ko-ch'ing. <u>Nan Mei-Chou lü Hsing Chi,</u> Shanghai,
Hsin Wên i Ch'u pan Shê, 1957, 150p.
(A Book of Travel of South America)

79 王央樂　　拉丁美洲文学　　北京
作家出版社

Wang, Yang-lo. <u>La-ting-Mei-Chou Wên Hsüeh.</u>　Peking, Tso
Chia Ch'u Pan Shê, 1963, 2 +201p.
(Latin American Literature)

BRAZIL

80 陸達初　　認識巴西　　台北
中国文化公司 [1951]

Lu, Hsi-Chou. <u>Jên Shih Pa-hsi,</u>　Taipei, Chung Huo Wên
Hua Hung Ssu, 195-, 105p.
(Recognition of Brazil)

81 郑志　九颗红心向祖国　北京
作家出版社

Chêng, Chih. <u>Chiu K'o Hung Hsin Hsiang Tsnoko.</u> Peking,
Tso Chia Chiu Pan Shê, 1965, 5 - 96pp.
(Patriotic-Minded People Heading Toward
Motherland, Cuba)

82 路伟　英雄的古巴　北京
中国少年儿童出版社

Lu, Wei. <u>Ying Hsiung Ti Ku-pa.</u> Peking, Chung-kuo Shao Nien
Êrh T'ung Ch'u Pan Shê, 1961, 91p.
(Heroic Cuba)

83 邵宇　在英雄的古巴　北京
人民美术出版社　[1963]

Shao, Yü. <u>Tsai Ying Hsiung ti Ku-pa.</u> Peking, Jên Min
Ch'u Pan Shê, 1963, 63p.
(In Heroic Cuba)

84　世界知識出版社　　古巴人民的英勇斗争　　北京
　　世界知識出版社

　　Shih Chieh Chih Shih Ch'u Pan Shê. <u>Ku-pa Jên Min ti Ying</u>
　　　<u>Yung Tou Chêng</u>. Peking, Shih Chieh Chih Shih Ch'u Pan Shê,
　　1959, 164p.

　　　　　　　　　　　　　　　　　(Bravely Struggling People
　　of Cuba)

MEXICO

85　馮香生　　墨西哥绘画选　　北京
　　人民美術出版社

　　Fêng, Hsiang-Shêng. <u>Mo-hsi-ko Hui Hua Hsüan</u>. Peking,
　　　Jên Min Mei Shu Ch'u Pan Shê, 1957, 3+3pp. + 48 plates.
　　　　　　　　　(Selected Paintings of Mexico)

86　馮香生　　墨西哥版画选　　北京
　　人民美術出版社

　　Fêng, Hsiang-Shêng. <u>Mo-hsi-ko Pan Hua Hsuan</u>. Peking, Jên
　　　Min Mei Shu Ch'u Pan Shê, 1957, 247p. + 87plates.
　　　　　　　　　(Selected Wood-cut Paintings of Mexico)

ENGLISH-LANGUAGE ITEMS PUBLISHED IN MAINLAND CHINA
AND ON FORMOSA

LIBROS Y FOLLETOS EN INGLES, PUBLICADOS EN CHINA Y
TAIWAN

87   Asian Peoples' Anti-Communist League. Latin America's
Red Peril; a Factual Account of Chinese Communist Plots
in Central and South Americas. Taipei, 1961, 36p.

88   Chang, Ch'ŭn. Sino-Japanese Relations and America. Taipei,
Office of the Government Spokesman, 1952, 58p.

89   Chung-kuo Jên Nin Pao Wei Shih Chieh ho P'ing Wei Yüan Hui.
Commemoration of Chu Yuan, Nicolaus Copernicus, Francois
Rabelais, José Martí. Peking, Chinese People's Committee
for World Peace, 1963, 41p.

90   Declarations of Havana. Peking, Foreign Languages Press,
1962, 40p.

91   Lien Ho Kuo Chung-Kuo T'ung Chih Hui. News Letter. Taipei,
Chinese Association for the United Nations, 1949-

LATIN AMERICA

92　張一飛　　拉丁洲與大西洋三角形在單事訊粹
第15巻　第8号　第50頁

Chang, I-fei. "La-ting Mei-chou yǔ T'ai-hsi-yang San Chio
Hsing." Taipei, Chün shih i sui (15: 8), October 1966, p. 50.
　　　　　("On The Triangularity Formed by the Atlantic
Ocean and the Latin American Countries")

93　許華振訳　　拉丁美洲的経済結合與発展
在国際経済資料　第18巻　第4号　第52頁

Hsǔ, Hua-chên, tr. "La-ting Mei-chou ti Ching Chi Chieh
ho yǔ fa Chan." Taipei, Kuo chi ching chi tzǔ liao (18: 4),
April, 1967, p. 52.
　　　　　("The Development and Economic Unity
of Latin America")

94　徐国賀　　拉丁美洲的医療保険概説
在公保　第8巻　第4号　第20頁

Hsǔ, Kuo-pin. "La-ting Mei-chou ti Illiao pao Hsien Kai K'uang."
Taipei, Kung pao (8: 4), December 1966, p. 20.
　　　　　("General Condition of Medical Insurance in
Latin America")

95 仁澤　　透視拉丁美洲政治經濟情勢
　　情報知識　第5c卷　第10号　第8頁

Jên-tsê. "T'ou Shih La'ting Mei-chou Chêng Chin Ching Chi
　　Ch'ing Shih." Taipei, Ch'ing pao chih shih (5: 10), May,
　　1960, p. 8.
　　　　　("Clairvoyant View of Political and Economic
　　Situation in Latin America")

96 馬從單訳　　拉丁美洲的土地改革與農民就業問題
　　在國際經濟資料　第18卷　第6号　第56頁

Ma, Ts'ung-chủn, tr. "La-ting Mei-chou ti t'u ti Kai ko yử
　　Nung Min Chiu Yeh Wên t'i." Taipei, Kuo chi ching chi
　　tzů liao (18: 6), June, 1967, p. 56.
　　　　　　　　　　("Land Reform and Problems of
　　Farm Employment in Latin America")

97 美国總統（艾森豪）訪問拉丁美洲的重要演說　　台北
　　国際經濟資料月刊　第4卷　第3号　第84頁

"Mei-kuo Tsung T'ung Ai-Sên-Hao Fêng Wên La-ting Mei-Chou
　　ti Chung Yao Yen Shuo." Taipei, Kuo chi ching chi tzử
　　liao yửeh k'an (4: 3), March, 1960, p. 84.
　　("Important Speeches of President Eisenhower During his
　　Visits to Latin American Countries")

98 門羅主義全球化
　　在国際問題參考資料　第298号　第25頁

"Mên-Lo Chu i Ch'üan Ch'iu Hua." Taipei, Kuo chi wên t'i
　　ts'an k'ao tzử liao (298), January, 1966, p. 25.
　　("The Global Spread of Monroeism")

99
南美　三国之経済現説　台北
問題　研究　第5巻　第2号　第45頁

"Nan Mei ABC San Kuo Chih Ching Chi Hsien K'uang."
Taipei, <u>Wên t'i yü yen chiu</u> (5: 2), April, 1960, p. 45.
("Present Conditions in Argentina, Brazil, and Chile")

100
白水　拉丁美洲的軍事問題
在軍　訳粹　第15巻　第9号　第28頁

Pai, Shui. "La-ting Mei-chou ti Chûn Shih Wên T'i."
Taipei, <u>Chûn shih i sui</u> (15: 9), December, 1966, p. 28.
("Military Problems of Latin America")

101
白丁　拉丁美洲的問題
在民主憲政　第32巻　第15号　第6頁及第2号　第7

Pai, Ting. "La-ting Mei-chou ti Wên T'i." Taipei, <u>Min chu
hsien chêng</u> (32: 1), May, 1967, p. 6.
("Problems of Latin America")

102
德恂訳　拉丁美洲的真正革命
在国際現勢　第537号　第16頁

Tê-Hsün, tr. "La-ting Mei-chou ti Chên Chêng ko Ming."
Taipei, <u>Kuo chi hsien shih</u> (537), June 1966, p. 16.
("True Revolution in Latin America")

103　楊仁澤　從拉丁美洲結合運動說到我国與中南美洲之貿易往来　在中国会計　第13卷　第10号　第12頁

Yang, Jên-tsê. "Ts'ung La-ting Mei-chou Chieh ho Yün Tung
Shuo Tao wo Kuo yü Chung-Nan-Mei-Chou Chih Mao i Wang
Lai." Taipei, Chung-kuo k'uai chi (13: 10), December, 1966,
p. 12.
　　　　　　　("On the Effect of Unification Movements in
Latin America on our Foreign Trade with Latin American
Countries")

104　楊仁澤　從拉丁美洲協進聯盟說到中南美的経済與貿易　在貿易週刊　第171号　第7頁

Yang, Jên-tsê. "Ts'ung La-ting Mei-chou Hsieh Chin Lien
Mêng Shuo Tao Chung-Nan-Mei ti Ching Chi yü Mao i."
Taipei, Mao i chou k'an (171), April, 1967, p. 7.
　　　　　　　("On Economy and Foreign Trade of Central
and South America Viewed from the Standpoint of the Alliance
for Progress")

105　楊仁澤　從拉丁美洲協進聯盟說到中南美的経済與貿易　中中　在貿易週刊　第170号　第4頁

Yang, Jên-tsê. "Ts'ung La-ting Mei-chou Hsieh Chin Lien
Mêng Shuo Tao Chung-Nan-Mei ti Ching Chi yü Mao i."
Taipei, Mao i chou k'an (170), March, 1967, p. 4.
　　　　　　　("On Economy and Foreign Trade of Central
and South America Viewed from the Standpoint of the Alliance
for Progress")

106　朱新民　　阿根廷采風記
在旅行雜誌　第24号　第2頁

Chu, Hsin-min. "A-Kên-Ting Ts'ai Fêng Chi." Taipei,
Lü hsing tsa chi (24), May, 1967, p. 2.
　　　　　　("Sightseeing in Argentina")

BRAZIL

107　公共関係服務社　　巴西情況及其移民政策　　台北
中国一周　第518号　第28頁

Kung Kung Kuan Hsi fu wu Shê. "Pa-hsi Ch'ing K'uang Chi Ch'i
i min Chêng Ts'ê." Taipei, Chung-kuo i chou (518), March,
1960, p. 28.
　　　　　　　　("Condition of Brazil and its
Immigration Policy")

李洪鰲　　今日巴西　　台北
108　中國一周　第511号　第17頁

Li, Hung-ao. "Chin Jih Pa-hsi." Taipei, <u>Chung-kuo i chou</u>
　　(511), February, 1960, p. 17.
　　　　　("Brazil Today")

109　論巴西新政府搜捕共產的原則技術　　台北
国際半月刊　第1卷　第3号　第2頁

"Lun Pa-hsi Hsin Chêng fu Sou P'u Kung Tang ti Yǔan Tsê Chi
　　Shu." Taipei, <u>Kuo chi pan yüeh k'an</u> (1: 3), May, 1960, p. 2.
　("On Principal Techniques of the New Regime in Brazil on Checking
　Communism")

110　巴西爆発革命成功　　台北
国際現勢　第423号　第15頁

'Pa-hsi Pao fa ko Ming Ch'êng Kung." Taipei, <u>Kuo chi hsien
　　shih</u> (423), April, 1960, p. 15.
　("The Success of the Explosive Brazilian Revolution")

鄭千惠訳　　中美洲的経済結合
111　在国際経済資料　第18卷　第4号　第57頁

Cheng, Ch'ien-hui, tr. "Chung Mei-chou ti Ching Chi Chieh
ho." Taipei, <u>Kuo chi ching chi tzǔ liao</u> (18: 4), April, 1967,
p. 57.

("On Economic Unity of Central America")

112　徳愉訳　　中美洲的新景象
在国際現勢　第535号　第20頁

Tê-yü, tr. "Chung Mei-chou ti Hsin Ching Hsiang." Taipei,
<u>Kuo chi hsien shih</u> (535), June, 1966, p. 20.
("New Scenes in Central America")

COLOMBIA

蒯増模　　哥倫比亜対外貿易的策進與管理
113　在国際経済資料　第18卷　第3号　第26頁

K'uai, Tsêng-mo. "Ko-Lun-Pi-Ya Tui Wai Mao i ti Ts'ê Chin
yü Kuan li." Taipei, <u>Kuo chi ching chi tzǔ liao</u> (18: 3), March,
1967, p. 26.
("Control and Promotion of Foreign Trade
in Colombia")

徐国魂　今日古巴　台北
114　憲政論壇　第64号　第9頁

Hsü, Kuo-hun. "Chin Jih Ku-pa." Taipei, Hsien chêng lun t'an
(64), April, 1960, p. 9.
　　　("Cuba Today")

黄浦月刊社　論古巴反美　台北
115　黄浦月刊　第95号　第2頁

Huang P'u Yüeh K'an Shê. "Lun Ku-pa Fan Mei." Taipei, Huang
p'u yüeh k'an (95), March, 1960, p. 2.
　　　("On Anti-U.S. Movements in Cuba")

古巴進行肉彈攻勢
116　在国際現勢　第554　号　第28頁

"Ku-pa Chin Hsing Jo Tan Kung Shih." Taipei, Kuo chi hsien shih
(554), October, 1966, p. 28.
("Cuba Begins to Battle with Human Bullets Against her Enemy")

古巴人民生活実況
117　在国際現勢　第517　号　第28頁

"Ku-pa Jên Min Shêng Huo Shih K'uang." Taipei, Kuo chi hsien
shih (517), January, 1966, p. 22.
("Actual Living Conditions of the Cuban People")

118 古巴最近之新情勢　　台北
問題与研究　第4卷　第11号　第43頁

"Ku-pa Tsui Chin Chih Hsin Ch'ing Shih." Taipei, Wên t'i yü
yen chiu (4: 11), March, 1960, p. 43.
("Recent Trends in Cuba")

119 劉珍颺　卡斯楚統治下的古巴　　台北
建設　第8卷　第11号　第5頁

Liu, Chên-hun. "K'a-ssū-ch'u T'ung Chih Hsia ti Ku-pa."
Taipei, Chien shê (8: 11), April, 1960, p. 5.
("Cuba Under the Castro Regime")

120 自清訳　古巴激撃式
在軍事雑誌　第33卷　第10号　第14頁

Tzū-Ch'ing, tr. "Ku-pa yu Chi Chan." Taipei, Chün shih tsa
chih (33: 10), July, 1965, p. 14.
("Guerrilla Wars in Cuba")

121 袁道豐　古巴駆逐西班牙大使　　台北
新聞天地　第626号　第11頁

Yüan, Tao-fêng. "Ku-pa Ch'ü Chu Hsi-pan-ya ta Shih."
Taipei, Hsin wên t'ien ti (626), January, 1960, p. 11.
("Expulsion of the Spanish Ambassador from
Cuba")

DOMINICAN REPUBLIC

122 　白丁　　多明尼加会变成古巴第二嗎
　　　在民主憲政　第28卷　第5号　第7頁

Pai, Ting. "To-Ming-ni-Chia Hui Pien Ch'êng Ku-pa ti Êrh
　Ma?" Taipei, Min chu hsien chêng (28: 5), July, 1965,
　p. 7.
　　　　("Will the Dominican Republic Become a Second Cuba")

123 　德怡訳　　美国可以擺脱多明尼加内争的紛擾嗎
　　　在国際現勢　第536号　第17頁

Tê-I, tr. "Mei-Kuo K'o i Pait'o To-Ming-Ni-Chia Nei Chêng
　ti Fên Jao Ma?" Taipei, Kuo chi hsien shih (536), June
1966, p. 17.
　　　　("Can U. S. Quell the Internal Disturbance in the
Dominican Republic? ")

NICARAGUA

124 　富弘義　　尼加拉瓜行脚　　台北
　　　在旅行雜誌　第19号　第32頁

Fu, Hung-i. "Ni-Chia-la-Kua Hsing Chiao." Taipei, Lü hsing
　tsa chih (19), December, 1966, p. 32.
　　　　("Traveling in Nicaragua")

張文仲　　巴拿馬運河的前途
125　在軍事訳粹　第15卷　第9号　第20頁

Chang, Wên-Chung. "Pana-ma Yün Ho ti Ch'ien Tu." Taipei,
Chün shih i sui (15: 9), December, 1966, p. 20.
　　　　　　　　("The Future of the Panama Canal")

都本仁　　巴拿馬反美運動的経済　　台北
126　民主憲政　第17卷　第7号　第22頁

Tu, Pên-jên. "Pa-na-ma fan Mei Yün Tung ti Ching Wei."
Taipei, Min chu hsien chêng (17: 7), January, 1960, p. 22.
　　　　　　　("The Path of the Anti-U.S. Movements in
Panama")

楊春楼　　巴拉圭處女地
127　在民主憲政　第29卷　第1号　第23頁

Yang, Ch'un-lou. "Pa-La-Kuei -- Ch'u nü ti." Taipei, Min
chu hsien chêng (29: 1), January, 1966, p. 23.
　　　　　　　　("Paraguay -- The Virgin Land")

徐斌　　秘魯·利瑪　　台北
128　在旅行雜誌　第 19 号　第 46 頁

Hsü, Pin. "Pi-lu, Li-ma." Taipei, <u>Lü hsing tsa chih</u> (19),
December, 1966, p. 46.
　　　　　("Peru, Lima")

URUGUAY

蕭瑜　　在烏拉圭十三年看烏拉圭
129　在學粹　第 8 卷　第 4 号　第 19 頁

Hsiao, Yü. "Tsai Wu-La-Kuei Shih San Nien K'an Wu-La-Kuei."
Taipei, <u>Hsüeh sui</u> (8: 4), June, 1966, p. 19.
　　　　　("Watching the Progress of Uruguay During my
Thirteen Years' Stay in Uruguay")

INDIA

The Ph. D. degree in International Relations and Area
Studies, awarded by the Indian School of International
Studies in New Delhi, covers research on the Latin
American area, as well as on North America.

In this bibliography the English translation of the title of
each bibliographic item is to be found directly under the
title in the original language, and immediately following
the entire bibliographic description. Bengali, Hindi, Gujarati,
Malayalam, Marathi, Oriya, Telugu, and Urdu are the
principal languages of India. Following the transliteration
of each item there may be found, in parentheses the
corresponding Indian language.

El Doctorado en Asuntos Internacionales y Regionales,
otorgado por la Escuela Indiana de Estudios Internacionales,
situada en Nueva Delhi, abarca investigaciones sobre
Latinoamérica así como América del Norte.

En esta bibliografía la traducción inglesa del título de cada
asiento se encuentra directamente bajo el título de la lengua
original, seguida de la ficha entera. Bengalí, Hindi,
Gujarati, Malayalam, Marathi, Oriya, Telugu y Urdu son
las lenguas principales de India. Después de la transcripción
de cada asiento se encuentra, en paréntesis, el idioma
correspondiente de este país.

I. Books

LATIN AMERICA

130 Bagala, Sitaram, & Sarad Bagala

बागला, सीताराम और बागला, शरद

उत्तरी अमेरिका. कानपुर, किताब घर, १९६०.

१४, ४९६ पृ०, मानचित्र. २२सें० २०.००

Bagala, Sitaram, & Sarad Bagala. <u>Uttari Amerika.</u> Kanapur,
Kitabghar, 1960, 496p. (Hindi)
                                    (North America)
-Includes description of some Latin American countries.

131 Balakṛṣṇa Piḷḷa, Umayanallūr

Balakṛṣṇa Piḷḷa, Umayanallūr. <u>Māyanmārum Iṅkākaḷum.</u> Kōṭṭayam,
Sāhityapravarttaka Sahakaraṇasaṅgham, 1961, 282p. (Malayalam)
                                    (The Mayas and Incas)

132 Gauḍa, Kṛpāśaṅkar

गौड़, कृपाशंकर,

उत्तरी अमेरिका की भौगोलिक समीक्षा ।

वाराणसी, हिन्दी प्रचारक पुस्तकालय, १९६४.

८,५३० प०, निर्देशन. मानचित्र. २४.५ से० २५.००

Gauḍa, Kṛpāśaṅkar. <u>Uttarī Amérikā Kī Bhaugolika Samīkṣā,</u>
Benares, Hindi Pracharak Pustakalaya, 1964, 530p. (Hindi)
                        (Geographical Account of North America)
-Includes description of some Latin American countries.

133 Jog, D. V.

प्राणावरचा—प्रवास

Jog, D. V. <u>Prāṇāvarcā Pravās,</u> Bombay, Vora, 1960, 32p.
(Marathi)
          (Travel in South America)

134 Padmā Rājagopāl

प्राणावरचा   प्रवास

Padmā Rājagopāl. <u>Ulaka Vilaṅkukaḷ: Vataten Amerikka.</u>
Madras, Valluvar Pannai, 1958, 52p. (Marathi)
          (Animals of South America)

135 Peter, K. C.

പീറ്റർ, കെ. സി.
അപ്പുറത്തെ അമേരിക്ക (തെക്കേ അമേരിക്ക). തൃശൂർ, കറന്റ് ബുക്സ്,
1957. 338 പേ.

Peter, K. C. Appuratte Amēriykka (Tekke Amēriykka). Trichur, Current Books, 1957, 338p. (Malayalam)
(The America of the Other Side: South America)
-A Travelogue.

BRAZIL

136 Mathew, M. Kuziveli

മാത്യു എം. കുഴിവേലി
ബ്രസീൽ. തിരുവനന്തപുരം
ബാലൻ പബ്ലിക്കേഷൻസ്,
1964. 154 പേ.

Mathew, M, Kuziveli. Brazil. Tiruvanantapuram, Balan Publications, 1964, 154p. (Malayalam)
(Brazil)

137   Miśra, Godabariśa

ମିଶ୍ର , ଗୋଦାବରୀଶ

ମଧ୍ୟ ଆମେରିକା । ବ୍ରହ୍ମପୁର , ନିୟୁ ଷ୍ଟୁଡେଣ୍ଟସ୍ ଷ୍ଟୋର ନ୍ଃ, ୧୯୫୨

୍ୟ, ୪୦ପୃ:   P୮ ୧ଓ.ନି:   । ଯୁରୀ ୬୦.୧୬ [୪୦.ଓ୍] .

Miśra, Godabariśa. <u>Madhya Amerikā</u>. Brahmapur, New Students'
   Store, 1952, 40p. (Oriya)
                 (Central America)
-A Travelogue on Mexico.

138   Pāl, Mākhan

পাল, মাখন
বিপ্লবার বিপ্লব । কলিকাতা, লোকায়ত সাহিত্য চক্র, ৮ ১৯৬১ /
২, ৯০ পৃ: । ১৮ সেমি । ১.০০

Pāl, Mākhan. <u>Kubār Viplav.</u> Calcutta, Lokayat Sahitya Chakra,
   1961, 90p. (Bengali)
            (Cuba's Revolution)

139   Sen, Saurīn

সেন, সৌরীন
আমের স্বাদ নোনতা । কলিকাতা, মৈত্র প্রকাশনী,
১৯৬৫ । ২৯২ পৃ: । ২১.৩ সেমি । ৯.০০

Sen, Saurīn. <u>Ākher Svād Nonṭā.</u> Calcutta, Maitra Prakasani,
   1965, 292p. (Bengali)
            (The Sugarcane Tastes Salty)
-Fiction based on political events of Cuba.

MEXICO

140 Kumār, C. B.

കുമാർ, സി. ബി.
മെക്സിക്കൻ നാട്ടുകളിൽ. കോട്ടയം.
പി. എൽ. സരോജിനിദേവി;
വിതരണം നാഷണൽ ബുക്ക് സ്റ്റാൾ,
1959. 83 പു.

Kumār, C. B. Meksikkan Nātukalil, Kōttayam, P. L. Sarojini-devi; distributed by National Book Stall, 1959, 83p. (Malayalam)
(In Mexican Countrysides)
-A Travelogue.

141 Yādav, Rāmeśvaraprasād

यादव, रामेश्वरप्रसाद,
उत्तरी अमेरिका. लखनऊ, राष्ट्रधर्म प्रकाशन, १९५७.
१०, १७५ पृ०, मानचित्र. २१ सें०. ५.००

Yādav, Rāmeśvaraprasād. Uttari Amerikā. Lucknow, Rashtradharma, Prakashan 1957, 175p. (Hindi)
(North America)
-See: Mexico, pp. 119-120.

(Note: Due to the fact that English has been extensively spoken in India for over one hundred years, and in view of the dearth of materials from that nation with respect to Latin America, this English-language section has been added).

(Nota: Debido a que el inglés se habla en India por más de cientos de años, y en vista de la escasez de materiales, hemos incluido esta sección de inglés).

LATIN AMERICA

142   India (Republic) Indian Trade Delegation to Latin American Countries
       Report of Indian Trade Delegation to Latin American Countries: Brazil, Argentina, Chile, Bolivia, Peru, Colombia, and Venezuela, June-July 1964. New Delhi, Directorate of Commercial Publicity, Ministry of Commerce, Government of India, 1965, 50p.

143   Lal, Chaman. Hindu America, Revealing the Story of the Romance of the Srya Vanshi Indus and Depicting the Imprints of Hindu Culture on the Two Americas. 3d ed. Bombay, New Book Co., 1948, 267p.

144   Lal, Chaman. Who Discovered America? Bombay, New Book Co., 1951, 98p.

145   Rai, Lajpat. Latin America; a Socio-Economic Study. New Delhi, Institute for Afro-Asian and World Affairs, 1963, 233p.

CUBA

146   Dinesh, M. R. *Cuba Wins Freedom.* New Delhi, New Delhi
         Book Club, 1967, 137p.

147   Karanjia, Rustom Khurshedji. *Castro-storm over Latin America.*
         Bombay, Perennial Press, 1961, 159p.

MEXICO

148   India (Republic) Parliament. Joint Committee on the Prevention
         of Food Adulteration. *(Amendment) Bill, 1963.* New Delhi,
         Lok Sabha Secretariat, 1964, 46p.

WEST INDIES AND THE CARIBBEAN

Indian Institute of Foreign Trade. *India's Trade Prospect With
   West Indies, with Special Inference to Trinidad and Tobago.*
New Delhi, 1965, 50p.

INDONESIA

Although Indonesian universities offer no courses in Latin American Studies, The Indonesian Institute of World Affairs of the University of Indonesia in Djakarta concerns itself with Latin American affairs within its overall coverage of international matters. Cultural exchanges with Latin American nations are effected through the Foundation for Cultural Cooperation (Jajasan Kerdja-sama Kebudajaan) in Djakarta.

In this section the English translation of the title of each bibliographic item is to be found directly under the title in the original language, and immediately following the entire bibliographic description.

Aunque las universidades indonesianas no ofrecen cursos en Estudios Latinoamericanos, el Instituto Indonesiano de Asuntos Internacionales de la Universidad de Indonesia, en la ciudad de Djakarta, trata asuntos latinoamericanos dentro de sus intereses globales. Los intercambios culturales con los países latinoamericanos se llevan a cabo por medio de la Fundación para Cooperación Cultural (Jajasan Kerdja-sama Kebudajaan), en Djakarta.

En esta sección la traducción inglesa del título de cada asiento se encuentra directamente bajo el título de la lengua original, seguida de la ficha entera.

I. Books

LATIN AMERICA

150 Abdullah Bin Haji, Ismail. <u>Ilmu Alam Menengah II (Benua-benua Di-hemispiar Selatan)</u>. Revised by Abdul Rahman bin Mohd. Ali. Kota Bharau, Pustaka Aman Press, 1965.
(Geography for Secondary School II: Continents in the Southern Hemisphere)

CUBA

151 Jajasan, Pembaruan. <u>Viva Cuba.</u> Djakarta, 1963, 27p.

152 Sjariffudin, Amak. <u>Kuba Dengan Revolusinja.</u> Surabaya, Grip, 196-?, 88p.
(Cuba and its Revolution)

II. Periodical Articles

LATIN AMERICA

153 Fitzgibbon, Russell H. "Dictatorship dan Demokrasi di Amerika Latin." Djakarta, Siasat baru (15: 707), 1961, pp. 24-27.
("Dictatorship and Democracy in Latin America")

154 Samsuhaedi, M. L. "Hubungan Indonesia Dengan Amerika Latin." Djakarta, Utusan (3: 1), 1960, pp. 35-42.
("Relations Between Indonesia and Latin America")

CUBA

155 "Sekelumit Tjerita Tentang: 'Cuba por los Cubanos'." Djakarta, Berkala pembangunan (2: 3), 1961, pp. 31-42.
("An Impression of Cuba: 'Cuba for the Cubans'")

JAPAN

Because of long-standing Japanese emigration to Latin America
(mainly to Brazil) dating from the mid-19th century, there has
been continuous contact between Japan and Latin America.
However, the study of Brazil was begun in the early years
of the twentieth century at the School of Advanced Commercial
Studies in Kobe, Japan, where a Brazilian studies
association was established, which issued a journal. Before
World War II this institution was the only one which was
concerned with the study of Latin America.

Due to the interest of export-import firms and investors in the
opportunities available in Latin America following World War
II, economic studies were undertaken by the Japanese Government,
banks, firms and various universities. Research in the fields
of language, history, geography, and anthropology, among
other areas, was begun, and is continuing apace. Sophia
University in Tokyo had in 1967 inaugurated a Master's degree
program in Latin American Studies, and its Ibero-American
Institute publishes a newsletter. St. Paul's University
in Tokyo, and the Tokyo University of Foreign Study offer courses
on Latin America. Kobe University, which grew out of the
School of Advanced Commercial Studies in Kobe, inaugurated a chair
of Latin American economics after World War II, and subsequently
set up chairs of government and sociology. Kanagawa University
and other educational institutions have also instituted courses in
Latin American studies.

In addition to many cultural and social organizations concerned
with the Latin American countries, there has been established
a Latin American Association (Raten Amerika Kyokai), located
in the Maruzen Building, Number 6, 2-Chome, Nihonbashidori,
Chuo-ku, in Tokyo. University faculty members, advanced
students and others interested in the study of Latin America
in many disciplines contribute to the research of the Association,
which also sponsors conferences.

In 1964 the Raten America Kyokai published a 175-page annotated
bibliography in the Japanese language, entitled Nihon no Latin

America Chosa Kenkyusho Gaisetsu. This reference source covers materials on Latin America published in Japan through the year 1963. The books, pamphlets, documents and periodical articles to be found on the following pages of this section on Japan have been published since 1964, and readers desiring to locate items published in Japan prior to 1964 are directed to the above-mentioned publication of the Raten America Kyokai. On the following pages the English translation of the title of each bibliographic item is to be found directly under the title in the original language, and immediately following the entire bibliographic description.

Debido a la emigración japonesa a la América Latina (principalmente a Brasil) iniciada aproximadamente durante la quinta década del siglo XIX, han habido contactos continuos entre Japón y la América Latina. Los estudios sobre Brasil en Japón fueron inaugurados en la Escuela de Estudios Comerciales Superiores en la ciudad de Kobe, durante los primeros años del siglo XX. En esta Escuela se estableció una asociación de estudios brasileños, la cual publicó una revista. Antes de la Segunda Guerra Mundial, fué esta institución la única en Japón que se interesó por Estudios Latinoamericanos.

Después de la Segunda Guerra Mundial, debido al interés de compañías exportadoras e importadoras en las oportunidades comerciales en Latinoamérica, el Gobierno Japonés, así como bancos, firmas y varias universidades desempeñaron investigaciones económicas. También se iniciaron estudios en los campos de lenguas, historia, geografía y antropología, y actualmente se aumentan en cantidad. La Universidad Sophia en Tokyo inauguro en 1967 un nuevo programa de Licenciatura (o sea, título de Maestro en Artes) en Asuntos Latinoamericanos, y su Instituto Iberoamericano publica un noticiero. La Universidad San Pablo de Tokyo, y la Universidad de Estudios Extranjeros

en Tokyo ofrecen cursos sobre la América Latina. La
Universidad de Kobe, sucesora de la Escuela de Estudios
Comerciales Superiores, inauguró una cátedra de economía
Latinoamericana después de la Segunda Guerra Mundial, y
poco mas tarde estableció cátedras de ciencia política y
sociología. La Universidad de Kanagawa y otras instituciones
también ofrecen asignaturas de interés latinoamericano.

En Japón hay varias organizaciones culturales, sociales y
comerciales latinoamericanas. Catedráticos, estudiantes
universitarios y otros han establecido la Asociación Latinoamericana (Raten America Kyokai), situada en el Edificio
Maruzen, Número 6, 2-Chome, Nihonbashidori, Chuo-ku,
en Tokyo. Los miembros contribuyen a las investigaciones
dirigidas por parte de la Asociación, y participan en sus
conferencias regulares.

En 1964 publicó la Raten America Kyokai una bibliografía
que consta de 175 páginas en japonés, con el título, Nihon
no Latino America Chosa Kenkyusho Gaisetsu. Esta fuente
de consulta abarca materiales sobre Latinoamérica publicados
en Japón desde hace muchos años y hasta el año 1963. Los
libros, folletos, documentos y artículos de revista en las
páginas siguientes de este libro, en esta sección japonesa,
han sido publicados desde 1964. Los interesados en libros
publicados en Japón antes de 1964 se dirigen al mencionado
libro de la Raten America Kyokai. En las páginas siguientes
la traducción inglesa del título de cada asiento se encuentra
directamente bajo el título de la lengua original, seguida de
la ficha entera.

I. Books

LATIN AMERICA

156　アジア経済研究所
ラテン　アメリカの経済統合に関する
文献と雑誌　記事　東京　アジア経済研究所

Ajia Keizai Kenkyujo. <u>Raten Amerika no Keizai Togo ni Kansuro Bunken to Zasshi Kiji.</u> Tokyo, Ajia Keiz Kankyujo, 1964, 56p.

(Bibliography on Economic Integration in Latin America)

157　アジア経済研究所　ラテン.アメリカの経済　2
　　　東京　同所　1964 年　270 p.

Ajia Keizai Kenkyûjo. <u>Raten Amerika no Keizai 2.</u> Tokyo, 1964, 270p.

(Latin American Economy: 2)

158　アジア経済研究所　ラテン.アメリカの経済
　　　統合に関する文献と雑誌記事（II）
　　　東京　同所　1967 年　59 p

Ajia Keizai Kenkyûjo. <u>Raten Amerika no Keizaitôgô ni Kansuru Bunken to Zasshikiji (II).</u> Tokyo, 1967, 59p.

(Bibliography on Economic Integration in Latin America: II)

159 アジア租税研究会
ラテンアメリカ諸国の租税制度

東京 アジア経済研究所

Ajia Sozei Kenkyukai. <u>Raten Amerika Shokoku no Sozei Seido</u>. 5v.
Tokyo, Ajia Keizai Kenkyujo, 1966-67.
                    (Taxation Systems of Latin American
Countries)

160 外務省経済局ラテン.アメリカ課　アメリカ大陸の
口蹄疫に関する報告　東京　同課　1967 年
75 p.

Gaimusho Keizaikyoku Raten Amerikaka. <u>Amerika Tairiku no
Koteieki ni Kansuru Hokoku</u>. Tokyo, 1967, 75p.
(Report on the Hoof and Mouth Disease in the Western Hemisphere)

161 外務省経済局ラテン.アメリカ課　中南米 23 カ国
開発計画便覧　メキシコ．中米．カリブ海篇
東京　同課　1966 年　22 p.

Gaimusho Keizaikyoku Raten Amerikaka. <u>Chûnanbei 23 ka Koku
Kaihatsu Keikaku Binran Mekishiko, Chûbei, Karibukai Hen</u>.
Tokyo, 1966, 22p.
(Summary of Development Plans in the 23 Latin America Countries:
Mexico, Central America and Caribbean Countries)

162   外務省経済局ラテン．アメリカ課　中南米 23 カ国
　　　　　開発計画便覧　南米篇　東京　同課
　　　　　1966 年　**44** p.

Gaimusho Keizaikyoku Raten Amerikaka.　Chûnanbei 23 ka
Koku Kaihatsu Keikaku Binran Nanbei Hen.　Tokyo, 1966,
44p.
(Summary of Development Plans in the 23 Latin American
Countries)

163   外務省経済局ラテン．アメリカ課　ラフタ
　　　　　（**LAFTA**）便覧　東京　同課　**1967** 年　**152** p.

Gaimusho Keizaikyoku Raten Amerikaka.　LAFTA Binran.
Tokyo, 1967, 152p.

　　　　　　　　　　　　　　　　　(On LAFTA)

164   外務省経済局ラテン．アメリカ課　ラフタ域内
　　　　　貿易動向．相互補完協定に関する調査報告
　　　　　東京　**1965** 年　**54** p.

Gaimusho Keizaikyoku Raten Amerikaka.　LAFTA Ikinai Boeki
Dôkô, Sôgo Hokan Kyôtei ni Kansuru Chôsa Hôkoku.　Tokyo,
1965, 54p.
(Report on the Survey of Internal Trade and Mutual Trade
Cooperation Agreement of LAFTA)

165   外務省経済局ラテン.アメリカ課　最近の中南米
　　　　主要国経済．貿易の動向　東京　同課
　　　　1966年　54 p.

Gaimusho Keizaikyoku Raten Amerikaka. <u>Saikin no Chûnanbei</u>
<u>Shuyô Koku Keizai Boeki no Dôkô.</u> Tokyo, 1966, 54p.
(Recent Trend of the Economy and Trade in Principal Latin
American Countries)

166   外務省　経済局　ラテン.アメリカ課　わが国の
　　　　ラテン.アメリカ諸国からの主要品目別
　　　　輸入実績1963年　東京　同省
　　　　1964年　59 p.

Gaimusho Keizaikyoku Raten Amerikaka. <u>Wagakuni no Raten</u>
<u>Amerika Shokoku Karano Shuyô Hinmokubetsu Yunyû Jisseki</u>
<u>1963 Nen.</u> Tokyo, 1964, 59p.
(Japan's Imports from Latin American Countries by Principal
Commodity, 1963)

167   羽仁　進　羽仁　進, 左　幸子のアンデス旅行
　　　　東京　徳間書店　1966年　246　p.

Hani, Susumu. <u>Hani Susumu, Hidari Sachiko no Andesu Ryokô.</u>
Tokyo, Tokuma Shoten, 1966, 246p.
　　　　　　　　(A Trip to the Andes by Mr. and Mrs. Hani,
Motion Picture Director and Actress)

168 羽仁 進
左幸子 共著

羽仁 進・左幸子 のアンデス
旅行 東京 徳間書店
1966 246 p.

Hani, Susumu, & Sachiko Hidari. Hani Susumu Hidari Sachiko
no Andesu Ryokô. Tokyo, Tokuma Shoten, 1966, 246p.
(The Travel Records of Susumu
Hani and Sachiko Hidari)

169 石井貫一 わが国の中南米政策
東京 鹿島研究所出版会 1965年 260 p.

Ishii, Kan'ichi. Wagakuni no Chunambei Seisaku. Tokyo, Kajima
Kenkyusho Shuppankai, 1965, 260p.
(Japanese Policy Towards Latin America)

170 石井貫一。ラテンアメリカを訪ねて 東京 ラテン・アメリカ協会
Ishii, Kan'ichi. Raten Amerika o Tazunete. Tokyo, Raten
Amerika Kyôkai, 1965, 260p.
(On Visiting Latin America)

171 　　泉 靖一　アンデスの芸術　東京　中央公論
　　　　美術出版　1964 年　166 p.

Izumi, Seiichi. <u>Andesu no Geijutsu.</u> Tokyo, Chuokoron
Bijutsu Shuppan, 1964, 166p.
　　　　　　　　(Andean Arts)

172 　　泉　靖一編　世界の文化第16 中南米と
　　　　アンデス　東京　河出書房新社　1965 年

Izumi, Seiichi, ed. <u>Sekai no Bunka No. 16 Chūbei to Andesu.</u>
Tokyo, Kawade Shobo Shinsha, 1965, 167p.
　　　　　　　　　　(World Culture No. 16: Central America and
the Andes)

173 　　泉　靖一　佐藤　久編　世界の文化地理
　　　　第17 巻南アメリカ　東京　講談社
　　　　1965 年　375 p.

Izumi, Seiichi & Hisashi Sato, ed.　<u>Sekai no Bunka Chiri, No. 17:</u>
<u>Minami Amerika.</u> Tokyo, Kodansha, 1965, 375p.
　　　　　　　　　　　(World Cultural Geography
No. 17 [South America])

174 　　菅　泰子　秘境アンデスの四季　東京　潮文社
　　　　1966 年　226 p.

Kan, Yasuko. <u>Hikyô Andesu no Shiki,</u> Tokyo, Chobunsha, 1966,
226p.
　　　　　　(Four Seasons in the Andes)

175　北川　豊編　ラテン.アメリカの統計
　　　東京　アジア経済研究所　1965年　379 p.

Kitagawa, Yutaka, ed. Raten Amerika no Tôkei. Tokyo, Ajia
Keizai Kenkyûjo, 1965, 379p.
(Statistics on Latin America)

176　神戸大学経済経営研究所編　ラテン.アメリカ
　　　経済の諸問題　神戸　同所　1968年
　　　182 p.

Kobe Daigaku Keizai Keiei Kenkyûjo, ed. Raten Amerika
Keizai no Shomondai. Kobe, 1968, 182p.
(Problems of the
Latin American Economy)

177　熊本大学中南米事情研究所　中南米における漁業事業
Kumamoto Daigaku. Chûnanbei Jijô Kenkyûjo. Kumamoto,
Chûnanbei ni Okeru Gyogyô Jigyô, 1965.
(Fishing Industries of Central and South
America)

178　LAFTA調査チーム編　LAFTA調査チーム報告書
　　　東京　1966年　106 p.

LAFTA Chôsa Chiimu, ed. LAFTA Chôsa Chiimu Hôkokusho.
Tokyo, 1966, 106p.
(Report of the LAFTA Investigating
Team)

179　　日本シオス協会　ラテン．アメリカ経済の問題点
　　　東京　同会　1965年　60 p.

Nihon CIOS Kyokai.　Raten Amerika Keizai no Mondaiten.
　Tokyo, 1965, 60p.
(Problems of the Latin American Economy)

180　　大原美範編−アンヂス諸国の経済発展
　　　東京　アジア経済研究所　1965年　193 p.

Ohara, Yoshinori, ed.　Andesu Shokoku no Keizai Hatten.
　Tokyo, Ajia Keizai Kenkyusho, 1965, 193p.
　　　　　　　　　　　　(Economic Development in the Andean
Countries)

181　　大原美範編　ラテン．アメリカ自由貿易連合
　　　東京　アジア経済研究所　1966年　285 p.

Ohara, Yoshinori, ed.　Raten Amerika Jiyû Boeki Rengô.
　Tokyo, Ajia Keizai Kenkyusho, 1966, 285p.
　　　　　　　　　　　　(Latin American Free Trade Association)

182　　.大原美範編　ラテン．アメリカ経済統合と経済開発
　　　東京　アジア経済研究所　1968年　212 p.

Ohara, Yoshinori, ed.　Raten Amerika Keizaitôgô to Keizaikaihatsu.
　Tokyo, Ajia Keizai Kenkyusho, 1968, 212p.
　　　　　　　　　　　　(Economic Integration and Development
in Latin America)

183　大山勇　南アメリカ

Oyama, Isamu et al.　Minami Amerika.　Tokyo,
Nippon Hôsô Kyôkai, 1964, 270p.
(South America)

184　ラテン.アメリカ協会　米国における ラテン.
　　アメリカ研究センター ── その組織と
　　活動　東京　同会　1966年　43 p.

Raten Amerika Kyokai.　Beikoku ni Okeru Raten Amerika
　Kenkyû Sentâ--Sono Soshiki to Katsudô.　Tokyo, 1966, 43p.
(Latin American Research Centers in the U.S.A.: their
Organization and Activities)

185　ラテン.アメリカ協会　ラテン.アメリカ貿易
　　手帳　東京　同会　1967年　69 p.

Raten Amerika Kyokai.　Raten Amerika Bôeki Techô.　Tokyo,
　1967, 69p.
(Latin American Trade Memo)

186　ラテンアメリカ研究所　ラテンアメリカ事典　東京　ラテン.アメリカ研究所

Raten Amerika Kenkyûjo.　Raten Amerika Jiten.　Tokyo, Raten
　Amerika Kenkyûjo, 1964, 798p.
(Dictionary of Latin America)

187　ラテン・アメリカ経済委員会　ラテンアメリカ経済の躍進的政策

Raten Amerika Keizai Iinkai.　<u>Raten Amerika Keizai no</u>
<u>Yakushinteki Seisaku.</u>　Tokyo, Raten Amerika Kyokai,
1965, 131p.
(Progressive Economic Policies of Latin America)

188　ラテン アメリカ 協会
　　　ラテン アメリカ の 歴史 東京　中央公論社

Raten Amerika Kyokai.　<u>Raten Amerika no Rekishi.</u>　Tokyo,
Chûô Kôron Sha, 1964, 633p.
(History of Latin America)

189　ラテン.アメリカ協会　ラテン.アメリカ産業
　　　貿易統計集覧　1966年版　東京　同会
　　　1966年　139 p.

Raten Amerika Kyokai.　<u>Raten Amerika Sangyô Bôeki Tôkei</u>
<u>Shûran, 1966 Nenban.</u>　Tokyo, 1966, 139p.
(Collection of Statistics on Latin American Industry and Trade,
1966.

190　ラテン.アメリカ協会　ラテン.アメリカ諸国への
　　　日本人移住史　東京　同会　1965年
　　　145 p.

Raten Amerika Kyokai.　<u>Raten Amerika Shokoku eno Nihonjin Ijûshi.</u>
　Tokyo, 1965, 145p.
(History of Japanese Emigrants in Latin American Countries)

191 ラテン・アメリカ協会、ラテン・アメリカ諸国の　政党、
　　　続　ラテニ アメリカ協会

Raten Amerika Kyokai. <u>Raten Amerika Shokoku no Seitô</u>. Tokyo,
　　Raten Amerika Kyokai, 1965, 278p.
(Political Parties of Latin American Countries)

192　ラテン・アメリカ協会　ラテン・アメリカ諸国の
　　　　政党――アルゼンチン　ベルー　東京
　　　同会　1966年 162 p.

Raten Amerika Kyokai. <u>Raten Amerika Shokoku no Seitô</u>--
Aruzentin, Perû. Tokyo, 1966, 162p.
(Political Parties in Latin American Countries--Argentina
and Peru)

193　ラテン・アメリカ協会　ラテン・アメリカ諸国の
　　　　政党――コロンビア・メキシコ・イネズエラ
　　　東京　同会　1965年 278 p.

Raten Amerika Kyokai. <u>Raten Amerika Shokoku no Seitô</u>--
Coronbia, Mekishiko, Benezuera. Tokyo, 1965, 278p.
(Political Parties in Latin American Countries--Colombia,
Mexico and Venezuela)

194　ラテン・ア、リカ協会　研究部　ラテン・アメリカ
　　　東京　ラテン・アメリカ協会　1966年 211 p.

Raten Amerika Kyokai, Kenkyubu. <u>Raten Amerika</u>.   Tokyo,
　　Raten Amerika Kyokai, 1966, 211p.
(Latin America)

195　ラテン.アメリカ協会　ラテン.アメリカを訪ねて
　　　　東京　同会　1965年　260 p.

Raten Amerika Kyokai. <u>Raten Amerika wo Tazunete</u>. Tokyo,
1965, 260p.
(Impressions of Latin America)

196　佐藤信行　未開と文明の交点 —— 南米諸族の
　　　　人類学覚え書　東京　日本放送出版協会
　　　　1967年　219 p.

Sato, Nobuyuki. <u>Mikai to Bunmei no Kôten-Nambei Shozoku no</u>
<u>Jinruigaku Oboegaki</u>. Tokyo, Nihon Hoso Shuppan Kyokai,
1967, 219p.
(The Intersection of Barbarism and Civilization: Anthropological
Note on South American Tribes)

197　菅　泰子
　　　　秘境アンデスの四季
　　　東京　潮文社　1966 p.226

Suga, Yasuko. <u>Hikyô Andesu no Shiki</u>. Tokyo, Chôbun Sha,
1966, 226p.

(Four Seasons of the Andes)

198　高野　悠　ラテン.アメリカ－東京　日本放送
　　　出版協会　1968 年　313 p.

Takano, Hisashi. Raten Amerika.   Tokyo, Nihon Hoso
　　Shuppan Kyokai, 1968, 313p.
　　　　　　　　　　　(Latin America)

199　渡辺勇雄　中南米の風情と移民　札幌
　　　北書房　1966 年　240 p.

Watabe, Isao. Chûnanbei no Fuzei to Imin. Sapporo, Kita
　　Shoten, 1966, 240p.
　　　　　　　　(Feelings of Latin America and Its Immigrants)

200　山本省一　ラテン．アメリカの移住地－青森
　　　県出身者を訪ねて　青森　東奥日報社
　　　1967 年　172 p .

Yamamoto, Shoichi. Raten Amerika no Ijûchi--Aomori Ken
　　Shusshinsha wo Tazunete. Aomori, Toô Nipposha, 1967, 172p.
(Japanese Colonies in Latin America: Visiting the Emigrants
from Aomori Prefecture)

201　山本進　中南米　東京　岩波書店

Yamamoto, Susumu. Chûnambei. Tokyo, Iwanami Shoten, 1965,
　　150p.
　　　　　　　　　　(Central and South America)

202　淀川　正樹　訳

コロンビア・ベネズエラ

東京　時事通信社　1966.

160p.

Yodokawa, Masaki, tr. <u>Korombia, Benezuera</u>.　Tokyo, Jiji
Tsūshin Sha, 1966, 160p.

(Colombia,　Venezuela)

203　吉田　実　ラテン・アメリカ報告　東京　青林書院
新社　**1966**年　**360** p.

Yoshida, Minoru.　<u>Raten Amerika Hôkoku</u>.　Tokyo, Seirin
Shoin Shinsha, 1966, 360p.

(Latin American Report)

204 アジア租税研究会編　ラテン.アメリカ諸国の
租税制度 III （ アルゼンチン ）　東京
アジア経済研究所　1967 年　221 p.

Ajia Sozei Kenkyukai, ed. Raten Amerika Shokoku no
Sozeiseido III (Aruzentin). Tokyo, Ajia Keizai Kenkyûjo,
1967, 221p.
(Taxation Systems of Latin America, III: Argentina)

205 外務省経済局ラテン.アメリカ課　アルゼンチン
経済開発計画に関する報告　東京　同課
1964 年　119 p.

Gaimusho Keizaikyoku Raten Amerikaka. Aruzentin Keizai
Kaihatsu Keikaku ni Kansuru Hôkoku. Tokyo, 1964, 119p.
(Report on the Economic Development Plan of Argentina)

206 外務省経済局ラテン.アメリカ課　アルゼンチン
の信用構造　東京　同課　1967 年
113 p.

Gaimusho Keizaikyoku Raten Amerikaka. Aruzentin no Shinyo
Kôzô, Tokyo, 1967, 113p.
(Monetary Structure of Argentina)

207 　細野昭雄　アルゼンチンの経済発展　東京
　　　アジア経済研究所　1964 年　159 p.

Hosono, Akio. <u>Aruzenchin no Keizai Hatten</u>.　Tokyo, Ajia
　　Keizai Kenkyûjo,　1964, 159p.
　　　　　　　(Economic Development of Argentina)

208 　ライフ編集部

　　　アルゼンチン　東京
　　時事通信社　1966.　160p.

Raifu. <u>Henshûku Aruzenchin</u>.　Tokyo, Jiji Tsûshin Sha, 1966,
　160p.
(Life.　Editorial Department.　<u>Argentina</u>)

209 　篠沢恭助　パンパの発展と停滞
　　　東京　アジア経済研究所　1967 年　189 p.

Shinozawa, Kyosuke. <u>Pampa no Hatten to Teitai</u>.　Tokyo,
　　Ajia Keizai Kenkyûjo,　1967, 189p.
　　　　　　　(Development and Stagnation in the Pampas)

210 　大岩祥浩等　タンゴ入門　東京　音楽之友社
　　　1965 年　258 p.

Oiwa, Shoko, & C. <u>Tango Nyûmon</u>.　Tokyo, Ongaku no
　Tomosha, 1965, 258p.
　　　　　　　(Introduction to the Tango)

BRAZIL

211 アジア租税研究会編　ラテン・アメリカ諸国の
　　　　租税制度 I （ブラジル）　東京
　　　　アジア経済研究所　1965年　500 p.

Ajia Sozei Kenkyukai, ed. <u>Raten Amerika Shokoku no
　Sozeiseido I (Burajiru).</u> Tokyo, Ajia Keizai Kenkyûjo,
1965, 500p.
　　　　　　　　　　　　　　　(Taxation Systems of Latin America
　I: Brazil)

212 ブラジル 日本商工会議所　ブラジル経済辞典 1967
　　　Burajiru Nihon Shôkô Kaigisho. <u>Burajiru Keizai Jiten.</u>　Tokyo,
　　　Burajiru Nihon Shôkô Kaigisho, 1967.
　　　(Dictionary of Brazilian Economics)

213 飯山達雄　未知の裸族ラピチ　東京
　　　　朝日新聞社　1967年　284 p.

Iiyama, Tatsuo. <u>Michi no Razoku Rapichi.</u> Tokyo, Asahi
　Shinbun, 1967, 284p.
　　　　　　　　　(Unknown Naked Tribe: The Rapiti)

214　石川 之助

毒薬先生 アドヴエンチヤ

旅行　東京 大邑社 1966

251p.

Ishikawa, Motosuke. <u>Dokuyaku Sensei Adovencha Ryokô</u>.
Tokyo, Daikô Sha, 1966, 251p.
> (The Travel of the Poisons Doctor)

215　飯山達雄 ブラジル

Iiyama, Tatsuo. <u>Burajiru.</u>　Tokyo, Teikoku Shoin, 1964, 183p.
> (Brazil)

216　実吉達郎 ブラジル動物通信――野生の国の
　　　七年間 東京 弘文堂 1966年 202 p.

Jitsuyoshi, Tatsuro. <u>Burajiru Dôbutsu Tsûshin--Yasei no
Kuni no 7 Nenkan.</u> Tokyo, Kobundo, 1966, 202p.
> (News on Animals of Brazil: Seven Years
in the Wilderness)

217　海外技術協力事業団 ブラジル木材利用工業
　　　開発計画調査報告書 東京 同事団
　　　1966年 100 p.

Kaigai Gijutsu Kyoryoku Jigyodan. <u>Burajiru Mokuzai Riyô
Kôgyô Kaihatsu Keikaku Chôsa Hôkokusho.</u>　Tokyo, 1966, 100p.
> (Report on the Survey
for the Development of Forest Resources in Brazil)

218   海外技術協力事業団　東北ブラジル電力開発
　　　　計画基礎調査報告書　東京　同団　1967年
　　　　61 p.

Kaigai Gijutsu Kyoryoku Jigyodan. Tôhoku Burajiru Denryoku
Kaihatsu Keikaku Kiso Chôsa Hôkokusho. Tokyo, 1967, 61p.
　　　　　　　　　　　　　　　　　　(Report on Investigation of the
Electric Power Development Plan in Northeastern Brazil)

219   海外経済協力基金　調査部　ブラジル　東京
　　　　同部　1965年　395 p.

Kaigai Keizai Kyoryoku Kikin Chosabu. Burajiru, Tokyo,
1965, 395p.
　　　　　　　　　　　　　　　　(Brazil)

220   機械振興協会　経済研究所　ブラジルの機械
　　　　工業　東京　同所　1965年　132 p.

Kikai Shinko Kyokai Keizai Kenkyûjo. Burajiru no Kikai
Kôgyô. Tokyo, 1965, 132p.
　　　　　　　　　　　　　　(The Machine Industry
in Brazil: 1)

221   機械振興協会　経済研究所　ブラジルの
　　　　機械工業 (2)　東京　同所　1966年　120 p.

Kikai Shinko Kyokai Keizai Kenkyusho. Burajiru no Kikai
Kôgyô (2). Tokyo, 1966, 120p.
　　　　　　　　　　　　　　(The Machine
Industry in Brazil: 2)

222　熊本大学中南米事情研究所　ブラジルの工業化と水産加工

Kumamoto Daigaku. <u>Chûnanbei Jijô Kenkyûjo. Burajiru no
Kôgyôka to Suisan Kakô</u>, Kumamoto, 1965.
(Industrialization of Brazil and Processing Industries of Brazilian
Marine Products)

223　宮坂国人・在ブラジル日系人の現勢　東京
　　　日伯中央協会　1966年　24 p.

Miyasaka, Kunito. <u>Zai Burajiru Nikkeijin no Gensei</u>. Tokyo,
Nippaku Chuo Kyokai, 1966, 24p.
　　　　　　　　　(The Present Situation of the Japanese in Brazil)

224　実吉達郎，ブラジル動物通信　東京　弘文堂

Miyoshi, Tatsuo. <u>Burajiru Dôbutsu Tsûshin</u>. Tokyo,
Kôbundô, 1966, 202p.
　　　　　　　　　(Data on Brazilian Animals)

225　長尾武雄　拓けゆくアマゾン──その自然と生活
　　　東京　家の光協会　1965年　224 p.

Nagao, Takeo. <u>Hirakeyuku Amazon--Sono Shizen to Seikatsu</u>.
Tokyo, Ienohikari Kyokai, 1965, 224p.
　　　　　　　　　(The Developing Amazon: Its Nature and Life)

226 　長尾武雄
　　拓けゆく アマゾン　　東京　家の光協会

Nagao, Takeo. <u>Hirakeyuku Amazon</u>. Tokyo, Iei no Hikari
Kyôkai, 1965, 224p.
　　　　　　(On Developing the Amazon Valley)

227 　日本貿易振興会　ブラジルの塗料市場調査

Nihon Bôeki Shinkôkai. <u>Burajiru no Toryô Shijô Chôsa.</u>
Tokyo, Nihon Bôeki Shinkôkai, 1966.
　　　　　　(Market Survey for Paint in Brazil)

228 　日本貿易振興会　ジェトロ貿易市場シリーズ
　　　No. 29 ブラジル　東京　同会　1964年
　　　44 p.

Nihon Bôeki Shinkôkai. <u>JETRO Boeki Shijô Shirîzu No. 29,
Burajiru.</u> Tokyo, 1964, 44p.
　　　　　　(JETRO Trade Market Series, No. 29:
Brazil)

229 　日本綿花協会綿花経済研究所　ブラジルの
　　　綿花　大阪　同所　1967年 40 p.

Nihon Menka Kyokai Menka Keizai Kenkyûjo. 　<u>Burajiru no
Menka.</u> Osaka, 1967, 40p.
　　　　　　(Brazilian
Cotton)

230 日本専売公社　ブラジルのタバコ　東京　同社
　　1964 年　46 p.

Nihon Senbai Kosha. <u>Burajiru no Tabako</u>. Tokyo, 1964, 46p.
　　　　　　　　　　　(Brazilian Tobacco)

231 日伯中央協会　ブラジル事情講演集　東京　同会
　　1965 年　68 p.

Nippaku Chuo Kyokai. <u>Burajiru Jijô Kôenshu</u>. Tokyo, 1965, 68p.
　　　　　　　　　　　(Collection of Lectures on the Brazilian
Situation)

232 日伯協会　ブラジル　神戸　同会　　1965 年
　　138 p.

Nippaku Kyokai. <u>Burajiru</u>. Kobe, 1965, 138p.
　　　　　　　　(Brazil)

233 西向嘉昭　ブラジルの産業開発　東京　アジア経済研究所

Nishimukai, Yoshiaki. <u>Burajiru no Sangyô Kaihatsu</u>. Tokyo,
Ajia Keizai Kenkyûjo, 1966, 227p.
　　　　　　　　　　　(Industrial Development in Brazil)

234 西向嘉昭　ブラジルの工業化とインフレーション
　　東京　アジア経済研究所　1964 年　186 p.

Nishimukai, Yoshiaki. <u>Burajiru no Kôgyôka to Infurêshon</u>.
　Tokyo, Ajia Keizai Kenkyûjo, 1964, 186p.
　　　　　　　　　　(Industrialization and Inflation in
Brazil)

235   西向義昭編 ブラジルの産業開発
       東京 アジア経済研究所 1966年 227 p.

Nishimukai, Yoshiaki, ed. Burajiru no Sangyō Kaihatsu.
Tokyo, Ajia Keizai Kenkyusho, 1966, 227p.
                    (Industrial Development in Brazil)

236   農業拓植協会 アカラ植民地の創建 東京
       同会 1966年 110 p.

Nogyo Takushoku Kyokai. Akara Shokuminchi no Sōken. Tokyo,
1966, 110p.
                    (Foundation of the Acara Colony)

237   農業拓植協会 ブラジル──その農村と生活
       東京 同会 1965年 204 p.

Nogyo Takushoku Kyokai. Burajiru--Sono Nōson to Seikatsu.
Tokyo, 1965, 204p.
                    (Brazil--its Rural Communities and
Life)

238   農業拓植協会 イグアペ植民地 東京 同会
       1966年 135 p.

Nogyo Takushoku Kyokai. Iguape Shokuminchi. Tokyo,
1966, 135p.
                    (A Japanese Colony in Iguape)

239　農業拓殖協会　昭和初期におけるブラジル移住邦人
　　　の活躍　東京　同会　1966年　92 p.

Nogyo Takushoku Kyokai. Shôwa Shoki ni Okeru Burajiru
　Ijûhojin no Katsuyaku. Tokyo, 1966, 92p.
　　　　　　　　　　　　　(Activities of Japanese Emigrants
　in Brazil at the Beginning of the Showa)

240　農業拓殖協会　わが国ブラジル移民のあしあと
　　　東京　同会　1967年　103 p.

Nogyo Takushoku Kyokai. Wagakuni Burajiru Shokumin no
　Ashiato. Tokyo, 1967, 103p.
　　　　　　　　　　　　　(The Trail of Japanese Emigrants
　in Brazil)

241　桜井雅夫　ブラジルにおける外国資本の法　判政
　　　東京　アジア経済研究所

Sakurai, Masao. Burajiru ni Okeru Gaikoku Shihon no Hôseido.
　Tokyo, Ajia Keizai Kenkyûjo, 1965, 74p.
　　　　　　　　　　　　　(Laws and Legal System Pertaining to Foreign
　Capital in Brazil)

242　桜井稔夫　ブラジルにおける外国資本の法制度
　　　東京　アジア経済研究所　1965年　74 p.

Sakurai, Takao. Burajiru Niokeru Gaikoku Shihon no Hôseido.
　Tokyo, Ajia Keizai Kenkyûjo, 1965, 74p.
　　　　　　　　　　　　　(Legal Institutions Relating to Foreign Investment
　in Brazil)

243 白木 茂 訳
アマゾンに消えた探険隊　東京　偕成社

Shiraki, Shigeru, tr. <u>Amazon ni Kieta Tankentai</u>.　Tokyo,
Kaisei Sha, 1966, 220p.
(Expedition Lost in the Amazon Valley)

244　角田房子　ブラジルの日系人 - 東京　潮出版社
1967 年　252 p.

Tsunoda, Fusako. <u>Burajiru no Nikkeijin</u>.　Tokyo, Ushio
Shuppansha, 1967, 252p.
(Japanese Emigrants in Brazil)

245 外務省 経済局 ラテン.アメリア課 新しい
市場中米と経済統合 東京 同課
1964 年 109 p.

Gaimusho Keizaikyoku Raten Amerikaka. Atarashii Shijô
Chûbei to Keizaitôgô. Tokyo, 1964, 109p.
(Central America and its Integration)

246 外務省経済局ラテン.アメリカ課 中 米共同市場
のすべて 東京 同 1967 年 37 p.

Gaimusho Keizaikyoku Raten Amerikaka. Chûbei Kyôdô
Shijô no Subete. Tokyo, 1967, 37p.
(All About the Central American Common Market)

247 石田英一郎 マヤ文明 - 東京 中央公論社
1967 年 217 p.

Ishida, Eiichiro. Maya Bunmei. Tokyo, Chuokoronsha,
1967, 217p.

(Maya Civilization)

248 　海外経済協力基金 調査部　中南米6カ国の
経済開発計画　東京　同部　1965年
94 p.

Kaigai Keizai Kyoryoku Kikin Chosabu.　Chûnanbei 6 Kakoku no
Keizai Kaihatsu.　Tokyo, 1965, 94p.
(Economic Development Plans in the Six Central American
Countries)

249 　二宮　謙 訳

ハ゜ナハ゜・グアテマラ

東京　時事通信社　1966.
160p.

Ninomiya, Ken, tr.　Panama. Guatemara.　Tokyo, Jiji Tsûshin
Sha, 1966, 160p.

(Panama, Guatemala)

250 　大原美範編 - 中米共同市場
東京　アジア経済研究所　1967年　229 p.

Ohara, Yoshinori, ed.　Chûbei Kyôdo Shijô,　Tokyo, Ajia
Keizai Kenkyûjo,　1967, 229p.
(Central American Common Market)

251   世界文化社　世界文化シリーズ第16　中央
           アメリカ　東京　同社　1964年　146 p.

     Sekai Bunkasha. <u>Sekai Bunka Shirîzu No. 16, Chuô Amerika.</u>
       Tokyo, 1964, 146p.

                            (World Culture Series No. 16: Central America)

252   富山 妙子 中南米ひとりたび　東京　朝日新聞社

     Toyama, Taeko. <u>Chûnambei Hitori Tabi.</u>　Tokyo, Asahi Shimbun
       Sha, 1964, 207p.

                          (My Journey to Central America)

CHILE

253   アジア租税研究会編　ラテン.アメリア諸国の
　　　　租税制度　Ｖ　（チリ）　東京
　　　　アジア経済研究所　1967 年　184 p.

Ajia Sozei Kenkyukai, ed.　Raten Amerika Shokoku no Sozeiseido
v (Chiri).　Tokyo, Ajia Keizai Kenkyûjo,　1967, 184p.
　　　　　　　　　　　　　　　　（Taxation Systems of Latin America,
V: Chile)

254   海外技術協力事業団　チリ マイクロウエーブ
　　　　回線経建設計画調査報告書　東京　同庆団
　　　　1965 年　95 p.

Kaigai Gijutsu Kyoryoku Jigyodan.　Chiri Maikurowêbu
Kaisenmô Kensetsu Keikaku Chôsa Hôkokusho.　Tokyo,
1965, 95p.
　　　　　　　　　　　　　（Report on the Survey for
Chile's Microwave　Network Project)

255   日本貿易振興会　ジエトロ貿易市場シリーズ
　　　　No. 42 チリ　東京　同会　1966 年
　　　　44 p.
Nihon Bôeki Shinkôkai.　JETRO Boeki Shijo Shirizu No. 42,
Chiri.　Tokyo, 1966, 44p.
　　　　　　　　　　　　（JETRO Trade Market Series No. 42:
Chile)

256   海外技術協力事業団　コロンビア国 Patia 河電源
　　　　開発計画基礎調査報告書　東京　同団
　　　　1967 年　108 p.

Kaigai Gijutsu Kyoryoku Jigyodan. Koronbia Koku Patia Gawa
Dengen Kaihatsu Keikaku Kiso Chôsa Hôkokusho, Tokyo, 1967,
108p.
　　　　　　　　　　　　　　　　(Report on the Survey of the
Rio Patia Hydro-Electric Power Development Plan in Colombia)

257   海外技術協力事業団　コロンビア共和国鉱物
　　　　資源調査報告書第 2 次　東京　同所 1966 年
　　　　47 p.
Kaigai Gijutsu Kyoryoku Jigyodan. Koronbia Kyôwakoku
Kôbutsu Shigen Chôsa Hôkokusho Dai 2 ji. Tokyo, 1966, 47p.
　　　　　　　　　　　　　　　　(Report on the Second
Investigation of Ore Deposits in Colombia)

258   海外技術協力事業団　コロンビア共和国鉱物
　　　　資源調査報告書　東京　同社 1965 年
　　　　99 p.

Kaigai Gijutsu Kyoryoku Jigyodan. Koronbia Kyôwakoku
Kôbutsushigen Chôsa Hôkokusho. Tokyo, 1965, 99p.
　　　　　　　　　　　　　　　　(Report on the Investigation
of Ore Deposits in Colombia)

259 　海外経済協力基金 調査部　コロンビアの
　　　経済　東京　同部　1964 年　226 p.
Kaigai Keizai Kyoryoku Kikin Chosabu. Koronbia no Keizai.
　Tokyo, 1964, 226p.
　　　　　　　　　　　　　　　　　(The Colombian
Economy)

CUBA

260 　堀田善衞　キューバ紀行　東京　岩波書店
　　　　　1966 年　190 p
Hotta, Yoshie. Kyuba Kikô. Tokyo, Iwanami Shoten, 1966, 190p.
　　　(A Trip to Cuba)

261 　富岡倍雄
　　　キューバ革命　　東京　みすず書房
Tomioka, Masuo, tr. Kyûba Kakumei. Tokyo, Misuzu Shôbô,
　1966, 189p.
　　　　(The Cuban Revolution)

262   伊藤秀三　ガラパゴス諸島　東京　中央公論社
　　　1966 年　194 p.
Ito, Shuzo. Garapagosu Shotô.　Tokyo, Chuokoronsha, 1966,
194p.
　　　　　(The Galapagos Islands)

263   海外技術協力事業団　エクアドル共和国
　　　SANMIGUEL DE CAR 電源開発計画調査
　　　報告書　東京　同団　1966 年　125 p.

Kaigai Gijutsu Kyoryoku Jigyodan.　Ekuadoru Kyôwakoku San
Miguel de Cardengen Kaihatsu Keikaku Chôsa Hôkokusho.
Tokyo, 1966, 125p.
　　　　　　　　　　　　　(Report on the Survey of the
San Miguel de Car Hydro-Electric Power Development Plan in
Ecuador)

264   日本シオス協会　エクアドル経済　東京
　　　同課　1966 年　45 p.

Nihon CIOS Kyokai.　Ekuadoru Keizai.　Tokyo, 1966, 45p.
　　　　　(The Ecuadoran Economy)

265　　アジア租税研究会編　ラテン.アメリカ諸国の
　　　　租税制度 II （メキシコ）　東京
　　　　アジア経済研究所　1965 年　490 p.

Ajia Sozei Kenkyukai, ed. <u>Raten Amerika Shokoku no</u> ∧
<u>Sozeiseido II (Mekishiko)</u>.　Tokyo, Ajia Keizai Kenkyujo,
1965, 490p.
　　　　　　　　　　　　（Taxation Systems of Latin
America, II: Mexico)

266　　深作光貞　メキシコのすべて　東京
　　　　角川書店　1967 年　356 p.

Fukasa, Mitsusada. <u>Mekishiko no Subete</u>.　Tokyo, Kadokawa
Shoten, 1967, 356p.
　　　　　　　　　　（All About Mexico)

267　　外務省経済協力局技術協力課　メキシコ電気.通信
　　　　開発の現状と問題点　東京　同課　1966 年
　　　　81 p.

Gaimusho Keizai Kyoryoku Kyoku Gijutsu Kyoryokuka.
　<u>Mekishiko Denki Tsûshin Kaihatsu no Genjô to Mondaiten</u>.
Tokyo, 1966, 81p.
（Present Condition and Problems of Telecommunication
Development in Mexico)

268   外務省経済局ラテン.アメリカ課　メキシコに
       おける信用構造　東京　同課　1967年
       31 p.

Gaimusho Keizaikyoku Raten Amerikaka. <u>Mekishiko no Shinyô
Kôzô</u>. Tokyo, 1967, 31p.
                                        (The Monetary
Structure of Mexico)

269   海外技術協力事業団　メキシコ電気通信技術
       訓練センター実施調査団報告書　東京
       同団　1966年　162 p.

Kaigai Gijutsu Kyoryoku Jigyodan. <u>Mekishiko Denki Tsûshin
Gijutsu Kunren Sentâ Jisshi Chôsadan Hôkokusho</u>. Tokyo,
1966, 162p.
                                (Report on the Survey of
a Telecommunication Training Center in Mexico)

270   長尾みのる　ソンブレロは風まかせ――メキシコ
       旅日記　東京　朝日新聞社　1966年
       257 p.

Nagao, Minoru. <u>Sonburero wa Kaze Makase- Mekishiko Tabinikki</u>.
Tokyo, Asahi Shinbunsha, 1966, 257p.
                       (Sombrero and Wind-Mexican Travel Diary)

271   中川和彦　メキシコ会社法および信用証券ならび
       に活動一般法　東京　ラテン.アメリカ協会
       1966年　160 .

Nakagawa, Kazuhiko. <u>Mekishiko Kaishahô Oyobi Shinyô Shôken
Narabini Katsudô Ippan Hô</u>. Tokyo, Raten Amerika Kyokai,
1966, 160p.
                       (Corporation Law and General Law on
Credit Activities in Mexico)

272 日本貿易振興会　ジェトロ貿易市場シリーズ
No. 38　メキシコ（改訂版）　東京　同会
1965 年　46 p.

Nihon Bôeki Shinkôkai.　JETRO Boeki Shijô Shirîzu No. 38
Mekishiko (Kaiteiban).　Tokyo, 1965, 46p.
(JETRO Trade Market Series No. 38:
Mexico, Revised Edition)

273 世界文化社　世界文化シリーズ第 15　メキシコ．
カナダ　東京　同社　1965 年　146 p.

Sekai Bunkasha.　Sekai Bunka Sirîzu No. 15: Mekishiko,
Kanada.　Tokyo, 1965, 146p.
(World Culture Series No. 15: Mexico and
Canada)

274 利根山　光人　メキシコ　東京　雪華社

Toneyama, Mitsuto.　Mekishiko.　Tokyo, Sekka Sha, 1964,
257p.
(Mexico)

275   海外技術協力事業団 パラグアイ植林計画
       調査報告書 東京 同団 1966年 100 p.

Kaigai Gijutsu Kyoryoku Jigyodan. Paraguai Shokurin
Keikaku Chôsa Hôkokusho. Tokyo, 1966, 100p.
                         (Report on the Survey for the
Afforestation Project in Paraguay)

276   毎日新聞社 人口問題調査会 パラグアイに
       おける集団移民 東京 同会 1964年
       29 p.

Mainichi Shinbunsha Jinko Mondai Chosakai. Paraguai ni
Okeru Shûdan Imin. Tokyo, 1964, 29p.
                         (Collective
Emigration to Paraguay)

PERU

277 アジア租税研究会編　ラテン.アメメカ諸国の
租税制度　IV -(ペルー)　東京
アジア経済研究所　1967 年　12■ p.

Ajia Sozei Kenkyukai, ed.　Raten Amerika Shokoku no Sozeiseido
IV (Perû).　Tokyo, Ajia Keizai Kenkyûjo,　1967, 128p.
(Taxation Systems of Latin America
IV: Peru)

278 外務省経済局ラテン.アメリカ課　最近のペルー
経済の動向　東京　同課　1967 年　38 p.

Gaimusho Keizaikyoku Raten Amerikaka.　Saikin no Perû Keizai
no Dôkô.　Tokyo, 1967, 38p.
(Recent Trends of
the Peruvian Economy)

279 泉　貴美子　インカ探検記　東京　徳間書店
1965 年　205 p.

Izumi, Kimiko.　Inka Tanken Ki.　Tokyo, Tokuma Shoten,
1965, 205p.
(An Inca Expedition)

280 氣　靖一
　　　イン力帝国　　東京
　　　岩波書店　1966　296 P.

Izumi, Seiichi. Inka Teikoku. Tokyo, Iwanami Shoten,
1966, 296p.
　　　　　　　(Inca)

281 海外技術協力事業団　ペルー共和国包蔵水力
　　　調査報告書　東京　同所団 1965 年　198 p.

Kaigai Gijutsu Kyoryoku Jigyodan. Peru Kyôwakoku Hôzô
Suiryoku Chôsa Hôkokusho. Tokyo, 1965, 198p.
　　　　　　　　　　　(Report on the Survey
of Water Power Resources in Peru)

282 海外技術協力事業団　ペルー共和国プノ県
　　　電化計画調査報告書　東京　同会団 1967 年
　　　123 p.

Kaigai Gijutsu Kyoryoku Jigyodan. Peru Kyôwakoku Puno
Ken Denka Keikaku Chôsa Hôkokusho. Tokyo, 1967, 123p.
(Report on the Survey of the Puno Electrification Project
in Peru)

283 加藤　幸編　アンヂスの白い鷹―芝浦工大
　　　ペルー．アンヂス遠征記録　東京
　　　あかね書房　1967 年　285 p.

Kato, Ko, ed. Andesu no Shiroi Taka-Shibaura Kôdai Perú,
Andesu Ensei Kiroku. Tokyo, Akane Shobo, 1967, 285p.
　　　　　　　(White Hawk in the Andes: Record of the
Peruvian Andes Expedition of the Shibaura University of
Technology)

284   見砂直照　ラテンリズム入門　東京　東亜音楽社
　　　　　1967年　344 p.

Misago, Masaaki. <u>Raten Rizumu Nyûmon</u>.　Tokyo,　Toa
Ongakusha, 1967, 344p.
　　　　　　　　　　(Guide to Latin Rhythms)

285   三浦和一　訳
　　　　　ペルー・チリ　　東京
　　　　　時事通信社　　1966　　160p.

Miura, Kazuichi, tr.　<u>Perû, Chiri</u>.　Tokyo, Jiji Tsûshin Sha,
1966, 160p.
　　　　　　　　　　(Peru, Chile)

286   中屋健一
　　　　　ラテン・アメリカ史　東京　　中央公論社　1964

Nakaya, Ken'ichi.　<u>Raten Amerika Shi</u>.　Tokyo, Chûô Kôron Sha,
1964, 232p.
　　　　　　　　　　(History of Latin America)

287   南米経済使節団編　1965年　南米経済使節団
　　　　　報告書　東京　同　1965年　221 p.

Nanbei Keizai Shisetsudan, ed. <u>1965 Nen Nanbei Keizai Shisetsudan</u>
<u>Hôkoku Sho</u>.　Tokyo, 1965, 221p.
　(Report of the Economic Mission to South America in 1965)

288 日本貿易振興会 ジエトロ貿易市場シリーズ
No. 55 ペルー 東京 同会 1967年
39 p.

Nihon Bôeki Shinkôkai. JETRO Boeki Shijô Shirîzu No. 55,
Perû. Tokyo, 1967, 39p.
(JETRO Trade Market Series No. 55:
Peru)

289　外務省経済局ラテン．アメリカ課　トリニダッド
　　　トバゴの経済情勢と工業開発の将来性
　　　東京　同課　1966年　30 p.

Gaimusho Keizaikyoku Raten Amerikaka.　Torinidaddo-
　Tobago no Keizai Jôsei to Kôgyô Kaihatsu no Shôrai.
Tokyo, 1966, 36p.
(Economic Situation of Trinidad-Tobago and the Future
of its Industrial Development)

290　海外技術協力事業団　トリニダード：トバゴ
　　　国ナリバ地域湿地開発計画調査報告書
　　　東京　同団　1967年　145 p.

Kaigai Gijutsu Kyoryoku Jigyodan.　Torinidaddo-Tobago Koku
　Nariba Chiiki Shicchi Kaihatsu Keikaku Chôsa Hôkokusho.
Tokyo, 1967, 145p.
　　　　　　　　　　　　　(Report on the Survey of the
Agricultural Development Project for the Nariva Swamp in
Trinidad and Tobago)

291　ラテン．アメリカ協会　トリニダッド・トバゴ事情
　　　東京　同会　1966年　48 p.

Raten Amerika Kyokai.　Torinidaddo-Tobago Jijô.　Tokyo,
　1966, 48p.
　　　　　　　　　　　　(Situation of Trinidad-Tobago)

292　　海外技術協力事業団　ベネエラ　カラカス市
　　　都市交通網整備計画調査報告書　東京
　　　同原版 1965 年　127 p.

Kaigai Gijutsu Kyoryoku Jigyodan.　Benezuera Karakasu Shi
Toshi Kôtsûmô Seibi Keikaku Chôsa Hôkokusho.　Tokyo,
1965, 127p.
　　　　　　　　　　　　　　　　　(Report on the Survey of
Traffic in Caracas, Venezuela)

WEST INDIES

293　　N H K 特別取材班　カリブ海の国ぐに
　　　　東京　日本放送出版協会　1964 年　271 p.

NHK Tokubetsu Shuzaihan.　Karibu Kai no Kuniguni.　Tokyo,
Nihon Hoso Shuppan Kyokai, 1964, 271p.
　　　　　　　　　　　　　　　(Countries in the Caribbean Sea)

LATIN AMERICA

294 米花 稔 ラテン・アメリカにおけるわが国企業
経営 東京 アジア経済《7：6）6。1966，
68～79

Beika, Minoru. "Raten Amerika Niokeru Wagakuni Kigyôkeiei."
Tokyo, Ajia keizai (7: 6), June 1966, pp. 68-79.
("Management of Japanese Enterprises in
Latin America")

295 土井光輝生 ラテン・アメリカにおける国際商事
仲裁制度の発達 東京 ラテン・アメリカ研究
（1）11。1962，17～25

Doi, Teruo. "Raten Amerika Niokeru Kokusai Shôji Chûsai
Seido no Hattatsu." Tokyo, Raten Amerika kenkyu (1),
November 1962, pp. 17-25.
("Development of the International Commercial
Arbitration System in Latin America")

296 土井輝生 対ラテン・アメリカ企業進出の法律問題
東京 ラテン・アメリカ研究（3）11，1963，
71～87

Doi, Teruo. "Tai Raten Amerika Kigyô Shinshutsu no Hôritsu
Mondai." Tokyo, Raten Amerika kenkyu (3), November 1963,
pp. 71-87.
("Legal Problems of Business Investments
in Latin America")

297   藤田正寛　低開発国における資本変動の一考察—
　　　　ラテン．アメリカを中心として　神戸
　　　　経済経営研究年報（17：2）1966，85-111

Fujita, Masahiro. "Teikaihatsukoku Niokeru Shihon Hendô
no Ichi Kôsatsu--Raten Amerika wo Chûshintoshite." Kobe,
<u>Keizai keiei kenkyu nenpo</u> (17: 2), 1966, pp. 85-111.
　　　　　　　　　　　　　　("A View on Capital Movements in the
Developing Countries: The Case of Latin America")

298   原　正行　カルボ条項の効力　東京　ラテン．
　　　　アメリカ研究（5）12，1964，59-73

Hara, Masayuki. "Karubo Jôkô no Kôka." Tokyo, <u>Raten Amerika</u>
<u>kenkyu</u> (5), December, 1964, pp. 59-73.
　　　　　　　　　　　　　("The Effect of the Calvo Clause")

299   細野昭雄　プレビッシュ理論の核心と意義　東京
　　　　国際経済（16）9，1965，207-224

Hosono, Akio. "Purebisshu Riron no Kakushin to Igi." Tokyo,
<u>Kokusai keizai</u> (16), September 1965, pp. 207-224.
　　　　　　　　　　　　　("Core and Significance of the Prebisch Theory")

300   細野昭雄　プレビッシュの経済思想　東京
　　　　アジア経済（6：3）3，1965，17-38

Hosono, Akio. "Purebisshu no Keizai Shisô." Tokyo, <u>Ajia keizai</u>
(6: 3), March 1965, pp. 17-38.
　　　　　　　　　　　　　("Economic Thought of Raúl Prebisch")

301　細野閑雄　ラテン・アメリカの「構造学派」
　　　　東京　アジア経済（6：1）1, 1965。62～69

Hosono, Akio. "Raten Amerika no Kôzôgakuha." Tokyo,
　Ajia keizai (6: 1), January 1965, pp. 62-69.
　　　　　　　("'Structuralist School' in Latin America")

302　石井　章　アンデスにおける土地所有の変遷と社会
　　　　変化　東京　アジア経済（5：8）8。1964,
　　　39～48

Ishii, Akira. "Andesu Niokeru Tochi-Shoyû no Hensen to
　Shakaihenka." Tokyo, Ajia keizai (5: 8), August 1964, pp. 39-48.
　　　　　　　("Social Change, and Changes in Land Tenure
in the Andean Countries")

303　井上忠勝　ラテンアメリカにおける米国バナナ企業
　　　　の経験　神戸　経済経営研究年報（16：2）
　　　1966, 75～107

Inoue, Tadakatsu. "Raten Amerika Niokeru Beikoku Banana
　Kigyô no Keiken." Kobe, Keizai keiei kenkyu nenpo (16: 2),
　1966, pp. 75-107.
　　　　　　　("Experiences of U. S. Banana Companies
in Latin America")

304　泉　靖一．松沢亜生　中央アンデスにおける無土器
　　　　神殿文化——コトシュ・ミト期を中心として
　　　　東京　ラテン・アメリカ研究（8）8, 1967,
　　　39～67

Izumi, Seiichi, & Asei Matsuzawa. "Chûô Andesu Niokeru
　Mudoki Shinden Bunka-Kotoshu Mito ki wo Chûshin Toshite."
Tokyo, Raten Amerika kenkyu (8), August 1967, pp. 39-67.
　　　　　　　　　　("Early Pre-ceramic
Cultist Culture of the Central Andes: on the Kotosh Mito Phase")

305   泉 靖 一　ラテン．アメリカの地域社会　東京
　　　　世界経済（15 : 4）4, 1960。2~15

Izumi, Seiichi. "Raten Amerika no Chiiki Shakai." Tokyo,
  Sekai keizai (15: 4), April 1960, pp. 2-15.
　　　　　　　　　("Regional Societies in Latin America")

306   賀川俊彦　ラテン．アメリカにおけるナショナリズム
　　　　東京　アジア経済（5 : 9）9。1964。16~26

Kagawa, Toshihiko. "Raten Amerika Niokeru Nashonarizumu."
  Tokyo, Ajia keizai (5: 9), September 1964, pp. 16-26.
　　　　　　　　　　("Nationalism in Latin American Countries")

307   鴨沢 巌　ラテン．アメリカ共同市場をめぐる角逐
　　　　東京　思想（479）5。1964。154~160

Kamozawa, Iwao. "Raten Amerika Kyôdô Shijô wo Meguru
  Kakuchiku." Tokyo, Shiso (479), May 1964, pp. 154-160.
　　　　　　　　　("Competition in a Latin American Common
Market")

308   川上太郎　ラテンアメリカと国際私法の法典化
　　　　神戸　国際経済研究年報（10）1, 1960。
　　　　169~194

Kawakami, Taro. "Raten Amerika to Kokusai Shihô no Hôtenka."
  Kobe, Kokusai keizai kenkyu nenpo (10), January 1960, pp.
169-194.
　　　　　　　　　("Codification of International Private Law
in Latin America")

309 木田和雄　米州大統領宣言と中南米共同市場　東京
　　　　　経済 (42) 10, 1967, 183-193

Kida, Kazuo. "Beishû Daitôryô Sengen to Chûnanbei Kyôdôshijô."
Tokyo, <u>Keizai</u> (42), October 1967, pp. 183-193.
　　　　　　　　　　("Declaration of the Presidents of the Western
Hemisphere Nations on the Latin American Common Market")

310 木田和雄　ラテン・アメリカにおける土地所有形態
　　　の特質　吹田　関西大学商学論集 (9：1) 4,
　　　1964, 59-84

Kida, Kazuo. "Raten Amerika Niokeru Tochishoyû Keitai
no Tokushitsu." Suita, <u>Kansai daigaku shogaku ronshu</u>
(9: 1), April 1964, pp. 59-84.
　　　　　　　　　　("Characteristics of Forms of Land Tenure
in Latin America")

311 木田和男
　　　ラテン・アメリカにおける土地所有形態の特質
　　　関西大学商学論集　第九巻第一号　大阪　1964

Kida, Kazuo. "Raten Amerika ni Okeru Tochi Shoyû Keitai
no Tokushitsu." Osaka, <u>Kansai daigaku shôgaku ronshû</u> (9: 1),
1964.
　　　　　　　　　　("The Characteristics of Land Tenure in Latin
American Countries")

312   小林　新　ラテン・アメリカ経済の不均衡　東京
　　　　　国際経済 (8) 9. 1956. 163~166

Kobayashi, Arata. "Raten Amerika Keizai no Fukinkô."
　Tokyo, <u>Kokusai keizai</u> (8), September 1956, pp. 163-166.
　　　　　　　("Imbalance in the Latin American
Economy")

313   近藤四郎，友枝啓泰　アンデス原住民の生態と高地
　　　　　適応能　東京　ラテン・アメリカ研究 (8)
　　　　　8. 1967. 31~37

Kondo, Shiro, & Hiroyasu Tomoeda. "Andesu Genjûmin no
　Seitai to Kôchi Tekiônô." Tokyo, <u>Raten Amerika kenkyu</u>
(8), August 1967, pp. 31-37.
　　　　　　　　　　("Ecology and Adaptability
to Highland Conditions of the Andean Aborigines")

314   増田義郎　アンデス地方のクロニスタ　東京
　　　　　ラテン・アメリカ研究 (1) 11. 1962. 95~112

Masuda, Yoshio. "Andesu Chihô no Kuronisuta." Tokyo,
<u>Raten Amerika kenkyu</u> (1), November 1962, pp. 95-112.
　　　　　　　　　("Chroniclers in the Andes")

315   増田義郎　後古典期から植民地時代へ ― エスノヒス
　　　　　トリーの可能性　東京　ラテン・アメリカ研究 ―
　　　　　(8) 8. 1967. 119~154

Masuda, Yoshio. "Kô-Kotenki Kara Shokuminchi Jidai e-
　Esunohisutorii no Kanôsei." Tokyo, <u>Raten Amerika</u>
<u>kenkyu</u> (8), August 1967, pp. 119-154.
　　　　　　　("From Post-Classic to Colonial Period:
the Possibility of Ethnohistory")

316   笑濃部亮吉　ラテン・アメリカの経済――後進国の
      経済的発展における一つの実例　東京
      経済学論集（東大）（25：1-2）12，1965，
      65~88

Minobe, Ryokichi. "Raten Amerika no Keizai--Kôshinkoku
  no Keizaiteki Hatten Niokeru Hitotsuno Jitsurei." Tokyo,
  Keizaigaku ronshu (Tokyo University) (25: 1-2), December
  1956, pp. 65-88.
                    ("Latin American Economy; One Example
  in Economic Development of Less-Developed Countries")

317   水野　一　LAFTA の現状と問題点　東京　アジア経済
      （5：9）9，1964，42~53

Mizuno, Hajime. "LAFTA no Genjô to Mondaiten." Tokyo,
  Ajia keizai (5: 9), September 1964, pp. 42-53.
                    ("LAFTA: Present Condition and Problems")

318   森山和夫　ラテンアメリカにおけるアメリカ帝国主義
      の支配――資本輸出を中心にして　東京
      アジア・アフリカ研究（5：5）6，1965，
      13~30

Moriyama, Kazuo. "Raten Amerika Niokeru Amerika Teikokushugi
  no Shihai--Shihon Yushutsu wo Chûshinnishite." Tokyo, Ajia
  afurika kenkyu (5: 5), June 1965, pp. 13-30.
                    ("Domination of U. S. Imperialism in Latin
  America, with Special Reference to its Capital Exports")

319   中川和彦　経済統合の法律的諸問題 ― LAFTA を
       中心として　東京　アジア経済 (8 : 9) 9,
       1967, 80~92

Nakagawa, Kazuhiko. "Keizaitôgô no Hôritsuteki Shomondai-
    LAFTA wo Chushintôshite." Tokyo, Ajia keizai (8: 9),
    September 1967, pp. 80-92.
                    ("Some Legal Problems of Economic
    Integration, with Special Reference to LAFTA")

320   中曽根悟郎　ラテン．アメリカの経済成長とインフレ
       東京　ラテン．アメリカ研究 (2) 4, 1963,
       86~96

Nakasone, Goro. "Raten Amerika no Keizai Seichô to Infure."
    Tokyo, Raten Amerika kenkyu (2), April 1963, pp. 86-96.
                    ("Economic Growth and Inflation in Latin
    America")

321   中屋健一　干渉と不干渉の史的概観 ― 米国の
       対ラテン．アメリカ政策　東京　ラテン．
       アメリカ研究 (7) 1, 1966, 1~30

Nakaya, Kenichi. "Kanshô to Fukanshô no Shiteki Gaikan--
    Beikoku no tai Raten Amerika Seisaku." Tokyo, Raten
    Amerika kenkyu (7), January 1966, pp. 1-30.
                    ("General Survey on a History of Intervention
    and Non-intervention in U. S. Policy Towards Latin America")

322   西俣昭生　ラテン．アメリカ諸国と大陸棚の法理
       東京　ラテン．アメリカ研究 (3) 11, 1963,
       55~70

Nishimata, Akio. "Raten Amerika Shokoku to Tairikudana
    no Hôri." Tokyo, Raten Amerika kenkyu (3), November
    1963, pp. 55-70.
                    ("Latin American Countries and Legal
    Principles of the Continental Shelf")

323　西向嘉昭　ラテン・アメリカの戦後の経済思想
　　　東京　国際経済 (18) 10, 1967, 154～162

Nishimukai, Yoshiaki. "Raten Amerika no Sengo no Keizai
　Shisô." Tokyo, <u>Kokusai keizai</u> (18), October 1967, pp. 154-162.
　　　　　　　　　　　("Post-war Economic Thought in
Latin America")

324　西向嘉昭　米洲開発銀行の現状と問題点　東京
　　　世界経済評論 (9：8) 8, 1965, 22～29

Nishimukai, Yoshiaki. "Beishû Kaihatsu Ginkô no Genjô to
　Mondaiten." Tokyo, <u>Sekai keizai hyoron</u> (9: 8), August
1965, pp. 22-29.
　　　　　　　　　("The Inter-American Development
Bank: Present Condition and Problems")

325　西向嘉昭　「構造派」のインフレーション分析
　　　神戸　国民経済雑誌 (109：1) 1, 1964,
　　　67～76

Nishimukai, Yoshiaki. "Kôzôha no Infurêshon Bunseki."
　Kobe, <u>Kokumin keizai zasshi</u> (109: 1), January 1964, pp. 61-76.
　　　　　　　　　("Analysis of Inflation of the 'Structuralist
School'")

326　西向嘉昭　LAFTA の域内貿易の現状と課題 (1～2)――
　　　ブラジルとコロンビアの事例から　東京
　　　アジア経済 (8：5) 5, 1967, 13～27 ; (8：8)
　　　8, 1967, 45～54

Nishimukai, Yoshiaki. "LAFTA no Ikinai Bôeki no Genjô to
　Kadai (1-2)--Burajiru to Korombia no Jirei Kara." Tokyo,
<u>Ajia keizai</u> (8: 5), May 1967, pp. 13-27; (8: 8), August 1967,
pp. 45-54.
　　　　　　　　　　　("Present Condition and Tasks of Intra-
Regional Trade in LAFTA; the Cases of Brazil and Colombia [1-2]")

327　西向嘉昭　ラテン・アメリカ自由貿易連合（LAFTA）
　　　の現状と課題　神戸　国民経済雑誌（111：1）1，
　　　1965，71-86

Nishimukai, Yoshiaki. "Raten Amerika Jiyû Bôeki Rengô
  (LAFTA) no Genjô to Kadai." Kobe, Kokumin keizai zasshi
  (111: 1), January 1965, pp. 71-86.
                          ("Latin American Free Trade Association
[LAFTA]: Present Condition and Tasks")

328　西向嘉昭　ラテン・アメリカの貿易と国際収支
　　　神戸　経済経営研究年報（15：2）3，1965，
　　　114-142

Nishimukai, Yoshiaki. "Raten Amerika no Bôeki to Kokusaishûshi."
Kobe, Keizai keiei kenkyu nenpo (15: 2), March 1965, pp. 114-142.
                          ("Trade and Balance of Payments of
Latin America")

329　西向嘉昭　ラテン・アメリカ共同市場と域内企業
　　　神戸　国民経済雑誌（115：3）3，1967，65-81

Nishimukai, Yoshiaki. "Raten Amerika Kyôdô-Shijô to Ikinai
  Bungyô." Kobe, Kokumin keizai zasshi (115: 3), March
1967, pp. 65-81.
                          ("A Latin American Common Market
and Regional Specialization")

330　大原美範　ラテン・アメリカ経済統合の効果と
　　　その条件　東京　アジア経済（7：6）6，
　　　1966，2-21

Ohara, Yoshinori. "Raten Amerika Keizaitôgô no Kôka to Sono
  Jôken." Tokyo, Ajia keizai (7: 6), June 1966, pp. 2-21.
                          ("Effects of and Conditions for Latin
America's Economic Integration")

331 　大原美範　ラテン・アメリカにおける資本蓄積の
　　　現状と問題点　東京　アジア経済（5：4）4,
　　　1964。37～50
Ohara, Yoshinori.　"Raten Amerika Niokeru Shihon Chikuseki
　no Genjô to Mondaiten."　Tokyo, Ajia keizai (5: 4), April
1964, pp. 37-50.
　　　　　　　　　　　　　　("Accumulation of Capital in Latin America:
Present Condition and Problems Involved")

332 　大原美範　ラテン・アメリカ経済発展の条件　東京
　　　アジア経済（5：9）9, 1964。2～15
Ohara, Yoshinori.　"Raten Amerika Keizai Hatten no Jôken."
Tokyo, Ajia keizai (5: 9), September 1964, pp. 2-15.
　　　　　　　　　　　　　("Conditions for Economic Development
of Latin America")

333 　大原美範　ラテン・アメリカの金融機関　東京
　　　アジア経済（4：5）5。1963, 32～42
Ohara, Yoshinori.　"Raten Amerika no Kinyû Kikan."　Tokyo,
Ajia keizai (4: 5), May 1963, pp. 32-42.
　　　　　　　　　　　　　("Financial Institutions in Latin America")

334 　大原美範　低開発地域における経済統合の目的と
　　　動機—特にラテン・アメリカの場合を中心と
　　　して　東京　アジア経済（8：9）9, 1967。
　　　50～64
Ohara, Yoshinori.　"Teikaihatsu Chiiki ni Okeru Keizaitôgô
　no Mokuteki to Dôki--Tokuni Raten Amerika no Baai wo
Chûshintoshite."　Tokyo, Ajia keizai (8: 9), September
1967, pp. 50-64.
　　　　　　　　　　　　　("Purposes and Motives of Economic
Integration in the Underdeveloped Areas: the Case of Latin
America")

335   大貫良夫 中央アンデスにおける形成期および古典期
         後古典期の生態学的背景 東京 ラテン・
         アメリカ研究 (8) 8, 1967, 71~100

Onuki, Yoshio. "Chûô Andesu Niokeru Keiseiki Oyobi Kotenki,
   Kô-Kotenki no Seitaigakuteki Haikei." Tokyo, Raten Amerika
kenkyu (8), August 1967, pp. 71-100.
                  ("Ecological Backgrounds of the Formative,
Classic and Post-Classic Periods of the Central Andes")

336   大貫良夫, 狩野千秋 中央アンデスの人類学的研究
         のための文献目録 東京 ラテン・アメリカ
         研究 (8) 8, 1967, 213~312

Onuki, Yoshio, & Chiaki Kano. "Chûô Andesu no Jinruigakuteki
   Kenkyû no Tameno Bunken Mokuroku." Tokyo, Raten Amerika
kenkyu (8), August 1967, pp. 213-312.
                  ("Bibliography for Anthropological
Studies of the Central Andes")

337   斎藤志郎 LAFTA の進行速度を図る 東京
         アジア経済 (7：6) 6, 1966, 112~116

Saito, Shiro. "LAFTA no Shinkô Sokudo wo Hakaru." Tokyo,
   Ajia keizai (7: 6), June 1966, pp. 112-116.
                  ("LAFTA: How Fast is it Going?")

338   坂本重太郎 ラテン・アメリカ自由貿易連合
         (LAFTA) について 東京 外務省調査月報
         (4：6) 6, 1963, 22~55

Sakamoto, Jutaro. "Raten Amerika Jiyû Bôeki Rengô (LAFTA)
   Nitsuite." Tokyo, Gaimusho chosa geppo (4: 6), June 1963,
pp. 22-55.
                  ("On the Latin American Free Trade
Association [LAFTA]")

339　佐々木高明　中部アンデスにおける村落共同体の
　　　　地理学的意義　京都　史林（42：1）1，1959，
　　　　51~78

Sasaki, Takaaki. "Chūbu Andesu Niokeru Sonraku Kyōdōtai
　no Chirigakuteki Igi. " Kyoto, Shirin (42: 1), January 1959,
pp. 51-78.
　　　　　　　　　("Geographical Implications of the Rural
Community in the Central Andes")

340　佐藤　久　アンデス高原地形　東京　ラテン●
　　　　アメリカ研究（8）8，1967，3~30

Sato, Hisashi. "Andesu Kōchi no Kōgen Chikei. " Tokyo,
Raten Amerika kenkyu (8), August 1967, pp. 3-30.
　　　　　　　　　("Topography of the Andean Highlands")

341　佐藤　久　ラテン・アメリカの自然　東京
　　　　ラテン・アメリカ研究（5）12，1964，5~10

Sato, Hisashi. "Raten Amerika no Shizen. " Tokyo, Raten
Amerika kenkyu (5), December 1964, pp. 5-10.
　　　　　　　　　("Nature in Latin America")

342　佐藤和男　ラテン・アメリカ経済統合の背景と
　　　　実現過程　東京　ラテン・アメリカ研究（6）
　　　　6，1965，72~103

Sato, Kazuo. "Raten Amerika Keizaitōgō no Haikei to Jitsugen
Katei. " Tokyo, Raten Amerika kenkyu (6), June 1965, pp. 72-103.
　　　　　　　　　("Backgrounds and Process of Economic
Integration in Latin America")

343 佐藤信行 中央アンデスの社会人類学 東京
ラテン・アメリカ研究 (8) 8, 1967, 115~182

Sato, Nobuyuki. "Chūō Andesu no Shakai Jinruigaku."
Tokyo, Raten Amerika kenkyu (8), August 1967, pp. 155-182.
("Social Anthropology of the Central Andes")

344 妹尾正毅 米国の対ラテン・アメリカ援助政策
東京 ラテン・アメリカ研究 (3) 11, 1963,
88~106

Seno, Masatake. "Beikoku no Tai Raten Amerika Enjo Seisaku."
Tokyo, Raten Amerika kenkyu (3), November 1963, pp. 88-106.
("U. S. Aid Policy Towards Latin America")

345 巣山靖司 ラテン・アメリカ研究の諸問題 ── アジア
アフリカ研究所の分析視角を中心にして
名古屋 法政論集 (37) 1, 1967, 1~38

Suyama, Yasushi. "Raten Amerika Kenkyū no Shomondai--
Ajia Afurika Kenkyusho no Bunseki Shikaku wo Chūshintoshite."
Nagoya, Hosei ronshu (37), January 1967, pp. 1-38.
("Problems in Latin American Studies:
Analytical View of the Asia-Africa Institute")

346 高木秀樹
ラテン・アメリカの単一栽培と大土地所有制
山 徳島大学学芸紀要 第10巻 徳島 1961

Takaki, Hideki. "Raten Amerika no Tan'ichi Saibai to Dai Toshi
Shoyūsei." Tokushima, Tokushima daigaku gakugei kiyō
(10), 1961.
("The Single Plantation System and Large-
Scale Land Tenure in Latin America")

347 田中拓男　一次産品の輸出構造 ── 東南アジアと
　　　ラテン・アメリカとの比較　東京　世界経済評論
　　　(8：11) 12，1964，56～66

Tanaka, Takuo. "Ichijisanpin no Yushutsu Kōzō-Tōnan Ajia
to Raten Amerika to no Hikaku." Tokyo, <u>Sekai keizai</u>
<u>hyoron</u> (8: 11), December 1964, pp. 56-66.
　　　　　　　("Export Structure of Primary Commodities:
Comparison of Southeast Asia and Latin America")

348 寺田和夫　中央アンデス海岸における古代文化の
　　　展開　東京　ラテン．アメリカ研究 (8) 8，

Terada, Kazuo. "Chūō Andesu Kaigan Niokeru Koten Bunka
no Tenkai." Tokyo, <u>Raten Amerika kenkyu</u> (8), August
1967, pp. 101-118.
　　　　　　　("Development of Ancient Cultures in the
Central Coast of the Andean Region")

349 東井金平　ラテン．アメリカの農業問題と単一共同
　　　市場創設案　東京　農業総合研究 (14) 5，1967，
　　　9～38

Toi, Kinpei. "Raten Amerika no Nōgyō Mondai to Tanitsu
Kyōdōshijō Sōsetsuan." Tokyo, <u>Nogyo sogo kenkyu</u> (14),
May 1967, pp. 9-38.
　　　　　　　("Agricultural Problems and a Proposed
Common Market in Latin America")

350 藪忠綱　ラテン．アメリカの人口問題　東京
　　　外務省調査月報 (8：6) 6，1967，36～68

Yabu, Takatsuna. "Raten Amerika no Jinkō Mondai." Tokyo,
<u>Gaimusho chosa geppo</u> (8: 6), June 1967, pp. 36-68.
　　　　　　　("Population Problems of Latin America")

351   山崎禎一　南米の工業化とその地理的基礎　神戸
       国民経済雑誌（93：1）4, 1956, 17〜33

Yamazaki, Teiichi. "Nanbei no Kōgyōka to Sono Chiriteki Kiso."
    Kobe, <u>Kokumin keizai zasshi</u> (93: 1), April 1956, pp. 17-33.
                    ("The Industrialization of South America
and its Geographical Foundations")

352   山崎禎一　南米の交通の地理的特色　神戸　国民経済
       雑誌（100：5）11, 1959, 515〜532

Yamazaki, Teiichi. "Nanbei no Kōtsūmō no Chiriteki
    Tokushoku." Kobe, <u>Kokumin keizai zasshi</u> (100: 5),
November 1959, pp. 515-532.
                    ("Geographical Features of the Traffic
Network in South America")

353   山崎禎一　南米の経済地理的パターン　神戸
       国民経済雑誌（102：1）7, 1960, 38〜59

Yamazaki, Teiichi. "Nanbei no Keizai Chiriteki Patân."
    Kobe, <u>Kokumin keizai zasshi</u> (102: 1), July 1960, pp. 38-59.
                    ("Economic-Geographic Pattern of
South America")

354 　浜田滋郎　アルゼンチン民謡の本態　東京
　　　ラテン・アメリカ研究 (4) 5. 1964. 79〜92

Hamada, Jiro. "Aruzentin Minyô no Hontai." Tokyo, <u>Raten
Amerika kenkyu</u> (4), May, 1964, pp. 79-92.
　　　　　　　　("The Heart of Argentine Folksongs")

355 　細野昭雄　アルゼンチンの外国貿易と経済発展
　　　　東京　アジア経済 (5 : 1) 1. 1964. 34〜50

Hosono, Akio. "Aruzentin no Gaikoku Bôeki to Keizai Hatten."
Tokyo, <u>Ajia keizai</u> (5: 1), January 1964, pp. 34-50.
　　　　　　　　("Foreign Trade and Economic Development
of Argentina")

356 　三谷 弘　アルゼンチンにおける政党の発展　東京
　　　ラテン・アメリカ研究 (3) 11. 1963. 1〜19

Mitani, Hiroshi. "Aruzentin Niokeru Seitô no Hatten."
Tokyo, <u>Raten Amerika kenkyu</u> (3), November 1963, pp. 1-19.
　　　　　　　　("Development of Political Parties in Argentina")

357 　中川和彦　アルゼンチン会社法改正の動き　東京
　　　ラテン・アメリカ研究 (1) 11. 1962. 38〜46

Nakagawa, Kazuhiko. "Aruzentin Kaishahô Kaisei no Ugoki."
Tokyo, <u>Raten Amerika kenkyu</u> (1), November 1962, pp. 38-46.
　　　　　　　　("Reform of Corporation Law in Argentina")

358　中川和彦　アルゼンチンにおける株式会社に対する
　　　行政的監督制度　東京　アジア経済（5：9）
　　　9，1964。27～41

Nakagawa, Kazuhiko. "Aruzentin Niokeru Kabushikigaisha
　Nitaisuru Gyôseiteki Kantoku Seido." Tokyo, <u>Ajia keizai</u>
　(5: 9), September 1964, pp. 27-41.
　　　　　　　　　　　　　("The System of Administrative
Supervision Over Corporate Business in Argentina")

359　大原栄一　アルゼンチン社債法における企業担保
　　　制度　東京　ラテン．アメリカ研究（1）
　　　11．1962．26～37 ；（2）4，1963．26～42

Ohara, Eiichi. "Aruzentin Shasaihô Niokeru Kigyô Tanpo
　Seido (1-2)." Tokyo, <u>Raten Amerika kenkyu</u> (1), November
1962, pp. 26-37; (2), April 1963, pp. 26-42.
　　　　　　　　　　　　("The Company Guarantee System in the
Debenture Law of Argentina")

360　篠沢恭助　アルゼンチンにおけるインフレ財政の
　　　諸問題　東京　アジア経済（7：6）6，1966，
　　　22～47

Shinozawa, Kyosuke. "Aruzentin Niokeru Infure Zaisei no
　Shomondai." Tokyo, <u>Ajia keizai</u> (7: 6), June 1966, pp. 22-47.
　　　　　　　　　　　　　("Problems of Inflationary Public
Finance in Argentina")

361 アンドウ．ゼンパチ　ブラジルつ地域社会の分化と
特色　東京　ラ＝ン．アメリカ研究（4）5,
1964, 48〜62
Ando, Zenpachi. "Burajiru no Chiiki Shakai no Bunka to
Tokushoku." Tokyo, <u>Raten Amerika kenkyu</u> (4), May
1964, pp. 48-62.
("Specialization and Characteristics
of Regional Societies")

362 米花　稔　ブラジルの地域開発　神戸　国民経済
雑誌（114 ： 5）11, 1966, 19〜36
Beika, Minoru. "Burajiru no Chiiki Kaihatsu." Kobe,
<u>Kokumin keizai zasshi</u> (114: 5), November 1966, pp. 19-36.
("Regional Development Problems of
Brazil")

363 米花　稔　在外企業と国際経営問題 ― ブラジルの
場合を中心に　神戸　国民経済雑誌（113 ： 4）
4, 1966, 35〜52
Beika, Minoru. "Zaigai Kigyō to Kokusai Keiei Mondai--
Burajiru no Baai wo Chūshinni." Kobe, <u>Kokumin keizai
zasshi</u> (113: 4), April 1966, pp. 35-52.
("Management Problems in Overseas
Operation: The Case of Brazil")

364　土井輝生　Banco do Brasil 事件と国際通貨基金
加盟国の公序　東京　ラテン．アメリカ研究
(6) 6. 1965, 27~40

Doi, Teruo. "Banco do Brasil Jiken to Kokusai Tsûka Kikin
Kameikoku no Kôjo." Tokyo, Raten Amerika kenkyu (6),
June 1965, pp. 27-40.
　　　　　　　("The Case of Banco do Brasil and the Public
Policy of Member Countries of the International Monetary
Fund")

365　藤井孝四郎　ブラジル農業の現状と将来　東京
農業構造研究 (17) 8. 1967. 26~37

Fujii, Koshiro. "Burajiru Nôgyô no Genjô to Shôrai."
Tokyo, Nogyo kozo kenkyu (17), August 1967, pp. 26-37.
　　　　　　　("The Present Condition and the Future
of Brazilian Agriculture")

366　小林利郎　クルゼイロとブラジル経済　東京
アジア経済 (7：6) 6. 1966. 87~94

Kobayashi, Toshiro. "Kuruzeiro to Burajiru Keizai."
Tokyo, Ajia keizai (7: 6), June 1966, pp. 87-94.
　　　　　　　　　　　　　("The Cruzeiro and the Brazilian Economy")

367　黒沢　清　ブラジルのインフレおよび会計事情
東京　会計 (90：1) 7. 1966. 167~171

Kurosawa, Kiyoshi. "Burajiru no Infure Oyobi Kaikei Jijô."
Tokyo, Kaikei (90: 1), July 1966, pp. 167-171.
　　　　　　　　　　　("Inflation and the Situation of Public
Accounting in Brazil")

368   西向嘉昭　ブラジルの外資導入政策の問題点　神戸
　　　　経済経営研究年報 (16 : 2) 1966, 44~74

Nishimukai, Yoshiaki. "Burajiru no Gaishi Dônyû Seisaku
   no Mondaiten." Kobe, Keizai keiei kenkyu nenpo (16: 2),
1966, pp. 44-74.
                         ("Problems of Foreign Capital
Policy of Brazil")

369   西向嘉昭　ブラジルの経済開発計画の問題点　神戸
　　　　国民経済雑誌 (113 : 1) 1, 1966, 48~64

Nishimukai, Yoshiaki. "Burajiru no Keizai Kaihatsu
   Keikaku no Mondaiten." Kobe, Kokumin keizai zasshi
(113: 1), January 1966, pp. 48-64.
                         ("Problems of Programa de Ação
in Brazil")

370   西向嘉昭　ブラジルの経済発展と地域問題　神戸
　　　　国民経済雑誌 (107 : 1) 1, 1963, 76~95

Nishimukai, Yoshiaki. "Burajiru no Keizai Hatten to Chiiki
   Mondai." Kobe, Kokumin keizai zasshi (107: 1), January
1963, pp. 76-95.
                         ("Economic Development and Regional
Problems in Brazil")

371   西向嘉昭　ブラジルの工業化と外国資本 — 対外利
　　　　送金制限法をめぐつて (1~2) 東京
　　　　アジア経済 (6 : 11) 11, 1965, 27~37 ; (6 :
　　　　12) 12, 1965, 20~30

Nishimukai, Yoshiaki. "Burajiru no Kôgyôka to Gaikoku Shihon--
   Taigai Rijun Sôkin Seigenhô wo Megutte (1-2)." Tokyo, Ajia
keizai (6: 11) November 1965, pp. 27-37; (6: 12), December
1965, pp. 20-30.
                         ("Brazilian Industrialization and
Foreign Capital: Law for Restricting Profit Remittances")

372   西向嘉昭　ラテン．アメリカ自由貿易連合（**LAFTA**）
　　　　　　におけるブラジルの立場（1~2）東京
　　　　　　アジア経済《6：2）2．1965，39~50；（6：3)
　　　　　　3，1965．39~50

Nishimukaı, Yoshiaki.　"Raten Amerika Jiyūbōeki Rengō
(LAFTA) Niokeru Burajiru no Tachiba (1-2)."　Tokyo,
<u>Ajia keizai</u> (6: 2), February 1965, pp. 39-50; (6: 3), March
1965, pp. 39-50?
　　　　　　　　　　　　　　("Position of Brazil in the Latin
American Free Trade Association [LAFTA]")

373   斎藤広志　ブラジルにおける外国移民の研究　東京
　　　　　　ラテン．アメリカ研究（**6**）6，1965．41~71

Saito, Hiroshi.　"Burajiru Niokeru Gaikoku Imin no Kenkyū."
Tokyo, <u>Raten Amerika kenkyu</u> (6), June 1965, pp. 41-71.
　　　　　　　　　　　　　("The Study of Immigrants in Brazil")

374   斎藤広志　ブラジルにおける邦人移住者の地域移動
　　　　　　神戸　国際経済研究年報（**10**）1．1960．
　　　　　　195~247

Saito, Hiroshi.　"Burajiru Niokeru Hōjin Ijūsha no Chiikiidō."
Kobe, <u>Kokusai keizai kenkyu nenpo</u> (10), January 1960, pp. 195-247.
　　　　　　　　　("Regional Movement of Japanese Emigrants
in Brazil")

375   斎藤広志　ブラジルのナショナリズム　東京
　　　　　　ラテン．アメリカ研究（4）5，1964，1~29

Saito, Hiroshi.　"Burajiru no Nashonarizumu."　Tokyo, <u>Raten
Amerika kenkyu</u> (4), May 1964, pp. 1-29.
　　　　　　　　　　　　　("Nationalism in Brazil")

376 斎藤広志　ブラジル政界最近の動向　東京
ラテン・アメリカ研究 (1)　11, 1962, 1~16

Saito, Hiroshi. "Burajiru Seikai Saikin no Dōkō." Tokyo,
Raten Amerika kenkyu (1), November 1962, pp. 1-16.
("The Recent Political Situation in Brazil")

377 桜井雅夫　ブラジルにおける公益事業の国家独占
東京　アジア経済 (4：10) 19, 1963, 30~43

Sakurai, Takao. "Burajiru Niokeru Kōeki Jigyō no Kokka
Dokusen." Tokyo, Ajia keizai (4: 10), October 1963, pp. 30-43.
("State Monopoly of Public Utilities in Brazil")

378 桜井雅夫　ブラジルにおける対外利潤送金制限法の
立法過程　東京　アジア経済 (4：5) 5,
1963, 44~66

Sakurai, Takao. "Burajiru Niokeru Taigai Rijun Sōkin Seigenhō
no Rippō Katei." Tokyo, Ajia keizai (4: 5), May 1963, pp.
44-66.
("The Process of Enactment of a Restrictive
Law on Foreign Profit Remittances from Brazil")

379 桜井雅夫　低開発国における国際投資の法的保障 ---
ブラジルを中心として　東京　アジア経済 (7：6)
6, 1966, 48~67

Sakurai, Takao. "Teikaihatsukoku Niokeru Kokusai Tōshi
no Hōteki Hogo-Burajiru wo Chūshintoshite." Tokyo,
Ajia keizai (7: 6), June 1966, pp. 48-67.
("Legal Protection of International Investment
in a Developing Country: The Case of Brazil")

380   佐野泰彦　ブラジル憲法史試論　東京　ラテン．
アメリカ研究（3）11．1963，20～39

Sano, Yasuhiko. "Burajiru Kenpôshi Shiron. " Tokyo, <u>Raten Amerika kenkyu (3)</u>, November 1963, pp. 20-39.
                ("Essay on the History of Constitutions in Brazil")

381   佐々木専三郎　ブラジル労資関係の性質　東京
ラテン．アメリカ研究（4）5，1964，30～47

Sasaki, Senzaburo. "Burajiru Rôshi Kankei no Seisitsu. " Tokyo, <u>Raten Amerika kenkyu</u> (4), May 1964, pp. 30-47.
                ("Features of Capital and Labor Relations in Brazil")

382   高橋勝之　ブラジルの経済の特徴　東京　経済（9）
6，1964，142～151

Takahashi, Katsuyuki. "Burajiru no Keizai no Tokuchô. " Tokyo, <u>Keizai</u> (9), June 1964, pp. 142-151.
                ("Characteristics of the Brazilian Economy")

383   中川和彦　中米経済統合の法律上の諸問題　東京
        アジア経済 (7 : 6) 6, 1966, 80-86

Nakagawa, Kazuhiko. "Chūbei Keizaitōgō no Hōritsujō no
   Shomondai." Tokyo, <u>Ajia keizai</u> (7: 6), June 1966, pp. 80-86.
                    ("Legal Problems Concerned with the
Economic Integration of Central America")

384   中曽根悟郎　中米共同市場について　東京
        外務省調査月報 (5 : 5) 5, 1964, 1-43

Nakasone, Goro. "Chūbei Kyōdō Shijō ni Tsuite." Tokyo,
   <u>Gaimusho chosa geppo</u> (5: 5), May 1964, pp. 1-43.
                    ("On the Central America Common Market")

385   佐藤和男　中米共同市場の発展　東京　世界経済
        評論 (11 : 9) 9, 1967, 41-47

Sato, Kazuo. "Chūbei Kyōdō Shijō no Hatten." Tokyo, <u>Seikai
   keizai hyoron</u> (11: 9), September 1967, pp. 41-47.
                    ("The Development of the Central American
Common Market")

386 　田中 薫　チリー領パタゴニアのリオ．バケル地で
　　　　における土地と民生　神戸　経済学研究
　　　　（神戸大）（7）7，1960，45-83

Tanaka, Kaoru. "Chirii Ryô Patagonia no Rio Bakeru Chiku
　Niokeru Tochi to Minsei. " Kobe, <u>Keizaigaku kenkyu</u> (Kobe
University) (7), July 1960, pp. 45-83.
　　　　　　　　("Land and Life at Rio Baker in Chilean
Patagonia")

CUBA

387 　後藤政子　キューバの工業発展政策について
　　　　東京　アジア．アフリカ研究（7：8）8，1967，
　　　　49-57

Goto, Masako. "Kyûba no Kôgyô Hatten Seisaku Nitsuite. "
　Tokyo, <u>Ajia Afurika kenkyu</u> (7: 8), August 1967, pp. 49-57.
　　　　　　　　("On the Industrial Development Policy of Cuba")

388 　水野　一　革命後のキューバ経済発展　東京
　　　　アジア経済（6：11）11，1965，76-83

Mizuno, Hajime. "Kakumei go no Kyûba Keizai Hatten. "
　Tokyo, <u>Ajia keizai</u> (6: 11), November 1965, pp. 76-83.
　　　　　　　　("Economic Development in Post-Revolution
Cuba")

389　大原美範　キューバの経済計画　東京　世界経済
　　　　評論 (9 : 10) 10, 1965, 25~32

Ohara, Yoshinori. "Kyûba no Keizai Keikaku." Tokyo,
<u>Sekai keizai hyoron</u> (9: 10), October 1965, pp. 25-32.
　　　　　　　　　("Economic Planning in Cuba")

390　吉沢末男　キューバ革命と経済建設の動向　東京
　　　　経済 (9) 6, 1964, 125~132

Yoshizawa, Sueo. "Kyûba Kakumei to Keizai Kensetsu no
Dôkô." Tokyo, <u>Keizai</u> (9), June 1964, pp. 125-132.
　　　　　　　　("The Cuban Revolution and Trends in
Economic Development")

DOMINICAN REPUBLIC

391　横田一太郎　ドミニカ共和国における土地登記制度
　　　　東京　ラテン．アメリカ研究 (7) 1, 1966,
　　　　31~40

Yokota, Ichitaro. "Dominika Kyôwakoku Niokeru Tochi
Tôkiseido." Tokyo, <u>Raten Amerika kenkyu</u> (7), January
1966, pp. 31-40.
　　　　　　　　("The Land Registration Law in the Dominican
Republic")

392 木田和雄　グアテマラ🔲🔲領における藍産業　東京
　　　ラテン．アメリカ研究 (5) 12。1964，20-39

Kida, Kazuo. "Guatemara Sōtokuryō Niokeru ai Sangyō. "
Tokyo, <u>Raten Amerika kenkyu</u> (5), December 1964, pp. 20-39.
　　　　　("The Indigo Industry in Colonial Guatemala")

MEXICO

393　　石井　章　メキシコにおける土地所有形態の歴史的
　　　　変遷　東京　アジア経済 (6：12) 12。1965。
　　　　45-61

Ishii, Akira. "Mekishiko Niokeru Tochi Shoyū Keitai no
Rekishiteki Hensen. " Tokyo, <u>Ajia keizai</u> (6: 12), December
1965, pp. 45-61.
　　　　　　　("Changes in the Forms of Land Tenure in
Mexican History")

394　　賀川俊彦　ロペス．マテオス大統領と現代メキシコ
　　　　の政治　東京　ラテン．アメリカ研究 (3) 11，
　　　　1963，40-54
Kagawa, Toshihiko. "Ropesu Mateosu Daitōryō to Gendai
Mekishiko no Seiji. " Tokyo, <u>Raten Amerika kekyu</u> (3),
November 1963, pp. 40-54.
　　　　　　　　("President Lopez Mateos and the
Politics of Modern Mexico")

395   毛利　亮　メキシコの北方国境地帯とホアレス市
        東京　早稲田商学 (185) 12, 1965, 99～121

Mori, Toru. "Mekishiko no Hoppō Kokkyō Chitai to Hoaresu
    Shi." Tokyo, Waseda Shogaku (185), December 1965,
    pp. 99-121.
                ("The Northern Border Area of Mexico and
    Ciudad Juarez")

PERU

396   斎藤広志　ペルー在住日系人の人口と家族　東京
        ラテン・アメリカ研究 (2) 4, 1963, 1～25

Saito, Hiroshi. "Perū Zaijū Nikkeijin no Jinko to Kazoku."
    Tokyo, Raten Amerika kenkyu (2), April 1963, pp. 1-25.
                ("Population and the Families of Japanese
    Emigrants in Peru")

397   田嶋　久　ペルーにおける大土地所有と小作制変
        の事例　東京　ラテン・アメリカ研究 (8) 8,
        1967, 183～211

Tajima, Hisashi. "Perū Niokeru Daitochishoyū to Kosakuseibo
    no Jirei." Tokyo, Raten Amerika kenkyu (8), August 1967,
    pp. 183-211.
                ("Some Examples of Large Landholdings
    and Land Tenure in Peru")

398

ベネズエラ人民は かれの歌を作る
平和と社会主義の諸問題
第8巻 第5号

"Benezuera Jimmin wa Kare no uta o Tsukuru." Tokyo,
　Heiwa to Shakaishugi no sho mondai (8: 5), May, 1965.
("The People of Venezuela are Composing his Song")
-About President Betancourt

Hankuk University of Foreign Studies in Seoul grants a
Bachelor of Arts degree in Spanish and Portuguese,
and a Master of Arts degree in Latin American Area
Studies. Courses in these fields are under the supervision of the Department of Spanish at the University.

In this bibliography the English translation of the title
of each bibliographic item is to be found directly under
the title in the original language, and immediately
following the entire bibliographic description.

———————

La Universidad Hankuk de Estudios Internacionales en
la ciudad de Seoul otorga Bachillerato en el campo de
Lenguas Español y Portugués, y título académico de
Maestro en Artes en Asuntos Latinoamericanos. El
Departamento de Lengua Español de la Universidad
administra los cursos en estos campos.

En esta bibliografía la traducción inglesa del título
de cada asiento se encuentra directamente bajo el
título de la lengua original, seguida de la ficha entera.

I. Books

LATIN AMERICA

399 金東成　中南美紀行　서울　원문각

Kim, Tong-Sŏng. <u>Chungnammi Kihaeng</u>. Seoul, Wŏnmun'gak,
1954, 191p.
　　　　　　(A Trip to Central and South America)
-Report of the author's visit to Latin American countries as a
special envoy in 1949.

400 吳應瑞　移民　中南美案内　서울　向文社

O, Ŭng-so. <u>Imin-gwa Chungnammi Anne</u>. Seoul, Hyangmun-sa,
1964, 189p.
　　　　　　(Immigration and a Guide to Central and South
America)
-Information about Latin American countries and related
immigration problems for applicants hoping to emigrate;
description of Latin American political geography.

401 외무부　諸國移民協定　서울　외무부

Oemubu. <u>Chekuk Imin Hyŏpchŏng</u>. Seoul, Oemubu, 1960, 81p.
(Korea. Ministry of Foreign Affairs. <u>Immigration Pacts
Among the Nations</u>)
-Contents. 1. Brazil-Italy immigration pact.
　　　　　　2. Brazil-Netherlands immigration pact.
　　　　　　3. Japan-Paraguay immigration pact.

402　외무부　　中南美地域経済調査団綜合報告書

　　　　서울　　외무부

Oemubu.　Chungnammi Chiyŏk Kyŏngje Chosadan Chonghap
Pokosŏ.　Seoul, Oemubu, 1960, 37p.
(Korea.　Ministry of Foreign Affairs.　A Report of an Economic
Inquiry Section in Latin America)

403　외무부　　라틴아메리카経済概観　　서울　　외무부

Oemubu.　Latin America Kyŏngje Kaekwan.　Seoul, Oemubu, 1959.
(Korea.　Ministry of Foreign Affairs.　An Outline of Economies of
Latin America)

404　외무부　　美洲地域観書　慶祝使節団綜合報告書

　　　서울　　외무부

Oemubu.　Miju Chiyŏk Ch'inŏn-Mit Kyŏngch'uk Sajŏltan Chonghap
Pokoso.　Seoul, Oemubu, 1962, 138p.
(Korea.　Ministry of Foreign Affairs.　A Report of the Goodwill
Mission to America)
-Report of the goodwill mission which went to inform the Latin
American countries of the meaning and inevitability of the May
16 military revolution in Korea, and for the promotion of friendship
between Korea and Latin American countries. Issuing a joint
communiqué, Korea entered into permanent political and economic
relations with them.

405 외 무 부   정 무 국   中南美政治概觀   서 울   외무

Oemubu Chŏngmukuk. Chungnammi Chŏngch'i Kaekwan.
  Seoul, Oemubu, 1961, 374p.
(Korea. Ministry of Foreign Affairs. Bureau of Political
Affairs. Political Outline of Central and South America)
-Description of the history and the political problems of the
Latin American countries and OAS.

406 외 무 부   정 무 국   큐 바 의 카 스 트 로 政權   서 울

Oemubu Chŏngmukuk. Cuba-ui Castro Chongkwon. Seoul,
  Oemubu, 1962, 37p.
(Korea. Ministry of Foreign Affairs. Bureau of Political
Affairs. Cuba Under the Castro Government)
-The government under Castro has tried to destroy the
stable governments of Latin American nations.

407 외 무 부 정 무 국   南美大陸에对한我國移民計画
     서 울   외무부

Oemubu Chŏngmukuk. Nammi Taeryug-e Taehan Aguk Imin
  Kyehoek. Seoul, Oemubu, 1960, 76p.
(Korea. Ministry of Foreign Affairs. Bureau of Political
Affairs. The Korean Immigration Plan to the South American
Continent)
-Brazil is the best country in the South American continent for
immigration in terms of climate, industry and social conditions.
Summaries of climate, population, political and economic conditions
in each country in South America are given.

외무부 통상국   執務參考資料各國便覽

408

서울   외무부 책

Oemubu T'ongsang'guk. Chipmu Ch'amgo Charyo, Kakuk
P'yŏnlam. Seoul, Oemubu, 1959-1960.
(Korea. Ministry of Foreign Affairs. Bureau of Economic
Affairs. Reference Materials for Official Work: Handbooks for
Each Country)
-Each book contains data on the political geography, government,
culture, and foreign policy of the country. Books on each of the
following 15 countries: Argentina (33p.), Bolivia (66p.), Chile (42p.),
Cuba (29p.), Ecuador (40p.), Haiti (31p.), Mexico (44p.), Nicaragua
(18p.), Honduras (15p.), Salvador, Guatemala (20p.), Peru (26p.),
Paraguay (29p.), Uruguay (38p.), and Venezuela (28p.).

외무부   통상국   中南美地域諸國의共同市場發展

409

의重要性

Oemubu T'ongsang'guk. Chungnammi Chiyŏk Chaegug-ŭi
Kongdong Sijang Palchŏn-ŭi Chungyosong. Seoul, Oemubu,
1961, 89p.
(Korea. Ministry of Foreign Affairs. Bureau of Economic Affairs.
Importance of the Development of the Common Market in Central
and South American Countries)
-An underdeveloped country will be confronted with difficulties if
it makes plan only for itself. The expansion of markets develops
a form of enterprise.

외무부   통상국   라틴아메리카自由貿易聯合

410

서울 외무부

Oemubu T'ongsang'guk. Latin America Chayumuyŏk Yonhap.
Seoul, Oemubu, 1965, 236p.
(Korea. Ministry of Foreign Affairs. Bureau of Economic
Affairs. Latin American Free Trade Association)
-Survey of the economic condition of Latin America, as a reference
for trade with Latin American countries. Study of the Latin
American economy and a view of LAFTA in Korean. Montevideo
treaty in appendix in English.

411 외무부 통상국 라틴 아메리카 經濟槪觀

年度 서울 외무국

Oemubu T'ongsang'guk. <u>Latin America Kyŏngje Kaekwan, 1959
Nyŏndo</u>. Seoul, Oemubu, 148p.
(Korea. Ministry of Foreign Affairs. Bureau of Economic
Affairs. <u>Economy of Latin America in 1959</u>)
-Trade was in a serious state of depression in 1959. The national
incomes decreased over 1%.

412 朴東烈 移民問題 와南美各国의槪況 서울 利文

Pak, Tong-Yŏl. <u>Imin Munje-wa Nammi Kakug-ŭi Kaehwang</u>.
Seoul, Imun'gak, 1962, 416p.
(The Immigration Question and the Conditions
of South American Countries)
-A guide to overseas immigration. Study of South American
countries' situations: Brazil, Argentina, Uruguay, Paraguay,
Chile and Peru.

413 中央情報部　　브라질 聯邦共和国　서울　中央情報部

Chungang Chŏngbobu. Brazil Yŏnbang Konghwaguk. Seoul, Chungang
　Chŏngbobu, 1965, 224p.
(Korea. Central Intelligency Agency. United States of Brazil)
-Record of the history, climate, social, political and economic conditions
and industry in Brazil.

414 韓治養　鄭之柄　基礎브라질語入門　新文化社

Han, Ch'i-sŏn. Chŏng, Ŭl-pyŏng. Kich'o Brazil Ŏ ipmun.
　Seoul, Sinmunhwa-sa, 1961, 233p.
　　　　　　　　　　　　　　　(Primeras Licões
de Portugués)
-A guide to Brazilian language: grammar and conversation.

415 보건 사회부　브라질 移民手帖　서울　보건 사회부

Pogŏn Sahoebu. Brazil Imin Such'ŏp. Seoul, Pogŏn Sahoebu,
　1963, 60p.
(Korea. Ministry of Health and Social Affairs. Handbook for Immigration
to Brazil)
-Guide for Korean emigrants upon landing in Brazil, and information
on Brazilian agricultural conditions.

CENTRAL AMERICA

416 주 멕시 코   한국 대사관   中美共同市場研究

서울   외무부

Chu Mexico Han'guk Taesakwan. Chungmi Kongdong Sijang Yŏn'gu.
  Seoul, Oemubu, 1965, 91p.
(Korea. Embassy in Mexico. A Study of the Central American Free Tr.
Association)
-Record of the background of unification of the Central American
common market and a view of CAFTA.

CUBA

417 외 무 부   서 울   외 무 부

Oemubu. Cuba Crisis. Seoul, Oemubu, 1962.
(Korea. Ministry of Foreign Affairs. Cuban Crisis)

MEXICO

418 외 무 부   서 울   외 무 부

Oemubu. A Manual of Mexico and a Statement of the Principal
Laws of Mexico. Seoul, Ministry of Foreign Affairs)

PARAGUAY

419 吳杓 南美 의 오 아 시 스 파 라 파 이   서 울   파 한   협 회

O, P'yo. Nammi-ui Oasis Paraguay. Seoul, P'ahan Hyop'hoe,
1966, 212p.
          (Paraguay, Oasis in South America)
-Guide to Paraguay for people hoping to emigrate. Introduction
to the history, economy, government and culture.

LATIN AMERICA

비 지 네 스 사   中南美経済를吟味한다   서울
420
비 지 네 스   젼 회 년 월

Business Sa. "Chungnammi Kyŏngje-rŭl Ŭmmi-handa."
    Seoul, <u>Business</u> (II: 2), February 1962, p. 17.
            ("An Inquiry into Central and South American
    Economies")

鄭然權   開拓의 망中南美와韓國移民   서 울
421
비 지 네 스 젼 회 년 월

Chŏng, Yŏn-Kwŏn. "Kech'ŏg-ŭi Ttang, Chungnammi-wa Han'guk
    Imin." Seoul, <u>Business</u> (II: 8), August 1962, pp. 2-7.
            ("Land Clearing, Central and South America,
    and Korean Emigration")
    -Study of the Latin American countries where Koreans can immigrate
    and the Korean conditions for emigration.

鄭然權   南美経済이 모 저 모 서 울   비 지 네 스
422

Chŏng, Yŏn-kwŏn.   "Nammi Kyŏngje Imochŏmo." Seoul,
    <u>Business</u> (I: 11), November 1961, pp. 20-23.
            ("Facets of South American Economy")
    -The economies in Latin America depend on their own unique
    products. Foreign capital comprises 90% of all capital investment.

423 韓鍾元 　서울　한국외국어 대학 논문집　년 월

Han, Chong-wŏn. "America Latina, La Tierra de Promisión. "
Seoul, Han'guk Oegug O Taehak Nonmunjip. April 1964, pp.
375-451.
　　　　　　　　　　　　("Latin America, Land of Promise")
- The writer has been in Mexico for half of his life and has traveled
throughout Latin America. He describes the residents' way of
thinking, the feeling of life and general problems in Latin America.
In Spanish.

424 韓國銀行　海外経済秒錄　서 울　조 사 월 보

Han'guk Ŭnhaeng. "Haeoe Kyŏngje Ch'orok. " Seoul, Chosa wolbo,
1947-
("Korea. Bank of Korea. Current Economic Events Abroad")
-Every number contains information on world economic conditions,
including Latin American countries.

425 한 국 은 행　해 외 경제 동 향　서 울　세 계 경제)

Han'guk Unhaeng. "Haeoe Kyŏngje Tonghyang. " Seoul, Segye kyongje,
1951-
("Korea. Bank of Korea. Trends of World Economy")
- This journal often has articles containing references to Latin
America, country by country.

426 金滋東　南美의 現勢와 美國의 政策　서울　新世界

Kim, Cha-tong. "Nammi-ŭi Hyŏnse-wa Migug-ŭi Chŏngch'aek."
Seoul, <u>Sinsegye</u> (I: 1), November 1962, pp. 159-166.
                    ("The Present Condition of South America
and the Policy of the U.S.A.")
- The U.S.A. has aided the South American countries by one
billion dollars since the OAS was organized, but South American
peoples still remain in poverty and under ineffective goverments.

427 金鈺　南美 시장　서울 무역진흥 호 년 월

Kim, Ok. "Nammi Sijang." Seoul, <u>Muyŏk chinhŭng</u> (4: 5), May,
July 1963, pp. 55-61, 152-155.
                    ("Markets in South America")
-Study of the economy of Latin America, country by country,
in relation to trade with Korea.

428 金永熙　南美의 두 單事革命　서울　世代 진호 년 월

Kim, Yŏng-hi. "Nammi-ŭi tu Kunsa Hyŏkmyŏng." Seoul,
<u>Sedae</u> (I: 6), November 1963, pp. 328-330.
                    ("Two Revolutions in South America")
- The main cause of the coup d'état in the Dominican Republic
was that the officers were desirous of power. The coup d'état in
Honduras had no meaning. It was a revolution among officers.

429 文一英 "中美美의 政治気象図" 서울 時事 호 년 월

Mun, Ill-yŏng. "Chungnammi-ŭi Chŏngch'i Kisangdo." Seoul,
Sisa (23), June 1963, pp. 42-51.
("The Political Anticipation in Central and
South America")
-Revolutions occured in Central and South America during the 4 years
since Cuba's Revolution in 1960. Accomplishment of the
Cuban Revolution shows that a small country in Latin America can
defy the United States.

朴武昇 "軍事쿠데타와 貧困의 南美" 서울
430
思想界 권호 년 월

Pak, Mu-sŭng. Kunsa Coup d'état-wa Pin'gon-ŭi Nammi."
Seoul, Sasanggye (XI: 2), February 1963, pp. 220-227.
("Military Coup d'état and Poverty Stricken
South America")
-The U.S. Government must reconsider its Latin American
policy, and fix a realistic policy for Latin America based on
political stability and economic prosperity.

思想界社 "搖動하는 라틴" 아메리카政局
431
서울 思想界

Sasanggye Sa. "Yotong-hanŭn Latin America Chŏng'guk."
Seoul, Sasanggye (XIII: 7), July 1965, pp. 154-156.
("Troubled Latin America")
-Coups d'état in Latin American countries are briefly treated.

432 李相舜 "美洲에 浸透하는 새로운 帝國主義"

서울 공군 호 년 월

Yi, Sang-sun. "Miju-e Ch'imt'u-hanŭn Saeroun Chaekukchuŭi."
Seoul, <u>Kong'gun</u> (75), June 1963, pp. 20-26.
                    ("The New Imperialism Invading the Americas")
- The American success against Castroism depends upon economic
development of Latin American countries.

433 柳鍾玄 "世界의 地域別共同市場圈近況"

서울 무역 진흥 권호 년월

Yu, Chong-hyon. "Segye-ui Chiyŏk-pyŏl Kongdong Sijang-kwon-
      LAFTA CACM P'yŏn." Seoul, <u>Muyŏk chinhung</u> (IV: 21), May
1965, pp. 44-48.
                    ("The Current State of Regional Common Markets
in the World - LAFTA, CACM-")
-One of a series of articles on world common markets. The writer,
who works at the Bureau of Economic Affairs in the Ministry of
Foreign Affairs, believes all Latin American countries will join
LAFTA.

ARGENTINA

434 "駐알젠틴韓國大使館" 알젠틴에 대한

韓國輸出可能品目調査

Chu Argentina Han'guk Taesakwan. "Argentina-e Taehan Han'guk Such'ul Kanung P'ummok Chosa." Seoul, Muyok chinhung (IV: 21), May 1965, pp. 52-55.
(Korean Embassy, Argentina. "Investigation of Articles Possible to Export to Argentina")
-Written to assist Korean businessmen who wish to trade with Argentina: 14 articles.

435 金庚哲 "알젠틴의貿易과關稅制度" 서울 무역진흥

Kim, Kyŏng-ch'ŏl. "Argentina-ŭi Muyŏk-gwa Kwanse Chedo." Seoul, Muyŏk chinhung (IV: 22), June 1965, pp. 74-78.
("The Trade of Argentina and the Tariff Policy")
-The trade of Argentina is in the black. Main export articles are agricultural products, and imported articles machinery.

436 文鍾律 "알젠틴 의經濟槪況" 서울 무역진흥 권호 년월

Mun, Chong-yul. "Argentina-ŭi Kyŏngje Kaehwang." Seoul, Muyŏk Chinhung (III: 9), April 1964, pp. 49-55.
("An Outline of Economy in Argentina")
-The writer is an officer at the Korean Embassy in Argentina. He explains Argentina's economy industry by industry.

외무부 통상국 "알젠틴의 財政問題"

437

서울 국제경제 권호 년월

Oemubu T'ongsang'guk. "Argentina-ŭi Chaejŏng Munje."
　Seoul, <u>Kukche kyŏngje</u> (II: 7), July 1960, pp. 103-109.
(Korea. Ministry of Foreign Affairs. Bureau of Economic
Affairs. "The Financial Problems of Argentina")
-Argentina needs foreign funds and technical assistance in
order to overcome the current economic emergency.

438　외무부 통상국 "알젠틴의 貿易과 関税制度"

서울 국제 경제 월보

Oemubu T'ongsang'guk. "Argentina-ŭi Muyŏk-gwa Kwanse."
　Seoul, <u>Kukche kyŏngje wolbo</u> (III: 3), March 1964, pp. 25-29.
(Korea. Ministry of Foreign Affairs. Bureau of Economic
Affairs. "Argentine Trade and Tariff")
-Argentine trade depends upon agricultural products and oil.
Tariff rates are low for industrial articles.

BRAZIL

439 비 지 니 스 사 "브 라 질 經濟는 어 디 로 가 나" 서 울 비 지 니 스

Business Sa. "Brazil Kyongje-nun Odiro Kana." Seoul,
Business (II: 5), May 1962, pp. 88-89.
(Business Co. Where is Brazil's Economy Going? ")

440 비 지 니 스 사 "브 라 질 未來를約束하는開發計劃

서 울 베 지 니 스

Business Sa. "Brazil, Mire-rŭl Yaksok-hanŭn Kaepal Kyehoek."
Seoul, Business (II: 3), March 1962, pp. 12-14.
(Business Co. "Brazil, the Development Plan Bringing a
Promising Future")

441 張幸勳 "右側으로 핸들을 꺾은 브 라 질革命"

서 울 世代

Chang, Haeng-hun. "Uch'ŭg-ŭro Handle-rŭl Kkŏkkŭn Brazil Hyŏkmyŏng."
Seoul, Sedae (II: 5), May 1964, pp. 277-281.
("The Turn to the Right in the Brazilian
Revolution")
-Description of the political conditions in Brazil prior to the
military revolution on April 1, 1964. Brazilians, like many other Latin
American peoples, are likely to interpret close relations with
the United States as dependence.

韓國關稅協会 〝브 라 질 의經済近況〞

442

　　서 울　關稅 와貿易

Han'guk Kwanse Hyop'hoe. "Brazil-ui Kyongje Kunhwang."
　Seoul, Kwanse-wa Muyok (I: 2, 3), February, March 1965,
　pp. 37-39, 70-71.
(Korea. Korea Customs Association. "The Present Economy
of Brazil")
-Review of Brazilian economy for those interested in emigration
policy.

443 金昌順 〝브 라 질政変 이 收拾 되기 까지〞서울 해군

Kim, Ch'ang-sun. "Brazil Chŏngbyŏn- i Susŭp-toeki Kkaji."
　Seoul, Haegun (107), November 1961, pp. 32-35.
　　　　　　　　　　("Until the Brazilian Political Crisis was
Controlled")
-There is no political party in Brazil supported by most of
the people. The National Assembly reformed the government
into a parliamentary system.

444 金永文 〝브 라 질移民 의 實態 를 直視 하 라〞서 울　財務

Kim, Yŏng-mun. "Brazil Imin-ui Silte-rul Chiksi-hara." Seoul,
Chaemu (105), September 1964, pp. 64-72.
　　　　　　　　　　("Look the Actual Condition of Emigration
to Brazil in the Face")
-The result of emigration to Brazil is discontent. The government
must plan on emigration outlets and administration of emigration.

445 金永文 "브라질로分家가는 우리 겨레" 서울 財務

Kim, Yŏng-mun. "Brazil-lo Pun'ga-ganŭn Uri Kyŏre. "
   Seoul, <u>Chaemu</u> (85), January 1963, pp. 64-72.
                    ("The Korean Emigrating to Brazil")
   -Korean emigration to Brazil is the first experience, and
   so it must be successful emigration. Emigration policy
   is accomplished with official support.

446 南振祐 "브라질移民의合理化에対하여" 서울 最高会議報

Nam, Chin-u. "Brazil Imin-ui Hamnihwa-e Taehayo. "
   Seoul, <u>Chóego-hoeŭibo</u> (16), January 1963, pp. 136-142.
                ("For the Rationalization of Emigration
   to Brazil")
   - The course of emigration negotiations and the Brazilian
   character. We must study the history and political
   conditions of the nation where Koreans plan to emigrate.

447 南振祐 "伯國의情勢와 우리移民의展望" 서울 最高会議報

Nam, Chin-u. "Paegug-ŭi Chŏngse-wa Uri Imin-ŭi Chŏnmang. "
   Seoul, <u>Ch'oego hoeuibo</u> (18), March 1963, pp. 85-87.
                    ("The Situation of Brazil and a View of Korean
   Emigration")
   -Recording the real condition of the emigrants in Brazil:
   Koreans should be permitted to emigrate to Brazil in the
   near future.

448　외 무 부　통 상 국 "브 라 질 의 貿易 및 關稅" 서 울
百屠 以屋 以논

Oemubu T'ongsang'guk. "Brazil-ŭi Mŭyok-mit **Kwanse.**"
　Seoul, Kukche kyŏngje wolbo (III: 1), January 1964, pp. 96-100.
(Korea. Ministry of Foreign Affairs. Bureau of Economic
Affairs. "The Trade of Brazil and the Customs")
-International payments are "in the red". The government
has a general economic improvement plan.

449　白 玉彬 "브 라 질 軍部革命 과僑胞" 서 울　思想界

Paek, Ok-pin. "Brazil Kunbu Hyokmyŏng-gwa Kyop'o."
　Seoul, Sasanggye (XII: 7), July 1964, pp. 226-229.
　　　　　　　　("Military Revolution in Brazil and Koreans Abroad")
-Korean life in Brazil and the bad effects of Brazil's revolution.

450　白 玉彬 "브 라 질 의 歡喜" 서 울　思想界

Paek, Ok-pin. "Brazil-ŭi Hwanhi." Seoul, Sasanggye (XII: 1),
　January 1964, pp. 146-148.
　　　　　　　　("Delight in Brazil")
-Recording Korean life in Brazil and nostalgia for Korea.

451 　白玉杉 "鄕愁를달러며" 서을 思想界

Paek, Ok-pin. "Hyangsu-rŭl Talemyŏ." Seoul, <u>Sasanggye</u>
(XII: 5), May 1964, pp. 176-181.
                              ("Longing for my Home")
-Diary of a Korean's first year in Brazil.

452 　朴武昇 "쿠비체크의政治理念" 서을 思想界

Pak, Mu-sung. "Kubitschek-ŭi Chongch'i Inyŏm." Seoul,
<u>Sasanggye</u> (XII: 9), September 1964, pp. 177-180.
                              ("Kubitschek's Political Ideology")
-Kubitschek is a statesman of merit. He proposes a Pan-
American working plan.

453　申用淳 "中南美紀行" 서울　新東亜

Sin, Yong-sun. "Chungnammi Kihaeng." Seoul, <u>Sindonga</u>
(1), September 1964, pp. 245-249.
　　　　　　　　("A Trip to Central and South America")
- The writer is a reporter on the Dong- A newspaper in Korea.
He treats the social conditions and the national characteristics
of Central American nations. There is no food problem,
and so people are idle.

454　方鉐柱 "美國과中美六個國頂上会談의 意義"

　　　서울　最高会議報

Pang, P'il-ju. "Migug-gwa Chungmi 6 Kaeguk Chongsang
Hoetam-ui Uiui." Seoul, <u>Ch'oego hoeuibo</u> (19), April 1963,
pp. 119-121.

　　　　　　　　(" The Meaning of the Summit Conference
Between U.S.A. and six Central American Countries")
- Are the Central American countries able to quarantine Cuba
and so weaken Castroism, or will they be assimilated by
Castroism? .

455　新思潮社 "連鎖反應的中南美쿠데타" 서울　新思潮

Sinsajo Sa. "Yŏnsoe Panŭng-chŏk Chungnammi Coup d'état."
Seoul, <u>Sinsajo</u> (II: 9), November 1963, pp. 152-154.
(Sinsajo Co. Chain Reaction of Coups d'état in Central and
South America")
- It treats the aim of coups d'état in the Dominican Republic,
Venezuela, Brazil and Honduras. One aim is expansion of
military power for the government.

456 新世界社 "政變地帶의 波動, 中南美의 새 쿠 데타"
　　　서울 新世界

Sinsegye Sa. "Chongpyŏn Chitae-ŭi P'adong, Chungmi-ui
　　Sae Coup d'état. " Seoul, <u>Sinsegye</u> (II: 10), November
1963, pp. 169-170.
(Sinsegye Co. "Effects of Political Change: New Coups d'état
in Central and South America")
- The Coup d'état in the Dominican Republic occurred because
the military had misgivings about the internal political situation
and the danger of Castroism. The Coup d'état of Honduras had no
meaning.

金二培 "콜럼비아 一般經濟事情과貿易制度"

457

서울 무역진흥

Kim, I-pae. "Colombia Ilpan Kyŏngje Sajŏng-gwa Muyok Chedo."
Seoul, Muyŏk chinhŭng (V: 34), June 1966, pp. 62-67.
　　　　　　("Economic Condition of Colombia and the Trade
System")
- The economic situation of Colombia is not good, and a few
financial interests hold economic power.

458　외무부 통상국 "콜럼비아 의經濟開發策" 서울 국제 경제

Oemubu T'ongsang'uk. "Colombia-ŭi Kyŏngje Kaepal
Ch'aek." Seoul, Kukche kyŏngje (II: 9), September
1960, pp. 79-81.
(Korea. Ministry of Foreign Affairs. Bureau of Economic
Afairs. "The Economic Development Plan of Colombia")
- The Colombian Government is developing its industry
positively. Foreign trade is decreasing.

459　외무부 통상국 "콜럼비아 의經濟事情" 서울 국제 경제

Oemubu T'ongsang'guk. "Colombia-ŭi Kyŏngje Sajŏng."
Seoul, Kukche kyŏngje (II: 1), January 1960, pp. 104-109.
(Korea. Ministry of Foreign Affairs. Bureau of Economic
Affairs. "Economic Condition of Colombia")
-Colombia is improving its economic situation in foreign trade.

CHILE

460　金庚哲 "칠리의 貿易과 関税制度" 서울　무역 진흥

Kim, Kyŏng-Ch'ŏl. "Chile-ŭi Muyok-gwa Kwanse Chedo."
　　Seoul, Muyŏk chinhŭng (IV: 26), October 1965, pp. 44-47.
　　　　　　　　　　　("Chile's Trade and Tariff Policy")
- The trade condition of Chile is better this year (1965) than
last year. Korea has not exported Korean articles, but has
imported chemicals from Chile.

461　외 무 부　통 상 국 "칠 리 의 財政近況" 서 울　국제 경제

Oemubu T'ongsang'guk. "Chile-ŭi Chaejŏng Kŭnhwang."
　　Seoul, Kukche kyongje (II: 7), July 1960, pp. 94-98.
　(Korea. Ministry of Foreign Affairs. Bureau of Economic Affairs.
"The Present Condition of the Finance of Chile")
- Policies that the government has planned in order to improve
the financial condition of the country.

CUBA

462 崔南俊 "퀴바의 武器는 果然撤去되었는가" 서울 時事

Ch'oe, Nam-jun. "Cuba-ŭi Mugi-nŭn Kwayŏn Ch'ŏlkŏ- Toeŏssnŭm'g
Seoul, Sisa (20), March 1963, pp. 68-71.
                    ("Are the Weapons in Cuba Really Withdrawn?")
- The danger in Cuba is not missiles but the hot-bed of Communism
for Latin America.

463 林芳鉉 "퀴바革命 카리브海의 붉은叛逆" 서울 世代

Im, Pang-hyŏn. "Cuba Hyŏkmyŏng, Carib Hae-ŭi Pulkŭn
Panyŏk." Seoul, Sedae (III: 3), April 1965, pp. 104-109.
                    ("Cuban Revolution, the Communists in the
Caribbean Sea")
- Cuba is a hot-bed of Communism for the American continent.

464 국무원 사무처 "퀴바의 事態解剖" 서울 情報

Kukmuwŏn Samuch'ŏ. "Cuba-ŭi Sat'e Haebu." Seoul, Chongbo,
August 1960, pp. 137-141.
(Korea. Ministry of Government Administration. "Study of
Cuban Situation")
- The fundamental U.S. policy towards Cuba is to localize
Castroism in Cuba.

465 외무부 통상국 "큐바의 貿易近況" 서울 국제 경제

Oemubu T'ongsang'guk. "Cuba-ŭi Muyŏk Kŭnhwang."
  Seoul, Kukche kyŏngje (II: 9), September 1960, pp. 48-51.
(Korea. Ministry of Foreign Affairs. Bureau of Economic
Affairs. "The Present Condition of Trade of Cuba")
- The Cuban government further tightens the controlled economy,
and it is taking over American enterprises.

466 嚴基衡 "爆發直前에서 큐바는어디로" 서울 時事

Ŏm, Ki-hyŏng. "Pokpal Chikchŏn-esŏ Cuba-nŭn Ŏdiro."
  Seoul, Sisa (16), November 1962, pp. 24-31.
                ("Cuba's Way at the Critical Moment")
- The U. S. A. could force the withdrawal of missiles but not
of Communism. The success of the blockade against Cuba
shows that the military power of the U. S. A. is stronger than
that of the U. S. S. R.

467 方弼柱 "큐바는共産化할것인가" 서울 코메트

Pang, P'il-ju. "Cuba-nŭn Kongsan-hwa Halkŏsin'ga." Seoul,
  Comet (48), November 1961, pp. 91-98.
          ("Is Cuba Communized? ")
- The writer is a member of an advisory committee of the
Korean Broadcasting System. Wise policy and patience are
needed in order to regenerate liberty and democracy in Cuba.

468 新世界社 "世界 의 耳目 은 큐 바 로" 서 을 新世界

Sinsegye Sa. "Segye-ŭi Imog-ŭn Cuba-ro." Seoul, <u>Sinsegye</u>
(I: 1), November 1962, pp. 147-150.
(Sinsegye Co. "Cuba, A Matter of Concern to the World")
- The blockade against Cuba showed unity among the western
nations.

GUATEMALA

469 외 무 부 통 상 국 "과 레 말 라 의 經濟事情" 서 을 국제 경제

Oemubu T'omgsang'guk. "Guatemala-ŭi Kyŏngje Sajŏng."
Seoul, <u>Kukche kyŏngje</u> (II: 7), July 1960, pp. 79-81.
(Korea. Ministry of Foreign Affairs. Bureau of Economic
Affairs. "The Economic Condition of Guatemala")
- The economic condition of Guatemala changes for the worse.

徐東九 〝하이티 도미니카 紛料의実体〟

서 울 最高会議報

470

Sŏ, Tong-ku. "Haiti Dominca Pun'gyu-ŭi Silch'e." Seoul,
Shoego hoeŭibo (21), June 1963, pp. 110-113.
                    ("The Facts on the Trouble between Haiti
and the Dominican Republic")
-Recording the origin and history of the disagreement
between Haiti and the Dominican Republic.

471 張基安 "멕시코의 經濟近況" 서울 진흥

Chang, Ki-an. "Mexico-ŭi Kyŏngje Kŭnhwang. " Seoul,
Muyŏk chinhŭng (7), November 1963, pp. 66-70.
("Economy of Mexico")
- The economy of Mexico in 1962 took a more favorable turn
than in 1961, but the government cannot cover the deficit.

472 외무부 통상국 "멕시코의 經濟動向" 서울 국제 경제 월보

Oemubu T'ongsang'guk. "Mexico-ŭi Kyŏngje Tonghyang. "
Seoul, Kukche kyŏngje wŏlbo (III: 3), March 1964, pp. 13-17.
(Korea. Ministry of Foreign Affairs. Bureau of Economic Affairs
"Trend of Mexico's Economy")
-Mexico imports more than it exports, but exports are steadily
increasing.

외무부 통상국 "멕시코의 1960 년 上半期貿易狀況"

473

서울 국제 경제

Oemubu T'ongsang'guk. "Mexico-ŭi 1960 nyŏn Sangban'gi Muyŏk
Sanghwang. " Seoul, Kukche kyŏngje (II: 10), October 1960,
pp. 45-49.
(Korea. Ministry of Foreign Affairs. Bureau of Economic
Review. "The Foreign Trade Condition of Mexico in the First Half
of 1960.')
-A review of the Mexican economy, with the conclusion that the
economic condition of Mexico is worse than the last year.

大韓損害再保險会社 "世界各國의保険市場概況

474

멕시코篇" 서울

Taehan Sonhae Chaepohŏm Kongsa. "Segye Kaggug-ŭi Pohŏm
 Sijang Kaehwang-Mexico Pyŏn." Seoul, <u>Sonhae pohŏm wŏlbo</u>
(25), June 1965, pp. 35-38.
(Korea. Korean Reinsurance Corporation. "Insurance Markets
of the World-Mexico")
-Insurance history and the present insurance conditions are
treated. Insurance market is growing rapidly.

車政錫 "一九六五年度 의 페루 市場動向"

475

서울 무역진흥　손해 보험 월보

Cha'a, Chŏng-sŏk. "1965 Nyŏndo-ŭi Sijang. Tonghyang."
Seoul, Muyŏk chinhŭng (V: 32), April 1966, pp. 37-41.
("Trend of Marketing in Peru in 1965")
- The principal imports are machinery, and the exports
are minerals.

476　車政錫 "페루 전전지" 서울 무역 진흥

Ch'a, Chŏng-sŏk. "Peru, Kŏnjŏnji." Seoul, Muyŏk chinhŭng
(V: 31), March 1966, pp. 53-58.
("Peru; Batteries")
- Investigation of market conditions for batteries in Peru for the
purpose of exporting Korean products. One of a series on trade
possibilities in Peru.

477　車政錫 "페루 라디오" 서울 -무역진흥

Ch'a, Chŏng-sŏk. "Peru, Radio." Seoul, Muyŏk chinhŭng
(V: 29), January 1966, pp. 120-124.
("Peru, Radios")
- Investigation of market conditions for radios in Peru for the
purpose of exporting Korean products. One of a series on trade
possibilities in Peru.

478 車政錫 " 피루 의류 " 서울 무역 진흥

Ch'a, Chŏng-sŏk. "Peru, Ŭiryu." Seoul, Muyŏk chinhŭng
   (IV: 27), November 1965, pp. 111-121.
                 ("Peru; Clothing")
-Investigation of market conditions for clothing in Peru for
the purpose of exporting Korean products, articles. The Peruvians
want standard items rather than new articles.

479 외 무 부 통 상 국 "피 루 의 經濟安定 "

서울 국제 경제 월보

Oemubu T'ongsang'guk. "Peru-ŭi Kyŏngje Anjŏng." Seoul,
   Kukche kyŏngje (II: 7), July 1960, pp. 70-76.
(Korea. Ministry of Foreign Affairs. Bureau of Economic
Affairs. "Economic Stability in Peru")
-Finance is stable, and the government is trying to improve
financial strength.

480 외 무 부 통 상 국 "피루의貿易收支 " 서울 국제 경제

Oemubu T'ongsang'guk. "Peru-ŭi Muyŏk Suji." Seoul, Kukche
   kyŏngje (II: 9), September 1960, pp. 53-56.
(Korea. Ministry of Foreign Affairs. Bureau of Economic
   Affairs. "The Trade of Peru")
-The most important element of improvement in the foreign
trade situation is stability in the money market.

大韓貿易振興会社 " 페루의 貿易과 關稅制度 "

481

서울 무역진흥

Taehan Muyŏkchinhŭng Kongsa. "Peru-ŭi Muyŏk-gwa
    Kwanse-cheto." Seoul, <u>Muyok chinhŭng</u> (III: 15),
November 1964, pp. 76-81.
(Korean Traders Association. "The Trade of Peru and
Tariff Policy")
- The condition of Peru's foreign trade is taking a favorable
turn.   Tariff rates on capital goods are low.

VENEZUELA

482   비지네스 사 " 베네주엘라 ,"   예산의 7활을 개발에

서울 비지네스

Business Sa. "Venezuela, Yesan-ŭi 7 Hal-rŭl Kaepal-e."
    Seoul, <u>Business</u> (II: 3), March 1962, pp. 10-11.
(Business Co. "Venezuela, 70% of the Budget for Development")
-A four-year development plan is delayed because the key industries
are lacking and the government is unstable.

PHILIPPINES

Geographically and in terms of language, the
Philippines are located in the non-western world,
specifically six hundred miles southeast of the
mainland of Asia, in the Malay Archipelago. In the
rural areas of the Philippines, over 70 native
languages are spoken, the official one being Tagalog.
For these reasons the Philippines are included in
this bibliography. Since the islands comprised a
significant part of the empire of Spain for several
centuries, Spanish civilization is reflected in family
names, religion, customs, and language. Spanish,
English and Tagalog are the official languages.
Subsequent to the Spanish-American War, with the
advent of occupation by the United States, Anglo-Saxon
culture has made important inroads into the prepon-
derantly Spanish-Catholic heritage. In 1946 the
Philippines won independence as a sovereign nation.

Although comparatively little publishing is undertaken
in the native languages of the Philippines, it should be
of interest to observe Philippine attitudes toward the
Latin American nations (for both were formerly
colonies of Spain), as reflected in the publications of
the Philippines. This, in addition to the fact that
geographically the Philippines lie in the non-western
world, dictates the inclusion of a Philippine section
herein, despite the fact that almost all items are in
English, with a few in Spanish.

The final argument for inclusion rests on the fact that
the Philippine National Archives contain a host of
materials in Spanish, vital for research on Latin
America during its colonial period.

With respect to courses on Latin America in educational
institutions, the University of Manila, which grants a
Bachelor of Science degree in Foreign Service, offers
courses in Latin American literature and in "Political
and Diplomatic History of Latin America."

Geograficamente, y en cuanto al idioma, las Filipinas
están situadas en el mundo no-occidental, especifi-
camente seiscientas millas al sureste del continente
asiático, en el Archipiélago Malayo. En las regiones
rurales de las Filipinas, se hablan más de 70 lenguas
indígenas, siendo la principal Tagalog. Por estas
razones se incluyen las Filipinas en esta bibliografía.
Puesto que las Islas formaron una parte significante
del Imperio Español por varios siglos, la civilización
española influye mucho en apellidos, religión, costum-
bres y idioma. Español, inglés y tagalog son las
lenguas principales. Después de la Guerra Española-
Norteamericana, con la conquista de las Filipinas por
las fuerzas de los EEUU, la cultura anglo-sajona ha
tenido mucha importancia en la civilización católica-
española. En 1946 las Filipinas ganaron la independencia como una nación soberana.

Aunque se publica poco en las lenguas nativas, debería
ser de sumo interés observar las actitudes filipinas
hacia las naciones latino-americanas (puesto que
ambas fueron colonias españolas), como se reflejan
en las publicaciones filipinas. En adición al hecho
que geograficamente las Filipinas se encuentran en
el mundo no-occidental, el interés en conocer las
ideas filipinas con respecto a Latinoamérica requiere
la inclusión de esta sección, a pesar de que casi todos
los asientos están redactados en inglés, con algunos
en español.

El argumento final para la inclusión de esta sección
se basa en el hecho que hay disponibles en el Archivo
Nacional de las Filipinas una gran cantidad de materiales
sobre Latinoamérica colonial.

Con respecto a cursos sobre Latinoamerica en instituciones avanzadas, la Universidad de Manila, la cual
otorga Bachillerato en Ciencia en Servicio Extranjero
(o sea, Diplomacia), ofrece cursos en letras latinoa-
americanas y en "Historia Política y Diplomática de
Latinoamérica. "

I. Books

LATIN AMERICA

483   Garcia, Eusebio Y. Specimen Under the Microscope. Manila,
    167p.

484   Retana, W. E. Aparato Bibliográfico de la Historia General de
    Filipinas. 3v. Manila, Pedro B. Ayuda y Cía. , 1964.
                (Bibliography of the General History of the
Philippines)

485   Villanueva, H. A. The Diplomacy of the Spanish-American
    War. Quezon City, University of the Philippines Press, 1949-51.

II. Periodical Articles

LATIN AMERICA

486   Ford, P. L. "Alliance for Progress." Manila, Weekly graphic (30: 43), April 15, 1964, p. 27.

487   "Latin America: Evolution or Revolution?" Manila, Mirror, June 3, 1961, pp. 20-21.

488   Sanchez, L. A. "Latin America--Old-New States." Manila, Comment (13), 2d quarter, 1961, pp. 82-91.

489   "What's Wrong With Latin America?" Manila, Sunday times magazine (17: 42), May 27, 1962, pp. 50-51.

490   "Why Latin Americans Mistrust the U. S." Manila, Sunday times magazine (17: 29), February 25, 1962, pp. 36-37.

491   Wilson, Dick. "Asia and Latin America: Prospects and Parallels." Hong Kong, Asia magazine (3: 2), January 13, 1963, pp. 5-7.

ARGENTINA

492   "The Argentine Republic: Optimism, Political Order Back in the
       Land of Gauchos." Manila, _Examiner_, 61st issue, August 12,
       1963, p. 13.

493   Brisard, Pierre. "Argentina." Manila, _Mirror_, December 3,
       1960, pp. 28-29.

494   "Integrated Development Plans for Argentina." Quezon City,
       Philippine architecture, engineering and construction record
       (10: 8), July 31, 1962, p. 24.

495   Sherman, George. "Powder Keg in Argentina." Manila, _Sunday
       times magazine_ (17: 44), June 10, 1962, pp. 28-31.

496   "A South American Country in Distress." Manila, _Sunday times
       magazine_ (13: 19), December 22, 1957, pp. 52-53.

BOLIVIA

497   Vega, Luis. "Bolivian Revolution Seeks Second Wind." Manila, Philippines herald magazine, January 23, 1965, p. 9.

BRAZIL

498   "Brazil: Its Past and Present." Manila, Mirror, November 12, 1960, pp. 16-17.

499   Maceda, José. "Latin Qualities in Brazil and the Philippines." Quezon City, Asian studies (2: 2), August, 1964, pp. 223-230.

500   Sionil, José F. "Where Revolution Fails, the Samba Succeeds." Manila, Sunday times magazine (16: 13), November 6, 1960, pp. 34-37.

501   Wilson, Dick. "Brasilia: a Concrete Fact in the Primeval Jungle." Hong Kong, Asia magazine (2: 45), November 11, 1962, pp. 4-8, 17-18.

502   Zaragosa, J. M. "Brasilia: Its Building Pattern Is Like That of the Philippine National Capital Site." Manila, Sunday times magazine (16: 15), November 20, 1960, pp. 28-29.

CENTRAL AMERICA

503   "Agreement for Establishment of the Central American Monetary Union and its Regulations." Manila, <u>Central bank news digest</u> (16: 45), November 3, 1964, pp. 2-9.

504   "Central American Integration Program." Manila, <u>Central bank news digest</u> (16: 49), December 1, 1964, pp. 6-7.

COLOMBIA

505   Kipper, Anna. "Where is Colombia Heading to?" Manila, <u>Mirror</u>, November 26, 1960, pp. 36-37.

CUBA

506   Alba, Victor. "The Americans Without Cuba." Manila, Sunday times magazine (17: 33), March 25, 1962, pp. 36-39.

507   Allemann, F. R. "Puerto Rico's 'Third Way'." Manila, Mirror, May 20, 1961, pp. 22-23.

508   "Caution Before Khruschchev Creates New Incidents." Quezon City, Weekly graphic (29: 22), November 21, 1962, pp. 22-23.

509   Cruz, E A. "Economics in the News." Manila, Commerce (57: 2), September, 1960, pp. 6, 38.

510   "Cuba: Tropical Paradise With a Violent History." Manila, Mirror, July 16, 1960, p. 38.

511   Dacanay, A. R. "Turmoil in Cuba." Quezon City, Weekly graphic (27: 45), May 3, 1961, p. 10.

512   Dewart, Leslie. "Christianity and Revolution: the Lesson of Cuba." Manila, Philippine studies (13: 2), April, 1965, pp. 395-398.

513   "The Failure in Cuba." Manila, Sunday times magazine (16: 41), May 21, 1961, pp. 16-17.

514   "The First Exclusive Photos of a Locked-in Cuba." Manila, Mirror, January 12, 1963, pp. 36-39.

515 León, Bernardo de. "The Cuban Debacle." Manila, _Mirror_, May 6, 1961, pp. 22-23.

516 León, Bernardo de. "The Errors of U.S. Interventionist Policy in the Americas." Manila, _Weekly graphic_ (31: 54), July 7, 1965, pp. 10-12.

517 "The Lesson of Cuba." Manila, _Philippines free press_ (54: 23), June 10, 1961, p. 3, pp. 49-50, 52.

518 Licuanan, F. H. "The Cuban Crisis." Quezon City, _Philippine journal of education_ (41: 6), November, 1962, p. 387.

519 Locsin, T. M. "Clash Over Cuba." Manila, _Philippines free press_ (55: 44), November 3, 1962, pp. 2-3, 71.

520 Locsin, T. M. "The 'Chicken' Game." Manila, _Philippines free press_ (55: 45), November 10, 1962, pp. 2, 80.

521 Locsin, T. M. "The Man in Havana." Manila, _Philippines free press_ (54: 17), April 29, 1961, pp. 2-3, 78.

522 Locsin, T. M. "The Moment of Truth." Manila, _Philippines free press_ (54: 18), May 6, 1961, pp. 2-3, 74.

523 Madariaga, Salvador de. "Cuba: the West's Gravest Setback." Manila, _Comment_ (13), 2d quarter, 1961, pp. 28-30.

524 Marlow, James. "Reds Delaying Berlin Showdown." Manila, _Philippines herald magazine_, October 6, 1962, pp. 18-19.

525   Morfett, Keith. "1984 in Cuba." Manila, <u>Mirror</u>, November 3, 1962, pp. 44-45.

526   Morfett, Keith. "Red Star Over Cuba." Manila, <u>Mirror</u>, October 13, 1962, pp. 14-15.

527   Myers, Lawrence. "U. S. Support of World Sugar Agreements." Manila, <u>Sugar news</u> (37: 11), November, 1961, pp. 612-614.

528   "New Cuban Crisis." Manila, <u>Philippines free press</u> (55: 43), October 27, 1962, p. 48.

529   Olivera, B. T. "Warning From Cuba." Quezon City, <u>Kislap graphic</u> (25: 34), February 18, 1959, p. 10.

530   Pacis, V. A. "Cuba: Russia's Dagger vs. America." Quezon City, <u>Weekly graphic</u> (29: 16), October 10, 1962, pp. 11, 60

531   Patacsil, A. C. "Castro Scares the World." Manila, <u>Examiner</u> (1: 21), November 2, 1962, pp. 4-5.

532   "The Politics of Mercy. (Editorial)." Manila, <u>Philippines free press</u> (54: 17), April 29, 1961, p. 8.

533   "Q and A-- Inside Castro's Cuba." Manila, <u>Sunday times magazine</u> (15: 15), July 24, 1960, pp. 12-13.

534   "Rebellion in Cuba." Manila, <u>This week</u> (13: 19), May 11, 1958, pp. 7-8.

535   "Revolt in Cuba." Manila, _Mirror_, January 24, 1959, p. 17; Manila, _This week_ (14: 4), January 25, 1959, pp. 18-21.

536   "Russian--Cuban Agreement. (Editorial)." Manila, _Sugar news_ (36: 2), February, 1960, p. 62.

537   Ryan, W. L. "Hope Dies Hard Among Cuban Exiles." Manila, _Philippines herald magazine_, May 4, 1963, pp. 14-15.

538   Salonga, J. R. "The Meaning of Cuban Crisis." Manila, _Lyceum of the Philippines law review_ (7: 3), December, 1962, pp. 120-125.

539   Sauvage, Leo. "Cuba and the United States." Manila, _Mirror_, October 29, 1960, pp. 14-15.

540   "Seven Days That Shook the World." Manila, _Philippines herald magazine_, November 3, 1962, pp. 10-11.

541   Shields, R. H. "Cuba and Extension of Sugar Act." Manila, _Sugar news_ (36: 4), August, 1960, pp. 174-176.

542   Shields, R. H. "Who Will Fill America's Sugar Bowl Tomorrow?" Manila, _Sugar news_ (36: 6), June, 1960, pp. 276-282.

543   "Sour Notes in the Sugar World: Cuba's Loss is Philippines' Gain." Manila, _Sunday times magazine_ (16: 5), September 11, 1960, pp. 14, 16.

544   Tetlow, Edwin. "Inside Cuba." Manila, _Philippines herald magazine_, September 29, 1962, pp. 14-16.

545   Tupas, R. G. "Cuba Crisis Proves Strength Is Argument
        Communists Understand--Pelaez." Manila, Mirror, November
        10, 1962, pp. 10-11.

546   Villasanta, J. F. "A Filipino in the Cuban Fiasco." Quezon City,
        Weekly graphic (27: 48), May 24, 1961, pp. 8-9, 23.

547   Villasanta, J. F. "Castro Selling Human Beings for Sorely Needed
        Dollars." Manila, Philippines herald magazine, May 26, 1962,
        pp. 10-11.

548   "When Cuba Sparked a Crisis." Manila, Philippines herald
        magazine, December 29, 1962, pp. 20-21.

DOMINICAN REPUBLIC

549   Kennewick, R. E. "The Dominican Revolt." Manila, Philippines
        free press (58: 20), May 15, 1965, pp. 7, 87.

550   Peterson, L. H. "Death of a Dictator." Quezon City, Weekly
        graphic (28: 3), July 12, 1961, pp. 18-19, 22.

HAITI

551   "The 'Calm' After the Haiti Disorder. " Manila, <u>Sunday times</u> <u>magazine</u> (13: 2), August 25, 1957, pp. 14-16.

552   Eder, Richard. "Autocracy of Descending Expectations. " Manila, <u>Philippines herald magazine</u>, February 6, 1965, pp. 46-47.

553   Smith, Julie. "Haiti: Paradise Rediscovered. " Manila, <u>Sunday</u> <u>times magazine</u>, March 14, 1965, pp. 46-47.

MEXICO

554   Avena, M. R. "Federal Republic, South of the Rio Grande. " Quezon City, Examiner, 71st issue, October 27, 1963, p. 15.

555   Bernal, Rafael. "The Mexican Heritage in the Philippines." Manila, Unidas, revista de cultura y vida universitaria (37: 2), June, 1964, pp. 292-300.

556   Berry, Madeleine. "Sojourn in Mexico. " Manila, Mirror, December 17, 1960, pp. 34-35.

557   Brillantes, G. C. "Visitor From Mexico. " Manila, Philippines free press (55: 43), October 27, 1962, pp. 6, 87.

558   "DM, Mateos Bolster Philippine Islands, Mexico Ties. " Quezon City, Examiner (1: 20), October 26, 1962, p. 8.

559   Espino, F. L "The Mexican Influence in the Philippines. " Manila, Mirror, October 20, 1962, pp. 20-21.

560   "Excerpts on the Report on Evaluation of the Mexican Peso to $12.50 per U.S. Dollar. " Manila, Philippine economy review (2: 8), March, 1956, pp. 18-19.

561   Gomez, M. O. "The Foreign Policy of Mexico. " Manila, Unidas, revista de cultura y vida universitaria (37: 4), December, 1964, pp. 597-606.

562   "Handicrafts and Dollars for Mexico. " Manila, Sunday times magazine (12: 51), August 4, 1957, pp. 44-46.

563   Hernandez, P. D. "Mexico, the Mexicans and me." Quezon City, Weekly graphic (28: 1), June 28, 1961, pp. 28, 51.

564   "Mexicans: a Story in Pictures." Manila, This week (14: 7), February 15, 1959, pp. 30-32, 34-35.

565   "Mexico Chief's State Visit Revives Relations with Philippine Islands." Quezon City, Weekly graphic (29: 18), October 24, 1962, p. 3.

566   "Mexico Head Sees Parallels in Philippine Islands." Quezon City, Weekly graphic (29: 19), October 31, 1962, p. 5.

567   Paguio, B. B. "Philippine-Mexican Ambassadors of Good-Will." Manila, Mirror, October 31, 1964, pp. 6-7.

568   Palma, Fé. "Holy Week in Mexico." Manila, This week (14: 12), March 22, 1959, p. 40.

569   "Philippine Islands, Mexico Have Close Ties." Quezon City, Examiner (1: 19), October 19, 1962, p. 17.

570   Rebamontan, L. M. "Filipino-Mexican Ties Today Unfettered by Colonial Bondage." Manila, Mirror, February 15, 1964, pp. 16-17.

571   Rosario, C. R. del. "Filipino-Mexican Friendship Year." Quezon City, V. P. today (2: 4), September, 1964, pp. 31-33.

572   Wilson, Dick. "Mexico." Hong Kong, Asia magazine (2: 50), December 16, 1962, pp. 6-9, 12-13.

PERU

573   Allred, W. M. "System of Government in Peru." Manila, <u>Philippine journal of public administration</u> (4: 1), January, 1960, pp. 46-60.

574   Brun, Albert. "The Problems That Plague Peru." Manila, <u>Mirror</u>, December 10, 1960, pp. 28-29.

575   "Peru." Manila, <u>Mirror</u>, September 30, 1961, pp. 36-41.

PUERTO RICO

576   Arquisola, S. M. "We Can Learn From Puerto Rico's Fomento Plan." Manila, <u>Sunday times magazine</u> (15: 34), April 3, 1960, pp. 20-23.

577   Espino, H. R. "Report on Sugarcane Hybridization in Puerto Rico, Florida and Hawaii." Manila, <u>Philippine Sugar Institute quarterly</u> (2), 2d quarter, June, 1956, pp. 35-55.

578   Taffe, A. J. "People, Jobs and Economic Development: a Case History of Puerto Rico." Manila, <u>Economic research journal</u> (7: 3), December, 1960, pp. 170-172.

VENEZUELA

579   Adam, Felix. "Venezuela's Literacy Campaign." Manila, Philippines herald magazine, September 5, 1964, p. 25.

580   Leiva, José. "Venezuela and its Future." Manila, Mirror, November 19, 1960, pp. 22-23.

581   "Oil Boom in Venezuela." Manila, Sunday times magazine (12: 33), March 31, 1957, pp. 42-43.

582   Venezuela--Nation on a Tightrope." Manila, Sunday times magazine (18: 21), December 30, 1962, pp. 14-15.

THAILAND

Although neither Chulalongkorn nor Thammasat Universities
in Bangkok offer courses in the languages and area studies
of Latin America, Latin America is treated generally with
other world regions in such courses as comparative world
economics, comparative literature, world and regional
geography, etc. No organizations concerned with Latin
America exist in Thailand.

Prior to World War II Thailand's exports to Latin America
consisted of comparatively small shipments of rice to
Colombia, Cuba and Peru. For further details on commercial,
political and cultural relations between the Far East and
Latin America, see Bradley, Anita. Trans-Pacific relations
of Latin America (New York, Institute of Pacific Relations,
1942, 120p.).

In this section the English translation of the title of each
bibliographic item is to be found directly under the title
in the original language, and immediately following the
entire bibliographic description.

Aunque no se ofrecen ni en la Universidad Chulalongkorn,
ni en la Universidad Thammasat (ambas situadas en Bangkok),
cursos en las lenguas y estudios regionales de Latinoamérica,
se estudia Latinoamérica, con otras regiones del mundo, en
las materias tales como economía comparativa mundial, literatura comparativa, geografía universal y regional, etc. No
existen organizaciones con intereses latinoamericanos en
Tailandia.

178

Antes de la Segunda Guerra Mundial Tailandia exportó pocas
cantidades de arroz a Colombia, Cuba y Perú. Para datos
adicionales sobre los contactos comerciales, políticas y
culturales entre las naciones asiáticas y Latinoamérica,
se dirige el lector a la obra de Anita Bradley, <u>Trans-Pacific</u>
<u>relations of Latin America</u> (Nueva York, Institute of Pacific
Relations, 1942, 120p.).

En esta sección la traducción inglesa del título de cada
asiento se encuentra directamente bajo el título de la
lengua original, seguida de la ficha entera).

LATIN AMERICA

583 ปิยวิทยาการ. หลวง. ภูมิศาสตร์ว่าด้วยทวีปอเมริกาใต้. พระนคร, โรงพิมพ์ศรีหงส์,
พ.ศ. ๒๔๗๓. ๑๙ หน้า.
เป็นหนังสือแบบเรียนภูมิศาสตร์สำหรับชั้นมัธยมตอนกลาง ให้รายละเอียดเกี่ยวกับ
ภูมิศาสตร์ทวีปอเมริกาใต้โดยย่อ

Piyawidthajaakaan, Luang. Phuumisaad Waa Duaj Thaweeb Ameerikaat
Pranakhoon, Roongphim Seehong, Paw Saw 2473, 19 naa.
-Pen Nangsyy Baab Rain Phuumisaad Samrab Chan Madthajom
Toonklang Haj Raaj La-iad Kiaw Kab Phuumisaad Thaweeb
Ameerikaataaj Dooj Joo.
(Biyavitayakar, Luang. Latin American Geography. Bangkok,
Srihong Press, 1930, 19p.)
-This is a Textbook for Thai High School Students, Written in Thai.
It Gives a Brief General Geography of the Continent.

584 คารโดนา. เฟาสต์. ประวัติศาสตร์บราซิลโดยสังเขป. พระนคร, ฉัตราการพิมพ์,
พ.ศ. ๒๕๐๔. ๑๑๙ หน้า.
ประวัติศาสตร์การค้นพบอเมริกา การก่อตั้งประเทศบราซิล และการพัฒนาการ
ของประเทศนี้ ในระหว่างปี ค.ศ. ๑๔๙๒-๑๙๔๒.

Kardona, Fauth. Prawadsaad Braasil Dooj Sangkheeb. Pranakhoon,
Chadtra Kaanphim, Paw Saw 2504, 119 naa.
-Prawadsaad Kaan Khonphob Ameerikaa, Kaan Koo Tang Pratheed
Braasil Laa Kaan Phadthanaakaan Khoong Pratheed Nie Naj
Rawaang Pee Kaw Saw 1492-1942.
(The Brief History of Brazil. Bangkok, Chatra Press, 1961, 119p.)
-This Book is Written in Thai and the Title Here is Translated. It
Tells About the History of the Discovery of America, the Establishment
of Brazil and its Development from 1492 to 1942.

THE ARAB WORLD

While no courses in the field of Latin American Studies
per se are offered in the universities of the United Arab
Republic, courses are available in Spanish language and in
the geography of Latin America at the University of
Alexandria. The School of Languages in Cairo offers a
Bachelor of Arts degree in the Spanish language. Spanish
language courses are also offered at the American University
in Cairo.

With respect to additional nations in the Arab World, Spanish
is also taught at Mohammed V University in Rabat, Morocco,
at the Bourguiba Institute of Modern Languages in Tunis,
Tunisia, and at the Translators' School of the University
of Algeria in Algiers. The University of Algiers also houses
an Institute of Geography, which concerns itself with Latin
America as part of its overall interest in world regions.

"Mahjar" (meaning "immigrant" or "new home") literature,
composed by Arabs residing in the Latin American countries,
has been assuming ever-increasing importance in the
twentieth century (see items #590 and #594 in this section).
Works in prose and poetry have been and are being produced,
mainly in Argentina and Brazil. For further data on Mahjar
literature, the reader is referred to Brockelmann, C.
Geschichte der arabischen litteratur. v. 3, supplement.
Leiden, Brill, 1942, pp. 448-.

In this bibliography the English translation of the title of
each bibliographic item is to be found directly under the
title in the original language, and immediately following
the entire bibliographic description.

Aunque no se enseñan cursos en el campo de Estudios
Latinoamericanos per se en las universidades de la República
Arabe Unida, la Universidad de Alexandria ofrece asignaturas
de lengua española así como geografía de Latinoamérica.
La Escuela de Idiomas de Cairo otorga título académico de
Bachiller en Artes en Lengua Española, y se enseña español
también en la Universidad Americana, en Cairo.

En cuanto a los otros países árabes, la Universidad Muhamed
V en la ciudad de Rabat, Marruecos, ofrece cursos de
Español. También se enseña español en el Instituto
Bourguiba de Lenguas Modernas de Tunis, Tunisia, y en la ⌐
Escuela de Traductores de la Universidad de Argelia, en
Argel. Existe, además, en la Universidad de Argelia, un
Instituto de Geografía, el cual trata, dentro de sus intereses
mundiales generales, la región Latinoamericana.

"Mahjar" (lo que significa "inmigrante", o "nueva casa")
se aplica a la literatura arábiga escrita por parte de personas
de origen árabe, residentes en los países latinoamericanos.
Obras significativas en prosa y poesía, producidas por mayor
parte en la Argentina y en el Brasil (vea las fichas números
590 y 594 en esta sección), llaman la atención desde los
comienzos del siglo XX. Para datos adicionales el lector
se dirige a Brockelmann, C. Geschichte der arabischen
litteratur. v. 3, suplemento. Leiden, Brill, 1942, pp. 448-.

En esta bibliografía la traducción inglesa del título de cada
asiento se encuentra directamente bajo el título de la lengua
original, seguida de la ficha entera.

LATIN AMERICA

585

أبو الليل ، موسى
جغرافية الأمريكتين • القاهرة ، مطبعة الأميرية ١٩٤٨ •
الجزء الأول (أمريكا الجنوبية) •

Abu-al-Layl, Mūsā. Jughrāfiyat al-Amrīkatayn; al-Juz'
al-Awal Amrīkā al-Janūbīyah. Cairo, Matba'at al-Amīrīyah,
1948.
(The Geography of the Two Americas-
pt. 1: South America)

586

العروسي ، أحمد فهمي
أربع محاضرات في التربية في إنجلترا وأمريكا ومقارنتها بالتربية
عند الأمم اللاتينية • القاهرة ، مطبعة شركة مصر ، الطبعة الثانية،
١١٢٦ ، ١٣٣ ص •

Al-'Amrusi, Ahmad Fahmy. Arba' Muhādarāt fī al-Tarbīyah
fī Injlitirā wa-Amrīkā wa-Muqaranatihā bi-al-Tarbīyah 'ind
al-Umam al-Lātīnīyah. Cairo, Matba' at Shirkat Misr, al-
Tab' ah al-Thānīyah, 1926, 133p.
(4 Lectures on Education in
England and the U. S. A. and Their Comparisons with Education
in the Latin American Countries)

587

البلدى ، حسن
عشت في أمريكا اللاتينية • القاهرة ، دار القومية للطباعة
والنشر ، ١٩٦٠-١٩٦٣ • ١٣٥ ص •

Al-Baladī, Hasan. 'Isht fī Amrīkā al-Lātīnīyah. Cairo,
al-Dār al-Qawmīyah lil-Tibā 'ah wa-al-Nashr, 1960-1963,
135p.

(I Lived in Latin America)

588

الفرا ،جمال
دنيا المغتربين ،بيروت ،دار الكتب الجديد ،١٩٦٢ •
١٣٤ ص•

Al-Farrā, Jamāl. Dunyā al-Mughtaribīn. Beirut, Dār al-
Kutub al-Jadīd, 1962, 134p.
(The World of the Immigrants)

589

الملثم ،بدوي
الناطقون بالضاد في أمريكا الجنوبية • بيروت،دار
الريحاني للطباعة والنشر ،١٩٦٥ • جزئين •

Al-Multhim, Badawī. Al-Nātiqūn bi-al-dād fī Amrīkā al-
Janūbīyah. Beirut, Dar al-Rihāni lil-Tibā 'ah wal-Nashr,
1965.
(The Arabic-Speaking People in South
America)

590

الناعوري ،عيسى
أدب المهجر • القاهرة ،دار المعارف ،١٩٥٩ •
٦٢٨ ص•

Al-Nā 'ūri, Isā. Adab al-Mahjar. Cairo, Dār al-Ma 'rif,
1959, 628p.
(Mahjar Literature: Arabic Literature in Latin America)

591

الشرقاوي ، محمد عبد المنعم
هذا العالم • القاهرة ،دار المعارف ، الطبعة الرابعة ،
١٩٥٩ • ص ١٥٠ـ١٥٣ وص٢٢٣ـ٢٢٧ وص٢٧٥ـ٢٧٩
وص٣٤٢ وص٣٨٨ـ ٤٠٢ وص٤٢٨ـ٤٣١ وص ٤٣٨ـ٤٤١•

Al-Sharqāwī, Muhammad 'Abd-al-Mun 'im. Hadhā al-'Alam.
Cairo, Dar al-Ma 'ārif, al-Tab'ah al-Rābi'ah, 1959, pp.
150-153; 223-227; 275-279; 342; 388-402; 428-431; 438-441.
(Geography
of Latin America)

2

Al-Shāmī, Salah al-Dīn

امريكا اللاتينية، علاقة النقل بالتعمير والاستغلال الاقتصادى .
تأليف صلاح الدين الشامى . القاهرة، مكتبة الأنجلو المصرية
1963. ١٩٦٣،

Al-Shāmī, Salah al-Dīn. Amerika Allatiniyah, Alakat
Alnakl Bittamir Walistiklal Aliktisadi, Cairo, Maktabat
Alandjelu Almisriyyah, 1963, 267p.
        (Latin America: the Relationship
Between Communications, Development and Economic
Consumption)

3

الطاهر،أحمد زكى
الأرض والفلاح فى أمريكا اللاتينية (ملحق يوزع مع عدد أول
يوليو ١٩٦٥) . القاهرة،مطابع مؤسسة الأهرام،١٩٦٥ .
٤٨ ص.

Al-Tāhir, Ahmad Zaky. Al-Ard wāl-Fallāh fī Amrīkā Al-
Lātīnīyah (Mulhaq Yūwaza' ma' 'Adad Awil Yūlyū 1965).
Cairo, Matābi' Mū 'Asasat al-Ahrām, 1965, 48p.
        (The Land and the Peasant in Latin
America)

داود،أنيس
الطبيعة فى شعر المهجر . القاهرة،الدار القومية للطباعة
والنشر،دون تاريخ . ١٨٤ص.

Dāwūd, Anīs. Al-Tabī'ah fī Shi'r al-Mahjar. Cairo, al-Dār
al-Qawmīyah lil-Tibā'ah, dūn Tārikh (n. d.), 184p.
(Nature in the Mahjar Poetry: Arabic Poetry in Latin America)

595   Hashīmah, ʿAbd Allāh.

من ارض الغد ‏[تاليف]‏ عبد الله حشيمه. بيروت، المطبعة
الكاثوليكية ‏[1962]‏

Hashīmah, ʿAbd Allāh. <u>Min Ard Alghad,</u> Beyrouth, Al-Matbaah
Al-Kathu-Likiyyah, 1962, 186p.
(From the Land of Tomorrow)

596   Institut Dominicain d'Etudes Orientales. <u>Mélanges.</u> Cairo,
1957? -
-Bibliography of books published in U. A. R.

597

صلاح الدين ، على السامى
أمريكا اللاتينية ؛ علاقة النقل بالتعمير والإستغلال الإقتصادى ،
القاهرة ، مكتبة الأنجلو المصرية ، ١٩٦٣ ، ٢٧٦ ص.

Salāh al-Dīn, Alī al-Sāmī. <u>Amrīkā al-Lātīnīyah; Alāqat al-Naql
bi-al-taʾmīr wa-al-Istighlāl al-Iqtisādī.</u> Cairo, Maktabat al-
Anglu al-Misrīyah, 1963, 267p.
(Latin America, the Relationship
Between Transportation, Reclamation and Financial Exploitation)

598

ثابت ، محمد
جولة فى ربوع الدنيا الجديد ، بين مصر والأمريكتين .
القاهرة ، مكتبة النهضة المصرية ، الطبعة الثالثة ، ١٩٤٨ ،
١٦٦ ص .

Thābit, Muhammad. <u>Jawlah fī Rubuʾ al-Dunyā al-Jadīdah, Bayna
Misr wa-al-Amrīkatayn.</u> Cairo, Maktabat al-Nahdah al-
Misrīyah, al-Tabʾah al-Thālithah, 1948, 166p.
(A Trip Around the New World, from Egypt
to the Americas)

ARGENTINA

599

شمعون، ودیع
تاریخ الأرجنتین • القاهرة،مطبعةالسلام، ١٩١١ •
١٦٢ ص•

Sham'ūn, Wadī'. Tārīkh al-Arjintīn. Cairo, Matba'at al-
Salām, 1911, 162p.
(History of Argentina)

BRAZIL

600

Al-Farrā, Jamāl

دنيا المغتربين، تأليف، جمال الفرا، الطبعة الأولى، بيروت،
دار الكتاب الجديد، 1962،

Al-Farrā, Jamāl. Dunyya el-Mightaribin, Beyrouth, Dar
al-Kitab al-Jadid, 1962, 134p.
(The World of the Immigrants to the West)

CENTRAL AMERICA

601

عبد المجيد، محمد فايد
أمريكا الوسطى • القاهرة ، دار النهضة المصرية ،
١٩٦٧ • ٢٠٧ ص•

'Abd-al-Majīd, Muhammad Fāyīd. Amrīkā al-Wūstā. Cairo,
Dār al-Nahdah al-Misrīyah, 1967, 207p.
(Central America)

187

CUBA

602

محمد ،أحمد

ثورة كوبا · القاهرة ، الدار القومية للطباعة والنشر ،
۱۹۵۹ · ۵۳ ص ·

Muhammad, Mahmūd. <u>Thawrat Kūbā</u>. Cairo, al-Dār al-Qawmīyah
lil-Tibā'ah wa-al-Nashr, 1959, 53p.

(The Revolution in Cuba)

603

صبرى ، موسى

ثورة كاسترو · القاهرة ، دار المعرفة ، ۱۹۶۱ · ۱۵۵ ص ·

Sabrī, Mūsā. <u>Thawrat Kāstrū</u>. Cairo, Dār al-Ma'rifah, 1961,
155p.

(Castro's Revolution)

604

سعيد ،أحمد

عائداً من كوبا · القاهرة ،الدار القومية للطباعة والنشر ،
۱۹۶۱ · ۵۳ ص ·

Sa'īd, Ahmad. <u>'Āydan min Kūbā</u>. Cairo, al-Dār al-Qawmīyah
lil-Tibā'ah wa-al-Nashr, 1961, 53p.

(A Returnee from Cuba)

605

بقطر، جبرائيل
عربى فى المكسيك،أو مناظره بينالأهرامات. القاهرة،
دار الأدباء للطباعة والنشر،دون تاريخ • الجزء الأول •

Buqtur, Jabrā'īl. Arabī fī al-Miksīk, aw Munāzarah Bayna
al-Ahrāmāt. Cairo, Dār al-udabā' lil-Tibā 'ah wa-al-
Nashr, dūn Tārīkh (n. d.).
      (An Arab in Mexico, or Glances Among
the Pyramids)

606

Hatem, Anouar.
اساطير مكسيكية، تأليف انور حاتم • دمشق، مكتبة اطلس،
1962، ١٩٦٢

Hatem, Anouar. Asatir Meksikiyyah. Damascus, Makhtabat
Atlas, 1962, 204p.
      (Mexican Anecdotes)

607

محفوظ، محمد
تقرير مقدم من حضرة صاحب العزة الأستاذ الدكتور محمد
محفوظ بك عن رحلته الى بلاد المكسيك مندوباً عن الجامعات
المصرية • القاهرة، جامعة فاروق الأول،دون تاريخ، ٥١ ورقة •

Mahfūz, Muhammad. Taqrīr Muqaddam min Hadrit Sāhib
al-'izah al-Ustādh al-Duktūr Muhammad Mahfūz 'an
Rihlatihi ilā Bilād al-Miksīk Mandūban 'an al-Jami' āt al-
Misrīyah. Cairo, Jāmi' at Fārūq al-Awal, dūn Tārīkh
(n. d.) 51p.
      (Report Presented by the Honorable
Dr. Muhammad Mahfuz About his Trip to Mexico as a
Representative of the Egyptian Universities)

PUERTO RICO

608

    Ghallāb, Abd al-Karīm.

صحفى فى امريكا ,بالبخم عبد الكريم غلاب. ,الدار البيضاء، ,1962

    Ghallāb, Abd al-Karīm.   Sahafi fi-Amerika. Casablanca, 1962, 108p.

          (A Journalist in America)

VENEZUELA

609

    Al-Dabʻ, Wadīʻ

بوليفار، سيرته، بقلم وديع الضبع. القاهرة، مكتبة النهضة المصرية، 1957.

    Al-Dabʻ, Wadīʻ Bolivar, Siratuhu. Cairo, Al-Nahzah, 1957, 274p.

        (Biography of Bolivar)

II. Periodical Articles

LATIN AMERICA

510

" الأزمات التى تجتاح القارة " ، القاهرة ، **الأهرام** ،
٣ مايو ١٩٦٢ ،ص٢ .

"Al-Azamāt al-Latī Tajtāh al-Qārah. " Cairo, <u>al-Ahrām,</u>
May 3, 1962, p. 2.
("The Crises which Shake the Continent")

511

" البيض فى أفريقيا وأمريكا اللاتينية " ، القاهرة ، **الأهرام**
الاقتصادى ، ١ يناير ١٩٦٢ ،ص٢٠ .

"Al-Bīd fī Ifrīqyā wā-Amrīkā al-Lātīniyah. " Cairo, <u>al-Ahrām</u>
<u>al-Iqtisādī</u>, January 1, 1962, p. 20.
("The Whites in Africa and Latin America")

612

" البرازيل والمكسيك تعلنان عدم التدخل فى شئون الدول
الأخرى " ، القاهرة ، **الجمهورية** ، ١٢ فبراير ١٩٦٢ ،
ص٢ .

"Al-Brāzīl wal Miksīk tu'Linān 'Adam al-Tadakhul fī Shu'ūn
al-duwal al-'Ukhrā. " Cairo, <u>al-Jumhūrīyah,</u> February 12,
1962, p. 2.
("Brazil and Mexico Declare their non-Interference in the
Affairs of other States")

613

السيطرة الإحتكارية الأمريكية ، القاهرة ، المساء ،
١٠ يوليو ١٩٦٢ ،ص ٢٠

"Al-Sayṭarah al-Ihtikārīyah al-Amrīkīyah. " Cairo, al-Misā,̓
July 10, 1962, p. 2.
("American Monopolistic Domination")

614

الولايات المتحدة تفقد تأثيرها سياسياً عليها ،
القاهرة ،المساء ، ١٠ فبراير ١٩٦٢ ،ص ٢٠

"Al-Wilāyāt al-Muttaḥidah Tafqid tā' Thīrahā Siyāsiyan 'Alayhā."
Cairo, al-Misā,̓ February 10, 1962, p. 2.
("The U. S. A. Loses her Political Influence Over Latin America")

615

أمريكا اللاتينية في مفترق الطرق ، القاهرة، الهلال ،
مارس ١٩٦٢ ، ص ١٥٢٠

"Amrīkā al-Lātīnīyah fī Miftaraq al-Ṭuruq." Cairo, al-Hilāl,
March 1962, p. 152.
("Latin America with a Diversity of Decisions")

616

أثار أزمة الأرجنتين على السياسة الأمريكية تجاه أمريكا
اللاتينية ، القاهرة ، الأهرام ، ٢٥ مارس ١٩٦٢ ،
ص ٢٠

"Athār Azmat al-Arjintīn 'alā al-Siyāsah al-Amrīkīyah
Tijāh Amrīkā al-Lātīnīyah." Cairo, al-Ahrām, March 25,
1962, p. 2.
("The Influence of the Argentine Crisis on U. S. Policy Towards
Latin America")

617

" أزمة أمريكا اللاتينية "، القاهرة ، الأهرام الإقتصادي ،
١ فبراير ١٩٦٢ ،ص١٢ .

"Azmat Amrīkā al-Lātīnīyah. " Cairo, al-Ahrām al-Iqtiṣādī,
February 1, 1962, p. 12.
("The Crisis of Latin America")

618

غالى ، بطرس

منظمة الدول الأمريكية ، " مجلة الأقتصاد والسياسة والتجارة ،
يوليو — ديسمبر ١٩٥٧ ،ا لسنة الخامسة ،ر١٨ — ص ١٤٥.

Ghāli, Butrus. "Munaẓamat al-Duwal al-Amrīkīyah." Cairo,
Mijalat al-Iqtiṣād wa-al-Siyāsah wa-al-Tijārah (5), July-
December 1957, pp. 89-145.
                ("The Organization of American States")

619

" إتجاه الريح فى أمريكا اللاتينية "، القاهرة ، الكاتب ،
مايو ١٩٦٢ ، ص١٧٣ .

"Itijāh al-Rīh fī Amrīkā al-Lātīnīyah. " Cairo, al-Kātib,
May 1962, p. 173.
("Whither Latin America")

620

" إتهام كاسترو بتشجيع ثورات أمريكا اللاتينية "،القاهرة ،
الأخبار ، ٥ يونيو ١٩٦٢ ،ص٢ .

"Ittihām Kāstrū bi-Tashjiʼ Thawrāt Amrīkā al-Lātīnīyah. "
Cairo, al-Akhbār, June 5, 1962, p. 2.
("Accusing Castro of Encouraging Revolutions in Latin America")

193

621
" إزدياد عدد الشيوعين "، القاهرة ، الجمهورية ١٠٦
أبريل ١٩٦٣ ،ص٢٠

"Izdiyād 'Adad al-Shuyū 'Iyīn. " Cairo, al-Jumhūrīyah, April
10, 1963, p. 2.
("Increase of the Number of Communists")

622
" إزدياد الشعور المعادى للولايات المتحدة "، القاهرة ،
أخبار اليوم، ٥ فبراير ١٩٦٢، ص٢٠

"Izdiyād al Shu' ūr al-mu'ādī lil-Wilāyāt al-Muttaḥidah. "
Cairo, Akhbār-al-Yawm, February 5, 1962, p. 2.
("Increase of Anti-U. S. Sentiment")

623
" موجة الإنقلابات "، القاهرة ، الجمهورية ، ١٤ أكتوبر
١٩٦٣ ، ص٢٠

"Mawjat al-Inqilābāt. " Cairo, al-Jumhūrīyah, October 14, 1963,
p. 2.
("A Wave of Coups d'Etat")

624
" مؤتمر وزراء خارجية الدول الأمريكية "،القاهرة ،الأهرام
الاقتصادى، ١ فبراير ١٩٦٢ ،ص٢٣٠

"Mū'Tamar Wūzarā' Khārijīyat al-Dūwal al-Amrīkīyah. "
Cairo, al-Ahrām al-Iqtiṣādī, February 1, 1962, p. 23.
("Conference of Foreign Ministers of the American Nations")

625
" عفو شامل للذين إشتركوا نى حركات ثورية منذ (١٩٥٨)،
القاهرة ، الأخبار ، ١٤ سبتمبر ١٩٦٣، ص ٤٠

"'Afw Shāmil lil-Ladhīn Ishtarakū fī Harakāt Thawrīyah Mundh
(1958). " Cairo, al-Akhbār, September 14, 1963, p. 4.
("Full Pardon fon all who Participated in Revolutionary
Activities Since 1958")

626
" الأرجنتين تلغى عقود البترول مع ١٢ شركة " ، القاهرة ،
المسا° ، ١٧ نوفمبر ١٩٦٣، ص ١٠

"Al-Arjintīn Talghī 'Uqūd al-Bitrūl ma' 12 Shirkah. " Cairo,
al-Misā, November 17, 1963, p. 1.
("Argentina Cancels Oil Contracts with 12 Gompanies")

627
" الأرجنتين تعلن قطع علاقاتها مع كبا " ، القاهرة، الأخبار ،
٩ فبراير ١٩٦٢، ص ٢٠

"Al-Arjintīn tu 'lin qat' 'Alāqātihā ma' Kūbā. " Cairo, al-Akhbār,
February 9, 1962, p. 2.
("Argentine Severs Relations with Cuba")

628
" الحكومة العسكرية تواجه ثورة بركان " ، القاهرة ،
الأهرام ملحق ، ٢ سبتمبر ١٩٦٦، ص ١٠

"Al-Ḥukūmah al-'Askarīyah Tuwājih Thawrat Burkān. "
Cairo, al-Ahrām Mulḥaq, September 2, 1966, p. 10.
("The Military Government is Facing a Volcanic Revolution")

629 ‏• الإنقلاب الذى جاء بدستور جديد • ‏، القاهرة ،الأهرام :
‏ملحق ، ٨ يوليو ١٩٦٦، ص١٢•

"Al-Inqilāb al-Ladhī jā' bi-Dustūr Jadīd. " Cairo, al-Ahrām:
mulḥaq, July 8, 1966, p. 12.
("The Coup Which Came with a New Constitution")

630 ‏• الإستعمار الإقتصادى نى الأرجنتين • ، القاهرة ،
‏أخبار اليوم ، ٢ نونبر ١٩٦٣، ص٩•

"Al-Isti 'mār al-Iqtiṣādī fī al-Arjintīn. " Cairo, Akhbār al-
yawm, November 2, 1963, p. 9.
("Financial Imperialism in Argentina")

631 ‏• النظام الجديد يهدف للقضاء على أنصار بيرون • ، القاهرة،
‏المساء ، ١١ مارس ١٩٦٣، ص٢•

"Al-Nizām al-Jadīd Yahdif lil-Qaḍā' 'alā Anṣār Bīrūn. "
Cairo, al-Misā', March 11, 1963, p. 2.
("The New System Aims at Destroying Peron's Followers")

632 ‏• القضاء على المعارضة السياسية • ،القاهرة ،الأهرام ،
‏٥ يوليو ١٩٦٦ ،ص٤•

"Al-Qaḍā' 'Alā al-mu'Āradah al-Siyāsīyah. " Cairo, al-
Ahrām, July 5, 1966, p. 4.
("Suppression of the Political Opposition")

633

" الطبيب أرتورو إيليا يصبح رئيساً " ، القاهرة ، الأخبار ،
١٣ أكتوبر ١٩٦٣ ، ص ٧٠

"Al-Ṭabīb Artūrū Īlīyā Yuṣbiḥ ra'īsan." Cairo, al-Akhbār,
October 13, 1963, p. 7.
("The Physician, Arturo Illia, Becomes President")

634

" الوزارة : تتألف من خمسة وزرا " " ، القاهرة ، الجمهورية ،
٥ يوليو ١٩٦٦ ، ص ٤٠

"Al-Wizārah: Tatā'Ilaf min Khamsat Wuzarā'." Cairo,
al-Jumhūrīyah, July 5, 1966, p. 4.
("The Government is Composed of 5 Ministers")

635

" أنصار بيرون ما زالوا قوة " ، القاهرة ، الأهرام ، ٧ فبراير
١٩٦٣ ، ص ٣٠

"Anṣār Bīrūn mā-Zālū Quwwah." Cairo, al-Ahrām,
February 7, 1963, p. 3.
("Peron's Followers are Still Powerful")

636

" أين تذهب الأموال الأمريكية المخصصة لمساعدتها " ،
القاهرة ، المسا ، ٨ مايو ١٩٦٢ ، ص ٢٠

"Ayna Tadhhab al-Amwāl al-Amrīkīyah al-Mukhaṣaṣah li-Musā
'Adatihā." Cairo, al-Misā, May 8, 1962, p. 2.
("Where Does the American Money, Intended for Aid, go
in Argentina?")

637

" حل البرلمان تمهيداً لإجراء الإنتخاب " ، القاهرة ،
المساء ، ٨ سبتمبر ١٩٦٢ ، ص١ .

"Ḥal al-Barlamān Tamhīdān li-Ijrā' al-Intikhāb. " Cairo,
al-Misā', September 8, 1962, p. 1.
("Dissolving the Parliament, a Step Toward Elections")

638

" حكام الولايات من العرب " ، القاهرة ، الجمهورية ،
٦ سبتمبر ١٩٦٢ ، ص٧ .

"Ḥukkām al-Wilāyāt min al-'Arab. " Cairo, al-Jumhūrīyah,
September 6, 1962, p. 7.
("Arab Governors of Argentina States")

639

" إضطراب ١٧٥ ألف عامل بسبب النزاع على الأجور " ،
القاهرة ، الجمهورية ، ٢٢ مايو ١٩٦٢ ، ص٨ .

"Iḍṭirāb 175 Alf 'Āmil bi-Sabab al-Nizā' 'alā al-Ujūr. "
Cairo, al-Jumhūrīyah, May 22, 1962, p. 8.
("A Disturbance by 175, 000 Laborers Because of the Conflict
Over Wages")

640

" إنقلابها فرق العلاقات بين دول أمريكا اللاتينية " ، القاهرة ،
الأهرام ، ٤ أغسطس ١٩٦٦ ، ص٥ .

"Inqilābuhā Farraqa al-'Alāqāt Bayna Duwal Amrīkā al-
Lātīnīyah. Cairo, al-Ahrām, August 4, 1966, p. 5.
("Her Revolution has Spoiled Argentine-Latin American
Relations")

198

"إنقسام خطير بالجيش " ، القاهرة ، العساء ، ٢٠ سبتمبر
١٩٦٢ ، ص١٠

"Inqisām Khaṭīr bil-Yaysh. " Cairo, <u>al-Misā,</u> September
20, 1962, p. 1.
("Dangerous Split in the Army")

"إشتباكات داخل البرلمان بسبب مرسوم فض المجلس " ،
القاهرة ، العساء ، ٢٣ مايو ١٩٦٢ ، ص١٠

"Ishtibākāt Dākhil al-Barlamān bi-Sabab Marsūm Faḍ
al-Majlis. " Cairo, <u>al-Misā,</u> May 23, 1962, p. 1.
("Clashes in the Parliament Because of the Decree Dissolving
the Council")

"إتهام الحكومة بالرجعية ودعوة العمال الى إستئناف
المظاهرات" ،القاهرة ،الأهرام ، ٥ أكتوبر ١٩٦٦،
ص ٥٠

"Ittihām al-Ḥukūmah bil-Raj 'Iyah wa-da 'wat al-'umāl ilā
Isti' naf al-Muẓāharāt. " Cairo, <u>al-Ahrām,</u> October 5,
1966, p. 5.
("The Government is Accused of Being Reactionary and the
Workers are Called upon to Continue the Demonstrations")

44

"إتهام واشنطون بالتدخل فى شئونها " ، القاهرة ،
الأهرام ، ١٠ أغسطس ١٩٦٦ ،ص٤٠

"Ittihām Wāshintūn bil-Tadakhul fī shu' Ūnihā. " Cairo,
<u>al-Ahrām,</u> August 10, 1966, p. 4.
("Accusing Washington of Interfering in her Affairs")

645   " جوان كارلوس أونجانيا " ، القاهرة ، <u>الجمهورية</u> ، ٧ يوليو
             ١٩٦٦ ،ص ٦ .

"Juān Kārlūs Awngānyā. "   Cairo, <u>al-Jumhūrīyah</u>, July 7,
    1966, p. 6.
("Juan Carlos Onganía")

646   " خلاف بين القوات المسلحة " ، القاهرة ، <u>الأهرام</u> ،
             ٢٠ فبراير ١٩٦٣ ،ص ٢ .

"Khilāf Bayna l-Quwāt al-Musalaḥah. "   Cairo, <u>al-Ahrām</u>,
    February 20, 1963, p. 2.
("Differences Within the Armed Forces")

647   " مركز أنصار بيرون " ،القاهرة ، <u>الأهرام ملحق</u> ، ١٢ أبريل
             ١٩٦٢ ،ص ١٠

"Markaz Anṣār Bīrūn. "   Cairo, <u>al-Ahrām mulḥaq</u>, April
    12, 1962, p. 10.
("The Position of Peron's Followers")

648   " مظاهرة معادية للولايات المتحدة " ،القاهرة ، <u>الأخبار</u> ،
             ٢٣ أكتوبر ١٩٦٣ ،ص ٢ .

"Muẓāharah mu' Ādīyah lil-Wilāyāt al-Muttaḥidah. "
    Cairo, <u>al-Akhbār</u>, October 23, 1963, p. 2.
("Anti-American Demonstration")

" قطع المعونة عن الأرجنتين " ، القاهرة ، الأهرام ،
١٨ نوفمبر ١٩٦٣ ، ص ١ .

"Qaṭ' al-ma 'Ūnah 'an al-Arjintīn. " Cairo, al-Ahrām,
November 18, 1963, p. 1.
("U. S. Aid to Argentina Stopped")

" رفض إستقبال سفير إسرائيل " ، القاهرة ، الأهرام ، ٧ يوليو
١٩٦٦ ، ص ٤ .

"Rafd Istiqbāl Safīr Isrā'īl." Cairo, al-Ahrām, July 7,
1966, p. 4.
("Refusing to Receive New Israeli Ambassador")

" سحب الأمريكى القبيح من الأرجنتين " ، القاهرة ،
الأهرام ، ١٥ ديسمبر ١٩٦٣ ، ص ٢ .

"Saḥb al-Amrīkī al-Qabīḥ min al-Arjintīn." Cairo, al-Ahrām,
December 15, 1963, p. 2.
("Withdrawing the Ugly American from Argentina")

" ثورة عسكرية لإجبار فروند يزى على الإستقالة " ، القاهرة ،
الأخبار ، ١٨ مارس ١٩٦٢ ، ص ١ .

"Thawrah 'Askarīyah li-Ijbār Frūndīzī 'alā al-Istiqālah. "
Cairo, al-Akhbār, March 28, 1962, p. 1.
("Military Revolution to Compel Frondizi to Resign")

653

• ثورة فى الأرجنتين إحتجاجا على قطع العلاقات مع كوبا •
القاهرة ، الجمهورية ، ١٠ فبراير ١٩٦٢ ،ص ١ •

"Thawrah fī al-Arjintīn Iḥtijājan 'alā qat' al-'Alāqāt ma' Kūbā. "
Cairo, al-Jumhūrīyah, February 10, 1962, p. 1.
("Revolution in Argentina in Protest of the Severing of
Relations with Cuba")

654

• وند تجارى أرجنتينى يصل بيروت • ،القاهرة ،الجمهورية ،
١٧ مايو ١٩٦٢ ،ص ٤ •

"Wafd Tujārī Arjintīnī Yaṣil Bayrūt. " Cairo, al-Jumhūrīyah,
May 17, 1962, p. 4.
("Argentine Commercial Mission Arrives in Beirut")

BOLIVIA

655

• الموقف يهدد بالإنفجار وأمريكا تتدخل لإطلاق سراح رعاياها •
القاهرة ،الأهرام، (١٠ ديسمبر ١٩٦٣ ،ص ٢) (١٢
ديسمبر ١٩٦٣ ، ص ٢) (١٦ ديسمبر ١٩٦٣ ، ص ٢) •

"Al-Mawqif Yuhadid bi-al-Infijār wā-Amrīkā Tatadakhal
li-Iṭlāq Saraḥ ra'Āyāhā. " Cairo, al-Ahrām, December
10, 1963, p. 2; December 12, 1963, p. 2; December 16,
1963, p. 2.
("The Situation is Explosive and the U. S. Intervenes to
Protect its Citizens")

656

* الوزارة : إستقالة الوزارة بكامل هيئتها * ، القاهرة ،
الأخبار ، ٨ يناير ١٩٦٢ ،ص٢ •

"Al-Wizārah: Istiqālat al-Wizārah Bikāmil Hay'atihā. "
Cairo, al-Akhbār, January 8, 1962, p. 2.
("Complete Government Resignation")

657

* رئاسة الجمهورية : لإنتخاب رين بارينتوس رئيسا * ،
القاهرة ،الأهرام ، ٥ يوليو ١٩٦٦ ، ص٤ •

"Ri'āsat al-Jumhūrīyah: Intikhāb Ryn Bāryantūs ra' Īsan. "
Cairo, al-Ahrām, July 5, 1966, p. 4.
("Presidency of the Republic: Election of René Barientos")

BRAZIL

658

*أحدث عاصمة مهددة بالإنقراض (برازيليا) ،القاهرة ،
الأهرام ، ١٤ سبتمبر ١٩٦٢ ،ص١١ •

"Aḥdath 'Āṣimah Muhadadah bi-al-inqirāḍ Brāzīlīa. "
Cairo, al-Ahrām, September 14, 1962, p. 11.
("The New Capital is Threatened by Oblivion: Brasilia")

659

* البرازيل تستولي على شركة أمريكية * ، القاهرة ، الأهرام ،
١٨ فبراير ١٩٦٢ ، ص٢ •

"Al-Brāzīl Tastawlī 'alā Shirkah Amrīkīyah. " Cairo,
al-Ahrām, February 18, 1962, p. 2.
("Brazil Confiscates a U.S. Company")

660

" البرازيل تعود إلى النظام الرئاسى " ، القاهرة ، الأهرام ،
الإقتصادى ، ١٥ مارس ١٩٦٢ ، ص ٢٢ .

"Al-Brāzīl Ta'ūd ilā al-Nizām al-ri'āsī. " Cairo, al-Ahrām
al-Iqtiṣādī, March 15, 1962, p. 22.
("Brazil Returns to the Presidential System")

661

" البرازيل تحاول أن تتحرر من سيطرة الإحتكارات الإقتصادية
الأمريكية " ، القاهرة ، المسا، ، ١٠ يناير ١٩٦٢ ،
ص ٢ .

"Al-Brāzīl Tuḥāwil an Tataḥarar min Sayṭarat al-Ihtikārat
al-Iqtiṣadīyah al-Amrīkīyah. " Cairo, al-Misā', January
10, 1962, p. 2.
("Brazil is Trying to Liberate Itself from American Financial
Monopolies")

662

" الحكومة لن تتجه إلى اليسار " ، القاهرة ، الأخبار ،
٩ مارس ١٩٦٢ ، ص ٢ .

"Al-Ḥukūmah lan Tatajih Ilā al-Yasār." Cairo, al-Akhbār,
March 9, 1962, p. 2.
("The Government Does not Have Leftist Tendencies")

663

" الجيش البرازيلى يحتل المراكز الرئيسية " ، القاهرة ،
الجمهورية ، ١٦ سبتمبر ١٩٦٢ ، ص ٢ .

"Al-Jaysh al-Brāzīlī Yaḥtal al-Marākiz al-ra' Īsīyah. "
Cairo, al-Jumhūrīyah, September 16, 1962, p. 2.
("The Brazilian Army Occupies Key Positions")

64   " الجيش يطالب بحل الأزمة السياسية " ، القاهرة ،
الأخبار ، ٨ يوليو ١٩٦٢ ،ص ٢ .

"Al-Jaysh Yuṭālib bi-ḥal al-Azmah al-Siyāsīyah. " Cairo,
     al-Akhbār, July 8, 1962, p. 2.
("The Army Demands a Solution to the Political Crisis")

65   " النظام الرئاسى يعود إليها (رئاسة الجمهورية) ،
القاهرة ، الأخبار ، ٢٤ يناير ١٩٦٣ ،ص ٢ .

"Al-Niẓām al-ri' Āsī ya'ūd Īlayha (Ri'āsat al-Jumhūrīyah). "
     Cairo, al-Akhbār, January 24, 1963, p. 2.
("The Presidential System Returns")

66   " الرئيس يكلف وزير العمل السابق بتشكيل الحكومة
الجديدة " ، القاهرة ، المساء ، ١٧ سبتمبر
١٩٦٢ ، ص ١ .

"Al-Ra'īs Yukallif Wazīr al-'Amal al-Sābiq bi-Tashkīl al-
     Ḥukūmah al-Jadīdah. " Cairo, al-Misā', September 17,
     1962, p. 1.
("The President Asks the Former Minister of Labor to
Form a New Government")

67   " الرجعية والإقطاع تعوق التقدم " ، القاهرة ، المساء ،
٣ سبتمبر ١٩٦٢ ، ص ٢ .

"Al-Raj'īyah wal-Iqtā' Ta'ūq al-Taqadum. " Cairo, al-Misā',
     September 3, 1962, p. 2.
("Reaction and Feudalism Blocking Progress")

668

" إعلان حالة الطوارى' بين الجيش بسبب الأزمة السياسية " ،
القاهرة ، الأخبار ، ١٥ يوليو ١٩٦٢ ،ص٢٠

"I'lān Ḥālat al-Ṭawāri' Bayna al-Jaysh bi-Sabab al-Azmah
al-Siyāsīyah." Cairo, al-Akhbār, July 15, 1962, p. 2.
("Imposing Emergency Status in the Army Because of the
Political Crisis")

669

" إنقلاب ١٢ سبتمبر سنة ١٩٦٢ الفاشل = فشل الثورة
العسكرية "والقاهرة "والاخبار، ١٣ سبتمبر ١٩٦٣، ص٥٠

"Inqilab 12 Sibtimbar 1962 al-Fashil: Fashal al-Thawrah al-
'Askariyah." Cairo, al-Akhbār, September 13, 1963, p. 5.
("The Abortive Coup of September 12, 1962; Failure of the
Military Revolt")

670

" إستفتاء عام فى ٦ يناير حول شكل الحكومة التى تحكم البلاد "،
القاهرة ،والأخبار ، ١٦ سبتمبر ١٩٦٢ ،ص٢٠

"Istifta' 'ām fī 6 Yanāyir Ḥawla Shakl al-Ḥukūmah al-Latī
Taḥkum al-Bilād." Cairo, al-Akhbār, September 16, 1962,
p. 2.
("General Referendum on the 6th of January as Regards
the Form of Government Which Rules the Country")

671

" خلاف على سلطة رئيس البرازيل مع البرلمان " ، القاهرة ،
المساء ،١٣ سبتمبر ١٩٦٢ ،ص١٠

"Khilāf 'alā Sulṭat ra' īs al-Brāzīl ma' al-Barlamān."
Cairo, al-Misā', September 13, 1962, p. 1.
("Dispute Concerning the Power of the Brazilian President
over the Parliament")

72

" منع عقد مؤتمر مناصر لكوبا " ، القاهرة ، الأهرام ،
٢٧ مارس ١٩٦٣ ، ص ٢ .

"Man' 'Aqd mū'Tamar Munāṣir li-Kūbā. " Cairo, <u>al-Ahrām,</u>
March 27, 1963, p. 2.
("Prevention of a Pro-Cuban Conference")

73

" تكليف سنتياجو دانتاس بتشكيل الوزارة ، القاهرة ، الأهرام
٢١ يونيو ١٩٦٢ ، ص ٢ .

"Taklīf Santyājū Dāntās bi-Tashkīl al-Wizārah. " Cairo,
<u>al-Ahrām,</u> June 21, 1962, p. 2.
("Asking Santiago Dantas to Form a Government")

74

" ٣٩٨ مليون دولار قرض للبرازيل " ،القاهرة،الأهرام ،
٢٦مارس ١٩٦٣ ،ص ٢ .

"398 Milyūn Dūlār Qard lil-Brāzīl. " Cairo, <u>al-Ahrām,</u>
March 26, 1963, p. 2.
("398 Million Dollar Loan to Brazil")

75

" ١٢ مليون عامل يضربون " ، القاهرة ، الأهرام ،
١٦ سبتمبر ١٩٦٢ ، ص ٢ .

"12 Milyūn 'Āmil Yuḍribūn. " Cairo, <u>al-Ahrām,</u> September
16, 1962, p. 2.
("12 Million Workers Strike")

COLOMBIA

676

خسارة مالية ضخمة سببتها أمريكا لكولومبيا بسبب خفض
أسعار البن "، القاهرة ، الجمهورية ٢٥، فبراير
١٩٦٢ ،ص٢٠

"Khusārah Māliyah Ḍakhmah Sababathā Amrīkā li-Kūlūmbyā
Bisabab Khafḍ as 'ār al-Bun." Cairo, al-Jumhūrīyah,
February 25, 1962, p. 2.
("The U. S. A. Causes Colombia Great Financial Loss by
Lowering the Price of Coffee")

CENTRAL AMERICA

677

تقدم فرانشسكو أورليش في إنتخابات الرياسة "، القاهرة ،
الأخبار ، ٦ فبراير ١٩٦٢،ص٢٠

"Taqadum Frānshiskū Aūrlīsh fī Intikhābāt al-Riyāsah."
Cairo, al-Akhbār, February 6, 1962, p. 2.
("Francisco Orlich Presents Himself as a Candidate in the
Presidential Elections")

CUBA

678

أكبر ميزانية في تاريخ كوبا مقدارها ١، ٨ بليون دولار "،
القاهرة، الأهرام ، ٧ يناير ١٩٦٢، ص٢٠

"Akbar Mizānīyah fī Tārikh Kūbā Miqdāruhā 1, 8 Bilyūn
Dūlār." Cairo, al-Ahrām, January 7, 1962, p. 2.
("The Greatest Budget in Cubas' History, 1. 8 Billion
Dollars")

679 ، " الحرب بين أنصار كاسترو وخصومه في أمريكا اللاتينية " ،
القاهرة ، الجمهورية ، ٢١ أكتوبر ١٩٦٣ ،ص٢ .

"Al-Ḥarb Bayna Anṣār Kāstrū wa Khuṣūmihi fī Amrīkā
al-Lātīnīyah. " Cairo, al-Jumhūrīyah, October 21, 1963,
p. 2.
("War Between Castro's Supporters and Enemies in Latin
America")

680 " العيد الثالث للثورة " ، القاهرة ، الأخبار ، ١ يناير
١٩٦٢ ، ص٦ .

"Al-'Īd al-Thālith lil-Thawrah. " Cairo, al-Akhbār,
January 1, 1962, p. 6.
("The Third Anniversary of the Revolution in Cuba")

681 " الإهتمام بالحزب الذي أسسه كاسترو " ، القاهرة ، الأهرام ،
٢٠ يوليو ١٩٦٦ ،ص٤ .

"Al-Ihtimām bi-al-Ḥizb al-Ladhī Assasahu Kāstrū. "
Cairo, al-Ahrām, July 20, 1966, p. 4.
("Significance is Attached to the Party Founded by Castro")

682 " الكوبيون في أمريكا يطالبون حكومتها بأسلحة للرد على
تسليح روسيا لكوبا " ، القاهرة ، الأهرام ، ٤ سبتمبر
١٩٦٢ ، ص٢ .

"Al-Kūbiyyūn fī Amrīkā Yuṭalibūn Ḥukumatihā bi-Aslihah lil-
rad 'alā Taslīḥ Rūsyā li-Kūbā. " Cairo, al-Ahrām, September
4, 1962, p. 1.
("Cubans in the U. S. A. Ask for Weapons as a Reaction to Russia's
Arming of Cuba")

683

* اللاجئون يقطعون علاقتهم بحكومة كيدى * ، القاهرة ،
الأخبار ، ١٢ أبريل ١٩٦٢ ، ص٢٠

"Al-Lāgi' ūn Yaqta' ūn 'Alāqātihim bi-Ḥukūmat Kinīdī. "
Cairo, al-Akhbār, April 12, 1962, p. 2.
("Cuban Refugees Sever Their Relations with the Kennedy
Administration")

684

* المخابرات الأمريكية تستخدم السفن فى مهاجمة كوبا * ،
القاهرة ، المسا* ، ٣١ أكتوبر ١٩٦٣ ،ص١

"Al-Mukhābarāt al-Amrīkīyah Tastakhdim al-Sufun fī Muhājamat
Kūbā. " Cairo, al-Misā, October 31, 1963, p. 1.
("The C. I. A. Uses Vessels to Attack Cuba")

685

* المنظمات المعادية لكاسترو تعلن أنها ستطلق النار على
كل سفينة شيوعيه فى مياهها * ، القاهرة ، المسا* ،
٨ سبتمبر ١٩٦٢ ، ص١

"Al-Munaẓamāt al-mu'Ādīyah li-Kāstrū tu'lin Anahā
Satutliq al-nār 'alā Kul Safinah Shuyū 'Īyash fī Miyāhihā. "
Cairo, al-Misa, September 8, 1962, p. 1.
("The Anti-Castro Organizations Declare that they Will
Set Fire to Each Communist Ship in Cuban Waters")

686

* القائمة الأمريكية السودا* للسفن التى تتعامل مع كوبا * ،
القاهرة ، الأهرام ، ١٤ سبتمبر ١٩٦٣ ، ص٢٠

"Al-Qā' Imah al-Amrīkīyah al-Sawdā' lil-Sufun al-Latī Tata'
Āmal ma' Kūbā. " Cairo, al-Ahrām, September 14, 1963, p. 2.
("U. S. Blacklist of Ships Dealing with Cuba")

687

* القصة الحقيقية للصواريخ الروسية " ، القاهرة ،

أخبار اليوم ، ١٤ ديسمبر ١٩٦٣، ص ٥٠

"Al-Qisah al-Ḥaqīqīyah lil-Ṣawārikh al-Rūssīyah. " Cairo,
Akhbār al-Yawm, December 14, 1963, p. 5.
("The Real Story About the Russian Missiles")

688

* السفن الغربية تحمل إليها البضائع تحت أعلام أجنبية ،

القاهرة ، الأخبار ، ١٤ سبتمبر ١٩٦٢، ص ٦

"Al-Ṭayyār al-Amrīkī i'Taraf bi-Anahu ya'mal li-Ḥisāb
al-Mukhābarāt al-Amrīkīyah. " Cairo, Akhbār al-Yawm,
November 25, 1963, p. 2.
("American Pilot Confesses that he Was Working for the
C. I. A. ")

689

* الطيار الأمريكي اعترف بأنه يعمل لحساب المخابرات

الأمريكية ، القاهرة ، أخبار اليوم ، ٢٥ نوفمبر ١٩٦٣،

ص ٢٠

"Al-Sufun al-Gharbīyah Taḥmil Ilayhā al-Badā Taḥt a'lām
Ajnabīyah. " Cairo, al-Akhbār, September 14, 1962, p. 6.
("Western Vessels Carry Cuban Merchandise Under Foreign
Flags")

690

* اليابان لا تقاطع كوبا تجارياً " ، القاهرة ، الأهرام ،

٧ فبراير ١٩٦٢، ص ٢٠

"Al-Yābān lā Tuqāṭi' Kūbā Tujāriyan. " Cairo, al-Ahrām,
February 7, 1962, p. 2.
("Japan will not Boycott Cuba Commercially")

691 ° أمريكا لن تجد وقتاً للدفاع عن نفسها اذا حاولت الغزو
(كاسترو) ، القاهرة ، الأخبار ، ١١ أبريل ١٩٦٢ ،

"Amrīkā lan Tajid Waqtan lil-Difā' 'an Nafsihā Idhā
Hāwalat al-Ghazw (Kāstrū). " Cairo, al-Akhbār, April
19, 1962, p. 2.
("The U.S.A. will not Find Time to Defend Herself if she
Attempts an Invasion")

692 °أمريكا تفرض عقوبات إقتصادية على كوبا ° ، القاهرة ،
الجمهورية ، ١ فبراير ١٩٦٤ ،ص٢٠

"Amrīkā Tafriḍ 'Uqūbāt Iqtiṣādīyah 'alā Kūbā. " Cairo,
al-Jumhūrīyah, February 9, 1964, p. 2.
("The U.S.A. Imposes Financial Penalties on Cuba")

693 ° أمريكا تحتجز أربع سفن كوبية ° ،القاهرة ،الأهرام ،
٥ فبراير ١٩٦٤ ،ص٤٠

"Amrīkā Taḥtajiz Arba' Sufun Kūbīyah. " Cairo, al-Ahrām,
February 5, 1964, p. 4.
("The U.S.A. Confiscates 4 Cuban Vessels")

694 ° أمريكا تعد جيشاً في هندوراس لغزو كوبا ° ،القاهرة ،
الأهرام ، ٢٤ فبراير ١٩٦٢ ،ص٢٠

"Amrīkā Ta'ud Jayshan fī Hundūrās li-Ghazw Kūbā. "
Cairo, al-Ahrām, February 24, 1962, p. 2.
("The U.S.A. is Preparing an Army in Honduras for the
Invasion of Cuba")

695

" أمريكا تحاول شراء البرازيل ضد كوبا " ، القاهرة ، الأخبار ،

١٩ يناير ١٩٦٢ ، ص ٢

"Amrīkā Tuḥāwil Shirā' al-Brāzīl ḍid Kūbā. " Cairo, al-
Akhbār, January 19, 1962, p. 2.
("America Tries to Bribe Brazil to Oppose Cuba")

696

" أمريكا تعلن أن كوبا تكتل خطر عليها " ، القاهرة ،

الأهرام ، ٤ يناير ١٩٦٢ ، ص ١

"Amrīkā tu'lin Anna Kūbā Takattul Khaṭar 'Alayhā. "
Cairo, al-Ahrām, January 4, 1962, p. 1.
("The U.S.A. Declares that Cuba Constitutes a Danger to
Her")

697

" أمريكا تشجع العمل ضد كاسترو داخل كوبا " ، القاهرة ،

المساء ، ٢٥ أبريل ١٩٦٢ ، ص ٢

"Amrīkā Tushaji' al-'Amal ḍid Kāstrū Dākhil Kūbā. " Cairo,
al-Misā', April 25, 1962, p. 2.
("The U.S.A. Encourages Anti-Castro Activities Within
Cuba")

698

" أزمة بين بريطانيا وأمريكا بسبب كوبا " ، القاهرة ، أخبار

اليوم ، ٣١ مارس ١٩٦٢ ، ص ٢

"Azmah Bayna Brītāniyā wa Amrīkā bi-Sabab Kūbā. "
Cairo, Akhbār al-Yawm, March 31, 1962, p. 2.
("Crisis Between Britain and the U.S.A. Because of Cuba")

" باع كاسترو الأسرى بلغ ٦٢ مليون دولار " ، القاهرة ،
الأهرام ، ٤ مايو ١٩٦٢ ،ص ٠١

"Bā' Kāstrū al-Asrā bi-Mablagh 62 Milyūn Dūlār." Cairo,
al-Ahrām, May 4, 1962, p. 1.
("Castro Sold Prisoners for 62 Million Dollars")

" بريطانيا تطالب كاسترو بالإعتذار لمهاجمة جزيرة
أنجويلا " ، القاهرة ، الأهرام ، ١٤ سبتمبر
١٩٦٣ ،ص ٢٠

"Brīṭanyā Tuṭālib Kāstrū bi-al-i' Tidhār li-Muhājamat
Jazīrat Anjūwīlā." Cairo, al-Ahrām, September 14,
1963, p. 2.
("Britain Demands an Apology from Castro for the
Attack on Anguilla Island")

" بريزنيف يقول أى هجوم عليها سيؤدى للحرب " ،القاهرة ،
الأخبار ، ٢٨ سبتمبر ١٩٦٢ ،ص ٢٠

"Brīznyiv Yaqūl ay Hujūm 'Alayhā Sayū' Adī lil-Ḥarb."
Cairo, al-Akhbār, September 1962, p. 2.
("Brezhnev Says any Attack on Cuba will Lead to War")

" دراسة تشريحية للثورة " ،القاهرة ، الجمهورية ، ١٥٤
سبتمبر ١٩٦٦ ،ص ١٦٠

"Dirāsah Tashrīḥīyah lil-Thawrah." Cairo, al-Jumhūrīyah,
September 15, 1966, p. 16.
("Analytical Study of the Revolution in Cuba")

703 · نرنسا تتحدى أمريكا وتترك سفنها تعمل مع كوبا · ،
القاهرة ، الأهرام ، ٢٠ سبتمبر ١٩٦٣ ،ص٩ ·

"Fransā Tataḥadā Amrīkā wa-Tatruk Sufunahā Ta'Mal ma²
Kūbā." Cairo, al-Ahrām, September 20, 1963, p. 9.
("France Warns the U. S. A. and Lets her Ships Deal with
Cuba")

704 · هل وقعت محاولة لا غتياله · ، القاهرة ،
الجمهورية ، ١ أبريل ١٩٦٢ ،ص٢ ·

"Hal Waqa 'at Muḥāwalah li-Ightiyālihi." Cairo, al-Jumhūrīyah,
April 1, 1962, p. 2.
("Did an Attempt to Murder Fidel Castro Take Place?")

705 · حقها في إختيار نظامها السياسي · ، القاهرة ،
الأهرام ، ٢٠ يناير ١٩٦٢ ،ص١ ·

"Ḥaquhā fī Ikhtiyār Niẓāmihā al-Siyāsy." Cairo, al-Ahrām,
January 20, 1962, p. 1.
("Cuba's Right to Choose her Own Political System")

706 · إبادة ٦٠٪ من أعداء حكومة كاسترو · ، القاهرة ،
الأهرام ، ١ أبريل ١٩٦٢ ،ص٢ ·

"Ibādat 60% min a'dā' Ḥukūmat Kāstrū." Cairo, al-Ahrām,
April 1, 1962, p. 2.
("Elimination of 60% of the Enemies of Castro's Government")

707

« إضطراب العلاقات بين القارتين الأمريكيتين بسبب كوبا » ،
القاهرة ، <u>الجمهورية</u> ، ٥ فبراير ١٩٦٢ ، ص٢ .

"Idṭirāb al-'Alāqāt Bayna al-Qāratayn al-Amrīkīyatayn
bi-Sabab Kūbā. " Cairo, <u>al-Jumhūrīyah</u>, February 5,
1962, p. 2.
("Disturbance in the Relations Between the Two Americas
Because of Cuba")

708

« إغارات للمنفيين » ، القاهرة ، <u>الأهرام</u> ، ١١ سبتمبر
١٩٦٣ ، ص٢ .

"Ighārāt lil-Manfīyīn. " Cairo, <u>al-Ahrām,</u> September 11,
1963, p. 2.
("Raids by Exiled Cubans")

709

« إخفاء طائراتها الميج تحت الأرض » ، القاهرة ،
<u>الجمهورية</u> ، ١٦ يوليو ١٩٦٢ ، ص٢ .

"Ikhfā' ṭā' Irātuhā al-Mīj Taḥt al-Arḍ. " Cairo, <u>al-Jumhūriyah,</u>
July 16, 1962, p. 2.
("Hiding her Mig Planes Underground")

710

« إستئناف العلاقات » ، القاهرة ، <u>الجمهورية</u> ، ١٥ يناير
١٩٦٤ ، ص٨ .

"Isti' Nāf al-'Alāqāt. " Cairo, <u>al-Jumhūrīyah,</u> January 15,
1964, p. 8.
("Resumption of Relations with Morocco")

" إستمرار المحاولات لمنع نقل الأسلحة إليها " ، القاهرة ،
الأخبار ، ١٦ سبتمبر ١٩٦٢ ، ص٢ .

"Istimrār al-Muḥāwalāt li-man' Naql al-Asliḥah Ilayhā."
Cairo, al-Akhbār, September 16, 1962, p. 2.
("The Continuation of the Efforts to Prevent Transporting
Weapons to Cuba")

" إتهام أمريكا بضرب احدى المدن " ،القاهرة، الأهرام،
٧ سبتمبر ١٩٦٣ ،ص ١ .

"Ittihām Amrīkā bi-Ḍarb Iḥda al-Mudum." Cairo, al-Ahrām,
September 7, 1963, p. 1.
("Accusing America of Bombing a Town")

" إتهام أمريكا برفع أعلام الدول الأخرى على السفن التى
تهاجم كوبا " ، القاهرة ، الأهرام ، ١ نوفمبر ١٩٦٣ ،
ص٢ .

"Ittihām Amrīkā bi-raf' a'lam al-duwal al-Ukhrā 'alā al-
Sufun Allatī Tuhājim Kūbā." Cairo, al-Ahrām, November 1,
1963, p. 2.
("Accusing America of Using Other Countries' Flags on Vessels
Attacking Cuba")

" إتهام كوبا بالتآمر عليها " ، القاهرة ،أخبار اليوم ،
١ فبراير ١٩٦٤ ،ص٢ .

"Ittihām Kūbā bi-al-ta' Āmur 'Alayhā." Cairo, Akhbār
al-Yawm, February 1, 1964, p. 2.
("Honduras Accuses Cuba of Conspiring Against her")

715 * جيش في جواتيمالا ينظمه أعداء * كاسترو * ، القاهرة ،
الأخبار ، ٢٠ نبراير ١٩٦٢، ص ٢.

"Jaysh fī Juwātīmālā Yunazimuhu a 'da' Kāstrū. " Cairo,
al-Akhbār, February 20, 1962, p. 2.
("The Enemies of Castro are Organizing an Army in Guatemala")

716 * كندا ترفض سياسة الحصار الإقتصادى الأمريكى * ، القاهرة ،
الجمهورية ، ١٠ نبراير ١٩٦٤، ص ٢.

"Kanadā Tarfuḍ Sīyāsat al-Ḥiṣār al-Iqtiṣādī al-Amrīkī. "
Cairo, al-Jumhūrīyah, February 10, 1964, p. 2.
("Canada Rejects the Policy of the U. S. Financial Blockade")

717 * كاسترو يقول كوبا لم تجع رغم حصار الاستعماريين * ، القاهرة ،
أخبار اليوم ، ١١ مايو ١٩٦٢، ص ٢.

"Kāstrū Yaqūl Kūbā lam Taju' Ragham Ḥiṣār al-Isti'
Mārīyyīn. " Cairo, Akhbār al-Yawn, May 19, 1962,
p. 2.
("Castro Declares that Cuba will not Starve Despite
the Imperialist Blockade")

718 * كاسترو يهاجم المعارضين للخط الشيوعى المستقل فى
كوبا * ، القاهرة ، الجمهورية ملحق ، ٣٠ سبتمبر ١٩٦٦،
ص ١٦.

"Kāstrū Yuhājim al-mu'Āridīn lil-Khat al-Shuyū' i al-
Mustaqīl fī Kūbā. " Cairo, al-Jumhūrīyah mulḥaq,
September 30, 1966, p. 16.
("Castro Attacks Those Who Oppose an Independent
Communist Plan for Cuba")

719

* كاسترو يعلن فشل أمريكا فى إسقاطه * ، القاهرة ،
أخبار اليوم ، ٢ نوفمبر ١٩٦٣ ، ص٢٠

"Kāstrū yu'lin Fashal Amrīkā fī Isqāṭihi. " Cairo,
Akhbār al-Yawm, November 2, 1963, p. 2.
("Castro Declares U.S. Failure in Efforts to Remove Him")

720

* كيف يتحول ثوار الجبال إلى رجال فى مكاتب حكومية * ،
القاهرة،آخر ساعة، ١١ يوليو ١٩٦٢ ،ص١٦ ٠

"Kayfa Yataḥawal Thūwwār al-Jibāl ilā Rijāl fī Makātib
Ḥukūmīyah. " Cairo, Ākhir Sā'ah, July 11, 1962, p. 16.
("How the Mountain Rebels Become Government Officials")

721

* خطرها على القارة الأمريكية * ، القاهرة ، الجمهورية ،
٢٢ فبراير ١٩٦٣ ،ص٢٠

"Khaṭaruha 'alā al-Qārah al-Amrīkīyah. " Cairo, al-
Jumhūrīyah, February 22, 1963, p. 2.
("The Danger of Cuba to the American Continent")

722

* خروشوف ينذر بسياستها ضد كوبا * ، القاهرة ،
الأهرام ، ٢٢ يناير ١٩٦٤، ص٥٠

"Khrūshūf Yundhir bi-Siyāsatihā ḍid Kūbā. " Cairo,
al-Ahrām, January 22, 1964, p. 5.
("Khrushchev Warns U.S.A. About the Anti-Cuban Policy")

• خوسيه مارتى رائد الثورة الفكرية • ، القاهرة ،، الكاتب ،
فبراير ١٩٦٢، (عدد ٤٠)

"Khūsīh Mārtī rā'id al-Thawrah al-Fikrīyah." Cairo,
al-Kātib, February 1962, 40th Issue.
("José Martí, Pioneer of the Intellectual Revolution")

• كنيدى يهدد بإتخاذ إجراءات جديدة • ، القاهرة ،
الأهرام ، ٢١ أبريل ١٩٦٢ ، ص٢ •

"Kinīdī Yahadid bi-Itikhādh Ijrā'āt Jadīdah." Cairo,
al-Ahrām, April 21, 1962, p. 2.
("Kennedy Threatens with New Reprisals")

• كوبا تشكو أمريكا ومجلس الأمن يستمع • ، القاهرة ،
الأهرام ، ١١ مارس ١٩٦٢، ص٢ •

"Kūbā Tashkū Amrīkā wa Majlis al-amn Yastami'."
Cairo, al-Ahrām, March 19, 1962, p. 2.
("Cuba Complains Against the U.S.A. and the U.N. Security
Council Listens")

• كوبا تتهم المنظمة بتدبير عدوان عليها • ، القاهرة ،
المساء ، ٢٦ يناير ١٩٦٢ ، ص١ •

"Kūbā Tattahim al-Munaẓamah bi-Tadbīr 'Udwān 'Alayhā."
Cairo, al-Misā', January 26, 1962, p. 1.
("Cuba Accuses the O.A.S. of Preparing Aggression Against
her")

* كوبا تتهمها بوضع الألغام فى مياهها *، القاهرة ،
أخبار اليوم ، ۳۰ ديسمبر ۱۹٦۳، ص ٥٠

"Kūbā Tattahimuhā bi-waḍ' al-Alghām fī Miyāhihā. "
  Cairo, <u>Akhbār al-Yawm</u>, December 30, 1963, p. 5.
("Cuba Accuses U.S.A. of Placing Mines in her Waters")

* كوبا تثير قلق أمريكا بتوسيع تجارتها مع أوربا الغربية *،
القاهرة ، الأهرام ، ۲۲ يناير ۱۹٦٤، ص ٦٠

"Kūbā Tuthīr Qalaq Amrīkā bi-Tawsī' Tijāratihā Ma'
  Awrubā al-Gharbīyah. " Cairo, <u>al-Ahrām</u>, January 22,
  1964, p. 6.
("Cuba Causes U.S.A. Unrest Through her Widening
Trade with Western Europe")

* كوبا وحلف وارسو *، القاهرة ، الأهرام الإقتصادى ،
۱٥ يناير ۱۹٦۲، ص ۲۰

"Kūbā wa-Ḥilf Wārsū. " Cairo, <u>al-Ahrām al-Iqtiṣādī</u>,
  January 15, 1962, p. 20.
("Cuba and the Warsaw Pact")

* مجلس الأمن يرفض بحث شكوى كوبا ضد أمريكا *، القاهرة ،
الأهرام ، ۱ مارس ۱۹٦۲، ص ۱۰

"Majlis al-Amn Yarfud Bahth Shakawā Kūbā ḍid Amrīkā. "
  Cairo, <u>al-Ahrām</u>, March 1, 1962, p. 1.
("The Security Council Refuses to Discuss Cuba's
Complaints Against the U.S.A. ")

731

* ماكميلان يناشد شركات الملاحة منع نقل الأسلحة الشيوعية
إليها * ، القاهرة ، الجمهورية ، ١٦ سبتمبر ١٩٦٢ ،
ص ٢ .

"Makmīllān Yunāshid Sharikāt al-Milāhah Man'Naql al-Aslihah
al-Shuyū 'Īyah Ilayhā. " Cairo, al-Jumhūrīyah, September
16, 1962, p. 2.
("Macmillan Asks Shipping Companies not to Transport
Soviet Weapons to Cuba")

732

* معنى زيارته لروسيا * ، القاهرة ، الأهرام ، ١٨ أبريل
١٩٦٢ ،ص ٢ .

"Ma' nā Ziyāratuhu li-Rūsyā. " Cairo, al-Ahrām, April
18, 1962, p. 2.
("The Meaning of Castro's Visit to Russia")

733

* منع سفن اليونان من التعامل معها * ، القاهرة ،
الأهرام ، ٢٥ سبتمبر ١٩٦٣ ، ص ٢ .

"Man' Sufun al-Yūnān Min al-ta'āmul ma'ahā. " Cairo,
al-Ahrām, September 25, 1963, p. 2.
("Greek Vessels Forbidden to Deal with Cuba")

734

* مطارات سرية بها * ،القاهرة ،الأخبار ، ١٦ يوليو ١٩٦٢ ،
ص ٢ .

"Matārāt Sirrīyah Bihā. " Cairo, al-Akhbār, July 16,
1962, p. 2.
("Secret Airports in Cuba")

735

مذكرات احتجاج من كوبا عن انتهاك المجال الجوي والبحري ٠
٠ ، القاهرة المصري ، ٣ يناير ١٩٦٢ ، ص ١ .

"Mudhakarat Iḥtijāj Min Kūbā 'an Intihāk al-Majāl al-
Jawwī wa-al-Baḥarī. " Cairo, al-Miṣā, January 3, 1962,
p. 1.
("Cuban Protest About the Violation of her Air Space and
Territorial Waters")

736

٠ نهرو يعارض أى عدوان على كوبا ٠ ، القاهرة ، الأهرام ،
٢٤ يناير ١٩٦٢ ، ص٢ ٠

"Nihrū yu'Ārid ay 'Udwān 'alā Kūbā. " Cairo, al-Ahrām,
January 24, 1962, p. 2.
("Nehru Opposes any Aggression Against Cuba")

737

٠ رد كاسترو على قرار طرد كوبا من المنظمة ٠ ،القاهرة ،
الأهرام ، ٥ فبراير ١٩٦٢ ،ص٢ ٠

"Rad Kāstrū 'alā Qarār Ṭard Kūbā Min al-Munaẓamah. "
Cairo, al-Ahrām, February 5, 1962, p. 2.
("Castro's Answer to the Decree Expelling Cuba from
the OAS")

738

٠ روسيا تحذر من إتخاذ إجراءات ضد كوبا ٠ ، القاهرة ،
الجمهورية ، ٧ فبراير ١٩٦٤ ، ص٢ ٠

"Rūsyā Tuḥadhir min Itikhādh Igrā' āt ḍid Kūbā. " Cairo,
al-Jumhūrīyah, February 7, 1964, p. 2.
("Russia Warns Those who Take Anti-Cuban Measures")

223

739

رویسا وكوبا تعلمان بوجود خطة جديدة للغزو "،القاهرة،،
الأخبار، ٢١ أبريل ١٩٦٢ ،ص٢.

"Rūsyā wa Kūbā ta'Lamān bi-Wujūd Khiṭṭah Jadīdah lil-
Ghazw." Cairo, al-Akhbār, April 21, 1962, p. 2.
("Russia and Cuba Know of a New Plan for an Invasion")

740

صواریخ لكوبا تستطیع أصابة أهداف أمريكية ، أكبر ترسانة
حربیة فی أمريكا اللاتينية "،القاهرة ، الأهرام ، ٧
نبرایر ١٩٦٢ ،ص٢.

"Ṣawārīkh li-Kūbā Tastaṭī' Iṣābat Ahdāf Amrīkīyah;
Akbar Tirsānah Ḥarbīyah fī Amrīkā al-Latīnīyah."
Cairo, al-Ahrām, February 7, 1962, p. 2.
("Cuban Missiles can Strike any American Target; Biggest
Military Arsenal in Latin America")

741

١٦ قاذفة أمريكية أسقطتها كوبا خلال الغزو الفاشل " ،
القاهرة ، الأخبار ، ٤ أبريل ١٩٦٢ ، ص٢.

"16 Qādhifah Amrīkīyah Asqaṭathā Kūbā Khilāl al-Ghazw
al-Fāshil." Cairo, al-Akhbār, April 4, 1962, p. 2.
("16 U.S. Bombers Shot Down by Cuba During the Unsuccessful
Invasion")

742

سياسة أمريكية لخنق كوبا بالتدريج "،القاهرة ، الجمهورية ،
٥ مايو ١٩٦٢ ،ص٤.

"Siyāsat Amrīkīyah li-Khanq Kūbā bil-Tadrīj." Cairo,
al-Jumhūrīyah, May 5, 1962, p. 4.
("U.S. Policy for the Gradual Strangulation of Cuba")

743

" تحول كبير في موقف الولايات المتحدة من كاسترو " ،
القاهرة «المساء» ، ٢٤ أبريل ١٩٦٢ ص ٢ .

"Taḥawul Kabīr fī Mawqif al-Wilāyāt al-Muttaḥidah min
Kāstrū." Cairo, al-Misā', April 24, 1962, p. 2.
("Great Change in U. S. Attitude Toward Castro")

744

"طرد الكوبيين من أمريكا عمل غير إنساني (كاسترو) " ،
القاهرة « الأهرام » ، ١٥ فبراير ١٩٦٤ ص ٤ .

"Ṭard al-Kūbīyyīn min Amrīkā 'Amal Ghayr Insānī (Kāstrū)."
Cairo, al-Ahrām, February 15, 1964, p. 4.
("Expelling Cubans from the U. S. A. is an Inhuman Act: Castro")

745

" ٣ ملايين دولار تقدمها الأمم المتحدة لها " ، القاهرة ،
المساء ، ١٤ فبراير ١٩٦٣ ، ص ١ .

"3 Milyūn Dūlār Tuqadimuhā al-Umam al-Muttaḥidah
Lahā." Cairo, al-Misā', February 14, 1963, p. 1.
("3 Million Dollars Offered to her by the United Nations")

746

" تركيا توقف التبادل التجاري بناء على طلب أمريكا " ،
القاهرة «المساء» ، ٢٨ سبتمبر ١٩٦٢ ص ١ .

"Turkiyā Tūqif al-Tabādul al-Tujārī Binā' 'Alā Ṭalab
Amrīkā." Cairo, al-Misā', September 28, 1962, p. 1.
("Turkey Stops Commercial Exchanges with Cuba Upon
U. S. Request")

747 • ٢٧ ألف سوفيتى فى كوبا • ، القاهرة ،الجمهورية، ١٢
فبراير ١٩٦٣، ص ٢ •

"27 Alf Suvyīty fī Kūbā. " Cairo, <u>al-Jumhūrīyah,</u>
February 12, 1963, p. 2.
("27 Thousand Russians in Cuba")

748 • عملاء المخابرات الأمريكية يعرضهم التليفزيون فى كوبا •
القاهرة ،أخبار اليوم، ٤ نوفمبر ١٩٦٣ ،ص ٢ •

"Umalā al-Mukhābarāt al-Amrīkīyah ya'Riḍuhum al-Tilīvizyūn
fī-Kūbā. " Cairo, <u>Akhbār al-Yawm</u>, November 4, 1963, p. 2.
("Accomplices of the C. I. A. Shown on Cuban Television")

749 • وزير دفاع أمريكا يهاجم كاسترو • ، القاهرة ، المساء •
٢٠ يناير ١٩٦٢، ص ١ •

"Wazīr Difā' Amrīkā Yuhājim Kāstrū. " Cairo, <u>al-Misā</u>,
January 20, 1962, p. 1.
("The U. S. Secretary of Defense Attacks Castro")

750 •وزارة الدفاع الأمريكية تنفى وجود أسلحة ذرية فيها •
القاهرة ، المساء ، ٢ فبراير ١٩٦٣ ،ص ٢ •

"Wizārat al-Difā' al-Amrīkīyah Tanfi Wujūd Asliḥah
Dharīyah Fīhā. " Cairo, <u>al-Misā</u>, February 2, 1963,
p. 1.
("U. S. Department of Defense Denies Existence of Atomic
Weapons in Cuba")

" زوارق طوربيد سوفيتية تظهر فى هافانا " ، القاهرة ،الأهرام ،
٨ سبتمبر ١٩٦٢ ،ص ١ ٠

"Zawāriq Ṭūrbīd Sūvyītīyah Taẓhar fī Hāvānā. " Cairo,
al-Ahrām, September 8, 1962, p. 1.
("Soviet Torpedo-Boats Appear in Havana")

" جونسون يطلب من هيوم وقف التجارة مع كوبا " ،القاهرة ،
الجمهورية ، ١٤ فبراير ١٩٦٤ ،ص ٢ ٠

"Zhūnsūn Yaṭlub min Hyūm Waqf al-Tijārah ma'Kūbā. "
Cairo, al-Jumhūrīyah, February 14, 1964, p. 2.
("Johnson Asks Hume to Stop Trading with Cuba")

DOMINICAN REPUBLIC

" أمريكا وإنقلاب الدومينيكان " ، القاهرة ، المساء ، ٢٥
يناير ١٩٦٢ ،ص ٢ ٠

"Amrīkā wā-Inqilāb al-Dūmīnīkān. " Cairo, al-Misā',
January 25, 1962, p. 2.
("The U.S.A. and the Dominican Coup d'Etat")

" مؤامرة لقلب الحكومة وإعادة تروحيللو " ، القاهرة ،الجمهورية ،
١٥ يناير ١٩٦٢ ،ص ٢ ٠

"Mu' Āmarah Liqalb al Ḥukūmah wa-i 'Ādat Trūhillū. "
Cairo, al-Jumhūriyah, January 15, 1962, p. 2.
("Conspiracy to Overthrow the Government and Bring
Trujillo Back")

755

" مظاهرات معادية فى دومنيكا ضد أمريكا " ، القاهرة ،
الجمهورية ، ١٤ يناير ١٩٦٢، ص٢.

"Muẓāharat mu'Ādiyah fi Dūminīka ḍid Amrīkā." Cairo,
al-Jumhūrīyah, January 14, 1962, p. 2.
("Anti-U.S. Demonstrations in the Dominican Republic")

GUATEMALA

756

" إستمرار المظاهرات ضد الحكومة لتزوير الإنتخابات " ،
القاهرة ، الأخبار، ٢٧ أبريل ١٩٦٢ ،ص٢.

"Istimrār al-Muẓāharāt ḍid al-Ḥukūmah li-Tazwīr al-
Intikhābāt." Cairo, al-Akhbār, April 27, 1962, p. 2.
("Continuation of Anti-Government Demonstrations for
Election Frauds")

757

" طائرات جواتيمالا تغرق سفينة لكوبا " ، القاهرة ، الجمهورية ،
١ مايو ١٩٦٢ ،ص١.

"Ṭā'Irāt Juwātīmālā Tughriq Safīnah li-Kūbā." Cairo,
al-Jumhūrīyah, May 1, 1962, p. 1.
("Guatemala's Planes Sink a Cuban Vessel")

MEXICO

758

" محادثات تيتو ني المكسيك "، القاهرة ، الجمهورية، ٨
أكتوبر ١٩٦٣، ص ٢.

"Muḥādathāt Tītū fī al-Miksīk." Cairo, al-Jumhūrīyah,
    October 8, 1963, p. 2.
("Tito's Discussions in Mexico")

PERU

759

" الثورة فيها "، القاهرة ، المساء ، ٢٥ يوليو ١٩٦٢،
ص ٢.

"Al-Thawrah Fīhā." Cairo, al-Misā', July 25, 1962, p. 2.
("The Revolution in Peru")

760

" إعلان الأحكام العرفية بعد إكتشاف مؤامرة شيوعية ،
القاهرة ، الأهرام ، ٦ يناير ١٩٦٣ ، ص ٩.

"I'Lān al-Aḥkām al-'Urfīyah Ba'd Iktishāf mu'Āmarah
    Shuyū 'Iyah." Cairo, al-Ahrām, January 6, 1963, p. 9.
("Declaration of Martial Law After the Discovery of a
Communist Conspiracy")

" ثورة جديدة ضد الإقطاع"، القاهرة ، السا" ، ١٠ يناير
١٩٦٣ ،ص ٢٠

"Thawrah Jadīdah did al-Iqtā'." Cairo, al-Misā', January
10, 1963, p. 2.
("New Revolution Versus Feudalism")

VENEZUELA

"إتهام كوبا بتهريب الأسلحة الى العصابات "، القاهرة ،
الأهرام ، ٣٠ نوفمبر ١٩٦٣ ، ص ٢٠

"Ittihām Kūbā bi-Tahrīb al-Aslihah Ilā al-Iṣābāt." Cairo,
al-Ahrām, November 30, 1963, p. 2.
("Accusing Cuba of Supplying Rebels with Weapons")

"نسف أنابيب البترول التابعة لشركات أمريكية" ،القاهرة ،
الأهرام ، ٧ نوفمبر ١٩٦٣ ،ص ٢٠

"Nasf Anābīb al-Bitrūl al-Tābi 'ah li-Sharikāt Amrīkīyah."
Cairo, al-Ahrām, November 7, 1963, p. 2.
("Destroying the Oil Pipe Lines Belonging to U.S. Companies")

764   * راؤل ليونى يفوز بالرياسة * ، القاهرة ، الأهرام ،
٤ ديسمبر ١٩٦٣، ص ٧ •

"Rā'ūl Liyūnī Yafūz bi-al-Riyāsah." Cairo, al-Ahrām,
December 4, 1963, p. 7.
("Raúl Leoni is Elected President")

765   * ثورة عسكرية فى فنزويلا * ، القاهرة ، أخبار اليوم ،
٥ مايو ١٩٦٢، ص ١ •

"Thawrah 'Askarīyah fī Vinizuwīlā." Cairo, Akhbār
al-Yawm, May 5, 1962, p. 1.
("Military Revolt in Venezuela")

766   * تطالب بفرض حصار على كوبا * ، القاهرة ، الأهرام ،
٥ ديسمبر ١٩٦٣، ص ٧ •

"Tuṭalib bi-Farḍ Ḥiṣār 'alā Kūbā." Cairo, al-Ahrām,
December 5, 1963, p. 7.
("Asks for the Imposition of a Blockade on Cuba")

ISRAEL

In the Autumn of 1967 the Hebrew University in Jerusalem, Israel inaugurated a new Department of Spanish and Latin American Studies. The Head of the new Department is Dr. Moshe Lazar, Professor of Romance Languages. Bachelor of Arts and Master of Arts degrees are being granted through the new Department, which offered the following courses during the 1967-68 school year: Latin American Literature; Portuguese and Spanish Language; Introduction to the History of Latin America; The Colonial Period; Simon Bolivar's Policy and Leadership; The Mexican Revolution; Spain on the Eve of the Discoveries; Political Movements in Latin America. Additionally, special lectures and seminars on the social, political and economic structures of Brazil, Mexico and Venezuela were scheduled.

The new Department plans to offer a broad program of courses covering all regions of Latin America, with stress on language literature, history, political science, economics and social trends. Independent research on current Latin American problems will be encouraged. Tel Aviv University also offers course work.

Also located in Jerusalem is the Information Center for Latin America (6 Sokolov Street), an organization which exchanges information, publications and exhibits between Israel and the Latin American countries, and assists individuals from Latin America, Spain and Portugal by arranging visits to Israel.

(In this section of the bibliography on Israel, the English translation of the title of each bibliographic item is to be found directly under the title in the original language, and immediately following the entire bibliographic description.

Note: Although this section is devoted to items published in Hebrew, there are many items written in Yiddish, the popular language of Jews the world over.)

En el otoño de 1967 la Universidad Hebrea en Jerusalén inauguró
un nuevo Departamento de Español y Estudios Latinoamericanos.
El Jefe del nuevo Departamento es el Dr. Moshe Lazar, Profesor
de Lenguas Romances. Se otorgan títulos de Bachiller y Maestro
en Artes, y se ofrecen las siguientes asignaturas durante el año
escolar 1967-68: Literatura Latinoamericana; Lengua Portuguesa,
así como Lengua Española; Introducción a la Historia de Latinoamérica; Historia Colonial; la importancia de la Jefatura de Simón
Bolívar; la Revolución Mexicana; España en las vísperas de los
Descubrimientos; Movimientos Políticos en Latinoamérica.
Adicionalmente, se proyectaron conferencias y seminarios
especiales sobre las estructuras sociales, políticas y económicas
de Brasil, México y Venezuela.

El nuevo Departamento espera ofrecer un programa bastante
amplio abarcando todas las regiones de Latinoamérica, con
énfasis en lenguas y letras, historia, ciencias políticas y
económicas y sociología. Se fomentan investigaciones en
cuanto a problemas actuales de la América Latina.

El Centro de Información para Latinoamérica está situado en
la Calle Sokolov, # 6, en Jerusalén. Esta organización canjea
información, publicaciones y exhibiciones entre Israel y los
países latinoamericanos, y arregla visitas a Israel para
latinoamericanos, españoles y portugueses.

(En esta sección de la bibliografía sobre Israel, la traducción
inglesa del título de cada asiento se encuentra directamente bajo
el título de la lengua original, seguida de la ficha entera.

Nota: Aunque en esta sección se encuentran asientos publicados
en hebreo, hay muchas fichas escritas en Idish, la lengua
popular de los judíos en todos los países del mundo.)

I. Books

LATIN AMERICA

767　　בעלער, יעקב. **איבער צוואנציק לאטיין-**
אמריקאנער לענדער**.** בוענאס-איירעס,
339 ע'.

Beller, Yacov. _Iber Zvanzik Latin Amerikaner Lender._
Buenos Aires, 1953, 339p.
(About Twenty Latin-American Countries)

768　　ביסטריצקי, נתן. **על היהדות והציונות באמריקה**
הלטינית. ירושלים, הלשכה הראשית של
הקרן הקיימת לישראל, תש"ז. 94 ע'.

Bistritzky, Natan. _Al Ha'yahadut Ve'ha' Zionut Be'America_
Ha'Latinit. Jerusalem, Ha'Lishka Ha'Roshit Shel Ha'Keren
Ha'Kayemet Le'Israel, 1947, 94p.
(About Judaism and Zionism in Latin
America)

769　　Bistritzky, Natan. **ספרית. מרחביה. קסמי יבשת. רשמי מסע באמריקה הדרומית.**
פועלים.
Kisme Yabeshet, Rishmei Masa be-Amerika
Hadromit. Merhavya, Israel, Sifriyat Poalim, 1948, 245p.
(Fascinations of a Continent, Impressions of
a Journey in South America)

770　　דייקסעל, שמואל. **אינדיאנישע דערציילונגען.**
(ניו יארק, 1959) 281 ע'.

Deiksel, Shmuel. _Indianishe Dertzeilungen._ New York, 1959,
281p.
(Indian Stories)

771　　גמזו, חיים. **שירת הקוצאל; רשמי מסע**
באמריקה הלטינית. תל-אביב, "מסדה", תש"ט.
309 ע'.

Gamzu, Haim. _Shirat Ha'Quetzal; Rishmei Masa Be'America_
Ha'Latinit. Tel Aviv, "Massadah", 1949, 309p.
(The Song of the Quetzal; Impressions of
Journey in Latin America)

772 • גלרטר, מנחם• יהדות ביבשת מסוערת•
ירושלים, תשכ"ג• 50 ע'•

Gelerter, Menahem. Yahadut Be'Yabeshet Me'Soeret. Jerusalem,
1963, 50p.

(Jewry in a Stormy Continent)

773 גורדול, ישכר בר בן יחיאל מיכל• ספר שבילי
עולם חדש• ווארשא, תרל"א-1870• 146 ע'•

Gordon, Yisachar B. Sefer Shvilei Olam Hadash. Warsaw,
1870, 146p.

(Paths of the New World)

774 • גאטליב, יצחק• יידן אין לאטיין אמריקע•
ניו-יארק, 1960• 240 ע'•

Gotlib, Yitzhak. Yidden in Latin Amerike. New York, 1960,
240p.

(Jews in Latin America)

775 הקונגרס היהודי העולמי• הישוב היהודי
באמריקה הלטינית• ירושלים, תש"ך• 48 ע'

Ha'Congress Ha'Yehudi Ha'Olami. Ha'yshuv Ha'Yehudi Ba'
America Ha'Latinit. Jerusalem, 1960, 48p.
(World Jewish Congress. Jewish Communities in Latin
America)

776 הירשביין, פרץ• פון ווייטע לענדער•
ניו-יארק, בלי שם המדפיס, 1916• 256 ע'•

Hirshbein, Peretz. Fun Veite Lender. New York, 1916, 256p.
(From Far-Away Countries)

235

ירושלים.האוניברסיטה העברית.הפקולטה למדעי
הרוח.החוג לגאוגרפיה. חומר לשעורים ולתרגילי.
ירושלים, תשט"ו- מס. 1-

Jerusalem. Ha'Universita Ha'Ivrit. Ha'Faculta Le'Madaei
Ha'Ruah. Ha'Hug Le'Geographia. Homer Le'Shiurim Ule'
Targilim. Jerusalem, 1956.
(Jerusalem. Hebrew University. Faculty of Humanities.
Geography Department. Lectures and Exercise Material)

778 קראנץ, פיליפ. אמעריקא פאר קאלאמבוס;
ניו-יארק, אינטערנאציונאלע ביבליאטעק,
חש"ד (1904). 169 ע'.

Kranz, Philip. America Far Colombus. New York, Internazionale
Bibliotek, 1904, 169p.
(America Before Columbus)

779 קריינין, מ. די איינוואנדערונגס-
מעגליכקייטן קיין דרום-אמריקע און די
דורטיגע יידישע ישובים; ארגענטינע,
בראזיליע, אורוגווי. בערלין "היאס-
עמיגדירעקט", 1928. 59 ע'

Kreinin, M. Di Einvonderungs-Meglichkeiten Kein Drom-Amerike
Un Di Dortige Yiddishe Yshuvim: Argentine, Brazilie, Uruguay.
Berlin "Hias-Emigdirect", 1928, 59p.
(Possibilities for Jewish Immigration to South
America and the Jewish Communities in Argentina, Brazil and
Uruguay)

780 לאטצקי, ו. די איינוואנדרונג און די
יידישע ישובים אין דרום-אמריקע.
בערלין "עמיגדירעקט", 1926. 48 ע'.

Latsky, W. Di Einvonderung un di Yiddishe Yshuvim in Drom-
Amerike. Berlin, "Emigdirect", 1926, 48p.
(Immigration and the Jewish Communities of
South America)

781 לשצ'ינסקי, יעקב. די לאגע פון יידן אין
לאטיין-אמעריקאנער לענדער. ניו-יורק,
אינסטיטוט פאר יידישע עניינים, 1948.

Lestschinsky, Jacob. Di Lage fun Yidden in Latin-Amerikaner
Lender. New York, Institute far Yiddishe Inyonim, 1948,
60p.
(The Position of Jews in the South
American Countries)

782   מכון מרכזי ליחסי תרבות ישראל-אמריקה האיברית,
      ספרד ופורטוגל.   תזכיר מס. 1-   ירושלים,1956-

Machon Merkazi Le'Yahasei Tarbut Israel America Ha'Iberit,
    Sefarad U'Portugal. <u>Tazkir. No. 1</u>- Jerusalem, 1956-
(Central Institute for Cultural Relations Israel-Ibero America,
Spain and Portugal. <u>Memorandum</u>)

783   שאשקעס, חיים.   <u>מיט ײדן צװישן אינדיאנער,</u>
      <u>נעגער און אראבער.</u>   תל-אביב, 1960.
                      373 ע'.

Shashkes, Haim. <u>Mit Yidden Tzevishen Indianer, Neger un</u>
  <u>Araber.</u> Tel-Aviv, 1960, 373p.
            (With Jews Among Indians, Negroes and Arabs)

784   שאצקי, יעקב.   <u>ײדישע ישובים אין לאטין-</u>
      <u>אמעריקע.</u> בוענאס-איירעס, אמעריקאנער
      ײדישער קאמיטעט, חש"ב.   206 ע'.

Shatzky, Jacob. <u>Yiddishe Yshuvim in Latin Amerike.</u> Buenos
Aires, Amerikaner Yiddisher Comitet, 1952, 206p.
          (Jewish Communities in Latin America)

785   שר, דניאל.   <u>קדמוניות אמריקה;</u> תרבויות-הקדם
      של אדומי העור וקורותיהן...   תל-אביב,
      "מסדה", חש"ח.   253 ע'.

Sher, Daniel. <u>Kadmoniyut America; Tarbuyot Ha'Kedem Shel</u>
  <u>Adumey Ha'or Ve'Korotehen...</u> Tel Aviv, "Massadah",
1948, 253p.
         (Ancient Events of America; The Ancient Cultures
of the Red-Skin Peoples and Their History)

786   <u>סופרים יהודים מאמריקה הלטינית מספרים.</u>
      ירושלים, משרד החינוך והתרבות, המרכזיה
      הפדגוגית, חש"ך.   26 ע'.
Sofrim Ye'Hudim Me'America Ha'Latinit Mesaprim. Jerusalem,
  Misrad Ha'Hinuch Ve'ha'Tarbut, Ha'Mercazia Ha'Pedagogit,
1960, 26p.
(Jewish Writers from Latin America Tell)

787   **א ײדישער כלל טוער אין ארגענטינע.**
     בוענאס-אײרעס, 1943. 124, 34 ע'.

.A Yiddisher Klal Toer in Argentine. Buenos Aires, 1943, 124+34p.
(A Jewish Communal Worker in Argentina)

788   **אקרוטני, יוסף. א שטײן צוקאפנס.**
     בוענאס-אײרעס, תשכ"א-1960.
     381 ע'.

Akrotni, Yosef. A Shtein Zukopens. Buenos Aires, 1960, 381p.
(A Stone to Put your Head On)

789   **אל פערסאן, מרדכי. קאלאניע מאאוריציא**
     דרייסיג יעהריגע יק"א קאלאניזאציע
     אין ארגענטינע. בוענאס-אײרעס,
     דרוק קופערשמיד, 28–1922. באנד 3- 1

Alperson, Mordechay. Colonie Maorizia Dreising Yerige
ICA Colonizazia in Argentine. 3v. Buenos Aires, Druk Kupershmid,
1922-1928.

                  (Mauricio Colony, Thirty Years' ICA
Colonization in Argentina)

790   **אלפערסאן, מרדכי. דרייסיג יאר אין**
     ארגענטינע. (בערלין) 28–1923.
     3 כרכים.

Alperson, Mordechay. Dreisig Yor in Argentine. 3v. Berlin,
1923-1928.

             (Thirty Years in Argentina)

791   ‫ארגענטינא... דאס לאנד... אינדוסטריע‬
       ‫וכו׳.   ווארשא, תרנ"א–1891.   24 ע׳.‬

Argentina...dos Land... Industria,etc. Warsaw, 1891, 24p.
(Argentina...the Country...Industry etc.)

792   ‫ארגענטינע,פופציג יאר יידישער ישוב.‬
       ‫בוענאס–איירעס, די פרעסע, 1938.   690 ע׳.‬

Argentine. Fufzig Yor Yiddisher Yshuv. Buenos Aires, Di
    Presse, 1938, 690p.
(Argentina, Fifty Years of Jewish Community)

793   ‫ארגענטינער יידישער קונסט–געזעלשאפט.‬
       ‫"איפט" ביולעטין.   בוענאס–איירעס,‬
          ‫1957.   64 ע׳.‬

Argentiner Yiddisher Kunst-Gezelshaft. IFT Bulletin. Buenos
    Aires, 1957.
(The Argentine Jewish Society of Art. IFT Bulletin)

794   ‫אסאסיאציאן איזראעליטא דע בענעפיסענסיא.‬
       ‫באריכט–באלאנס פונעם 26–טן ארבעטס‬
       ‫פעריאד תרפ"ח–תרפ"ט... ראזאריא (תרפ"ט).‬
          ‫40 ע׳.‬

Asociación Israelita de Beneficencia. Baricht-Balance Funem
    26 Ten Arbets Period 1928-1929. Rosario, 1929, 40p.
(Asociación Israelita de Beneficencia. Statement for
the 26th Working Period,1928-1929)

795 בליץ, צאלעל. <u>טריט אף סאן-מארטינישער ערד</u>
<u>ערד</u>. בוענאס-איירעס, 1961. 188 ע'.

Blitz, Zalel. <u>Trit af San-Martinisher Erd</u>. Buenos Aires, 1961, 188p.
(Trodding the Soil of San Martín)

795 בוענוס איירס.קהלה. <u>הקהלה דבואנוס איירס;</u>
אפיה הדמוקרטי ופעולתה המסועפת.
(בוענוס איירס, 1959) 28 ע'.

Buenos Aires. Kehila. <u>Ha'Kehila de Buenos Aires; Ofya Ha'Democrati</u>
<u>u'Peulata Ha'Mesoefet</u>. Buenos Aires, 1959, 28p.
(Buenos Aires. Community. <u>The Community of Buenos Aires;</u>
<u>Its Democratic Nature and Diversified Activities</u>)

797 בוענאס-איירעס.ועד הקהלות בארגנטינה.
<u>פראטאקאלן פונעם קאנגרעס פון די</u>
<u>קהלות פון דער ארגענטינער רעפובליק...</u>
בוענאס-איירעס, תשי"ג-

Buenos Aires. Va'Ad Ha'Kehilot Be'Argentina. <u>Protocolen Funem</u>
<u>Congress Fun di Kehilot fun der Argentiner Republic</u>... Buenos
Aires, 1953-
(Communities Committee in Argentina. <u>Protocol</u>
<u>of the Argentine Republic Communities' Congress)</u>

798 בוענאס-איירעס.יידישע קהלה. <u>פנקס פון</u>
<u>דעם קהלה אין בוענאס-איירעס, 62–1956.</u>
בוענאס-איירעס, קולטור-דעפארטאמענט ביי
דער קהלה אין בוענאס-איירעס, 1963. 712 ע'.

Buenos Aires. Yiddishe Kehile. <u>Pinkas fun der Kehile in</u>
<u>Buenos Aires, 1956-1962</u>. Buenos Aires, Kultur-Departament by
der Kehile in Buenos Aires, 1963, 712p.
(Buenos Aires. Jewish Community. <u>Note-Book of the Community in</u>
<u>Buenos Aires, 1956-1963</u>)

בוענאס-איירעס.יידישע קהלה. סטאטוטען
פראיעקט פאר דער יידישער קהלה אין
בוענאס-איירעס. בו ענאס איירעס, 1926.
32 ע'.

Buenos Aires. Yiddishe Kehile. Statuten-Proyect far der Yiddisher
Kehile in Buenos Aires. Buenos Aires, 1926, 32p.
(Buenos Aires. Jewish Community. A Statutes Project for the
Jewish Community in Buenos Aires)

בוענאס-איירעס.יידישע קהלה. יארבוך...
בוענאס-איירעס, די יידישע קהלה, תשי"ד

Buenos Aires. Yiddishe Kehile. Yorbuch... Buenos Aires,
Di Yiddishe Kehile, 1954-
(Buenos Aires. Jewish Community. Yearbook...)

צענטראל פארבאנד פון פוילישע יידן אין
ארגענטינע. פוילישע יידן אין דרום-
אמריקע. בוענאס-איירעס, 1941. 450 ע'.

Central Farband fun Poilishe Yidden in Argentine. Poilishe
Yidden in Drom-Amerike, Buenos Aires, 1941, 450p.
(Central Organization of Polish-Jews in Argentina. Polish
Jews in South-America)

די קהלה אין בוענאס-איירעס. יארבוך.
1954, 1956. 2 באנד.

Di Kehile in Buenos Aires. Yorbuch, 1954, 1956.
(The Jewish Community in Buenos Aires. 2v. Buenos Aires,
Yearbook, 1954, 1956)

803 די פרעסע. ארגענטינע; פופציק יאר יידישער
     ישוב, צוואנציק יאר די פרעסע. בוענאס-
     איירעס, דפוס "די פרעסע", 1938. 690ע.

Di Presse. Argentine; Fufzik yor Yiddisher Yshuv, Zvanzik
yor Di Presse. Buenos Aires, Defus "Di Presse", 1938, 690p.
(The Press. Argentina; Fifty Years of Jewish Community, Twenty
Years of "The Press")

804 עלסלאנדער, י.פ. א באזוך אין א מודערנער
     שולע. בוענאס-איירעס, 1921. 36 ע׳.

Elslander, Y. F. A Bazuch in a Moderner Shule. Buenos
Aires, 1921, 36p.
                    (A Visit in a Modern School)

805 פינקעלשטיין, חיים. אנאליטישע לערן-פראגראם
     פאר א זעקס קלאסיקער צוגאב-שול...
     בוענאס-איירעס, 1943. 293 ע׳.

Finkelstein, Haim. Analitishe Lern-Program far a Zeks Klasiker
Zugabshul... Buenos Aires, 1943, 293p.
                    (Analytical Study Program for a Sixth Grade
Complementary School)

806 פרוכטער, נתן. די געשיכטע פון ארגענטינע.
     בוענאס-איירעס (דפוס י. קאופמן) 1944.
     2 באנד.

Fruchter, Natan. Di Geschichte Fun Argentine. 2v. Buenos Aires
(Defus J. Kaufman), 1944.
                    (The History of Argentina)

807   **גענעראל סאן מארטן דער** ‎.‏פרוכטער, נחן
‎   **באפרייער.** בוענאס-איירעס, פארייץ
‎   ה.ד. נאמבערג, 1950. 196 (12) ע'.

Fruchter, Natan. General San Martin der Bafrayer. Buenos
Aires, Farein H. D. Nomberg, 1950, 196+12 p.
                (General San Martín, the Liberator)

808   **די ארגאניזאציע פון אונדזער** ‎.‏גלאזמאן, י
‎   **ישוב.** בוענאס-איירעס, "פועלי ציון
‎   צעירי ציון", 1940. 16 ע'.

Glozman, Y. Di Organizazie Fun Undzer Yshuv. Buenos Aires,
"Poaley Zion, Zeirey Zion", 1940, 16p.
                (The Organization of our Community)

809   **די יידן אין ארגענטינע אין** ‎.‏גאלדמאן, דוד
‎   **דער פערגאנגענהייט און אין דער געגענווארט**
‎   **אין ווארט און אין בילד, פון 1914.**
‎   בוענאס-איירעס, ארלאפ, תש"ד. 211 ע'.

Goldman, David. Di Yidden in Argentine in der Fergangenheit un
in der Gegenvort, in Vort un in Bild fun 1914. Buenos Aires,
Arlap, 1940, 211p.
                (The Jews in Argentina Past and Present, In
Word and Picture Since 1914)

810   **יידישע קאלאניזאציע אין** ‎.‏הויכמאן, ברוך
‎   **אגראר-קאאפעראציע אין ארגענטינע.**
‎   בוענאס-איירעס, תשכ"א. 166 ע'.

Hoichman, Baruch. Yiddishe Colonizazie un Agrar-Cooperazie
in Argentine. Buenos Aires, 1961, 166p.
                (Jewish Colonization and Agricultural-
Cooperation in Argentina)

811　　　הורביץ, ס.　קאלאניע לוסיינוויל; צו דער
　　　　גשיכטע פון דער אנטסטייאונג און
　　　　אנטוויקלונג פון דער קאלאניע, אין
　　　　פראווינס ענטרע ריוס, במשך פון 37 יאר צייט.
　　　　בוענאס-איירעס. 1932.　137 ע.'

Hurwitz, S.　Colonie Lucienville; Zu der Geschichte fun der Antshteiung
　　un Antvikelung fun der Colony, in Province Entre Rios, Bemeshech fun
　　37 yor Zeit.　Buenos Aires, 1932, 137p.
　　　　　　　(Lucienville Colony; on the History of the Establishment
　　and Development of the Colony in the Province of Entre Rios,
　　During 37 Years)

812　　　קאצאוויטש, נח.　מאזעסווילער בראשית
　　　　"זכרונות".　בוענאס-איירעס, יידישער
　　　　וויסנשאפטלעכער אינסטיטוט, 1947.
　　　　231 ע.'　(סעריע "מאטעריאלן צו דער
　　　　גשיכטע פון דער יידישער קאלאניזאציע אין
　　　　ארבעגטינע")

Katzavitsh, Noah.　Mosesviler Bereshit "Zichronot".　Buenos
　　Aires, Yiddisher Visenshaftlecher Institut, 1947, 231p.
　　　　　　　(Serie, "Materialen zu der Geschichte fun der
　　Yiddisher Colonizazie in Argentine")
　　　　　　　(Mosesville: Early "Memoirs". Series, Materials
　　on the History of the Jewish Settlement in Argentina)

813　　　קהלה און פאלק... ביולעטין פון ועד
　　　　הקהלות... בוענאס-איירעס, 1956-

Kehile un Folk... Bulletin fun Va'ad Ha'kehilot... Buenos Aires
　　1956-
　　(Community and People... Bulletin of the Community Committee)

814   מאיערן-לאזער, מנחם. ס'איז שוין צייט.
בוענאס-איירעס (דפוס י. גלאזמאן)
1945. 23 ע'.

Mayern-Lazer, Menahem. S'is Shoin Zeit. Buenos Aires
(Defus J. Glasman) 1945, 23p.
                       (It's About Time)

815   פארישעווסקי, מארקוס. דזשונגלס און שטעט.
בוענאס-איירעס, יידישער ליטעראטן און
זשורנאליסטן פאריין "ה.ד. נאָמבערג"
אין ארגענטינע, 1951. 268, 276 ע'.

Porishewsky, Marcus. Jungels un Shtet. Buenos Aires,
Yiddisher Literaten un Journalisten Farein "H. D. Nomberg"
in Argentina, 1951, 268+276p.
                    (Jungles and Cities)

816   ראזשאנסקי, שמואל. דאס יידישע געדרוקטע
ווארט און טעאטער אין ארגענטינע...
בוענאס-איירעס (דפוס י. גלאזמאן) 1941.
263 ע'. (געזאמלטע שריפטן, באנד 1)

Razshansky, Shmuel. Dos Yiddishe Gedrukte Vort un Teater
in Argentine... Buenos Aires (Defus Glozman), 1941, 263p.
(Gezamelte Shriften, Band 1)
              (The Jewish Written Word and Theater
in Argentina... Collected Works, v. 1)

817   ראזשאנסקי, שמואל, מלקט. פון ארגענטינע
לאנד און ישוב. בוענאס-איירעס, אלטער
ראזענטאל-פאנד פאר יידישער קינדער
ליטעראטור, 1960. 150 ע'.

Razshansky, Shmuel, ed. Fun Argentiner Land un Yshuv.
Buenos Aires, Alter Rosental-Fund far Yiddisher Kinder
Literatur, 1960, 150p.
             (From Argentine Land and Community)

818   Rollansky, Samuel, ed.

פון ארגענטינע, לאנד און ישוב; פאעזיע, פראזע, פובליצסטיק,
בילדער. רעדאקטירט פון שמואל ראזשאנסקי. בוענאס-איירעס,
אלטער ראזענטאל-פאנד. 1960.

Rollansky, Samuel, ed. <u>Foon Argentine, Land don Yishuv, Fazeyeh,
Frazeh, Publitzistik, Bilder</u>. Buenos Aires, Alter Rosental-Fund,
1960, 150p.

(From Argentina; Land and People: Statements,
Publicity, Photographs)

819   ראיאל מאיל ליין. סניף וואַרשא. <u>ארגענטינא</u>.
וואַרשא, "ראיאל מאיל ליין", 1923.
32 ע'.

Royal Mail Line. Snif Varsha. <u>Argentina</u>. Warsaw, "Royal
Mail Line", 1923, 32p.

(Argentina)

820   <u>ספר ארגענטינה</u>. בואנוס אירס, קבוצת עברים
ליד "דרום", תשט"ו. 335 ע'.

<u>Sefer Argentina</u>. Buenos Aires, Kvuzat Ivrim le'Yad "Darom",
1956, 335p.
(Book of Argentina)

821   שוחט, יחזקאל. <u>בלעטלאך צו דער געשיכטע
פון נארסיס לעווען</u>. בוענאס-איירעס,
ייִדישער וויסנשאפטלעכער אינסטיטוט-
יווא, 1953. 120 ע' (ארגענטינער
יווא-ביבליאטעק, נ. 11)

Shohat, Yehezkel. <u>Bletlach Zu der Geshichte Fun Narciso
Leven</u>. Buenos Aires, Yiddisher Visenshaftlecher Institut
IVO, 1953, 120p. (Argentiner IVO Bibliotek, No. 11)
(Some Contributions to the Story of Narciso Leven)

822   סאקאל, שאול. <u>ארגענטינען; די אנטי
פעראניסטישע רעוואלוציע</u>. ניו-יורק,
1957. 28 ע'.

Sokol, Shaul. <u>Argentine; di Anti-Peronistishe Revoluzie</u>. New
York, 1957, 28p.
(Argentina; the Anti-Peron Revolution)

823   ווילה, חיים.   האט דער ארגענטינער ייִדישער
יישוב טאקע אזא פנים? בוענאס-איירעס,
תשט"ו. 18 ע'. (ווארט און קלאנג)

Vila, Chaim. Hot der Argentiner Yiddisher Yshuv Take
Aza Ponim? Buenos Aires, 1956, 18p. (Vort un Klong)
(Does the Argentine Jewish Community
Really Look Like That? Word and Sound)

824   וולברג, יהושע. לסיכויי העליה מארגנטינה.
ירושלים, תשכ"ד, 1963. 15 ע'.

Wolberg, Yehoshua. Le'Sikuyei Ha'Alia Me'Argentina.
Jerusalem, 1963, 15p.
(Prospects of Immigration from Argentina)

825   יעדוואבניק, יעקב. דיא רייזע נאך
ארגענטינא. ווארשא, דפוס האחים
שולדבערג, תרנ"ב. 54 ע'.

Yedvovnik, Jacob. Di Reize Noch Argentina. Warsaw, Defus
Ha'Ahim Shuldberg, 1892, 54p.
(The Trip to Argentina)

826   יארבוך פאר ליטעראטור, קונסט און געזעל-
שאפטלעכקייט פון ייִדישן יישוב אין
ארגענטינע. בוענאס-איירעס, תש"ח.
328, 14 ע'.

Yorbuch far Literatur, Kunst un Gezelshaftlechkeit fun Yiddishen
Yshuv in Argentine. Buenos Aires, 1948, 328+14p.
(Yearbook for Literature, Art and Social Organization of the
Jewish Community in Argentina)

827   יובל-בוך; סך הכל'ן פון 50 יאר יידיש
לעבען אין ארגענטינע. בוענאס-איירעס,
געזעלשאפטלעכער יובל-קאמיטעט, 1940.
656, 110 ע'.

Yovel-Buch; Sach Ha'Colen fun 50 yor Yiddishe Leben in Argentine.
Buenos Aires, Gezelshaftlecher Yovel-Comitet, 1940, 656+110p.
(Jubilee-Book; The Sum of 50 Years of Jewish Life in Argentina.

828   צוקער, נחמיה. אויף נייע רעלסן.
בוענאס-איירעס, געזעלשאפטלעכער קאמיטעט
צום זעכציקסטן געבורסטאג פון מחבר,
1958. 235 ע'.

Zuker, Nehemia. Oif Naye Relsen. Buenos Aires, Gezelshaftlecher
Comitet Zum Sechziksten Geburstog fun Mehaber, 1958, 235p.
(On a New Road)

829   ברזיל.שגרירות,ישראל.מחלקת ההסברה. <u>כמה מלים</u>
<u>על...ברזיל...נתונים כל**לי**ם.הסטוריה.ערי</u>
<u>ברזיל...</u> (תל-אביב) מחלקת ההסברה של
שגרירות ברזיל בישראל (תשכ"ו). 8 ע'.

Brazil. Shagrirut. Israel. Machleket Hasbarah. <u>Kama Milim</u>
<u>al Brazil; Netunim Klaliyim, Historia, Arei Brazil.</u>   Tel-Aviv,
1966, 8p.
(Brazil. Embassy. Israel. Information Department. <u>A few</u>
<u>Words on Brazil; History, General Features, Cities of Brazil</u>)

830   "בראזקאר".   <u>"בראזקאר" צו זיין צווייטן</u>
<u>לאנדס-צוזאמענפאר.</u> ריו דה זשאניירא,
צענטראל קאמיטעט "בראזקאר", 1934.
29 ע'.

"Brazkar".   <u>Brazkar zu Zein Zveiten Lands-Zuzamenfar.</u>   Rio
de Janeiro, Zentral Comitet "Brazkar", 1934, 29p.
(The "Brazkar", Its Second Conference)

831   כהן, משה.   <u>יידן אין דער אנטשטייאונג פון</u>
<u>ברזיל.</u> סאו-פאולא, 1955. 105 VI ע'.

Cohen, Moshe. <u>Yidden in der Antshteiung fun Brazil.</u> São
Paulo, 1955, 105p.
                (The Role of the Jews in the Development
of Brazil)

832 דותן, אלכסנדר. ברזיל. ירושלים, משרד
החינוך והתרבות ומוסד סאלד למען הילד
והנוער, תשכ"ה, 1964. 76 ע'.
(הספריה למדריך)

Dotan, Alexander. Brazil. Jerusalem, Misrad Ha'Hinuch
Ve'ha'Tarbut U'Mosad Szold Le'Ma'an Ha'Yeled Ve'ha'Noar,
1964, 76p. (Ha'Sifria Le'Madrich)
(Brazil)

833 אילון, דבורה (רבינוביץ). על פני ברזיל.
תל-אביב, תשכ"א, 1960. 156 ע'.

Eilon, Dvora (Rabinowitz). Al Pney Brazil. Tel-Aviv, 1960, 156p.
(Over Brazil. Travel Impressions).

834 ארגון יהודים דתיים.ריו דה ז'נירו. דרכנו.
(ריו דה ז'נירו) תשי"ג. 42 ע'.

Irgun Yehudim Datiyim, Rio de Janeiro. Darkenu. Rio
de Janeiro, 1953, 42p.
(Religious Jews Organization, Rio de Janeiro. Our Way)

835 ישראל.משרד החוץ.המחלקה לשתוף בינלאומי.
דו"ח ביניים על בעיות פיתוח ישוב חקלאי
בפטרולנדיה-ברזיל... (ירושלים) 1962.
50 ע'.
Israel. Misrad Ha'huz. Ha'Mahlaka Le'Shituf Benle'ummi.
Doh Benaim al Ba'yot Pituah Yshuv Haklai Be'Petrolandia-
Brazil,..Jerusalem, 1962, 50p.
(Israel. Ministry of Foreign Affairs. International Cooperation
Department. Interim report on Agricultural Settlement Development
Problems in Petrolandia, Brazil)

836   קאראקושאנסקי, שבת. אספעקטן פונעם ייִדישן
לעבען אין בראזיל. ריו דה זשאנײרא,
("מאנטע סקאפוס") 1957-1956. 2 באנד.

Karakushansky, Shabat . <u>Aspecten Funem Yiddishen Leben</u>
in Brazil. Rio de Janeiro, "Monte Scopus", 1956-1957.
              (Aspects of Jewish Life in Brazil)

837   קוטשינסקי, מאיר. <u>נוסח ברזיל</u>. תל-אביב,
י.ל. פרץ, 1963. 185 ע'.

Kutshinsky, Meir. <u>Nusah Brazil.</u> Tel-Aviv, Y. L. Perez, 1963,
185p.
              (Brazil Style)

838   נחומי, מרדכי. <u>בראזיל ארץ הסתירות</u>.
תל-אביב, דפוס "הדפוס החדש", 1959.
126 ע'.

Nahumi, Mordechai. <u>Brazil Eretz Ha'Stirot.</u> Tel-Aviv,
Defus Ha'Defus Ha'Hadash, 1959, 126p.
              (Brazil, Land of Contradictions)

839   רייזמאן, יצחק. <u>געשיכטע פון ייִדן אין</u>
<u>אין בראזיל</u>. סאו פאולא, "בוך און
פרעסע", 1935. 116 ע'.

Reizman, Yitzhak. <u>Geschichte fun Yidden in Brazil.</u> São Paulo,
"Buch un Presse", 1935, 116p.
              (History of Jews in Brazil)

CHILE

840   פארבאנד פון פוילישע יידן. טשילע.
טעטיקייטס-באריכט... סאנטיאגא, 1957 -

Farband fun Poilishe Yidden. Chile. Tetikeits-Baricht...
   Santiago, 1957-
(Union of Polish Jews. Chile. Report of Activities...)

841   שענדערריי, משה. די געשיכטע פון דעם
יידישן ישוב אין טשילע. סאנטיאגא,
1956. 360 ע'.

Shenderey, Moshe. Die Geschichte fun dem Yiddishen Yshuv
   in Chile. Santiago, 1956, 360p.
                (The History of the Jewish Community
   in Chile)

CUBA

842   Lapide, Phinn E.
קובה—להבה בלב אמריקה. תל-אביב, קרני.
97p.

Lapide, Phinn E. Cuba-Lehavah be-lev Amerika. Tel Aviv,
   Karni, 1963, 97p.
                (Cuba: Flame in the Heart of America)

843   קאהאן, סאלאמאן. בריוו וועגן דער
מעקסיקאנער יידישער סטודענטנשאפט.
מעקסיקע, 1953. 23 ע'.

Cohen, Solomon. Briv Vegen der Mexikaner Yiddisher
Studentenschaft. Mexico, 1953, 23p.
(Letters About the Mexican Jewish Students)

844   קאהאן, סאלאמאן. מעקסיקאנער ווידערקלאנגען.
מעקסיקע, "זלבסטהילף", 1951. 289 XV ע'.

Cohen, Solomon. Mexikaner Viderklongen. Mexico, "Zelbsthilf",
1951, 289p.
(Mexican Echoes)

845   קאהאן, סאלאמאן. מעקסיקאנישע רעפלעקסן.
מעקסיקע, "זלבסטהילף", 1954. 312 ע'.

Cohen, Solomon. Mexikanishe Reflexsen. Mexico, "Zelbsthilf",
1954, 312p.
(Mexican Reflections)

846   קאהאן, סאלאמאן. יידיש-מעקסיקאניש.
מעקסיקע, "זעלבסטהילף", 1945. 304 ע'.

Cohen, Solomon. Yiddish-Mexikanish. Mexico, "Zelbsthilf",
1945, 304p.
(Mexican Yiddish)

847   בולעטין פון דער   מעקסיקע.אשכנזישע קהלה.
אשכנזישע קהלה אין מעקסיקע. (ארויסגעגעבן
דורך דעם יוגנט-דעפארטמענט).   מעקסיקע,
ד.פ., 1961-   נומ' 1-

Mexike. Ashkenazishe Kehile. Buletin Fun Der Ashkenazishe
    Kehile in Mexike. (Aroisgegeben Durch Dem Yugent-Department).
Mexico, 1961- No. 1-
(Mexico. Ashkenazi Community. Bulletin of the Ashkenazi Community
in Mexico. Issued by the Youth-Department)

848   איר און אייער   מעקסיקע.אשכנזישע קהלה.
קהלה.   מעקסיקע, ד.פ. (דפוס
1961.   24 ע'.

Mexike. Ashkenazishe Kehile. Ir un Ayer Kehile. Mexico,
    (Defus Imprenta Moderna), 1961, 24p.
(Mexico. Ashkenazi Community. You and your Community)

849   מעקסיקע.אשכנזישע קהלה "נדחי ישראל".
טעטיקייט-באריכט פון דער קהלה פארן
יאר...   מעקסיקע, 1957-

Mexike. Ashkenazishe Kehile "Nidahei Israel". Tetikeit-
    Baricht Fun Der Kehile, Faren Yor...Mexico, 1957-
(Mexico. Ashkenazi Community "Nidahei Israel". Report of
Activities of the Community, for the Year...1957)

850   "מופלאות המאייה";   אוסטרי-דן, ישעיהו.
תל-אביב, אל"ף, תשי"ג,   מכסיקו הקדמונית.
1962.   223 ע'.

Ostri-Dan, Yeshayahu. Muflaot Ha'Maya; Mexico Ha'Kadmonit.
    Tel-Aviv, Alef, 1962, 223p.
                     (Wonders of the Maya; Ancient Mexico)

851   ראפאפארט, מאיר.   מעקסיקאנער יידן
.1956 ,.פ.ד ,מעקסיקע ...צווישן בערג
.ע' 324

Rapoport, Meir. <u>Mexikaner Yidden Zevishen Berg</u>...Mexico,
1956, 324p.

        (Mexican Jews in the Mountains...)

852   רובינשטיין, משה. מעקסיקאנער טעמעס.
.1940-41 "מעקסיקע, "אונזער לעבן
.ע' 253

Rubinstein, Moshe. <u>Mexikaner Temes</u>. Mexico, "Undzer
Leben", 1940-1941, 253p.
        (Mexican Topics: "Our Life")

853   סוראסקי, לעאן. מאטעריאלן צו דער
,געשיכטע פון יידישן ישוב אין מעקסיקע
.ע' 312 .1959 ,מעקסיקע <u>1942-1917</u>

Suraski, Leon. <u>Materialen Zu Der Geshichte Fun Yiddishen
Yshuv in Mexike, 1917-1942</u>. Mexico, 1959, 312p.
        (Materials on the History of the Jewish Community
in Mexico, 1917-1942)

854   ווייסבוים, אברהם. <u>אין מעקסיקאנער גן-עדן</u>.
.ע' 328 .1959-ר"חש ,מעקסיקע

Veisboim, Avraham. <u>In Mexikaner Gan-Eden</u>. Mexico, 1959,
328p.
        (In Mexican Paradise)

855
וייסבוים, אברהם. מעקסיקאנער זיגזאגן.
מעקסיקע, ד.פ. "ווייסן", 1947. 410 ע'.

Veisboim, Avraham. <u>Mexikaner Zigzagen</u>. Mexico,
1947, 410p.

          (The Mexican Zigzag Path)

856
יארבוך פון מעקסיקאנער יידנטום...
מעקסיקע, ד.פ., יידישער וועלט קאנגרעס,
1952-

Yorbuch Fun Mexikaner Yiddentum...Mexico, Yiddisher
   Velt Congress, 1952-
(Yearbook of Mexican Jewry...)

857
יובל-בוך; צוואנציק יאר יידישע שול אין
מעקסיקע, 1924-1944. 536 ע'.

Yovel Buch; Zvanzik yor Yiddishe Shul in Mexike, 1924-1944,
   Mexico, 1944? 536p.
(Jubilee Book. Twenty Years of Jewish Schools in Mexico)

PERU

858
סוכנות ארץ ישראלית למסחר וחקלאות. פרו.
תל-אביב, דפוס "תל-אביב", 1940. 16 ע'.

Sochnut Eretz-Yisraelit Le'Mishar Ve'Haklaut. <u>Peru</u>, Tel-
   Aviv, Defus "Tel-Aviv", 1940, 16p.
(Palestine Agency for Trade and Agriculture. <u>Peru</u>)

256

859   ‏היאס–ייקא–עמיגדירעקט, אורורוויין; טעטיקייט
‏פאר די יארן 1927-1930.   מאנטעווידעא,
‏1930.   34 ע.

Hias-ICA-Emigdirect, Uruguay. Tetikeit far di Yoren 1927-1930.
   Montevideo, 1930, 34p.
(Hias-ICA-Emigdirect, Uruguay. Activities During the Years
1927-1930)

860   ‏מאנטעווידעא.יידישע קהלה.   די מאנטעווידעא
‏יידישע קהלה...   מאנטעווידעא, 1940–
‏בעריכט 1938-39 ; 1945- 47.

Montevideo. Yiddishe Kehile. Di Montevideo Yiddishe Kehile...
   Montevideo, 1940- Bericht 1938-1939; 1945-1947.
(Montevideo. Jewish Community. The Montevideo Jewish
Community 1940-. Report 1938-39; 1945-47)

861   ‏וויינשענקער, איציק.   בויערס און מיטבויערס
‏פון יידישן ישוב אין אורוגוויי.
‏מאנטעווידעא, 1957.   280 ע.

Veinshenker, Itzik. Boyers un Mitboyers fun Yiddishen Yshuv
   in Uruguay. Montevideo, 1957, 280p.
                  (Builders and Co-builders from the
Jewish Community in Uruguay)

VENEZUELA

862   **יְדִיעוֹת מוֹנצוּאֶלה**; עלונה של שגרירות ונצואלה.
ירושלים, 1961-

Ye'Diot Mi'Venezuela; Alona Shel Shagrirut Venezuela.   Jerusalem,
   1961-
(News from Venezuela; Embassy of Venezuela Bulletin)

II. Periodical Articles

LATIN AMERICA

863

גליקובסקי, משה. "ײדן אין לאטײן אמעריקע".
נױ-יארק, <u>ײדישער קעמפער</u>. (באנד 28) יולי
1947. ‏ע׳ 5-6. (באנד 29) פעברואר 1948.
ע׳ 7-9.

Glikowsky, Moshe. "Yidden in Latin Amerike". New York,
<u>Yiddisher Kemfer</u> (28), July 1947, pp. 5-6; (29), February
1948, pp. 7-9.

("Jews in Latin America")

864

לאצקי, ו. "די דרום-אמעריקאנישע לענדער און
די ײדישע אײנװאנדערונג". בערלין,
<u>די ײדישע אימיגראציע</u>. (נומער 9) אוקטובער
1925. ע׳ 1-12.

Latzky, W. "Di Drom Amerikanishe Lender un Di Yiddishe
Einvonderung". Berlin, <u>Di Yiddishe Imigrazie</u> (9),
October 1925, pp. 1-12.

("South American Countries and Jewish Immigration")

865

לאצקי, ו. "מאטעריאלן פון דער אײנװואנדערונג
קאלאניזאציע און די ײדישע ישובים אין
דרום-אמעריקע". בערלין, <u>די ײדישע אימיגראציע</u>
(נומער 9) אוקטובער 1925. ע׳ 12-22.
(נומער 10) נובעמבר 1925. ע׳ 13-15.

Latzky, W. "Materialen Fun Der Einvonderung Colonizazie
un di Yiddishe Yshuvim in Drom-Amerike". Berlin, <u>Di
Yiddishe Imigrazie</u> (9), October 1925, pp. 12-22; (10), November
1925, pp. 13-15.

("Facts on Immigration, Colonization and the Jewish
Communities in South America")

866   רוביז, יוסף.   "החינוך היהודי בדרום-
אמריקה".   תל-אביב, הפועל הצעיר.
(כ' 22) 21 באוגוסט 1951.

Rubin, Yosef. "Ha'Hinuch Ha'Yehudi Be'Drom-America".
Tel-Aviv, Ha'Poel Ha'Zair (22), August 21, 1951.
           ("Jewish Education in South America")

867   סירליז, ג. און שיפריז ד.   "די פארמינדערונג
פון דער טובערקולוזקראנקייט אין די לעצטע
צעז יאר".   בוענאס איירעס, ארגענטינישער
יווא שריפטז.   (באנד 6) 1955.   עז' 121-99.

Sirlin, G., & D. Shifrin. "Di Farminderung fun der Tuberculozkrankeit
in di Lezte Zen Yor". Buenos Aires, Argentinisher Yivo
Shriften (6), 1955, pp. 99-121.
                       ("The Decrease in Incidence of
Tuberculosis in the Last Ten Years")

868   שטארקמעט, ח.   "די לאגע אין דרום-אמעריקאנישע
לענדער".   בערליז, די יידישע אימיגראצי-ע.
(נומער 15) ספטעמבר 1927.   עז' 14-6.
Starkmet, H. "Di Lage in Drom-Amerikanishe Lender".
Berlin, Di Yiddishe Imigrazie (15), September
1927, pp. 6-14.
               ("The Situation in South American Countries")

ARGENTINA

869

אקון, א.   "די קליינהענדלער-קאאפעראציע
בא יידן אין ארגענטינע".   בוענאס
אײרעס, <u>ווירטשאפט און לעבן</u>.
(נומער 13) נאוועמבער 1930.   עע' 47-53.

Akon, I. "Di Kleinhendler-Cooperazie ba Yidden in Argentine".
Buenos Aires, <u>Virtshaft un leben</u> (13), November
1930, pp. 47-53.
         ("Retail Cooperatives Among Jews in Argentina")

870

"די ארבעט פונעם ארגענטינער פאראייניגטן
אימיגראציע קאמיטעט".   בערלין,
<u>די יידישע אימיגראציע</u>.   (נומער 19)
יאנואר 1928.   עע' 35-39.

"Di Arbet Funem Argentiner Fareingten Imigrazie-Comitet".
Berlin, <u>Di yiddishe imigrazie</u> (19), January 1928,
pp. 35-39.
("The Work of the Argentine United Immigration Committee")

871

"די אימיגראציע קיין ארגענטינע".
בערלין, <u>די יידישע אימיגראציע</u>.
(נומער 4) מאי 1925.   עע' 29-30.

"Di Imigrazie Kein Argentine". Berlin, <u>Di yiddishe imigrazie</u>
(4), May 1925, pp. 29-30.
("Immigration into Argentina")

872   "די קהילות אין לאנד". בוענאס איירעס,
יארבוך פון דער יידישער קהילה אין בוענאס
איירעס, 1954. ע"ז 351-377.

"Di Kehilot in Land". Buenos Aires, <u>Yorbuch fun der Yiddisher
Kehile in Buenos Aires</u> 1954, pp. 351-377,
("The Jewish Communities in Argentina")

873   פײבלוקעס, חיים. "שטערבליכקײט בײַ די
יידן פון דער שטאָט בוענאס איירעס, 1928-
1917". בוענאס איירעס, ארגענטינער
יוואָ שריפטן. (נומער 1) מערץ 1941.

Favelukes, Haim. "Sterblechkeit bei di Yidden fun der Shtot
Buenos Aires, 1917-1928". Buenos Aires, <u>Argentinisher
Yivo shriften</u> (1), March 1941.
                   ("Mortality Among the Jews in the City
of Buenos Aires, 1917-1928")

874   פוגל, ק. "די דײטשע יידן אין בוענאס איירעס"
בוענאס איירעס, ארגענטינישער יוואָ שריפטן.
(נומער 4) 1947.

Fogel, K. "Di Deitche Yidden in Buenos Aires". Buenos Aires,
<u>Argentinisher Yivo shriften</u> (4), 1947.
             ("German Jews in Buenos Aires")

875   גאביס, אברהם. "די אנטוויקלונג און דער
איצטיקער מצב פון דער היגער יידישער איקא
קאָלאָניזאַצ'ע". בוענאס איירעס, יארבוך פון
דער יידישער קהילה אין בוענאס איירעס,
1954. ע"ז 113-131.

Gabis, Abraham. "Di Antviklung un der Iztiker Mazav fun der
Higer Yiddisher ICA Colonizazie". Buenos Aires, <u>Yorbuch
fun der Yiddisher Kehile in Buenos Aires</u> 1954, pp. 113-131.
                 ("The Development and Present Condition
of Local Jewish ICA Colonization")

876   גאביס, אברהם.   "50 יאר קאָלאָניע "באַרון
הירש".   בוענאָס איירעס, יאָרבוך פון דער
ייִדישער קהילה אין בוענאָס איירעס, 1956.
עז' 191-211.

Gabis, Abraham. "50 yor Colonie Baron Hirsch". Buenos
Aires, <u>Yorbuch fun der Yiddisher Kehile in Buenos Aires</u>,
1956, pp. 191-211.

                          ("50 Years of the Baron Hirsch Colony")

877   הררי, י.   "הישוב היהודי בארגנטינה".
ירושלים, סוגיות. (ספרית פועלים) 1956.

Harari, J. "Ha'Yshuv Ha'Yehudi Be'Argentina". Jerusalem,
<u>Sughiot</u> (Sifriat Poalim) 1956.
                       ("The Jewish Community in Argentina")

878   הררי, י.   "יהדות ארגנטינה".   ירושלים,
בתפוצות הגולה. (שנה ב' מס. 3-4)
אפריל-יוני 1960.

Harari, J. "Yahadut Argentina". Jerusalem, <u>Bitfuzot ha'gola</u>
(2d Year, Number 3-4) April-June 1960.
                     ("Argentine Jewry")

879   הורוביץ, מ.   "ייִדישע קאָלאָניזאַציע אין
אַרגענטינע".   בוענאָס איירעס, אַרגענטינישער
ייִוואָ שריפטן (באַ נד 5) 1952. עז' 145-148.

Horowitz, M. "Yiddishe Colonizazie in Argentine". Buenos
Aires, <u>Argentinisher Yivo shriften</u> (5), 1952, pp.
145-148.
                 ("Jewish Colonization in Argentina")

880

הורביץ, ס.י.   "די קאאפעראטיבן אין די
 יידישע קאלאניעס אין ארגענטינע".
בוענאס איירעס, <u>ארגענטינישער ייוא</u>
<u>שריפטן</u>. (באנד 1) 1941. עז 59-116.

Hurwitz, S. J. "Di Cooperativen in di Yiddishe Colonies in
   Argentine". Buenos Aires, <u>Argentinisher Yivo shriften</u>
   (1), 1941, pp. 59-116.

                      (Cooperatives in the Jewish Colonies in Argentina")

881

איסאייב, ב.   "די ספרדים אין בוענאס איירעס".
בוענאס איירעס, <u>ארגענטינישער ייוא שריפטן</u>.
(באנד 1), מערץ 1941. עז 168-176.

Issayev, B. "Di Sephardim in Buenos Aires". Buenos Aires,
   <u>Argentinisher Yivo shriften</u> (1), March 1941, pp. 168-176.
                ("The Sephardim in Buenos Aires")

882

איסייב, ב.   "משהו על היהדות הספרדית
בארגנטינה". תל-אביב, <u>קמה</u>, 1948.
עז 319-324.

Issayev, B. "Ma'Shehu al Ha'Yahadut Ha'Sephardit Be'Argentina".
   Tel-Aviv, <u>Kama</u> 1948, pp. 319-324.
                ("Notes on Sephardic Jewry in Argentina")

883

זיטניצקי, ל.   "יידן אין בוענאס איירעס
לויט דער מוניציפאלער ציילונג פון 1936".
בוענאס איירעס, <u>ארגענטינישער ייוא שריפטן</u>.
(נומער 3) 1945.

Jitnitzky, L. "Yidden in Buenos Aires Loit der Munizipaler
   Zeitung fun 1936". Buenos Aires, <u>Argentinisher Yivo shriften</u>
   (3), 1945.

                    ("Jews in Buenos Aires According to the Municipal
Census of 1936")

884   תל-אביב,   ."ארגענטינע"   לעשצ׳ינסקי, יעקב.
.1960 יוני (37 נומער) .<u>די גולדענע קייט</u>

Lestschinsky, Jacob. "Argentine". Tel-Aviv, <u>Di goldene keit</u> (37), June 1960.
                        ("Argentina")

885   ."יידן אין ארגענטינע"   .לוין, ח
,3 באנד) .<u>געדאנק און לעבן</u> ,ניו-יארק
.1946 ינואר-מערץ (4 נומער
.193-213 ׳עע

Levin, H. "Yidden in Argentine". New York, <u>Gedank un leben</u> (3: 4), January-March 1946, pp. 193-213.
                  ("Jews in Argentina")

886   "וועגן דעם יידישן ישוב אין   .פינס, ל
.<u>דער וועג</u> ,בערלין ."ארגענטינע
.24-40 ׳עע .1922 (2-1 נומער)

Pines, L. "Vegen dem Yiddishen Yshuv in Argentine". Berlin, <u>Der veg</u> (1-2), 1922, pp. 24-40.
         ("On the Jewish Community in Argentina")

887   -"די יידישע יוגנט און ספּאָרט   .פּאָלאָטיצקי, י
בוענאָס ."באַוועגונג אין בוענאָס איירעס
.<u>איירעס, ארגענטינישער יוואָ שריפטן</u>
.1945 (3 נומער)

Polotitzky, J. "Di Yiddishe Yugent un Sport-Bavegung in Buenos Aires". Buenos Aires, <u>Argentinisher Yivo shriften</u> (3), 1945.
            ("The Jewish Youth and Sports Movement in Buenos Aires")

888   רבינוביץ, זינה.   "על החינוך בארגנטינה".
        ניו-יורק, הדאר.   (כ' 30) אוקטובר
                      ע.

Rabinowitz, Zina. "Al Ha'Hinuch Be'Argentina". New York,
Ha'Doar (30), October 1950, pp. 1088-1089.
                 ("On Education in Argentina")

889   רגלסקי, מ.   "ארגענטינע אלס איינוואנ-
        דערונגס לאנד".   בערלין, די יידישע
        אימיגראציע.   (נומער 23) מאי 1928.
                    עע' 7-1.

Regalsky, M. "Argentine Als Einvonderungs Land". Berlin,
Di yiddishe imigrazie (23), May 1928, pp. 1-7.
             ("Argentina as a Country of Immigration")

890   "רשימה פון ארגענטינער יידישער און יידיש-
     ספאנישע פובליקאציעס פאר די יארן 1956-1951".
     בוענאס איירעס, ארגענטינישער יוואָ שריפטן.
                 (באנד 7)   עע' 222-169.

"Reshima fun Argentiner Yiddisher un Yiddish-Spanishe
   Publicazies far di Yoren 1951-1956". Buenos Aires,
Argentinisher Yivo shriften (7), pp. 169-222.
("List of Yiddish and Yiddish-Spanish Publications in Argentina
for the Years 1951-1956")

891   טרטקובר, אריה.   "יהדות ארגנטינה".
        ניו-יורק, מבוע.   (כ' 14) 1954.
                  עע' 446-433.

Tartakower, Arieh. "Yahadut Argentina". New York, Mabua
(14), 1954, pp. 433-446.
                ("Argentine Jewry")

892 "ווּעגן דער איינוואנדערונג קיין ארגענטינע".
בערלין, די יידישע אימיגראציע.
(נומער 11) אפריל 1926. זע 37-31.

"Vegen der Einvonderung Kein Argentine".   Berlin, Di yiddishe
   imigrazie. (11), April 1926, pp. 31-37.
("On Immigration into Argentina")

893 ווינבערג, מ.   "האַרצקראנקייט ביי ייִדן
אין בוענאס איירעס".   ניו-יאָרק,
יוואָ בלעטער. (באַנד 23) 1944.
זע 281-280.

Weinberg, M.   "Hartzkrankeit Bei Yidden in Buenos Aires".
   New York, Yivo bleter   (23), 1944.
               ("Heart Disease Among the Jews in Buenos Aires")

267

BRAZIL

894

"די יידישע שטאטישע ישובים אין בראזיליע".

בערלין, די יידישע אימיגראצסיע.   (נומער 1-2)

מערץ 1925.   ע' 18-19.

"Di Yiddishe Shtatishe Yshuvim in Brazilie". Berlin, Di
yiddishe imigrazie (1-2), March 1925, pp. 18-19.
("Jewish Urban Communities in Brazil")

895

אייזנברג, יצחק.   "פורטו אלגרה ויהודיה".

בואנוס איירס, דרום.   (כ' 17, מס' 8-7)

אוגוסט-ספטמבר 1954   ע' 79-80.

Eisenberg, Yitzchak. "Porto Alegre Ve'Yehudeha". Buenos
Aires, Darom (17: 7-8), August-September 1954, pp. 79-80.
("The Jews of Porto Alegre")

896

הלפרן, מנשה.   "די יידן אין בראזיליע".

בערלין, די יידישע אימיגראצסיע.   (נומער 8-6)

אוגוסט-אוקטובר 1929.   ע' 328-336.

Halpern, Menashe. "Di Yidden in Brazilie". Berlin, Di
yiddishe imigrazie (6-8), August-October 1929, pp. 328-336.
("The Jews in Brazil")

897   "קופרשטיין, ל.   "החינוך היהודי בברזיל.
תל-אביב, <u>עם הספר</u>.   אוגוסט 1954.
עע' 30-37.

Kuperstein, L. "Ha'Hinuch Ha'Yehudi Be'Brazil". Tel-Aviv,
<u>Am ha'sefer</u>, August 1954   pp. 30-37.
("Jewish Education in Brazil")

898   אהל, י.   "החינוך היהודי בסן-פאולו
(ברזיל)".   תל-אביב, <u>החינוך</u>.
(כ' 27, מס' 3) אפריל 1955.   עע' 311-317.

Ohel, Y. "Ha'Hinuch Ha'Yehudi Be'San-Paulo (Brazil)".
Tel-Aviv, <u>Ha'Hinuch</u> (27: 3), April 1955, pp. 311-317.
("Jewish Education in São Paulo")

<u>CENTRAL AMERICA</u>

899   הלוי, מרדכי.   "החינוך העברי בארצות
אמריקה המרכזית".   תל-אביב, <u>מגילות</u>.
(כ' 6) אוגוסט 1951.   עע' 153-251.

Halevy, Mordechay. "Ha'Hinuch Ha'Ivri Be'Arzot America Ha'
Mercazit". Tel-Aviv, <u>Megilot</u> (6), August 1951, pp. 153-251.
("Hebrew Education in Central America")

CHILE

900
"דער ייִדישער ישוב אין טשילע".
‫בערלין‬, די ייִדישע אימיגראַצּיע. (נומער 2-1)
מערץ 1925. עע' 18-15.

"Der Yiddisher Yshuv in Chile". Berlin, Di yiddishe imigrazie
(1-2), March 1925, pp. 15-18.
("The Jewish Community in Chile")

901
קויפמן, מ.   "על יהדות צ'ילה".
תל-אביב, קמה.   1948.   עע' 313-303.

Kaufman, M. "Al Yahadut Chile". Tel-Aviv, Kama   1948, pp.
303-313.
("On the Jews of Chile")

902
וואלאבסקי, מאוריצי.   "די ייִדן אין טשילע".
בערלין, די ייִדישע אימיגראַצּיע.
(נומער 14) פעברואר 1927.   עע' 52-50.

Wolowsky, Mauricy. "Di Yidden in Chile". Berlin, Di
yiddishe imigrazie   (14), February 1927, pp. 50-52.
("The Jews in Chile")

MEXICO

903   הורביץ, י.   "צו דער פראגע וועגן
אימיגראציע קיין מעקסיקע".
בערלין, <u>דער וועג</u>. (נומער 3) 1923. עע' 30-21.

Hurwitz, J. "Zu der Frage Vegen Emigrazie Kein Mexike".
Berlin, <u>Der veg</u> (3), 1923, pp. 21-30.
                 ("The Question of Immigration into Mexico")

904   קאהן, סאלאמאן.   "מעקסיקאנער יידישער
ישוב".   ניו-יארק, <u>געדאנק און לעבן</u>.
אפריל 1945.

Kahn, Solomon. "Mexikaner Yiddisher Yshuv". New York,
<u>Gedank un leben</u> April, 1945.
                 ("The Mexican Jewish Community")

905   מייזל, ט.   "יידן אין מעקסיקע".
ניו-יארק, <u>יידישער קעמפפר</u>.
(באנד 28) 1947. עע' 12-10.

Lazdeisky, Haim. "Yidden in Mexike". New York, <u>Yiddisher</u>
<u>kemfer</u> (28), 1947, pp. 10-12.
                 ("Jews in Mexico")

906   מייזל, ט.   "יידן אין מעקסיקע".   ניו-יארק,
         <u>ייוא אננואל.</u> (באנד 27, נומער 2). 1946.

      Maizel, T. "Yidden in Mexike". New York, <u>Yivo annual</u>
      (27: 2), 1946.
          ("Jews in Mexico")

907   מירקין, מ.   "יידן אין מעקסיקע".   ווארשא,
         <u>יידישע אקונאמיק</u>. (באנד 2) 1938.
         ע' 285-286.

      Mirkin, M. "Yidden in Mexike". Warsaw, <u>Yiddishe economic</u>
      (2), 1938, pp. 285-286.
          ("Jews in Mexico")

908   שרפשטיין, צבי.   "החינוך היהודי במקסיקו".
         תל-אביב, <u>שבילי החינוך</u>. (כ' 14)
         אוקטובר 1953. ע' 40-44.

      Sharfstein, Zvi. "Ha'Hinuch Ha'Yehudi Be'Mexico". Tel-Aviv,
      <u>Shviley Ha'hinuch</u> (14), October 1953, pp. 40-44.
          ("Jewish Education in Mexico")

909   שרפשטיין, צבי.   "היהודים במקסיקו".
         ניו-יורק, <u>הדאר</u>. (כ' 34) 27 באוגוסט
         1954. ע' 692-693.

      Sharfstein, Zvi. "Ha'Yehudim Be'Mexico". New York,
      <u>Ha'Doar</u> (34), August 27, 1954, pp. 692-693.
          ("The Jews in Mexico")

910   טשער, א.   "דער יידישער ישוב אין מעקסיקע".
       בערלין, די יידישע אימיגראציע. (נומער 4)
                      יוני 1929.   עע' 201-193.

Tcher, A. "Der Yiddisher Yshuv in Mexike". Berlin,
Di yiddishe imigrazie   (4), June 1929, pp. 193-201.
              ("The Jewish Community in Mexico")

PERU

911   קעלמאן, ס.   "יידישע אימיגראנטן אין פערו".
       בערלין, די יידישע אימיגראציע. (נומער 14)
              פעברואר 1927.   עע' 54-52

Kelman, S. "Yiddishe Imigranten in Peru". Berlin, Di yiddishe
imigrazie   (14), February 1927, pp. 52-54.
              ("Jewish Immigrants in Peru")

URUGUAY

"אלגעמיינע קאלאניזאציע תנאים אין אורוגווי".
בערלין, <u>די יידישע אימיגראציע</u>. (נומער 7-8)
יולי-אוגוסט 1925. עז' 38-43.

"Algemeine Colonizazie T'Naim in Uruguay". Berlin, <u>Di yiddishe
imigrazie</u> (7-8), July-August 1925, pp. 38-43.
("General Colonization Conditions in Uruguay")

שעכטער, בן-ציון. "די יידן אין אורוגווי".
בערלין, <u>די יידישע אימיגראציע</u>. (נומער 13)
ספטעמבר 1926. עז' 40-42.

Shechter, Ben-Zion. "Di Yidden in Uruguay". Berlin, <u>Di yiddishe
imigrazie</u> (13), September 1926, pp. 40-42.
("The Jews in Uruguay")

PERSIA (IRAN)

The English translation of the title of each bibliographic item is to be found directly under the title
in the original language, and immediately following
the entire bibliographic description.

La traducción inglesa del título de cada asiento se
encuentra directamente bajo el título de la lengua
original, seguida de la ficha entera.

I. Books

ARGENTINA

914   احمد توکلی

نظری به آرژانتین

تهران ۱۳۳۷

Tavakkoli, Ahmad.   Nazari Be Argentin.   Teheran,
1958, 57p.

(A Glance at Argentina)

TURKEY

The English translation of the title of each bibliographic item is to be found directly under the title
in the original language, and immediately following
the entire bibliographic description.

(La traducción inglesa del título de cada asiento se
encuentra directamente bajo el título de la lengua
original, seguida de la ficha entera).

I. Books

LATIN AMERICA

915   Amerikan Haberler Merkezi. <u>Birleşmiş Devletler</u>
<u>Istikbali Kuruyor. Unicef Lâtin Amerika'da.</u> Ankara,
Doğuş Ltd., O. Matbaasi, 1952, 13p.
(U. S. Information Service. <u>The United Nations Plans</u>
<u>the Future. Unicef in Latin America</u>)

916   Anamur, Reşid. <u>Orta ve Güney Amerika.</u> Ankara, Doğuş
Basimevi, 1945, 210p.
           (Central and South America)

917   Duran, Faik Sabri. <u>Beş Kit'a Coğrafyasi. Şimalî ve Cenubî</u>
<u>Amerika.</u> Istanbul, Hilmi Kitabevi, 1930, 128p.
           (The Geography of Five Continents.
North and South America)

918   Duran, Faik Sabri. <u>Şimalî ve Cenubî Amerika. Ortamektep</u>
<u>Sinif: 2.</u> Istanbul, Hilmi Kitabevi, 1930, 128p.
           (North and South America for Junior
High School Second Class)

919   Petrof, Lüben. <u>Defolun Sömürgeciler!</u> Sofia, Narodna Prosveta,
1959, 102p.
           (Colonialists, Go Home)

920   Posta, Telgraf ve Telefon Umum Müdürlüğü. <u>Buenos-Aires</u>
<u>Evrensel Posta Kongresi Kararlari.</u> Izmir, Demiryollar
Basimevi, 1942, 410p.
(The Postal Telegraph and Telephone General Directorate.
<u>Proceedings of the Buenos Aires International Postal</u>
<u>Congress</u>)

921   Şaman, Bedri Tahir. <u>Amerika Kültür Tarihi. Yeni Dünyanin</u>
       <u>Eski Medeniyeti.</u> Lâtin Amerika Tarihi, V. 1. Ankara,
Ulus Basimevi, 1949, 244p.
                          (American Cultural History. The Old
Civilization of the New World. Latin American History)

922   Selen, Hâmit Sadi. <u>Coğrafya Dersleri (Cenubî Amerika). Sinif:</u>
      <u>7.</u> Istanbul, Tefeyyüz Kitabevi, 1930, 48p.
                    (Geography Lessons [South America], for the
Seventh Grade)

ARGENTINA

923   Arif, Hikmet. <u>Arjantin Mektep Gemisinin Istanbulu Ziyaretinde</u>
      <u>Tatbik Edilecek Program.</u> Ankara, Genelkurmay Basimevi,
1937, 16p.
              (The Program that will be Carried out During the
Visit of the Argentine Training-Ship to Istanbul)

BRAZIL

924   Ali. _Brezilya._ Istanbul, Ebüzziya Basimevi, 1932, 201p.
      (Brazil)

925   Atay, Falih Rifki. _Brezilya Seyyahati._ Istanbul, Devlet
      Basimevi, 1929.
                          (Brazilian Voyage)

926   Brezilya Kahvesi Türk Anonim Şirketi. _Esas Mukavelenamesi._
      Istanbul, Kâatcilik ve Matbaacilik A. Ş., 1933, 24p.
      (Turkish Brazilian Coffee, Inc. _Basic Contract_)

CUBA

927   Ilhami Bekir. _Küba._ Istanbul, Sinan Basimevi, 1962.
      "Bir Şairin Mektuplari No. 5"
                          (Cuba. No. 5 in the Series: "Letters of a Poet")

II. Periodical Articles

LATIN AMERICA

928   Dorsay, Şevki. "Güney Amerikali Yediler." Ankara, TMO
       dergisi (V: 59), February 1, 1960, pp. 9-12, 59-61.
              ("Seven South Americans")

929   Zengin, Coşkun. "Lâtin Amerika Edebiyati." Istanbul, Yelken (56),
       October 1961, pp. 24-25.
              ("Latin American Literature")

CUBA

930   Aksoy, Suat. "Küba ve Misir'da Toprak Reformu." Ankara,
       Forum (XIII: 162), January 1, 1961, pp. 8-10.
              ("Land Reform in Cuba and Egypt")

931   Kovaci, Nef'i. "Kübanin Iktisadi ve Malî Durumu." Istanbul,
       Istanbul Ticaret odasi gazetesi (III: 128), October 27, 1960, pp. 3-4.
              ("Cuba's Economic and Financial Condition")

MEXICO

932   Uzunoğlu, Bahtiyar. "Meksika'da Iktisadi Durum." Istanbul,
Istanbul Ticaret odasi gazetesi (III: 137), December 29, 1960,
p. 4.

                  ("The Economic Condition of Mexico")

PERU

933   Izer, Sadi Faik. "Kitalar Tarihi." Istanbul, Yeni insan (3: 3),
March 1965, pp. 26-40.

                  ("Peruvian History")

BULGARIA

The Spanish language is taught at the University of Sofia, which also contains a Faculty of Foreign Trade. There is also a Geographical Society located in Sofia. There is, however, no organized field of Latin American Studies in Bulgarian universities.

In this section the English translation of the title of each bibliographic item is to be found directly under the title in the original language, and immediately following the entire bibliographic description.

Se enseña español en la Universidad de Sofia, donde existe también una Facultad de Comercio Internacional. La Sociedad Geográfica está situada también en la ciudad de Sofia. Sin embargo, no existen Estudios Latinoamericanos como campo organizado en las universidades búlgaras.

En esta sección la traducción inglesa del título de cada asiento se encuentra directamente bajo el título de la lengua original, seguida de la ficha entera.

I. Books

LATIN AMERICA

934   Анастасов, Илия. Англо-Американските Противоречия в
Латинска Америка. София, Национален Комитет за
Защита на Мира, 1955, 60 стр.

Anastasov, I. <u>Anglo-Amerikanskite Protivorečija v
Latinska Amerika.</u> Sofia, Nacionalen Komitet za Zaštita na
Mira, 1955, 60p.
             (Conflicts of Interest Between Britain and
the U.S. in Latin America)

935   Андрейчин, Ерик. Латинска Америка (Политическо-
Икономически Очерк). София, Българска Комунистическа
Партия, 1956, 68 стр.

Andrejčin, E. <u>Latinska Amerika (Političesko-Ikonomičeski
Oček).</u> Sofia, Bǎlgarska Komunističeska Partija, 1956, 68p.
           (Latin America: Politico-Economic Outline)

936   Арие, Едуард, Калчев, Добри. Борбата на Трудещите се в
Латинска Америка за Независимост, Хляб и Мир. София,
Българска Комунистическа Партия, 1953, 184 стр.

Arie, Eduard, & Dobri Kalčev <u>Borbata na Trudeštite se v
Latinska Amerika za Nezavisimost, Hljab i Mir.</u> Sofia, Bǎlgarska
Komunističeska Partija, 1953, 184p.
                 (The Struggle of the Workers in
Latin America for Independence, Bread and Peace)
-Note: Contains a large bibliography on Latin America

937   Бешков, Ан., Динев, Л., Борисов, Здр. История на

Географията и Географските Открития. София, Наука и

Изкуство, 1966, 256 стр.

Beškov, A., et al. Istorija na Geografijata i Geografskite
Otkritija. Sofia, Nauka i Izkustvo, 1966, 256p.
(History of Geography and Geographical
Discoveries)

938   Бешков, Ан., Динев, Л., Маринов, Хр. Икономическа

География на Страните. Част Първа (На Капиталистическите

Страни). София, Народна Просвета, 1958, 440 стр.

Beškov, A., et al. Ikonomičeska Geografija na Stranite.
Čast Parva (Na Kapitalističeskite Strani). Sofia, Narodna
Prosveta, 1958, 440p.
(Economic Geography of the Nations.
Part I [Capitalist Countries])

939   Борбата на Колониалните и Зависими Народи за Национална

Независимост, Мир и Демокрация. София, Национален

Съвет на Отечествения Фронт, 1952, 28 стр.

Borbata na Kolonialnite i Zavisimi Narodi za Nacionalna
Nezavisimost, Mir i Demokracija. Sofia, Nacionalen
Savet na Otecestvenija Front, 1952, 28p.
(The Struggle of the Colonial and Dependent Nations for
National Independence, Peace and Democracy)

940   Ценков, Тодор. Борбата на Народите от Латинска Америка за

Свобода и Национална Независимост. София, Национален

Съвет на Отечествения Фронт, 1960, 48 стр.

Cenkov, T. Borbata na Narodite ot Latinska Amerika za
   Svoboda i Nacionalna Nezavisimost. Sofia, Nacionalen Săvet
na Otečestvenija Front, 1960, 48p.
                    (The Struggle of the Peoples of Latin America
   for Freedom and National Independence)

941   Цветанов, Л. Намесата на САЩ във Вътрешните Работи на

Другите Страни (Материал за Доклади). София,

Национален Съвет на Отечествения Фронт, 1957, 16 стр.

Cvetanov, L. Namesata na SAStț văv Vătrešnite Raboti na
   Drugite Strani (Material za Dokladi). Sofia, Nacionalen
Săvet na Otečestvenija Front, 1957, 16p.
                    (U.S. Intervention in the Internal Affairs of
   Foreign Countries: Handbook for Public Speakers)

942   Цветанов, Любен. Южна Америка под Гнета на Северо-

Американския Монополистичен Капитал. София, Национален

Съвет на Отечествения Фронт, 1957, 160 стр.

Cvetanov, L. Južna Amerika pod Gneta na Severo-
   Amerikanskija Monopolističen Kapital. Sofia, Nacionalen
Săvet na Otečestvenija Front, 1957, 160p.
                    (South America Oppressed by North
   American Monopolistic Capital)

943 Данилевич, М. Положението на Трудещите се Селяни от
Латинска Америка и Тяхната Борба Против Империалистическия
Гнет и Феодалната Реакция. София, Български Земеделски
Народен Съюз, 1952, 112 стр.

Danilevič, M. Položenieto na Trudeštite se Seljani ot
 Amerika i Tjahnata Borba Protiv Imperialističeskija Gnet i
Feodalnata Reakcija. Sofia, Bălgarski Zemedelski Naroden
Săjuz, 1952, 112p.
     (The Position of the Peasant-Workers of Latin
America and their Struggle Against Imperialist Oppression and
Feudal Reaction)

944 Димитров, Тодор. Латинска Америка Против Империализма
на САЩ. София, Национален Съвет на Отечествения Фронт,
1962, 32 стр.
Dimitrov, T. Latinska Amerika Protiv Imperializma na
 SASt. Sofia, Nacionalen Săvet na Otečestvenija Front,
1962, 32p.
     (Latin America vs. U. S. Imperialism)

945 Димитров, Тодор. Тройно Безразсъдство. Империали-
стическата Политика на САЩ в Африка, Азия и Латинска
Америка. София, Национален Съвет на Отечествения Фронт,
1964, 36 стр.
Dimitrov, T. Trojno Bezrazsădstvo. Imperialističeskata
 Politika na SASt v Afrika, Azija i Latinska Amerika. Sofia,
Nacionalen Săvet na Otečestvenija Front, 1964, 36p.
     (Triple Madness: Imperialistic Politics of the
United States in Africa, Asia and Latin America)

946   Гловня, М., Димитров, Д. Физическа География на
Континентите. София, Народна Просвета, 1955^2,
240 стр., 1958^3, 255 стр.

Glovnja, M., & D. Dimitrov. Fiziĉeska Geografija na
Kontinentite. Sofia, Narodna Prosveta, 1955, 240p.;
1958, 225p.

(Physical Geography of the
Continents)

947   Иванов, Б., Даков, В. Икономическа География на
Капиталисти-ческите Страни. София, Наука и Изкуство,
1967, 660 стр.

Ivanov, B., & V. Dakov. Ikonomiĉeska Geografija na
Kapitalistiĉeskite Strani. Sofia, Nauka i Izkustvo, 1967, 660p.

(Economic Geography of the Capitalist
Countries)

948   Йорданов, Т., Маринор, Хр. Икономическа География на
Капиталистическите Страни. София, Наука и Изкуство,
1955, 429 стр.

Jordanov, T., & H. Marinov. Ikonomiĉeska Geografija na
Kapitalistiĉeskite Strani. Sofia, Nauka i Izkustvo, 1955,
429p.

(Economic Geography of the
Capitalist Countries)

949   Караиванова, П., Джерекаров, В., Костов, Вл. Младежки

Паралели. Очерци за Живота на Младежта в Извън-
социалисти ческите Страни. София, Народна Младеж, 1966,
176 стр.

Karaivanova, P., et al. Mladežki Paraleli, Očerci za Života
 na Mladežta v Izvănsocialističeskite Strani, Sofia, Narodna
Mladez, 1966, 176p.

                        (Youth in Other Lands: Sketches of the
Life of Young People in the Non-Socialist Countries)

950   Кесяков, Б., Манолов, М. От Захарните Плантации на

Куба до Ляносите на Венецуела. София, Народна Просвета,
1962, 66 стр.

Kesjakov, B., & M. Manolov. Ot Zaharnite Plantacii na Kuba do
 Ljanosite na Venecuela, Sofia, Narodna Prosveta, 1962, 66p.
                        (From the Sugar Plantations of
Cuba to the Llanos of Venezuela)

951   Крумова-Йовева, М. Национално-Освободителното Движение

в Света в Наши Дни. Препоръчителен Списък на Книги и
Статии. Перник, Окръжна Библиотека, 1961, 8 стр.

Krumova-Joveva, M. Nacionalno- Osvoboditelnoto Dviženie v
 Sveta v Naši Dni, Preporăčitelen Spisăk na Knigi i Statii,
Pernik, Okrăžna Biblioteka, 1961, 8p.
                        (The National Liberation Movement in the
Modern World: Recommended List of Books and Articles)

952   Материали по История на Международното Работническо и
       Комунистическо Движение. София, Българска Комунис-
       тическа Партия, 1959, 899 стр.

       Materiali po Istorija na Meždunarodnoto Rabotničesko i
       Komunističesko Dviženie. Sofia, Bǎlgarska Komunističeska
       Partija, 1959, 899p.
       (Materials on the History of the International Labor and
       Communist Movement)

953   Международна Политика. Библиографски Списъци.
       София, Димитровски Съюз на Народната Младеж,
       1957, 44 стр.

       Meždunarodna Politika. Bibljografski Spisǎci. Sofia,
       Dimitrovski Sǎjuz na Narodnata Mladež, 1957, 44p.
       (International Politics: Bibliographic Notes)

954   Митев, Ст., Ковачев, Хр. Партизанската Война. София,
       Държавно Военно Издателство, 1966, 184 стр.

       Mitev, S., & H. Kovačev. Partizanskata Vojna. Sofia,
       Dǎržavno Voenno Izdatelstvo, 1966, 184p.
                          (Guerrilla Warfare)
       -Note: Bibliography, pp. 181-182 on Cuba and Venezuela.

955   Панайотов, Иван Ал. Календар на Географските Открития и
       Изследвания. София, Народна Просвета, 1958, 288 стр.

       Panajotov, I. Kalendar na Geografskite Otkritija i
       Izsledvanija. Sofia, Narodna Prosveta, 1958, 288p.
                          (Calendar of Geographical Discoveries and
       Research)

956   Петровски, Боньо. Нефтените Монополи през Епохата на
Империализма. София, Наука и Изкуство, 1961, 175 стр.

Petrovski, B. Neftenite Monopoli Prez Epohata na
Imperializma. Sofia, Nauka i Izkustvo, 1961, 175p.
(Giant Oil Companies During the Era of
Imperialism)

957   Пирински, Георги. Битка за Мир из Три Континента
(Америка, Азия и Европа). София, Национален Комитет
за Защита на Мира, 1960, 152 стр.

Pirinski, G. Bitka za Mir iz Tri Kontinenta (Amerika,
Azija i Evropa). Sofia, Nacionalen Komitet za Zaštita na
Mira, 1960, 152p.
(Struggle for Peace Throughout Three Continents:
America, Asia and Europe)

958   Пописаков, Григор. Международна Търговия – Част III:
Външна Търговия на Народна Република България. София,
Наука и Изкуство, 1959, 264 стр.

Popisakov, G. Meždunarodna Targovija - Čast III: Vănšna
Tărgovija na Narodna Republika Bălgarija. Sofia, Nauka i
Izkustvo, 1959, 264p.
(International Trade - Part III: Foreign Trade
of the People's Republic of Bulgaria)

959   Попов, Станчо. Латинска Америка Ше Победи! София,
Българска Комунистическа Партия, 1966, 96 стр.

Popov, S. Latinska Amerika Šte Pobedi! Sofia, Bălgarska
Komunističeska Partija, 1966, 96p.
(Latin America will Win!)

960 Съдебни, Консулски и Други Договори на Народна Република
     България. (Сборник, Съставили: Илиев, Сп., Главов, Н.).
     София, Наука и Изкуство, 1966, 332 стр.

     Sădebni, Konsulski i Drugi Dogovori na Narodna Republika
       Bălgarija (Sbornik, Săstavili: Iliev, Sp., Glavov, N.).
       Sofia, Nauka i Izkustvo, 1966, 332p.
     (Jurisdictional, Consular and Other Treaties of the People's
       Republic of Bulgaria: articles and essays by Sp. Iliev and N. Glavov

961 Сестримски, Вл. Тайните на Империалистическата "Помощ".
     София, Българска Комунистическа Партия, 1966, 71 стр.

     Sestrimski, V. Tajnite na Imperialističeskata "Pomošt".
     Sofia, Bălgarska Komunističeska Partija, 1966, 71p.
                      (The Secrets of Imperialistic "Assistance")

962 Трендафилов, Тончо. Американският Неоколониализъм.
     София, Национален Съвет на Отечествения Фронт, 1961,
     44 стр.

     Trendafilov, T. Amerikanskijat Neokolonializăm. Sofia,
     Nacionalen Săvet na Otečestvenija Front, 1961, 44p.
                      (American Neocolonialism)

963 Трифонова, Слава. С Книгата по Света. Препоръчителна
     Библиография на Художествена и Научно-Популярна Лите-
     ратура. Пловдив, Народна Библиотека "Иван Вазов", 1960,
     48 стр.

     Trifonova, S. S Knigata po Sveta. Preporăčitelna Bibliografija
       na Hudožestvena i Naučno-Populjarna Literatura. Plovdiv,
     Narodna Biblioteka "Ivan Vazov", 1960, 48p.
                    (Around the World with a Book: Recommended
     Bibliography in Belletristic and Popular-Scientific Literature)

964   Вълчев, Тодор. За Разширяване на Търговията Между
       Страните от Двата Световни Пазара. София, Национален
    Съвет на Отечествения Фронт, 1955, 48 стр.
    Vǎlčev, T. Za Razširjavane na Tǎrgovijata Meždu Stranite
     ot Dvata Svetovni Pazara, Sofia, Nacionalen Sǎvet na
    Otečestvenija Front, 1955, 48p.
            (Toward the Expansion of Trade Between the Countries
    of the Two World Markets)

ARGENTINA

965   Петров, Станьо. Аржентина. София, Наука и Изкуство,
      1961, 192 стр.
    Petrov, S. Aržentina. Sofia, Nauka i Izkustvo, 1961, 192p.
        (Argentina)

BOLIVIA

966   Цачева, Виктория. Боливия (Политическо-Географски Очерк).
     София, Национален Съвет на Отечествения Фронт, 1962, 56 стр.
    Cačeva, V. Bolivija (Političesko-Geografski Očerk). Sofia,
     Nacionalen Sǎvet na Otečestvenija Front, 1962, 56p.
        (Bolivia: A Politico-Geographic Sketch)

967   Георгиев, Любен. Бразилия (Политическо-Географски
Очерк). София, Национален Съвет на Отечествения Фронт,
1967, 68 стр.
Georgiev, L. Brazilija (Političesko-Geografski Očerk).
Sofia, Nacionalen Săvet na Otečestvenija Front, 1967, 68p.
(Brazil: A Politico-Geographic Sketch)

968   Игнатиев, О. Бразилия - Гигантът на Тропика. Бележки
на Един Кореспондент. София, Национален Съвет на
Отечествения Фронт, 1964, 148 стр.
Ignatiev, O. Brazilija - Gigantăt na Tropika. Beležki na Edin
Korespondent. Sofia, Nacionalen Săvet na Otečestvenija
Front, 1964, 148p.
(Brazil- Giant of the Tropics: Notes of a
Correspondent)

969   Меворах, Нисим. Семейно Право. София, Наука и Изкуство,
1962, 254 стр.
Mevorah, N. Semejno Pravo. Sofia, Nauka i Izkustvo, 1962,
254p.
(Domestic Law)

970   Тилев, Христо. Островна и Средна Америка. София,
       Наука и Изкуство, 1960, 258 стр.

   Tilev, H. Ostrovna i Sredna Amerika. Sofia, Nauka i
   Izkustvo, 1960, 258p.
              (Central America and the Caribbean Islands)

CHILE

971 Андрейчин, Ерик. Чили. София, Българска Комунистическа
Партия, 1954, 46 стр.

Andrejčin, E. Čili. Sofia, Bălgarska Komunisticeska Partija,
1954, 46p.

  (Chile)

972 Димитров, Тодор. Чили (Политическо-Географски Очерк).
София, Национален Съвет на Отечествения Фронт, 1966,
84 стр.

Dimitrov, T. Čili (Politicesko-Geografski Ocerk). Sofia,
Nacionalen Săvet na Otecestvenija Front, 1966, 84p.

  (Chile: A Politico-Geographic Sketch)

973 Канев, Диньо. Чили (Географски Очерк). София, Наука и
Изкуство, 1962, 120 стр.

Kanev, D. Čili (Geografski Ocerk). Sofia, Nauka i Izkustvo
1962, 120p.

  (Chile: A Geographical Sketch)

COLOMBIA

974   Шишов, А. , Бенбасат, Н. Колумбия (Политическо-
     Географски Очерк). София, Национален Съвет на
     Отечествения Фронт, 1966, 60 стр.
Šišov, A., & N. Benbasat. <u>Kolumbija (Političesko-Geografski</u>
     <u>Očerk).</u> Sofia, Nacionalen Săvet na Otečestvenija Front,
     1966, 60p.
                         (Colombia: A Politico-Geographic
   Sketch)

975   Аржентински, Иван. Непокорна Куба. София, Национален

Съвет на Отечествения Фронт, 1961, 32 стр.

Aržentinski, I. Nepokorna Kuba. Sofia, Nacionalen Săvet
na Otečestvenija Front, 1961, 32p.
(Obstinate Cuba)

976   Аржентински, Иван. Зелената Перла (Впечатления от

Революционна Куба). София, Държавно Военно Издателство,
1961[1], 252 стр.,1962[2], 256 стр.

Arzentinski, I. Zelenata Perla (Vpečatlenija ot Revoljucionna
Kuba). Sofia, Dăržavno Voenno Izdatelstvo, 1961, 252p.;
1962, 256p.
(The Green Pearl: Impressions of Revolutionary
Cuba)

977   Българанова, Ана. Куба, Колко Хубава Си, Куба! София,

Национален Съвет на Отечествения Фронт, 1962, 36 стр.

Bălgaranova, A. Kuba, Kolko Hubava Si, Kuba! Sofia,
Nacionalen Săvet na Otečestvenija Front, 1962, 36p.
(Cuba, How Beautiful You Are!)

978   Боровик, Хенрих.   От Искрата се Разгоря Пламък. Епизоди

от Борбата на Кубинския Народ. София, Държавно Военно

Издателство, 1961, 120 стр.

Borovik, H. Ot Iskrata se Razgorja Plamǎk. Epizodi ot
  Borbata na Kubinskija Narod, Sofia, Dǎrzavno Voenno
Izdatelstvo, 1961, 120p.
              (From the Spark is Kindled a Flame: Episodes
from the Struggle of the Cuban People)

979   Давидов, Нешо.   Репортаж от Куба. София, Българска

Комунисти- ческа Партия, 1965, 60 стр.

Davidov, N. Reportaž ot Kuba. Sofia, Bǎlgarska Komunisti-
  češka Partija, 1965, 60p.
              (Report from Cuba)

980   Дунавец, Михаил.   Биографията на Една Революция

(Революцията в Куба).   Варна, Държавно Издателство,

1963, 228 стр.

Dunavec, M. Biografijata na Edna Revoljucija (Revoljucijata
  v Kuba). Varna, Dǎrzavno Izdatelstvo, 1963, 228p.
              (The Biography of a Revolution: The Cuban
Revolution)

982   Калчев, Камен.   Куба. Островът на Свободата. София,

Национален Съвет на Отечествения Фронт, 1963, 52 стр.

Kalčev, K. Kuba, Ostrovǎt na Svobodata. Sofia, Nacionalen
Sǎvet na Otečestvenija Front, 1963, 52p.
              (Cuba: The Island of Freedom)

982   Мудров, Д., Малчев, Н., Николов, Н. Куба, Ние Сме с
        Тебе! София, Държавно Военно Издателство, 1962, 127 стр.

Mudrov, D., et al. Kuba, Nie Sme s Tebe! Sofia, Dǎržavno
Voenno Izdatelstvo, 1962, 127p.
          (Cuba, We Are with You!)

983   Ошеверов, Георги. Фидел Кастро. София, Българска
        Комунисти- ческа Партия, 1961, 31 стр.

Oševerov, G. Fidel Kastro. Sofia, Bǎlgarska Komunističeska
Partija, 1961, 31p.
          (Fidel Castro)

984   Телалов, Константин. Куба - Да! Янки - Не! Варна,
        Държавно Издателство, 1961, 96 стр.

Telalov, K. Kuba - Da! Janki - Ne! Varna, Dǎržavno
Izdatelstvo, 1961, 96p.
          (Cuba - Si! Yanqui - No!)

ECUADOR

985   Николов, Емил. Еквадор (Политическо-Географски Очерк).
София, Национален Съвет на Отечествения Фронт, 1963,
52 стр.

Nikolov, E. <u>Ekvador (Političesko-Geografski Očerk),</u> Sofia,
Nacionalen Săvet na Otečestvenija Front, 1963, 52p.
(Ecuador: A Politico-Geographic Sketch)

GUATEMALA

986   Димитров, Тодор. Гватемала (Политическо-Географски
Очерк). София, Национален Съвет на Отечествения Фронт,
1967, 79 стр.

Dimitrov, T. <u>Gvatemala (Političesko-Geografski Očerk).</u>
Sofia, Nacionalen Săvet na Otečestvenija Front, 1967, 79p.
(Guatemala: A Politico-Geographic Sketch)

MEXICO

987   Мелнишки, Любен. Мексико. София, Наука и Изкуство, 1961, 220 стр.

Melniški, L. _Meksiko,_ Sofia, Nauka i Izkustvo, 1961, 220p.
(Mexico)

PANAMA

988   Димитров, Тодор. Панама (Политическо-Географски Очерк). София, Национален Съвет на Отечествения Фронт, 1964, 68 стр.

Dimitrov, T. _Panama (Političesko-Geografski Očerk)._ Sofia, Nacionalen Săvet na Otecestvenija Front, 1964, 68p.
(Panama: A Politico-Geographic Sketch)

PERU

989   Николов, Емил. Перу (Политическо-Географски Очерк).
София, Национален Съвет на Отечествения Фронт,
1964, 60 стр.

Nikolov, E. Peru (Političesko-Geografski Očerk). Sofia,
Nacionalen Săvet na Otečestvenija Front, 1964, 60p.
(Peru: A Politico-Geographic Sketch)

URUGUAY

990   Димитров, Тодор. Уругвай (Политическо-Географски Очерк).
София, Национален Съвет на Отечествения Фронт,
1965, 52 стр.

Dimitrov, T. Urugvaj (Političesko-Geografski Očerk). Sofia,
Nacionalen Săvet na Otečestvenija Front, 1965, 52p.
(Uruguay: A Politico-Geographic Sketch)

991   Георгиев, Любен. Венецуела (Политическо-Географски
       Очерк). София, Национален Съвет на Отечествения Фронт,
       1965, 72 стр.

Georgiev, L. Venecuela (Politicesko-Geografski Ocerk).
Sofia, Nacionalen Săvet na Otecestvenija Front, 1965, 72p.
              (Venezuela: A Politico-Geographic Sketch)

992   Наумов, Любен. Венецуелски Патриоти с Българска Кръв
       (Разказ за Тримата Братя Теодоро, Любен и Мирослав
       Петкови, Участници във Венецуелската Съпротива). София,
       Национален Съвет на Отечествения Фронт, 1965, 128 стр.

Naumov, L. Venecuelski Patrioti s Bălgarska Krăv (Razkaz
      za Trimata Bratja Teodoro, Ljuben i Miroslav Petkovi,
Ucastnici văv Venecuelskata Săprotiva). Sofia, Nacionalen
Săvet na Otecestvenija Front, 1965, 128p.
              (Venezuelan Patriots of Bulgarian Descent:
Story of the Three Brothers Teodoro, Luben and Miroslav Petkov,
Participants in the Venezuelan Resistance)

993   Панайотов, Ив., Мелнишки, Л. Венецуела (Географски Очерк).
       София, Наука и Изкуство, 1963, 128 стр.

Panajotov, I., & L. Melniški. Venecuela (Geografski Ocerk).
Sofia, Nauka i Izkustvo, 1963, 128p.
                    (Venezuela: Geographic Sketch)

CZECHOSLOVAKIA

Spanish Language and Literature are taught at Palacky
University in Olomouc, and at Purkyné University, in
Brno. In Prague, Spanish History and Spanish and Latin
American Literature are offered at Charles University,
while the College of Economics offers courses in Foreign
Trade. Charles University has a Latin American Center.

Two Czech anthropologists are worthy of mention.
Professor Cestmir Loukotka (deceased), a noted
specialist on South American Indian languages, was
a colleague of the internationally-renowed French
linguistic anthropologist, Dr. Paul Rivet, with whom
he often collaborated. The Latin American Center
at UCLA in 1968 published his Classification of South
American Indian Languages, a volume which represents
his life-work.

Dr. Miloslav Stingl, is a young Czech scholar in the field
of anthropology with many books to his credit. These
include: Indiani Bez Tomhavku (Indians Without Tomahawks),
Indiani, Černoši a Vousaci: Antropologie Kuby (The Indians,
the Negroes and the Bearded Ones: Antropology of Cuba),
and Indiánský Bězěc-Sport, a Hry ve Starém a Novem Mexiku
(The Indian Runner: Sports and Games in the Old and New
Mexico), all published in Prague in 1968. The Directorship
of the Division of American Anthropology and Ethnohistory
of the Czechoslovak Academy of Sciences, formerly held by
Professor Loukotka, is currently administered by Dr. Stingl.

In this section the English translation of the title of each
bibliographic item is to be found directly under the title
in the original language, and immediately following
the entire bibliographic description.

Se enseñan lengua y literatura española en la Universidad Palacky en la ciudad de Olomouc, y en la Universidad Purkyné en Brno. En Praga la Universidad Charles ofrece cursos en historia española así como en letras españolas y latinoamericanas. En Praga también se enseñan cursos en comercio internacional, en el Colegio de Economía. Hay Centro Latinoamericano en la Charles.

Dos antropólogos checos se mencionan aquí. El Profesor Cestmir Loukotka (fallecido), experto en las lenguas indígenas suramericanas, fué colega del notable antropólogo francés, el Dr. Paul Rivet, con quien colaboró. En 1968 el Centro Latinoamericano de la UCLA publicó su Classification of South American Indian Languages, volumen que representa su trabajo de toda la vida.

Dr. Miloslav Stingl es joven antropólogo checo quien ya escribió una cantidad de libros, y entre ellos: Indiani Bez Tomhavkú (Indígenas sin Tomahawkes), Cernosi a Vousaci: Antropologie Kuby (los Indígenas, los Negros y los Barbudos: Antropología Cubana), Indiánský Bezec-Sport, a Hry ve Starém a Novem Mexiku (El Corredor Indígena: Deportes y Juegos en México Antiguo y Nuevo), todos publicados en Praga en 1968. La gerencia de la División de Antropología y Etnohistoria Americanas de la Academia Checa de Ciencias, antes la responsabilidad del Profesor Loukotka, es actualmente al cargo del Dr. Stingl.

En esta sección la traducción inglesa del título de cada asiento se encuentra directamente bajo el título de la lengua original, seguida de la ficha entera.

I. Books

LATIN AMERICA

994 Bartos, Lubomír. Úvod do Dějin, Společénskeho Zřízení
a Kultury Španělské Ameriky. Prague, SNPL, 1964, 68p.
(An Introduction to History, Social Institutions,
and Culture of Spanish America)

995 Basl, Josef. Amerika Jižní, Spoužitím Nejnovejsích Spisů
Batesa, Gildenmeistera, Hellwalda, Hübnera, Iheringa,
Lendenfelda, Regela, Rodtové, Röthlisbergera, Scobela,
Sieverse, Sokolowskyho, Schutz-Holzhausena, Vlacha, Vráze,
Wheelera a Jiných. Prague, J. L. Kober, 1931, 501p.
(South America. With Material From the Most
Recent Works of Bates, Gildenmeister, Hellwald, Hübner,
Ihering, Lendenfeld, Regel, Rodtov, Röthlisberger, Scobel,
Sievers, Sokolowsky, Schutz-Holzhausen, Vlach, Vráz, Wheeler
and Others)

996 Brancovský, Miroslav. Problémy Ekonomického Vyvoje
Některých Zemí Latinské Ameriky. K Některým Otázkám
Strategie a Taktiky Komunistichých Stran Latinské Ameriky.
Prague, Čsl. Společnost PVZ, 1965, 31 + 25p.
(Problems of Economic Evolution in
Some Countries of Latin America. Notes to Some Questions
Regarding Strategy and Tactics of Communist Parties in
Latin America)

997 Čech-Vyšata, František. Patnáct Let v Jižní Americe.
Prague, Kvasnička a Hampl, 1927. Díl I, v Žáru Pamp,
216p. Díl II, Divokým Hájem, 222p.
(Fifteen Years in South America.
Vol. I: in the Heat of Pampas. Vol. II: Across a Wild Forest)

998 Čech-Vyšata, František. Středem Jižní Ameriky. Prague,
Čsl. Grafická Unie, 1936, 260p.
(Cutting Through the Middle of
South America)

999   Čemus, Jan K. Pod Klenbou Pralesa, Pouť Českého Hocha
Napríč Jižní Amerikou, Dobrodružný Román Pro Mládež.
Prague, O. Šeba, 1941, 133p.
                (Under the Vault of a Virgin Forest. The Journey
of a Czech Boy Across South America: An Adventurous Novel for
Youth)

1000   Danilevič, M. Boj Rolníků Latinské Ameriky Proti Imperialistickému
Utisků a Feudální Reakci, Brno, Rovnost, 1951, 39p.
                (Struggle of Latin American Farmers with Imperialistic
Oppression and Feudal Reactionaries)

1001   Danilevič, M. Dělnicka Třída Latinské Ameriky v Boji Za
Nezávislost a Demokracii, Brno, Rovnost, 1950, 34p.
                (Working Class of Latin America in Fight for Independence
and Democracy)

1002   Danilevič, M. Latinská Amerika; Informační Politická Příručka,
Prague, Nakl. Politické Literatury, 1965.
                (Latin America; Manual of Political Information)

1003   Denis, Pierre. Jižní Amerika. 2v. Prague, 1929-1930.
                (South America)

1004   Dokumenty a Materialy k Otázce Latinské Ameriky, Prague,
SNPL, 1962, 521p.
(Documents and Sources on the Latin American Question)

1005   Domin, Karel. Nové Příspěvky k Poznáni Kapradin Tropické
Jižní Ameriky a Ostrovu Západoindických, Prague, Nákladem
Vlastním, 1941, 7p.
                (New Contributions to Recognition of the Ferns in
Tropical South America and West Indies. Prague, Published by
Author)

1006   Drda, Jan. <u>Horká Puda.</u> 1st ed. Prague, Ceskoslovenský
       Spisovatel, 1955, 257p.
           (Burning Land)

1007   Dvorský, Viktor. <u>Amerika Střední a Jižní a Australie s Okeanií.</u>
       Prague, SPKI, 1926, 143p.
           (Central and Latin America and Australia with
   Oceania)

1008   Erben, Josef L. <u>Po Stopach Dobyvatelu, Osvoboditelu a Diktátoru.</u>
      <u>Cesty Jiho-Americkým Zemědílem.</u> Prague, Československá
      Grafická Unie, 1937, 396p.
           (In the Footprints of Conquerors, Liberators
   and Dictators: Routes over the South American Continent)

1009   Flos, František. <u>Lovci Orchidejí.</u> Prague, SNDK, 1955, 193p.
           (Hunters of Orchids)

1010   Frič, Alberto V. <u>Dlouhý Lovec. Dobrodružství u Indianu Kaďuveju.</u>
       Prague, SNDK, 1955, 177p.
           (The Tall Hunter: An Adventure with Kaduwei
   Indians)

1011   Frič, Alberto V. <u>Hadí Ostrov, Dobrodružství s Hady, Žraloky</u>
      <u>a Lidmi Pralesa.</u> Prague, SNDK, 1959, 198p.
           (The Island of Serpents, Adventures with Snakes,
   Sharks and People of the Virgin Forest)

1012   Frič, Alberto V. <u>Indiáni Jižní Ameriky.</u> Prague, Mladá Fronta,
       1946, 211p.
           (Indians of South America)

1013   Frič, Alberto V. <u>Krajané v Cizině.</u> Smíchov, Nákladem Vlastním, 1920, 11p.

          (Countrymen Abroad. Published by Author)

1014   Frič, Alberto V. <u>Mezi Indiány.</u> Vinohrady, Koníček, 1918, 220p.

          (Among Indians)

1015   Frič, Alberto V. <u>Zákon Pralesa, Indiánskó Pohádky Pro Děti od Sesti do Sedesáti Let.</u> Prague, Zátiší, 1921, 85p.

          (Law of the Virgin Forest. Indian Stories for Children from six to sixty)

1016   Hanzelka, Jiří. <u>Pres Kordillery,</u> 1st ed. Prague, Orbis, 1957, 306p.

          (Unworked Cordilleras)

1017   Hanzelka, Jiří, & Miroslav Zikmund. <u>Jizní Amerikou Výbor Pro Mládež.</u> Prague, SNDK, 1959, 350p.

          (Across South America: Selection for Youth)

1018   <u>Informační Politická Příručka,</u> Prague, SNPL, 1965, 342p.

          (A Handbook of Political Information)

1019   Janecek, Ladislav. <u>Amerikou s Jabloneckým Sklem.</u> Liberec, Krajské Nakladatelství, 1958, 139p.

          (Journey in America with the Glass of Jablonec)

1020   Jungbauer, Radomír. Ekonomické Důsledkv EHS pro Latinskou Ameriku. In <u>Zapado-Europska Integrace,</u> Sbornik. Prague, SNPL, 1963, 208p.

          (Economic Consequences of the European Common Market for Latin America. An Article in: <u>West European Integration,</u> a Collection of Essays)

1021   Kahoun, František. Hospodářský a Politický Zeměpis USA a
       Latinské Ameriky. Prague, Vysoká Škola Politických a
       Hospodářských Věd, 1950, 29p.
                        (Economic and Political Geography of the
       USA and Latin America)

1022   Kolář, Jaroslav. Přehled Zeměpisu Státu Latinské Ameriky.
       Prague, SPN, 1963, 123p.
                        (Synopsis of Geography of Latin American Countries)

1023   Kovář, Blahoslav. Asie, Afrika, Latinská America; Bibliografie
       Českých a Slovenských Knih, 1961-1964. Prague, Národní
       Knihovna, 1964, 78p.
                        (Asia, Africa and Latin America; Bibliography
       of Czech and Slovak Books, 1961-1964)

1024   Krátký, Karel. Program Spojenectví Pro Pokrok. Prague,
       SNPL, 1965, 124p.
                        (Program of the Alliance for Progress)

1025   Krobot, Antonín. Z Buenos Aires k Panamskému Průplavu. Mé
       Příhody z Cest po Jižní Americe. Žamberk, Naše Zájmy, 1939,
       29p.
                        (From Buenos Aires to the Panama Canal. My
       Adventures on Trips to South America)

1026   Kubín, Miroslav. Latinská Amerika- Kontinent Pohybu. Prague,
       SNPL, 1962, 145p.
                        (Latin America- The Continent in Motion)

1027   Kunosi, Alexander. Predstavujeme Vám Latinskú Ameriku.
       Bratislava, Osveta, 1955, 34p.
                        (We Introduce you to Latin America)

1028   Kybal, Vlastimil. **Jižní Amerikou. Přehled Hospodářský, Obchodní a Politický.** Prague, Vesmír, 1935, 157p.
             (Across South America: Economic, Trade, and Political Survey)

1029   Kybal, Vlastimil. **Jižní Amerika a Československo, S. Přehledem Obchodní, Finanční a Emigrační Činnosti Jiných Národů,** Prague, Merkur, 1928, 228p.
             (South America and Czechoslovakia. With a Survey of Trade, Financial and Emigration Activity of Other Nations)

1030   Kybal, Vlastimil. **Jižní Amerika ve Světovém Hospodářství,** Prague, Česká Společnost Národohospodářská, 1934, 34p.
             (South America in World Economy)

1031   Kybal, Vlastimil. **Naše Práce v Mexiku a Střední Americe 1935-1938.** Mexico, 1939.
             (Our Work in Mexico and in Central America)

1032   Kybal, Vlastimil. **Po Československých Stopách v Latinské Americe.** Prague, Česká Akademie Věd a Umění, 1935, 90p.
             (Czechoslovak Footprints in Latin America)

1033   Kybal, Vlastimil. **Velikáni Španělských Dějin,** Prague, Jednota Českých Matematiku a Fyziků, 1935, 76p.
             (Giants of Spanish History)

1034   Loukotka, Čestmír. **Slovníky Indianskych Řečí. Z Rokopisné Pozustalosti Cestovatele E. St. Vráze.** Prague, Král, Česká Spol, Nauk, 1943, 18p.
             (Vocabularies of Indian Languages, from Hand-Written Material Left by the Traveller, E. St. Vráz)

1035   Mocko, Zdenko. Ekonomická Geografia Latinskej Ameriky.
        Bratislava, SPN, 1957, 69p.
                    (Economic Geography of Latin America)

1036   Müller, Karel, & Augustin Bartík. Neznámo Pod Sivým Kondorem.
        Prague, Orbis, 1934, 192p.
                    (Unknown under a Dove-Coloured
        Condor)

1037   Náčrt z Dějin Jižní Ameriky. Prague, Čsl. Bolivijská Společnost,
        1937, 18p.
        (Sketch from the History of South America)

1038   Nástin Ekonomiky Rozvojových Zemí Oblasti Latinské Ameriky.
        Prague, Vysoká Skola Ekonomická, 1964, 200p.
        (A Sketch of Economies of Developing Lands in South America)

1039   Národy Latinské Ameriky v Boji Proti Americkému Imperialismu.
        Sborník Statí. Prague, SNPL, 1953, 486p.
        (Latin American Nations in Struggle with American Imperialism.
        Collection of Essays)

1040   Polisénský, Josef. Úvod do Studia Dějin a Kultury Španielska a
        Latinské Ameriky. Prague, SPN, 1963, 114p.
                        (An Introduction to Study of History and Culture
        of Spain and Latin America)

1041   Prausek, M. Dobrodružství v Jižní Americe. Klimkovice, 1936,
        39p.
                    (An Adventure in South America)

1042   Samhaber, Emil. Jižní Amerika. Tvář-Duch-Dějiny. Prague,
        Čin, 1941, 741p.
                        (South America: Face-Spirit-History)

1043 Šnejdávek, Antonín. Bibliografie Pracio Latinské Americe. Prague, 1963-

(A Working Bibliography of Latin America)

1044 Stingl, Miloslav. Indiani Bez Tomhavků. Prague, Svoboda, 1968, 622p.

(The Indians without Tomahawks)

1045 Stölting, Inge. Žena Letí Přes Andy. Prague, Čes. Graf. Unie, 1941, 175p.

(A Woman is Flying over the Andes)

1046 Šumavský, Jan, et al. Kontinent Před Bouří. Prague, NV, 1965, 148p.

(Continent Before the Storm)

1047 Šustr, Vladimír. Rudí a Bílí. Brno, Brněská Knihtiskárna, 1949, 150p. (O Kolonisaci Jižní Ameriky v 16. Stol.)

(The Red and the White Ones. [About Colonization of South America in the 16th Century])

1048 Višváder, František. Latinská Amerika - Nepokojný Kontinent. Bratislava, SNPL, 1963, 384p.

(Latin America - A Restless Continent)

1049 Vráz, Enrik S. Napříč Rovníkovou Amerikou. Prague, Jelínek, 1925, 421p.

(Across Equatorial America)

1050 Vráz, Enrik S. Za Poklady El Dorado, Napříč Rovníkovou Amerikou. Prague, Toužimský a Moravec, 1938, 867p.

(After the Treasure of El Dorado, Across Equatorial America)

1051   Za Dynamiku Rozvoje Latinské Ameriky. Prague, Vysoká Škola
        Ekonomická, 1964, 106p.
        (For Dynamics of Progress of Latin America)

ARGENTINA

1052   Baar, Oskar. Z mé Cesty do Argentiny. Třeboň, Nákladem
        Vlastním, 1911, 16p.
                        (From my Journey to Argentina. Published
        by the Author)

1053   Elstner, František A. Tango Argentino; Dobrodružství, Dlouhé
        36000 Kilometrů, Které Prožili,don Francisco a Dva Gringos
        v Semiargentionské. 3rd ed. Prague, J. Albert, 1947, 200p.
                        (Argentine Tango; Adventures Along
        36,000 Kilometers...)

1054   Flos, František. V Bažinách Argentinských, Prague, 1947.
                        (In the Bogs of Argentina)

1055   Forejt, Alan. Pampa Florida. Prague, Pražská Akciová Tiskárna,
        1943, 233p.
                        (Pampa Florida)

1056   Frič, Alberto V. Strýček Indián. Dobrodružství Lovce v Gran
        Chacu. Prague, SNDK, 1956, 177p.
                        (Uncle Indian: An Adventure of a Hunter in Gran
        Chaco)

1057   Hanzelka, Jiří, & Miroslav Zikmund. Tam za Řekouje Argentina,
        Prague, SNPL, 1956, 384p.
                        (There Behind the River
        is Argentina)

315

BOLIVIA

1058 Južnič, Stane. _Bolivija._ Belgrade, Instituta Zame Dunarodnu
Politiku i Privredu, 1963, 176p.
(Bolivia)

BRAZIL

1059 Flos, František. _Vzducholodí do Srdce Brasilie._ Prague, 1929.
(Trip by Airship into the Heart of Brazil)

1060 Loukotka, Čestmír. _Do Brazilie za Indiány._ Prague, Lidová
Demokracie, 1962, 209p.
(Into Brazil Beyond the Indians)

CENTRAL AMERICA

1061 Bert, Zdeněk, & Arnost Tauber. _Pod Sopkami Střední Ameriky._
Prague, SNPL, 1959, 192p.
(Under Volcanoes of Central
America)

1062 Hanzelka, Jiří. _Mezi Dvěma Oceany._ 2d ed. Prague, Orbis,
1961, 351p.
(Between Two Oceans)

1063   Stingl, Miloslav. _Angatar: Indian z Chile._ Prague, SNDK, 1964, 56p.
(Angatar: the Indian from Chile)

1064   Veselý, Miloš. _Země Zadávená Anacondou; Dnešní Chile._ Prague,
Nakl. Politické Literatury, 1962, 108p.
(Country Reports- Anaconda; Today's Chile)

COLOMBIA

1065   Schecker, Frieda. _Šťastné Savany. Kolumbijské Cesty._ Prague,
Orbis, 1944, 237p.
(Happy Savannas: Trips in Colombia)

CUBA

1066   Bělič, Oldřich. O. Kubánské Literaturé. 1st ed. Prague,
Nakl. Politické Literatury, 1964, 247p.
(On Cuban Literature)

1067   Bukovčan, Ivan. Kuba Bez Brady. Bratislava, Slovenský
Spisovatel', 1963, 170p.
(Cuba without Beards)

1068   Bulletin Klubu Přatel Kuby. Prague, Nos. 1-3, 1962-1964-
(Bulletin of the Club of Friends of Cuba)

1069   Civrný, Lumir. Ostrov Mladé Svobody; Zapiský z Pobytuna
Kubě v Únoru 1961. 1st ed. Prague, Československý
Spisovatel', 1961, 125p.
                (Island of Young Freedom; Notes from a Visit
to Cuba in February, 1961)

1070   Hochman, Jiří. Patria ó Muerte; Reportáže z Kuby. 1st ed.
Prague, Státní Nakl. Politické Literatury, 1961, 73p.
          (Homeland or Death; Report on Cuba)

1071   Holler, Josef. S Fidelem Castrem Napříc Kubou. 1st ed.
Prague, Mladá Fronta, 1961, 111p.
          (Fidel Castro Redresses Cuba)

1072   Kubiček, Ivan. Loviti Žraloky Dovoleno; Sedmnáct Reportáž iz
Kuby. Prague, Nakl, Politické Literatury, 1964, 169p.
          (Hunting Sharks on a Holiday; 7th Report on Cuba)

1073   Landovský, Vladimír. <u>Kuba.</u> 1st ed. Prague, Státní Nakl.
        Politické Literatury, 1960, 111p.
                    (Cuba)

1074   Neuman, Stanislav. <u>Neexotická Kuba.</u> 1st ed. Prague,
        Státní Nakl. Politické Literatury, 1961, 187p.
                    (Unexotic Cuba)

1075   Polišenský, Josef V. <u>Stručné Dějiny Kuby; Předpoklady</u>
        <u>Kubánské Revoluce.</u> Prague, Nakl. Politické Literatury, 1964,
        221p.
                    (Traditional Instigators in Cuba; Assumptions
        of the Cuban Revolution)

1076   Prague. Mestská Lidová Knihovna. <u>Kuba-Territorio Libre de</u>
        <u>America; Ukázky z Poezie a Výbérová Bibliografie.</u> Prague,
        1961, 42p.
                    (Cuba-Free Territory
        of America: Excerpts from Poetry, and Selected Bibliography)

1077   Stingl, Miloslav. <u>Indiani Černoši a Vousaci (Antropologie</u>
        <u>Kuby).</u> Prague, 1968, 168p.
                    (The Indians, the Negroes and the Bearded
        ones: Anthropology of Cuba)

1078   Volaŕík, Josef. <u>Taková je Kuba.</u> 1st ed. Prague, Naše
        Vojsko, 1961, 165p.
                    (This is Cuba)

DOMINICAN REPUBLIC

1079   Fukatsch, Josef. <u>Trujilliáda.</u> 1st ed. Bratislava, Vydavatel'stvo Politickej Literatury, 1962, 139p.
(Trujillo Story)

ECUADOR

1080   Flos, František. <u>V Pralesích Ecuadoru,</u> Prague, 1941.
(In the Virgin Forests of Ecuador)

1081   Hanzelka, Jiří, & Miroslav Zikmund. <u>Cez Kordillery,</u>
Bratislava, SVPL, 1960, 338p.

(Across the Cordilleras)

1082   Hanzelka, Jiří, & Miroslav Zikmund. <u>Za Lovci Lebek.</u> Prague, Orbis, 1958, 266p.

(Behind Headhunters)

MEXICO

1083   Feýd, Norbert. <u>Mexiko Je v Americe</u>. Prague, Práce;
Vydavatelstvo Rotl, 1952, 173p.
(Mexico Exists in America)

1084   Kisch, Egon E. <u>Objevy v Mexiku</u>. 1st ed. Prague, Svoboda,
1947, 228p.
(Discovery in Mexico)

1085   Stingl, Miloslav. <u>Indiánský Běžěc-Sport, a Hry ve Starém a
Novem Mexiku</u>. Prague, Olympia, 1968, 38p.
(The Indian Runner: the Sports and Games
in the Old and New Mexico)

1086   Stingl, Miloslav. <u>Za Poklady Mayských Měst: Architektura Mayů</u>.
Prague, Svoboda, 1968, 220p.
(After the Treasures of the Mayan Cities:
the Architecture of the Mayans)

1087   Zeman, Kamil. <u>Dobyvatel</u>. 5th ed. Prague, Naše Vojsko, 1964,
489p.
(The Conqueror)

NICARAGUA

1088   Stingl, Miloslav. <u>Nicaragua.</u> Prague, Strojopis, 1952, 148p.
(Nicaragua)

PANAMA

1089   Galský, Desider. <u>Panamské Dobrodružstvi.</u> Prague, Nakl.
Politické Literatury, 1963, 150p.
(Panamanian Adventures)

PERU

1090   Kotal, V. <u>V Zemi Zlata a Utrpení.</u> Pelhřimov, 1930, 152p.
(In the Land of Gold and Suffering)

1091   Vráz, Enrik S. <u>O Zemi Zlata a Inku.</u> Prague, Toužimský
a Moravec, 1939, 374p.
(About the Land of Gold and Incas)

VENEZUELA

1092   Vesely, Miloš. <u>Cesty K Eldorádu; Dnešní Venezuela</u>. Prague,
        Státní Nakl. Politické Literatury, 1961, 122p.
        (Honor to El Dorado: Today's Venezuela)

II. Periodical Articles

LATIN AMERICA

1093   Adámek, Josef. "Hospodářsko-Politický Profil Latinské
Ameriky. Přehled Jednotlivých Zemí." Prague, Zahraniční
obchod (7: 5), 1953, pp. 223-227.
("The Economic - Political Profile of Latin
America: A Survey of the Individual Countries")

1094   Adžubej, A. "50.000km Latinskou Amerikou." Prague, Svět
sovětů (25: 14), 1962, p. 2.
("A 50,000 kilometer Long Journey Through Latin
America")

1095   Badura, B. "První Konference Skupiny pro Hutnickou Ameriku.
(Při Historickém Ústavu ČSAV)." Prague, Věstník ČSAV (72: 3),
1963, pp. 379-381.
("The First Conference of the Metallurgical Group of
America, at the Historical Institute of the Czechoslovak Academy
of Sciences")

1096   Badura, B. "První Konference Skupiny pro Latinskou Ameriku:
Při Historickém Ústavu ČSAV 15. Ledna 1963." Prague,
Český časopis historický (II: 3), 1963, pp. 411-412.
("The First Conference of the Group for Latin
America, Held by the Historical Institute of the Czechoslovak
Academy of Sciences on January 15, 1963")

1097   Barrera, Hernán. "Imperialistická Politika USA v Latinské
Americe." Prague, Otázky míru a socialismu (6: 10),
1963, pp. 78-79.
("Imperialist Politics of the USA in Latin
America")

1098   Barrera, Hernán. "Spiknutí Imperialistů a Solidarita Národů."
         Prague, Otázky míru a socialismu (6: 5), 1963, pp. 56-57.
                 ("The Conspiracy of Imperialists and
      Solidarity Among Nations")

1099   Bočkarjov, J. "Opět Vojenské Junty." Prague, Nová doba
         (21: 41), 1963, pp. 10-11.
              ("Again, Military Juntas")

1100   Bočkarjov, J. "Politické Ovzduší na Jih od Rio Grande." Prague,
         Nová doba (21: 52), 1963, pp. 13-15.
              ("Political Situation South of Rio Grande")

1101   "Bouřlivé Udalosti v Latinské Americe." Prague, Rudé právo,
         March 9, 1962, p. 2.
      ("Stormy Events in Latin America")

1102   Bradáč, Zdeněk. "Politika Velké Hole Již Neprojde." Prague,
         Rudé právo, October 31, 1962, p. 5.
              ("The Big Stick's Politics will not Succeed")

1103   Čapek, Abe. "Jorge Amado v Boji za Mír a Kulturu v Latinské
         Americe." (Zpráva o Stavu z Léta 1953). Prague, Literární
      noviny (2: 40), 1953, p. 8.
              ("Jorge Amado in Struggle for Peace and Culture
      in Latin America:" Report from Summer 1953)

1104   Čapek, Abe. "Národy Latinské Ameriky Bojují za Mír a
         Svobodu." Prague, Mír (5: 12), 1953, p. 232.
              ("Latin American Nations Fight for Peace and
      Freedom")

1105   Čapek, Abe. "Stín Dolaru nad Latinskou Amerikou. " (Reportáž z Cyklu: Tak Vypadá Americký Způsob Života). Prague, Svět v obrazech (9: 44), 1953, p. 14.
         ("Shadow of the Dollar Upon Latin America": A Report from the Series, This is the American Way of Life)

1106   Dankovičová, Inge. "Integrační Tendence v Latinské Americe. " Prague, Politická ekonomie (10: 10), 1962, pp. 905-910.
         ("Integrating Tendencies in Latin America")

1107   Drda, Jan. "Horká Půda. Z Jihoamerického Zápisníku. " (Oslavy k 50. Narozeninám Pabla Nerudy). Prague, Literární noviny (3: 38), 1954, pp. 1-7.
         ("The Hot Soil: From the Latin American Notebook") (Celebrations of the 50th Birthday Anniversary of Pablo Neruda)

1108   Elstner, F. A. "Besedujeme o Dalekých Cestách. " Prague, Svět motoru (8: 9-10), 1954, pp. 311-312.
         ("We Talk About Far-Away Trips")

1109   Fedullo, Mario. "Katolická Církev a Latinská Amerika. " Prague, Mezunárodní politika (6: 10), 1962, pp. 446-449.
         ("Catholic Church and Latin America")

1110   Fišer, Drago. "O Plánovaní v Latinské Americe. " Prague, Politická ekonomie (10: 8), 1962, pp. 722-725.
         ("Planning in Latin America")

1111   Gonionskij, S. "Koloniální Útlak Spojených Státu v Latinské Americe. " Prague, Nová doba (8), 1954, pp. 14-18.
         ("Colonial Oppression of the United States in Latin America")

1112   Gonionskij, S. "Wallstreetsky Žralok v Latinské Americe."
        (Recenze Knih Guatemal-Ského Politika Juan José Arévalo,
        'Fábula del Tiburón y las Sardinas'). Prague, Nová doba (11),
        1957, pp. 28-29.
                        ("The Shark of Wall Street in Latin America").
        (Review of the Book of the Guatemalan Politician, Juan José Arévalo,
        'The Fable of the Shark and the Sardines')

1113   Gvozdev, J. "Nebezpečný Eksém." (Vojenskó Zakladny USA v
        Latinsko-Amerických Zemích). Prague, Nová doba (18),
        1963, pp. 19-21.
                        ("Military Bases of the USA in Latin American
        Countries")

1114   Hampejs, Zdeněk. "Latinská Amerika o Juliu Fučíkovi."
        (Soubor Zprav o Ohlase Díla a Osobnosti J. Fučika v Literatuře
        Latinské Ameriky). Prague, Časopis pro moderní filologii (35: 4),
        1953, pp. 235-236.
                        ("Latin America About Julius Fučík").
        (Collection of Reports on Works and Personality of Julius Fučík
        Echoed in Latin American Literature)

1115   Hochman, Jiří. "Další Lekce pro Latinskou Ameriku." Prague,
        Rudé právo, March 23, 1963, p. 3.
                        ("A Further Lesson for Latin America")

1116   Hoffmeister, Adolf. "U Miliardářu." Prague, Československý
        výbor obráncu míru (10), 1963, pp. 76-77.
                        ("At a Visit of Multi-Millionaires")

1117   "Jednota Pracujícich Proti Snahám Reakce. Fronta Lidové
        Mobilizace." Prague, Rudé právo, October 16, 1963, p. 1.
        ("Union of Workers Against Efforts of Reactionaries: People's
        Mobilization Front")

1118   "Jihoameričkti Zemědělci Proti Monopolum. " Prague, Odborář
        (16: 8), 1963, pp. 381-383.
        ("South American Farmers Against Monopolies")

1119   Jiroudková, Kamila. "Beseda s Uruguayským Spisovatelem.
        Alfredo Graviňa o Kulturní Situaci v Zemích Latinské
        Ameriky. " Prague, Literární noviny (2: 43), 1953, p. 3.
                        ("A Chat with an Uruguayan Writer: Alfredo
        Graviňa Speaks About Situation of Culture in Latin American
        Countries")

1120   Kincl, Jiří. "Project Jihoamerického Pruplavu. Spojujícího
        Reky Orinoco, Negro, Madeira-Guaparé Nebo Tapajoz,
        Paraguay, Parná, La Plata. " Prague, Sborník československé
        společnosti zemepisné (62: 3), 1957, pp. 259-260.
                        ("Project of a South American Canal: To Connect
        the Rivers of Orinoco, Negro, Madeira-Guaparé or Tapajoz,
        Paraguay, Paraná, La Plata")

1121   Kubín, Miroslav. "Protikomunistický Teror v Latinské Americe. "
        Prague, Rudé právo, November 30, 1963, p. 5.
                        ("Anti-Communist Terror in Latin America")

1122   "Latinská Amerika Proti Wall Streetu. " Prague, Lidé a zeme
        (2: 6), 1963, p. 236.
        ("Latin America Against Wall Street")

1123   Ledesma, Luis. "Zotročující Vojenské Pakty USA se Zememi
        Latinské Ameriky. O Knize Dr. Marcose A. Hardyho 'Dvoustranné
        Pakty o Vojenské Pomoci'. Vydáne v Buenos Aires r. 1953. "
        Prague, Za trvalý mír (29), 1954, p. 4.
                        ("Enslaving Military Pacts of the USA with Latin
        American Countries: About the Book of Dr. Marcos A. Hardy,
        Bilateral Pacts Concerning Military Support, Published in Buenos
        Aires in 1953")

1124   "Lid Latinské Amerike Pevné na Strané Kuby." Prague, Rudé
právo, March 23, 1963, p. 6.
("People of Latin America Firmly on Cuban Side")

1125   "Lid Latinské Ameriky v Boji." Prague, Rudé právo, March 4,
1962, p. 5.
("People of Latin America in Struggle")

1126   Lima, Pedro Motta. "Agrární Problém Latinské Ameriky."
Prague, Mezunárodní politika (6: 10), 1962, pp. 443-445.
("Agrarian Problem of Latin America")

1127   Listov, V. "Diplomaté s Hákovým Křížem. Pronikání NSR do
Zemí Latinské Ameriky." Prague, Nová doba (31), 1963,
pp. 17-18.
        ("Swastika's Diplomats: NSR Penetration into
Latin American Countries")

1128   Lohr, George. "Od Rio Grande po Tierra del Fuego. O
Pronikání Kapitálu USA do Jižní Ameriky." Prague, Rovnost,
June 6, 1957-
        ("From the River Rio Grande up to the Tierra
del Fuego: Penetration of US Capital into South America")

1129   M. "Úpadek Zemědělství v Zemích Latinské Ameriky. Z Časopisu
Pravda." Prague, Za socialistické zemědělství (3: 6), 1953,
pp. 741-743.
        ("Decline of Agriculture in Latin American Countries: From
the Newspaper Pravda")

1130   Menezes, Lauro. "Boj za Mír v Latinské Americe." Prague,
Rudé právo, September 30, 1953-
        ("Struggle for Peace in Latin America")

1131   Mocko, Zdenko. "Hospodárske Pomery Krajín Latinskej
            Ameriky. " Prague, Dejepis a zemepis v škole (5: 2), 1962-
        1963, pp. 46-51.
                        ("Economic Situation of Latin American
        Countries")

1132   Mrzeha, Karel. "Omyl Miltona Eisenhowera. Snahy Latinské
            Ameriky o Znárodnění Cizích Akciových Společností a Postoj
        USA. " Prague, Literární noviny (3: 5), 1954, p. 8.
                        ("Mistake of Milton Eisenhower: Efforts of
        Latin America to Nationalize the Foreign Joint-Stock Companies,
        and Attitude of the USA")

1133   Nibaut, G. "Eisenhower a Jižní Amerika - Historie Rostoucích
            Rozporu. Překlad z Revue 'Defence de la Paix'. " Prague,
        Mír (5: 6), 1953, pp. 110-111.
                        ("Eisenhower and South America, A History of
        Growing Discords: Translation from the Periodical, 'Défence
        de la Paix'")

1134   "Obchodní Válka v Latinské Americe. Národohospodářské
            Poznámky. " Prague, Nová doba (23), 1953, pp. 28-29.
        ("Trade War in Latin America: Political Economy Notes")

1135   Obst, František. "Národy Latinské Ameriky v Boji za Mír,
            Svobodu a Národní Nezávislost. " Prague, Nová svoboda,
        September 18, 1954-
                        ("Latin American Nations in Struggle for
        Peace, Freedom, and National Independence")

1136   Ondráček, Mojmír. "Program 'Spojenectví za Pokrok' Jako
            Výraz Nové Etapy Americké Pomoci Zemím Latinské
        Ameriky. " Prague, Finance a úvěr (4), 1963, pp. 289-294.
        ("Alliance for Progress Program as Expression of a New
        Stage of American Help to Latin American Countries")

1137   Orlov, Radim. "Latinská Amerika a Druhá Světová Válka."
Prague, Mezinárodní politika (7: 5), 1963, pp. 236-237.
("Latin America and World War II")

1138   "Ostrá Kritika Politiky USA v Latinské Americe." Prague,
Rudé právo, September 15, 1963, p. 3.
("Sharp Critique of US Politics in Latin America")

1139   Pérez, Víctor. "Lid Latinské Ameriky je na Stráži Před
Machinacemi Imperialistu." Prague, Rudé právo, December
1, 1961, p. 5.
("People in Latin America are on Guard
Against Trickery of Imperialists")

1140   Pérez, Víctor. "Špatný Lék na Nemoci Latinské Ameriky.
Politický a Hospodářský Nátlak USA." Prague, Rudé
právo, September 3, 1962, p. 3.
("Wrong Medicine for Latin American
Illness: Political and Economic Pressure of the USA")

1141   Píriz, Hernán. "Latinská Amerika, 'Nejkritičtější Oblast'–
Spojenectví pro Pokrok." Prague, Rudé právo, November
2, 1963, p. 5.
("Latin America, 'The Most Critical Area':
Alliance for Progress")

1142   Píriz, Hernán. "Latinská Amerika Odmítá Plány Amerických
Imperialistu. Zpráva Waynea Morscho a Bourkea Hickenloopera
Senátní Komisi pro Zahranicní Styky." Prague, Rudé právo,
March 28, 1962, p. 5.
("Latin America Refuses Plans of American
Imperialists: Report of Wayne Morse and Bourke Hickenlooper
to the Senate Committee on Foreign Relations")

1143   Píriz, Hernán. "Problém Jihoamerického Rolnictva Nevyřeší
        Pseudoreformy. " Prague, Rudé právo, January 30, 1963, p. 3.
                ("Problem of South American Farmers will
        not be Solved by Pseudo-Reforms")

1144   Píriz, Hernán. "Vojenské Aspekty 'Pomoci USA'. Ohlas v
        Latinské Americe. " Prague, Rudé právo, July 18, 1963, p. 3.
                ("Military Aspects of 'United States Help':
        Echo in Latin America")

1145   Polišenský, Josef. "Novější Práce k Dějinám Latinské
        Ameriky. " Prague, Český časopis historický (II: 1),
        1963, pp. 81-85.
                ("Recent Contributions to the History of
        Latin America")

1146   "Přátelé a Nepřátelé Latinské Ameriky. Poselství N. S. Chruščova. "
        Prague, Nová doba (14), 1963, pp. 1-2.
        ("Friends and Enemies of Latin America: Message of N. S.
        Khrushschev")

1147   Pušová, Jitka. "Hudební Sezóna v Jižní Americe. " Prague,
        Hudební rozhledy (10), 1957, pp. 417-418.
                ("Musical Season in South America")

1148   "Rozhovor s Jihoamerickými Spisovateli. Fernando Santiván,
        Jorge Zalamea a Jorge Enrique Adoun. " Prague, Československsnký
        voják (2: 2), 1953, p. 11.
        ("Interview with South American Writers: Fernando Santiván,
        Jorge Zalamea, and Jorge Enrique Adoun")

1149   Schulz, Arnošt. "Filmy z Afriky a Jižní Ameriky. " Prague,
        Svět práce (3: 2), 1953, p. 8.
                ("Films from Africa and South America")

1150   "Sedmdesát Milionu Dosp̌elých v Latinské Americe Neumí Číst Ani Psát. 3. Mezi-Americká Konference Ministru Školství v Bogotě. " Prague, Rudé právo, August 7, 1963, p. 5. ("Seventy Million Adults in Latin America do not Know how to Read and Write: The Third Pan-American Conference of Ministers of Education in Bogotá")

1151   Šelder, Alois. "Mezi Učiteli Latinské Ameriky. " Prague, Učitelské noviny (13: 31), 1963, pp. 4-5. ("Among Teachers of Latin America")

1152   Settner, V. "Neúspěch Amerických Plánu v Latinské Americe na 10. Konferenci Pan-Americké Unie v Caracásu. " Prague, Rudé právo, March 26, 1954- ("Failure of American Plans in Latin America at the Tenth Pan-American Conference in Caracas")

1153   Síp, Emil. "Hrozí Okleštení Práv Latinskoamerického Lidu. " Prague, Rudé právo, March 18, 1963, p. 3. ("Curtailment of Rights Threatens the Latin American People")

1154   Síp, Emil. "Kto je Odpovědný za Vojenské Puče v Latinské Americe?" Prague, Rudé právo, October 10, 1963, p. 3. ("Who is Responsible for Military Overthrows in Latin America?")

1155   Síp, Emil. "Latinská Amerika Směruje k Socialismu a Neutralitě. " Prague, Rudé právo, September 27, 1962, p. 5. ("Latin America Goes Towards Socialism and Neutrality")

1156   "Současník (pseud.) "Neklidný Kontinent. Protikomunistický Teror v Latinské Americe. " Prague, Nová doba (47), 1963, pp. 1-3. ("Restless Continent: Anti-Communist Terror in Latin America")

1157   Staněk, Pavel. "Aliance Proti Pokroku." Prague, Mezunárodní
        politika (6: 3), 1962, pp. 109-113.
                    ("Alliance Against Progress")

1158   Staněk, Pavel. "Banánová Chobotnice. Fakta o Monopolech.
        United Fruit Company." Prague, Mezunárodní politika (7: 3),
        1963, pp. 119-121.
                    ("Bananas in the Trunk of an Elephant. Facts
        About Monopoly: United Fruit Company")

1159   Štrafelda, Miroslav. "Spiknutí 'Goril'. Ultrareakční
        Fašismus Financovaný USA." Prague, Rudé právo, March 26,
        1963, p. 3.
                    ("Conspiracy of 'Gorillas': Ultra-
        Reactionary Fascism Financed by the United States of America")

1160   Štrafelda, Miroslav. "Zase Převraty v Latinské Americe."
        Prague, Rudé právo, October 29, 1963, p. 3.
                    ("New Coup d'États in Latin America")

1161   Šulgovskij, A. "Nová Taktika Spojených Státu v Latinské Americe."
        Prague, Mezunárodní politika (7: 8), 1963, pp. 337-342.
                    ("New Tactics of the United States of America
        in Latin America")

1162   Švamberk, Jaromír. "Kolonie, o Níž Washington Nechce Vědět."
        Prague, Mladá fronta, November 16, 1963, p. 2.
                    ("A Colony About which Washington Does
        not Want to Hear")

1163   Svoboda, Bohumil E. "Mírové Hnutí v Latinské Americe."
        Prague, Československý výbor obráncu míru (10: 3),
        1963, pp. 41-42.
                    ("Peace Movement in Latin America")

1164   Uhlíř, Kamil. "Boj o Kladného Hrdinu v Současném Latinsko-
americkém Románu. Několik Poznámek k Problematice
Socialistického Realizmu v Současné Pokrokové Próze Latinské
Ameriky. " Prague, Časopis pro Moderní Filologii (35: 4),
1953, pp. 193-208.
                ("Struggle for a Positive Hero in the Contemporary
Latin American Novel. Some Notes on the Problem of Social
Realism in the Contemporary Progressive Prose of Latin America")

1165   "V Latinskoamerických Zemích Sílí Odpor Proti Plánu 'Spojenectví
pro Pokrok'. " Prague, Rudé právo, March 2, 1962, p. 3.
("Resistance Against 'Alliance for Progress' Program Gains
Momentum in Latin American Countries")

1166   Vokrouhlický, Zbyněk. "Latinská Amerika a Monopoly USA. "
Prague, Dvacáté Století, 1962, pp. 269-280.
                ("Latin America and US Monopoly")

1167   Vorobjov, S. "Národy Latinské Ameriky Zesilují Boj za Mír. "
Prague, Sovětské informační zprávy (8: 29), 1953, p. 14.
                ("Nations of Latin America Intensify Struggle for
Peace")

1168   Votrubec, Ctibor. "O Vrázově Cestě Jizní Amerikou. "
Prague, Lidé a země (3: 9), 1954, pp. 416-420.
                ("Vráz's Journey Through South America")

1169   Vyškovský, Jan. "Partyzánská Akce v Latinské Americe. "
Prague, Mezinárodní politika (7: 6), 1963, pp. 268-270.
                ("Partisan Activity in Latin America")

1170   Wičaz, J. "Otázka Pudy - Nejožehavejsí Problém Latinské
Ameriky. " Prague, Zemědělské noviny, August 11, 1954-
                ("Question of the Land-The Most Pressing Problem
in Latin America")

1171   Winter, Kamil. "Spojenectví pro Pokrok. Vojenské Puče v
        Latinskoamerických Zemích." Prague, <u>Svoboda,</u> October
        12, 1963, p. 2.
                  ("Alliance for Progress: Military Coup d'États
in Latin American Countries")

1172   Žívný, Š. "Amerika Američanum." Prague, <u>Hospodářské</u>
        <u>noviny</u> (7: 11), 1963, p. 10.
          ("America for the Americans")

ARGENTINA

1173   "Argentina Před Vážným Rozhodnutím. " Prague, Rudé právo
(9), 1963, p. 4.
("Argentina is Facing a Serious Decision")

1174   "Argentina; Vláda Nehodlá Ustoupit od Zrušení Naftových Výhod.
Též Hnutí Proti Represivním Zákonum. " Prague, Rudé
právo (9), 1963, p. 3.
("Argentina: The Government Does not Intend to Rescind
Annulment of Oil Concession. Also: Movement Against Oppressive
Laws")

1175   Goldman, Luis. "Vřeni v Argentine. " Prague, Rudé práve, July
3, 1963, p. 5.
("Something Boiling in Argentina")

1176   Kašík, Václav. "Argentinské Rozcestí. " Prague, Mezinárodní politika
(7: 10), 1963, pp. 465-467.
("The Crossroads of Argentina")

1177   Kubín, Miroslav. "Anonymní Kandidát v Argentických Volbách. "
Prague, Rudé právo, July 12, 1963, p. 3.
("An Anonymous Candidate in Argentine
Elections")

1178   Kubín, Miroslav. "Strach z Jednoty Lidu v Argentině. Perzekuce
Komunistu a Peronistu. " Prague, Rudé právo, June 3, 1963, p. 3.
("Fear of Unification of People in Argentina:
Persecution of Communists and Peronists")

1179   Pérez, Víctor. "Argentina s Novou Vládní Soustavou. " Prague,
        Rudé právo, October 10, 1963, p. 3.
                ("Argentina with a New Governmental Structure")

1180   Pérez, Víctor. "Boj Lidových Sil v Argentině. Vítezství Nad
        t. zv. Gorilisty. " Prague, Rudé právo, October 11, 1962, p. 5.
                ("Struggle of People's Forces in Argentina:
        Victory Over So-Called Black Gorillas")

1181   Pérez, Víctor. "O Koho se Opře Illíava Vláda. " Prague,
        Rudé právo, October 26, 1963, p. 3.
                ("From Whom Does the Government of Illía
        Get Support? ")

1182   "První Výsledky Voleb v Argentině. " Prague, Rudé pravo, July
        9, 1963, p. 4.
        ("First Electoral Results in Argentina")

1183   "Rozhodnutí Argentinské Vlády o Zrušení Naftových Dohod
        Uvítáno Lidem. " Prague, Rudé právo, November 19, 1963,
        p. 3.
        ("Decision of the Government in Argentina Concerning Cancellation
        of Oil Agreements Welcomed by People")

1184   Sedý, Milan. "Armáda - Proti Komu? Rozpravy o Argentinské
        Armádě. " Prague, Obrana lidu (13: 22), 1963, p. 3.
                ("An Army - Against Whom? Discussions About
        Argentina's Army")

1185   Simon, Kamil. "Argentinské Intermezzo. " Prague, Mladá
        fronta, June 16, 1963, p. 4.
                ("Argentine Interlude")

BOLIVIA

1186   Pleskotová, Eva. "Indiáni Žijí v Bolívii." Prague, Mladá
fronta, November 3, 1963, p. 3.
           ("Indians Live in Bolivia")

BRAZIL

1187   Bouček, Jaroslav. "Latinská Amerika Před Bouří. V Kraji
Cangaceiru. " Prague, Rudé právo (May 25, 1963, p. 3;
May 27, 1963, p. 3; June 3, 1963, p. 3; June 17, 1963, p. 3;
June 24, 1963, p. 3; July 1, 1963, p. 3; July 15, 1963, p. 7;
July 29, 1963, p. 3).
                ("Latin America is Facing a Storm: In
the Land of Cangaceiros")

1188   "Brazílie Odmítá Násilí v Mezinárodní Politice. " (Obsah
Poselství J. Goularda Kongresu). Prague, Rudé právo,
March 18, 1963, p. 3.
("Brazil Refuses Force as Tool in International Politics":
The Summary of the Message to the Congress of President
João Goulart)

1189   "Brazilská Komunistická Strana Žádá: Energicky Bojovat
Proti Reaksi. " Prague, Rudé právo, October 9, 1963,
p. 6.
("Brazilian Communist Party Demands: Energetic Fight
Against Reaction")

1190   "Brazilský President Jmenoval Další Ministry. " Prague,
Rudé právo, June 19, 1963, p. 5.
("Brazilian President Appointed Additional Ministers")

1191   "Brazilští Pracující Požadují Sociální Reformy. " Prague,
Rudé právo, May 26, 1963, p. 5.
("Brazilian Workers Demand Social Reforms")

1192   "Další Změny v Brazilské Vládě." Prague, Rudé právo, June
        21, 1963, p. 4.
        ("Further Changes in the Brazilian Government")

1193   Dvořák, Jiří. "Brazílie Dneška." Prague, Pravda, October 13,
        1963, p. 2.
        ("Brazil of Today")

1194   Goulart, João. "Západní Velmoci Mají Vinu na Vážnó Hospodářské
        Situaci v Brazilii." Prague, Rudé právo, October 23, 1963,
        p. 1.
                    ("Western Powers are Responsible for the
        Serious Economic Situation in Brazil")

1195   Janáček, Vít. "Obnovení Presidentského Systému v Brazílii."
        Prague, Mezunárodní Politika (7: 3), 1963, pp. 124-125.
                    ("Renewal of the Presidential System in Brazil")

1196   Kamynin, L. "Nové Perspektívy Brazílie." Prague, Nová
        doba (20: 10), 1963, pp. 19-20.
                    ("New Perspectives of Brazil")

1197   "Kritický Postoj Brazílie k Hospodářské Politice USA v
        Latinské Americe." Prague, Rudé právo, November 16,
        1963, p. 5.
        ("Critical Position of Brazil Towards Economic Policies
        of the USA in Latin America")

1198   Lima, Pedro Motta. "Brazílie. Též Vnitřní Situace." Prague,
        Mezunárodní politika (6: 12), 1962, pp. 543-545.
                    ("Brazil: Internal Situation")

1199   "Před Reorganizací Vlády v Brazílii." Prague, Rudé právo,
        June 14, 1963, p. 4.
        ("Reorganization of the Government in Brazil Imminent")

341

1200   "President Goulart Varuje Reakci. "   Prague, <u>Rudé právo,</u>
        October 4, 1963, p. 3.
        ("President Goulart Gives Warning to Reactionaries")

1201   "Protiimperialistické Hnutí v Brazílii Sílí. "   Prague, <u>Rudé právo,</u>
        February 26, 1963, p. 5.
        ("Anti-Imperialistic Movement in Brazil Grows")

1202   Šimon, Kamil. "Kříže na Rio de Janeirem. "   Prague, <u>Mladý</u>
        <u>svět</u> (5: 10), 1963, p. 3.
               ("The Crosses over Rio de Janeiro")

1203   Štrafelda, Miroslav. "Brazilský Problem Č. I. Zemědělská Reforma.
        Prague, <u>Rudé právo,</u> May 30, 1963, p. 5.
                    ("Brazilian Problem No. 1: The Agrarian
        Reform")

1204   "Urputný Boj Brazilských Pracujících. Generální Stávka, 30. 10.
        v Sao Paolu. "   Prague, <u>Rudé právo,</u> November 1, 1963, p. 1.
        ("Headstrong Struggle of Brazilian Workers: General Strike of
        October 30 in São Paulo")

1205   "USA Vydírají Brazílii. "   Prague, <u>Rudé právo,</u> March 20,
        1963, p. 3.
        ("The United States Extorts Brazil")

1206   "Vměšování USA do Brazilských Záležitostí. "   Prague, <u>Rudé</u>
        <u>právo,</u> March 19, 1963, p. 4.
        ("Interference of the United States in Brazilian Affairs")

1207   Volařík, Josef. "Brazílie. Viva Julião. Bojovník za Práva
        Brazilských Rolníku a Bezzemku. "   Prague, <u>Mladý svět,</u>
        (5: 12), 1963, p. 4.
                ("Brazil, Viva Julião: Warrior for the
        Rights of Brazilian Farmers and the Landless")

1208   Zeman, Stanislav. "Indiáni Chaca. "   Prague, Lidé a země
         (3: 10), 1954, pp. 452-456.
                    ("Chaco Indians")

CENTRAL AMERICA

1209   Kašík, Václav. "Banánové Republiky ve Stínu Dolarů a Diktatorů. "
         Prague, Svoboda, March 19, 1963, p. 2.
                    ("Banana Republics in the Shadow of Dollars and
      Dictators")

CHILE

1210   Cademártori, José. "Chile a Latinsko-Americké Sdružení
Volného Obchodu." Prague, Otázky míru a socialismu
(6: 6), 1963, pp. 35-41.
         ("Chile and the Latin American Free
Trade Association")

1211   Kruglyj, I. "U Chilských Horníku." Prague, Nová doba (19),
1963, pp. 26-28.
         ("A Visit to the Chilean Miners")

1212   Orlov, Radim. "Perspektívy v Chile. Vzrust Moci Levicových
Sil." Prague, Mezunárodní politika (7: 10), 1963, pp. 464-465.
         ("Perspectives in Chile: Growth of Leftist
Forces")

1213   Stanek, Pavel. "Chile. Hospodářství a Politika. Přehled."
Prague, Mezunárodní politika (6: 10), 1962, pp. 473-476.
         ("Chile. Economy and Politics: Survey")

COSTA RICA

1214   Noskov, G. "Jankeeové v Kostarice." Prague, Nová doba
(20: 12), 1963, pp. 12-13.
         ("Yankees in Costa Rica")

1215   "Reakce Připravuje Puč v Kostarice." Prague, Rudé právo,
October 13, 1963, p. 5.
("Reactionaries Prepare Coup d'État in Costa Rica")

CUBA

1216   Domkář, Zdeněk. "Revoluční Kubě Solidarita Činú." Prague,
Mladá fronta, April 21, 1963, p. 5.
("Solidarity of Deeds in Rebelling Cuba")

1217   Dymov, V., & G. Ušakov. "Pravda o Invazi Na Playa Girón."
Prague, Nová doba (20: 17), 1963, pp. 23-26.
("Truth About Invasion at Playa Girón")

1218   Gonzaga de Oliveira Leite, Luis. "Latinsko-Americký Lid na
Obranu Kuby." Prague, Práce, March 28, 1963, p. 2.
("Latin American People
for Defense of Cuba")

1219   Hochman, Jiří. "Kuba - Příklad, Symbol, Zkušenost." Prague,
Rudé právo, April 19, 1963, p. 5.
("Cuba - An Example, Symbol, Experience")

1220   Ignatjev, Oleg. "Bráaní Ostrov Svobody." Prague, Nová doba,
1963, pp. 11-12.
("Defense of the Island's Freedom")

1221   "Kongres Solidarity s Kubou Zahajuje." Prague, Rudé právo,
March 29, 1963, p. 5.
("The Congress of Solidarity with Cuba Opens")

1222   "Kubánsky Lid Má Zájem na Zachovaní Míru. Obsah Projevu
F. Castra na I. Sjezdu Federace Kubánských Žen v Havane."
Prague, Rudé právo, October 3, 1963, p. 6:
("Cuban People Wants to Preserve Peace: Summary of the
Speech of F. Castro on the First Convention of the Federation
of Cuban Women in Havana")

1223   Martín, Luis M. "Jdeme Sklízet Kávu. Mládež Kubánská. "
         Prague, <u>Mladá fronta,</u> October 20, 1962, p. 2.
                        ("We Are Going to Harvest Coffee: Cuban Youth")

1224   Mašek, Jaromír. "Tak Dýchá Revoluce. Výstavba Socialismu. "
         Prague, <u>Svobodné slovo,</u> October 18, 1962, p. 2.
                     ("Revolution Breathes this Way: Building of
      Socialism")

1225   "Na Straně Kuby Stojí Všechen Pokrokový Lid, Přípravy
         Latinskoamerického Kongresu Solidarity. ČTK. " Prague,
         <u>Rudé právo,</u> March 27, 1963, p. 4.

      ("On the Cuban Side Stand all Progressive People: Preparations for
      Latin American Solidarity Congress")

1226   "Playa Girón. " Prague, <u>Nová doba</u> (16), 1963, p. 4.
      ("Playa Girón")

1227   Plojhar, Josef. "Solidarita s Revoluční Kubou. " Prague,
         <u>Lidová demokracie,</u> March 31, 1963, p. 1.
                  ("Solidarity with Revolutionary Cuba")

1228   Štrafelda, Miroslav. "Kuba Není Sama. " Prague, <u>Práce,</u>
         May 1, 1963, p. 3.
                     ("Cuba is not Alone")

DOMINICAN REPUBLIC

1229   Kašík, Václav. "Napětí na Hispaniole. Politika Presidenta H. Duvalier." Prague, Mezunárodní politika (7: 11), 1963, pp. 514-515.

                ("Tension at Hispaniola: Politics of President H. Duvalier")

1230   Nikolajev, N. "Omyl Presidenta Boscha. Vojenský Převrat v Dominikánské Republice." Prague, Nová doba (21: 43), 1963, pp. 20-21.

                ("Mistake of President Bosch. Military Coup D'Etat in the Dominican Republic")

ECUADOR

1231   Brinke, Josef. "Ecuador." Prague, Lidé a země (3),
1963, pp. 103-107.
("Ecuador")

1232   Gvozdev, J. "V Ústí Řeky Guayasu." Prague, Nová doba (11),
1963, pp. 25-26.
("In the Delta of the Guayasu River")

1233   Hernández, Rubén. "Tragédie Ecuadoru." (Vláda Vojenské
Junty). Prague, Nová doba (46), 1963, p. 17.
("Tragedy of Ecuador: Government of the
Military Junta")

1234   Lorenzo, Ventura. "Zločiny 'Obráncu Demokrace' v Ecuadoru."
Prague, Otázky míru a socialismu (11), 1963, pp. 82-83.
("Crimes of 'Defenders of Democracy' in
Ecuador")

1235   Píriz, Hernán. "Ecuador Pod Vládou 'Goril'." Prague,
Rudé právo, October 6, 1963, p. 5.
("Ecuador Under Government of 'Gorillas'")

1236   "Pronasledování Pokrokových Sil v Ecuadoru Podle Plánu FBI."
Prague, Rudé právo, June 24, 1963, p. 3.
("Persecution of Progressive Forces in Ecuador According to
Plans of FBI")

GUATEMALA

1237   Galich, Manuel. "I v Guatemale Existuje Opět Mírové Hnutí."
    Prague, Československý výbor obráncu míru (10: 3), 1963,
    p. 42.
                     ("The Peace Movement Exists Again in
Guatemala")

1238   Tzul, C. "Síla Bratrské Solidarity. Propuštění Guatemalských
    Vlastencu z Vězení pod Tlakem Solidarity." Prague, Otázky
míry a socialismu (8: 10), 1963, p. 95.
                  ("Strength of Brotherly Solidarity. The Guatemalan
Patriots Released from the Prison due to the Pressure of
Solidarity")

GUYANA

1239   Síp, Emil. "Pozadí Spiknutí Proti Jaganově Vládě." Prague,
    Rudé právo, May 29, 1963, p. 3.
                  ("Background of the Plot Against Jagan's Government")

1240   Kašik, Václav. "Haiti - Ráj a Peklo. " Prague, Kvety (13: 22), 1963, p. 9.

                    ("Haiti: Paradise and Hell")

1241   "Námorní a Letecké Mise USA má Opustit Haiti. Obsah Tiskové Konference 15. 5 v Port -au-Prince. " Prague, Rudé právo, May 17, 1963, p. 6.
("Naval and Aeronautical Missions of the USA to Leave Haiti: Summary of a Press Conference Held on May 15 in Port-au-Prince")

1242   "Napětí Mezi Haiti a Dominikánskou Republikou. " Prague, Rudé právo, May 1, 1963, p. 8.
("Tension Between Haiti and Dominican Republic")

1243   Šeda, Josef. "Haiti. " Prague, Svět v obrazech (19: 22), 1963, p. 9.

                    ("Haiti")

1244   Síp, Emil. "Přibližuje se Konec Dalšího Diktátora, Haiti. " Prague, Rudé právo, May 3, 1963, p. 3.

                    ("The End of the Other Dictator is Imminent: Haiti")

1245   "Zostření Napětí Mezi Haiti a Dominikánskou Republikou. " Prague, Rudé právo, May 7, 1963, p. 6.
("Aggravation of Strain Between Haiti and Dominican Republic")

HONDURAS

1246   "Vojenský Puč v Hondurasu. " Prague, <u>Rudé právo,</u> October
4, 1963, p. 4.
("Military Coup d'État in Honduras")

JAMAICA

1247   Bára, František. "Jamajka. " (Hospodářský Přehled). Prague,
<u>Zahraniční obchod</u> (10), 1962, pp. 17-20.
("Jamaica": An Economic Survey ")

MEXICO

1248   Aragón, Eliseo. "Zahraniční Politika Mexika." Prague, Nová doba (20: 20), 1963, pp. 20-22.
("Foreign Policy of Mexico")

1249   Pavlenko, A. "Mezi Mexickými Dělníky." Prague, Nová doba (46), 1963, pp. 22-24.
("Among Mexican Workers")

NICARAGUA

1250   "Nicaragua - Základna Agrese Proti Kubě." Prague, Rudé právo, July 25, 1963, p. 5.
("Nicaragua: Base of Aggression Against Cuba")

1251   Šulc, Ota. "Nicaragua." Prague, Mladá fronta, March 21, 1963, p. 4.
("Nicaragua")

PERU

1252   Bes (pseud.)   "Peru: Je to Spiknutí? "   Prague, <u>Mladý svět</u> (5: 12), 1963, pp. 4-5.
      ("Peru: Is this a Conspiracy?")

1253   Gómez, Manuel.   "Politická Situace v Peru. "   Prague, <u>Nová doba</u> (21: 44), 1963, pp. 18-19.
      ("Political Situation in Peru")

1254   Stanek, Pavel.   "Republika Peru. "   Prague, <u>Mezunárodní politika</u> (6: 10), 1962, p. 452.
      ("Republic of Peru")

1255   Sumar, J.   "Na Obranu Peruánských Vlastencu. "   Prague, <u>Otázky míru a socialismu</u> (6: 3), 1963, p. 92.
      ("For Defense of Peruvian Patriots")

1256   Trnka, Jan.   "Peru 1963.   Politická Situace, Komentář. "   Prague, <u>Mezunárodní politika</u> (7: 5), 1963, 219-220.
               ("Peru in the Year of 1963:   Political Situation, a Commentary")

VENEZUELA

1257   Bouček, Jaroslav. "Venezuelská Varianta Zapálení Řísskeho Sněmu. " (Betancourtův Terror Proti Opozici). Prague, Rudé právo, October 8, 1963, p. 3.
("Venezuelan Variance of Burning Reichstag": The Terror of Betancourt Against Opposition)

1258   "Devět v Anzoategui. " (Rozhovor s Mladými Venezuelskými Revolucionáŕi, Kteří Unesli Lod Anzoategui). Prague, Svět v obrazech (19: 24), 1963, p. 9.
("The Nine in the Anzoategui": An Interview with the Young Venezuelan Revolutionaries who Carried away the Ship Anzoategui)

1259   Faria, Jesús. "Pravda o 'Nové' Pracovní Smlouvě Venezuelských Naftových Dělníku. " Prague, Otázky míru a socialismu (6: 11), 1963, pp. 41-44.
("Truth About a 'New' Labor Contract of Venezuelan Oil Workers")

1260   Mancera, E. "Co se Děje ve Venezuele? " Prague, Otázky míru a socialismu (6), 1963, pp. 55-58.
("What is Happening in Venezuela? ")

1261   "Protilidové Represálie ve Venezuele. " Prague, Rudé právo, November 20, 1963, p. 4.
("Retaliations Against People in Venezuela")

1262   Siblin, P. "Proč Jel Betancourt do Spojených Státu. " Prague, Nová doba (11), 1963, pp. 27-29.
("Why Betancourt Went to the United States")

1263   Šiblin, P. "Vnitropolitický Boj ve Venezuele." Prague, Nová doba (47), 1963, pp. 18-19.
("Internal Political Struggle in Venezuela")

1264   "Vlna Teroru vo Venezuele." Prague, Rudé právo, October 22, 1963, p. 1.
("Wave of Terror in Venezuela")

1265   Vorobjov, S. "Porázka v Caracasu. Neúspěchy Politiky USA v Latinské Americe." Prague, Nová doba (14), 1954, p. 7-12.
("Defeat in Caracas: Failure of U.S. Policy in Latin America")

1266   "Za Nastolení Demokratického Režimu ve Venezuele." Prague, Rudé právo, November 20, 1963, p. 6.
("For Installation of a Democratic Regime in Venezuela")

FINLAND

While no social science courses on Latin America per se
are offered in the universities of Finland, one may study
Spanish and Portuguese language and literature as a
specialty within the broad field of Romance philology.
There are two organizations in Finland concerned with
Latin America: the Ibero-American Association of Finland
(founded in Helsinki in 1964), and the Ibero-American
Institute of Finland, located at Oksasenkatu 7 A 6, Helsinki
10. Founded in 1963, the Ibero-American Institute of
Finland acts as an information center for all fields and areas
of activity with respect to Spain, Portugal and Latin America.

In the United States of America it is not generally realized that
the Swedish language is utilized in Finland (in addition to the
Finnish language), to a great extent. Not only are many books
published in Finland in Swedish, but in addition, periodicals
of scholarly as well as general interest are published throughout
the country. Hence some entries to be found in this section
for Finland have been published in Swedish.

The Finnish Academy of Sciences, located in Helsinki, publishes
various series, including its Annals, Commentationes Humanarum
Litterarum, a Yearbook, as well as its proceedings (Acta).
The fact that many of its publications are issued in languages
other than Finnish will explain the inclusion of a comparatively
small amount of the total of the items (presented in this section)
in English.

In this section the English translation of the title of each
bibliographic item is to be found directly under the title in
the original language, and immediately following the entire
bibliographic description.

———

Aunque no se ofrecen asignaturas en las ciencias sociales sobre Latinoamérica en las universidades finlandesas, es posible estudiar español y portugués, así como las letras de las mismas lenguas, como especialidad del campo de filología romance.

En Finlanda hay dos organizaciones con intereses latinoamericanos: la Asociación Iberoamericana de Finlandia (establecida en Helsinki en 1964), y el Instituto Iberoamericano de Finlandia, situada en la calle de Oksasenkatu 7 A 6, en Helsinki.

Fundada en 1963, el Instituto Iberoamericano de Finlanda es centro de información para cada campo y actividad en Finlanda con respecto a España, Portugal y Latinoamérica.

En los Estados Unidos de América generalmente no se realiza que el idioma sueco se usa mucho en Finlandia, además del sueco. Se publican en Finlanda libros en sueco, así como revistas de interés general así como científico. Por eso, se encuentran en esta sección de Finlanda algunos asientos publicados en sueco.

La Academia Finlandesa de Ciencias, situada en Helsinki, publica varias series, incluyendo Annales, Commentationes Humanarum Litterarum, Acta y un libro anual. El hecho de que muchas de sus publicaciones se imprimen en lenguas además del finlandés explicará la inclusión de una pequeña cantidad comparativa de fichas inglesas.

En esta sección la traducción inglesa del título de cada asiento se encuentra directamente bajo el título de la lengua original, seguida de la ficha entera.

I. Books

LATIN AMERICA

1267   Alfthan, G. E. von. En Utflykt till Antipoder. Helsinki, G. W.
        Edlund, 1887, 172p.
                            (A Voyage to the Antipodes: Uruguay,
        Argentina)

1268   Dalén, Lennart. Andien Valtiot. (In Maat ja Kansat. Helsinki,
        Otava, 1953, pp. 60-104).
        (The States of the Andes)

1269   Donner, Arno, & Ossi Donner. Matkustus Argentinassa ja
        Uruguayssa. Helsinki, K. E. Holm, 1891, 249p.
                            (A Voyage in Argentina and Uruguay)

1270   Hagman, Tyko C. Amerikka, sen Löytö, Valloitus ja Kehitys.
        Porvoo, W. Söderström Oy, 1892, 182p.
                            (America, Its Discovery, Conquest and
        Evolution)

1271   Hannikainen, O. Löytöretket. (In Maailmanhistoria. Helsinki,
        Tietosanakirja Oy, 1920, pp. 755-810).
                            (The Voyages of Discovery)

1272   Hausen, Hans. Över Kontinenter och Oceaner; en Geolog ser på
        Världen. Helsinki, Söderström & Co., 1945, 461p.
                            (Through Continents and Oceans; a Geologist
        Looks at the World: Argentina, Uruguay, Chile, The Caribbean)

1273   Hornborg, Eirik. Hernando Cortes. Porvoo, W. Söderström Oy,
        1919, 100p.

1274   Juutilainen, Matti. *Sellainen oli Retkemme; "Suomen Joutsenen"*
         Matkat Maailman Merillä. 3d ed. Helsinki, Tu li Oy, 1952,
         216p.
                (Such Was Our Voyage; the Voyages of the
         Finnish Training Ship "Suomen Joutsen" on the Oceans of the
         World, Mainly Around South America)

1275   Karsten, Rafael. *Addenda to My "Notes on South American*
         Arrow Poison". Helsinki, Societas Scientiarum Fennica
         (Commentationes Humanarum Litterarum, VI:7), 1935, 12p.

1276   Karsten, Rafael. *Ceremonial Games of the South American*
         Indians. Helsinki, Societas Scientiarum Fennica (Commen-
         tationes Humanarum Litterarum, III;2), 1932, 38p.

1277   Karsten, Rafael. *The Couvade or Male Child-Bed Among the*
         South American Indians. Helsinki, Societas Scientiarum Fen-
         nica (Öfversigt af Finska Vetenskaps-Societetens Förhandlingar,
         LVII, 1914-1915, B:3), 1915, 33p.

1278   Karsten, Rafael. *The Head-Hunters of Western Amazonas; the Life*
         and Culture of the Jibaro Indians of Eastern Ecuador and Peru.
         Helsinki, Societas Scientiarum Fennica (Commentationes Huma-
         narum Litterarum, VII), 1935, 598p.

1279   Karsten, Rafael. *Huvudjägare och Soldyrkare i Sydamerika.* Hel-
         sinki, Söderström & Co., 1929, 190p.
                (Head-Hunters and Sun Worshippers in South
         America: Ecuador, Peru, Bolivia, Argentina)

1280   Karsten, Rafael. *Indian Dances in the Gran Chaco (South America).*
         Helsinki, Societas Scientiarum Fennica (LVII (1914-15, B:6),
         1915, 35p.

1281   Karsten, Rafael. Indian Tribes of the Argentine and Bolivian
        Chaco; Ethnological Studies. Helsinki, Societas Scientiarum
        Fennica (Commentationes Humanarum Litterarum, IV:1), 1932,
        236p.

1282   Karsten, Rafael. Indianernas Rättsliga Ställning i Spanska
        Amerika. Helsinki, Societas Scientiarum Fennica (Årsbok -
        Vuosikirja XXIX,1950-51, B:2), 1950, 14p.
                        (The Legal Position of the Indians in Spanish
        America)

1283   Karsten Rafael. Notes on South American Arrow-Poison.
        Helsinki, Societas Scientiarum Fennica (Commentationes
        Humanarum Litterarum, VI:4), 1935, 15p.

1284   Karsten, Rafael. Some Critical Remarks on Ethnological
        Field-Research in South America. Helsinki, Societas
        Scientiarum Fennica (Commentationes Humanarum Litterarum,
        XIX:5), 1954, 32p.

1285   Karsten, Rafael. Studies in South American Anthropology. I.
        Helsinki, Societas Scientiarum Fennica (Översikt av Finska
        Vetenskaps-Societetens Förhandlingar, LXII, 1919-20, B:2),
        1920, 232p.

1286   Karsten, Rafael. Studies in the Religion of the South-American
        Indians East of the Andes. Ed. by A. Runeberg and M. Webster.
        Helsinki, Societas Scientiarum Fennica (Commentationes Huma-
        narum Litterarum, XXIX:1), 1964, 256p.

1287   Kujala, Arvi H. "Suomen Joutsenen" Näköaloja: Etelä-Amerikan
        Matka 1932-1933. Helsinki, W. Söderström Oy, 1934, 86p.
                        (Vistas of the Training Ship "Suomen Joutsen":
        the Voyage to South America, 1932-1933)

1288   Lindgren, Gunnar. <u>La Platan Maat</u>. (In <u>Maat ja Kansat</u> I.
Helsinki, Otava, 1953, pp. 9-59).
(The La Plata Countries)

1289   Nyman, Väinö. <u>Maailmanrannalla; Tosikuvaus Siirtolaisen</u>
<u>Kokemuksista ja Seikkailuista Mailla ja Merillä.</u> Helsinki,
Kustannus Oy Kirja, 1920, 293p.
(Travel Around the World: Description of the
Experiences and Adventures of an Immigrant in North and South
America)

1290   Paavolainen, Olavi. <u>Lähtö ja Loitsu.</u> Jyväskylä, K. J. Gummerus,
1937, 382p.
(A Voyage to South America)

1291   Peitso, Jukka. <u>Mahdollisuuksien Maanosassa; Matkakirja Sodan-</u>
<u>aikaisesta Latinalaisesta Amerikasta.</u> Helsinki, Kansankirja,
1945, 116p.
(The Continent of Possibilities; Description of
a Voyage in Wartime Latin America)

1292   Rislakki, Ensio. <u>Mazamorra; Matkani Etelä-Amerikkaan.</u>
Helsinki, Otava, 1948, 240p.
(Mazamorra; My Voyage to South America)

1293   Salovaara, Hannes. <u>Löytöretkeilijöitä.</u> Helsinki, Otava, 1925,
192p.
(Explorers: Columbus, Magalhães, Cortez,
Pizarro, etc.)

1294   Savonlahti, Reino. <u>Valaanpyytäjänä Etelämerellä.</u> Porvoo,
W. Söderström Oy, 1922, 127p.
(Memoirs of a Whaler: Argentina, Uruguay)

1295   Simonen, Seppo. Elämää ja Raunioita Tyynen Meren Rannalla.
Helsinki, Pellervo-Seura, 1953, 288p.
            (Life and Ruins by the Pacific: Description of
a Voyage in South America)

1296   Talvitie, Simo. Itää ja Länttä Suomalaisin Silmin. Helsinki,
Kirjapaja, 1965, 142p.
            (East and West through Finnish Eyes: Jamaica,
Peru, Chile, Argentina, Brazil)

1297   Virkki, Niilo. On the Cytology of Some Neotropical Cantharoids
(Coleoptera): El Salvador, Puerto Rico. Helsinki, Suomalai-
nen Tiedeakatemia (Academia Scientiarum Fennica, Annales
Academiae Scientiarum Fennicae, A IV:65), 1963, 16p.

1298   Zilliacus, Konni. Vandringsår. Helsinki, Söderström & Co.,
1920, 288p.
            (Years of Roving: South America)

ARGENTINA

1299   Antokoletz, Daniel. _Julkaisuja Argentiinan Tasavallasta._ Helsin-
        ki, Öflund & Pettersson, 1912, 140p.
        (Information about the Republic of Argentina)

1300   _Argentina._ Helsinki, Finska Ångfartygs Ab, 1927, 20p.
        (An Anonymous Publication for Emigrants)

1301   Auer, Väinö. _The Pleistocene of Fuego-Patagonia. Part I: The
        Ice and Interglacial Ages._ Helsinki, Suomalainen Tiedeakatemia
        (Academia Scientiarum Fennica, Annales Academiae Scientiarum
        Fennicae, A III:45, 1956), 226p. + 189 Plates.

1302   Auer, Väinö. _The Pleistocene of Fuego-Patagonia. Part II: The
        History of the Flora and Vegetation._ Helsinki, Suomalainen
        Tiedeakatemia (Academia Scientiarum Fennica), Annales Academiae
        Scientiarum Fennicae, A III:50, 1958), 239p.

1303   Auer, Väinö. _The Pleistocene of Fuego-Patagonia. Part III:
        Shoreline Displacements._ Helsinki, Suomalainen Tiedeakatemia
        (Academia Scientiarum Fennica , Annales Academiae Scientiarum
        Fennicae, A III:60),1959, 247p.

1304   Auer, Väinö. _The Pleistocene of Fuego-Patagonia._ Part IV: Bog
        Profiles. Helsinki, Suomalainen Tiedeakatemia (Academia Scienti-
        arum Fennica , Annales Academiae Scientiarum Fennicae, A III:80),
        1965, 165p.

1305   Auer, Väinö. Tulimaata Tutkimassa. Kuvia ja Kuvauksia Suomalai-
        sen Tulimaaretkikunnan Matkoilta Tulimaassa ja Patagoniassa.
        Helsinki, Otava, 1929, 313p.
                (Studying Tierra del Fuego; a Description about the
        Voyage of the Finnish Expedition in Tierra del Fuego and Patagonia)

1306   Auer, Väinö, & Martti Salmi, & Kyllikki Salminen. Pollen and Spore
        Types of Fuego-Patagonia. Helsinki, Suomalainen Tiedeakatemia
        (Academia Scientiarum Fennica,   Annales Academiae Scientiarum
        Fennicae, A III:43), 1955, 14 + 11p.

1307   Kranck, E. H. De Slocknade Eldarnas Land; Minnen Från en Forsk-
        ningsfärd Till Amerikas Sydända. Helsinki, Söderström & Co.,
        1930, 199p.
                (The Land of Extinct Fires; Reminiscences of an
        Exploring Expedition to the Southern Part of South America)

1308   Rosberg, J. E. Falkland-Saaret. (In Maapallo. Helsinki, Otava,
        1924, pp. 202-204).
                (The Falkland Islands)

                            BOLIVIA

1309   Karsten, Rafael. Bolivia. (In Maapallo. Helsinki, Otava, 1924,
        pp. 205-220).

1310   Karsten, Rafael. The Toba Indians of the Bolivian Gran Chaco.
        Turku, Åbo Akademi, Acta Academiae Aboensis, Humaniora 4,
        1923, 126p.

BRAZIL

1311   Hiisivaara, Tapio. Myrkkynuolia, Kahvia, Banaaneja;
Seikkailuja ja Kokemuksia Brasilian Kuuman Auringon Alla.
Helsinki, W. Söderström Oy, 1945, 380p.
(Poisoned Arrows, Coffee, and Bananas)
Adventures and Experiences under the Hot Sun of Brazil)

1312   Ingelius, Hugo H. En Sjöman For Till Rio. Turku, Åbo
Tryckeri och Tidnings Ab, 1932, 145p.
(A Sailor Went to Brazil)

1313   Jouskari, Lyyli. Heräävan Jättiläisen Maassa. Helsinki,
W. Söderström Oy, 1958, 247p.
(In the Country of the Awakening Giant:
Brazil)

1314   Lindgren, Gunnar. Amazonin ja Orinocon Maat. (In Maat ja
Kansat I. Helsinki, Otava, 1953, pp. 105-165).
(The Countries of the Amazonas and
Orinoco)

1315   Siirala, Reino. Ekonomi Etelänristin Valtakunnassa. Helsinki,
W. Söderström Oy, 1945, 336p.
(An Economist Looks at Brazil)

1316   Tolvanen, Viljo. Brasilia. (In Maapallo. Helsinki, Otava,
1924, pp. 9-86).
(Brazil)

1317   Uuskallio, Toivo. Matkalla Kohti Tropiikin Taikaa. Helsinki,
Otava, 1929, 128p.
(A Voyage Towards the Tropics: Brazil)

1318   Wainio, Edvard A. Matkustus Brasiliassa. Helsinki, K. E.
        Holm, 1888, 283p.
                (A Naturalist's Travels in Brzil)

1319   Vastari, Eva. Xingú; Matka Kivikauden Maailmaan.
        Helsinki, W. Söderström Oy, 1966, 153p.
                (Xingú; a Voyage to the World of the Stone Age)

BRITISH HONDURAS

1320   Tolvanen, Viljo. Belize eli Brittiläinen Honduras. (In Maapallo V.
        Helsinki, Otava, 1926, pp. 81-82).
                (Belize, or British Honduras)

CENTRAL AMERICA

1321   Dalén, Lennart. Kahden Mantereen Välissä. (In Maat ja Kansat I.
        Helsinki, Otava, 1953, pp. 166-221).
                (Between Two Continents: Central America)

1322   Mörne, Håkan. Den Förgyllda Fattigdomen; en Resa i Central-
        amerika. Helsinki, Holger Schild, 1949, 388p.
                (The Gilded Misery; a Voyage in Central America)

1323   Rosberg, J. E. Väli-Amerikka. (In Maapallo. Helsinki, Otava,
        1926, pp. 11-12).
                (Middle America)

CHILE

1324   Fieandt, Einar, et al. Chile. (In Maapallo. Helsinki,
        Otava, 1924, pp. 177-200).

COSTA RICA

1325   Rosberg, J. E. Costa Rica. (In Maapallo. Helsinki, Otava,
        1926, pp. 89-92).

CUBA

1326   Aminoff, Eva. Vallankumouksen Valtakunta; Suomalaisen Lehti-
        naisen Viisi Kuuban Kuukautta. Helsinki, Viikkosanomat Oy,
        1961, 299p.
                (The Realm of Revolution; Five Months in Cuba
        as a Finnish Female Journalist)

1327   Tolvanen, Viljo. Kuuba. (In Maapallo. Helsinki, Otava, 1926,
        pp. 102-122).
                (Cuba)

ECUADOR

1328   Karsten, Rafael. _Bland Indianer i Ekvadors Urskogar; Tre års Resor och Forskningar._ Helsinki, Söderström & Co. , 1920-21, 404p.

    (Among the Indians in the Forests of Ecuador; Three Years of Travel and Studies)

1329   Karsten, Rafael. _Blodshämnd, Krig och Segerfester Bland Jibaroindianerna i Östra Ecuador._ Helsinki, Holger Schildt, 1920, 167p.

    (Blood Revenge, War, and Feasts of Victory among the Jíbaro Indians in Eastern Ecuador)

1330   Karsten, Rafael. _Intiaanien Parissa Ecuadorin Aarniometsissä._ _pts. 1-2._ Helsinki, Otava, 1920-21, 392p.

    (Among the Indians in the Forests of Ecuador)

1331   Rosberg, J. E. _Ecuador._ (In _Maapallo._ Helsinki, Otava, 1924, pp. 242-260).

1332   Rosberg, J. E. San Salvador. (In Maapallo. Helsinki, Otava, 1926, pp. 77-80).

1333   Virkki, Niilo. Chromosomes of Certain Anthribid and Brentid Beetles from El Salvador. Helsinki, Suomalainen Tiedeaka-temia (Academia Scientiarum Fennica,, Annales Academiae Scientiarum Fennicae, A IV:83), 1965, 9p.

1334   Virkki, Niilo. Chromosomes of Certain Meloid Beetles from El Salvador. Helsinki, Suomalainen Tiedeakatemia (Academia Scientiarum Fennica, Annales Academiae Scientiarum Fennicae, A IV:57), 1962, 11p.

1335   Virkki, Niilo. Non-Conjugation and Late Conjugation of the Sex Chromosomes in the Beetles of the Genus Alagoasa (Chryso-melidae; Alticinae); El Salvador. Helsinki, Suomalainen Tiede-akatemia (Academia Scientiarum Fennica , Annales Academiae Scientiarum Fennicae, A IV:54), 1961, 22p.

1336   Virkki, Niilo. On the Cytology of Some Neotropical Chrysomelids (Coleoptera): El Salvador. Helsinki, Suomalainen Tiedeakatemia (Academia Scientiarum Fennica , Annales Academiae Scientiarum Fennicae, A IV:75), 1964, 24p.

GUATEMALA

1337   Rosberg, J. E. Guatemala. (In Maapallo. Helsinki, Otava, 1926,
pp. 71-76).

GUYANA

1338   Rosberg, J. E. Guayana. (In Maapallo. Helsinki, Otava, 1924,
pp. 288-294).

HAITI

1339   Rosberg, J. E. Haiti. (In Maapallo. Helsinki, Otava, 1926,
pp. 123-128).

HONDURAS

1340   Tolvanen, Viljo.   Honduras.   (In Maapallo.   Helsinki, Otava,
         1926, pp. 83-85).

JAMAICA

1341   Tolvanen, Viljo.   Jamaika.   (In Maapallo.   Helsinki, Otava,
         1926, pp. 129-133).

1342   Hagman, Tyko C.   Mexikon Valloitus.   Porvoo, W. Söderström
        Oy, 1892, 115p.
                        (The Conquest of Mexico)

1343   Hirvonen, Uuno.   Nauravan Kuoleman Maa; Matkakuvia Meksi-
        kosta, Helsinki, Otava, 1954, 178 p.
                        (The Land of Laughing Death; Sketches of My
        Travels in Mexico)

1344   Hornborg, Eirik.   Hernando Cortes och Erövringen av Mexico;
        ett Fyrahundraårigt Hjälteminne.   Helsinki, Holger Schildt,
        1921, 132p.
                        (Hernando Cortes and the Conquest of Mexico)

1345   Jalas, Aarno.   Meksikko.   (In Maapallo.   Helsinki, Otava,
        1926, pp. 13-70).
                        (Mexico)

1346   Koroleff, Herman.   Mexicoresan.   Helsinki, Söderström & Co.,
        1956, 155p.
                        (A Voyage to Mexico)

1347   Lilius, Aleko.   Bland Vilda Krigare i Mexiko.   Helsinki, Holger
        Schildt, 1925, 173p.
                        (Among Wild Warriors in Mexico)

1348   Lilius, Aleko.   Resor och Äventyr i Mexiko.   Stockholm,
        Froléen & Comp., 1924, 146p.
                        (Travels and Adventures in Mexico)

1349   Simpson, Briitta.   Unelmajunalla Meksikoon.   Helsinki, W. Söderström Oy, 1965, 227p.
(A Voyage in Mexico)

NICARAGUA

1350   Tolvanen, Viljo.   Nicaragua.   (In Maapallo.   Helsinki, Otava,
1926, pp. 86-88).

PANAMA

1351   Parvela, A. A.   Panama.   (In Maapallo.   Helsinki, Otava,
1926, pp. 93-101).

PARAGUAY

1352   Sulin, T. Z.   Paraguay.   (In Maapallo.   Helsinki, Otava, 1924,
pp. 87-99).

PERU

1353   Karsten, Rafael. Inkareligionen i det Gamla Peru. Helsinki,
      Societas Scientiarum Fennica, Societas Scientiarum Fennica:
      Årsbok - Vuosikirja III (1924-25): 2, 1925, 15p.
             (The Inca Religion in Ancient Peru)

1354   Parvela, A. A. Peru. (In Maapallo. Helsinki, Otava, 1924,
      pp. 221-241).

1355   Paavolainen, Olavi. Risti ja Hakaristi; Uutta Maailmankuvaa
      Kohti. Jyväskylä, K. J. Gummerus, 1938, 358p.
             (The Cross and the Swastika; Towards a
    New Picture of the World: Comparison between the Inca Civilization
    and the Third Reich)

PUERTO RICO

1356   Rosberg, J. E. Portoriko (Puerto Rico). (In Maapallo. Hel-
      sinki, Otava, 1926, pp. 134-136).

URUGUAY

1357   Lindholm, John O. Uruguay. (In Maapallo III. Helsinki,
      Otava, 1924, pp. 100-107).

VENEZUELA

1358   Rosberg, J. E.   <u>Venezuela</u>.   (In <u>Maapallo</u>.   Helsinki, Otava, 1924, pp. 276-287).

1359   Hubendick, Bengt.   <u>Filippin och Antipod</u>.   Helsinki, Forum, 1954, 205p.
       (The Philippines and the Antipodes: Venezuela)

WEST INDIES AND THE CARIBBEAN

1360   Rosberg, J. E.   <u>Bahama-saaret</u>.   (In <u>Maapallo</u>.   Helsinki, Otava, 1926, pp. 149-150)
       (The Bahama Islands)

1361   Rosberg, J. E.   <u>Vähät-Antillit</u>.   (In <u>Maapallo</u>.   Helsinki, Otava, 1926, pp. 137-148).
       (The Lesser Antilles)

II. Periodical Articles

LATIN AMERICA

1362   Auer, Väinö. "Aavikkopaholainen". Helsinki, <u>Terra</u> (47:1),
        1935. pp. 8-21.
        ("The Devil of the Wasteland")

1363   Auer, Väinö. "Etelä-Amerikan Jääkausista". Helsinki, <u>Suo-
        malainen tiedeakatemia: Esitelmät ja pöytäkirjat 1958, 1959</u>,
        pp. 129-176.
        ("About Glacial Periods in South America")

1364   Auer, Väinö. "Finländsk Geologisk Forskning i Sydamerika".
        Helsinki, <u>Nordenskiöld-samfundets tidskrift 24</u>, 1964, pp.
        3-20.
        ("Finnish Geological Research in South America")

1365   Auer, Väinö. "Late Glacial and Postglacial Displacements in
        South America as Established by Tephrachronology, Compared
        with Displacements of the Baltic Shorelines". Helsinki, <u>Fennia</u>
        (89:1), 1964, pp. 51-55.

1366   Bonsdorff, Johan von. "USA Omistaa Latinalaisessa Amerikassa.
        Yhdysvaltojen Investoinnit Kontrolloivat 40 % Koko Latinalaisen
        Amerikan Bruttokansantuotteesta". Helsinki, <u>Ydin</u> (2:1), 1968,
        pp. 3-6.
        ("The Possessions of the USA in Latin
        America - U.S. Investments Control 40% of the Gross National
        Product of Latin America")

1367   Hausen, Hans. "Snett Över Etthundra Breddgrader: Hangö-
        Köpenhamn-Bremen-Antwerpen-Lissabon-Rio de Janeiro -
        Rio de la Plata". Helsinki, <u>Finlandia 1920-21</u>, pp. 229-245.
        ("Across One Hundred Degrees of Latitude:
        Hango-Copenhagen-Bremen-Antwerp-Lisbon-Rio de Janeiro-
        Rio de la Plata")

1368   Hult, R. "Cristoforo Colombo". Helsinki, Geografiska förening-
        ens tidskrift 5, 1893, pp. 1-19.
                ("Christopher Columbus")

1369   Junnila, Eila. "Ministeri Eino Wälikankaan Eteläamerikkalainen
        Kokoelma Helsingin Yliopiston Kirjastossa". Helsinki, Biblio-
        philos (22:3), 1963, pp. 45-50.
                ("The South American Book Collection of Eino
        Walikangas in the Helsinki University Library")

1370   Karsten, Rafael. "Nio års etnologiska Fältforskningar i Sydame-
        rika". Helsinki, Nordenskiöld-samfundets tidskrift 13/1953,
        1954, pp. 68-89.
                ("Ethnological Field Research During Nine
        Years in South America")

1371   Karsten, Rafael. "Sydamerikanska Indiankulturer". Helsinki,
        Nordenskiöld-samfundets tidskrift 1, 1941, pp. 22-39.
                ("Indian Cultures of South America")

1372   Koljonen, Jouko. "Massa- ja Paperiteollisuudesta Latinalaisessa
        Amerikassa". Helsinki, Suomen puutalous (43:2), 1961, pp. 49-
        51, 54, 56.
                ("On Paper and Pulp Industry in Latin America")

1373   Koljonen, Jouko. "Piirteitä Latinalaisen Amerikan Paperiteolli-
        suuden Kehityksestä". Helsinki, Paperi ja puu (44:4), 1962, pp.
        267-270.
                ("An Outline of the Development of the Latin
        American Paper Industry")

1374   Leopold, Irene. "Kolonial-Arkitekturen i det Spanska Amerika".
        Helsinki, Finsk tidskrift 105, 1928, pp. 111-128.
                ("Colonial Architecture in Spanish America")

1375   Levón, Martti. "Etelä-Amerikan Aarniometsissä ja Pampalla".
        Helsinki, Paperi ja puu A (33:3), 1951, pp. 67-69.
                ("In the Forests and on the Pampas of South
        America")

1376   Niklander, Arne. "Pappersindustrien i Sydamerika". Helsinki,
        Pappers- och trävarutidskrift för Finland (13:11), 1931, pp.
        493-498.
                ("Paper Industry in South America")

1377   Öhman, Axel. "Monroe-Doktrin i Dollar - USA tar Krafttag för
        Latinamerika". Helsinki, Mercator 56, 1961, pp. 165-167.
                ("The Monroe Doctrine in Dollars - the U.S.
        Exercises Policy of Power in Latin America")

1378   Procopé, Victor. "Ekonomiska Integrationssträvanden i Latin-
        amerika". Helsinki, Mercator 55, 1950, pp. 556, 568.
                ("Attempts at Economic Integration in Latin
        America")

1379   Rosberg, J.E. "Amerikas Upptäcktshistoria". Helsinki, Geogra-
        fiska Föreningens tidskrift 14, 1902, pp. 239-250.
                ("The History of the Discovery of America")

1380   Rosberg, J.E. "Sydamerikas Folk". Helsinki, Geografiska
        Foreningens tidskrift 14, 1902, pp. 299-304, 337-340.
                ("The Peoples of South America")

1381   Rosberg, J.E. "Sydamerikas Fysiska och Biogeografi". Helsinki,
        Geografiska Foreningens tidskrift 14, 1902, pp. 251-298.
                ("The Physical Geography and Biogeography of
        South America")

1382   Rosberg, J. E. "Sydamerikas Stater". Helsinki, Geografiska
        Foreningens tidskrift 14, 1902, pp. 341-357.
        ("The Nations of South America")

1383   Sihvonen, Lauri. "Meksikosta Argentiinaan - Mitä on Tapahtunut
        ja Mitä on Tapahtuva Latinalaisessa Amerikassa?" Helsinki,
        Sosialistinen aikakauslehti 1, 1964, pp. 26-29, 42.
                    ("From Mexico to Argentina - What Has
        Happened and What Will Happen in Latin America?")

1384   Söderström, Bertel. "Kvalitativ Undernäring och Monokulturer -
        Latinamerikas Problem". Helsinki, Mercator 56, 1961, pp. 543-552.
                    ("Qualitative Undernourishment and Mono-
        cultures - the Problems of Latin America")

1385   Taipale, Ilkka. "Sotilaskaappaukset Latinalaisessa Amerikassa".
        Helsinki, Ydin (2:1), 1968, pp. 38-39.
                    ("The Coups-d'état of Soldiers in Latin America,
        in the 20th Century")

1386   Tammekann, August. "Etelä-Amerikan Manteren Tektonisesta
        Rakenteesta". Helsinki, Terra 65, 1953, pp. 45-55.
                    ("The Tectonics of the Continent of South
        America")

1387   Tiililä, Osmo. "Matkalta Etelä-Amerikkaan". Helsinki, Teolo-
        gia ja Kirkko 7, 1960, pp. 98-109.
                    ("From a Voyage to South America")

1388   Törnqvist, Erik. "Latinamerikansk Frihandel - en Nödvändig-
        het". Helsinki, Mercator 55, 1960, pp. 767-768.
                    ("Latin American Free Trade - a Necessity")

1389　　Törnqvist, Erik. "Tullfrihet inom Latinamerika". Helsinki,
　　　　Mercator 56, 1961, pp. 3-4.
　　　　　　　("Exemption from Duties in Latin America")

1390　　Väisälä, Vilho. "Atlantilla ja Vähän Etelä-Amerikassakin". Hel-
　　　　sinki, Terra 53, 1941, pp. 132-144.
　　　　　　　("On the Atlantic and in South America")

1391　　Vattulainen, Aulis. "Andien Forelleja Tavoittamassa". Helsinki,
　　　　Metsästys ja kalastus 48, 1959, pp. 337-340.
　　　　　　　("Catching Trout in the Andes")

ARGENTINA

1392　　Auer, Väinö. "Jääkausi ja sen Jälkeinen Aika Patagoniassa".
　　　　Helsinki, Suomalainen tiedeakatemia: Esitelmät ja pöytäkirjat,
　　　　1946, pp. 125-126.
　　　　　　　("The Pleistocene and Post-Glacial Period in Tierra
　　　　del Fuego".

1393　　Auer, Väinö. "Kuvia ja Kuvauksia Patagonian Retkikunnan Mat-
　　　　koilta". Helsinki, Suomalainen tiedeakatemia: Esitelmät ja
　　　　pöytäkirjat 1938, 1939, pp. 93-99.
　　　　　　　("Pictures and Descriptions of the Patagonian
　　　　Expedition")

1394   Auer, Väinö. "Suomalainen Tutkimus Tulimaassa ja Patagoni-
assa". Helsinki, Terra (66:1), 1954, pp. 1-21.
("Finnish Research in Terra del Fuego and
Patagonia")

1395   Auer, Väinö. "Tarkistustutkimukset ja Matkani Patagoniaan v.
1956-57". Helsinki, Terra 75, 1963, pp. 297-320.
("Control Studies and My Journey to Patagonia,
1956-57")

1396   Backman, E. H. "Våra Nybyggare i Argentina". Helsinki, Terra
29, 1917, pp. 161-166.
("Our Settlers in Argentina")

1397   Brusiin, Otto. "Carlos Cossio - an Argentine Jurist". Turku,
Finsk tidskrift (152:4), 1952, pp. 182-187.

1398   Enström, Gustaf. "Argentina och Dess Folk". Helsinki, Geografiska Föreningens tidskrift 4, 1892, pp. 129-151.
("Argentina and Its People")

1399   Hausen, Hans. "En Geologisk Resa i den Argentinska Delen av
Puna de Atacama Sommaren och Hösten 1923". Helsinki,
Terra 36, 1924, pp. 68-76.
("A Geological Expedition to Puna de Atacama,
Argentina, in Summer and Autumn, 1923")

1400   Hausen, Hans. "Ett Oceanografiskt Institut i Argentina". Helsinki, Terra 29, 1917, pp. 153-156.
("An Oceanographic Institute in Argentina")

1401   Hausen, Hans. "Suomalaisten Luona Misionesissa". Helsinki,
Terra 30, 1918, pp. 89-102.
("Visiting the Finns in Misiones")

1402   Kalela, Aarno. "Aro- ja Autiomaakasvillisuudesta Patago-
        niassa". Helsinki, Suomalainen tiedeakatemia: Esitelmät
        ja pöytäkirjat 1945, 1946, pp. 133-145.
                          ("Vegetation on the Plains and Deserts of
        Patagonia")

1403   Kalela, Aarno. "Lisiä Patagonian Kasviston Tuntemiseen,
        I-III". Helsinki, Suomalainen tiedeakatemia: Esitelmät ja
        pöytäkirjat 1940, 1941, p. 130.
                          ("Addenda to the Knowledge About Vegetation
        in Patagonia, I-III")

1404   Kalela, Erkki K. "Metsien Perääntymisestä ja Puulajinvaih-
        doksista Ita-Patagoniassa". Helsinki, Terra 53, 1941, pp.
        145-154.
                          ("Forestry Changes in Eastern Patagonia")

1405   Kalela, Erkki K. "Tutkimuksia Puulajien Kasvusta Eri Metsä-
        tyypeillä Itä-Patagoniassa". Helsinki, Suomalainen tiedeaka-
        temia: Esitelmät ja pöytäkirjat 1941, 1943, pp. 171-172.
                          ("Research on Various Types of Trees in
        Different Kinds of Forests in Eastern Patagonia")

1406   Kalela, Aarno, & Erkki K. Kalela. "Selostus Patagonian
        Retkikunnan Pohjoisen Ryhmän Tutkimusmatkoista". Helsinki,
        Suomalainen tiedeakatemia: Esitelmät ja pöytakirjat 1938, 1939,
        pp. 27-29.
                          ("Report on the Expedition
        to Northern Patagonia")

1407   Kranck, E. H. "Färder i den Eldslänska Cordilleren. Intryck
        från Geografiska Sällskapets Eldslandsexpedition 1928-29".
        Helsinki, Terra 42, 1930, pp. 129-150.
                          ("Travels on the Cordilleras of Tierra del Fuego:
        Impressions from the Expedition to Tierra del Fuego of the Geo-
        graphical Society")

1408   Kranck, E. H. "Om Forekömsten av Nyttiga Mineral i Magal-
        lanesländerna". Helsinki, Terra 42, 1930, pp. 30-44.
                ("On the Mineral Deposits of the Magallanes
        Territory")

1409   Levón, Martti. "Argentiinan Metsåtalous". Helsinki, Paperi
        ja puu B (33:4a), 1951, pp. 94-98.
                ("The Forestry of Argentina")

1410   Lunnasvaara, V. "Colonia Finlandeѕa, Misioneksen Suomalais-
        siirtola". Helsinki, Terra 44, 1932, pp. 1-29.
                ("Colonia Finlandesa, the Finnish Colony
        in Misiones")

1411   Nordenskjöld, Otto. "I Eldslandet och Sydpatagonien". Hel-
        sinki, Geografiska Föreningens tidskrift 12, 1900, pp. 137-
        157.
                (In Tierra del Fuego and South Patagonia")

1412   Öhman, Axel. "Argentina, Framtidsland på Gungfly". Hel-
        sinki, Mercator 58, 1963, pp. 17-18, 20.
                ("Argentina, Land of the Future")

1413   Pallasvirta, Åke. "Argentiinan Paperiteollisuudesta". Hel-
        sinki, Suomen puutalous (38:1), 1959, pp. 13-14.

                ("On the Paper Industry of Argentina")

1414   Roivainen, H. "Darwinin Joulu Tulimaan Intiaanien Parissa".
        Helsinki, Pellervo 60, 1959, pp. 982-983.
                ("Darwin among the Indians of Tierra del
        Fuego One Christmas")

1415   Salmi, Martti. "Patagonian Andien Postglasiaalisesta Tulivuo-
        ritoiminnasta". Helsinki, Terra 56, 1944, pp. 20-30.
        ("On the Post-glacial Volcanic Activity in the
        Patagonian Andes")

1416   Salmi, Martti. "Patagonian ja Tulimaan Postglasiaaliset Vul-
        kaaniset Tuhkakerrostumat". Helsinki, Suomalainen tiede-
        akatemia: Esitelmät ja pöytäkirjat 1941, 1943, pp. 161-162.
                        ("Post-Glacial Volcanic Ash Layers in Pata-
        gonia and Tierra del Fuego")

                              BRAZIL

1417   Björklund, Nils. "Några Synpunkter på Utländska Investeringar
        i Brasilien". Helsinki, Mercator 55, 1960, pp. 763-764, 780.
        Helsinki, Mercator 55, 1960, pp 763-764, 780
                        ("Some Points of View about Foreign Invest-
        ments in Brazil")

1418   Essen, Georg von. "Brasiliansk Utveckling". Helsinki, Finsk
        tidskrift 124, 1938, pp. 40-51.
                        ("Brazilian Development")

1419   Essen, Georg von. "Brasilien". Helsinki, Suomen paperi- ja
        puutavaralehti(16:16), 1939, pp. 692-694.
                        ("Brazil")

1420   Harmston, J. W. "En Dag i den Brasilianska Vildmarken".
        Helsinki, Turisttidskrift (5:4) , July 1916, pp. 76-79.
        ("A Day in the Brazilian Wilderness")

1421   Hirvonen, R. A   "Brasilian Retkikunta". Helsinki, Suoma-
        lainen tiedeakatemia: Esitelmät ja pöytakirjat 1948, 1949,
        pp. 119-127
                        ("Expedition to Brazil")

1422   Järnefelt, Kari. "Kaksi Kaupunkia, Parati ja Brasilia".
        Helsinki, Arkkitehti - Arkitekten 43, 1963, pp. 8-12.
                        ("Two Cities, Parati and Brasilia")

1423   Kåhlman, V. A. "Från Republiken Brasilien; Reseanteck-
        ningar". Helsinki, Finsk tidskrift 36, 1894, pp. 444-453,
        37, 1894, pp. 25-54.
                        ("From the Republic of Brazil; Impressions
        of Travel")

1424   Karsten, Rafael. "Den Finländsk-Svenska Amazonas-Expedit-
        ionen". Helsinki, Nordenskiöld-samfundets tiedskrift
        7/1947, 1948, pp. 49-51.
                        ("The Finnish-Swedish Amazonas Expedition")

1425   Karsten, Rafael. "Från en Resa Till Amazonfloden". Hel-
        sinki, Nordenskiöld-samfundets tidskrift 3, 1943, pp. 106-
        120.
                        ("About an Expedition to the Amazon River")

1426   Kolbe, Pirkko. "Valmet to Brasil, Eteläisin Traktoriteh-
        taamme". Helsinki, Suomen kuvalehti (44:35), 1960, pp. 32-33.
                        ("Valmet to Brasil, the Southernmost
        Finnish Tractor Factory")

1427   Lemberg, Bertel. "Amazonområdets Kautschukskogar och
        Deras Exploitering". Helsinki, Terra 37, 1925, pp. 17-28.
                ("The Rubber Forests of the Territory
        of Amazonas and Their Exploitation")

1428   Levón, Martti. "Eräitä Havaintoja Brasilian Metsätaloudes-
        ta". Helsinki, Paperi ja puu (34:1), 1952, pp. 11-14.
                ("Some Aspects of the Forestry of Brazil")

1429   Londén, Åke. "Tabaré - ett Sydamerikanskt Epos". Turku,
        Finsk tidskrift (140:5), 1946, pp. 237-243.
                ("Tabaré, a South American Epos")

1430   Ojasti, Juhani. "Havaintoja Orinokon Alueen Luonnosta ja
        sen Ekologisista Piirteistä". Helsinki, Luonnon tutkija 67,
        1963, pp. 137-146.
                ("Some Observations on the Nature of the
        Orinoco Territory and Its Ecological Features")

1431   Pasanen, Erkki, & Kauko Tiihonen. "Brasilia - Brasili-
        anskt". Helsinki, Arkkitehti - Arkitekten, 1956, pp. 150-
        157.
                ("On Brasilia: Brazil-
        ian Architecture")

1432   Saalas, Uunio. "Reinhold Ferdinand Sahlbergin Brasilian
        Matka v. 1849-51". Helsinki, Luonnon tutkija 58, 1954,
        pp. 33-42.
                ("Reinhold Ferdinand Sahlberg's Voyage to
        Brazil in 1849-51")

1433   Tammekann, August. "Amazonaksen Trooppisen Sademetsän
        Ulkoraja Brasiliassa". Helsinki, Terra 70, 1958, pp.
        204-207.
                ("The Outside Limits of the Tropical
        Forest of Amazonas in Brazil")

CENTRAL AMERICA

1434   Barck, Katarina. "Det Oroliga Centralamerika". Helsinki,
Nya Argus 54 , 1961, pp. 97-99.
           ("Unruly Central America")

1435   Konow, R. von. "Orsaken Till Istiderna, Eller är Orsaken
Till de Stora Geologiska Klimatväxlingarna en Följd av
Centralamerikas Orogenetiska Förändringar?". Helsinki,
Terra 59, 1947, pp. 122-128.
           ("Are the Great Geological Variations
of Climate Attributable to the Orogenetic Changes in Central
America?")

1436   Londén, Åke. "Centralamerika - ett Finländskt Exporttomrum".
Helsinki, Mercator 59, 1964, pp. 295, 322.
           ("Central America, an Area for Finnish Ex-
port")

1437   Rossi, Matti. "Mennyttä Loistoa Kadonneen Kulttuurin Rau-
nioilla". Helsinki, Uusi kuvalehti 23, 1960, pp. 35-37.
           ("Vanished Glory on the Ruins of a Bygone
Culture of the Mayas")

CHILE

1438   Hartman, Lars. "Asiantuntijana Chilessä". Helsinki,
Suomen puutalous (36:2), 1954, pp. 74-77.
("Forestry Expert in Chile")

1439   Kauko, Yrjö. "Piirteitä Chilen Metsätaloudesta". Helsinki,
Metsätaloudellinen aikakauslehti 68, 1951, pp. 209-210.
("Some Features of Forestry in Chile")

1440   Nylander, John W. "En Berättelse om ett Kors". Helsinki,
Från Nord Till syd (Kalender utg. af Geografiska För-
eningen i Finland), 1899, pp. 117-136.
("A Story about a Cross: Travel Sketch
from Chile")

COLOMBIA

1441   Sariola, Sakari. "Juomatavoista Colombian Maaseudulla".
Helsinki, Alkoholipolitiikka 25. 1960, pp. 158-162.
("On Drinking Habits in the Rural Districts
of Colombia")

COSTA RICA

1442   Virkki, Niilo. "Talamancan Pilvimetsissä ja Paramoilla".
        Helsinki, Luonnon tutkija 65, 1961, pp. 129-139.
                    ("In the Rain Forests of Talamanca, Costa
        Rica")

CUBA

1443   Harmston, J. W. "En Fård Till det Inre av Cuba". Hel-
        sinki, Turisttidskrift (5:6), December 1916, pp. 124-127.
                    ("A Voyage to the Interior of Cuba")

1444   Hildén, Kaarlo. "Kuuba Maailmantaloudessa". Helsinki,
        Terra (63:1), 1951, pp. 4-18.
                    ("Cuba's Place in World Economy")

1445   Raatikainen, Erkki. "Kuubalainen Jeremiaadi, eli Mitä,
        Miksi, Milloin ja Etenkin Miksi". Helsinki, Sosialistinen
        aikakauslehti 11/12, 1962, pp. 10-13, 61-62.
                    ("The Cuban Jeremiad, or What, Why,
        When, and Particularly Why")

1446   Ripatti, Viljo. "Amerikan Musta Lammas Fidel Castro".
        Helsinki, Sosialistinen aikakauslehti 11/12, 1960, pp. 20-21.
                    ("A Presentation of Fidel Castro")

ECUADOR

1447   Karsten, Rafael. "Matka Päiväntasaajan Maasta". Helsinki,
        Finlandia 1919 , 1920, pp. 89-100.
                ("A Journey in Ecuador")

EL SALVADOR

1448   Virkki, Niilo. "Conquistadorien Jäljillä Salvadorissa".
        Helsinki, Luonnon tutkija 67, 1963, pp. 65-81.
             ("Tracing the Conquistadors in El Salvador")

1449   Virkki, Niilo. "Salvadorin Instituto Tropical". Helsinki,
        Luonnon tutkija 65. 1961, pp. 5-9.
             ("The Instituto Tropical of El Salvador")

1450   Virkki, Niilo. "Tulivuorten Tuttavana". Helsinki, Luonnon
        tutkija 68, 1964, pp. 36-48.
           ("A Voyage in El Salvador")

GUATEMALA

1451   Sariola, Sakari. "Havaintoja Guatemalasta". Helsinki,
Suomalainen Suomi (22:6), 1954, pp. 346-349.
("Some Observations on Guatemala")

MEXICO

1452   Kaarlehto, P. "Maatalousnäkymiä Meksikossa". Helsinki,
Pellervo 62, 1961, pp. 1012-1015.
("Some Aspects of Farming in Mexico")

1453   Kråkström, Erik. "Meksikolainen Rapsodia - Mexikansk
Rapsodi". Helsinki, Arkkitehti - Arkitekten, 1958, pp.
118-122.
("A Mexican Rhapsody")

1454   Lehtonen, Maija. "Meksikon Runoutta". Helsinki, Suomalainen Suomi (22:7), 1954, pp. 444-447.
("Mexican Poetry")

1455   Paloheimo, F. K. "Meksikon Tienrakennuksesta". Helsinki,
Teknillinen aikakausl ehti 49, 1959, pp. 65-67.
("On Road Building in Mexico")

1456   Sjöberg, W. "Raser och Folk i det Moderna och Antika
        Mexico". Helsinki, Terra 28, 1916, pp. 323-333.
                ("Races and Peoples in Modern and Old
        Mexico")

1457   Tigerstedt, Ornulf. "Chichen Itza; ett Övergivet Mekka".
        Helsinki, Finsk tidskrift 98, 1925, pp. 197-206.
                ("Chichen Itza; a Rejected Mecca")

PARAGUAY

1458   Ehrman, Erik. "Paraguay" Helsinki, Geografiska För-
        eningens tidskrift 19, 1907, pp. 279-294.

1459   Karsten, Rafael. "El Gran Chaco, Stridsäpplet Mellan tre
        Republiker". Helsinki, Terra 47, 1935, pp. 22-30.
                ("El Gran Chaco, the Point of Discord
        Between Three Republics")

1460   Karsten, Rafael. "Något om Gran Chaco, Dess Natur och
        Folk". Helsinki, Terra 27, 1915, pp. 23-37.
                ("Something about Gran Chaco, Its
        Nature and People")

1461   Saari, Eino. "Paraguayn Metsäteollisuus ja sen Kehittämis-
        mahdollisuudet". Helsinki, Paperi ja puu (35:11), 1953,
        pp. 449-458.
                ("The Forest Industry in Paraguay and the
        Possibilities for Its Development")

PERU

1462   Karsten, Rafael. "Inkarikets Kultur och Dess Geografiska
         Förutsättningar". Helsinki, Terra 43, 1941, pp. 104-118.
                          ("Inca Culture from a Geographic Point
         of View")

PUERTO RICO

1463   Mikola, Peitsa. "Puerto Rico - Esimerkki Tropiikin
         Metsätaloudesta". Helsinki, Metsätaloudellinen aika-
         kauslehti 80, 1963, pp. 447-450, 454-455.
                          ("Puerto Rico - an Example of Tropical
         Forestry")

1464   Stewen, Kaarle. "Puerto Rico - Kehitysmaa Dollarien
         Varjossa". Helsinki, Suomen kuvalehti (47:7), 1963,
         pp. 24-26, 43.
                          ("Puerto Rico - an Underdeveloped
         Country in the Shadow of Dollars")

VENEZUELA

1465 Lavretzky, Ivan. "Teresa Carreño; Minnen Från Konst-
    närsbanan". Helsinki, Finsk tidskrift 78, 1915, pp. 446-
    454.
        ("Teresa Carreño, a Venezuelan Pianist;
    Reminiscences from the Career of an Artist")

WEST INDIES AND THE CARIBBEAN

1466 Favorin, H. "Tanskalaisen Länsi-Intian Geologisista
    Oloista". Helsinki, Geografiska Föreningens tidskrift 22,
    1910, pp. 163-168.
        ("On the Geological Conditions of the Danish
    West Indies")

1467 Törngren, Adolf. "Västindien och Centralamerika som
    Kolonisationsland". Helsinki, Finsk tidskrift 109, 1930,
    pp 275-281.
        ("The West Indies and Central America
    as a Territory for Colonization")

1468 Vattulainen, Aulis. "Sukelluskalastuksesta Karibialla".
    Helsinki, Metsästys ja kalastus 52, 1963, pp 511-514.
        ("On Sub-surface Fishing in the
    Caribbean")

GREECE

Although Latin American Studies as a field is non-existent in Greek universities, the Latin American area is being given attention by Greek scholars in many disciplines. Within its world-wide interests, the Athens Center for Ekistics has focused attention on urbanization problems in Latin America. One of the researchers at the Center is Guillermo Luna, a Mexican citizen, who has written on the problems of cities in his native land (see Ekistics, volume 24, number 140, July 1967, pp. 19-20).

A United States citizen, and a professor at the California State College at Hayward, Dr. Virgil Salera (a noted specialist on the economics of Latin America), has conducted research at the Center of Economic Research in Athens. The Center is operated under auspices of the University of California.

Also located in Athens is the Social Sciences Center, supported by Unesco and operated under the auspices of the Greek Ministry of Education. The Center supervises social science research carried out in Greece, and promotes international cooperation between social scientists in Greece and abroad.

In this section the English translation of the title of each bibliographic item is to be found directly under the title in the original language, and immediately following the entire bibliographic description.

Aunque no existe el campo de Estudios Latinoamericanos en las universidades de Grecia, especialistas grecos en muchas disciplinas profesionales ponen atención a la región latino-americana. Dentro de sus intereses mundiales, el Centro de Ekistics en Atenas ha desempeñado estudios en muchos problemas aliados con el proceso de urbanización en Latinoamérica. Sr. Guillermo Luna, investigador en este Centro y ciudadano mexicano, ha escrito sobre los problemas de las ciudades mexicanas (vea Ekistics, volumen 24, número 140, Julio de 1967, pp. 19-20).

El Doctor Virgil Salera, ciudadano estadounidense, Profesor en el California State College, situada en la ciudad de Hayward, California, es experto en la economía latinoamericana. El Doctor Salera desempeño investigaciones en el Centro de Investigaciones Económicas en Atenas; este Centro funciona bajo auspicios de la Universidad de California.

También en Atenas hay el Centro de Ciencias Sociales, sostenido por la Unesco y dirigido por el Ministerio de Educación de Grecia. El Centro supervisa investigaciones en los campos de las ciencias sociales que se desarrollan en Grecia, y fomenta cooperación internacional entre científicos sociales en Grecia y en ultramar.

En esta sección la traducción inglesa del título de cada asiento se encuentra directamente bajo el título de la lengua original, seguida de la ficha entera.

I. Books

LATIN AMERICA

1469   Ἀφτιάς, Ἰωαννής. Ἔρευνα ἐμπορευμάτων: Βραζιλία, Οὐρουγουάη, Ἀργεντινή, Χιλή, Κεντρικῆς Ἀμερικῆς, Περοῦ, Κολόμβια, Ἰσημερινος, Δημοκρατία τοῦ Παναμᾶ, Μεξικό, καί Βενεζουέλα ἀπό τόν Ἀπρίλη μέχρι τόν Ἰούλιο, 1959. Ἀθῆναι, Ἐκδ. Ἐθνική Ἑλληνική Ἐπιτροπή Διεθνοῦ Ἐμπορικου Ἐπιμελητηρίου, 1960, 78 ς.

Aftias, Ioánnes. Ehrevna Emborevmaton: Brazēlēa, Ourouyoūae, Argentēnē, Hēlē, Volivia, Kentrikēs Ahmerēkēs, Perou, Kolomvia, Esemēhrēnos, Dēmokratēa Tou Panama, Mehxēko, Keh Benezouela Apo ton Aprēle Mehri ton Ioulēo, 1959. Athens, Greek National Committee of the International Chamber of Commerce, 1960, 78p.
        (Market Research: Brazil, Uruguay, Argentina, Chile, Bolivia, Central America, Peru, Colombia, Ecuador, Panama, Venezuela, Mexico, During April-July, 1959)

1470   Ἀφτιάς, Ἰωάννης. Ἐργασία στον Καναδά, Ἰαμάικα, καί Τρινιταντ. Ἀθῆναι, Ἐκδ. Ἐθνικῆς Ἑλληνικῆς Ἐπιτροπή Διεθνούς Ἐμβορικοῦ Ἐπιμελετηρίου, 1963, 20 ς.

Aftias, Ióannes. Ehrghasea Ston Kahahda, Iahmahēka, Keh Trinitant. Athens, Ekd. Ethnikē Ehlēnikē Ehpitropē Diethnous Emborikous Ehpimēhlētēriou, 1963, 20p.
        (Employment Opportunities in Canada, Jamaica and Trinidad)

1471   Χριστοδουλίδης, Μ. Συγκριτική παγκόσμιος ἱστορια. Ἐκδ. Τριφινάτου, Λευκωσία, 1963, 48 ς.

Christontolos, M. Sēgritēkē Pangosmios Istoria. Athens, Ekd. Triphēnatou, 1963, 48p.
        (Comparative World History)

1472　　"Εκδοσις Διεθνοῦς Ἐμπορικοῦ Ἐπιμεκητηρίου. Ἐθνικῆς
　　　　'Ελληνικῆς Ἐπιτροπῆς. 'Αργεντινή καί Χιλή άπό
　　　　οἰκονομικῆς ἀπόψεως. 'Αθῆναι, 1961, 18 ς.

Ehkdosis Diethnous Emborikou Ehpēmeh-lētēriou. Ehthnikēs
Ehlēnikēs Ehpitropēs. Argentēnē Keh Hēlē apo Ēkonomēkēs
Apopseos. Athens, 1961, 18p.
(International Chamber of Commerce. Greek National
Committee. Argentina and Chile from an Economic Viewpoint)

1473　　"Εκδοσις Διεθνοῦς Ἐμπορικοῦ Ἐπιμελητηρίου. Ἐθνικῆς
　　　　'Ελληνικῆς Ἐπιτροπῆς. Περοῦ, Οὐραγουάη, καί
　　　　Παραγουάη άπό οἰκονομικῆς ἀπόψεως. 'Αθῆναι, 1962,
　　　　24 ς.

Ehkdosis Diethnous Emborikou Ehpēmeh-lētēriou. Ehthnikēs
Ehlēnikēs Ehpitropēs. Pehrou, Ourayouaē, Keh Parayouaē
Apo Ēkonomēkēs Apopseos. Athens, 1962, 24p.
(International Chamber of Commerce. Greek National
Committee. Peru, Uruguay, and Paraguay from an Economic
Viewpoint)

1474　　"Εκδοσις Διεθνοῦς Ἐμπορικοῦ Ἐπιμελητηρίου. Ἐθνικῆς
　　　　'Ελληνικῆς Ἐπιτροπῆς. Μέξικον, Κοῦβα, Δομινική
　　　　Δημοκρατία, καί Αἱτή άπό οἰκονομικῆς ἀπόψεως.
　　　　'Αθῆναι, 1962, 20 ς.

Ehkdosis Diethnous Emborikou Ehpēmeh-lētēriou. Ehthnikēs
Ehlēnikēs Ehpitropēs. Mexikon, Kouva, Dominēkē Dēmokratia,
Keh Aētē. Apo Ēkonomēkēs Apopseos. Athens, 1962, 20p.
(International Chamber of Commerce. Greek National Committee.
Mexico, Cuba, Dominican Republic, and Haiti from an Economic
Viewpoint)

1475   "Εκδοσις Διεθνοῦς ;Εμπορικοῦ 'Επιμελητηρίου. 'Εθνικῆς
         'Ελληνικῆς 'Επιτροπῆς. Βενεζουέλα, Κολόμβια,
         'Ισημερινός, καί Βολίβια ἀπό οἰκονομηκῆς ἀπόψεως.
         'Αθῆναι, 1962, 24 ς.

      Ehkdosis Diehthnous Emborikou Ehpēmeh-lētēriou. Ehthnikēs
      Ehlēnikēs Ehpitropēs. Benezouela, Kolombia, Esēmehrinos,
      Keh Bolivia apo Ēkonomēkēs Apopseos. Athens, 1962, 24p.
      (International Chamber of Commerce. Greek National Committee.
      Venezuela, Colombia, Ecuador and Bolivia from an Economic
      Viewpoint)

1476   Γαμβρέσεας, Παν. Μεγάλη παγκόσμιος γεωγραφία καί ἄτλας.
         'Αθῆναι, 'Εκδ. Π. Δημητράκος, 1924.

      Gambreese, Pan. Mehgalē Pangosmios Geographēa Keh Atlas.
      Athens, Ekd. P. Dēmētrahkou, 1924.
               (Unabridged World Geography and Atlas)

1477   Γκορτζῆ, Ν. 'Αμερική καί 'Αμερικανοί. 'Αθῆναι, 'Εκδ.
         Ραφτάνη Παπαγεωργίου, 1907, 95 ς.

      Gortze, N. Ahmehrēkē Keh Ahmehrēkanē. Athens, Ehkdosis
      Raftanē Papagehorgiou, 1907, 95p.
               (The Americas and their Inhabitants)

1478   Λυγιδάκης, Νίκος. Παγκόσμιος Ναυτική γεωγραφία.
         'Αθῆναι, 1964, 124 ς.

      Legedakis, Nikos. Pangosmios Naftēkē Geographēa. Athens,
      1964, 124p.
               (World Oceanic Geography)

BRAZIL

1479   ῎Εκδοσίς Διεθνοῦσ ᾿Εμπορικοῦ ᾿Επιμελητηρίου. ᾿Εθνικῆς
᾿Ελληνικῆς ᾿Επιτροπῆς. Βραζιλία ἀπό οἰκονομηκῆς
ἀπόψεως. ᾿Αθῆναι, ᾿Ιουνίου 1961, 16 ς.

Ehkdosis Diethnous Emborikou Ehpēmeh-lētēriou. Ehthnikēs
Ehlēnikēs Ehpitropes. Brazilēa apo Ēkonomēkēs Apopseos.
Athens, 1961, 16p.
(International Chamber of Commerce. Greek National Committee.
Brazil from an Economic Viewpoint)

1480   Γαρουφαλιάς, Δημητρής. Τό μαργαριτάρι τοῦ
Γκουαναμπάρα. ᾿Αθῆναι, 1961, 40ς.

Garoufallias, Jim. To Margahrētarē tou Guouanambahra. Athens,
1961, 40p.

(The Pearl of the Amazon)

CENTRAL AMERICA

1481   ῎Εκδοσις Διεθνοῦς ᾿Εμπορικοῦ ᾿Επιμελητηρίου. ᾿Εθνικῆς
᾿Ελληνικῆς ᾿Επιτροπῆς. ῾Η Δημοκρατία τοῦ Παναμᾶ
καί αἱ χῶραι τῆς Κεντρικῆς ᾿Αμερικῆς ἀπό οἰκονομικῆς ἀπόψεως. ᾿Αθῆναι, 1962, 22 ς.

Ehkdosis Diethnous Emborikou Ehpēmeh-lētēriou. Ehthnikēs
Ehlēnikēs Ehpitropēs. E Dēmokratia tou Panama keh eh
Horeh tēs Kentrēkēs Amerēkēs apo Ēkonomēkēs Apopseos.
Athens, 1962, 22p.
(International Chamber of Commerce. Greek National Committee.
Panama and the Nations of Central America)

1482   Μπελεγρῆς, Κωνσταντίνοσ. Ἡ Δομινική Δημοκρατία.
          Ἀθῆναι, 1957, 40ς.

     Belegre, Constantine. Ē Dominikanikē Dēmokratia. Athens,
     1957, 40p.
                         (The Dominican Republic)

MEXICO

1483   Βαρελείκος, Π. Ἡ ποίησι στό Μεξικό. Πάτραι, 1911,
          37 ς.

     Varehleikos, P. Ē Pēésē Sto Mehxēko. Patras, 1911, 37p.
                         (The Poetry of Mexico)

II. Periodical Articles

LATIN AMERICA

1484   Δημητριάδου, Ραΐν. 'Εντυπώσεις μετανάστου. 'Αθῆναι,
1908, σ. 44-48, 79-86, 147-152, 305-314, 407-412,
544-552 , καί 604-611.

Dēmētriadou, Raēn. Ehntiposis metanahstou. Athens, 1908,
pp. 44-48, 79-86, 147-152, 305-314, 407-412, 544-552, 604-601.
("Impressions of a Traveler upon his Return
Home")

1485   'Ελληνική Πολιτική καί Κοινωνική Βιβλιοθήκη. " 'Η
Σοβιετική οἰκονομικη κατάστασις--Δυτικός καί
'Ανατολικός κόσμος." 'Αθῆναι, 'Ο Κομμουνισμός
στή Ρωσσία (Β: ἀρ. 17), 1963, 56 ς.

"Ehllēnikē Polētēkē Keh Kēnonikē Bibleothēkē. E Sovietēke Ekonomeakē
Katastasis. Thetēkos Keh Anatolēkos Kosmos. " Athens, O Kommounisme
stē possea (II: 17), 1963, pp. 1-56.
(Greek Political and Economic Library. "The Soviet Economic Position
with Respect to North and South America")

1486   Κρήσσας, Π. "'Αρχαῖοι 'Αμερικανικοί λαοί. " Νέα
'Υόρκη, 'Η Νίκη (ἀρ. 27), 1913, σ. 5-7;
(ἀρ. 28), 1913, σ. 6-7.

Krēssas, P. "Ahrhaiē Amehrikanēkē Laē." New York, E nēkē
(27), 1913, pp. 5-7; (28), 1913, pp. 6-7.
("Ancient American Civilizaticns")

GUATEMALA

1487   Δρακόπυλος, Κ. Α. " Ἡ Δημοκρατία τῆς Γουατεμάλας. "
       'Αθῆναι, Ὁ Κόσμος (ἀρ. 33), 1916.

Drakopoulos, K. A. "Ē Dēmokratia tēs Yuahtehmalas."
Athens, O kosmos (33), 1916.
                   ("The Guatemalan Democracy")

MEXICO

1488   Κρήσσας, Π. . "Αἱ Ἀρχαιότητες τῆσ Γιουκατάν."
Νέα Ὑόρκη, Εἰκονογραφημένη Ἀτλαντίς (Β;ἀρ. 9),
1911.

Krēssas, P. "Eh Arhiotētehs Tēs Yioukatan." New York,
Ēkonographimenē atlantis (B: 9), 1911.
("The Antiquities of Yucatan")

1489   Κρήσσας, Π. . " Ἕνα βλέμμα ἐπί τοῦ Μεξικοῦ. "
Νέα Ὑόρκη, Ἀτλαντίς (Δ: ἀρ. 9), 1910.

Krēssas, P. "Ehna Vlema Ehpi Tou Mehxekou." New York,
Atlandētha (D: 9), 1910.
("A Glimpse of Mexico")

1490   Κρήσσας, Π. "Τά Μνημεῖα τῆς Γιουκατάν." Ἀθῆναι,
Πινακοθήκη (ΙΒ:), 1912, ς 79-80.

Krēssas, P. "Ta Mnēmēa tēs Yioukatan." Athens, Pēnakothēke
(XII), 1912, pp. 79-80.
("The Remains of Yucatan")

1491   Βλάστος. Σ. " Τό Μέξικον μέ τοῦς Ἰνδούς του. Ἡ
ἱστορία ἑνος Ἰνδικοῦ πολέμου. " Νέα Ὑόρκη,
Εἰκονογραφημένη Ἀτλαντίς (Β: ἀρ. 1), 1911.

Vlastos, S. "To Mehxēkon Meh Tous Indous Tou. Ē Istoria
Ehnos Ēndēkou Polehmou. " New York, Ēkonographēmehnē
atlantis (II: 1), 1911.
("Mexico and its Indians: the History of an Indian
War")

HUNGARY

Dr. Tibor Wittman holds the Chair of Latin American History in the Faculty of Philosophy of Attila József University in Szeged, in which Institution he has also established an Institute of Medieval and Latin American History. Several monographs by Dr. Wittman have been published at the Institute.

At Eötvös Loránd University in Budapest, courses in the Spanish and Portuguese literatures of Latin America are offered under the aegis of the Chair of Italian language and literature. Within the courses on literature mention is made wherever applicable of Latin American topics in the social sciences and humanities. At Kossuth Lajos University in Debrecen, the Americas are treated in a course entitled "Introduction to Ethnic Anthropology."

The Hungarian Academy of Sciences, which grants doctoral and "Kandidat" degrees, will accept university work done in the field of Latin American Studies. However, inasmuch as Latin American Studies as a field was instituted in Hungarian universities only as recently as 1961, no degrees within this specialization have been granted as yet, although some dissertations are currently being prepared (as of 1968).

In this bibliography the English translation of the title of each bibliographic item is to be found directly under the title in the original language, and immediately following the entire bibliographic description.

———————

El Dr. Tibor Wittman tiene la Cátedra de Historia
Latinoamericana en la Facultad de Filosofía de la
Universidad Attila József en la ciudad de Szeged.
En la misma Institución estableció el Dr. Wittman
un Instituto de Historia Medieval y Latinoamericana.
El Instituto ya publicó varias obras monográficas del
Dr. Wittman.

En la Universidad Eötvös Lórand de Budapest, bajo
la administración de la cátedra de lengua y literatura
italianas, se ofrecen cursos en las lenguas y letras
españolas y portuguesas. Se mencionan, dentro de
las materias de las asignaturas de letras, tópicos
latinoamericanos en las ciencias sociales y humanidades.
Se tratan las Américas en la asignatura, "Introducción
a Antropología Etnica", de la Universidad Kossuth
Lajos, situada en la ciudad de Debrecen.

La Academia Húngara de Ciencias, la cual otorga títulos
académicos de Doctor y Kandidat, acepta estudios
desempeñados en el campo de Estudios Latinoamericanos.
Visto que se instituyó este ramo profesional en las
universidades húngaras unicamente desde el año 1961,
todavía no otorgó la Academia cualquier título en Estudios Latinoamericanos. Actualmente (1968) se preparan
tésis en este campo.

En esta bibliografía la traducción inglesa del título de
cada asiento se encuentra directamente bajo el título
de la lengua original, seguida de la ficha entera.

I. Books

LATIN AMERICA

1492   Ács, Tivadar. Magyarok Latin Amerikában. Budapest,
Officina Képeskönyvek, 1944, 37p.
(Hungarians in Latin America)

1493   Ajtai, Kálmán. Az Őserdők Királya. Budapest, Szt.
István Társulat, 1941, 116p.
(The Jungle King, Novel)

1494   András, László. Dél keresztje. Latin-Amerikai Költők
versei. Vál., bev. és a jegyzeteket irta, ford. András
László, Devecseri Gábor, stb. Budapest, Európa, 1957,
315p.
                   (The Southern Cross.
Poems of Latin American Poets. Selected and Annotated
by Laszlo Andras. Tr. by Laszlo Andras, Gabor Devecseri, etc.)

1495   Babarczy, Jenő. Dél-Amerikai Emlékek. Arad, Aradi Ny.,
1909, 86p.
                 (South American Reminiscences)
- Travel book

1496   Balázs, Gábor. Utazásom Dél-Amerikában. Kolozsvár,
K. Papp Miklós, 1876, 166p.
(My Journey in South America)

1497   Bangha, Béla. Dél Keresztje Alatt... Budapest, Pázmány
P. Irod. Társ., 1934, 243p.
                 (Under the Southern Cross: Notes of a
Missionary Tour of South America)

1498   Békessy, Imre. Az uj Népvándorlás. Délamerika.
Budapest, May Ny., 1939, 243p.
               (The new Migration: South America)

1499   Brazilia-Argentina. Kiadja a Magyar Kereskedelmi
         Kamara Piac- és Konjunkturakutató Főosztálya. Budapest,
         Fővárosi Ny., 1959, 18p.
         (Brazil-Argentina. Edited by the Hungarian Chamber of
         Commerce: Foreign Trade Guide)

1500   A Chilei, Boliviai, es Perui Köztársaságok Kulturális és
         Közgazdasági Viszonyainak Valamint az Osztrák-Magyar
         Monarchia Ottani Érdekeinek Rövid Ismertetése. Bécs,
         Ny. n., 1902, 23p.
         (A Short Survey on the Cultural and Economic Conditions of
         Chile, Peru and Bolivia, as Well as on the Austro- Hunga-
         rian National Interests There)

1501   Colombia, República de Colombia. (Ecuador, República
         del Ecuador.) Budapest, Közgazdasági és Jogi Kk., 1956,
         140p. (Külkereskedelmi utmutató)
         (Republics of Colombia and Ecuador: Foreign Trade Guide)

1502   Csuday, Jenő. Dél-Amerika. Budapest, Hornyánszky,
         1909, 24p.
                        (South America)
         - Guide book.

1503   Délamerika Első Magyar Családi Naptára. Buenos Aires,
         Magyar Szo., 1924.
         (The First Hungarian Family Calendar in South America)

1504   Délamerikai Magyar Hirlap. Diario Hungaro Nagy Kepes
         Naptara. Szerk. Orban Leo. São Paulo, Délamerikai
         Magyar Hirlap, 1930.
         ("Hungarian Journal" of South America. The big Illustrated
         Calendar of the "Diario Hungaro". Ed. by Leo Orban)

1505   Az Evangélium Útja Délamerikában. Budapest, Gyarmati-
         Bosz Ny., 1941, 16p.
         (The Spread of the Gospel in South America)

1506   Forrongó Latin-Amerika. Budapest, Kossuth Kk., 1958,
         46p.
         (Latin America in Revolt)

1507   Futó, József. Közép- és Dél-Amerika. Budapest, Gondolat
         Kk., 1965, 306p.
                            (Central and South America)
         -Guide book

1508   Futó, József. Közép- és Dél-Amerika. 2d ed.   Budapest,
         Gondolat Kk., 1967, 304p.
                            (Central and South America)
         -Guide book

1509   Gáspár, Ferenc. Délamerika. Budapesttől-Hamburgon,
         a Kanári Szigeteken át Délamerika Körül-Colonig.
         Budapest, Singer & Wolfner, 1906, 588p.
                            (South America. From Budapest via
         Hamburg, Canary Islands, Around South America to
         Cologne)

1510   Guatemala. República de Guatemala. El Salvador.
         República de El Salvador. Honduras. República de
         Honduras; Külkereskedelmi útmutató. Budapest,
         Közgazdasági és Jogi Kk., 1957, 137p.
         (The Republics of Guatemala, El Salvador, Honduras:
         Guide to Foreign Trade)

1511 Kalchbrenner, Károly. Szibériai es Délamerikai Gombák.
      Fungi e Sibiria et America Australi; Értekezések a
      természettudományok köréből. 8. köt. 16. sz. Budapest,
      MTA, 1878, 23p.
                          (Siberian and South American
      Fungi. Dissertations in Natural Sciences, v. 8, no. 16)

1512 Kálmár, Gusztáv. Vihar az Orinoko Földjén. Budapest,
      Szt. István Társulat, 1941, 172p.
                          (Storm on the Land of Orinoco)
      -Wars of Independence of the Latin American States in
      the 19th Century

1513 Karczag, Gábor. Latin Amerika a Kubai Forradalom
      Után. Budapest, Kossuth Kk., 1968, 203p.
                          (Latin America After the Cuban
      Revolution)

1514 Kibédy, Albert. Az Ezüst Oroszlán. Utazás a Trópuson.
      Budapest, Szépirodalmi Kk., 1957, 467p.
                          (The Silver Lion. a Trip in the Tropics)
      - Travel book

1515 Kogutowicz, Mano. Dél-Amerika Politikai Térképe.
      Budapest, Magyar Földrajzi Intézet.
                          (Political map of South America)

1516 Lendl, Adolf. Uti Levelek két Vilagrészből. Budapest,
      1911, 157p.
                          (Travel Letters From two Continents)

1517   Mikes, György. Dél-Akerika Papucsban.
São Paulo, Livr. Bródy, 1962, 190p.
(Tango: a Solo Across South America)
-Latin American customs

1518   Nicaragua, República de Nicaragua. Costa Rica. Rep.
de Costa Rica. Panama. Rep. de Panama; Külkeres-
kedelmi utmutató. Budapest, Közgazdasági es Jogi
Kk., 1957, 139p.
(The Republics of Nicaragua, Costa Rica and Panama:
Guide to Foreign Trade)

1519   Peru. República del Peru. Bolivia. Republica de
Bolivia. Paraguay. República del Paraguay; Kül-
kereskedelmi utmutató. Budapest, Közgazdasági es
Jogi Kk., 1957, 154p.
(The Republics of Peru, Bolivia and Paraguay: Foreign
Trade Guide)

1520   Rónay, Gyula Z. Budapest-Buenos Aires.
Utazás a Spanyol es Portugálnyelvü Ó- és Ujvilágban.
Budapest, Arany J. Ny., 1927, 94p.
(Budapest-Buenos Aires:
Traveling in Spanish and Portuguese Speaking Old and
New Worlds)

1521   Schröder, Béla. Fehér Rabszolgák. Bevándorlók Sorsa
Délamerikában. Egy Világcsavargó Naplójából.
Budapest, Világosság Ny., 1913, 102p.
(White Slaves: The Situation of
Emigrants in South America. From a Globetrotter's
Diary)

1522   Temesy, Győző. A Föld Felfedezői és Meghóditói (v. 4:
Dél-Amerika Felfedezése és Meghóditása. Budapest,
Révai, 1938, pp. 319-441).
(Discoverers and Conquerers of the
World: The Discovery and Conquest of South America, v. 4)

1523   Tóbiás, Áron. Latin-Amerika Irodalma. Ajánló bibliográ-
fia. Kiadja a Fővárosi Szabó Ervin Könyvtár. Budapest,
Állami Ny., 1967, 199p.
(Latin American Literature, Select
Bibliography. Ed. by the Municipal Szabo Ervin Library)

1524   Toldy, Lászlo. A Föld és Népei. Föld és népismereti
kézikönyv. Hellwald Frigyes és más egyéb irók nyomán.
Kidolgozta Toldy László. Előszóval bevezette Hunfalvy
János. 1. köt. Eszak, Közép- és Dél-Amerika Földrajzi
és Népismereti Leirása. Budapest, Mehner, 1879, 456p.
(The Earth and its Peoples, Geographical
and Folkloristic Handbook. Compiled and With Preface
by Janos Hunfalvy, From the Writings of F. Hellwald and
Others. v. 1: Geographical and Folkloristic Description
of North, Central and South America)

1525   Vécsey, Zoltán. Elpusztult Népek, Elpusztult Kulturák.
Budapest, Mora Kk., 1966, 243p.
(Devastated Peoples, Destroyed Cultures)
-Cultural history

1526   Venezuela. Estados Unidos de Venezuela. Brit Guyana.
British Guiana. Francia Guyana. Guyana Française.
Holland Guyana. Surinam; Külkereskedelmi útmutató.
Budapest, Közgazdasági és Jogi Kk., 1958, 157p.
(Venezuela, British Guiana, French Guiana, Dutch Guiana:
Foreign Trade Guide)

1527   Zalai, Györgyné. Latin-Amerika. Budapest, Egyetemi
Ny., 1954, 35p.
(Latin America)
-Guide book

ARGENTINA

1528   Sikabonyi, Antal, comp. Argentinai Magyarok Könyv-
tárának Cimjegyzéke. Budapest, Pátria Ny., 1928, 90p.
(Catalog of Hungarians Residing
in Argentina)

1529   Elkán, Pál, & Rudolf Wodianer. Argentiana Leirása és
Ismertetése Magyar Nyelven. Magyar Spanyol Kézi-
szotar. Budapest, Elkán, 1928, 160p.
(A Description and
Survey of Argentina in Hungarian. Hungarian-Spanish
Dictionary)

1530   Facsády, Kálmán H. & Egon Lajos-Morenberger.
Argentina. Republica Argentina; Külkereskedelmi
útmutató. Budapest, Közgazdasági es Jogi Kk., 1962, 119p.
(Argentina: Foreign Trade Guide)

1531   Náday, Bela. Argentinában. 1920 Február-Március-
Aprilis. Budapest, Budapesti Hirlap Ny., 1920, 64p.
(Argentina: February-March-April 1920)

1532   Tatár, Imre. Argentina, a Sovány Peonok és a Kövér
        Tehenek Országa. Budapest, Kossuth Ny., 1962, 56p.
        (Argentina, the Land of the Thin "Peons" and the fat Cows)
        -Guide to national policy

1533   Worschitz, Frighes. Argentina Erdőgazdasági Vázlata.
        Budapest, Stádium, 1937, 10p.
                        (Forest Sketch of Argentina)

                        BOLIVIA

1534   Szokoly, Endre. Hét év Bolíviában. 2d ed. Budapest,
        Gondolat K., 1963, 294p.
                        (Seven Years in Bolivia)
        -Travel book

                        BRAZIL

1535   Aranyszemecskék, Jegyzetek a Braziliai Magyar Segély-
        egylet Működéséről. São Paulo, 1931, 24p.
        (Golden Pearls: Notes About the Function of the Hungarian
        Relief Society in Brazil)

1536   Boglár, Lajos. Trópusi Indiánok Között. Braziliai Utijegy-
       zetek. Budapest, Gondolat Kk., 1966, 158p.
                    (Among the Indians of the Tropics. Brazilian
    Travel Notes)

1537   Boldog, Gyula, A Légnedvesség Eloszlása Braziliában.
       Budapest, Állami Ny., 1933, 19p.
                    (The Dispersion of Humidity in Brazil)

1538   Brazilia. Estados Unidos de Brazil; Külkereskedelmi
       útmutató. Budapest, Közgazdasági és Jogi Kk., 1955,
       112p.
    (Brazil: Foreign Trade Guide)

1539   Braziliai Magyarok. Vázlatok a Braziliai Magyar Élet
       Kialakulásáról a Magyarok 2. Világkongresszusára.
       São Paolo, Délamerikai Magyar Újság, 1938, 130p.
    (Brazilian Hungarians: Sketches on the way of Life of
    Hungarians in Brazil. A Report Submitted to the Second
    World Congress of Hungarians)

1540   Migend,Dezso. Magyarok Braziliában. Békéscsaba, Körös-
       vidék Rt., 1925, 96p.
                    (Hungarians in Brazil)

1541   Molnár, Gábor. A Dzsungel Doktora. Vital Brazil Élete.
       Budapest, Gondolat Kk., 1967, 359p.
                    (The Jungle's Doctor; the Life of Vital Brazil)
    -Novelized biography

1542   Molnár, Gábor. Az Óriás Kigyók Földjén. Vadászuton
       Brazilia Őserdőiben. 4th ed. Budapest, Gondolat Kk.,
       1964, 301p.
                    (In the Land of Pythons: Boa Constrictor.
    A Hunting Trip in the Jungles of Brazil)

1543   Molnár, Gábor. <u>Barátom a Vadon.</u> <u>Braziliai Vadász-</u>
       <u>kalandok.</u> Budapest, Móra Kk., 1967, 280p.
                   (My Friend, the Wilderness: Brazilian
      Hunting Adventures)

1544   Németh, András. <u>Brazilia.</u> Budapest, Kossuth Kk., 1963,
       172p.
                   (Brazil)
      -Guide book

1545   Sikabonyi, Antal, comp. <u>Braziliai Magyarok Könyvtárának</u>
       <u>Cimjegyzéke.</u> Budapest, Pátria, 1928, 90p.
                   (Union Catalogue of the Library
      of Hungarians in Brazil)

1546   Steinen, Karl von den. <u>Közép Brazilia Természeti Népei</u>
       <u>Között. A Második Singu-Expedició (1887-88) útjának</u>
     <u>Vázolasa és Eredményei.</u> Átdolgozta Bátky Zsigmond.
      Budapest, Lampel, 1913, 275p.
                   (Among Native Peoples of Central
      Brazil. Sketches From the Route of the Second Singu
      Expedition (1887-1888) and its Results. Revised by
      Zsigmond Batky)

1547   Szabó, Pál. <u>Brazilia.</u> Budapest, Szikra, 1956, 184p.
                   (Brazil)
      -Guide to national policy

1548   Székely, Tibor. <u>Brazilia Őserdeiben.</u> Noviszád, Testvériség
       Egység Kk., 1955, 160p.
                   (In the Jungles of Brazil)
      -Novel

CHILE

1549   Chile, Republica de Chile; Külkereskedelmi utmutató,
Budapest, Közgazdasági és Jogi Kk., 1955, 68p.
(Republic of Chile: Foreign Trade Guide)

1550   Somlyó, György. Az Enciklopédikus Költő (A Költészet
Évadai. Budapest, Magvető, 1963, pp. 176-193).
(The Encyclopedic Poet, in his The
Seasons of Poetry, pp. 176-193)
-About Pablo Neruda

CUBA

1551   Csoóri, Sandor. Kubai Napló. Budapest, Magvető Kk.,
1965, 206p.
(Cuban Diary)

1552   Fenyő, Bela. Kolumbustól Kastróig. Budapest, Kossuth Kk.,
1960, 163p.
(From Columbus to Castro)
-Guide to national policy

1553   Fenyő, Béla. <u>Kuba nem Alkuszik</u>. Budapest, Kossuth Kk.,
        1961, 55p.
                        (Cuba Doesn't Admit)
        - Guide to national policy

1554   Salgó, László. <u>Ostromlott Sziget. Kubai Utijegyzetek.</u>
        Budapest, Kossuth Kk., 1964, 281p.
                        (Besieged Isle: Cuban Travel Diary)

1555   Tolnai, Gábor. <u>A Tenger és a Szél. Kubai Krónika.</u>
        Budapest, Magvető, 1964, 281p.
                        (The sea and the Wind. A Cuban Chronicle)
        - Travel book

1556   Várkonyi, Tibor. <u>A Kubai Válság Háttere</u>. Budapest,
        Kossuth Kk., 1963, 39p.
                        (The Background of the Cuban Crisis)

GUATEMALA

1557   Réti, Ervin. <u>Háború a Banánok Földjén</u>. Budapest, 1954,
        39p.
                        (War in the Land of Bananas)
        - Guide to national policy

MEXICO

1558   Banó, Jenő. Bolyongásaim Amerikában. Utleirások a
        Trópusok Vidékéről, a Mexikói Köztársaság Tüzetes
        Ismeretetésével. Budapest, Athenaeum, 1906, 344p.
                    (Wanderings in America. Travel Notes From
        the Tropics, With a Thorough Survey of Mexico)

1559   Banó, Jenő. Mexiko és Utazásom a Trópusokon. Budapest,
        Singer & Wolfner, 1896, 204p.
                    (Mexico and my Journey in the Jungles)

1560   Juhász, Vilmos. Az Inkák Birodalma. Budapest, Athenaeum,
        1936, 311p.
                    (The Empire of the Incas)

1561   Mocsáry, Beláné, & Maria Fay. Mexikoï Utazásom. Uti
        Jegyzetek. Budapest, Pesti Kny., 1905, 37p.
                                (My Journey in Mexico:
        Travel Notes)

1562   Pawlowszki, Ede, R. Miksa Csaszár Mexikói
        Szerencsétlen Expediciójanak Leirása. Kiváló Tekintet-
        tel Querétaro 70 Napig Tartó Ostomára. Mexikói Élet.
        Utazási Élmények. 2d ed. Budapest, Heisler, 1894, 218p.
                                (The Account of Emperor
        Maximilian's Unsuccessful Expedition in Mexico, With
        Special Attention to the Siege of 70 Days at Querétaro)

1563   Dadányi, György. Csordás Voltam Paraguayban. Budapest,
Stádium, 1939, 336p.
              (I was a Cowboy in Paraguay)
-Novelized travel book

1564   .   Migray, József. Egy Keresztényszociális Állam Története.
A Jezsuiták Köztársasága Paraguayban (1609-1768).
Budapest, Népszava, 1923, 71p.
              (The History of a Christian Social State:
The Jesuit Republic of Paraguay, 1609-1768)

PERU

1565   Gaal, József. Peru Fölfedezése és Elfoglalása. 2d ed.
Budapest, Heckenast G., 1872, 112p.
              (The Discovery and Occupation of Peru)

1566   Wittman, Tibor. La Riqueza Empobrece. Problemas de
Crisis del Alto Peru Colonial en la "Guia" de P. V.
Cañete y Dominguez. Los Metales Preciosos de América
y la Estructura Agraria de Hungaria a los Fines del Siglo
XVI. Szeged, Szegedi Ny., (Acta Universitatis
Szegediensis de Attila József Nominatae: Acta historica,
Studia Latinoamerica, 24), 1967, 35p.
              (Wealth Impoverishes: Problems of the
Crisis of Colonial "Alto Peru" in the "Guide" of P. V.
Cañete y Dominguez. The Precious Metals of America
and the Agrarian Structure of Hungary at the end of the
16th Century)

URUGUAY

1567   <u>Szemelvények Magyarország és az Uruguay-i Köztársaság</u>
       <u>Közti Kereskedelemről.</u> Statisztikai adatok a kereskede-
       lemről és pénzügyről. Uruguay kivitelképessége fagyasztott
       valamint fajbeli is vagoallatokban. Fiume, 1910, 18 & 8pp.
       (The Trade Between Hungary and the Republic of Uruguay.
       Statistical Data on Trade and Finance. Uruguay's Export
       Possibilities for Chilled Beef and Cattle for Slaughter)

1568   <u>Uruguay. República Oriental de Uruguay</u>; Külkereskedelmi
       útmutató. Budapest, Közgazdasági és Jogi Kk., 1956, 58p.
       (Uruguay)
       -Foreign trade guide

II. Periodical Articles

LATIN AMERICA

1569 Ács, Tivadar. "Délamerikai Magyar Utazók a XVII. és
XVIII. Században. " Budapest, A földgömb (IX: 4), April,
1938, pp. 150-153.
   ("Hungarian Travellers in South America
in the 17th and 18th Centuries")

1570 Ádám, György. "A Truman-Elv Latinamerikában. " Budapest,
Gazdaság (II), 1947, pp. 529-536.
   ("The Truman Doctrine in Latin America")

1571 Árkus, István. "A Dél-Amerikai Katolicizmus Válsága -
Közelről. " Budapest, Világosság (IV: 7-8), 1963, pp.
415-422.
   ("The Crisis of South American Catholicism -
on Close Inspection")

1572 "Az Aymara-Indusok Bolivia és Peruban. " Pest, Természet
(III), 1871, pp. 88-92.
("Aymara Indians in Bolivia and Peru")

1573 Balogh, Kálmán. "A Talaj és az Éghajlat Befolyása az
Ember Művelődésére (Mexikó és Peru). " Budapest,
Természettudományi közlöny (III), 1871, pp. 218-224.
   ("The Influence of Soil and Climate on
Civilization: Mexico and Peru")

1574   "Beszélgetés a Latin-Amerikai Nemzeti Burzsoázia
Szerepéről és Politikájáról. " Budapest, Nemzetközi
szemle (IV: 2), February 1960, pp. 30-38.
("A Talk About the Role and Policy of the Latin American
Burgeoisie")

1575   Boglár, Lajos. "XVIII. Századi Magyar Utazók Dél-Amerikában. "
Budapest, Ethnográphia (LXIII: 3-4), 1952, pp. 450-462.
("Hungarian Travellers of the 18th Century
in South America")

1576   Cholnoky, Jenő. "Argentina és Bolivia Határvidékeiről. "
Budapest, Földrajzi közlemények (XXXIII: 5), May 1905,
pp. 177-180.
("The Frontier Zones of Argentina and
Bolivia")

1577   Csikós, Mihály. "A Közlekedés Fejlődésének Néhány
Jellemző Adata Latin-Amerikában. " Budapest,
Közlekedéstudományi szemle (XV: 7), 1965, pp. 301-306.
("Some Characteristics of the Development
of Traffic in Latin America")

1578   Daday, Jenő. "A Délamerikai Halakban Élősködő Paramphistomida
Fajok Anatómiai és Szövettani Viszonyai. " Budapest,
Mathematikai és természettudományi értesitő (XXIV), 1906,
pp. 560-618.
("Anatomical and Hystological Properties of
Paramphistomida Parasite Species in South American
Fishes")

1579   Daday, Jenő. "Délamerikai Halakban Élősködő Trematodák. "
Budapest, Mathematikai és természettudományi értesitő
(XXIV), 1906, pp. 503-559.
("Trematode Parasites in South American
Fishes")

1580   Domán, Miklós. "Latinamerika Gazdasági Problémái. "
        Budapest, Külügyi szemle (XVII: 6), 1940, pp. 501-507.
        ("Economic Problems of Latin America")

1581   Goncol, György. "A Latinamerikai Népek Harca a Wall
        Street Gyarmatositó Politikája Ellen. A Caracasi Pánamerikai
        Ertekezlet. " Budapest, Társadalmi szemle (IX: 4), 1954,
        pp. 148-156.
                ("The Struggle of Latin American Peoples
        Against the Colonizing Policy of Wall Street: The Pan-American
        Conference in Caracas")

1582   Győrffy, Tibor. "Gazdaság és Politika Latin-Amerika
        Országaiban. " Budapest, Pártélet (IX: 12), 1964, pp. 113-119.
                ("Economic and Political Life in Latin
        America")

1583   Horváth, Lajos. "A Dél-Amerikai Őserdők Titokzatos Madara,
        a Hratzin. " Budapest, Élet és tudomány (XVIII: 6), 1963,
        pp. 181-184.
                ("Hratzin, a Mysterious Bird of the South
        American Jungles")

1584   Kádár, Béla. "Gazdasági Együttműködési Kisérletek Latin-
        Amerikában. " Budapest, Külkereskedelem (V: 12), 1961,
        pp. 1-3.
                ("Economic Cooperation Attempts in Latin
        America")

1585   Kádár, Béla. "Latin-Amerika Néhány Gazdasági és Külkereskedelmi
        Problémája. " Budapest, Külkereskedelem (V: 1), 1961,
        pp. 8-12.
                ("Some Economic and Foreign Trade Problems
        in Latin America")

1586   Kádár, Lajos. "A Latinamerikai Népek Harca a Demokráciáért
és a Függetlenségért. " Budapest, Magyar-Szovjet közgazdasági
szemle (VIII: 1), 1954, pp. 62-75.
("The Struggle of Latin American Peoples for
Democracy and Independence")

1587   Karcag, Gábor. "A Latin-Amerikai 'Közös Piac' Problémája. "
Budapest, Társadalmi szemle (XV: 2), 1960, pp. 103-109.
("The Problem of the Latin American Common
Market")

1588   Kilényi, Gyula. "Délamerikai Levelek. " Budapest, Magyar
figyelő (V: 1), 1915, pp. 287-291; (V: 2), 1915, pp. 140-145,
296-301; (V: 3), 1915, pp. 216-222.
("South American Letters: Travel Notes")

1589   "Latin-Amerika és "Che" Mitoszai. (Kerekasztal-Beszélgetés).
Paul Noirot, Georges Fournial, Albert-Paul Lentin, Carlos
Quijano. " Budapest, Nemzetközi szemle (XII: 3), 1968,
pp. 47-61.
("Latin America and the Myths of 'Che': Round-Table Talk
with Paul Noirot, Georges Fournial, Albert-Paul
Lentin, Carlos Quijano")

1590   "A Latinamerikai Irodalom Propagandája Europában. "
Budapest, Literatura (IV), 1929, p. 45.
("The Diffusion of Latin American Literature in Europe")

1591   Milesz, Béla. "Utiképek Délamerikából." Pest, Tarka
        világ és képes regélő (I), 1869, p. 90.
                ("Travel Notes from South America")

1592   Papp-Váry, Árpád. "A Közép és Dél-Amerikai Indián
        Osztálytársadalmak Térképészeti Ismeretei." Budapest,
        Geodézia és kartográfia (XIX: 6), 1967, pp. 440-443.
                ("The Cartographic Contributions
        of the Central and South American Indian Class-Societies")

1593   Puja, Frigyes. "A Latin-Amerikai Forradalom Néhány
        Kérdése." Budapest, Nemzetközi szemle (X: 4), 1966,
        pp. 26-36.
                ("Some Questions of the Revolution in
        Latin America")

1594   Réti, Ervin. "Szövetség a Haladás Ellen. Az Egyesult Államok
        Uj Latinamerikai Politikájának Ellentmondásai." Budapest,
        Társadalmi szemle (XXI: 10), 1966, pp. 62-72.
                ("Alliance Against Progress. Contradictions of
        the USA's New Latin American Policy")

1595   Rosty, Pál. "Délamerikai Képek." Pest, Uj Magyar Muzeum
        (I), 1860, p. 261.
                ("South American Sketches")

1596   Simor, András. "A Latin-Amerikai Irodalom Ujabb
        Könyvkiadásunkban." Budapest, A könyv (II: 6), 1962,
        pp. 14-15.
                ("Latin American Literature in Our
        Recent Publications")

1597   Sutó, Gábor. "A Latin-Amerikai Szolidaritási Szervezet
        Első Értekezlete. A Latin-Amerikai Forradalmak Stratégiája."
        Budapest, Nemzetközi szemle (XI: 10), 1967, pp. 12-20.
                ("The First Conference of the Latin American
        Solidarity Organization. The Strategy of the Latin American
        Revolutions")

1598   Sütő, Gábor. "Latin-Amerika Népeinek Harca az Egyesült
        Államok Imperialista Politikája Ellen. " Budapest,
        Társadalmi szemle (XIV: 1), 1959, pp. 71-79.
                        ("The Struggle of the Latin American People
        Aginst the Imperialist Politics of the USA")

1599   Szeberthy, János. "A Délamerikai Kivándorlás és a
        Magyarság. " Budapest, Az ország útja (II: 5), 1938,
        pp. 312-323.
                        ("Emigration to South America and the
        Hungarians")

1600   Szuhay-Havas, Ervin. "Istenek Születése - Vagy a Világ
        Keletkezése a Közép-Amerikai Maja-Kicsé Nép Mitológiájában. "
        Budapest, Világosság (IV: 11), 1963, pp. 665-667.
                        ("The Birth of Gods - or the Creation
        in the Mythology of South American Maya-Quiché People")

1601   Tarján, Imre. " Latin-Amerika, az Egyház "Elmaradt"
        Földrésze. " Budapest, Világosság (I: 2), 1960, pp. 34-38.
                        ("Latin America, a 'Backward' Continent
        of the Church")

1602   Zombory, István. "Indiánok Között. " Budapest, Uj idők
        (XXIII: II), 1917, pp. 407-409.
                        ("Among Indians: Latin American
        Ethnography")

1603   Zombory, István. "Napsugaras Tájak Felé. " Budapest,
        Uj idők (XXIV: I), 1918, pp. 304-306.
                        ("Towards Sun-Kissed Regions: South
        American Travel Notes ")

ARGENTINA

1604   "Az Argentin Köztársaság Mezőgazdasága." Budapest,
        Mezőgazdasági közlöny (XI: 12), 1938, pp. 536-538.
        ("The Agriculture of the Argentine Republic")

1605   Bánát, Lajos. "Argentina és Vasútja." Budapest, Vasút
        (XIII: 6), 1963, pp. 14-15.
        ("Argentina and its Railway")

1606   Marky-Mattyasovszky, Jenő. "Magyarok Élete Argentinában."
        Budapest, Uj idők (LIII), 1947, pp. 10-11.
                                    ("The Lives of Hungarians
        in Argentina")

1607   "Milyen Változások Mennek Végbe a Munkásosztály Strukturájában?"
        Budapest, Béke és szocializmus (IV: 4), 1961, pp. 112-135.
        ("What Changes Occur in the Structure of the Working Class?")

1608   "Rabszolgavásár Argentinában." Budapest, Magyar Figyelő
        (III: 4), 1913, pp. 478-480.
        ("Slave-Market in Argentina")

1609   Topál, Gyorgy. "Weight-Data of Birds Collected. The Zoological
        Results of Gy. Topál's Collectings in South Argentina."
        Budapest, Vertebrata Hungarica Musei Historico-Naturalis
        Hungarici (VII: 1-2), 1965, pp. 79-84.

BOLIVIA

1610   "Bolivia Népe Folytatja Harcát a Nemzeti Függetlenségért.
(Levél La Pazból). " Budapest, Tartós Békéért (30),
1953, p. 6.
("The Bolivian People Continues Struggle for National
Independence: Letter from La Paz")

1611   "A Boliviai Partizánmozgalom a Nép Harcának Egyik
Formája. Beszélgetés a Boliviai Kommunista Párt
Képviselőjével (Aldo Floressal). " Budapest, Nemzetközi
szemle (XI: 8), 1967, pp. 83-84.
("The Bolivian Guerilla Movement, a Model of the People's
Struggle: Interview with Aldo Flores, a Representative of
the Bolivian Communist Party")

1612   Futó, József. "Bolivia. " Budapest, Élet és tudomány
(XXI: 22), 1966, pp. 1031-1036.
("Bolivia")

BRAZIL

1613   Balogh, Kalmán. "A Talaj és az Éghajlat Befolyása az
Ember Művelődésére. Észak-Amerikai Egyesült Államok
és Brazilia. " Budapest, Természettudományi közlöny (III),
1871, pp. 417-425.
("The Influence of Soil and Climate on the
Civilization in the U. S. A. and Brazil")

1614 Boglár, Lajos. "Urn Burial of the Brazilian Indians. "
Budapest, <u>Acta Ethnographica</u> (VI), 1958, pp. 347-355.

1615 Csaba, László, & Ipoly Farkas. "Brazil Epitészet. "
Budapest, <u>Magyar épitőipar</u> (XII: 10), 1953, pp. 442-446.
("Brazilian Architecture")

1616 Futó, József. "A Világ Legnagyobb Folyója. " Budapest,
<u>Élet és tudomány</u> (XXI: 14), 1966, pp. 647-652.
("The Largest River of the World, the Amazon")

1617 Halmos, István. "Melody and Form in the Music of the
Nambicuara Indians (Mato Grosso, Brazil). " Budapest,
<u>Studia Musicologica Scientiarum Academiae Hungaricae</u>
(VI: 3-4) 1964, pp. 317-356.

1618 Kordás, Ferenc. "A Braziliai Magyarok. " Budapest,
<u>Magyar szemle</u> (XXXV: 2), 1939, pp. 177-179.
("Brazilian Hungarians")

1619 Kozma, Lajos. "Brazilia Epitészete és az Uj Formanyelv. "
Budapest, <u>Tér és forma</u> (XIX), 1946, pp. 161-166.
("Brazilian Architecture and the New Form
of Expression")

1620 Markos, János. "Magyarok Braziliaban. "Budapest,
<u>Uj éiet</u> (IX: 2), 1940, pp. 65-70.
("Hungarians in Brazil")

1621 Márky-Mattyasovszky, Jenő. "Hogyan Élnek a Magyar
Telepesek Braziliában?" Budapest, <u>Uj idők</u> (LIII),
1946, pp. 716-718.
("How Do the Hungarian
Settlers Live in Brazil?")

1622   Matolay, Tibor. "Szubtropikus Brazil Őserdők Klimája. "
        Budapest, Buvár (V: 1), 1939, pp. 21-25.
                        ("The Climate of the Subtropical Brazilian
        Jungles")

1623   Mora Valverde, E. "Latin Amerika Gazdasági Helyzete
        és a Latinamerikai Forradalom Fejlődése. " Budapest,
        Béke és szocializmus 8, 1965, pp. 60-73.
                        ("The Latin American Economic Situation
        and Latin American Revolutionary Progress")

1624   Rónai, Pál. "Találkozás a Brazil Irodalommal. " Budapest,
        Nagyvilág (X: 5), 1965, pp. 757-764.
                        ("An Encounter with Brazilian Literature")

1625   Sőtér, István. "Brazil Impresszió. (Részlet Egy Utinaplóból). "
        Budapest, Uj irás (I: 8), 1961, pp. 729-735.
                        ("Impressions from Brazil: Selections from a
        Travel Book")

1626   "A Sveiciak Uj Gyarmata Braziliában. " Pest, Tudományos
        gyüjtemény (I), 1821, p. 119.
        ("New Swiss Colony in Brazil")

1627   Tavaszy, Sándor. "A Mai Brazil Regény. " Budapest,
        Nagyvilág (VII: 9), 1962, pp. 1388-1391.
                        ("The Brazilian Novel of Today")

1628   Wallner, Ernő. "Brazilia Gazdasági Élete. " Budapest,
        Földrajzi közlemények (XI: 4), 1963, pp. 335-346.
                        ("Brazil's Economic Life")

1629   Wartha, Vincze. "Akik Adót Nem Fizetnek. (Brazilia
        Bakairi Néptörzse). " Budapest, Természettudományi
        közlöny (XXVII), 1895, pp. 569-577.
                        ("Those Who Don't Pay Any Taxes: Brazilian
        Bakairi Tribe")

1630   Weinstein, Pál. "Északamerikai és Braziliai Tanulmányút. "
Budapest, Orvosok lapja (IV), 1948, pp. 1128-1131.
("North American and Brazilian Study-
Tour: Brazilian Public Health")

1631   Zimányi, Károly. "Phenakit Braziliából. " Budapest,
Akadémiai Értesitő (XX: 234-235), 1909, pp. 386-387.
("Phenacite from Brazil: Mineralogy")

CHILE

1632   Balassa, András. "Az Elveszett Városok Völgye. " Budapest,
Élet és tudomány (XIX: 7), 1964, pp. 291-294.
("The Valley of the Lost Towns: Archaeology")

1633   Bódogh, Endre. "Rövid Ismertetés Magellánesz Chilei Megyéről
és Annak Geológiájáról. " Budapest, Földtani kutatás (X: 2),
1967, pp. 66-70.
("A Short Review of the Chilean Magallanes
Region and its Geology")

1634   Loksa, Imre, & I. Rubio. "Collembolen Aus Chile, Norte Grande.
l. " Budapest, Acta Zoologica Academiae Scientiarum Hungaricae
(XII: 3-4), 1966, pp. 323-330.
("Collembola from Chile, Norte
Grande")

1635   Matolay, Tibor. "A Chilei Földrengés. " Budapest, Buvar
(V: 2), 1939, pp. 90-94.
("The Chilean Earthquake")

1636   Pekár, Dezső. "A Geofizikai Kutatás Magyar Halottja Chilében."
           Budapest, Természettudományi közlöny (LXVIII), 1936,
           pp. 18-23.
                    ("Hungarian Martyr of Geophysical Research
           in Chile")

1637   "Polgárháború Chilében." Budapest, Budapesti szemle,
           (LXIX), 1892, pp. 111-118.
           ("Civil War in Chile")

COLOMBIA

1638   A. G. (pseud.) "Kolumbia Költészete." Budapest,
           Budapesti szemle (XXI), 1864, pp. 204-219.
                   ("Poetry of Colombia")

1639   Vadasdi, Károly. "Columbia." Budapest, Külkereskedelem
           (IV: 7), 1960, p. 16.
                   ("Colombia. Foreign Trade")

CUBA

1640   "Adatok a Kubai Köztársasághoz Tartozó Pinos Sziget Talajának
           Biológiai Jellemzéséhez." (Irta), Szegi, József, Maria
           Rodriguez, stb. Budapest, Agrókémia és talajtan (XVI: 3),
           1967, pp. 434-440.
           ("Data Concerning the Biological Characteristics of the Isle of
           Pines, Cuba by József Szegi, Maria Rodriguez, etc. ")

1641   Berndorfer, Alfréd. "Kuba Egészségügye." Budapest,
        Orvosi hetilap (CV: 20), 1964, pp. 938-940.
                    ("Public Health in Cuba")

1642   Bojthe, Tamás. "Kubai Képek." Budapest, Magyar
        epitőművészet (4), 1963, pp. 38-43.
                    ("Cuban Pictures. Architecture")

1643   Dobozy, Imre. "Védadó." Budapest, Élet és irodalom
        (VII: 36), 1963, pp. 1-2.
                    ("Cuban Sociography")

1644   Gara, Judit. "A Kubai Forradalom Gazdasági Vonatkozásai."
        Budapest, Közgazdasági szemle (IX: 5), 1962, pp. 606-628.
                    ("The Economic Aspects of the Cuban Revolution")

1645   Hajtó, Béla. "Diesel-Mozdonyok Kuba Részére." Budapest,
        Járművek mezőgazdasági gépek (XIV: 8), 1967, pp. 281-285.
                    ("Diesel Engines for Cuba")

1646   Járainé Komlódi, Magda. "A Tengerpart és a Mocsárvilág
        Növényzete Kubában." Budapest, Élővilág (IX: 3), 1964,
        pp. 3-13.
                    ("The Flora of the Seaside and
        the Marsh in Cuba")

1647   Járainé Komlódi, Magda. "Trópusi Vegetációtanulmányok
        Kubában." Budapest, Botanikai közlemények (LI: 2-3),
        1964, pp. 143-168.
                    ("Studies on Cuban Tropical
        Vegetation")

1648   Kmetty, Gyula. "Kuba Szeszesitalipara." Budapest,
        Szeszipar (XII: 4-5), 1964, pp. 95-97.
                    ("The Cuban Distilling Industry")

1649   Kollár, Zoltán. "A Kubai Köztársaság Külkereskedelme."
        Budapest, Külkereskedelem (IX: 3), 1965, pp. 79-82.
                        ("The Foreign Trade of the Cuban Republic")

1650   Komját, Irén. "Forradalom és Állam Kubában." Budapest,
        Társadalmi szemle (XVII: 4), 1962, pp. 34-51.
                        ("Revolution and State in Cuba")

1651   "Kuba. (A Kubai Irodalom Antológiája)." Budapest, Magvető
        almanach (3), 1965, pp. 7-123.
        ("Cuba: Cuban Literary Anthology")

1652   "Kuba Cellulóz- és Papiripara." Budapest, Papiripar
        (VIII: 4), 1964, pp. 141-142.
        ("Cellulose and Paper Industry in Cuba")

1653   "Kuba Gazdasági és Kulturális Elete a Forradalom Győzelme
        Óta." Budapest, Statisztikai szemle (XLI: 6), 1963, pp.
        646-649.
        ("Economic and Cultural Life in Cuba After the Victory of
        the Revolution")

1654   "A Kubai Forradalom és a Latin-Amerikai Imperialistaellenes
        Front." (Irta) A. Ferrari, J. M. Fortuny, stb. Budapest,
        Béke és szocializmus (VIII: 1), 1965, pp. 53-66.
        ("The Cuban Revolution and the Anti-Imperialistic Front
        of Latin America")

1655   Lenkei, László. "A Kubai Forradalom Utja." Budapest,
        Magyar filozófiai szemle (VI: 2), 1962, pp. 217-226.
                        ("The Way of the Cuban Revolution")

1656   Marthy, Barna. "Mesztic Irodalom és Forradalmi Művészet.
(Nicolas Guillén Kuba Irodalmáról)." Budapest, Elet és
irodalom (III: 36), 1959, p. 6.
("Mestizo Literature and Revolutionary Art.
Nicolas Guillén on Cuban Literature")

1657   Mikola, Anikó. "A Kubai Irodalom 200 Eve." Budapest,
Irodalmi szemle (X: 2), 1967, pp. 160-161.
("200 Years of Cuban Literature")

1658   Mlynarik, János. "A Kubai Húsipar Helyzete." Budapest,
Húsipar (XI: 2), 1962, pp. 72-76.
("The Situation of Cuban Meat Trade
Industry")

1659   Salgó, László. "A Kubai Forradalom és a Monroe-Doktrina."
Budapest, Párttörténeti kozlemények (IX: 2), 1963, pp. 57-69.
("The Cuban Revolution and the Monroe
Doctrine")

1660   Salgó, László. "Bandungtól a Havannai Trikontinentális
Ertekezletig." Budapest, Nemzetközi szemle (X: 3),
1966, pp. 6-21.
("From Bandoeng to the Tri-Continental
Conference in Havana")

1661   Sobieski, Artur. "Ezer Kilóméter Kuba Fölött." Budapest,
Elet és tudomány (XXI), 1966, pp. 1317-1323.
("A Thousand Kilometers Over Cuba")

1662   Szenthegyi, István, & Iván Vitányi. "Kubai Balett."
Budapest, Muzsika (IV: 6), 1961, pp. 18-20.
("Cuban Ballet")

1663 Szigethy, Károly. "A Kubai Gazdaság és a Magyar-Kubai
    Kereskedelmi Kapcsolatok Fejlődése." Budapest,
    Külkereskedelem (VII: 7), 1963, pp. 10-13.
        ("Cuban Economics and the Development
  of Hungarian-Cuban Commercial Relations")

1664 Temesi, Alfréd. "Közoktatási Reform Kubában." Budapest,
    Pedagógiai szemle (XI: 7-8), 1961, pp. 712-719.
        ("Reform in Public Education in Cuba")

1665 Timmer, József. "Kuba Sajtója." Budapest, Magyar sajtó
    (VII: 10), 1966, pp. 313-314.
        ("The Press of Cuba")

1666 Wallner, Ernő. "Kuba." Budapest, Földrajzi közlemények
    (XI: 1), 1963, pp. 51-57.
        ("Cuba: Sociography")

1667 Wittman, Tibor. "A Kubai Gazdaság Válaszuton, 1700-1762."
    Budapest, Századok (XCIX: 4-5), 1965, pp. 782-804.
        ("The Cuban Economy in Dilemma, 1700-1762")

1668 Zombory, István. "Ahol Még Akad Jó Szivar." Budapest,
    Uj idők (XXIV: I), 1918, pp. 511-513.
        ("Where There May Still be Some Good
  Cigars: Tobacco Production")

DOMINICAN REPUBLIC

1669   Probáld, Ferenc. "Amerika Bölcsője: Dominika."
Budapest, Elet és tudomány (XXI: 8), 1966, pp. 347-352.
("America's Cradle: Dominican Republic")

1670   Probáld, Ferenc, & János Hajdu. "Az Egymilliárd Dolláros
Hitbizomány. A Dominikai Koztársaság." Budapest,
Természettudományi közlöny (X: 1), 1966, pp. 12-17.
("One Billion Dollars
Seized: The Dominican Republic")

ECUADOR

1671   Méhes, György. "A Szél Gyermekei." Marosvásárhely,
Igaz szó (XIV: 2), 1966, pp. 301-303.
("The Children of the Wind: About Jorge Icaza")

1672   Vánffy, Lajos. "Ecuador - Chimborazo." Pest, Család
könyve (I), 1855, p. 275.

EL SALVADOR

1673   "San Salvador Elpusztulása. " Pest, Család könyve (I),
1855, p. 239.
("The Devastation of San Salvador")

GUATEMALA

1674   Gomori, Endre. "Mi Történt Guatemalában?" Budapest,
Propagandista (III: 8), 1954, pp. 43-46.
("What Happened in Guatemala?")

1675   Simor, András. "Budapesti Beszélgetés Asturiassal. "
Budapest, A könyv (IV: 12), 1964, pp. 421-422.
("A Talk with Asturias in Budapest")

GUYANA

1676   Bonyhádi, Jenő. "Brit-Guayana. " Budapest, Természet
és technika (CXII: 11), 1953, pp. 681-682.
("British Guiana: Sociology")

1677   Gerster, Béla. "Brit Guayana és Venezuela Közti Határrendezés. "
           Budapest, Földrajzi közlemények (XXVIII), 1900, pp. 111-113.
                      ("Rectification of Frontiers Between British
        Guiana and Venezuela")

1678   "Kommunizmus Brit-Guayanában?" Budapest, Nemzetközi
           szemle (I: 10), 1957, pp. 91-92.
           ("Communism in British Guiana?")

HAITI

1679   Ágai, Agnes. "Haiti Történet. " Budapest, Nagyvilág
           (VIII: 5), 1963, pp. 784-785.
                    ("A Story from Haiti: About Jacques Stephan
        Alexis")

1680   Lyka, Károly. "Paul Gauguin, a Trópusok Festője. "
           Budapest, Élet és tudomány (XVII: 24), 1962, pp. 751-755.
                    ("Paul Gauguin, the Painter of the Tropics")

1681   Tavaszy, Sándor. "Haiti Modern Költészete. " Budapest,
           Nagyvilág (X: 12), 1965, pp. 1869-1870.
                    ("Modern Haitian Poetry")

1682   Boglár, Lajos. "Diego Rivera, a Mexikói Nép Festője. "
Budapest, Szabad művészet (IX: 10), 1955, pp. 466-471.
("Diego Rivera, the Painter of the Mexican
People")

1683   Inkey, Béla. "Mexico Vulkánjairól. " Budapest, Földrajzi
közlemények (XXXVI: 8), 1908, pp. 309-322.
("About Mexican Volcanoes")

1684   Jemnitz, János. "Az 1910-1917. Évi Mexikói Forradalom. "
Budapest, Élet és tudomány (XVII: 35), 1962, pp. 1091-1095.
("The Mexican Revolution of 1910-1917")

1685   Kalmár, Vera. "Mire Irtak Mexikó Őslakói?" Budapest,
Papiripar és magyar grafika (I: 7-8), 1957, pp. 150-151.
("What Did the Indians of Mexico Write on?")

1686   Mayerffy, István. "Mexikó Földirati Nevei Helyes Kimondásáról. "
Pest, Magyar Tudományos Akadémiai Ertesitő, 1857, p. 597.
("About the Correct Pronunciation of
Mexican Geographical Names")

1687   "Mexiko. " Arad, Alföldi kalauz (I), 1860, p. 76.
("Mexico")

1688   "Mexikóban Esős Időszak. " Budapest, Athenaeum Nagy
Képes Naptára (XV), 1874, pp. 46-56.
("Rainy Season in Mexico")

1689   "A Mexikói Küldöttség Miramaréban. " Pest, Emich Nagy
        Képes Naptára (VI), 1865, p. 123.
        ("Mexican Delegation in Miramar: Concerning Maximilian
        I of Mexico")

1690   Solymár, István. "David Alfaro Siqueiros. " Budapest,
        Művészet (II: 2), 1962, pp. 3-5.

1691   Solymár, István. "José Clemente Orozco (1883-1949). "
        Budapest, Művészet (II: 9), 1961, pp. 12-16.

1692   Tamás, Aladár. "Szétszórt Parázs. (Mexikóba Emigrált
        Baloldali Irókról). " Budapest, Nagyvilág (VII: 11),
        1962, pp. 1701-1707.
                        ("Scattered Glowing Embers: Leftist
        Writers Emigrate to Mexico")

1693   Vezérfi, Károly. "A Calpulli Rendszer Mexikóban. "
        Budapest, Élet és tudomány (XX: 8), 1965, pp. 352-356.
                        ("The Calpulli Tribe Communities in
        Mexico: Mexican Community in the 15th-16th Centuries")

1694   Zombory, István. "Egy Régi Mexikói Bányamágnás. "
        Budapest, Uj idők (XXIV: II), 1918, pp. 222-224.
                        ("An Old Mexican Mining Magnate")

1695   Zombory, István. "Minas Tapadas." Budapest, Uj idők
        (XXIII: II), 1917, pp. 525-528.
                        ("Mines Shut Down")

PANAMA

1696   Bogdánfy, Odon. "A Panama-Csatorna." Budapest,
        Természettudományi közlöny (LXVII), 1916, pp. 217-246.
        ("Panama Canal")

1697   Futó, József. "Panama-Csatorna." Budapest, Élet és
        tudomány (XIX: 12), 1964, pp. 550-555.
        ("Panama Canal")

1698   Gémes, Ferenc. "A Panama-Csatorna Története."
        Budapest, Természet-tudományi közlöny (IV: 1), 1960,
        pp. 20-23.
                    ("The History of Panama Canal")

1699   Hézser, Aurél. "A Panama-Csatorna Földrajzi Szempontból."
        Budapest, Földrajzi közlemények (XLII), 1914, pp. 99-102.
                    ("The Panama Canal from a Geographic
        Viewpoint")

1700   Somogyi, József. "A Panama Csatorna." Budapest,
        Külügyi szemle (XIX: V), 1942, pp. 375-381.
                    ("Panama Canal")

1701   Somogyi, József. "A Panama-Csatorna Közlekedésföldrajzi
        Jelentősége." Budapest, Földrajzi közlemények (LV),
        1927, pp. 214-227.
                    ("The Geographic Significance of the
        Panama Canal in Terms of Transportation")

1702   Tábori, Róbert. "A Délamerikai Uj Republikáról: A
Panama-Köztársaság. " Budapest, Uj idők (IX: II), 1903,
pp. 485-486.

                            ("A New Republic of South America:
Panama")

1703   Zellovich, Kornél. "A Panama-Csatorna Elso Terve. "
Budapest, Természettudományi közlöny (LVIII), 1926,
pp. 143-144.

                            ("The First Plan of the Panama Canal")

PARAGUAY

1704   Anisits, Izabella. "A Paraguayi Konyha. " Budapest,
Uj idők (XII), 1906, pp. 445-447.
                      ("Paraguayan Kitchen")

1705   Babarczyné Jósa, Jolán. "A Csipkecsodák Hazájából.
(Paraguay). " Budapest, Uj idők (XXIV: II), 1912, pp. 507-509.
                         ("From the Land of Lace Wonders:
Paraguay")

1706   Babarczyné Jósa, Jolán. "La Dulce Idioma Guarani. "
Budapest, Uj idők (XVII: II), 1911, pp. 481-483.
                         ("Sweet Guarani, Indian Language")

1707   Babarczyné Jósa, Jolán. "Paraguayból. " Budapest, Uj
idők (XIII: I), 1907, pp. 431-433.
                         ("From Paraguay: Travel Notes")

1708   Daday, Jenő. "Paraguay Mikrofaunájának Alaprajza."
         Budapest, Mathematikai és természettudományi
         értesitő (XXIII), 1905, pp. 312-355.
                  ("Sketch of the Micro-Fauna of Paraguay")

1709   "Fauna Paraguayensis. 1. Report on Collecting, by
         István Andrássy, János Balogh...etc." Budapest,
         Rovartani közlemények (XX: 16), 1967, pp. 297-308.

1710   Vezérfi, Károly. "A Paraguayi Jezsuita Utópia." Budapest,
         Világosság (VII: 3), 1966, pp. 167-173.
                  ("The Jesuit Utopia in Paraguay")

                              PERU

1711   Balogh, János. "New Oribatids from Eastern Peru."
         Budapest, Annales Historico-Naturalis Musei Nationalis
         Hungarici (LIV), 1962, pp. 405-417.

1712   Balogh, János. "Some New Lohmanniids from Peru."
         Budapest, Opuscula Zoologica Instituti Zoosystematici
         Universitatis Budapestinensis (IV: 2-4), 1962, pp. 59-61.

1713   Bogdánfy, Odon. "A Perui Madárszigetek." Budapest,
         Természettudományi közlöny (LIX), 1927, pp. 562-565.
                  ("Bird Islands in Peru")

1714   "A Perui Forradalomról." Budapest, <u>Athenaeum Nagy
        Képes Naptára</u> (XV), 1874, pp. 45, 54.
        ("The Revolution in Peru")

1715   Szamos, Sári. "Teljes Napfogyatkozás Peruban." Budapest,
        <u>A földgömb</u> (IX: 6), 1938, pp. 232-236.
        ("Full Solar Eclipse in Peru")

1716   Székely, András. "Peru Művészete." Budapest, <u>Rajztanitás</u>
        (IX: 5), 1967, pp. 26-29.
        ("The Art of Peru")

1717   Székely, Mária. "Utazás az Inkák Földjén." Budapest,
        <u>Elet és tudomány</u> (XXI: 49), 1966, pp. 2327-2332;
        (51), 1966, pp. 2435-2440.
                    ("Travel in the Land of the Incas")

1718   Széplaki, Erneszt. "Peru Legujabb Zendülése." Buda,
        <u>Tudománytár</u> (VI), 1835, pp. 76-86.
                    ("The Recent Revolution in Peru")

1719   Vécsey, Zoltán. "Ahol a Perui Lavina Lezudult."
        Budapest, <u>Elet és tudomány</u> (XVII: 5), 1962, pp. 131-135.
                    ("Where the Peruvian Avalanche Fell:
        Sociography")

PUERTO RICO

1720   "Portorikó az Amerikai Gyarmatositók Igájában. "
        Budapest, Tartós békéért, népi demokráciáért (48),
        1953, p. 4.
        ("Puerto Rico Under the Yoke of the American Colonizers")

URUGUAY

1721   "Latin-Amerikában Forradalom Előtti Helyzet van. Beszélgetés
        Rodney Arismendivel az Uruguayi Kommunista Párt
        Főtitkárával. " Budapest, Nemzetközi szemle (XII: 2),
        1968, pp. 63-66.
        ("Pre-Revolutionary Situation in Latin America: A Talk
        with Rodney Arismendi, General-Secretary of the Uruguayan
        Communist Party")

1722   "Uruguay. -Montevideo Kikötője. " Budapest, Földrajzi
        közlemények (I), 1873, p. 53.
        ("Uruguay - the Seaport of Montevideo")

VENEZUELA

1723   Kando, Ata. "Fényképezőgéppel a Makiritare Indiánok
Között." Budapest, Élet és tudomány (XX: 46-47),
1965, pp. 2184-2189; 2227-2234.
("With a Camera Among Makiritare Indians")

1724   Török, Aurél. "A Délamerikai Puszták Fiairól." Budapest,
Természettudományi közlöny (XII), 1880, pp. 158-160.
("About the Sons of South American
Prairies: Anthropology")

1725   Wallner, Ernő. "Venezuela." Budapest, Természettudományi
közlöny (VII: 1), 1963, pp. 24-28.

WEST INDIES AND THE CARIBBEAN

1726   Vass, Samu. "A Nyugat-Indiai Szigetek." Pest, Magyarhoni
földtani társulat munkálatai (II), 1863, p. 129.
("West Indies")

1727   Rapcsányi, László. "Kalózok a Karib-Tengeren." Budapest,
Élet és tudomány (XVII: 23), 1962, pp. 716-719.
("Pirates on the Caribbean Sea:
History")

POLAND

The Spanish language is taught at the Jagiellonian
University in Cracow (where there is an Institute
of Languages), at the University of Poznan, and at
the University of Warsaw (which offers a Seminar
on the Regional Geography of the Americas). Institutes
of Geography are also located at the University of
Lodz and at the Adam Mickiewicz University in
Poznan. Pertinent courses are also offered in the
Faculty of Foreign Trade of the College of Planning
and Statistics in Warsaw.

Diplomacy is taught at the Central Foreign Service
School in Warsaw, and studies with respect to
Latin America are carried out by the Polish
Institute of International Affairs, also located in
Warsaw.

In this section the English translation of the title of
each bibliographic item is to be found directly under
the title in the original language, and immediately
following the entire bibliographic description.

La lengua española se enseña en la Universidad
Jadzielloniana en la ciudad de Cracov (donde hay un
Instituto de Idiomas), en la Universidad de Poznan,
y en la Universidad de Varsovia, la cual ofrece un
Seminario sobre la Geografía Regional de las Américas.
Institutos de Geografía también forman parte de la
Universidad de Lodz y de la Universidad Adam
Mickiewicz en Poznan. Se enseñan cursos apropiados

en la Facultad de Comercio Internacional del Colegio
de Planeación y Estadística en Varsovia.

Se enseña diplomacia en la Escuela Central de Servicio
Extranjero en Varsovia, y se desempeñan estudios
sobre Latinoamérica en el Instituto Polaco de Asuntos
Internacionales, también situado en Varsovia.

En esta sección la traducción inglesa del título de
cada asiento se encuentra directamente bajo el título
de la lengua original, seguida de la ficha entera.

LATIN AMERICA

1728   Ameryka Łacińska. Poszczególne Kraje, Ich Rozwój, Teraźniej-
Szośo. Mexico, 1948, 241p.
(Latin America: Corresponding States, Their Development and
Present Situation)

1729   Ameryka Łacińska. Warsaw, Polska Agencja Prasowa PAP,
1961, 333p.
(Latin America)

1730   Ameryka Łacińska. Wazniejsze Dane o Rozwoju Gospodarczym
Ameryki Łacińskiej. Warsaw, Głowny Urzad Statystyczny,
1962, 51p.
(Latin America: Significant Data on Economic Development of
Latin America)

1731   Ameryki Odkrycie i Zdobycie Przez Kolumba, Pizara i Corteza.
Kraków, 1861, 52p.
(The Discovery and Conquest of America by Columbus, Pizarro
and Cortez)

1732   Azembski, Miroslaw. Inny Swiat. Warsaw, Nasza Księgarnia,
1966, 294p.
(The Other World)

1733   Barszczewski, Stefan. Na Szlaku Sławy, Krwi i Złota. Szkice z
Dziejów Odkrycia Ameryki. Warsaw, Gebethner i Wolff, 1928,
152p.
(On the Road of Fame, Blood and Gold: Excerpts From Deeds in Discovering America)

1734   Baity, Elisabeth (Chesley). Ameryka Przed Kolumbem.
Translated from English by Marian L. Pisark. Warsaw,
"Nasza Ksiegarnia", 1962, 163p.

                             (America Before Columbus)

1735   Campe, Joachim H. Odkrycie Ameryki, Dzieło Przeznaczone
Dla Oświecenia i Zabawy Młodziezy a Składajace Dalszy Ciag
Nowego Robinsona. 3v. Wroclaw, Naklad i Druk W. B. Korna,
1809.

                       (Discovery of America, Work Written
to Enlighten and Delight Youth, Also Composed Continuation of
New Robinson Crusoe)

1736   Cieszynski, Nikodem. W Cieniu Palm i Pinjorow. Potulice,
Seminarium Zagraniczne, 1935, 338p.

                       (In Shadows of Palms and Pinion Trees)

1737   Daszyński, Stefan W. Polska Wyprawa Alpinistyczno-
Naukowa w Góry Ameryki Południowej. Kraków, 1934,
24p.

                     (Polish Scientific Alpine Expedition
Into Mountains of South America)

1738   Dorawski, Jan K. Wysoko w Andach. Warsaw, Iskry,
1961, 295p.

                     (High in the Andes)

1739   Drabowski, Eugeniusz. Problemy Rozwoju Ameryki Łacińskiej.
Warsaw, Książka i Wiedza, 1963, 161p.

                     (Development Problems of Latin America)

1740   Drohojowski, Jan. Religie i Wierzenia w Życiu Ameryki Łacińskiej.
Warsaw, Wiedza i Życie, 1964, 126p.

                     (Religious Worship in Latin American Life)

1741   Dybczyński, Tadeusz. Ameryka Południowa, Wielka Geografia
Powszechna. v. 14. Warsaw, 1936.

                     (South America)

1742   Finkel, Ludwik. <u>O Odkryciu Ameryki Przez Krzysztofa Kolumba</u>.
Lwów, Macierz Szkolna, 1892, 56p.
(On Discovery of America by Christopher
Columbus)

1743   Gitlin, Jan. <u>Opowieści z Dżungli, Pustyni i Pampasów</u>. Warsaw,
Iskry, 1957, 181p.
(Stories from Jungle, Desert and Pampas)

1744   Iwaszkiewicz, Jaroslaw. <u>Listy z Podrozy do Ameryki Południowej</u>.
Kraków, Wydawnictwo Literackie, 1954, 305p.
(Letters From Travels in South America)

1745   Iwaszkiewicz, Jaroslaw. <u>Podróze.</u> Warsaw, Czytelnik, 1958, 467p.
(Travels)

1746   Krzemiński, Stanislaw. <u>Krzysztof Kolumb</u>. Warsaw, T. Paprocki,
1893, 68p.
(Christopher Columbus)

1747   Lazarusówna, Fryderyka. <u>Krzysztof Kolumb</u>. 2v. Warsaw,
Polska Zjednoczona, 1932.
(Christopher Columbus)

1748   Lepecki, Bohdan T. <u>W Miastach i Puszczach Ameryki
Południowej</u>. Warsaw, Instytut Wydawniczy, Biblioteka
Polska, 1934, 255p.
(In Cities and Jungles of South America)

1749   Lepecki, Mieczyslaw B. <u>Od Amazonki do Ziemi Ognistej,</u>
Warsaw, Ludowa Spóldzielnia Wydawnicza, 1958, 397p.
(From the Amazon to Tierra del
Fuego)

1750 Leszczyński, Jan N. Rozprawa Historyczna o Kolumbie, Czyli
   o Źródłach Jego Głównej Idei Robienia Nowych Odkryć na
   Zachodzie Europy. Z Pism w Obcnych Jezykach Zebrał. Warsaw,
   1843, 116p.
        (Historical Analysis of Columbus on
   Sources of his Main Idea of Probing Newly-Discovered Lands
   to the West of Europe)

1751 Mlynarski, Marian. Wśród Zararak i Grzechotników. Warsaw,
   Iskry, 1962, 158p.
        (Snake Bites and Rattlesnakes)

1752 Morawski, Zdzisław. Listy z Podróży do Ameryki Południowej.
   Kraków, 1886, 140p.
        (Letters from Travels in South America)

1753 Narkiewicz-Jodko, Konstanty. W Walce o Szczyty Andów.
   Warsaw, Glowna Księgarnia Wojskowa, 1935, 239p.
        (Conquering the Andes)

1754 Narody Ameryki Łacinskiej w Walce z Imperializmem Amerykanskim.
   Tłum, z Ros., Franciszka Wistreich i Michał Derenicz. Warsaw,
   Książka i Wiedza, 1954, 302p.
   (Peoples of Latin America in the Struggle with American
   Imperialism: Translation from Russian by Franciszka Wistreich
   & Michal Derenicz)

1755 Nocón, Rudolf H. Kobieta w Życiu Indian Ameryki Południowej.
   Katowice, Śląsk, 1964, 310p.
        (Woman in the Life of the South American Indian)

1756 Obroty Artykułami Rynkowymi Pochodzenia Przemysłowego
   Między Krajami Socjalistycznymi (RWPG) a Rozwijającymi
   Się Krajami Ameryki Łacinskiej, Afryki i Azji. Warsaw,
   Zakład Badań Koniuktur i Cen Handlu Zagranicznego, 1966, 134p.
   (Industrial Trading Between the Socialist Countries and Developing
   Countries of Latin America, Africa and Asia)

1757   Olcha, Antoni. **Różne Strony Czasu**. Warsaw, Ludowa Spółdzielnia
        Wydawnicza, 1961, 57p.
                (Different Edges of Time: Poems)

1758   Ostrowski, Jerzy. **Polscy Konkwistadorzy**. Warsaw, 1934, 95p.
                (Polish Conquistadors)

1759   Ostrowski, Wiktor. **Na Szczytach Kordyljerów, Wspomnienia
        z Polskiej Wyprawy Naukowo-Alpinistycznej w Kordyllera de
        Los Andes.** Warsaw, Panstwowe Wydawnictwo Książek Szkolnych,
        1935, 159p.
                        (Above the Cordilleras, Recollections from
        Polish Alpine Expedition into Andes Cordilleras)

1760   Ostrowski, Wiktor. **Na Szczytach Świata.** Warsaw, Gebethner
        i Wolff, 1938, 59p.
                (On Top of the World)

1761   Ostrowski, Wiktor. **Wyżej Niż Kondory.** Warsaw, Sport i
        Turystyka, 1959, 208p.
                        (Higher than the Condors)

1762   Pamiętniki, Emigrantów. **Ameryka Południowa.** Warsaw,
        Instytut Gospodarstwa Społecznego, 1939, 488p.
        (Diaries of Immigrants, South America)

1763   Peiper, Tadeusz. **Krzysztof Kolumb Odkrywca.** Warsaw,
        Czytelnik, 1949, 264p.
                        (Christopher Columbus, the Discoverer)

1764   Pepłowski, Stanisław S. **Jeszcze Polska nie Zginęła,
        Dzieje Legjonów Polskich. Opowieść Dziejowa z Lat
        1797-1806.** Kraków, Spółka Wydawnicza Polska, 1897, 228p.
        (Poland Has not Fallen Yet: Deeds of Polish Legions Abroad;
        Excerpts from 1797-1806)

1765   Poeche, Izydor. <u>Na Dalekim Oceanie, Późniejsze Wyprawy i</u>
<u>Odkrycia Kolumba i Innych Żeglarzy.</u> Słóczow, W. Zukerkandel,
1886, 89p.
                (On the Distant Ocean, Later Voyages and
Discoveries of Columbus and Other Sailors)

1766   Poeche, Izydor. <u>Pierwsza Morska Podróż Krzysztofa Kolumba</u>
<u>w Celu Odkrycia Przyszłej Ameryki.</u> Złoczów, W. Zukerkandel,
1886, 82p.
                (First Voyage of Columbus to Discover the
Future America)

1767   Polski Instytut Spraw Międzynarodowych, Warsaw, <u>"Sojusz dla</u>
<u>Potępu,"</u> Wykaz Wybranych Dokumentów i Literatury za Okres
<u>1961-1962,</u> Warsaw, 1963, 44p.
(Alliance for Depredation: Statement of Selected Documents and
Literature for the Period 1961-1962)

1768   Posadzy, Ignacy. <u>Drogą Pielgrzymów.</u> Wrażenia z Objazdu
<u>Kolonij Polskich w Południowej Ameryce.</u> Potulice, Seminarium
Zagraniczne, 1935, 344p.
                (Pilgrims' Road: Impressions from Travels
to Polish Colonies in South America)

1769   Potocki, Antoni. <u>O Krzysztofie Kolumbie i Odkryciu Ameryki.</u>
7th ed. Warsaw, Księgarnia Polska, 1925, 40p.
                (On Christopher Columbus and Discovery of
America)

1770   Rómmel, Waldemar, & Ignacy Sachs. <u>Jak Żyją Chłopi w Ameryce</u>
<u>Łacińskiej.</u> Warsaw, Książka i Wiedza, 1955, 78p.
                (How the Peasants Live
in Latin America)

1771   Rusinek, Michał. <u>Kolorowe Podróże, Wrażenia z Podróży do</u>
        <u>Ameryki Południowej (1957-1961) Do Ameryki Północnej (1958)</u>
        <u>i do Japonii (1961).</u> Warsaw, Ludowa Spółdzielnia Wydawnicza,
        1964, 261p.
                    (Colorful Travels, Impressions from Travels
        in South America [1957-1961], in North America [1958], and in
        Japan [1961])

1772   Rusinek, Michał. <u>Trylogia Historyczna o Krzysztofie Arciszewskim.</u>
        6th ed. Warsaw, Państwowy Instytut Wydawniczy, 1965, 771p.
                    (Trilogy on Christopher Arciszewski)

1773   Rusinek, Michal. <u>Wódz i Wygnaniec, O Krzysztofie Arciszewskim</u>
        <u>i Jego Czasach.</u> Warsaw, Ludowa Spółdzielnia Wydawnicza,
        1957, 297p.
                    (Chief in Exile, On Christopher Arciszewski
        and his Times)

1774   Serafińska, Janina, & Włodzimierz Serafiński. <u>Największe</u>
        <u>Zoo Świata. Zwierzęta Ameryki Południowej.</u> Warsaw,
        Państwowe Wydawnictwo Naukowe, 1962, 191p.
                                            (The Biggest
        Zoo in the World: Animals of South America)

1775   Siemiradzki, Józef. <u>Na Kresach Cywilizacji. Listy z Podróży</u>
        <u>po Ameryce Południowej, Odbytej W R. (1892).</u> Lwów, 1896,
        263p.
                    (On the Edges of Civilization, Letters from
        Travels in South America in 1892)

1776   Siemiradzki, Józef. <u>O Indianach Południowej Ameryki.</u> Kraków,
        Polskie Towarzystwo Geograficzne, 1924, 31p.
                    (On South American Indians)

1777   Sierzputowski, Jan. Ameryka Łacińska, In Rozmowy o Gospodarce.
Warsaw, 1964, pp. 225-322.
(Discussions on Latin American Economy)

1778   Skomorowski, Jan. Od Patagonji do Japonji. 20 Lat na Obczyźnie
1900-1920, Cz. 1, Ameryka Południowa. Warsaw, 1936, 81p.
(From Patagonia to Japan, 20 Years Abroad
1900-1920. Part I, South America)

1779   Slonimski, Antoni. Pod Zwrotnikami, Dziennik Okrętowy.
Warsaw, Gebethner i Wolff, 1925, 156p.
(In the Tropics, Ship's Log)

1780   Synoradzki, Michał. Żeglarz nad Żeglarze, Krzysztof Kolumb.
Warsaw, E. Koliński, 1896, 143p.
(Sailor Above Sailors, Christopher Columbus)

1781   Szczepański, Jan A. Wyprawa do Księżycowej Ziemi. 2d ed.
Warsaw, Państwowe Instytut Wydawniczy, 1957, 340p.
(Expedition to Moon Land)

1782   Urbaniak, Jan. Dryfujący Subkontynent. Warsaw,
Centralna Rada Związków Zawodowych, 1966, 264p.
(Drifting Subcontinent)

1783   USA i Kraje Ameryki Łacińskiej a Kuba. Warsaw, 1962, 61p.
(USA and Latin America with Cuba)

1784   Wasilewska, Wanda. Kryształowa Kula Krzysztofa Kolumba.
Warsaw, B. Drapczyńscy, 1934, 134p.
(Crystal Bag of Christopher Columbus)

1785   Wasserman, Jakób. Krzysztof Kolumb, Don Kchot Oceanu.
        Warsaw, J. Mortkowicz, 1931, 274p.
                        (Christopher Columbus, Don Quixote of
        the Ocean)

1786   Witowski, Hipolit. Krzysztof Kolumb Czyli Odkrycie Ameryki
        Skreślone Dla Ciekawej Młodzi. Lwów, H. W. Kallenbach,
        1853, 181p.
                        (Christopher Columbus on Discovery of
        America: Written for Interested Youth)

1787   Wojsznis, Justyn. Polacy na Szczytach Świata, Wybór Tekstów
        Uczestników Siedmiu Wypraw Alpinistycznych w Latach 1933-
        1939. Andy, Spitsbergen Atlas, Kaukaz, Ruwenzori, Himalaje.
        Warsaw, Sport i Turystyka, 1964, 549p.
                        (Poles on Top of the World: Selections of
        Texts of Participants of Seven Alpine Expeditions in the Years
        of 1933-1939: Andes, Spitsbergen, Atlas, Caucasus, Ruwenzori,
        Himalaya)

1788   W Skałach i Lodach, Świata. Polskie Wyprawy Górskie i
        Polarne, Dzieło Zespołowe Pod Red, Kazimierza Saysse-
        Tobiczyka. v. 2, Polskie Wyprawy Egzotyczne, Andy,
        Atlas... Warsaw, Wiedza Powszechna, 1961, 406p.
                        (In Mountains and Ice of the
        World, Polish Alpine, and Polar Expeditions; Collective Work,
        edited by Kazimierza Saysse-Tobiczyka. v. 2, Polish Exotic
        Expeditions: Andes, Atlas)

ARGENTINA

1789   Cynalewski, Stanisław. <u>List z Argentyny</u>. Kraków, W. Kornecki, 1900, 38p.

          (A Letter from Argentina)

1790   Dostal, Wacław. <u>Argentyna</u>. Warsaw, 1937, 86p.

          (Argentina)

1791   Fularski, Mieczysław. <u>Polskie Kolonie Rolnicze w Argentynie</u>. Warsaw, Polskie Tow. Emigracyjne, 1927, 39p.

          (Polish Farming Colonies in Argentina)

1792   Gitlin, Jan. <u>Nad Rio de la Plata</u>. Warsaw, Książka i Wiedza, 1958, 340p.

          (Over Rio de la Plata)

1793   Kocyba, Edward. <u>Porty Buenos Aires i Montevideo. Przepisy, Praktyka i Zwyczaje</u>. Warsaw, 1961, 76p.

          (Ports of Buenos Aires and Montevideo: Description, Practice and Customs)

1794   Lepecki, Mieczysław B. <u>Oceanem, Rzeką, Lądem. Przygody z Podróży po Argentynie</u>. Warsaw, Rój, 1929, 223p.

          (By Ocean, River and Land: Adventures During Travel in Argentina)

1795   Melcer, Wanda. <u>Nad Srebrną Rzeką. Argentyna</u>. Warsaw, Biblioteka Dzieł Wyborowych, 1927, 160p.

          (Over the Silver River, Argentina)

1796   Stołyhwo, Kazimierz. **W Sprawie Człowieka Kopalnego i Jego**
Poprzedników w Argentynie Oraz Sprawozdanie z Delegacji
na Kongres Naukowy Amerykański w Buenos Aires w r. 1910.
Warsaw, Societas Scientiarum Varsoviensis, 1911, pp. 22-41.
        (The Miner and his Predecessors in
Argentina; also Report from the Delegation to the American
Scientific Congress in Buenos Aires in 1910)

1797   **Wiadomości o Argentynie do Użytku Wychodźców Wraz z**
Samouczkiem Języka Hiszpańskiego. Warsaw, Syndykat
Emigracyjny, 1937, 100p.
(Information on Argentina for Immigrants, Together with
Self-Instruction Manual of Spanish)

1798   Wlodek, Józef. **Argentyna i Emigracja ze Szczególnem**
Uwzględnieniem Emigracji Polskiej. Warsaw, M. Arct,
1923, 513p.
        (Argentina and Immigration, with Particular
Attention to Polish Immigration)

461

BRAZIL

1799   Adamski, Józef. Polacy Jako Producenci Bananów w Brazylii.
        Warsaw, Miedzynarodowe Towarzystwo Osadnicze, 1938, 15p.
                (Poles as Banana Producers of Brazil)

1800   Breowicz, Wojciech. Slady Piasta Pod Piniorami, Szkice z
        Dziejów Wychodźstwa Polskiego w Brazylii. Warsaw, Polonia,
        1961, 256p.
                (Tracks of the Nave under Pinion Trees:
        Sketches from the Life of Polish Immigrants in Brazil)

1801   Breowicz, Wojciech. Wybór Utworów, T. 1, Wiersze, T. 2,
        Trzy Etapy, Pamiętnik, Oprac. i Wstępem Topatrzył
        Antoni Olcha. Warsaw, Ludowa Społdzielnia Wydawnicza,
        1956, 76 + 351p.
                (Collected Works; v. 1, Verse; v. 2,
        Three Part Diary, Edited with Introduction by Antoni Olcha)

1802   Bujwid, Odo. Rozpowszechnienie Trądu w Brazylii, Stosunek
        Tej Chroby do Polskich Osadników. Kraków, 1932.
                (The Spread of Skin Disease in Brazil, Relation
        of the Disease to Polish Settlers)

1803   Bujwid, Odo. Stosunki Zdrowotne Brazylii, Treściowe Wiadomości
        Dla Użytku Osadników... Warsaw, Naukowy Instytut Emigracyjny,
        1930, 93p.
                (Health Conditions in Brazil, Concrete Information
        for Immigrants)

1804   Bujwid, Odo. Zwalczanie Chorób Zakaźnych i Pasożytniczych w
         Brazylji. Warsaw, 1929.
                     (Fighting Against Contagious and Parasitic Diseases
     in Brazil)

1805   Caro, Leopold. Emigracja i Polityka Emigracyjna. Poznań,
         Księgarnia Św. Wojciecha, 1914, 392p.
                     (Emigration and Immigration Policy)

1806   Chełmicki, Zygmunt. W Brazylii, Notatki z Podróży, 2v.
         Warsaw, 1892.
                  (In Brazil, Notes from Travel)

1807   Chrostowski, Tadeusz. Paraná, Wspomnienia z Podróży w
         Roku, 1914. Poznań, Księgarnia Św. Wojciecha, 1922, 237p.
                    (Paraná, Recollection from Travels
     in 1914)

1808   Dygasinski, Adolf. Listy z Brazylii Specjalnego Delegata
         Kurjera Warszawskiego. Warsaw, 1891, 201p.
                  (Letters from Brazil of the Special
     Correspondent for "Kurjera Warszawskiego")

1809   Dygasiński, Adolf. Na Złamanie Karku. Powieść. Warsaw,
         Książka i Wiedza, 1952, 206p.
                  (Riding at Break-Neck Speed, Novel)

1810   Ekes, Roman. Brazylia Jako Źródło Zaopatrzenia Europy po
         Wojnie. Rio de Janeiro, Koło Pracowników i Ekonomistów
     Polskich Przy Tow., Polonia, 1944, 46p.
                  (Brazil as a Target of Europe After the War)

1811 Federowicz, Władyslaw. Z Biegiem Rzeki Tocantins, Kartki z
     Podróży na Północ, Przygody Polskiego Inżyniera w Puszczach
     i Stepach Północnej Brazylie. Curitiba, 1927, 187p.
           (Along the Tocantins River: Pictures
     from Travel to the North. Adventures of a Polish Engineer in
     Jungles and Prairies of North Brazil)

1812 Ficińska, Maria. Dwadzieścia Lat w Paranie. Warsaw, Biblioteka
     Polska, 1938, 119p.
        (Twenty Years in Paraná)

1813 Ficińska, Maria. Za Ocean do Parany. Płock, 1914, 53p.
        (Across the Ocean to Paraná)

1814 Fiedler, Arkady. Bichos, Moi Brazylijscy Przyjaciele. Poznań,
     Księg. Uniwersytecka, 1931, 106p.
        (Bichos, My Brazilian Friends)

1815 Fiedler, Arkady. Orinoko. Warsaw, Iskry, 1957, 418p.
        (Orinoco)

1816 Fiedler, Arkady. Rio de Oro, Na Ścieżkach Indian Brazylijskich.
     Warsaw, Nasza Księgarnia, 1950, 206p.
        (Rio de Oro, On the Tracks of Brazilian Indians)

1817 Fiedler, Arkady. Wśród Indian Koroadów. Poznań, 1932, 231p.
        (Among the Coroado Indians)

1818 Fiedler, Arkady. Wyspa Robinsona. 8th ed. Warsaw, Iskry, 1966,
     229p.
        (Robinson's Island)

1819   Gauze, Dan. Na Przełaj Przez Dżungle. 2d ed. Warsaw,
        Sporti Turystyka, 1961, 365p.
        (On the Return Through Jungles)

1820   Gauze, Jan. Brazylia Mierzona Krokami, Powieść. Warsaw,
        Sport i Turystyka, 1961, 362p.
        (Brazil Measured in Steps, Novel)

1821   Gitlin, Jan. Do Zobaczenia, Brazylio. Warsaw, Iskry, 1956,
        209p.
        (Til Next Time, Brazil)

1822   Głuchowski, Kazimierz. Materiały do Problemu Osadnictwa Pol-
        skiego w Brazylii. Warsaw, Instytut Naukowy do Badań
        Emigracji i Kolonizacji, 1927, 354p.
                        (Materials on the Problems of Polish
        Settlers in Brazil)

1823   Grabowski, Tadeusz S. Brazylia, In Polska i Polacy w
        Cywilizacjach Świata. v. 1. Warsaw, 1939, pp. 42-78.
                        (Brazil in Poland, and Poles in the
        Civilization of the World)

1824   Grabowski, Tadeusz S. Brazylia i Jej Dzieje. Kraków, S.
        Kamiński, 1947, 125p.
                        (Brazil and its Status)

1825   Gruszecki, Artur. Przygody Chlopca w Brazylii. Warsaw,
        M. Arct, 1912, 294p.
                        (Adventures of a Boy in Brazil)

1826   Hempel, Antoni. <u>Polacy w Brazylii, Przez Członka Wyprawy</u>
      <u>Naukowej dr. J. Siemiradzkiego do Brazylii i Argentyny.</u>
      Lwów, Kurier Lwowski, 1893, 178p.
                (Poles in Brazil, by the Member of a Scientific
      Expedition to Brazil and Argentina, Dr. J. Siemiradzky)

1827   Isaakowa, Michalina. <u>Polka w Puszczach Parany</u>. Poznań,
      Ksiegarnia Św. Wojciecha, 1936, 232p.
                (Polka in Jungles of Paraná)

1828   Iwaszkiewicz, Jaroslaw. <u>Opowieści Zasłyszane</u>. Warsaw,
      Państwowe Instytut Wydawniczy, 1954, 154p.
                (Of Tales Heard, Brazilian Stories)

1829   Klobukowski, Stanisław. <u>Wycieczka do Parany, Stanu Rzeczypos-</u>
      <u>politej Brazylii, Dziennik Podróży.</u> Lwów, Gubrynowicz,
      1909, 213p.
                (A Trip to Paraná, State of the
      Federal Republic of Brazil: Travel Diary)

1830   Konopnicka, Maria. <u>Pan Balcer w Brazylii.</u> Warsaw, Czytelnik,
      1955, 385p.
                (Mr. Balcer in Brazil)

1831   Korabiewicz, Wacław. <u>Mato Grosso.</u> 2d ed. Warsaw, Czytelnik,
      1959, 244p.
                (Mato Grosso)

1832   Kossobudzki, Szymon. <u>Odgłosy Parańskie.</u> Curitiba, 1927,
      122p.
                (Echoes of Paraná)

1833   Kubina, Teodor. <u>Wśród Polskiego Wychodźstwa w Ameryce</u>
      <u>Południowej.</u> Potulice, Seminarium Zagraniczne, 1938, 357p.
                (Among Polish Immigrants to South America)

1834   Kurcyusz, Aleksy. Brazylia. 2 v. Warsaw, Biblioteka
Dzieł Wyborowych, 1911.
(Brazil)

1835   Lepecki, Bohdan T. Czarni Brazyljanie. Warsaw, Rój,
1932, 61p.
(Black Brazilians)

1836   Lepecki, Mieczysław B. Matto Grosso, Dziki Zachód
Brazylji. Warsaw, Polskie Towarzystwo Emigracyjne,
1927, 43p.
(Mato Grosso, Wilderness of
Western Brazil)

1837   Lepecki, Mieczyslaw B. Na Cmentarzyskach Indjan,
Wrażenia z Podróży po Paranie. Warsaw, Biblioteka
Dzieł Wyborowych, 1926, 122p.
(In Indian Cemeteries: Impressions
of Travel in Paraná)

1838   Lepecki, Mieczysław B. Na Podbój Amazonki. Warsaw,
Rój, 1928, 61p.
(To Conquer the Amazon)

1839   Lepecki, Mieczyslaw B. Niknący Świat, Opowieść o
Podróży po Centralnej Brazylii. Warsaw, Iskry, 1965, 217p.
(Vanishing World, Recollections
from Traveling in Central Brazil)

1840   Lepecki, Mieczysław B. Opis Stanu Esperito Santo ze
Specjalnym Uwzględnieniem Terenów, Na Których Odbywa
Się Kolonizacja Polska. Warsaw, Liga Morska i Kolonjalna,
1931, 101p.
(Description of the State of Espírito
Santo, with Special Attention to Terrain, Where Polish
Colonization is Taking Place)

1841   Lepecki, Mieczysław B. Paraná i Polacy. Warsaw, Wiedza
Powszechna, 1962, 214p.
(Paraná and Poles)

1842   Lepecki, Mieczysław B. Po Bezdrożach Brazylii. Warsaw,
Ludowa Spółdzielnia Wydawnicza, 1961, 40lp.
(On the Dusty Roads of Brazil)

1843   Lepecki, Mieczysław B. W Krainie Jaguarów, Przygody Oficera
Polskiego w Dżunglach i Stepach Brazylji. Warsaw, 1925, 142p.
(In the Land of Jaguars: Adventures
of Polish Officers in Jungles and Prairies of Brazil)

1844   Lepecki, Mieczysław B. Z Gwiazdy na Gwiazdę, Podróż z
Brazylii do Polski. Warsaw, Iskry, 1960, 293p.
(From Star to Star: Travel from
Brazil to Poland)

1845   Lyp, Franciszek F. Brazylia. Kraj, Ludzie, Stosunki.
Warsaw, Naukowy Instytut Emigracyjny, 1930, 445 + 81p.
(Brazil: Country, Peoples, Conditions)

1846   Makarczyk, Janusz. Nowa Brazylia, Dżungla - Osiedla i
Ludzie. Warsaw, M. Arct, 1929, 184p.
(New Brazil: Jungle - Settlements and
People)

1847   Makarczyk, Janusz. Przez Morza i Dżungle. Lwów, Książnica
Atlas, 232p.
(Across the Seas and Jungles)

1848   Mariański J., & N. Bogusz. Brazylia, Warunki Życia i Pracy.
London, 1946, 124p.
(Brazil, Conditions of Life and Work)

1849   Migasiński, Emil L. Polacy w Paranie Współczesnej,
       Obrazy Kraju i Ludzi. Warsaw, Księgarnia "Kroniki
       Rodzinnej", 1923, 237p.
                           (Poles in Paraná, Description of
       Country and People)

1850   Mlynarski, Marian. Wśród Żararak i Grzechotników. Warsaw,
       Iskry, 1962, 159p.
                           (Amid Pestilence and Rattlesnakes)

1851   Mrówczyński, Bolesław. Bartochowe, Opowieść Brazylijska o
       Rodzie Śląskim, Który na Drugiej Półkuli Budował Nową, Ojczyznę.
       Katowice, Śląsk, 1965, 297p.
                           (Bartochovians, Story of a Silesian
       Family in Brazil Building a Second Home)

1852   Naganowski, Egon. Brazylia w Twórczości Jorge Amado.
       Warsaw, 1955, 23p.
                           (Brazil in the Art of Jorge Amado)

1853   Nikoden, Pawel. Pół Wieku Osadnictwa Polskiego w Brazylii.
       Curitiba, 1941.
                           (Half-Century of Polish Settlement in Brazil)

1854   Nostitz-Jackowski, Mieczysław. Maria Antonina, Humoreska
       Brazylijska na Tle Prawdziwej Przygody. Poznań, Księgarnia
       Św. Wojciecha, 1923-
                           (Maria Antonina, Humorous
       Story)

1855   Nostitz - Jackowski, Mieczysław. Tumba, Ojcze Nasz, Obrazki
       Brazylijskie. Poznań, Księgarnia Św. Wojciecha, 1928, 66p.
                           (Tumba, Our Father; Sketches
       of Brazil)

1856   Olcha, Antoni. <u>Szumią Dęby nad Iguassú</u>. Warsaw, Ludowa
Społdzielnia Wydawnicza, 1959, 247p.
(Rustling of Oaks over Iguassú)

1857   Ostrowski, Jerzy. <u>Brazylia</u>. Lwów, Książnica - Atlas, 1939,
111p.
(Brazil)

1858   Ostrowski, Jerzy. <u>Ziemia Świętego Krzyża</u>. Warsaw, Gebethner
i Wolff, 1929, 188p.
(The Land of the Holy Cross)

1859   Pankiewicz, Michał. <u>W Sprawie Wychodżstwa do Sau Paulo</u>.
Warsaw, Polskie Towarzystwo Emigracyjne, 1926, 102p.
(On Settling in Sao Paulo)

1860   Pankiewicz, Michał. <u>Z Parany i o Paranie</u>. Warsaw, Gebethner
i Wolff, 1916, 79p.
(Of and About Paraná)

1861   Pawlowicz, Bohdan. <u>Pionierzy, Powieść</u>. Warsaw, Pionier,
1930, 485p.
(Pioneers, Novel)

1862   Pawlowicz, Bohdan. <u>Pod Polską Banderą</u>. Curitiba, 1924,
88p.
(Under the Polish Banners)

1863   Piotrowski, Wieńczysław. <u>Opowiadania Parańskie</u>. Grodno, 1928.
(Paraná Tales)

1864   Piotrowski, Witalis. <u>Po Szczęście do Piekła, Opowiadanie
Przebytych Zdarzén i Wrażeń Wychodżcy do Parany</u>. Warsaw,
1912, 71p.
(To Hell with Luck: Recollection of Living
in Paraná)

1865   Polacy w Rio de Janeiro. Zbiór Materjałów Historyczno-Informa-
cyjnych z Okazji Powszechnej Wystawy Krajowej w r. 1929 w
Poznaniu. Rio de Janeiro, 1929, 124p.
(Poles in Rio de Janeiro: Collection of Information. Historical
Materials on the Occasion of an Exposition in Poznán in 1929)

1866   Potocki, Antoni. Listy z Brazylii Przez Wychodźców do Rodzin
Pisane. Warsaw, 1891, 55p.
                (Letters from Brazil by Emigrants to
Families at Home)

1867   Rafalski, Julian B. Badania nad Drewnem Piniora Brazylijskiego.. i Peroby Różowej.. Poznań, 1939, 36p.
             (Observations on the Wood of Brazilian
Pinion and Peroba Rosa Trees)

1868   Rómmel, Waldemar, & Ignacy Sachs. W Kraju Kawowych Plantacji.
O Stosunkach Rolnych w Brazylii. Warsaw, Ludowa Spółdzielnia Wydawnicza, 1955, 179p.
                 (Country of Coffee Plantations:
on Farming Conditions in Brazil)

1869   Rusinek, Michał. Zielone Złoto, Kartki z Podróży. Warsaw,
Iskry, 1960, 234p.
           (The Green Gold, Travel Post Cards)

1870   Sapieha, Leon. Lasy Ituri. Wspomnienia z Podróży. Kraków,
1928, 204p.
         (Forests of Ituri)

1871   Sieciński, Piotr. Echa z Brazylii, Utwory Wierszem. Curitiba,
1910, 52p.
         (Echoes from Brazil, Verses)

1872   Siemiradzki, Józef. <u>Szlakiem Wychodźców, Wspomnienia z Podróży po Brazylii.</u> 2pts. Warsaw, 1900.
          (The Road of Immigrants: Recollection from Travels in Brazil)

1873   Siemiradzki, Józef. <u>Za Morze, Szkice z Wycieczki do Brazylii.</u> Lwów, Jakubowski i Zadurowicz, 1894, 100p.
          (Across the Sea: Sketches from Travel to Brazil)

1874   Sosnowski, Paweł. <u>Brazylia, Jej Przyroda i Mieszkańcy.</u> 4th ed. Warsaw, 1917, 64p.
          (Brazil, its Nature and Inhabitants)

1875   Stańczewski, Józef. <u>Szlakiem Wychodźców, Wspomnienia.</u> Warsaw, 1910, 130p.
          (On the Road of Immigrants, Recollections)

1876   Stołyhwo, Kazimierz. <u>Sprawozdanie z Podróży po Brazylii w Sprawie Badań Antropologicznych w Paranie.</u> Warsaw, Nauk. Instytut Emigracyjny, 1931, 15p.
          (Observations on Travel in Brazil in Connection with Anthropological Studies in Paraná)

1877   Studnicki, Władysław. <u>Brazylia, Kraj Możliwości Osiedlania Się.</u> Rzym, 1946, 90p.
          (Brazil, Country of Possibilities and Settlement)

1878   Sujkowski, Boguslaw. <u>Dziewice Slonica.</u> 1st ed. Warsaw, Czytelnik, 1961, 271p.
          (Virgins of the Sun)

1879   Tatarkiewicz, Władysław. Architektura Barokowa w Brazylii.
        Warsaw, 1936, 24p.
                              (Baroque Architecture in Brazil)

1880   Turczyński, Juliusz. Nasza Odysseja, Obraz z Wychodźstwa
        Brazylijskiego. Lwów, Kurier Lwowski, 1894, 143p.
                              (Our Odyssey: Recollection from Brazilian
        Immigration)

1881   Tuszyńska, Anna. Brazylia. 2d ed. corr. Warsaw, Wiedza
        Powszechna, 1955, 193p.
                              (Brazil)

1882   Warchałowski, Kazimierz. Do Parany, Przewodnik dla Podróżują-
        cych i Wychodźców. Kraków, W. L. Anczyc, 1903, 52+54p.
                              (To Paraná, A Guide for Travellers
        and Immigrants)

1883   Warchałowski, Kazimierz. Na Wodach Amazonki. Warsaw,
        Liga Morska i Kolonjalna, 1938, 175p.
                              (On the Waters of the Amazon)

1884   Warchałowski, Kazimierz. Picada, Wspomnienia z Brazylii.
        Warsaw, Pionier, 1930, 201p.
                              (Picada, Recollection from Brazil)

1885   Wieluniak, Józef. Ciekawe Wiadomości z Brazylii. Warsaw,
        S. Zaleski, 1891, 32p.
                              (Interesting News from Brazil)

1886   Włodek, Ludwik. Ilustrowany Przewodnik po Brazylii Wraz ze
        Słowniczkiem Polsko-Portugalskim. Kraków, Polskie Towarzystwo
        Emigracyjne, 1909, 64p.
                              (Illustrated Guide of Brazil, with Polish-Portuguese
        Dictionary)

1887   Włodek, Ludwik. Polskie Kolonie Rolnicze w Paranie. 2d ed.
Warsaw, 1911, 148p.
(Polish Farming Colonies in Paraná)

1888   Wójcik, Władysław. Lubliniacy w Brazylii. Warsaw, Ludowa
Spóldzielnia Wydawnicza, 1963, 197p.
(Ex-Residents of Lublin, Poland, in Brazil)

1889   Wójcik, Władysław. Moje Życie w Brazylii. Warsaw, Ludowa
Spółdzielnia Wydawnicza, 1961, 287p.
(My Life in Brazil)

1890   Wójcik, Władysław. Po Obydwu Stronach Równika. Warsaw,
Ludowa Spółdzielnia Wydawnicza, 1966, 221p.
(In the Tropics)

1891   Wójcik, Władysław. Wojna Domodrążców, Brazylijski Romans
Historyczny z Epoki Kolonialnej. Curitiba, 1930, 147p.
(War of Domokregs, Brazilian Novel
from Colonial Era)

1892   Wójcik, Władysław. Zemsta Indjanina, Nowele Brazylijskie.
Curitiba, 1931, 40p.
(Indian Revenge, Novel of Brazil)

1893   Wojnar, Jan. Polsko-Brazylijskie Stosunki Handlowe, Dorobek
i Bilans Pierwszego Dziesięciolecia, 1921-1931. Warsaw,
Liga Morska i Kolonialna, 1933,· 42p.
(Polish-Brazilian Trade Relations, Profits and
Trade Balance of the Decade 1921-1931)

1894   Wolniewicz, Janusz. Ku Wybrzeżom Zielonej Kawy. Warsaw,
Min. Obrony Narodowej, 1960, 156p.
(Towards the Coast of Green Coffee)

1895 Nestorowicz, Stefan. W Brazylii i Argentynie. Warsaw, 1891, 49p.

      (In Brazil and Argentina)

1895 Żabko-Potopowicz, Bolesław. Osadnictwo Polskie w Brazylii. Warsaw, 1936, 228p.

      (Polish Settlements in Brazil)

1897 Zaniewicki, Zbigniew. Zielone Piekło, Z Przeżyć w Puszczy Brazylijskiej. Warsaw, Rój, 1929, 175p.

      (The Green Hell, From Travels in Brazilian Jungles)

1898 Zarychta, Apoloniusz. Wśród Polskich Conquistadorów, Wrażenia i Przygody z Podróży do Południowej Brazylii. Warsaw, L. Wolnicki, 1927, 239p.

      (Among Polish Conquistadors, Recollections and Adventures in Southern Brazil)

1899 Zarychta, Apoloniusz. W Szkole i Dżungli. Warsaw, Nasza Księgarnia, 1966, 254p.

      (In School and in Jungle)

1900 Bero, Józef. <u>Na Ziemiach Ajmarów i Araukanów, Opowieść</u>
<u>o Ignacym Domeyce</u>. Warsaw, Nasza Księgarnia, 1955, 194p.
    (In the Land of Aymaras and Araucanians:
Story of Ignacy Domeyc)

1901 Brzoza, Jan. <u>Ignacy Domeyko, Powieść Biograficzna</u>. Katowice,
Śląsk, 1961, 187p.
    (Ignacy Domeyc, Biography)

1902 Kutejščikova,V., & A. Štejn. <u>Pablo Neruda</u>. Tr. from Russian
by Marta Okołów-Podhorska. Warsaw, Wiedza Powszechna,
1953, 141p.
    (Pablo Neruda)

1903 Paryski, Witold H. <u>W Górach Atakamy. Wspomnienia z Polskiej</u>
<u>Wyprawy w Andy</u>. Warsaw, Nasza Księgarnia, 1957, 193p.
    (In the Mountains of Atacama, Recollection
from Polish Expedition into Andes)

1904 Szczepański, Jan A. <u>Druga Polska Wyprawa w Andy</u>.
<u>Sprawozdanie Tymczasowe; Próba Opisu Przeżyć</u>. Kraków,
1938, 31p.
    (Other Polish Expedition into Andes;
Attempt to Relate the Experiences)

COLOMBIA

1905 Brzeziński, Witold. **Kolumbia, Informacje o Kraju i Praktyczne Wskazówki.** Warsaw, 1965, 107p.
     (Colombia: Imformation About the Land and Practical Suggestions)

1906   Breza, Tadeusz. <u>Listy Hawańskie.</u> Warsaw, Czytelnik, 1961, 215p.

(Letters from Havana)

1907   Brzezińska, Helena. <u>Orkan Na Kubie.</u> Łódź, Towarzystwo Wydawnicze, Kompas, 1924, 140p.

(Anchor in Cuba)

1908   Burchard, Przemysław. <u>Wśród Mogotów i Krokodyli.</u> Warsaw, Wiedza Powszechna, 1963, 280p.

(Among the Crocodiles)

1909   Gelberg, Ludwik. <u>Kryzys Karaibski 1962, Problemy Prawa Między-narodowego.</u> Warsaw, Państwowe Wydawnictwo Naukowe, 1964, 203p.

(Caribbean Crisis of 1962, Problems of International Law)

1910   Giełżyński, Wojciech. <u>Desant na Playa Giron.</u> Warsaw, Ministerstwo Obrony Narodowej, 1963, 189p.

(Landing on Playa Giron)

1911   Krynicki, Marian. <u>Na Wyspach Atlantyku.</u> 2d ed. Warsaw, Wiedza Powszechna, 1957, 165p.

(On Islands of the Atlantic)

1912   Kurczok, Bernard, & Jerzy Figarski. Przepisy, Praktyka i
Zwyczaje Portów Kuby. Warsaw, 1965, 103p.
(Description, Practices
and Customs of Cuban Ports)

1913   Lidert, Mieczysław. Kuba a Stany Zjednoczone. Warsaw,
Książka i Wiedza, 1961, 252p.
(Cuba and the USA)

1914   Sierecki, Sławomir. Burzliwe Dzieje Perły Antyli. Warsaw,
Książka i Wiedza, 1963, 254p.
(Stormy Deeds of the Pearl of the Antilles)

1915   Słoński, Stefan. Kuba, Rewolucja a Rolnictwo. Warsaw,
Państwowe Wydawnictwo Rolnicze i Leśne, 1963, 106p.
(Cuba, Revolution and Agriculture)

DOMINICAN REPUBLIC

1916   Skalkowski, Adam. Polacy na San Domingo, 1802-1809.
        Poznań, 1921, 199p.
                            (Poles in Santo Domingo, 1802-1809)

1917   Przyborowski, Walery. Na San Domingo, Opowiadanie
          Legjonisty z Początków XIX w. Warsaw, J. Przeworski, 1939,
        235p.
                            (In Santo Domingo, Recollection of
        Legionnaire from Beginning of the Nineteenth Century)

1918   Przyborowski, Walery. Na San Domingo, Powieść dla Młodzieży.
        Warsaw, Ludowa Spółdzielnia Wydawnicza, 1958, 177p.
                            (In Santo Domingo, Novel for Youth)

1919   Wydrzyński, Andrzej. Ostatnia Noc w Ciudad Trujillo; Powieść.
        Katowice, Śląsk, 1962.
                            (Last Night in Ciudad Trujillo; Novel)

ECUADOR

1920   Siemiradzki, Józef. <u>Z Warszawy do Równika. Wspomnienia z</u>
        <u>Podróży po Ameryce Południowej, Odbytej w Latach 1882-1883.</u>
        2d ed. Lwów, H. Altenberg, 1895, 226p.
                        (From Warsaw to Ecuador; Recollections from
        Travels in South America in 1882-1883)

FRENCH GUIANA

1921   Jelski, Konstanty. <u>Popularno-Przyrodnicze Opowiadanie z</u>
        <u>Pobytu w Gujanie Francuskiej i po Części w Peru (Od r. 1865</u>
        <u>do 1871).</u> Kraków, J. Sowiński, 1898, 172p.
                        (Popular Nature Stories of Living in French
        Guiana and Parts of Peru, From 1865 to 1871)

GUATEMALA

1922   Fryd, Norbert. Uśmiechnięta Gwatemala. Tr. from Czech by
       Jadwiga Bułakowska. Warsaw, Wiedza Powszechna, 1958,
       379p.
                    (Smiling Guatemala)

1923   Wiśniowski, Sygurd. Pisma Wybrane. V. 2. w Kraju Czarnych
       Stóp Oraz Inne Nowele, Obrazki i Szkice Podróżnicze. Ed. by
       Julian Tuwin i Bolesław Olszewicz. Warsaw, Czytelnik, 1954,
       449p.
                    (Selection of Letters. v. 2: In the Land
       of Black Feet and Other Novels; Sketches and Recollections
       from Travels)

HAITI

1924   Kuźmiński, Boleslaw. Czarny Napoleon, Toussaint L'Ouverture.
       1st ed. Warsaw, Ksiażka i Wiedza, 1963, 239p.
                    (Black Napoleon, Toussaint L'Ouverture)

1925   Lepkowski, Tadeusz. Haiti, Poczatki Państwa i Narodu. 1st ed.
       Warsaw, Państwowe Wydawn. Naukowe, 1964, 501p.
                    (Haiti, The Beginnings of State and Nation)

JAMAICA

1926   Szyszło, Witold. <u>Małe Antylle i Jamajka</u>. Warsaw, St.
Sadowski, 1911, 252p.
          (Lesser Antilles and Jamaica)

1927   Bór, Andrzej. Prześladowanie Kościoła Katolickiego w Meksyku.
        Warsaw, Księgarnia Kroniki Rodzinnej, 1928, 103p.
                    (Persecution of the Catholic Church in Mexico)

1928   Dmochowski, Franciszek S. Mexik Opisany Pod Względem
        Jeograficznym, Statystycznym i Historycznym... Od Najdawniejszyc
        Czasów Aż Do Śmierci Cesarza Maxymiliana. Warsaw, 1867, 108p.
                    (Mexico Described from Geographical,
        Statistical and Historical Viewpoints, From Ancient Times until the
        Death of Maximilian)

1929   Drohojowski, Jan. Indianin Prezydentem Meksyku (Benito Juárez
        García). Warsaw, Książka i Wiedza, 1964, 238p.
                    (Indian: the President of Mexico, Benito Juárez
        García)

1930   Drohojowski, Jan. Meksyk Bogów, Krzyża i Dolarów. Warsaw,
        Ludowa Spółdzielnia Wydawnicza, 1962, 276p.
                    (Mexico of Gods, the Cross and Dollars)

1931   Drohojowski, Jan. Róg Obfitości. Warsaw, Ksiażka i Wiedza,
        1967, 272p.
                    (Cornucopia)

1932   Drohojowski, Jan. Wspomnienia Dyplomatyczne. Warsaw,
        Państwowe Instytut Wydawniczy, 1959, 415p.
                    (Diplomatic Recollections)

1933   Dunikowski, Emil H. Meksyk i Szkice z Podróży po Ameryce.
        Lwów, Przez Lądy i Morza, 1913, 552p.
                        (Mexico, and Sketches from Travels
        in the Americas)

1934   Hadyna, Stanislaw. Na Podbój Kontynentu. Warsaw, Iskry,
        1964, 415p.
                        (On the Conquest of the Continent)

1935   Jaszúński, Grzegorz. Szkice Amerykańskie: Reportaże.
        Warsaw, Państwowe Instytut Wydawniczy, 1950, 225p.
                        (American Sketches; Report)

1936   Jeżewska, Zofia. W Królestwie Pierzastego Węża, Z Podróży
        po Meksyku. Poznań, Wydawnictwo Poznańskie, 1964, 286p.
                        (In Kingdom of the Spotted Snakes, From
        Travels in Mexico)

1937   Korzycki, Antoni. Zapiski Meksykańskie. Warsaw, Ludowa
        Spóldzielnia Wydawnicza, 1965, 64p.
                        (Mexican Notes)

1938   Krzywicka-Adamowicz, Helena. Meksyku, Orzel, Wąż i
        Opuncja. Warsaw, Wiedza Powszechna, 1963, 277p.
                        (Mexico, Eagle and Snake)

1939   Lipińska, Anna. Meksyku, Analiza Rozwoju Gospodarczego i
        Perspektywy Stosunków Ekonomicznych z Polską. Warsaw,
        Zakład Badań i Koniunktur i Cen Handlu Zagranicznego,
        1966, 103p.
                        (Mexico, Analysis of Economic Development
        and Prospects of Relations with Poland)

1940   Merdinger, Zygmunt. <u>Meksyku</u>. Warsaw, 1936, 70p.
        (Mexico)

1941   <u>Meksyk i Kraje Ameryki Środkowej. Praca Zbiorowa Pod.</u>
        Ed. by Tadeusza Witt; pt. 1, <u>Meksyku</u>. Warsaw, Polskie
        Wydawnictwo Gospodarcze, 1951, 87p.
        (Mexico and States of Central America. Part I: Mexico)

1942   Niklewicz, Konrad. <u>Meksyk za Panowania Maksymiljana I.</u>
        2d ed. 2v. Warsaw, 1901.
                        (Mexico Under Maxmilian I)

1943   Niklewicz, Konrad. <u>Wspomnienia z Meksyku. Opowiadania</u>
        <u>Legjonisty.</u> Warsaw, Gebethner i Wolff, 1896, 339+293p.
                        (Recollections from Mexico Told by a
        Legionnaire)

1944   Sten, Maria. <u>Trzy Barwy Meksyku, Tłum, Tekstow Poetyckich,</u>
        <u>Konstanty Ildefons Gałczyński, Artur Międzyrzecki, Maria</u>
        <u>Sten.</u> Warsaw, Arkady, 1961, 81p.
                        (Three Colors of Mexico: Translation of Poetry
        by Konstanty Ildefons Galczynski, Artur Miedzyrzecki, and Maria
        Sten)

1945   Sujkowski, Bogusław. <u>Nie Bogowie, Powieść o Wyprawie Corteza.</u>
        Łódź, Wydawnictwa Łódzkie, 1958, 456p.
                        (Not of God, Novel on Cortez)

1946   Szygowski, Juliusz. <u>Starożytny Meksyku.</u> Warsaw, Tow.
        Wydawnicze Rój, 1933, 119p.
                        (Old Mexico)

1947   Szyszlo, Witold. <u>Meksyku.</u> Warsaw, Gebethner i Wolff, 1912,
        257p.
                    (Mexico)

1948   Wańkowicz, Melchior. <u>W Kościołach Meksyku.</u> Warsaw, Rój,
        1927, 180p.
                        (In the Churches of Mexico)

1949   Wodzicki, Stanisław. <u>Z Ułanami Cesarza Maksymiliana w
        Meksyku, Wspomnienia Oficera.</u> Kraków, D. E. Friedlein,
        1931, 163p.
                        (With Dragoons of Maximilian in Mexico:
        Recollection of an Officer)

1950   <u>Zdobycie. Meksyku. Przełum, z Azteckiego i Opracował
        Tadeusz Milewski.</u> Wrocław, Zakład Narodowy im. Ossolińskich,
        1959, 94+160pp.
                        (Conquest of Mexico. Translation from
        Aztec. Edited by Tadeusz Milewski)

NICARAGUA

1951   Fijałkowski, Wiesław. Awantury Karaibskie. Warsaw, Książka
        i Wiedza, 1965, 265p.
                    (Caribbean Adventures)

PANAMA

1952   Fijałkowski, Wiesław. Złota Droga. Warsaw, Ministerstwo
        Obrony Narodowej, 1966, 140p.
                    (The Golden Road)

1953   Krotoski, Ludwik. Kanał Panamski w Dyplomacji Stanów
        Zjednoczonych i Wielkiej Brytanii. Warsaw, 1934, 52p.
                        (Panama Canal in the Diplomacy of
        the USA and England)

1954   Venin, V. M. Panama i Kanał Panamski. Tr. from Russian
        by K. Więckowski. Warsaw, 1953, 75p.
                        (Panama and Panama Canal)

1955   Barszczewski, Stefan. Na Ciemnych Wodach Paragwaju.
        Wspomnienia z Podróży. Lwów, Książnica-Atlas, 1931,
        126p.
                          (In Dark Waters of Paraguay:
        Recollections from Travels)

1956   Lepecki, Mieczyslaw. W Selwasach Paragwaju. 2d. ed.
        Warsaw, Wiedza Powszechna, 1962, 269p.
                          (In Selvas of Paraguay)

1957   Wiadomości o Paragwaju Dla Użytku Wychodźców.   Warsaw,
        Syndykat Emigracyjny, 1937, 92p.
        (Information on Paraguay for Immigrants)

1958   Bochdan-Niedenthal, Maria. Ucayali, Raj Czy Piekło Nad
Amazonką. Warsaw, 1935, 165p.
(Ucayali, Paradise or Hell over
Amazon)

1959   Fiedler, Arkady. Ryby Śpiewają w Ukajali. Warsaw, Iskry,
1957, 234p.
(Fish Sing in Ukajali)

1960   Freyd, Aleksander. Patologia Amazonji Peruwiańskiej. Warsaw,
Naukowy Instytut Emigracyjny, 1930, 44p.
(Pathology of the Peruvian Amazon)

1961   Gieysztor, Michał. Peru. Warsaw, Wyd. Rój, 1933, 63p.
(Peru)

1962   Kluger, Władysław. Listy z Peruwii, Skreślił... Inżynier
Rządowy i Profesor Szkoły Inżynierskiej w Limie. Kraków,
1877, 48p.
(Letters from Peru, Written by an
Engineer and Professor of School of Engineering in Lima)

1963   Kosidowski, Zenon. Królestwo Złotych Łez. 3d ed. Warsaw,
Iskry, 1961, 501p.
(Thousands of Golden Quarters)

1964   Nocón, Rodolf H. Dzieje, Kultura i Upadek Inków. Warsaw,
        Zakład Narodowy im. Ossolińskich, 1958, 377p.
                    (Deeds, Civilization and Downfall of the Incas)

1965   Oxiński, Tomasz. Peru, Opracowane na Polecenie Naukowego
        Instytuto Emigracyjnego i Kolonjalnego. 2d ed. Warsaw, 1939.
                    (Peru, Through the Institute of Immigration
        and Colonization)

1966   Oxiński Tomasz, & Roman Ciechanow. Augusto B. Leguia,
        Prezydent Republiki Peru. Warsaw, 1930, 25p.
                    (Augusto B. Leguia,
        President of Peru)

1967   Pankiewicz, Michał. Ustrój Społeczny Montanji Peruwjańskiej
        a Praktyczne Wskazania dla Osadnictwa Polskiego. Warsaw,
        1928, 23p.
                    (Social Conditions in Peru, and Practical
        Suggestions for Polish Settlers)

1968   Sztolcman, Jan. Peru, Wspomnienia z Podróży. 2v. Warsaw,
        Gebethner i Wolff, 1912.
                    (Peru, Recollections from Travel)

1969   Warchałowski, Kazimierz. Peru, Warunki Gospodarcze Montanji
        Peruwiańskiej. Warsaw, Nakł. Polonii Polskiej, 1930, 44p.
                    (Peru, Economic Conditions in Peru)

PUERTO RICO

1970 Szyszło, Witold. <u>Pod Zwrotnikami, Porto Rico.</u> 2 pts. Warsaw,
    Biblioteka Dzieł Wyborowych, 1911, 284p.
    (In the Tropics, Puerto Rico)

VENEZUELA

1971 Fiedler, Arkady. <u>Orinoko.</u> 4th ed. Warsaw, Iskry, 1961, 390p.
    (Orinoco)

1972 <u>Próba Oceny Potencjalnych Możliwości Eksportu do Wenezueli.</u>
    Warsaw, Polska Izba Handlu Zagranicznego, 1959, 128p.
    (Attempt at Evaluation of Potential Possibilities of Export to
    Venezuela)

WEST INDIES AND THE CARIBBEAN

1973 Budrewicz, Olgierd. <u>Romans Morza Karaibskiego.</u> 2d ed.
    Warsaw, Czytelnik, 1963, 238p.
        (The Romance of the Caribbean Sea)

1974 Łepkowski, Tadeusz. <u>Archipelagu Dzieje Niełatwe, Obrazy z
    Przeszłosci Antyli XV-XX w.</u> Warsaw, Wiedza Powszechna,
    1964, 302p.
        (Archipelago in Unsettled History, Excerpts
    from the Past of the Antilles: Fifteenth-Twentieth Centuries)

II. Periodical Articles

LATIN AMERICA

1975   Brodzki, Stanisław. "Daleko od Boga, Blisko U.S.A. " Warsaw,
        Argumenty (4: 26), 1960, p. 2.
                        ("Far Away from God, Close to the U.S. A.")

1976   C. K. (pseud.) "Integracja Gospodarcza Ameryki Łacińskiej. "
        Warsaw, Handel zagraniczny (6: 11), 1961, pp. 494-499.
                        ("Economic Integration of Latin America")

1977   Dobroczyński, Michal. "Integracja Gospodarcza Ameryki Łacińskiej. "
        Warsaw, Sprawy międzynarowe (14: 6), 1961, pp. 55-74.
                        ("Economic Integration of Latin America")

1978   Drohojowski, Jan. "Dialog z Ameryką Łacińska. " Warsaw, Nowa
        kultura (14: 14), 1963, pp. 1, 3.
                        ("Dialogue with Latin America")

1979   Drohojowski, Jan. "Odkrycie Ameryki Łacińskiej. " Warsaw,
        Prawo i życie (6: 15), 1961, pp. 6-7.
                        ("The Discovery of Latin America")

1980   Jakubik, Stefan. "Ameryka Łacińska Wczoraj i Dziś. " Warsaw,
        Problemy pokoju i socjalizmu (9), 1965, pp. 1-16, appendix.
                        (" Latin America Yesterday and Today")

1981   Jakubik, Stefan. "Kontynent 200 Milionow. " Warsaw, Wiedza
        i życie (29: 12), 1961, pp. 744-750.
                        ("Continent of 200 Million")

1982   Kozierkiewicz, Roman. "Inflacja a Wzrost Gospodarczy w Krajach
        Ameryki Łacińskiej." Warsaw, Handel zagraniczny zeszyty
        ekonomiczne (44), 1963, pp. 49-71.
                            ("Inflation and Economic Growth in
        Countries of Latin America")

1983   Kozierkiewicz, Roman. "O Zewnętrznym Finansowaniu Rozwoju
        Gospodarczego Ameryki Łacińskiej." Warsaw, Handel
        zagraniczny (9: 5), 1964, pp. 207-210.
                            ("Concerning External Outside
        Financing of the Economic Development of Latin America")

1984   Morawski, Dominik. "Przemiany w Ameryce Łacińskiej."
        Warsaw, Za i przeciw (4: 8), 1960, p. 2.
                            ("Changes in Latin America")

1985   Nencki, Boleslaw. "Stare i Nowe w Ameryce Łacińskiej."
        Warsaw, Tygodnik demokratyczny (8: 1), 1960, p. 306.
                            ("The Old and the New in Latin America")

1986   Orlewicz, Tadeusz. "Ruch Chłopski w Ameryce Łacińskiej.
        Aktualne Problemy w Kwestii Rolnej Ameryki Łacińskiej."
        Cracow, Wieści (9: 10/11), 1965, pp. 3-4.
                            ("The Farmers' Movement of Latin
        America: Current Problems cn the Agriculture of Latin America")

1987   Pasierbiński, Tadeusz M. "Ameryka Łacińska - Niespokojny
        Kontynent." Warsaw, Wojsko ludowe (3), 1962, pp. 37-45.
                            ("Latin America - Restless Continent")

1988   Piasecka, Anna. "Ważniejsze Dane o Rozwoju Gospodarczym
        Krajów Ameryki Łacińskiej." Warsaw, Sprawy międzynarodowe
        (16: 2), 1963, pp. 100-104.
                            ("The Most Important Data About Economic
        Development of the Countries of Latin America")

1989   Rommel, Waldemar. "Międzyamerykanski Bank Rozwoju. "
        Warsaw, Sprawy międzynarodowe (12: 11/12), 1959, pp. 94-99.
                        ("Inter American Development Bank")

1990   Rommel, Waldemar. "Plany Rozbrojeniowe w Ameryce Łacińskiej. "
        Warsaw, Sprawy międzynarodowe (13: 7/8), 1960, pp. 111-116.
                        ("Plans for Disarmament in Latin America")

1991   Rommel, Waldemar. "Zagadnienie Reformy Rolnej w Niektórych
        Krajach Ameryki Łacińskiej. " Warsaw, Sprawy międzynarodowe
        (14: 3), 1961, pp. 84-92.
                        ("The Question of Agricultural Reform in
        Some Countries of Latin America")

1992   Stanke, Ludwik. "Dokąd Zmierza Ameryka Łacińska?"
        Warsaw, Przegląd związkowy (16: 5), 1964 pp. 25-27.
                        ("Where is Latin America Going? ")

1993   Tomiczek, Jan, & Walenty Daszkiewicz. "Sprawy Ameryki
        Łacińskiej. " Warsaw, Sprawy międzynarodowe (15: 5),
        1962, pp. 102-111.
                        ("The Affairs of
        Latin America")

1994   Zaruk-Michalski, Aleksander. "Kolonie Francuzkie i Holenderskie
        w Ameryce Łacińskiej. " Warsaw, Sprawy międzynarodowe (16:
        5), 1963 pp. 93-103.
                        ("The French and Dutch Colonies
        in Latin America")

ARGENTINA

1995   Azembski, Mirosław. "Na Równinach Patagonii." Warsaw,
        Kontynenty (11), 1965, pp. 13-15.
                    ("On the Plains of Patagonia")

1996   Babad, Beata. "U Źródeł Konfliktów Argentyńskich." Warsaw,
        Nowe drogi (14: 1), 1960, pp. 110-123.
                    ("At the Source of Argentina's Conflicts")

1997   Bonasiewicz, Andrzej. "Argentyna - Kraj Wielkiej Hodowli."
        Warsaw, Geografia w szkole (13: 4), 1960, pp. 183-190.
                            ("Argentina - Country of Great Animal
        Breeding")

1998   Broniarek, Zygmunt. "Argentyna i Szersze Problemy."
        Warsaw, Trybuna ludu (15: 90), 1962, pp. 1-2, 8.
                            ("Argentina and Wider Problems")

1999   Ciechanowska, Maria. "O Teatrze w Argentynie." Warsaw,
        Teatr (16: 7), 1961, pp. 18-19.
                            ("About the Theatre in Argentina")

2000   Garztecki, Stanisław. "Współczesna Prasa Argentyńska."
        Warsaw, Prasa współczesna i dawna (1: 1-2), 1959, pp.
        207-214.
                    ("Modern Press in Argentina")

2001   Jabrzeński, Jerzy. "Na Tropach Bormana w Argentynie."
        Kracow, Przekrój (920), 1962, pp. 14-15.
                            ("Following the Steps of Borman in Argentina")

2002   Jarzembski, Jerzy. "Tacuara' Straszy w Argentynie."
        Warsaw, Zycie Warsżawy (19: 227), 1962, p. 4.
                    ("Taquara' is Haunting in Argentina")

2003   Marciniak, Bolesław. "List z Buenos Aires." Warsaw,
        Pszczelarstwo (17: 9), 1966, pp. 12-13.
                    ("A Letter from Buenos Aires")

2004   Michalski, Marian. "150 Lat Niepodległości Narodu Argentyńskiego."
        Warsaw, Życie Warszawy (17: 123), 1960, pp. 3-4.
                    ("150 Years of Independence of Argentina")

2005   Minkiewicz, Marian, & Edwin Zagorski. "Niektóre Problemy
        Handlu z Argentyną." Warsaw, Handel zagraniczny (5: 5),
        1960, pp. 200-203.
                                        ("Some of the
        Problems of Trade with Argentina")

2006   Ostrowski, Wiktor. "Niespodzianka Przed Szczytem."
        Warsaw, Poznaj świat (13: 6), 1965, pp. 11-13.
                    ("Surprise Before the Summit")

2007   P. G. A. (pseud.) "Jakie Wnioski Płyną z Wyborów w Argentynie?"
        Warsaw, Problemy pokoju i socializmu (1: 6), 1960, pp. 77-78.
                        ("What Conclusions can be Drawn from the
        Elections in Argentina? ")

2008   Piasecka, Anna. "Cień Perona nad Argentyna." Warsaw,
        Życie Warszawy (19: 81), 1962, p. 3.
                    ("The Shadow of Peron over Argentina")

2009   Pruss, Edmund. "La Pampa." Warsaw, Poznaj świat (9: 5),
        1961, pp. 18-21.
                    ("La Pampa")

2010   Radzymińska, Józefa. "Mapuche." Warsaw, Kontynenty (8),
        1965, pp. 26-27.

2011   Radzymińska, Józefa. "Ziemia 'Dobrego Powietrza'." Warsaw,
        Widnokręgi (9), 1963, pp. 48-50.
                    ("The Land of 'Good Air'")

2012   Rutowicz, Jerzy. "Argentyna, Partnerzy Handlowi Polski."
        Warsaw, Handel zagraniczny (9: 3), 1964, pp. 107-113.
                    ("Argentina, Commercial Partner of Poland")

2013   Starzeński, Antoni. "Argentyna - Kraj i Ludzie." Kracow,
        Wszechświat (7/8), 1962, pp. 181-184.
                    ("Argentina - the Country and the People")

2014   Starzeński, Antoni. "Pod Modrym Niebem Argentyny." Kracow,
        Wszechświat (9), 1961, pp. 218-221.
                    ("Under the Blue Sky of Argentina")

2015   Wolniewicz, Janusz. "Befsztyk po Argentyńsku." Warsaw,
        Kontynenty (8), 1964, pp. 18-19.
                    ("Beefsteak in Argentina's Way")

2016   Zabiełło, Stanisław. "Chroniczny Kryzys w Argentynie."
        Warsaw, Sprawy międzynarodowe (15: 6), 1962, pp. 76-78.
                    ("The Chronic Crisis in Argentina")

BOLIVIA

2017   Azembski, Mirosław. "Boliwia: Żebrak na Złotym Krzesle. " Łódz, Odgłosy (8: 27), 1965, p. 5.
("Bolivia: A Beggar on a Golden Chair")

2018   Azembski, Miroslaw. "Tajemnice Tiahuanaco. " Łodz, Odgłosy (8: 33), 1965, p. 4.
("The Secrets of Tiahuanaco")

2019   Babad, Beata. "'Idelogiczna' Podbudowa Interwencji. " Warsaw, Kontynenty (8), 1965, p. 31.
("'Ideological' Foundation of Interventions")

2020   Bartnicki, Andrzej. "Wojna Między Boliwią i Paragwajem 1932-1935. " Warsaw, Mowią wieki (8: 8), 1965, p. 3.
("War Between Bolivia and Paraguay, 1932-1935")

2021   Bogucki, Sławomir. "La Paz. " Warsaw, Poznaj świat (13: 3), 1965, pp. 23-28.
("La Paz")

2022   Budrewicz, Olgierd. "Boliwia: Dramat i Farsa. " Kracow, Przekrój (1020), 1964, pp. 5-6.
("Bolivia: Drama and a Farce")

2023   Budrewicz, Olgierd. "Nad Swiętym Jeziorem Inków. " Kracow, Przekrój (10: 18), 1964, pp. 5-6, 10.
("By the Sacred Lake of the Incas")

BRAZIL

2024   Albinowski, Stanislaw. "Quadros i Kennedy." Warsaw, Życie
Warszawy (18: 43), 1961, pp. 4, 7.
("Quadros and Kennedy")

2025   Azembski, Mirosław. "Favelado Przestaje Być Potulny."
Warsaw, Życie warszawy (22: 66), 1965, p. 6.
("Favelado Stops Being Submissive")

2026   Babad, Beata. "Brazylia. Swiatła i Cienie. --Dwie Kandydatury
Przed Wyborami na Prezydenta." Warsaw, Trybuna ludu
(13: 264), 1960, p. 8.
       ("Brazil. Lights and Shades. --Two Candidacies
Before the Presidential Election")

2027   Babad, Beata. "Geneologia J. Goularta." Warsaw, Kontynenty
(5), 1964, pp. 2-5.
("The Genealogy of J. Goulart")

2028   Biedroń, Antoni. "Wrażenia z Podróży do Brazylii. Projekty -
Problemy." Katowice, Biuletin biur projektów przemysłu
węglowego (8: 1/2), 1963, pp. 64-69.
       ("Impressions from a Trip to Brazil")

2029   Bonasewicz, Andrzej. "Brasilia - Stolica Brazylii." Warsaw,
Geografia w szkole (16: 4), 1963, pp. 185-187.
("Brasilia - Capital of Brazil")

2030   Budaszewski, Jan. "Brasilia Rewelacją Techniki Budownictwa
XX Wieku." Warsaw, Przegląd techniczny (81: 28), 1960,
pp. 4-5.
       ("Brasilia, the Revelation of Architectural
Techniques of the 20th Century")

2031   ECK (pseud.) "Jan Macumba". Kracow, Przekrój (930),
        1963, pp. 5-6.
        ("Juan Macumba")

2032   Gawron, Witold. "Szkolnictwo Wyższe w Brazylii. " Warsaw,
        Życie szkoly wyższej (14: 7/8), 1966, pp. 198-204.
        ("Higher Education in Brazil")

2033   H. K. (pseud.) "J. Quadros. " Warsaw, Widnokręgi (1), 1961,
        pp. 90-91.
        ("J. Quadros")

2034   Hajduk, Ryszard. "Niemcy Znów w Siodle. " Warsaw, Polityka,
        (8: 33), 1964, p. 9.
        ("The Germans are in the Saddle Again ")

2035   Kacer, R. W. "Budownictwo w Brazylii - Kilka Informacji. "
        Warsaw, Przegląd budowlany i budownictwo mieszkaniowe
        (34: 10), 1962, pp. 619-620.
        ("Building in Brazil: Little Information")

2036   Kobryner, Jan. "Republika Stanów Zjednoczonych Brazylii. "
        Warsaw, Handel zagraniczny (7: 8), 1962, pp. 349-350.
        ("The Republic of the United States of Brazil")

2037   Krasicki, Ignacy. "Arcybiskup Câmara na Czele Antyfaszystowskiej
        Opozycji w Brazylii. " Warsaw, Życie Warszawy (23: 203),
        1966, p. 6.
        ("Archbishop Câmara at the Head of the
        Anti-fascist Opposition in Brazil")

2038   Krupińska, Aniela. "Wojskowy Reżim Brazylii Prześladuje
        Intelektualistów. " Warsaw, Życie Warszawy (21: 303),
        1964, p. 2.
        ("The Military Regime of Brazil is
        Persecuting the Intellectuals")

2039   Kula, Marcin. "Brazylijska Plantacja Cukrowa XVI-XVIIw. "
        Warsaw, Kwartalnik historii kultury materialnej (14: 4),
        1966, pp. 617-640.
                        ("Brazilian Sugar-cane Plantations of 16th -
        17th Centuries")

2040   Leonowicz, Halina. "Niebanalny Banał. " Warsaw, Widnokręgi
        (6), 1963, pp. 27-30.
                        ("Not a Triviality")

2041   Leonowicz, Halina. "Złoto. " Warsaw, Widnokręgi (5),
        1962, pp. 55-56.
                        ("Gold")

2042   Lewinowa, Sabina. "Brazylia. Oświata i Wychowanie w
        Innych Krajach. " Warsaw, Kwartalnik pedagogiczny (7: 2),
        1962, pp. 305-309.
                        ("Brazil: Education and Child Care
        in Other Countries")

2043   Lewinowa, Sabina. "Kilka Słów o Przedszkolach w Brazylii. "
        Warsaw, Wychowanie w przedszlolu (15: 5), 1962, pp. 237-
        241.
                        ("Few Words about the Pre-schools in
        Brazil")

2044   Lewinowa, Sabina. "Migawki ze Szkól Brazylijskich. "
        Warsaw, Nowa szkoła (3), 1962, pp. 37-41.
                        ("Snapshots from Brazilian Schools")

2045   Lidert, Mieczysław. "Brazylia, Batalia o Reformy w Decydujacej
        Fazie. " Warsaw, Tygodnik demokratyczny (12: 14), 1964,
        pp. 3, 7.
                        (" Brazil, Battle for Reforms in its
        Decisive Phase")

2046   Małkim, Borys. "W Dżunglach Rio Gurupi." Warsaw, Poznaj
świat (12: 9), 1965, pp. 3-7.
("In the Jungle of Rio Gurupi")

2047   Nowicz, Wiktor. "Watykan i Ameryka Łacińska. Przykład Brazylii. "
Warsaw, Zeszyty argumentów (4), 1964, pp. 92-96.
("Vatican and Latin America: The Example
of Brazil")

2048   Osmańczyk, Edmund. "Brazylijska Niagara. " Warsaw,
Polityka (8: 8), 1964, p. 10.
("The Brazilian Niagara")

2049   Osmańczyk, Edmund. "Napieta Sytuacja w Brazylii. " Warsaw,
Trybuna Ludu (17: 94), 1964, pp. 1-21.
("Tense Situation in Brazil")

2050   Osmańczyk, Edmund. "Różancowe Bojówki z Bêlo Horizonte. "
Warsaw, Kontynenty (5), 1964, pp. 4-5.
("The Struggles of the Rosary with Bêlo
Horizonte")

2051   Osmańczyk, Edmund. "Walki w Brazylii nie Ustały. " Warsaw,
Zycie Warszawy (21: 83), 1964, pp. 1-2.
("The Fights in Brazil did not Cease")

2052   Pankiewicz, Michał. "Z Dziejow Szkolnictwa Polskiego w
Brazilii. " Warsaw, Przegląd historyczno oswiatowy
(2: 2), 1959, pp. 163-173.
("From the History of Polish Education
in Brazil")

2053   Piasecka, Anna. "Brazylia na Rozdrożu." Warsaw,
        Życie Warszawy (18: 218), 1961, pp. 3-4.
        ("Brazil on the Cross-road")

2054   Piasecka, Anna. "Od Vargasa do Goularta." Warsaw,
        Życie Warszawy (21: 82), 1964, p. 2.
        ("From Vargas to Goulart")

2055   Piasecka, Anna. "Strach Przed Brazylijskim Fidelem."
        Warsaw, Życie Warszawy (19: 70), 1962, p. 3.
        ("The Fear of a Brazilian Fidel")

2056   Prembiński, Aleksander. "Szkolnictwo Wyższe w Brazylii."
        Warsaw, Życie szkoły wyższej (11: 6), 1963, pp. 81-86.
        ("Higher Education in Brazil")

2057   Prembiński, Aleksander. "O Szkolnictwie Zawodowym w
        Brazylii." Warsaw, Szkoła zawodowa (4), 1962, pp. 55-57.
                        ("About Vocational Education in
        Brazil")

2058   Rabsztyn, Jerzy, & Sikora Włodzimierz. "Niektóre Uwagi
        Dotyczące Brazylijskiego Przemysłu Węglowego." Katowice,
        Biuletin biur projektów przysłu węglowego (8: 1/2), 1963, pp.
        61-64.
                                ("Some Comments
        Regarding the Brazilian Coal Industry")

2059   Raciborski, Jan. "Olbrzym Znad Amazonki." Warsaw, Za
        wolność i lud (13: 11), 1961, pp. 6-7.
                ("The Giant from the Amazon")

2060   Rajski, Jerzy. "Jeszcze o Prawie Brazylijskim." Warsaw, Tamże (8: 20), 1963, pp. 6-7.
                ("About Brazilian Law")

2061   Rommel, Waldemar. "O Ruchu Chłopskim w Brazylii." Warsaw, Wieś współczesna (6: 2), 1962, pp. 105-115.
                ("About the Farmers' Movement in Brazil")

2062   Sacks, Ignacy. "Na Marginesie Wydarzeń Brazylijskich." Warsaw, Nowe drogi (15: 10), 1961, pp. 55-61.
                ("On the Margin of the Brazilian Happenings")

2063   Sachs, Ignacy. "Niektóre Aspekty Rozwoju Gospodarczego w Brazylii." Warsaw, Ekonomista (1), 1962, pp. 119-138.
                ("Some of the Aspects of the Economic Development of Brazil")

2064   S. F. (pseud.) "Perspektywy Polsko-Brazylijskiej Wymiany Handlowej." Warsaw, Życie gospodarcze (16: 22), 1961, p. 7.
                ("The Prospects for Polish-Brazilian Trade")

2065   Stefanowicz, Janusz. "Wydarzenia w Brazylii. Tło i Przyczyny." Warsaw, Sprawy międzynarodowe (17: 6), 1964, pp. 42-60.
                ("Occurrences in Brazil: Background and Causes")

2066   Szczypińska, Hanna. "Sztuka Prymitywów Brazylijskich." Kracow, Tygodnik powszechny (20: 27), 1966, p. 4.
                ("The Art of the Brazilian Primitives")

2067   Tomaszewski, Jan. "Okruchowe Złoża Cyny w Dorzeczu Rio São Laurence." Katowice, Rudy i metale nieżelazne (11: 7), 1966, pp. 377-382.
                ("Crumbled Beds of Tin in the Basin of Rio São Laurenço")

2068   Urbaniak, Jan. "Karnawał w Rio." Warsaw, Trybuna ludu
        (17: 54), 1964, p. 6.
                    ("The Carnival in Rio")

2069   Urbaniak, Jan. "Za Szańcami Wstecznej Konstytucji."
        Warsaw, Trybuna ludu (16: 175), 1963, p. 2.
                    ("Behind the Ramparts of a Backward
        Constitution")

2070   Urusek, Leszek. "Zródła Neutralismu Brazylijskiego."
        Warsaw, Sprawy międzynarodowe (15: 5), 1962, pp. 9-19.
                    ("The Origins of the Brazilian Neutralism")

2071   Wiśniewski, Eugeniusz. "Prawda o Ustawodawstwie Brazylii."
        Warsaw, Prawo i życie (8: 19), 1963, p. 6.
                        ("The Truth About the Legislature
        of Brazil")

2072   Wojcik, Władysław. "Indianie Asymiluja się." Warsaw,
        Kontynenty (11), 1966, pp. 23-25, 32.
                        ("Indians Assimilate Themselves")

2073   Wróblewski, Piotr. "Karnawał w Mato Grosso." Warsaw,
        Tygodnik kulturalny (9: 8), 1965, pp. 2-3.
                        ("The Carnival in Mato Grosso")

2074   Zabiełło, Stanisław. "Brazylia w Roku 1961." Warsaw,
        Żicie i myśl (12: 1/2), 1962, pp. 104-114.
                        ("Brazil in the Year 1961")

2075   Zabiełło, Stanisław. "Walka o Orientację Polityczną
        Brazylii." Warsaw, Sprawy międzynarodowe (15: 12),
        1962, pp. 83-92.
                        ("A Struggle for Political Orientation
        in Brazil")

CHILE

2076   A. (pseud.) "Rozwój Rybołówstwa w Chile." Gdynia,
        Technika i gospodarka morska (15: 7), 1965, pp. 275-276.
        ("Development of Fishing in Chile")

2077   Azembski, Mirosław. "Chilijska Współczesność." Warsaw,
        Argumenty (8: 38), 1964, p. 7.
        ("The Chilean Modernism")

2078   Babad, Beata. "Chile na Skrzyżowaniu Dróg." Warsaw,
        Nowe drogi (20: 4), 1966, pp. 81-98.
        ("Chile on a Crossroad")

2079   Budrewicz, Olgierd. "Kraj Zwariowanej Geografii."
        Kracow, Przekrój (1037), 1965, pp. 5-7.
        ("A Country of Insane Geography")

2080   Czartoryski, Paweł. "Inflacja w Chile." Warsaw, Ekonomista
        (6), 1963, pp. 1195-1205.
        ("Inflation in Chile")

2081   Gizycki, L. "Huachipato, Huta na Brzegach Oceanu."
        Warsaw, Poznaj świat (9: 12), 1961, p. 33.
        ("Huachipato, Smelting House on the Coast")

2082   Kobryner, Jan. "Chile. Partnerzy Handlowi Polski." Warsaw,
        Handel zagraniczny (7: 11), 1962, pp. 490-493.
        ("Chile, Commercial Partner of Poland")

2083 Piasecka, Anna. "Chile pod Znakiem Wyborów." Warsaw,
Życie Warszawy (21: 210), 1964, p. 2.
      ("Chile under the Sign of Elections")

2084 Piasecka, Anna. "Pomruk Wulkanu w Chile." Warsaw,
Życie Warszawy (21: 92), 1964, p. 2.
      ("Murmur of a Volcano in Chile")

2085 Senkowski, Henryk. "Chile." Warsaw, Poznaj świat (11: 9),
1963, pp. 37-38.
      ("Chile")

2086 Sienkiewicz, Edward. "Przeżyłem Trzęsienie Ziemi w
Chile." Kracow, Przekrój (822), 1961, pp. 14-16.
      ("I Lived Through an Earthquake
in Chile")

2087 Urbaniak, Jan. "Chile Broni Zasady Nieinterwencji."
Warsaw, Trybuna ludu (15: 351), 1962, p. 2.
      ("Chile Guards the Principle of Non-
intervention")

2088 Urbaniak, Jan. "Na Wyspie Między Pacyfikiem i Andami."
Warsaw, Trybuna ludu (16: 264), 1963, p. 6.
      ("On an Island Between Pacific and Andes")

2089   Drohojowski, Jan. "Wrzenie w Kraju Orchidei." Warsaw,
        Prawo i życie (7: 9), 1962, p. 6.
                        ("Ferment in the Land of Orchids")

2090   Hrankowski, H. "Andyjska Kraina Kawy." Warsaw, Trybuna
        ludu (16: 53), 1963, p. 4.
                        ("Coffee Land of the Andes")

2091   Klimowicz, Jolanta. "Kolumbią Rządzi Kawa." Warsaw,
        Kontynenty (11), 1966, p. 14.
                        ("Colombia is Ruled by Coffee")

2092   Kowalska - Lewicka, Anna. "Indianie znad Rzeki Arato."
        Warsaw, Poznaj świat (12: 8), 1965, pp. 15-16.
                                ("Indians from the River
        Arato")

2093   Kwiatek, Jerzy. "Kolumbia." Warsaw, Poznaj świat (12: 2),
        1964, pp. 37-38.
                        ("Colombia")

2094   Owczarck, Mieczysław. "Kolumbia: Gdy Gwałt Rodzi Gwałt."
        Warsaw, Kontynenty (1), 1966, pp. 22-23.
                        ("Colombia: When Violence Creates
        Violence")

2095   Urbaniak, Jan. "Krwawa 'Violencia' w Kolumbii." Warsaw,
        Trybuna ludu (20: 305), 1963, p. 6.
                        ("Bloody 'Violencia' in Colombia")

COSTA RICA

2096   Grabecki, Stanisław. "Tanie Bandery." Gdańsk, Tygodnik
        morski (9: 33), 1966, pp. 1, 4.
                            ("Cheap Banners")

CUBA

2097   A. A. (pseud.) "Fidel Castro." Warsaw, Widnokręgi (10),
        1960, pp. 72-73.
                            ("Fidel Castro")

2098   Albinowski, Stanislaw. "Kubański Drogowskaz." Warsaw,
        Widnokręgi (8), 1961, pp. 58-61.
                            ("The Cuban Road-Sign")

2099   Albinowski, Stanislaw. "Kubanczycy Wiedzą co Robią."
        Warsaw, Życie Warszawy (17: 263), 1960, pp. 3-4.
                            ("The Cubans Know What They are
        Doing")

2100   Babad, Beata. "Burzliwa Młodość Rewolucji." Warsaw,
        Argumenty (8: 1), 1964, pp. 6-7.
                            ("The Stormy Youth of the Revolution")

2101   Breza, Tadeusz. "Wieczór z Fidelem Castro." Warsaw,
        Przegląd kulturalny (10: 30), 1961, pp. 1, 4-5.
                    ("An Evening with Fidel Castro")

2102   Burchard, Przemysław. "Guantanamo." Warsaw, Poznaj
        świat (10: 12), 1962, pp. 15-16.
                    ("Guantanamo")

2103   Burchard, Przemysław. "Pożyteczne Nietoperze." Warsaw,
        Poznaj świat (10: 10), 1962, pp. 7-8.
                    ("The Useful Bats")

2104   Chmielewska, Teresa. "José Marti." Warsaw, Kontynenty
        (5), 1966, pp. 38-39.

                    ("José Marti")

2105   Daszkiewicz, Walenty. "Międzynarodowa Sytuacja Kuby."
        Warsaw, Sprawy międzynarodowe (15: 10), 1960, pp. 3-38.
                    ("The International Situation of
        Cuba")

2106   Daszkiewicz, Walenty. "Wizyta A. Mikojana na Kubie."
        Warsaw, Sprawy międzynarodowe (13: 4), 1960, pp. 81-88.
                    ("The Visit of A. Mikoyan to Cuba")

2107   Dobrowolski, Władysław J. "Narodziny Tragedii."
        Warsaw, Teatr (21: 4), 1966, pp. 10-12.
                    ("The Birth of Tragedy")

2108   Doman, Piotr. "Po Kryzysie Kubańskim - Wnioski, Nadzieje."
        Warsaw, Wieś współczesna (7: 2), 1963, pp. 3-12.
                    ("After the Cuban Crisis - Inferences, Hopes")

2109   E. K. (pseud.) "Rozwój Drobiarstwa na Kubie. " Warsaw,
        Drobiarstwo (14: 4), 1966, p. 22.
                ("The Development of Poultry in Cuba")

2110   Fiedorowicz, Maciej. "Kuba Wyspa Jak Wulkan Gorąca. "
        Warsaw, Przegląd techniczny (100: 34), 1966, pp. 10-11.
                ("Cuba, an Island as Hot as Volcano")

2111   Gałkiewicz, Tadeusz. "Szkic Geologii Kuby. " Katowice,
        Rudy i metale nieżelazne (6: 8), 1961, pp. 362-364.
                ("A Sketch of the Geology of Cuba")

2112   Garztecka, Ewa. "Współczesne Malarstwo Kubańskie. "
        Warsaw, Trybuna ludu (15: 291), 1962, p. 8.
                ("Contemporary Cuban Painting")

2113   Gelberg, Ludwik. "Kryzys Kubański a Współczsne Prawo
        Międzynarodowe. " Warsaw, Sprawy Międzynarodowe (16: 1),
        1963, pp. 20-39.
                ("The Cuban Crisis and Contemporary
        International Law")

2114   Giełżynski, Wojciech. "Niespokojna Las Villas. " Warsaw,
        Dookoła świata (7: 49), 1960, pp. 10-11.
                ("Restless Las Villas")

2115   "Gospodarka Morska Kuby na Starcie. " Szczecin, Tygodnik
        morski (4: 32), 1961, pp. 1-2.
        ("Origin of the Marine Economy of Cuba")

2116   G. P. (pseud.) "Guantanamo. " Gdynia, Przegląd morski
        (14: 9), 1961, pp. 72-81.
                ("Guantanamo")

2117   Gradziński, Ryszard. "W Jaskiniach Kuby. " Warsaw,
        Wszechświat (12), 1962, pp. 302-307.
                            ("In the Caves of Cuba")

2118   Ikonowicz, M. "Na Kubie - Spokój i Opanowanie. " Warsaw,
        Trybuna ludu (17: 41), 1964, pp. 1-2.
                            ("On Cuba, Peace, and Control")

2119   Jakus, Julian. "Rozwój Kubańskiej Żeglugi Handlowej. "
        Gdynia, Technika i gospodarka morska (16: 8/9), 1966,
        pp. 290-292.
                            ("The Development of the Cuban Commercial
        Fleet")

2120   Janczewski, Jerzy. "Mała Historia Kubańskiej Kinematografii. "
        Warsaw, Ekran (7: 2), 1963, pp. 7, 10.
                            ("Short History of the Cuban Cinema")

2121   Kapuścinski, W. J. "Osiągnięcia i Potrzeby Służby Zdrowia
        na Kubie. " Warsaw, Służba zdrowia (14: 30), 1962, p. 5.
                            ("The Achievements and the Needs
        of the Cuban Health Services")

2122   Kerner, Samuel. "Rewolucja Kubańska. " Warsaw, Nowe
        drogi (14: 7), 1960, pp. 126-140.
                            ("The Cuban Revolution")

2123   Konieczny, Jerzy R. "Lotnictwo Cywilne na Kubie. " Warsaw,
        Wojskowy przegląd lotniczy (19: 6), 1965, pp. 81-85.
                            ("Civilian Air Force in Cuba")

2124   Kowalewski, Jerzy. "Uwagi o Wspołistnieniu. " Warsaw,
        Nowe drogi (17: 1), 1963, pp. 49-56.
                            ("Comments About Co-existence")

2125   Krasicki, Ludwik. "Universidad Oriente." Warsaw, Trybuna
        ludu (19: 86), 1966, p. 6.
                ("Universidad Oriente")

2126   Krupińska, Aniela. "Kuba - Kraj Niklu." Warsaw, Życie
        Warszawy (22: 135), 1965, p. 4.
                ("Cuba, a Country of Nickel")

2127   Krupińska, Aniela. "Kubańska 'Casa de las Americas'."
        Warsaw, Kontynenty (9), 1965, pp. 22-23.
                ("Cuban 'Casa de las Americas'")

2128   Krupińska, Aniela. "Kuba Uczy Się Techniki." Warsaw,
        Życie Warszawy (21: 299), 1964, p. 2.
                ("Cuba is Learning Technology")

2129   Krupińska, Aniela. "Nagrody 'Casa de las Americas'."
        Warsaw, Życie Warszawy (22: 36), 1965, p. 6.
                ("Rewards 'Casa de las Americas'")

2130   Kucharek, Zygmunt. "Szkolnictwo Okrętowe na Kubie."
        Gdańsk, Przegląd ekonomiki przemysłu okrętowego
        (3: 1), 1966, pp. 55-56.
                ("Maritime Education in Cuba")

2131   Kuczyński, Maciej. "Podziemne Miasto Nietoperzy."
        Warsaw, Problemy (18: 9), 1962, pp. 622-628.
                ("The Underground City of Bats")

2132   Kwarciak, Stefan. "Szkolnictwo na Kubie." Warsaw,
        Szkoła sawodowa (4), 1961, pp. 53-55.
                ("Education in Cuba")

2133   Łaska-Mierzejewska, Teresa. "Badania Antropologiczne na
Kubie. " Poznań, Przegląd Antropologiczny (30: 2), 1965,
pp. 358-361.
                            ("Anthropological Research
in Cuba")

2134   Łaska-Mierzejewska, Teresa. "Wstepne Informacje o Rozwoju
Dzieci i Młodzieży Kubańskiej. " Warsaw, Wychowanie
fizyczne i sport (9: 4), 1965, pp. 459-477.
                     ("Introductory Information
About the Development of Cuban Children and Teenagers")

2135   Łętowska, Ewa. "Zagadnienia Gospodarczo-ustawodawe
Rewolucyjnej Kuby. " Warsaw, Prawo i życie (8: 23), 1963,
p. 6.
                   ("The Economic and Legislative Problems
of the Revolutionary Cuba")

2136   Lewin, Leopold. "Migawki Kubańskie. " Kracow, Życie
literackie (15: 9), 1965, pp. 1, 9.
                ("Cuban Snapshots")

2137   Lidert, Mieczysław. "Kuba a Stany Zjednoczone. " Warsaw,
Sprawy międzynarodowe (15: 6), 1962, pp. 103-107.
                 ("Cuba and the United States")

2138   Lidert, Mieczysław. "Kuba - 3 Lat Rewolucji. " Warsaw,
Geografia w szkole (15: 5), 1962, pp. 55-60.
                  ("Cuba-Three Years of the Revolution")

2139   Lubiński, D. "5-Letni Układ Handlowy NRD - Kuba. "
Warsaw, Trybuna Ludu (13: 348), 1960, p. 6.
                ("The Five Year Trade Agreement, East
Germany - Cuba")

2140   M . (pseud.) "Malarstwo Kubańskie. " Kracow, <u>Życie literackie</u>
            (12: 44), 1962, pp. 6.
            ("Cuban Painting")

2141   Mąka, Henryk. "Monokultura nie Popłaca. " Warsaw, <u>Poznaj</u>
            <u>świat</u> (10: 4), 1962, pp. 34-36.
            ("Monoculture Doesn't Pay")

2142   Malecki, Ignacy. "Año de la Educacione i Technika. "
            Warsaw, <u>Trybuna ludu</u> (14: 49), 1961, p. 4.
            ("Year of Education and Technology")

2143   Mroziewicz, Robert. "Cień nad Kuba. " Warsaw, <u>Mowią</u>
            <u>wieki</u> (8: 12), 1965, pp. 1-4.
            ("A Shadow over Cuba")

2144   Multański, A. "Szkolnictwo i Oświata na Kubie. " Warsaw,
            <u>Ruch pedagogiczny</u> (3: 2), 1961, pp. 118-121.
            ("Education and Learning in Cuba")

2145   Oboleński, Mikołaj. "Z Zagadnien Budownictwa Socjalistycznego
            na Kubie. " Warsaw, <u>Gospodarka planowa</u> (19: 6), 1964, pp. 55-59.
                  ("About the Problems of Building Socialism
      in Cuba")

2146   Okoński, Stanisław. "Rybołowstwo Kuby. " Gdynia, <u>Technika</u>
            <u>i gospodarka morska</u> (15: 2), 1966, pp. 47-49.
            ("Cuban Fishing")

2147 Babad, Beata. "Era Trujillo: Krew, Tortury, Mordy Skrytobójcze
i... Pieczątki na Paszporcie." Warsaw, Życie Warszawy
(17: 140), 1960, pp. 4, 7.
      ("Trujillo's Era: Blood, Tortures, Secret
Murders and... a Stamp on the Passport")

2148 Babad, Beata. "'Marines' w Dominikanie." Warsaw,
Kontynenty (7), 1965, pp. 14-15.
      ("'Marines' in Dominican Republic")

2149 Brodzki, Stanisław. "Smierć na San Domingo." Warsaw,
Świat (15: 20), 1965, pp. 4-5.
      ("Death in San Domingo")

2150 Broniarek, Zygmunt. "Byłem w Santo Domingo." Warsaw,
Kultura (3: 30), 1965, pp. 1-2.
      ("I Was in Santo Domingo")

2151 Broniarek, Zygmunt. "Irytacja Białego Domu po Przemówieniu
Fulbrighta 'Interwencja w Dominikanie Była Błedem'."
Warsaw, Trybuna ludu (18: 258), 1965, p. 6.
      ("Irritation of the White House After
Fulbright's Speech, 'Intervention in the Dominican Republic
was a Mistake'")

2152 Broniarek, Zygmunt. "Wyprawa do Santo Domingo." Kracow,
Przekrój (1058), 1965, pp. 5-6.
      ("Excursion to Santo Domingo")

2153   Dembiński, Ludwik. "Czy Koniec Ery Trujillo?" Kracow,
        Tygodnik powszechny (14: 35), 1960, p. 2.
                    ("The End of Trujillo's Era?")

2154   Dembiński, Ludwik. "Polityka 'Grubego Kija'." Kracow,
        Tygodnik powszechny (19: 20), 1965, p. 3.
                    ("The Policy of the 'Big Stick'")

2155   Kowzan, Tadeusz. "Kraj w Którym Cień i Zdrowie są z Łaski
        Dyktatora." Warsaw, Za wolność i lud (12: 10), 1960, pp.
        6-7.
                    ("Country in Which Shadow and Health
        are Favors from the Dictator")

2156   Krupińska, Aniela. "Ludowe Powstanie w Dominikanie."
        Warsaw, Życie Warszawy (22: 101), 1965, p. 2.
                    ("People's Uprising in the Dominican
        Republic")

2157   Krupińska, Aniela. "Oburzenie Ameryki Łacińskiej." Warsaw,
        Życie Warszawy (22: 105), 1965, p. 4.
                    ("Indignation of Latin America")

2158   Krupińska, Aniela. "Sprawa Republiki Dominikańskiej."
        Warsaw, Zbiór dokumentów (21: 7/8), 1965, positions 144-145:
        (21: 5/6), 1965, positions 110-126.
                    ("The Dominican Republic Affair")

2159   "O Doswiadczeniach Walki Zbrojnej w Republice Dominikańskiej."
        Warsaw, Problemy pokoju i socjalizmu (6), 1964, pp. 52-54.
        (" On the Experiences of Armed Battles in the Dominican Republic")

2160   Piasecka, Anna. "Amerykanie i Spadkobierca Trujillo."
        Warsaw, Życie Warszawy (22: 160), 1965, p. 2.
                    ("The Americans and the Heir of Trujillo")

2161   Piasecka, Anna. "Interwencja i co Dalej." Warsaw,
        Życie Warszawy (22: 126), 1965, p. 2.
                        ("Intervention and What Next")

2162   Piasecka, Anna. "Pośmiertne Rządy Trujillo." Warsaw,
        Życie Warszawy (18: 208), 1961, pp. 3-4.
                        ("Posthumous Rule of Trujillo")

2163   Piasecka, Anna. "Za Kulisami Konfliktu Dominikana -
        Haiti." Warsaw, Życie Warszawy (20: 109), 1963, p. 2.
                        ("Behind the Scenes of the Conflict
        Between the Dominican Republic and Haiti")

2164   Urbaniak, Jan. "'Doktryna Johnsona' i Jej Korzenie."
        Warsaw, Trybuna ludu (18: 123), 1965, p. 6.
                        ("'Johnson's Doctrine' and its Roots")

2165   Urbaniak, Jan. "Przewrót w Dominikanie." Warsaw,
        Trybuna ludu (16: 264), 1963, p. 6.
                        ("The Revolt in the Dominican Republic")

ECUADOR

2166   Dembiński, Ludwik. "Przewrót w Ekwadorze." Kracow,
        Tydodnik powszechny (15: 48), 1961, p. 2.
                        ("The Revolt in Ecuador")

2167   Krupińska, Aniela. "Ekwador w Okowach Terroru." Warsaw,
        Życie Warszawy (20: 298), 1963, p. 4.
                        ("Ecuador in Chains of Terror")

519

2168   Krupińska, Aniela. "Upadek Dyktatury w Ekwadorze."
Warsaw, Życie Warszawy (23: 77), 1966, p. 2.
("The Fall of the Dictatorship in
Ecuador")

2169   Kubiatowicz, Lucjan. "Ekwador." Warsaw, Poznaj świat
(12: 7), 1964, pp. 37-38, 48.
("Ecuador")

2170   M. B. (pseud.) "Równikowy Kraj." Warsaw, Widnokręgi
(4), 1961, pp. 38-40.
("A Country of the Equator")

2171   Osmańczyk, Edmund. "Pijany Prezydent i Trzeźwe Monopole."
Warsaw, Przegląd kulturalny (11: 43), 1962, p. 2.
("A Drunken President and Sober
Monopolies")

2172   Piasecka, Anna. "Po Argentynie - Ekwador." Warsaw,
Życie Warszawy (19: 90), 1962, p. 4.
("After Argentina - Ecuador")

2173   Urbaniak, Jan. "Od Morza Karaibskiego po Andy." Warsaw,
Trybuna ludu (14: 312), 1961, p. 2.
("From the Caribean Sea to the Andes")

2174   Urbaniak, Jan. "W Andach na Równiku." Warsaw, Trybuna
ludu (15: 97), 1962, p. 8.
("In the Andes on the Equator")

EL SALVADOR

2175   Kubiatowicz, Lucjan. "Salwador." Warsaw, Poznaj świat (12:7),
1965, pp. 37-38.
("San Salvador")

GUATEMALA

2176   Budrewicz, Olgierd. "Buenos Dias, Gwatemala! " Kracow,
Przekrój, Special Edition (1961), pp. 8-9.
("Buenos Dias, Guatemala")

2177   Budrewicz, Olgierd. "W Przeszłości Bez Wehikułu Czasu. "
Kracow, Przekrój (866), 1961, pp. 10-11.
("In the Past Without the Vehicle of
Time")

2178   Drohojowski, Jan. "Drwale na Rozdrożu. " Warsaw,
Prawo i życie (7: 4), 1962, p. 6.
("Wood-Cutters on a Crossroad")

2179   Giełżynski, Wojciech. "Rekin i Sardynki. Quetzal Ginie
w Niewoli. " Warsaw, Dookoła świata (8: 11), 1961, p. 6.
("A Shark and a Sardine: Quetzal
Perishes in Captivity")

2180   J. U. (pseud.) "Gwatemala." Warsaw, Trybuna ludu (16: 92),
        1963, p. 2.
                ("Guatemala")

2181   Krupińska, Aniela. "Ojczyzna Quetzala w Niewoli." Warsaw,
        Życie Warszawy (21: 41), 1964, p. 4.
                ("The Fatherland of Quetzal in Captivity")

2182   Ossowski, Ksawery. "Gwatemala." Warsaw, Poznaj świat (13: 1),
        1965, pp. 21-25, 48.
                ("Guatemala")

2183   Paszt, Adam. "Bananowa Republika." Warsaw, Polityka (5: 24),
        1961, p. 8.
                ("The Banana Republic")

GUYANA

2184   Budrewicz, Olgierd. "W Gujanie." Kracow, Przekrój (835),
        1961, pp. 6-7.
                ("In Guiana")

2185   Dembiński, Ludwik. "Gujana." Kracow, Tygodnik powszechny
        (20: 24), 1966, p. 2.
                ("Guiana")

2186   Dembiński, Ludwik. "Gujana Jeszcze Brytyjska." Kracow,
        Tygodnik powszechny (18: 24), 1964, p. 2.
                        ("Still British, Guiana")

2187   Fiedler, Arkady. "Na Początku Gujany Było Słowo." Warsaw,
        Kontynenty (5), 1965, pp. 12-13.
                        ("There Was a Word Before Guiana")

2188   Hajnicz, Artur. "Gujana Niepodległa." Warsaw, Życie Warszawy
        (23: 126), 1966, p. 2.
                        ("Independent Guiana")

2189   Małkin, Borys. "Wśród Indian w Gujanie." Warsaw, Poznaj
        świat (12: 6), 1964, pp. 24-29.
                        ("Among Indians in Guiana")

2190   Prószyński, Stanisław. "Gujany." Warsaw, Poznaj świat
        (8: 6), 1960, pp. 37-38.
                        ("Guianas")

2191   Urbaniak, Jan. "Dziel i Rządź." Warsaw, Trybuna ludu (16: 163),
        1963, pp. 2, 6.
                        ("Divide and Rule")

2192   Urbaniak, Jan. "Gujana Brytyjska Przed Wyborami." Warsaw,
        Trybuna ludu (17: 323), 1964, p. 8.
                        ("British Guiana Before Elections")

2193   Żaruk-Michalski, Aleksander. "Gujana na Drodze do Niepodległości."
        Warsaw, Sprawy międzynarodowe (16: 10), 1963, pp. 130-139.
                        ("Guiana on its Way to Independence")

2194   Zdanowski, Henryk. "Kuba Wielkiej Brytanii, Gujana
        Brytyjska." Warsaw, Polityka (8: 30), 1964, p. 8.
                        ("Cuba of Great Britain, British Guiana")

HAITI

2195   Babad, Beata. "Rozprawa Trwa." Warsaw, Polityka (7: 32),
        1963, p. 6.
                        ("Debate Continues")

2196   Budrewicz, Olgierd. "Biała Plama Czarnej Republiki."
        Warsaw, Trybuna ludu (14: 214), 1961, p. 8.
                        ("The White Spot of the Black Republic")

2197   Kubiatowicz, Lucjan. "Haiti." Warsaw, Poznaj świat (12: 8),
        1965, pp. 37-38.
                        ("Haiti")

2198   Piasecka, Anna. "Za Kulisami Konfliktu Dominikana - Haiti."
        Warsaw, Życie Warszawy (20: 109), 1963, p. 2.
                        ("Behind the Scenes of the Conflict Between
        the Dominican Republic and Haiti")

HONDURAS

2199   Drohojowski, Jan. "Drwale na Rozdrożu." Warsaw, <u>Prawo</u> <u>i życie</u> (7: 4), 1962, p. 6.
            ("Wood-Cutters on a Crossroad")

2200   Krupińska, Aniela. "'Gusanos' Czyli Robaki." Warsaw, <u>Życie Warszawy</u> (22: 33), 1965, p. 4.
            ("'Gusanos' or Worms")

JAMAICA

2201   Budrewicz, Olgierd. "Jamajka..." Kracow, <u>Przekrój</u> (585), 1961, pp. 9-11.
            ("Jamaica")

2202   E. K. (pseud.) "Wyspa Źródeł." Warsaw, <u>Poznaj świat</u> (8: 9), 1960, p. 29.
            ("An Island of Springs")

2203   Żaruk-Michalski, Aleksander. "Niepodległość Jamajki i Trynidadu." Warsaw, <u>Sprawy międzynarodowe</u> (15: 11), 1962, pp. 89-96.
            ("The Independence of Jamaica and Trinidad")

2204   Adamowich, Helena. "Karnawał w Sierra Nevada." Warsaw,
Poznaj świat (11: 4), 1963, pp. 23-25.
("A Carnival in the Sierra Nevada")

2205   Anusz, Jan. "Meksyk. Partnerzy Handlowi Polski." Warsaw,
Handel zagraniczny (9: 4), 1964, pp. 165-167.
("Mexico: Trade Partner of Poland")

2206   Babad, Beata. "Meksyk Prezydenta Mateosa." Warsaw,
Polityka (6: 13), 1963, 1963, pp. 1, 6.
("The Mexico of President Mateos")

2207   Babad, Beata. "Źródła i Tendencje Polityki Zagranicznej
Meksyku." Warsaw, Sprawy międzynarowe (16: 9), 1963,
pp. 37-61.
("The Origins and the Tendencies of the
International Politics of Mexico")

2208   Błaszczyk, Stanisław. "Wystawy Sztuki Starozytnego
Meksyku w Poznaniu." Wrocław, Etnografia polska
(10), 1966, pp. 487-490.
("An Exhibit of the Arts of Ancient
Mexico in Posen")

2209   Bonkowska, Alicja. "Wspaniali Meksykanie." Warsaw,
Ruch muzyczny (9: 23), 1965, pp. 10-11.
("The Magnificent Mexicans")

2210   Drohojowski, Jan. "Meksyk Bogów, Krzyża i Dolarów."
        Warsaw, Swiat (10: 38), 1960, pp. 8-9, 21.
                        ("Mexico of Gods, the Cross and Dollars")

2211   Drohojowski, Jan. "Nowy Okres w Życiu Partii." Warsaw,
        Problemy pokoju i socjalizmu (9), 1960, pp. 57-59.
                        ("New Period in the Life of the Communist
        Party")

2212   Drohojowski, Jan. "O Meksyku, Dyplomacji itp." Lublin,
        Kamena (30: 8), 1963, pp. 4, 9.
                        ("About Mexico: Diplomacy")

2213   Drohojowski, Jan. "Przyjaźń Bez Chmur." Warsaw, Prawo
        i życie (9: 7), 1964, pp. 6-7.
                        ("A Friendship without Clouds")

2214   Garztecka, Ewa. "Sztuka Wspołczesnego Meksyku." Warsaw,
        Trybuna ludu (14: 149), 1961, p. 8.
                        ("The Art of Modern Mexico")

2215   Goryński, Juliusz. "Muzea i Mieszkania. 10 Dni w Ciudad
        Mexico." Warsaw, Życie Warszawy (21: 271), 1964, p. 3.
                        ("Museums and Lodgings. 10 Days in
        Mexico City")

2216   Gostowski, Zygmunt. "Socjologia w Meksyku." Warsaw,
        Kultura i społeczeństwo (7: 4), 1963, pp. 251-255.
                        ("Sociology in Mexico")

2217   Grzelecki, Stanisław. "Film Meksykański Czeka na Hasło."
        Warsaw, Film (17: 7), 1962, pp. 12-13.
                        ("The Mexican Cinema is Waiting for
        a Sign")

2218   Guze, Joanna. "Zgilotynowana Cywilizacja." Warsaw,
        Świat (11: 24), 1961, pp. 12-15.
                    ("The Guillotined Civilization")

2219   Jeżewska, Maria. "21 Krżyzów w Indiańskiej Wiosce
        Romerillo w Środkowym Meksyku." Warsaw, Problemy
        (19: 1), 1963, pp. 21-29.
                    ("21 Crosses in an Indian Village: Romerillo
        in Central Mexico")

2220   Karwot, Edward. "Nad Jeziorem Patzcuaro." Warsaw,
        Poznaj świat (9: 11), 1961, pp. 22, 26, 68.
                    ("By Lake Pátzcuaro")

2221   Klimowicz, Jolanta. "Kariera Miasta Guanajuato." Warsaw,
        Życie Warszawy (22: 327), 1965, p. 2.
                    ("The Role of the City of Guanajuato")

2222   Klimowicz, Jolanta. "Meksykańska Nafta w Rękach Narodu."
        Warsaw, Życie Warszawy (23: 74), 1966, p. 4.
                    ("Mexican Petroleum in the Hands of
        the Nation")

2223   Klimowicz, Jolanta. "Meksyk Krytykuje Postawę U.S.A..."
        Warsaw, Życie Warszawy (22: 120), 1965, p. 4.
                    ("Mexico is Criticizing the Position of the
        U.S.A.")

2224   Kossakowski, Mirosław, & Jerzy Birkkolc. "Rozwój Dróg
        i Motoryzacji w Meksyku." Warsaw, Drogownictwo (20: 10),
        1965, pp. 248-250.
                    ("The Development
        of Roads and Motoring in Mexico")

2225   Kowalska, Bożena. " W Zwiazku z Meksykańską Grafiką. "
        Warsaw, Przegląd Artystyczny (4), 1961, pp. 28-35.
                            ("In Connection with Mexican Graphic
        Arts")

2226   Kruk, Maria. "Meksyk. Stara Kultura i Nowa Oświata. "
        Głos nauczycielski (13), 1963, p. 3.
                    ("Mexico: Old Culture and New Education")

2227   Krzywicka-Adamowicz, Helena. "Meksyk. " Warsaw,
        Argumenty (8: 1), 1964, pp. 6-7.
                                    ("Mexico")

2228   Kurta, H. "W Sercu Ameryku - Meksyk. " Warsaw, Widnokręgi
        (2), 1962, pp. 59-62.
                    ("In the Heart of America - Mexico")

2229   Logart, Witold. "Szkolnictwo Wyższe w Meksyku. " Warsaw,
        Życie szkoły wyższej (14: 7/80), 1966, pp. 205-208.
                    ("Higher Education in Mexico")

2230   Machowski, Jacek. "Taxco. " Warsaw, Poznaj świat (12: 10),
        1964, pp. 2-5.
                        ("Taxco")

2231   Manteuffel, Ryszard. "Rolnictwo Meksykańskie - Jego Poziom,
        Ustrój i Organizacja. " Warsaw, Postępy nauk rolniczych
        (9: 4), 1962, pp. 47-104.
                                ("Mexican Agriculture Its Level,
        Structure and Organization")

2232   Michałek, Bolesław. "Dramat Meksykański. " Warsaw,
        Nowa kultura (11: 7), 1960, pp. 8-9.
                            ("Mexican Drama")

NICARAGUA

2233   F. K. (pseud.) "Mleczarstwo w Nikaragua." Warsaw,
        Przegląd mleczarski (10: 3), 1962, pp. 27-28.
        ("Dairy Industry in Nicaragua")

PANAMA

2234   Bielecki, Stanisław. "Kanal, Który Dzieli." Warsaw,
        Polityka (8: 3), 1963, pp. 6-7.
        ("Canal Which Divides")

2235   Fijałkowski, Wiesław. "Panama." Warsaw, Mowią wieki
        (8: 6), 1965, pp. 18-21.
        (Panama")

2236   Kosidowski, Zenon. "Skarby Panamskie." Warsaw, Przegląd
        Kulturalny (12: 2), 1963, p. 10.
        ("Panama's Treasures")

2237   Kwiatek, Jerzy. "Klamra Oceanów." Warsaw, Poznaj świat,
        1964, pp. 22-26.
        ("In the Grip of the Oceans")

2238   Kwiatek, Jerzy. "Panama." Warsaw, Geografia w szkole
        (17: 2), 1964, pp. 84-85.
                ("Panama")

2239   Ludynia, Władysław. "Pół Wieku Kanału Panamskiego."
        Wrocław, Czasopismo geografia (37: 1), 1966, pp. 62-65.
                ("Half a Century of Panama Canal")

2240   Senkowski, Henryk. "Stosunki Gospodarcze w Republice
        Panamskiej." Warsaw, Geografia w szkole (12: 6), 1959,
        pp. 330-331.
                        ("Economic Relations of the Republic
        of Panama")

PARAGUAY

2241   Bosanowicz, Andrzej. "Paragwaj." Warsaw, Poznaj świat
        (8: 5), 1960, pp. 37-38.
                ("Paraguay")

2242   Budrewicz, Olgierd. "Z Paragwaju." Kracow, Przekrój
        (1062), 1965, pp. 5-7.
                ("From Paraguay")

2243   Pasierbiński, Tadeusz. "Rewolta w Paragwaju." Warsaw,
        Polityka (4: 2), 1960, p. 10.
                ("A Revolt in Paraguay")

PERU

2244   Banatt, Stanisław. "Peru - Nowe Mocarstwo w Rybołówstwie
Morskim. " Gdynia, Tygodnik morski (7: 19), 1964, p. 4.
("Peru: New Power in Ocean Fishing")

2245   Budrewicz, Olgierd. "Machu Picchu - Umarłe Miasto
Inków. " Kracow, Przekrój (1115), 1966, pp. 1-11.
("Machu Picchu: Dead City of the
Incas")

2246   Budrewicz, Olgierd. "W Kraju Inków. " Kracow, Przekrój
(1113), 1966, pp. 4-7.
("In the Land of Incas")

2247   Bukowski, Zbigniew. "Miasta Inków w Andach Peruwiańskich. "
Warsaw, Acta archaeologica carpathica (2: 1/2), 1960, pp.
215-218.
("The Cities of the Incas in the Peruvian
Andes")

2248   Kowalska-Lewicka, Anna. "Peruwiańskie Zbiory Archeologiczne
z Kolekcji Władysława Klugera. " Wroclaw, Sprawozdania z
prac naukowych wydziału nauk społecznych PAN (8: 3), 1965,
pp. 51-54.
("Archeological Collections from
Peru, from the Collection of Władysław Kluger")

2249   Krupińska, Aniela. "Represje w Peru za Wspołpracę z
Partyzantami. " Warsaw, Życie Warszawy (22: 257), 1965,
p. 4.
("Repressions in Peru for Cooperation with
the Partisans")

2250   Kwiatek, Jerzy. "Rewolucja w Peruwiańskim Rybołowstwie
Morskim. " Warsaw, Geografia w szkole (18: 5), 1965,
pp. 236-237.
("Revolution in Peruvian Ocean Fishing")

2251   Urbaniak, Jan. "Peruwiański Dramat. " Warsaw, Trybuna
ludu (20: 311), 1963, p. 2.
("Peruvian Drama")

2252   Ziemilski, Andrzej. "Lima. " Warsaw, Życie Warszawy (21: 131),
1964, p. 4.
("Lima")

PUERTO RICO

2253   Budrewicz, Olgierd. "Operacja 'Ucho od Buta'. " Warsaw,
Trybuna ludu (14: 228), 1961, p. 8.
("Operation 'Ear from a Boot'")

TRINIDAD AND TOBAGO

2254 Budrewicz, Olgierd. "Trinidad, Calypso, Karnawał."
    Kracow, <u>Przekrój</u> (841), 1961, pp. 15-17.
        ("Trinidad, Calypso, Carnival")

2255 Zaruk-Michalski, Aleksander. "Niepodłegłość Jamajki i Trynidadu."
    Warsaw, <u>Sprawy międzynarodowe</u> (15: 11), 1962, pp. 89-96.
        ("The Independence of Jamaica and Trinidad")

URUGUAY

2256 Azembski, Mirosław. "Klopoty Zamorskiej Szwajcarii."
    Warsaw, <u>Kamena</u> (9: 23/24), 1965, pp. 8, 13.
        ("Problems of the Overseas
  Switzerland")

2257 Gołebiewski, Włodzimierz. "Urugway." Warsaw, <u>Trybuna</u>
    <u>ludu</u> (19: 170), 1966, p. 6.
        ("Uruguay")

2258 Krupińska, Aniela. "W 'Amerykańskiej Szwajcarii'. Wrzenie
    w Urugwaju." Warsaw, <u>Życie Warszawy</u> (22: 304), 1964,
    p. 2.
        ("In the 'American Switzerland': Ferment
  in Uruguay")

2259   Marzec, Zdzisław. "Cowboye z 'Ziemi Malowanych Ptaków'. "
        Warsaw, Światowid (22), 1961, pp. 16-17.
                        ("Cowboys from the 'Land of Painted
        Birds'")

2260   Stec, Tadeusz. "Kraj Osobliwości. " Warsaw, Argumenty
        (7: 20), 1963, p. 2.
                        ("The Land of Peculiarities")

2261   Urbaniak, Jan. "Tysiąclecie w Urugwaju. " Warsaw, Trybuna
        ludu (17: 111), 1964, pp. 4, 8.
                        ("Millenium in Uruguay")

                        VENEZUELA

2262   Andrzejewski, Wiesław. "La Guaira. " Gdynia, Tygodnik
        morski (6: 23), 1963, p. 6.
                        ("La Guaira")

2263   Budrewicz, Olgierd. "Hałasy na Placu Ciszy. " Warsaw,
        Dookoła świata (8: 40), 1961, pp. 3-5.
                        ("Noises in the Plaza of Silence")

2264   Czajka, W. "Wysokościowce w Caracas. " Warsaw, Miasto
        (11: 4), 1960, p. 4.
                        ("Skyscrapers in Caracas")

                            535

2265   Kostecki, Wieslaw. "Wenezuela - Rynek Przyszłości dla
        Polskiego Eksportu. " Warsaw, Handel zagraniczny (5: 2),
        1960, pp. 63-65.
                            ("Venezuela: Future Market for
        Polish Exports")

2266   Kowalewski, Zbigniew. "Ludzie Zielonej Oliwki. " Łodź,
        Odgłosy (7: 14), 1964, p. 4.
                            ("People of the Green Olive")

2267   Krupińska, Aniela. "Walka Trwa w Wenezueli. " Warsaw,
        Życie Warszawy (21: 262), 1964, p. 2.
                            ("Struggle Continues in Venezuela")

2268   Osmańczyk, Edmund. "Naród i Nafta Małej Wenezueli. "
        Warsaw, Przegląd kulturalny (12: 12), 1963, p. 2.
                            ("The Nation and the Petroleum of
        Small Venezuela")

2269   Paszt, Adam. "Zygzaki Betancourta. " Warsaw, Polityka
        (5: 2), 1961, p. 10.
                            ("Zigzags of Betancourt")

2270   Urbaniak, Jan. "Krytyka Polityki Zagranicznej Wenezueli. "
        Warsaw, Trybuna ludu (17: 14), 1964, p. 2.
                            ("A Criticism of the Foreign Policy of
        Venezuela")

WEST INDIES AND THE CARIBBEAN

2271   Dembiński, Ludwik. "Nowe Państwa Karaibskie." Kracow,
Tygodnik powszechny (16: 32), 1962, p. 2.
("New Caribbean Countries")

2272   Pasierbiński, Tadeusz M. "Ostatnie 'Confetti'. " Warsaw,
Polityka (6: 24), 1962, p. 10.
("The Last 'Confetti'")

2273   Ruth, K. A. "Wyspa Bezprawia. " Warsaw, Widnokręgi (4),
1963, pp. 27-29.
("An Island of Injustice")

2274   Zaruk-Michalski, Aleksander. "Sytuacja w Posiadłościach
Kolonialnych w Krajach Karaibskich. " Warsaw, Sprawy
międzynarodowe (15: 3), 1962, pp. 73-83.
("The Situation in the Colonial
Territories of the Caribbean Countries")

RUMANIA

Although Latin American Studies as such are not offered as a formalized unit in the universities of Rumania, Latin America is treated as world region in courses such as Comparative World Literature, and Contemporary World History, at Babes-Bolyai University in Cluj, and in the course in World History offered at the University of Bucharest, where Spanish is also taught. A course in World Literature is also offered at the Cuza University in Iasi. An Institute of Geography is maintained at the University of Cluj.

Cultural contacts with Latin America are handled by the Rumanian Institute for Cultural Relations with Foreign Nations, located in Bucharest.

In this section the English translation of the title of each bibliographic item is to be found directly under the title in the original language, and immediately following the entire bibliographic description.

Aunque no se enseñan per se asignaturas en Asuntos Latinoamericanos en las universidades rumanas, se estudia Latinoamérica como región mundial en los cursos de Literatura Comparativa Mundial e Historia Mundial Contemporánea, en la Universidad Babes-Bolyai, situada en la ciudad de Cluj, y en el curso de Historia Mundial ofrecido en la Universidad de Bucharest (donde también se enseña español). La Universidad Cuza en la ciudad de Iasi ofrece curso en Literatura Mundial, y la Universidad de Cluj mantiene un Instituto de Geografía.

Contactos culturales con Latinoamérica se arreglan por
el Instituto Rumano para Relaciones Culturales con Países
Extranjeros, con sede en Bucharest.

En esta sección la traducción inglesa del título de cada
asiento se encuentra directamente bajo el título de la lengua
original, seguida de la ficha entera.

I. Books

LATIN AMERICA

2275   America Latina; Îndreptar Politic-Economic. Bucharest, Ed.
Politicǎ, 1965, 280p.
(Latin America, Political and Economic Rectifier)

2276   Etnografia Continentelor; Studii de Etnografie Generalǎ. Date
Generale: Australia, şi Oceania, America, Africa. Ed. by
S. P. Tolstov. v. 1. Bucharest, Ed. Ştiinţificǎ, 1959, 452p.
(The Ethnography of the Continents: Studies of General Ethnography.
General Facts: Australia and Oceania, America, Africa)

2277   Nitescu, Lionel. La Sud de Rio Grande. Bucharest, Politischer
Verlag, 1964, 140p.
                (South of the Rio Grande)

2278   Pacurariu, Francisc. Schite Pentru un Portret al Americii
Latine. Bucharest, Editura Tineretului, 1966, 207p.
                 (Sketches for a Portrait of Latin
America)

2279   Racovita, Emil. Spre Sud; Prin Patagonia şi Spre Polul Sud.
Ed. by Dan Coman. 2d ed. Bucharest, Ed. Tineretului, 1959,
104p.
             (Southward, Through Patagonia, and Toward
the South Pole)

2280   Radulescu, Ion. Curs de Geografia Fizicǎ a Continentelor.
America de Nord, America Centralǎ. Bucharest, Ed.
Didacticǎ şi Pedagogicǎ, 1963, 148p.
(A Course in the Physical Geography of the Continents of
North and Central America)

2281   Roşca, Ion, & Simion Lugojan. La Orizont, Pǎmînt. Bucharest,
Ed. Ştiinţifica, 1963, 80p.
               (Land at the Horizon)

2282   Rosu, Alexandru, & Octavia Seitan. Prima Călătorie în Jurul
        Lumii. Bucharest, Ed. Stiintifică, 1964, 72p.
                                    (The First Journey Around
        the World)

BRAZIL

2283   Moraru, Nicolae. In Lumea Contrastelor, Brazilia. Bucharest,
        Editura Tineretului, 1958, 192p.
                            (In the World of Contrasts [Brazil])

CHILE

2284   Cricoveanu, Constantin. Chile. Bucharest, Editura
        Stiințifică, 1966, 19lp.
                            (Chile)

2285   Crisan, Romulus. Intre Anzi si Pacific Chile. Bucharest,
        Editura Politică, 1965, 144p.
                            (Between the Andes and the Pacific [Chile])

2286   Gavrilă, G. Chile. Bucharest, Editura Stiințifică, 1956, 95p.
                            (Chile)

CUBA

2287   Ghilia, Alecu I. Insula Sperantei. Bucharest, Ed. Pentru
        Literatură, 1963, 274p.
                    (The Island of Separation)

2288   Lascu, Petre. Cuba. Bucharest, Ed. Stiintifica, 1962, 240p.
                    (Cuba)

2289   Obîden, K. M. Cuba in Luptă Pentru Libertate şi Independenţsa.
        Bucharest, Ed. Politică, 1960, 112p.
                    (Cuba in the Fight for Liberty and Independence)

2290   Pop, Valeriu. La Sud de Tropicul Racului. Documentar Cuban.
        Bucharest, Editura Politica, 1964, 66p.
                        (To the South of the Tropic of Cancer: Cuban
        Documentary)

2291   Popovici, Titus. Cuba, Teritoriu Liber al Americii. Bucharest,
        Ed. Tineretului, 1962, 333p.
                        (Cuba, the Free Territory of America)

2292   Zentova, A. I. Cuba. Bucharest, Ed. de Stat Pentru Literatură
        Stiintifică, 1953, 47p.
                    (Cuba)

DOMINICAN REPUBLIC

2293   Evenimentele din Republica Dominicană. Bucharest, Comitetul
        de Stat Pentru Cultură şi Artă, Consiliul Pentru Răspîndirea
        Cunoştintelor Cultural-Stiintifice, 1965, 19p.
        (Events in the Dominican Republic)

ECUADOR

2294   Marek, Jiri. Tara de Sub Ecuator. Bucharest, E.S.P.L.A.,
        1960, 176p.
                (The Country South of the Equator)

GUATEMALA

2295   Badescu, S. Guatemala. Bucharest, Editura Stiintifică, 1957,
        119p.
                (Guatemala)

MEXICO

2296   Andries, Mihai G. <u>Mexic</u>. Bucharest, Ed. Ştiinţifică, 1958, 231p.

                    (Mexico)

2297   Şiperco, Al. <u>Note de Drum Din Suedia, Franţa, Italia şi Mexic.</u> Bucharest, Ed. Tineretului, 1959, 328p.

                  (Travel Diary from Sweden, France, Italy and Mexico)

URUGUAY

2298   Bucur, I. N. <u>Uruguay.</u> Bucharest, Ed. Ştiinţifică, 1967,
        175p.
                (Uruguay)

VENEZUELA

2299   Alexandru, D. <u>Venezuela.</u> Bucharest, Editura Ştiinţifică,
        1957, 98p.
                (Venezuela)

II. Periodical Articles

LATIN AMERICA

2300   Adrian, L. "Alianţa Împotriva Progresului. Politica Statelor
Unite Faţă de Ţările Americii Latine." Bucharest, Probleme
internaţionale April 3, 1962, pp. 35-44.
("The Alliance Against Progress: United States
Policy Towards the Latin American Countries")

2301   "America Latină. "Ce au Arătat Ultimele Alegeri?" Bucharest,
Probleme ale păcii şi socialismului (8: 5), May 1965, pp. 52-55.
("Latin America: What Did the Last Elections Show?")

2302   "America Latină Ieri şi Azi. Cronica Luptelor Politice." Bucharest,
Supplement to: Probleme ale păcii şi socialismului (8: 8),
August 1965, p. 16.
("Latin America, Yesterday and Today: Account of the Political
Fights")

2303   "America Latină, un Continent de 180 Milioane de Locuitori
se Ridică la Luptă." Bucharest, Mişcarea sindicală mondială
(8: 9), August-September 1960, pp. 4-13.
("Latin America a Continent of 180 Million Inhabitants Rises to
Fight")

2304   Antohi, Iosif, & Vintilă Panduru. "Unele Probleme Actuale
ale Învăţămîntului din America Latină." Bucharest, Revista
de pedagogie (13: 2), February 1964, pp. 100-112.
("Some Present Problems
of Education in Latin America")

2305   Bogdan, A. R. "America Latină pe Calea Denuclearizării."
        Bucharest, Pentru apărarea păcii (4), April 1967, pp. 12-13.
                ("Latin America on the Way to Denuclearization")

2306   Căliman, G. "America Latină: Zonele Denuclearizate."
        Bucharest, Pentru apărarea păcii (3), March 1964, pp. 18-19.
                ("Latin America: Denuclearized Zones")

2307   Călinescu, George. "Peru, Nicaragua, Cuba. Difuziunea Literaturii
        Spaniole în Aceste Țări. Cronica Optimistului." Bucharest,
        Contemporanul (30), July 24, 1964, pp. 1-2.
                        ("Peru, Nicaragua, Cuba: The Spreading
        of Spanish Literature in those Countries; the Optimists' Chronicle")

2308   Cioară, I. "Cronică Latino-Americană. Mişcarea de Eliberare
        din Țările Americii Latine." Bucharest, Probleme internaționale
        (11), 1959, pp. 64-72.
                        ("Latin American Commentary: Liberation
        Movement in Latin American Countries")

2309   Comorovski, Constantin. "Momente ale Afirmării Naționale
        în America Latină." Bucharest, Lumea (5: 31), July 27,
        1967, pp. 28-29.
                        ("Moments of National Affirmation
        in Latin America")

2310   Danielevici, M. "Forțele Motrice ale Luptei de Eliberare în
        America Latină." Bucharest, Lupta de clasă (15: 10),
        October 1960, pp. 93-104.
                        ("Motive Powers in the Fight for Liberation
        in Latin America")

2311   Desmireanu, Maria. "Formarea, Repartiția şi Folosirea
        Venitului National în Țările Americii Latine." Bucharest,
        Probleme economice (18: 1), January 1965, pp. 86-99.
                        ("Formation, Distribution and Utilization
        of the National Income in Latin American Countries")

2312   Dolgu, Gabriela. "Climatul Sud-american. Carnet Econo-
         mic." Bucharest, Contemporanul (24), June 20, 1958, p. 7.
                          ("South American Climate: Economic
         Note-Book ")

2313   Dragomirescu, S. "Conferința Regională Latino-Americană a
         Uniunii Internaționale de Geografie, Ciudad de Mexico, 3-8
         August 1966." Bucharest, Studii și cercetări de geologie, geo-
         fizică, geografie. Seria geografie (13:1), January-June 1966,
         p. 116.
                          ("South American Regional Conference of the
         International Union of Geography, Mexico City, August
         3-8, 1966 ")

2314   Firănescu, C. "Popoarele Americii Latine Luptă Împotriva
         Dictatului Monopolurilor din S. U. A. " Bucharest, Apăra-
         rea Patriei, (15:97), April 25, 1959, p. 3.
                          ("Latin American Peoples' Fight Against the Dictates of
         U.S. Monopolies")

2315   Georgescu, Paul A. "Privire Asupra Poeziei Hispano-Ame-
         americane. " Bucharest, Revista de filologie romanică și
         germanică (3:1-2), 1959, pp. 215-223.
                          ("Consideration of Latin American Poetry")

2316   "O Întamplare în Câmpie a Americii. Nuvelă. " Iași,
         Albina Românească, XII, 1841, pp. 67-68, 70-72, 74-76.
         ("Happening on the American Plain: A Short Story ")

2317   Ionescu, Andrei. "Cuadernos Americanos. Caiete Ameri-
         cane, Publicație din America Latină. " Bucharest, Seco-
         lul 20 (5), May 1965, pp. 183-185.
                          ("Cuadernos Americanos, a Latin American
         Publication ")

2318   Lazăr, S. "America Latină- Continent al Contrastelor Sociale. " Bucharest, Albina (64:750), May 9, 1962, p. 7.
            ("Latin America- a Continent of Social Contrasts ")

2319   " Luptele Muncitorești se Dezvoltă în Țările Americii Latine. "
Bucharest, Mișcarea sindicală mondială, January, 1962,
pp. 24-29.
        ("Labor Struggles Develop in Latin American Countries ")

2320   Matei, Mihai. "În America Latină : Generalii Contra Preșe-
dinților. " Bucharest, Lumea (4:32) , August 4, 1966,
pp. 12-13.
            ("In Latin America : Generals Against Presidents ")

2321   Mecu, C. "Economia Țărilor Americii Latine și 'Alianța
Pentru Progres'. " Bucharest, Probleme economice (19:2)
February 1966, pp. 107-120.
            ("Economy of Latin American Countries and the
'Alliance for Progress' ")

2322   Mieraș, F. & C. Medina. "Criza Structurilor și Căile de Ie-
șire din ea. Criza Sistemului Social-economic al Americii
Latine. " Bucharest, Probleme ale păcii și socialismului
(10:5-6), May-June 1967, pp. 99-100.
                            ("The Crisis of Structures and the
Ways to Avoid It. The Crisis of the Social-Economic System of
Latin America ")

2323   Murgescu, Costin. "Latifundii și Minifundii in America
Latină. " Bucharest, Orizonturi (11:131), April 1962, pp. 15-21.
                    ("Large Rural Estates and Very Small Land
Holdings in Latin America ")

2324   Nováceanu, Darie. "Ziua Indienilor din America Latină.
        Aspecte din Istoria și Viața Indiienilor." Bucharest,
        Lumea (2:16), April 16, 1964, pp. 18-20.
                        ("The Indians' Day in Latin America.
        Aspects of the History and Life of Indians")

2325   Onică, Petre, & Steliana Beciu. "Aspecte ale Agriculturii
        din America Latină." Bucharest, Revista de statistică (2:16),
        November 1964, pp. 60-68.
                        ("Aspects of Latin American
        Agriculture ")

2326   Oros, V. "Pe Meleagurile Americii Latine. Documentar."
        Bucharest, Pentru apărarea păcii, (7), July 1964, pp. 24-26.
                ("Rambling about Latin America: Documentary ")

2327   Oros, V. "Cuba și Fenomenele noi în America Latină."
        Bucharest, Probleme internaționale , (2), May 1963, pp. 93-98.
                ("Cuba and the New Phenomena in Latin America ")

2328   Păcurariu, Francisc. "Aspecte și Tendințe Actuale ale Poe-
        ziei Latino-americane." Bucharest, Gazeta literară, (10:25)
        June 20, 1963, p. 8.
                        ("Present-Day Aspects and Tendencies
        of Latin American Poetry ")

2329   Păcurariu, Francisc. "Carnaval, Uluitoare Răbufnire a Setei
        de Bucurie. Zile de Carnaval în America Latină." Bucharest,
        Flacăra (14:48), November 27, 1965, pp. 12-15.
                        ("Carnival, Astounding Outbreak of
        Craving for Joy: Carnival Days in Latin America ")

2330   Păcurariu, Doina. "Rubén Darío și America Latină."
        Bucharest, Secolul 20 (3), 1966, pp. 161-165.
                        ("Rubén Darío and Latin America ")

2331   Pinczés, Iuliu. "In Fața Unei Crize...Ascuțirea Contradicții ·
        lor Dintre Monopolurile Nord-Americane și Popoarele Țărilor
        Americii Latine." Cluj, Tribuna (7:31), August 1, 1963, p. 12.
                    ("Facing a Crisis...Intensification of the Contra-
        dictions Between the North American Monopolies and the Peoples
        of the Latin American Countries ")

2332   Porumbacu, Veronica. "Latin America Seen by Rumanian
        Writers." Bucharest, Rumania Today (6), June 1967, p. 36.

2333   "Probleme ale Creării Frontului Unic Antiimperialist. În
        Jurul Mesei Rotunde a Redacției 'Probleme ale Păcii și
        Socialismului'. Schimb de Păreri Organizat în Vara Anului 1962
        cu Marxiștii Dintr-o Serie de Țări din America Latină."
        Bucharest, Probleme ale păcii și socialismului (6:11), January
        1963, pp. 72-84.
        ("Problems of the Creation of a Single Anti-Imperialist Front.
        Around the Round Table of the Editorial Staff of the 'Probleme
        ale Păcii și Socialismului'. Exchange of Views, Organized
        in the Summer of 1962, with Marxists From Latin American
        Countries ")

2334   "Programul de Luptă Adoptat de Congresul Permanent de
        Unitate Sindicală Pentru Acțiunea Comună Oamenilor Muncii
        din America Latină." Bucharest, Mișcarea sindicală mondială
        (4), April 1964, pp. 4-5.
        ("Fighting Program Adopted by the Permanent Congress of
        Trade Union Unity for the Common Action of Laborers of
        Latin America ")

2335   Retegan, G. "Cercetarea Comparativă a Fertilității Popu-
        lației în 7 Țări ale Americii Latine." Bucharest, Revista
        de statistică (13:8), August 1964, pp. 85-86.
                    ("Comparative Investigation of Population Ferti-
        lity in 7 Latin American Countries ")

2336   Sreja, S.   "Mijloace de Informație în America Latină. "
        Bucharest, Presa noastră (11:9), September 1966, p. 45.
        ("Means of Information in Latin America ")

2337   Stănescu, N. S.   "America Latină în Căutarea Unei Politici
        de Dezvoltare. " Bucharest, Viața economică, (5:7),
        February 17, 1967, pp. 22-23.
                    ("Latin America In Search of a Development
        Policy. ")

2338   Stanciu, A.   "America Latină se Opune Imperialismului Yankeu. "
        Bucharest, Probleme Internaționale (9), 1958, pp. 47-54.
        ("Latin America Opposes Yankee Imperialism ")

2339   Vulpescu Romulus.   "Poezia Latino-americană. " Cluj,
        Steaua (12:1), January 1961, pp. 102-111.
                    ("Latin American Poetry ")

                            ARGENTINA

2340   Antip, Felicia.   "Criza din Argentina: de ce și Încotro? "
        Bucharest, Contemporanul (18), May 4, 1962, p. 8.
                    ("Crisis in the Argentine : Why and Whereto? ")

2341   Brand, Sergiu. "Doctrina 'Bleu'. Dreptul Armatei Argenti-
        niene de a Interveni cu Forţa în Treburile Statului. "
        Bucharest, Cronica (1:25), July 30, 1966, p. 12.
                    ("The 'Bleu' Doctrine. The Right of the Argen-
        tine Army to Intervene by Force Into State Business ")

2342   Cornu, Ştefan. "Buenos Aires: Mutări Noi pe Eşichierul
        Politic. " Bucharest, Lumea (3: 3), January 14, 1965, p. 10.
                    ("Buenos Aires: New Moves on the Political
        Chessboard ")

2343   Georgescu, Rodica. "Buenos Aires: Semnificaţia Grevei
        Generale." Bucharest, Lumea (2:52), December 24, 1964, p. 12.
                    ("Buenos Aires: Significance of the Ge-
        ral Strike ")

2344   Georgescu, Rodica. "Buenos Aires: Implicaţiile Acţiunilor
        Peroniste. " Bucharest, Lumea (3:44), October 28, 1965,
        pp. 8-9.
                    ("Buenos Aires: Implications of Peronist
        Actions")

2345   Ivănescu, Mircea. "Buenos Aires: Rezultate şi Tendinţe în
        Alegerile Parţiale Pentru Reînoirea Mandatelor din Camera
        Inferioară şi Alegerea Consiliilor Municipale din Provincie. "
        Bucharest, Lumea (3:12), March 18, 1965, p. 8.
                    ("Buenos Aires: Results and Tendencies in the Partial
        Elections for the Renewal of Mandates in the Lower House, and
        the Election of Provincial Municipal Councils ")

2346   Moraru, N. "Aspecte ale Artei Plastice Argentiniene (Fragment
        Dintr-un Volum în Curs de Apariţie.)" Bucharest, Arta Plastică
        (5), May 5, 1958, pp. 19-24.
                    ("Aspects of Argentine Plastic Art: A Fragment
        From a Volume in Press ")

2347   Moraru, N. "Drumul Complex al Unei Literaturi. Literatura
        Argentiniană. " Bucharest, Gazeta Literară (5:28), July 10, 1958,
        p. 2.
                    ("The Complex Course of a Literature: Argentine
        Literature")

2348   Moraru, N. "Drumul Teatrului Argentinian." Bucharest,
        Contemporanul (16), April 25, 1958, p. 8.
                    ("The Progress of the Argentine Theatre")

2349   Nicolăescu, V. "Interludiu Argentinian. " Bucharest, Flacăra
        (14: 15), April, 10, 1965, pp. 14-15.
                    ("Argentine Interlude")

2350   Pop, Eugen. "Buenos Aires: Cauzele Conflictelor Sociale. "
        Bucharest, Lumea (4: 51), December 15, 1966, pp. 10-11.
                    ("Buenos Aires: The Causes of Social Conflicts")

2351   Pop, Eugen. "Buenos Aires: Încordare Socială. Acţiuni
        Greviste în Argentina. " Bucharest, Lumea (2: 27), 1967,
        pp. 9-10.
                    ("Buenos Aires: Social Tension. Strikes in the
        Argentine ")

2352   Pop, Eugen. "Buenos Aires: Preţul 'Colaborării', Dintre
        Noul Regim Argentinean şi Conducători Sindicali Peronişti. "
        Bucharest, Lumea (4: 28), July 7, 1966, pp. 12-13.
                    ("Buenos Aires: The Price of 'Collaboration'
        Between the New Argentine Regime and the Peronist Syndicalist
        Leaders")

2353   Pop, Eugen. "Buenos Aires: Problema nr. 1 Situaţia Economică a
        Argentinei. " Bucharest, Lumea (3: 7), February 11, 1965,
        pp. 8-9.
                    ("Buenos Aires: Problem no. 1: Argentina's
        Economic Situation")

2354   Pop, Eugen. "Buenos Aires: 'Sincronizarea'." Bucharest,
        <u>Lumea</u> (5:2), January 5, 1967, pp. 6-7.
                ("Buenos Aires: 'Synchronization' ")

2355   Pop, Eugen. "Prolog Prelungit. Proiectul Forțelor Militare
        Interamericane Dezbătut la Conferința Militară Panamericană
        de la Buenos Aires." Bucharest, <u>Lumea</u> (4: 46), November 10,
        1966, pp. 11-12.
                ("The Project of the Inter-American Military Force
        Debated at the Buenos Aires Pan American Military Conference")

2356   Pop, Eugen. "Substratul Loviturii Militare?" Bucharest,
        <u>Lumea</u> (4:27), January 30, 1966, pp. 14-15.
                ("What Lies Behind the Military Coup d'Etat?")

2357   Stănoiu, Valeriu. " 150 de ani de la Nașterea Scriitorului Ar-
        gentinian Domingo Faustino Sarmiento (15 Februarie 1811-
        11 Septembrie 1888). Marile Manifestări Culturale ale Anului
        1961." Bucharest, <u>Călăuza Bibliotecarului</u> (4: 2), February 1961,
        pp. 37- 38.
                ("150 Years After the Birth of the Argentine Writer,
        Domingo Faustino Sarmiento (February 15, 1811- September 11,
        1888): Great Cultural Manifestations of 1961")

2358   Udriște, Ion. "Țara de Foc. Reportaj pe Glob." Bucharest,
        <u>Lumea</u> (2: 25), June 18, 1964, pp. 20-24.
                ("Terra del Fuego: World Feature Report")

BOLIVIA

2359 Crǎciun, Ion. "Bolivia: Cositor, Vulcani şi Dinamitǎ."
Bucharest, Magazin (9: 399), May 29, 1965, p. 3.
("Bolivia: Tin, Volcanoes and Dynamite")

2360 Dobran, Victor. "Sectorul Minier în Centrul Frǎmîntǎrilor."
Bucharest, Viaţa economicǎ (5: 30), July 28, 1967, p. 15.
("The Mining Sector in the Center of Unrest")

2361 Matei, Mihai. "La Paz: Generalul şi Minierii. Conflictul
Între Sindicatele Minerilor şi Generalul Barrientos."
Bucharest, Lumea (3: 22), May 27, 1965, pp. 8-9.
("La Paz: The General and the Miners. The
Conflict Between the Miners' Syndicates and General Barrientos.")

2362 Morǎceanu, Darie. "Bolivia în Preajma Alegerilor. Documentar."
Bucharest, Lumea (2: 22), May 28, 1964, pp. 21-22.
("Bolivia on the Eve of Elections : Documentary")

2363 Pop, Eugen. "La Paz: Jocul de-a Puterea." Bucharest, Lumea
(3: 2), January 7, 1965, p. 11.
("La Paz: The Power Game")

2364 Vǎlureanu, U. "Soarta Cositorului în Bolivia. Controversa
Politicǎ în Legǎturǎ cu Extracţia de Cositor." Bucharest,
Viaţa economicǎ (2: 23), June 5, 1964, p. 15.
("The Destiny of Tin: The Political Controversy
in Bolivia in Connection with the Extraction of Tin")

BRAZIL

2365   Adler, L. "Oscar Niemeyer şi Oraşul Brazilia." Bucharest,
Arhitectura RPR (11: 5), 1963, pp. 52-57.
("Oscar Niemeyer and Brasilia")

2366   Alexe, Anton. "Cumplita Exploatare a Ţărănimii Braziliene."
Bucharest, Agricultura Nouă (6: 561), September 11, 1959, p. 4.
("The Ferocious Explotation of Brazilian Peasantry ")

2367   Antip, Felicia, & Sergiu Brand. "Cine a Învins in Brazilia?
Semnificaţia Rezultatelor Referendumului din Ianuarie 1963 cu
Privire la Forma de Guvernămînt." Bucharest, Probleme
Internaţionale (1), February, 1963, pp. 67-70.
("Who Carried the Day in Brazil?
Significance of the Referendum Results of January 1963, with
Regard to the Form of Government ")

2368   "Brazilia: Datorii Pînă în Anul 2003..." Bucharest, Viaţa
economică (2: 25), June 19, 1964, p. 15.
("Brazil: Debts Until Year 2003...")

2369   Buzoianu, Anton. "Poligonul Secetei: Nord -estul Brazilian."
Bucharest, Lumea (5: 9), February 23, 1967, pp. 14-15.
("The Drought Polygon: The Brazilian
North-East ")

2370   "Cascada Diavolului. Producţie Braziliană." Bucharest,
Contemporanul (1: 8), February 2, 1964, p. 5.
("Devil's Waterfall, a Brazilian Production")

2371   Cornu, Ştefan. "Rio de Janeiro: Situaţie Complexă. Frămîntările
        Perioadei Preelectorale în Brazilia." Bucharest, <u>Lumea</u>
        (3: 32), August 5, 1965, pp. 9-10.
                    ("Rio de Janeiro: A Complex Situation. Stirrings
        During the Pre-Electoral Period in Brazil ")

2372   Diplan, Rodica. "Manu Militari. Conflictul Dintre Cele Două
        Puteri (Executivă şi Legislativă) din Parlamentul Brazilian."
        Bucharest, <u>Lumea</u> (4: 44), October 27, 1966, p. 11.
                    ("Manu Militari: The Conflict Between the
        Two Powers, Executive and Legislative, in the Brazilian Parliament'

2373   Dragotă, Ion. "Brazilia: Problema Agrară la Ordinea Zilei."
        Bucharest, <u>Lumea</u> (2: 12), March 19, 1964, pp. 10-11.
                    ("Brazil: Agrarian Problem is the Order of the Day")

2374   Georgescu, Rodica. "Brazilia: Măsuri Excepţionale." Bucharest,
        <u>Lumea</u> (3: 45), November 4, 1965, pp. 4-5.
                    ("Brazil: Exceptional Measures")

2375   "Împăratul DomPedro." Iasi, <u>Albina Românească</u> II, 1830, pp. 81-82.
        ("Emperor DomPedro")

2376   "Jungla Tragică. Producţie Cinematografică Braziliană."
        Bucharest, <u>Albina</u> (67: 925), September 16, 1965, p. 5.
        ("The Tragic Jungle, Brazilian Film Production ")

2377   Maiorescu, Toma G. "Febre pe Tropice. Santos - São Paulo.
        Note de Drum." Bucharest, <u>Flacăra</u> (14:28), July 10, 1965,
        pp. 15-17.
                    ("Fevers on the Tropics, Santos-
        São Paulo: Travel Notes ")

2378   Marian, Eugen B. "Rio Amazonas - Marea Dulce. Marile
        Fluvii ale Lumii." Bucharest, Flacăra (12: 16), April 20, 1963,
        p. 13.
                        ("Rio Amazonas - the Sweet-Water Sea: The
        Great Rivers of the World ")

2379   Mihăileanu, I. "Situaţia Agriculturii Braziliene." Bucharest,
        Albina (66: 859), June 11, 1964, p. 7.
                        ("State of Brazilian Agriculture")

2380   Mirică, Tudor. "Oraşul Brazilia." Bucharest, Amfiteatru
        (1: 11), November 11, 1966, p. 172.
                        ("The City of Brasilia")

2381   "Necrolog a lui Dom-Pedro." Iasi, Albina Românească V-VI,
        Supplement to no. 88, 1833-1834, pp. 1-2.
        ("Necrology of Dom-Pedro. ")

2382   Nedelcu, C. "Brazilia - Ţara Contrastelor." Bucharest,
        Ştiinţa şi tehnică (13: 11), November 1961, pp. 24-25, 29.
                        ("Brazil- the Country of Contrasts ")

2383   Novăceanu, Darie. "Anatomia Unei Iluzii. Consecinţele Epuizării
        Rapide a Zăcămîntului de Cristal de Stîncă Descoperit la
        Cristalina." Bucharest, Lumea (3: 17), April 22, 1965, p. 20.
                        ("The Anatomy of an Illusion: Consequences
        of the Rapid Exhaustion of the Rock-Crystal Deposit Discovered at
        Cristalina ")

2384   Novăceanu, Darie. "Brazilia - Alegeri Indirecte." Bucharest,
        Lumea (4: 40), September 29, 1966, pp. 12-13.
                        ("Brazil: Indirect Elections ")

2385   Novăceanu, Darie. "Brazilia: Eldorado a Fost Găsit? Despre
        Bogățiile Naturale Descoperite la Cristalina și Goana După
        Înavuțire. " Bucharest, Lumea (3: 13), March 18, 1965, pp. 10-11.
                ("Brazil: Has Eldorado Been Found? About
        the Natural Riches Discovered at Cristalina and the Rush for
        Riches")

2386   Novăceanu, Darie. "Puncte de Reper în Literatura Braziliană. "
        Bucharest, Secolul 20 (3: 4), April 1963, pp. 85-101.
                ("Landmarks in Brazilian Literature ")

2387   Novăceanu, Darie. "Rio de Janeiro: Influența Militarilor în Viața
        Politică Braziliană. " Bucharest, Lumea (2:51), December 17,
        1964, p. 10.
                ("Rio de Janeiro: Influence of the Military
        in Brazilian Political Life")

2388   Obrea, Eugeniu. "Brazilia: Înfruntare cu 'Durii'. " Bucharest,
        Lumea (3: 52), December 23, 1965, pp. 10-11.
                ("Brazil: Defying the 'Die-Hards'")

2389   Obrea, Eugeniu. "Brazilia: Înfruntari Electorale. " Bucharest,
        Lumea (3: 40), September 30, 1965, pp. 20-21.
                ("Brazil: Electoral Challenge")

2390   Oros, V. "Triunghiul Puterii' în Etapa Preelectorală din Brazilia. "
        Bucharest, Lumea (3: 26), June 24, 1965, pp. 18-19.
                ("The 'Power Triangle' in the Pre-Electoral Stage
        in Brazil")

2391   Pop, Eugen. "Rio de Janeiro: Itinerar Neprecis. Oscilarea
        Politicii Președintelui Castelo Branco. " Bucharest, Lumea
        (3: 8), February 18, 1965, pp. 11-12.
                ("Rio de Janeiro: Unspecified Itinerary: Vacillation
        of President Castelo Branco's Policy")

2392   Popescu, P. "Starea Culturei și Datinele în Brazilia. "
        Iasi, Icoana Lumei II, 1846, pp. 359-360, 363-364.
                    ("Condition of the Culture and Customs of Brazil")

2393   Răzvan, A. T. "Teritoriul Liber Irribe. " Bucharest, Albina
        (65: 827), October 31, 1963. p. 7.
                    ("The Free Territory of Irribe")

2394   Roman, Ana. "Bossa Nova nu e Numai Samba. Note Despre
        Cinematografia Braziliană." Bucharest, Flacăra (14: 14),
        April 3, 1965, pp. 16-17.
                    ("Bossa Nova is Not Merely Samba: Notes About
        Brazilian Cinematography")

2395   Roman, Ștefan. "Unele Observații de la Campionatele Mondiale
        Masculine de Volei din Brazilia, 1960. " Bucharest, Cultura
        fizică și sport (14: 1), 1961, pp. 30-35.
                    ("Some Observations from the World Volleyball
        Championships in Brazil, 1960")

2396   "Terenuri Împărțite Țăranilor Brazilieni. " Bucharest, Agricultura
        socialistă (2: 11), March 12, 1964, p. 16.
        ("Land Distributed to Brazilian Peasants")

2397   Vlad, Corneliu. "Brazilia: Victoria Opoziției și Implicațiile ei. "
        Bucharest, Lumea (3: 42), October 14, 1965, pp. 10-11.
                    ("Brazil: Oposition's Victory and its Implications")

CENTRAL AMERICA

2398   "America Mijlocie (Centrală) și Carrera 'Riga Indienilor'. "
        Brașov, Gazeta de Transilvania (V), 1842, pp 112, 116, 119-120.
        ("Middle (Central) America and Carrera, the King of Indians")

2399   Oros, V. "Mărul Discordiei: Conflict Între Honduras si
        Salvador din Cauza... Incăpătînării Unui Agricultor. " Bucharest,
        Scînteia tineretului (23: 5633), June 30, 1967, p. 4.
                    ("The Apple of Discord: Conflict Between Honduras
        and Salvador Due to the Stubborness of a Farmer")

CHILE

2400   Cioră, I. "Pamîntul și Cuprul Chilian." Bucharest, Viața
        economica (4: 6), February 11, 1966, p. 14.
                    ("Chilean Land and Copper")

2401   Crișan, Romulus. "Între Anzi si Pacific. Chile. " Bucharest,
        Lumea (3: 34), August 19, 1965, p. 24.
                    ("Between the Andes and the Pacific")

2402   Dobran, Victor. "Importante Măsuri Economice în Chile."
        Bucharest, Viaţa economică (4: 44), November 4, 1966, p. 15.
                ("Important Economic Measures in Chile")

2403   "Grevele din Chile." Bucharest, Lumea (4: 13), March 24, 1966,
        p. 4.
        ("The Strikes in Chile")

2404   Nestor, Aurelian. "Între Anzi şi Pacific. Reportaj de pe Glob."
        Bucharest, Lumea (5: 33), August 10, 1967, pp. 16-18.
                ("Between the Andes and the Pacific: World
        Feature Report")

2405   Nováceanu, Darie. "Santiago: Drumul lui Eduardo Frei."
        Bucharest, Lumea (2: 46), November 12, 1964, p. 12.
                ("Santiago: Eduardo Frei's Progress")

2406   Oros, V. "Realităti Chiliene." Bucharest, Lumea (2: 13),
        March 26, 1964, pp. 13-15.
                ("Chilean Realities")

2407   Pădureanu, I. "Chile: Alegerile Prezidenţiale şi Cuprul."
        Bucharest, Viaţa economică (2: 36), September 4, 1964, p. 14.
                ("Chile: Presidential Elections and Copper")

2408   Pop, Eugen. "Reforma Agrară din Chile." Bucharest, Lumea
        (5: 39), September 21, 1967, p. 19.
                ("Agrarian Reform in Chile")

2409   Preda, Eugen. "Operaţia ' Chilenizacion'." Bucharest, Viaţa
        economică (3: 29), July 16, 1965, p. 24.
                ("Operation 'Chilenization")

COLOMBIA

2410   Lazăr, S. "Realităţi Colombiene. Viaţa Grea a Ţăranilor din
Lumea Capitalului." Bucharest, <u>Albina</u> (65: 777), November 14,
1962, p. 7.

        ("Colombian Realities, the Peasants' Hard Life in the
Capitalist World")

2411   Novăceanu, Darie. "Bogota: Din Două Motive. Situaţia Social-
Economică şi Politică a Colombiei." Bucharest, <u>Lumea</u> (3: 6),
February 4, 1965, pp. 10-11.

        ("Bogota: From Two Motives. Social-Economic an
Political Situation of Colombia")

2412   Obada, I. "Unitatea: Ţel Major al Mişcării Sindicale din Colombia. "
Bucharest, <u>Munca</u> (23: 6092), June 13, 1967, p. 6.

        ("Unity: The Major Goal of the Colombian Trade Movement'

COSTA RICA

2413 Grigore, C. "Documentar - Costa Rica." Bucharest, Viața economică (4: 19), May 13, 1966, p. 16.
("Documentary - Costa Rica")

2414 Ionescu, Crăciun. "Costa Rica: Cafea, Banane, și... 'Monstrul Verde." Bucharest, Magazin (10: 437), February 19, 1966, p. 3.
("Costa Rica: Coffee, Bananas, and.. 'the Green Monster")

CUBA

2415 "Artiștii Cubani Graziella Pogolotte, Servando Cabrera Moreno și Raul Oliva, Care ne Vizitează Țara, Răspund Întrebărilor 'Contemporanului'." Bucharest, Contemporanul (30), July 27, 1962, p. 6.
("The Cuban Artists, Graziella Pogolotte, Servando Cabrera Moreno and Raul Oliva, who are Visiting Our Country: Answers to Questions Put by 'Contemporanul'")

2416   Balaş, Iolanda. "15 Zile Printre Prietenii Cubanezi. Însemnări de
        Călătorie." Bucharest, <u>Magazin</u> (7: 291), May 4, 1963, pp. 1, 2;
        and (292), May 11, 1963, pp. 1, 2.
                        ("15 Days Among Cuban Friends: Travel Notes")

2417   Baranga, Aurel. "Alături de Poporul Cuban. Săptămîna Solidari-
        tăţii cu Poporul Cuban. " Bucharest, <u>Gazeta literară</u> (8: 30),
        July 20, 1961, pp. 1, 6.
                        ("By the Side of the Cuban People: Week of
        Solidarity with the Cuban People")

2418   Cornu, Ştefan. "Havana: a 6-a Aniversare a Republicii Cuba. "
        Bucharest, <u>Lumea</u> (3: 21), January 7, 1965, pp. 10-11.
                        ("Havana: The Sixth Anniversary of the Cuban
        Republic")

2419   "Descriere Geografică a Cubei. " Iaşi, <u>Gazeta de Moldavia</u> (XXII),
        1850, p. 184.
        ("Geographical Description of Cuba")

2420   "Direcţii ale Dezvoltării Economice a Republicii Cuba. " Bucharest,
        <u>Viaţa economică</u> (2: 1), January 3, 1964, p. 7.
        ("Economic Development Direction of the Cuban Republic")

2421   Gălăţeanu, Ion. " 'Dulceata' Cubei'. Impresii de Călătorie. "
        Bucharest, <u>Viaţa economică</u> (3: 53), December 31, 1965, pp. 23-24.
                        (" 'The Sweetness' of Cuba, Travel Impressions")

2422   "O Giudecată de Despărţire. In Insula Cuba. Nuvelă. " Iaşi,
        <u>Albina Romînească</u> (XI), 1841, pp. 61-63, 66-68.
        ("A Separation Judgment. On the Island of Cuba. A Short Story")

2423 "Inima Cubei. Orașul Santa Clara, Capitala Provinciei Las Villas. "
Bucharest, Lumea (3: 31), July 29, 1965, p. 4.
("The Heart of Cuba: The Town of Santa Clara, Capital of Las
Villas Province")

2424 Jebeleanu, Eugen. "Scrisoare Deschisă lui Nicolas Guillen Poet
Cuban, cu Ocazia Eliberării Cubei și a Întoarcerii Sale In Patrie. "
Bucharest, Gazeta literară (6: 8), February 19, 1959, pp. 1, 2.
("Open Letter to Nicolas Guillen, Cuban Poet,
on the Occasion of Cuba's Liberation and of His Return to His
Fatherland")

2425 Miron, Radu. "Piesa Într-un Act. Noua Dramaturgie Revolutio-
nară Cubană. " Cluj, Tribuna (6: 9), March, 1, 1962.
("The One Act Play: The New Revolutionary Cuban
Drama")

2426 Pătrașcu, N. "Havana: 1965 - 'Anul Dezvoltării'. " Bucharest,
Lumea (3: 1), January 1, 1965, p. 27.
("Havana: 1965 - 'Years of Development")

2427 Pop, Simion. "Pieton in Cuba. " Bucharest, Luceafărul (6: 24),
1963, p. 2.
("A Pedestrian in Cuba")

2428 Popovici, Titus. "Dreptul Popoarelor de a Transforma Cazărmile in
Școli. (un Fragment din Cartea, Aflată sub Tipar, Despre
Cuba). " Bucharest, Contemporanul (49), December 8, 1961, p. 8.
("The Right of Peoples to Convert Barracks
into Schools, a Fragment of the Book About Cuba now in Press")

2429 Pora, Eugen A. "În Pădurile din Sierra Maestra. " Cluj, Tribuna
(11: 5), February 2, 1967, p. 8.
("In the Sierra Maestra Forests")

2430   Stanciu, N. "Dezvoltarea Economiei Nationale a Republicii Cuba. "
       Bucharest, Probleme economice (17: 1), January 1964, pp. 118-122.
                  ("Development of the National Economy of the Republic
       of Cuba")

2431   Vlad, Corneliu. "Zahărul, Aurul Cubei. " Bucharest, Lumea
       (4: 1), January 1, 1966, p. 16.
                  ("Sugar, Cuba's Gold")

DOMINICAN REPUBLIC

2432   Găină, Emilian. "Bilanț Dominican. " Bucharest, România
       liberă (25: 7051), June 20, 1967, p. 6.
                  ("Dominican Balance")

ECUADOR

2433 Lupaş, Ion. "Latitudinea 0° - 0' - 0". Însemnări din Ecuador."
Bucharest, Magazin (11: 498), April 22, 1967, p. 7.
("Latitude 0° - 0' - 0": Notes from Ecuador")

2434 Novăceanu, Darie. "Ecuador 1965. Răsunetul Demonstratiilor
Antiguvernamentale de la Quito şi Guyaquil." Bucharest, Lumea
(31: 32), August 5, 1965, pp. 18-19.
("Ecuador, 1965: Echo of Antigovernment
Demonstrations at Quito and Guayaqul")

2435 Pop, Eugen. "Quito: Provizoratul Permanent al Juntei Militare
la Conducerea Statului." Bucharest, Lumea (4: 43), October 20,
1966, pp. 14-15.
("Quito: The Provisional Site of the Military Junta
Ruling the Nation")

2436 Tătaru, Petre. "Quito: Represiuni Antidemocratice." Bucharest,
Lumea (11), March 12, 1964, pp. 8-9.
("Quito: Antidemocratic Repressions")

GUATEMALA

2437   Georgescu, Paul A., "Un Mare Romancier al Americii Latine: Miguel Angel Asturias." Bucharest, Revista de filologie, romanică şi germanică (5: 1), 1961, pp. 97-100.
         ("A Great Novelist of Latin America: Miguel Angel Asturias")

2438   Jebeleanu, Eugen. " 'Yo lo vi'. Despre Poezia lui Miguel Angel Asturias." Bucharest, Gazeta literară (9: 28), July 12, 1962, p. 8.
         (" 'Yo lo vi', About Miguel Angel Asturias' Poetry")

2439   Marian, Paul B. " 'Domnul Preşedinte'. Un Roman Tipic Pentru Dictaturile din America Latină al Scriitorului Guatemalez Miguel Angel Asturias." Bucharest, Luceafărul (2: 15), August 11, 1959, p. 13.
         (" 'Mister President', a Novel Typical of Latin American Dictatorships, by Guatemalan Writer Miguel Angel Asturias")

2440   "Menendez Montenegro Preşedinţele Guatemalei. Profil." Bucharest, Lumea (4: 21), May 19, 1966, p. 31.
     ("Menendez Montenegro, Guatemala's President: Profile")

2441   Pop, Eugen. "Ciudad de Guatemala: Militarii şi Alegerile." Bucharest, Lumea (4: 12), January 1, 1966, pp. 7-8.
         ("Guatemala City: The Military and the Elections")

HAITI

2442   Ionescu, Crăciun. "Haiti sub Calcîiul lui 'Tonton Macout'. Atlas
        Magazin." Bucharest, Magazin (10: 447), April 30, 1966, pp. 1, 3.
                            ("Haiti Under the Heel of 'Tonton Macout':
        Atlas Magazine")

2443   Novăceanu, Darie. "Coşmarul lui Papa Doc şi Urmările Sale."
        Bucharest, Lumea (3: 28), July 8, 1965, pp. 8-9.
                            ("Papa Doc's Nightmare and its Consequences")

2444   Oros, V. "Haiti: Termenii Dilemei." Bucharest, Scînteia
        (36: 7375), June 18, 1967, p. 6.
                    ("Haiti: the Conditions of the Dilemma")

MEXICO

2445   Barbu, V. "Dezbateri Privind Denuclearizarea. A 4-a Sesiune
        COPREDAL. Ciudad de Mexico, 31 Ianuarie 1967."
        Bucharest, Lumea (5: 6), February 2, 1967, p. 9.
                    ("Debates Concerning Denuclearization: The Fourth
        COPREDAL Sesion, Mexico City, January 31, 1967")

2446   Botezat, S. S. "Ferdinand Cortet." Iași, <u>Icoana Lumei</u> (I), 1841,
pp. 177-178.
("Hernán Cortéz")

2447   Cherebețiu, Gabriel. "Piramidele de la Teotihuacan. Însemnări din
Mexic." Bucharest, <u>Magazin</u> (11: 488), February 11, 1967, p. 3.
("The Teotihuacan Pyramids: Notes from Mexico")

2448   Cherebețiu, Anca, & Gabriel Cherebetiu. "Ciudad Universitaria de Mexi
Alma Mater XX." Bucharest, <u>Viața studentească</u> (11: 41), December 10,
1966, p. 11.
("University City of Mexico: Alma
Mater XX")

2449   "Curg Apele Tulburi. Film Mexican." Bucharest, <u>Film</u> (7),
1956, pp. 27-31.
("Muddy Waters are Flowing; a Mexican Film")

2450   Ignat, Nestor. "Prin Cetățile Vii și Moarte ale Mexicului. (I).
Note de Drum." Bucharest, <u>Flacăra</u> (14: 7), February 13, 1965,
pp. 9-11.
("Through Living and Dead Cities of Mexico (I):
Travel Notes")

2451   Marian, Eugen B. "Teatrul Mexican Contemporan." Bucharest,
<u>Teatrul</u> (10 : 1), January 1965, pp. 91-93.
("The Contemporary Mexican Theatre")

2452   Novăceanu, Darie. "Mexic. Documentar." Bucharest, <u>Lumea</u>
(10), March, 1964, pp. 12-15.
("Mexico, Documentary")

2453   Novăceanu, Darie. "Mexic: Mandatul Prezidenţial Încredinţat la 1
        Decembrie lui Gustavo Diaz Ordaz." Bucharest, Lumea (2: 50),
        December 10, 1964, pp. 16-17.
                            ("Mexico: Presidential Mandate Entrusted on
        December 1 to Gustavo Diaz Ordaz")

2454   "Romanul Mexican." Bucharest, Secolul 20 (1), January, 1961,
        pp. 212-214.
        ("The Mexican Novel")

2455   Tătaru, P. "Pe Plantaţiile de Bumbac din Mexic." Bucharest,
        Albina (66: 841), February 6, 1964, p. 7.
                            ("On the Cotton Plantations of Mexico")

2456   Voican, Anca. "Mexic. Tradiţie şi Actualitate." Bucharest, Lumea
        (5: 25), June 15, 1967, pp. 20-21.
                            ("Mexico, Tradition and Actuality")

NICARAGUA

2457   Galeriu, S. " 'Praf în Ochii Mulţimii'. 'Reforma Agrară' din Nica-
        ragua." Bucharest, Agricultura nouă (8: 833), April 20, 1962, p. 4.
                            (" 'Dust in Peoples' Eyes': 'Agrarian Reform' in
        Nicaragua")

2458   Ionescu, Crăciun. "Vulcani Nestinşi. Atlas Magazin." Bucharest,
Magazin (11: 488), February 11, 1967, p. 3.
("Unextinct Volcanoes, Atlas Magazine")

2459   Voican, Anca. "Managua: Dupā 'Tacho', 'Tachito'..."
Bucharest, Lumea (5: 6), February 2, 1967, p. 8.
("Managua: After 'Tacho', 'Tachito'...")

PANAMA

2460   Cetină, Elena. "Panama." Bucharest, Natura, geografia, geologia
(14: 4), July- August, 1962, pp. 66-69.
("Panama")

2461   Novăceanu, Darie. "Ciudad de Panama: Sub Semnul Întrebării
Existenţa Organizaţiei Statelor Americane." Bucharest, Lumea
(4: 15), January, 1966, p. 11.
("Panama City: Under the Sign of the Question
Mark: The Existence of the Organization of American States")

2462   Obrea, Eugeniu. "Panama şi... Panamale. Cum a Devenit Canalul
Panama o Posesiune a S. U. A. ?" Bucharest, Studii, revista de
istorie (5:3030), February 8, 1959, p. 2.
("Panama and Panama Bubbles: How Did the
Panama Canal Become U. S. Property? ")

PARAGUAY

2463   Dolgu, Gabriela. "Fluviul Însîngerat. Represiunile Antidemocratice
Întreprinse de Guvernul Di ctatorial al lui Stroesser în Paraguay. "
Bucharest, Contemporanul (50), December 15, 1961, p. 8.
("The Blood-Stained River: Antidemocratic
Repressions Undertaken by Stroesser's Dictatorial Government in
Paraguay")

2464   Găina, E.   "Paraguay - Tara Mizeriei şi Opresiunii. "
Bucharest, Magazin (7: 294), May 25, 1963, p. 2.
("Paraguay, the Country of Misery and Opression ")

2465   Ionescu, Crăciun.   "Dictatori, Latifundiari, şi Monopoluri
Straine. " Bucharest, Atlas magazin (10: 473), October 29,
1966, p. 3.
("Dictators, Large Landowners and
Foreign Monopolies")

PERU

2466   Block, L.   "O Pseudoreformă Agrară in Peru. " Bucharest, Albina
(66: 871), September 3, 1964, p. 7.
("An Agrarian Pseudo-Reform in Peru")

2467   Baconsky, A. E. "César Vallejo, Privire asupra Operei Poetului
        Peruvian. " Bucharest, Contemporanul (15), April 12, 1963, p. 2.
                    ("César Vallejo, Consideration of the Work of the
        Peruvian Poet")

2468   Diplan, Rodica. "Nu Numai la Toquepala... Mişcarea Antiguvernamen-
        tală şi Antiimperialistă a Maselor Populare Peruviene. "
        Bucharest, Lumea (4: 45), November 3, 1966, p. 21.
                        ("Not Only at Toquepala... Antigovernment and
        Anti-Imperialist Movement of Peruvian Popular Masses")

2469   Florea, Z. "Consecinţe ale Întîrzierii Reformei Agrare. Peru. "
        Bucharest, Viaţa economică (2: 28), July 10, 1964, p. 15.
                        ("Consequences of the Retardation of Agrarian Reform:
        Peru")

2470   "Lima: Situaţie Încărcată. Trimiterea de Forţe Militare Împotriva
        Partizanilor Peruvieni. " Bucharest, Lumea (3: 39), September 23,
        1965, p. 12.
        ("Lima: Strained Situation: Military Forces Sent Against the
        Peruvian Partisans ")

2471   Oros, V. "Confruntări Electorale în Peru si în Argentina. "
        Bucharest, Probleme internaţionale (4), August, 1963, pp. 64-69.
                    ("Electoral Confrontations in Peru and Argentina")

2472   "Parlamentul Peruvian a Naţionalizat Zacaminte Exploatate de o
        Companie Petrolieră Americană. " Bucharest, Scînteia (36: 7382),
        June 25, 1967, p. 6.
        ("The Peruvian Parliament Nationalized Wealth Exploited by an
        American Oil Company")

2473   Pop, Eugen. "Pămîntul Fierbinte al Anzilor. Despre Luptele de
        Partizani din Peru. " Bucharest, Albina (67: 922), August 26, 1965, p.
                        ("The Hot Land of the Andes: About the Battles of the
        Partisans in Peru")

URUGUAY

2474   "Note Despre Expoziția de Gravură Uruguayană din Sala 'Nicolae Cristea'." Bucharest, <u>Arta plastică</u> (9: 1), 1962, pp. 41-42. ("Notes About the Exibition of Uruguayan Graphic Art of the 'Nicolae Cristea' Hall")

2475   Novăceanu, Darie. "Montevideo: Marșurile Țăranilor Pentru Distribuirea Terenurilor Nefolosite." Bucharest, <u>Lumea</u> (2: 21), May 21, 1964, pp. 10-11.
                 ("Montevideo: The Peasants' March for the Distribution of Unused Lands")

2476   Popescu, N. "Montevideo: Tensiune în Uruguay." Bucharest, <u>Lumea</u> (3: 51), December 16, 1965, p. 11.
                 ("Montevideo: Tension in Uruguay")

2477   Szilágyi, Dezideriu. "Din Pampa în Avenida '18 de Julio'. Reportaj." Bucharest, <u>Lumea</u> (5: 26), June 22, 1967, pp. 16-18.
                 ("From Pampa to Avenida '18 de Julio': World Features Report")

2478   "Biografia lui Bolivar. " Iaşi, Albina Românească (I), 1829, p. 47.
("Bolivar's Biography")

2479   Block, Igor. "Reformă Agrară sau Colonizare? Comentarii pe
Marginea Reformei Agrare din Venezuela. " Bucharest, Albina
(67: 893), February 4, 1965, p. 7.
                ("Agrarian Reform or Colonization? Commentaries on the
Agrarian Reform in Venezuela")

2480   Cioara, I. "Venezuela: Simptomul de Criză. " Bucharest, Lumea
(2: 44), October 29, 1964, pp. 20-21.
                ("Venezuela: The Symptom of Crisis")

2481   Drîmba, Ovidiu. "Un Poet din Venezuela José Romeón Medina. "
Bucharest, Secolul 20 (2: 1), January 1962, pp. 185-187.
                ("A Poet from Venezuela, José Romeón Medina")

2482   Mironescu, Emil. "Operaţia San Carlos. " Bucharest, Scînteia
(36: 7385), June 28, 1967, p. 5.
                ("Operation San Carlos")

2483   Tudor, H. "Ce se Petrece în Venezuela. " Bucharest, Apărarea
patriei (14: 2), January 4, 1958, p. 4.
                ("What is Happening in Venezuela")

YUGOSLAVIA

Although no degrees are offered in Latin American Studies
by the Universities of Belgrade, Ljubljana, Skoplje and
Zagreb, students may register for courses in Spanish
language and literature in all of these institutions.   The
Faculty of Philology of the University of Belgrade teaches
a course in the History of Latin American Literature,
while the Department of Romance Languages and Literatures
of the University of Zagreb offers Portuguese.

While none of the aforementioned institutions offers social
sciences or humanities courses specifically with respect
to Latin America, courses which are by their nature global
in scope (e. g. , History of Civilization, General and
Regional World Ethnology, General and Regional Geography,
World Economic Geography, History of Art, Archaeology,
etc.) touch upon Latin America.

In this bibliography the English translation of the title of
each bibliographic item is to be found directly under the
title in the original language, and immediately following
the entire bibliographic description.

Aunque no se ofrecen títulos académicos en el campo de
Estudios Latinoamericanos en las Universidades de Belgrade,
Ljubljana, Skoplje y Zagreb, se permiten a los estudiantes
seguir asignaturas y especializarse en lengua y letras
españolas.   En la Facultad de Filología de la Universidad
de Belgrade se enseña curso de Historia de Letras Latinoamericanas, mientras que el Departamento de Lenguas

y Letras Romances de la Universidad de Zagreb ofrece
portugués.

Ninguna de estas Instituciones ofrece cursos de interés
latinoamericano en los ramos de ciencias sociales y
humanidades. Sin embargo, las asignaturas siguientes,
universales en su carácter intrínsico, tratan la América
Latina: Historia de Civilización; Etnología General Mundial
y Regional; Geografía General y Regional; Geografía
Económica Mundial; Historia de Arte; Arqueología.

En esta bibliografía la traducción inglesa del título de cada
asiento se encuentra directamente bajo el título de la
lengua original, seguida de la ficha entera.

I. Books

LATIN AMERICA

2484   Almuli, Jaša. <u>Vojnici Na Sceni Latinske Amerike</u>. Belgrade,
Sedma Sila, 1964, 64p.
(Soldiers on the Latin American Scene)

2485   Blum, Rudolf. <u>Zemlje i Narodi Latinske Amerike</u>. Belgrade,
Rad, 1955, 218p.
(The Countries and Peoples of Latin America)

2486   Cvjtanović, Alfonso. <u>U Prašumama Amazonije</u>. Zagreb,
Školska Knjiga, 1963, 136p.
(In the Amazon Jungles)

2487   <u>Evropa i SAD u Borbi za Tržista Latinske Amerike</u>. Zagreb,
Kultura, 1965, 66p.
(Europe and the United States in the Struggle for the Latin
American Market)

2488   Južnič, Stane. <u>Kam Gre Latinska Amerika?</u> Ljubljana, Komunist,
1965, 46p.
(Where is Latin America Going?)

2489   Južnič, Stane. <u>Latinska Amerika. Nastanak i Razvoj Društveno-
Ekonomskih Struktura</u>. Belgrade, Institut za Medjunarodnu
Politiku i Privredu, 1966, 284p.
(Latin America: Rise and Development of the Socio-Economic
Structure)

2490   **Kalemata, Ritomir.** Južna Amerika. Zagreb, Školska Knjiga,
        1951, 56p.
                        (South America)

2491   Komadinić, Slobodan. Latinsko-Američka Književnost u Jugoslaviji;
        Bibliografija. Belgrade, Savez Književnika Jugoslavije, 1963, 144p.
                        (Bibliography of Translations of Latin American
        Literature into Yugoslav Languages)

2492   Komunističke Partije Latinske Amerike. Belgrade, Institut Za
        Izučavanje Radničkog Pokreta, 1962, 28p.
        (The Communist Parties of Latin America)

2493   Koral, Vladimir. Usamljena Rijeka. Zagreb, Epoha, 1962, 245p.
                        (The Lonely River)

2494   Kulišić, Špiro. Život i Kultura Zaostalih Plemena Australije,
        Okeanije, Amerike i Afrike. Sarajevo, Veselin Masleša, 1960,
        152p.
                        (The Life and Culture of the Underdeveloped
        Tribes of Australia, Oceania, America and Africa)

2495   Latinska Amerika. Godišnji Privredni Izveštaj Za 1958. Belgrade,
        Institut za Spoljnu Trgovinu, 1959, pp. 41-42.
        (Latin America: Annual Economic Report for 1958)

2496   Latinska Amerika. Opšte Karakteristike Razvoja. Institut za
        Medunarodnu Politiku i Privredu. Godišnjak 1963. Belgrade,
        1964, pp. 473-503.
        (Latin America: General Characteristics of Development)

2497 Materijali o Latinskoj Americi. Belgrade, Institut za Medjunarodnu
Politiku i Privredu, 1963, 68p.
(Materials on Latin America)

2498 Pešić, Bogdan. Južna Amerika. Kuda, Kako, Zašto. Belgrade,
Sedma Sila, 1962, 64p.
(South America: Where, How, Why)

2499 Privreda Zemalja Latinske Amerike. "Godisnji Pregled Privrede za
1961 Godinu". Belgrade, Institut za Spoljnu Trgovinu, 1961, pp. 54-59.
(Economies of the Countries of Latin America: Annual Economic
Survey for 1961)

2500 Redžepagić, Sulejman. Omladinski Pokret u Latinskoj Americi.
Belgrade, Mladost, 1962, 136p.
(Youth Movement in Latin America)

2501 Redžepagić, Sulejman. Radnički i Narodni Pokreti Latinske
Amerike. Belgrade, Institut Za Izučavanje Radničkog Pokreta,
1965, 171p.
(Working Class and Peoples' Movements
in Latin America)

2502 Redzepagić, Sulejman. Sindikalni Pokret u Latinskoj Americi.
"Savremeni Medjunarodni Radnički Pokret". Zagreb, Naprijed,
1963, pp. 253-282.
(Trade Union Movement in Latin America)

2503 Redžepagić, Sulejman. Suvremene Koncepcije Komunističkih
Partija o Društvenom Preobražaju Zemalja Latinske Amerike.
Zagreb, Centar "Božidar Adžija", 1964, 132p.
(Contemporary Concepts of the Communist
Parties on the Social Transformation in the Countries of Latin America)

2504 Rijavec, Mirko. Južna Amerika; Dežela, Prebivalstvo, Zgodovina,
Kultura. Gorica, 1957, 83p.
(South America: Deserts, Conquests, Agriculture,
Civilization)

583

2505   Savnik, Dušan. Svet Nasprotij. Dvajset Držav Latinske Amerike.
       Ljubljana, Mladinska Knjiga, 1958, 296p.
                    (The World on the Other Side: Twenty Latin American
       Countries)

2506   Svetska Privreda 1954-1955, Belgrade, Institut za Medjunarodnu
       Politiku i Privredu, 1955, pp. 148-161.
       (World Economy 1954-1955)

2507   Vuković, Branislav. Latinska Amerika. Radnički Pokret u
       Nerazvijenim Zemljama, Belgrade, Visoka Skola Politickih
       Nauka, 1962, pp. 42-44.
                    (Latin America: Working Class Movement
       in Underdeveloped Countries)

2508   Vukušić, Branko. Latinska Amerika Juče i Danas. Belgrade,
       Kultura, 1956, 80p.
                    (Latin America Yesterday and Today)

2509   Vukušić, Branko. Organizacija Američkih Država. Belgrade,
       Institut za Medjunarodnu Politiku i Privredu, 1958, 154p.
                    (Organization of American States)

2510   Vukušić, Branko. Panamerikanizam i Latinska Amerika,
       Belgrade, Kultura, 1960, 180p.
                    (Panamericanism and Latin America)

2511   Vuličić, Melita. Umjetnost Predkonkvistadorske Amerike. Kratki
       Pregled. Zagreb, Tehnička Knjiga, 1957, 120p.
                    (Art of Pre-Conquest America: Brief Survey)

ARGENTINA

2512   A. I. (pseud.) "Argentina. " Medunarodni Radnički Pokret.
    Godisnji Pregled 1962. Belgrade,1963, pp. 17-23.
        ("Argentina")

BOLIVIA

2513   Južnic, Stane. Bolivija. Belgrade, Institut za Medjunarodnu
    Politiku i Privredu, 1963, 176p.
       (Bolivia)

2514   Savić, Velizar. Bolivija - Krov Južne Amerike. Belgrade, Sedma
    Sila, 1963, 64p.
        (Bolivia - The Roof of South America)

BRAZIL

2515 Almuli, Jaša. Brazil, Putevi Emancipacije, Belgrade,Sedma
Sila, 1963, 62p.
(Brazil: The Ways of Emancipation)

2516 Dragomanović, Vladimir. Brazil. Belgrade, Institut za
Medjunarodnu Politicu i Privredu, 1961, 172p.
(Brazil)

2517 Košta, Vjekoslav. Brasil (Estados Unidos do Brasil). Belgrade,
Izd. Institutaza Medunarodnu Politiku i Privredu, 1961, 172p.
(Brazil)

2518 Redžepagić, Sulejman. Društveno-Politička Struktura i Radnički
Pokret Brazila. Belgrade, Institut za Izučavanje Radničkog Pokreta,
1962, 98p.
(Socio-Political Structure and the Working
Class Movement of Brazil)

2519 Sekelj, Tibor. Kroz Brazilske Prašume do Divljih Indijanskih
Plemena. Zagreb, Glas Rada, 1953, 164p.
(Through Brazilian Jungles to the Wild Indian Tribes)

CHILE

2520   M. K. (pseud.) "Čile. " <u>Medunarodni Radnički i Progresivni</u>
<u>Pokreti. Godišnji Pregled 1964</u>. Belgrade, 1965, pp. 487-497.
("Chile")

2521   Paligorić, Ljubomir. <u>Čile. Društveno-Politički Profil</u> Belgrade,
Sedma Sila, 1963, 64p.
(Chile: Socio-Political Profile)

2522   Pribicevic, Natalija. <u>Čile.</u> Belgrade, Institut za Medjunarodnu
Politiku i Privredu. 1965, 150p.
(Chile)

COLOMBIA

2523 Košta, Vjekoslav. "Kolombija." <u>Medunarodni Radnički i Progresivni Pokreti. Godišnji Pregled 1964.</u> Belgrade, 1965, pp. 498-504.
("Colombia")

CUBA

2524 Julius, Djuka. <u>Kubanski Bunt, Koreni, Značaj i Budućnost...</u> Belgrade, Sedma Sila, 1962, 64p.
(The Cuban Revolution: Roots, Significance and Future)

2525 Košta, Vjekoslav. <u>Kuba.</u> Belgrade, Institut za Medjunarodnu Politiku i Privredu, 1962, 166p.
(Cuba)

2526 Muljačić, Žarko. "O Hrvatima na Kubi u 18 Stoljeću." <u>Pomorski Zbornik Društva za Proučavanje i Unapredjenje Pomorstva Jugoslavije.</u> 2d ed. Zadar, Društvo za Proučavanje i Unapredjenje Pomorstva Jugoslavije, 1964, pp. 725-731.
(On the Croats in Cuba in the 18th Century)

MEXICO

2527   Gajić, Vasa. <u>Meksiko i Civilizacija Maja</u>. Sarajevo, Narodna
        Prosvjeta, 1955, 100p.
              (Mexico and the Maya Civilization)

2528   Južnič, Stane. <u>Meksiko,</u> Belgrade, Sedma Sila, 1963, 64p.
              (Mexico)

2529   Krunić, Luka. "Meksiko". <u>Medunarodni Radnički Pokret</u>.
        <u>Godišnji Pregled 1962</u>. Belgrade,1963, pp. 237-245.
              ("Mexico")

2530   M. M. (pseud.) "Meksiko. " <u>Medunarodni Radnicki i</u>
        <u>Progresivni Pokreti. Godisnji Pregled 1964</u>. Belgrade,1965,
        pp. 521-534.
              ("Mexico")

URUGUAY

2531   Jaksić, Aleksandar. "Urugvaj. " <u>Medjunarodni Radnicki Pokret</u>.
        <u>Godisnji Pregled, 1960</u>. Belgrade,1961, pp. 497-505.
              (Uruguay)

2532   Jaksić, Aleksandar. "Urugvaj. " <u>Medunarodni Radnički Pokret</u>.
        <u>Godišnji Pregled,1962</u>. Belgrade,1963, pp. 375-382.
              ("Uruguay")

VENEZUELA

2533   Južnič, Stane. <u>Venecuela.</u> Belgrade,Institut za Medjunarodnu
      Politiku i Privredu, 1961, 131p.
           (Venezuela)

2534   Južnič, Stane. "Venecuela. " <u>Medunarodni Radnički Pokret.</u>
      <u>Godišnji Pregled 1962.</u> Belgrade, 1963, pp. 394-400.
           ("Venezuela")

2535   Južnič, Stane. "Venecuela. " <u>Medunarodni Radnički i Progresivni</u>
      <u>Pokreti. Godišnji Pregled 1964.</u> Belgrade, 1965, pp. 542-550.
           ("Venezuela")

2536   Južnič, Stane. "Venecuela. " <u>Medunarodni Radnički i Drugi</u>
      <u>Progresivni Pokreti. Godišnji Pregled 1965.</u> Belgrade, 1966,
      pp. 651-658.
           ("Venezuela")

II. Periodical Articles

LATIN AMERICA

2537   Adamović, Ljubiša. "Poljoprivredni Planovi Latinske Amerike."
Belgrade, Ekonomska politika (III: 107), 1954, pp. 315-316.
("Agricultural Projects of Latin America")

2538   Almuli, Jaša. "Latinskaja Amerika Bespokojnyj Materik." Belgrade,
Meždunarodnaja politika (VIII: 184), 1957, pp. 15-18.
("Latin America, Continent of Turmoil")

2539   Almuli, Jaša. "Previranja u Latinskoj Americi." Belgrade,
Socijalizam (VII: 7-8), 1964, pp. 993-1020.
("Turmoil in Latin America")

2540   Barišić, Marijan. "Društvena i Politička Kretanja u Latinskoj
Americi." Zagreb, Politička misao (II: I), 1965, pp. 111-118.
("Social and Political Movements in Latin
America")

2541   Bartulica, Miroslav. "Iseljeničke Novine u Južnoj Americi za
Prvograta." Zagreb, Matica (III: 1), 1953, pp. 8-9.
("Immigrant Newspapers in South America
During the First World War")

2542   Bartulica, Miroslav. "Južnoamerički Hrvati u Borbi Protiv
Austro-Ugarske Monarhije." Zagreb, Matica (V: 3), 1955,
pp. 58-59.
("South American Croats in the Struggle
Against the Austro-Hungarian Monarchy")

2543   Bebler, Aleš. "Pogled na Južnu Ameriku. " Belgrade,
Medunarodna politika (IX: 203), 1958, pp. 5-6.
("A Look at South America")

2544   Brilej, Jože. "Problemy i Processy v Latinskoj Amerike. "
Belgrade, Meždunarodnaja politika (X: 230), 1959, pp. 6-7.
("Problems and Developments in Latin America")

2545   Bruner, Mirko. "Problemi i Težnje Latinske Amerike. " Belgrade,
Medjunarodna politika (XVI: 561), 1965, pp. 18-19.
("Problems and Aspirations of Latin America")

2546   Dabčević, Gracije. "Oko Južne Amerike. " Rijeka, Pomorstvo
(VI: 8), 1951, pp. 256-257.
("Around South America")

2547   "Delavsko Gibanje v Latinski Ameriki. " Ljubljana, Naši razgledi
(IV: 8), 1955, pp. 180-181.
("Working Class Movement in Latin America")

2548   Deleon, Ašer. "Dviženie Stran Latinskoj Ameriki i Meždunarodnoe
Sotrudničestvo. " Belgrade, Meždunarodnaja politika (XI: 237),
1960, pp. 14-15.
("Latin American Countries and International
Cooperation")

2549   Deleon, Ašer. "Nekotorye Aspekty Latinoamerikanskogo
Sotrudičestva. " Belgrade, Meždunarodnaja politika (XI: 236),
1960, pp. 9-11.
("Some Aspects of Latin American Cooperation")

2550   Delia, Germán. "Latinskaja Amerika na Pereput'i. " Belgrade,
Meždunarodnaja politika (XI: 245), 1960, pp. 9-10.
("Latin America at the Crossroads")

2551   Djerdja, Josip. "Pod Znakom Nepreryvnogo Rasširenja Zony Mira. "
Nakanune Poseščenija Prezidentom Tita Tito Nekotoryh Stran
Latinskoj Ameriki." Belgrade, Meždunarodnaja politika (XIV: 322),
1963, pp. 1-3.
("Continuous Expansion of the Zone of Peace")

2552   Dordević, Veroslava. "Razvoj Industrije Pamučnog Tekstila u
Južnoj Americi. " Belgrade, Nedeljni Komentari Instituta za
Spoljnu Trgovinu (VII: 284), 1962, pp. 391-393.
("Development of the Cotton Textile
Industry in South America")

2553   Dragomanović, Vladimir. "Dva Proekta Ekonomičeskoga Ob'edinenija
u Latinskoj Amerike. " Belgrade, Meždunarodnaja politika (XIV: 318-
319), 1963, pp. 7-10.
("Two Economic Integration Projects in
Latin America")

2554   Dragomanović, Vladimir. "Latinska Amerika na Putu Ekonomske
Integracije. " Belgrade, Socijalizam (III: 5), 1960, pp. 70-96.
("Latin America on the Way to
Economic Integration")

2555   Dragomanović, Vladimir. "Pregled Privrede Latinske Amerike. "
Belgrade, Medjunarodni problemi (IX: 4), 1957, pp. 158-164.
("Survey of Latin America's Economy")

2556   Dragomanović, Vladimir. "SAD i Zemlje Latinske Amerike. "
Belgrade, Medunarodna politika (IX: 196), 1958, pp. 6-7.
("The United States of America and
the Countries of Latin America")

2557   Dragomanović, Vladimir. "Specifična Uloga Države u Razvoju
        Latino-američkog Kapitalizma. " Belgrade, Medunarodni
        problemi (XI: 1), 1959, pp. 1-25.
                                    ("The Specific Role of the State in the
        Development of Capitalism in Latin America")

2558   "Ekonomska Struktura Zemalja Latinske Amerike. " Zagreb,
        Informatice INGRA (4-5), 1949, pp. 3-19.
        ("Economic Structures of the Latin American Countries")

2559   "Elementi Osamosvojitve in Samostojnejšega Nastopanja Latinskoameričkih
        Dežel v Mednarodnih Odnosih. " Ljubljana, Teorija in praksa (I: 1),
        1964, pp. 115-124.
        ("Components of Independence and of Independent Action of Latin
        America in International Relations")

2560   Fabinc, Jvo. "Nova Etapa u Privrednom Integrisanju Latinske
        Amerike. " Belgrade, Nedeljni Komentari Instituta za Spoljnu
        Trgovinu (VI: 251), 1961, pp. 668-669.
                                    ("New Stage in the Economic Integration of
        Latin America")

2561   Gajinović, Vujica. "Ekonomičeskie Otnošenija so Stranami Latinskoj
        Ameriki. " Belgrade, Meždunarodnaja politika (XII: 290), 1962,
        pp. 26-27.
                                    ("Economic Relations with the Countries of
        Latin America")

2562   Garvanov, Velibor. "O Gledanjima na Probleme Razvitka Zemalja
        Latinske Amerike. " Sarajevo, Gledišta (III: 2), 1962, pp. 71-79.
                                    ("On the Way of Looking at the Problems of
        Latin America's Development")

2563   Indić, Trivo. "Pred Drugi Kongres Omladine Latinske Amerike. "
        Belgrade, Medunarodna politika (XV: 335), 1964, pp. 6-7.
                ("Before the Second Youth Congress in Latin America")

2564   "Iz Oblasti Radnog i Socijalnog Zakonodavstva Nekih Zemalja
        Latinske Amerike. " Belgrade, Socijalna politika (II: 1), 1952,
        pp. 35-40.
        ("From the Labour and Social Legislation of Some Latin American
        Countries")

2565   "Izveštaj sa Četvrtog Zasedanja Komiteta za Trgovinu Ekonomske
        Komisije UN za Latinsku Ameriku. " Belgrade, Spoljnopolitička
        dokumentacija (XVII: 1), 1965, pp. 25-42.
        ("Report of the IVth Session of the Trade Committee, Economic
        Commission of the United Nations for Latin America")

2566   Jakšic, Aleksandar. "Konsultativni Komitet Latinoameričkog
        Sekretarijata Socijalističke Internacionale. " Belgrade, Medjunarodni
        radnički pokret. Godisnji pregled (1960). 1961, pp. 520-523.
                    ("Consultative Committee of the Socialist
        International's Latin American Secretariat")

2567   Javorski, Mihajlo. "Na Putu Mira i Progresa. Predsednik Tito u
        Latinskoj Americi, SAD i Pred Generalnom Skupštinom. " Belgrade,
        Medunarodna politika (XIV: 326), 1963, pp. 1-3.
                    ("On the Way to Peace and Progress: President
        Tito in Latin America, in the United States and Before the General
        Assembly")

2568   Jevremović, Miodrag. "Južnoameričko Tržište. " Belgrade, Nova
        trgovina (VII: 4), 1954, pp. 235-238.
                    ("Latin American Market")

2569   Georgiev, A. "Panamerikanizam Kao Instrument Politike
        Ekspanzije. " Belgrade, Trideset dana (IV: 8), 1946, pp. 201-202.
        ("Panamericanism as an Instrument in Expansive Policy")

2570   Hrzić, Boris. "Pritisak na Nezavisnu Politiku u Latinskoj
        Americi. " Belgrade, Medunarodna politika (XV: 346), 1964,
        pp. 9-10.
                        ("Pressure on the Independence Policy of
        Latin America")

2571   Hubeni, Marijan. "Latinska Amerika i Evropa. " Belgrade,
        Ekonomska politika (II: 63), 1953, pp. 474-475.
                        ("Latin America and Europe")

2572   Hubeni, Marijan. "Izneverena Očekivanja - Ekonomska
        Konferencija Latinsko-Američkih Zemalja. " Belgrade,
        Medjunarodna politika (VIII: 180), 1957, pp. 11-13.
                        ("Unfulfilled Expectations: Economic
        Conference of Latin American Countries")

2573   Hubeni, Marijan, & Ladević, Dorde. "Latinska Amerika. "
        Belgrade, Svetska privreda, 1954, pp. 139-153.
                        ("Latin America")

2574   Ilesić, Svetozar. "Kontinenti Bodocnosti. " Ljubljana, Obzornik
        (VI: 2), 1951, pp. 95-103.
                        ("Continent of the Future")

2575   Indjić, Trivo. "Narodna Omladina Jugoslavije i Omladinski
        Pokreti Latinske Amerike. " Belgrade, Gledišta (III: 8),
        1962, pp. 53-65.
                        ("People's Youth of Yugoslavia and Youth
        Movements in Latin America")

2576   Južnič, Stane. "Proces Društveno-Ekonomskih i Političkih
        Promena u Latinskoj Americi. " Belgrade, Medjunarodni problemi
        (XIII: 3), 1961, pp. 23-53.
                ("The Process of Socio-Economic and Political
        Change in Latin America")

2577   Južnič, Stane. "Progresivna Kretanja i Radnički Pokret u
        Latinskoj Americi. " Belgrade, Gledišta (IV: 1), 1963, pp. 79-95.
                ("Progressive Activities and the Working Class
        Movement in Latin America")

2578   Južnič, Stane. "Uloga i Dejstvo Stranog Kapitala u Razvitku
        Latinske Amerike. " Belgrade, Naše teme (X: 1-2), 1966,
        pp. 70-108.
                ("The Role and Effect of Foreign Capital in the
        Development of Latin America")

2579   Južnič, Stane. "Vidovi Hegemonije i Oblici Otpora. Stare i Nove
        Komponente u Interameričkim Sistemu. " Belgrade, Medjunarodna
        politika (XVII: 384), 1966, pp. 11-13.
                ("Aspects of Hegemony and Forms of Resistance")

2580   Krešić, Ivan. "Problem Smeštaja Svjetske Industrije i Latinska
        Amerika. " Zagreb, Ekonomski pregled (VI: 10), 1955, pp. 834-836.
                ("Problem of Comparing World Industry and Latin
        America")

2581   Kristan, Cvetko A. "Kulturno-Prosvetno Delo Južnoameričkin
        Slovencev od Junija 1958 do Junija 1959. " Ljubljana, Slovenski
        iseljenski koledar, 1960, pp. 226-230.
                ("Cultural-Educational Activities of the South
        American Slovenes from June 1958-June 1959")

2582   Kukoč, Eduard. "Latinska Amerika u Jugoslovenskoj Spoljnoj
        Trgovini i Pomorskom Saobraćaju." Split, Mornarički glasnik
        (XIII: 6), 1963, pp. 760-765.
                        ("Latin America in Yugoslav Foreign Trade and
        Maritime Communication")

2583   Kunc, Marijan. "Razvoj Naših Poslijeratnih Trgovinskih Odnosa
        sa Zemljama Latinske Amerike." Belgrade, Nova trgovina (VI: 1),
        1953, pp. 28-32.
                        ("Development of our Post-War Commercial
        Relations with the Countries of Latin America")

2584   "Latinska Amerika u Procesu Zaostravanja Protivrecnosti."
        Belgrade, Medjunarodna politika (XIII: 290), 1962, pp. 5-6.
        ("Latin America in the Process of Intensified Contradictions")

2585   Lazić, Dušan. "Kineske Koncepcije o Zemljama i Pokretima
        Azije, Afrike i Latinske Amerike." Belgrade, Informativni
        pregled (1), 1966, pp. 22-29.
                        ("Chinese Concepts on the Countries and Movements
        of Asia, Africa and Latin America")

2586   Leontić, Ljubo. "Jugoslavenska Narodna Odbrana u Južnoj
        Americi." Zagreb, Matičin Iseljenicki Kalendar za, 1955,
        pp. 51-53.
                        ("Yugoslav National Defense in Latin America")

2587   M. O. (pseud.) "Latinska Amerika - Pogled Nazaj in Naprej."
        Ljubljana, Naši razgledi (I: 15), 1952, pp. 6-7.
                        (Latin America - A Look into the Future and into
        the Past")

2588   M. O. (pseud.) "Zrcalo Latinske Amerike." Ljubljana, Naši
        razgledi (IX: 6), 1960, p. 122.
                        ("The Mirror of Latin America")

2589   Milenković, Vladislav. "Borba za Tržišta Latinske Amerike. "
        Belgrade, Ekonomska politika (VI: 263), 1957, pp. 359-361.
                            ("Struggle for the Latin American
        Market")

2590   Milenković, Vladislav. "Panamerička Operacija. " Belgrade,
        Ekonomska politika (VIII: 373), 1959, pp. 530-531.
                            ("Operation Pan America")

2591   Milenković, Vladislav. "Privreda Latinske Amerike. " Belgrade,
        Ekonomska politika (IX: 434), 1960, pp. 706-707.
                            ("Latin American Economy")

2592   Milenković, Vladislav. "Tržište Latinske Amerike. " Belgrade,
        Nova trgovina (XI: 5), 1958, pp. 295-298.
                            ("The Market of Latin America")

2593   N. V. (pseud.) "Američki Imperijalizam i Latinska Amerika. "
        Zagreb, Djelo (I: 5), 1948, pp. 387-389.
                            ("American Imperialism and Latin America")

2594   "Naša Spoljnotrgovinska Razmena sa Zemljama Južne Amerike
        Izuzev Argentine i Brazilije. " Belgrade, Nedeljni komentari
        Instituta za spoljnu trgovinu (II: 41), 1957, pp. 241-243.
        ("Our Foreign Trade with the Countries of Latin America, Except
        for Argentina and Brazil")

2595   Nešić, D. "Zadrugarstvo u Privredi Zemalja Latinske Amerike. "
        Sarajevo, Pregled (XIV: 1, 4-5), 1962, pp. 346-350.
                            ("Cooperatives in the Economies of the Latin American
        Countries")

2596   P. D. (pseud.) "Trgovačka Razmjena Latinske Amerike sa
        Istočnoevropskim Zemljama. " Sarajevo, Pregled (XII: 1-2),
        1961, pp. 195-196.
                        ("Latin America's Trade with the East European
        Countries")

2597   Paligorić, Ljubomir. "Aktuelne Teme Socijalista Latinske
        Amerike. " Sarajevo, Pregled (X, II: 9), 1958, pp. 216-221.
                        ("Current Topics of Latin American
        Socialists")

2598   Paligorić, Ljubomir. "Koncepcije Radničkih i Drugih Progresivnih
        Partija i Pokreta o Osnovnim Pitanjima Društvenog Razvitka u
        Latinskoj Americi. " Sarajevo, Pregled (XVI, II: 7-8), 1964, pp.
        107-125.
                        ("Concepts of the Working Class and Other
        Progressive Parties on the Essential Questions for Social
        Development in Latin America")

2599   Paligorić, Ljubomir. "Latinska Amerika. Osnovne Karakteristike
        Društveno-Politickih Kretanja. " Belgrade, Medunarodni
        radnički i progresivni pokret. Godišnji pre gled 1964. 1965, pp.
        450-457.
                        ("Latin America: Main Characteristics of the
        Socio-Political Processes")

2600   Paligorić, Ljubomir. "O Konsultativnom Komitetu Socijalisticke
        Internacionale za Latinsku Ameriku. " Belgrade, Dokumentacioni
        bilten (II: 2), 1958, pp. 55-56.
                        ("On the Consultative Committee of the
        Socialist International for Latin America")

2601   Paligorić, Ljubomir. "Odnosi Medu Radničkim Partijama i
        Progresivnim Pokretima u Latinskoj Americi. " Zagreb,
        Naše teme (VIII: 11), 1964, pp. 1856-1870.
                        ("Relations Between the Workers' Parties
        and Progressive Movements in Latin America")

2602   Paligorić, Ljubomir. "Regionalne Sindikalne Organizacije
        Latinske Amerike (CTAL i ORIT). " Belgrade, Pregled,
        (XI, II: 11-12), 1959, pp. 466-472.
                        ("Regional Trade Union Organizations
        in Latin America (CTAL and ORIT)"

2603   Paligorić, Ljubomir. "Revolucionarna Prenja u Latinskoj
        Americi. " Belgrade, Socijalizam (III: 1), 1960, pp. 80-104.
                        ("Revolutionary Activities in Latin
        America")

2604   Partonić, Andreja. "Ekonomičeskie Otnošenija Jugoslavii i
        Latinskoj Ameriki. " Belgrade, Meždunarodnaja politika
        (VII: 150), 1956, pp. 14-15.
                        ("Yugoslavia's Economic Relations with
        Latin America")

2605   Partonić, Andreja. "Naši Ekonomski Odnosi sa Latinskom
        Amerikom. " Belgrade, Medjunarodna politika (VII: 150),
        1956, pp. 15-16.
                        ("Our Economic Relations with Latin
        America")

2606   Partonić, Andreja. "Opadanje Robne Razmene sa Zemljama
        Latinske Amerike. " Belgrade, Ekonomska politika (VI: 264),
        1957, pp. 370-371.
                        ("Decreasing Trade with the Countries
        of Latin America")

2607   "Penetracija Sovjetskog Saveza u Privredu Latinske Amerike. "
        Belgrade, Nedeljni komentari Instituta za spoljnu trgovinu
        (IV: 144), 1959, pp. 369-370.
        ("Penetration of the Soviet Union into Latin America's Economy")

2608   Petković, Natalija. "Dr. Carlos Rama: Reperkusije Kubanske
        Revolucije u Latinskoj Americi. " Belgrade, Medjunarodni
        problemi (XV: 2), 1963, pp. 153-156.
                ("Review of the Lecture, Repercussions of
        the Cuban Revolution in Latin America, given by Dr. Carlos Rama
        at the Institute for International Politics in Belgrade on April
        17, 1963")

2609   Petković, Ranko. "Dezatomizacija Latinske Amerike. " Belgrade,
        Medunarodna politika (XIV: 315), 1963,   p. 5.
                ("Denuclearization of Latin America")

2610   Petković, Ranko. "Zur Entatomisierung Lateinsamerikas. " Belgrade,
        Internationale politik (XIV: 315), 1963, pp. 6-7.
                ("Latin America: an Atom-free Zone")

2611   Petrić, S. "Posle Vargasa i Perona. " Belgrade, Medjunarodna
        politika (VI: 138), 1956, pp. 33-41.
                ("After Vargas and Peron")

2612   "Problemi Osnivanja Nove Banke za Razvoj Južne Amerike. "
        Belgrade, Nedeljni komentari Instituta za spoljnu trgovinu
        (III: 116), 1958, pp. 852-853.
        ("Problems of Establishing a New Bank for Latin America's
        Development")

2613   "Program Stabilizacije u Zemljama Južne Amerike. " Belgrade,
        Nedeljni komentari Instituta za spoljnu trgovinu (V: 217), 1960,
        pp. 991-992.
        ("Stabilization Program in the Countries of Latin America")

2614   Pudar, Momo. "Teškoće Interameričke Saradnje. " Sarajevo,
        Pregled (XVII, II: 11), 1965, pp. 473-491.
                ("Difficulties in Inter-American Cooperation")

2615   Radovanović, Ljubomir. "De Gaulles Vorstoss Nach Latinamerika. "
        Belgrade, Internationale politik (XV: 336), 1964, pp. 14-16.
                        ("De Gaulle's Visit to Latin America")

2616   Radovanović, Ljubomir. "Transformacija Mauroeve Doktrine. "
        Belgrade, Medunarodna politika (XIII: 288), 1962, pp. 12-14.
                        (" Transformation of the Monroe
        Doctrine")

2617   Rakić, Franjo. "Medjunarodna Saradnja i Ekonomski Razvoj
        Zemalja Latinske Amerike. " Belgrade, Medjunarodni
        problemi (VI: 3-4), 1955, pp. 159-162.
                        ("International Cooperation and Economic
        Development of Latin American Countries")

2618   Rakić, Sveto. "Dvostruko Pov Ećanje Robne Razmene Sa
        Zemljama Latinske Amerike. " Belgrade, Ekonomska
        politika (IV: 179), 1955, pp. 714-715.
                        ("Two-Fold Increase of Trade with Latin America")

2619   Redžepagić, Sulejman. "Latinska Amerika, Ekvador i Socijalistička
        Revolucija. " Belgrade, Dokumentacioni bilten (IV: 3-4), 1960,
        p. 37.
                        ("Latin America, Ecuador and the
        Socialist Revolution")

2620   Redžepagić, Sulejman. "Nova Strujanja u Latinskoj Americi. "
        Belgrade, Medunarodna politika (XI: 248-249), 1960, pp. 15-17.
                        ("New Trends in Latin America")

2621   Redžepagic, Sulejman. "Prva Konferencija Narodnih Partija
        Latinske Amerike. " Belgrade, Dokumentacioni bilten (IV: 3-4),
        1960, pp. 96-98.
                        ("The First Conference of the Popular
        Parties in Latin America")

2622   Šolman, Andelko. "Socijalizam na Tlu Latinske Amerike. "
Zagreb, Naše teme (VIII: 9), 1964, pp. 1482-1495.
("Socialism on the Soil of Latin America")

2623   Sretenović, Mladen. "Privredna Konferencija Zemalja
Latinske Amerike. " Belgrade, Nova trgovina (X: 11),
1957, pp. 651-653.
("Economic Conference of the Latin
American Countries")

2624   Stanovnik, Janez. "Ekonomske Teškoće Latinske Amerike. "
Belgrade, Naša stvarnost (XII: 11), 1958, pp. 550-553.
("Economic Difficulties of Latin America")

2625   Tito, Josip Broz. "Izjava o Cilju Posjete Zemljama Latinske
Amerike. " Belgrade, Medunarodna politika (XIV: 323),
1963, p. 20.
("On the Aim of Visiting Latin America")

2626   Todorović, Srbislav. "Jugoslovenska Razmena sa Zemljama
Latinske Amerike u 1961. " Belgrade, Nedeljni komentari
Instituta za spoljnu trgovinu (VI: 237), 1961, p. 392.
("Yugoslavia's Trade with the Countries
of Latin America in 1961")

2627   "Trgovina sa Zemljama Južne Amerike. Privredni Izveštaj za
1956 Godinu. " Belgrade, Institut za spoljnu trgovinu, 1957,
pp. 217-218.
("Trade with the Countries of Latin America: Economic
Report for 1956")

2628   Trnokopović, Dragoslav. "U Južnoj Americi Raste Tendencija
ka Multilaterarnosti Platnog Prometa. " Belgrade, Hempro
bilten (VI: 7-8), 1956, pp. 24-30.
("Increasing Tendency for Multilateral
Financial Transactions in Latin America")

2629   Vuković, Branislav. "Radnički Pokret i Društveno-Politički
        Uslovi u Nerazvijenim Zemljama." Belgrade, Sedma sila,
        1965, pp. 239-245, 279-290.
                    ("Working Class Movement and Social-
        Political Conditions in the Underdeveloped Countries")

2630   Vukušić, Branko. "Nova Strujanja u Latinskoj Americi."
        Belgrade, Medjunarodna politika (X: 223), 1959, pp. 11-13.
                    ("New Trends in Latin America")

2631   "Zaostavanje Konkurencije u Latinskoj Americi." Belgrade,
        Nova trgovina (X: 4), 1957, pp. 246-248.
        ("Intensification of Competition in Latin America")

2632   "Zemlje Južne Amerike." Belgrade, Zemlje i problemi (VI: 11),
        1958, pp. 1-48.
        ("The Countries of Latin America")

2633   Živančević, Miloš. "Akcija Zemalja EEZ za Pomoć Latinskoj
        Americi." Belgrade, Nedeljni komentari Instituta za spoljnu
        trgovinu (VIII: 339), 1963, pp. 555-557.
                    ("Action of the EEC Countries in Aiding
        Latin America")

2634   Živančević, Miloš. "Direktne Investicije SAD u Zemljama
        Latinske Amerike." Belgrade, Nedeljni komentari Instituta
        za spoljnu trgovinu (IX: 365), 1964, pp. 14-15.
                    ("Direct Investments of the USA in the
        Countries of Latin America")

2635   Živančević, Miloš. "Drugi Period Zasedanja Zemalja Latinsko-
        Američke Zone Slobodne Trgovine." Belgrade, Nedeljni
        komentari Instituta za spoljnu trgovinu (VIII: 324), 1963, pp. 167-168.
                    ("The Second Period of Sessions of the Latin
        American Free Trade Association")

2636 Živančević, Miloš. "Monetarna Politika Zemalja Latinske
Amerike u 1962. " Belgrade, Nedeljni komentari Instituta
za spoljnu politiku (VIII: 340), 1963, pp. 588-589.
("Monetary Policy of Latin America in
1962")

2637 Živančević, Miloš. "Multilateralan Sistem Financiranja
Izvoza u Zemljama Latinske Amerike. " Belgrade, Nedeljni
komentari Instituta za spoljnu trgovinu (VIII: 357), 1963, pp.
1017-1018.
("Multilateral System of Financing Exports
in Latin America")

2638 Živančević, Miloš. "Perspektive Razvoja Latinskoameričkog
Uvoza Mašina i Opreme. " Belgrade, Nedeljni komentari
Instituta za spoljnu trgovinu (IX: 371), 1964, pp. 178-180.
("Prospects for Furthering Latin
American Imports of Machines and Equipment")

2639 Živančević, Miloš. "Povećanje Nacionalnog Bruto Proizvoda
u Zemljama Latinske Amerike u Toku 1962. " Belgrade,
Nedeljni komentari Instituta za spoljnu trgovinu (VIII: 330),
1963, pp. 322-323.
("Increase of the Gross National Product
in the Countries of Latin America During 1962")

2640 Živančević, Miloš. "Privredni Razvoj Latinske Amerike i
Trgovinski Odnosi sa Jugoslavijom. " Belgrade, Problemi
spoljne trgovine i konjukture (4), 1963, pp. 31-43.
("Economic Development of Latin America
and its Commercial Relations with Yugoslavia")

2641 Živančević, Miloš. "Projekti u Latinskoj Americi Čiju će
Izgradnju Finansirati Posebni Fond Ujedinjenih Nacija. "
Belgrade, Nedeljni komentari Instituta za spoljnu trgovinu
(VIII: 326), 1963, pp. 219-220.
("Construction Projects in Latin America
Financed by the Special Fund of the United Nations")

2642   Živančević, Miloš. "Spoljnotrgovinska Razmena Izmedu
        Jugoslavije i Zemalja Latinske Amerike." Belgrade, Nedeljni
        komentari Instituta za spoljnu trgovinu (VII: 285), 1962, pp. 437-438.
                    ("Foreign Trade Between Yugoslavia and the
        Countries of Latin America")

2643   Živančević, Miloš. "Trgovinska Razmena Jugoslavije sa Zemljama
        Latinske Amerike u Toku Poslednjih pet Godina." Belgrade,
        Nedeljni komentari Instituta za spoljnu trgovinu (VI: 231), 1961,
        pp. 245-246.
                    ("Yugoslavia's Trade with the Countries of
        Latin America During the Last Five Years")

2644   Živančević, Miloš. "Zaključci Pregovora Zemalja Članica
        Slobodne Trgovinske Zone Latinske Amerike (LAFTA)."
        Belgrade, Nedeljni komentari Instituta za spoljnu trgovinu (VII: 272),
        1962, pp. 69-70.
                    ("Conclusions of the Negotiations Held Among
        the Members of the Latin American Free Trade Association")

2645   Živanović, Mihailo. "Potrošnja Naftinih Derivata u Zemljama
        Latinske Amerike." Belgrade, Nedeljni komentari Instituta
        za spoljnu trgovinu (VII: 311), 1962, pp. 1150-1152.
                    ("Expenditure of Naphtha Derivatives in
        Latin America")

2646   "Značajni Dogadaji u Radničkom i Oslobodilačkim Pokretima."
        Belgrade, Informativni pregled (1), 1966, pp. 49-52.
        ("Significant Events in the Working Class and Liberation Movements")

ARGENTINA

2647   "Argentina. " Belgrade, Zemlje i problemi (IV: 2), 1956, pp. 1-57. ("Argentina")

2648   "Argentina Dobila Kredit od Medunarodne Banke za Obnovu i Razvoj. " Belgrade, Nedeljni komentari Instituta za spoljnu trgovinu (I: 21), 1956, pp. 13. ("Argentina Obtained a Credit from the International Bank for Reconstruction and Development")

2649   "Argentina i Pariski Klub u 1958 Godini. " Belgrade, Nedeljni komentari Instituta za spoljnu trgovinu (IV: 133), 1959, p. 120. ("Argentina and the Paris Club in 1958")

2650   "Argentina i Svetsko Tržište. " Belgrade, Ekonomska politika (III: 119), 1954, p. 557. ("Argentina and the World Market")

2651   "Argentina Pristupila Konvenciji o Statusu Izbeglica. " Belgrade, Sluzbeni list FNRJ dodatak: Medjunarodni ugovori i drugi sporazumi (X: 5), 1962, pp. 103-104. ("Argentina Joined the Convention on the Status of Refugees")

2652   "Argentinska Proizvodnja Cementa. " Belgrade, Nedeljni komentari Instituta za spoljnu trgovinu (I: 17), 1956, pp. 7-8. ("Argentina's Cement Production")

2653   "Argentinska Proizvodnja Polivinil Hlorida. " Belgrade, Nedeljni komentari Instituta za spoljnu trgovinu (V: 203), 1960, p. 638. ("Polyvinyl Chloride Production in Argentina")

2654   Halfter, Rudolf. "Neonacionalsocijalizam u Argentini?." Belgrade, Trideset dana (X: 83), 1952, pp. 1021-1025.
("Neo-National Socialism in Argentina")

2655   Hubeni, Marijan. "Šta se Dešava u Argentini?" Belgrade, Ekonomska politika (II: 58), 1953, pp. 372-374.
("What is Happening in Argentina?")

2656   "Hustisijalizam - Socijalna Politika Bez Ekonomske Osnove." Belgrade, Ekonomska politika (IV: 183), 1955, pp. 797.
("Justicialism - Social Policy Without Economic Basis")

2657   Ivanović, Tadija. "Argentina Traži Mašine Alatljike." Belgrade, Nedeljni komentari Instituta za spoljnu trgovinu (VII: 296), 1962, pp. 752-753.
("Argentina in Search of Machine Tools")

2658   "Jugoslovensko-Argentinska Trgovinska Razmena u 1960." Belgrade, Nedeljni komentari Instituta za spoljnu trgovinu (V: 219), 1960, pp. 1044-1045.
("Yugoslav - Argentine Trade in 1960")

2659   Južnič, Stane. "Argentina." Belgrade, Medunarodni radnički pokret. Godišnji pregled 1961. 1962, pp. 25-32.
("Argentina")

2660   Južnič, Stane. "Argentina. Peronizam i Radnički Pokret." Belgrade, Medunarodni radnički pokret. Godišnji pregled 1960. 1961, pp. 458-467.
("Argentina, Peronism and the Working Class Movement")

2661   Južnič, Stane. "Argentina Posle Prošlogodišnjih Izbora. "
        Belgrade, Naša stvarnost (XV: 2), 1961, pp. 201-213.
                ("Argentina After Last Year's Elections")

2662   Južnič, Stane. "Izbori i Položaj Frondizija. " Belgrade,
        Medunarodna politika (XI: 241), 1960, pp. 8-9.
                ("Elections and Frondizi's Position")

2663   Južnič, Stane. "Peronizam za Vreme i Posle Perona. "
        Belgrade, Medunarodni problemi (XI: 2), 1959, pp. 68-79.
                ("Peronism During the Time of Peron and
        After")

2664   Kićović, Božidar. "Previranje u Argentini. " Belgrade, Medunarodna
        politika (VII: 150), 1956, pp. 17-18.
                ("Turmoil in Argentina")

2665   "Kriza Argentinskog Tržišta Stoke. " Belgrade, Nedeljni
        komentari Instituta za spoljnu trgovinu (I: 7), 1956, pp. 7-8.
        ("Crisis of Argentina's Livestock Market")

2666   Kukoleča, Stevan. "Argentina. " Belgrade, Uloga države u
        privredi, serija V, 1956, pp. 135-146.
                ("Argentina")

2667   Kukoč, Eduard. "Porast Učešca Argentinske Flote u Prevozu
        Robe za Južnu Ameriku. " Belgrade, Nedeljni komentari Instituta za
        spoljnu trgovinu (VII: 307), 1962, pp. 1047-1048.
                ("Increased Participation of the Argentine
        Merchant Marine in Shipping Goods to South America")

2668   Kunc, Marijan. "Argentina. " Belgrade, Medjunarodni radnički
        pokret. Godišnji pregled 1963. 1964, pp. 380-389.
                ("Argentina")

2669 Ličen, Mirko. "Življenje Naših Ljudi v Argentini." Ljubljana,
Tovariš (VIII: 52), 1952, pp. 1117-1118.
("The Lives of our People in Argentina")

2670 M. K. (pseud.) "Argentina." Belgrade, Medunarodni radnički
i drugi progresivni pokreti. Godišnji pregled 1965. 1966, pp.
75-87.
("Argentina")

2671 Marjanović, Filip. "Mogućnosti Ekonomske Saradnje sa
Argentinom." Belgrade, Medunarodna politika (IX: 196),
1958, pp. 14-15.
("Possibilities for Economic Cooperation
with Argentina")

2672 Matačić, Ive. "Što se Dešava u Argentini?" Belgrade, Medunarodna
politika (II: 10), 1953, pp. 21-22.
("What is Happening in Argentina? ")

2673 Mihovilović, Ive. "Nove Perspektive Argentine." Belgrade,
Medunarodna politika (IX: 194), 1958, pp. 11-13.
("Argentina's new Prospects")

2674 "Multilateralni Platni Ugovor Argentine." Belgrade, Nedeljni
komentari Instituta za spoljnu trgovinu (III: 82), 1958, pp. 82-83.
("Argentina's Multilateral Payment Agreement")

2675 "Napori Argentine za Prelaz na Multilateralizam." Belgrade,
Nedeljni komentari Instituta za spoljnu trgovinu (I: 2), 1956,
pp. 18-19.
("Argentina's Efforts to Turn to Multilateralism")

2676   Nikolić, Rade. "Prvi Nacionalni Filozofski Kongres u Argentini. "
        Zagreb, Filozofski pregled (I: 1), 1953, pp. 44-46.
                ("The First Philosophical Congress in Argentina")

2677   Olbina, Josip. "Argentinsko Tržište Sirovih Koža. " Belgrade,
        Preradivačka industrija (II: 7-8), 1951, p. 53.
                ("Argentina's Raw Leather Market")

2678   Opacić, Nine. "Staro i Novo u Argentini. " Belgrade, Medunarodna
        politika (XIV: 320-321), 1963, pp. 9-10.
                ("Old and New in Argentina")

2679   "Opadanje Argentinske Spoljne Trgovine. " Belgrade, Nedeljni
        komentari Instituta za spoljnu trgovinu (IV: 143), 1959, pp. 350-351.
        ("Decrease of Argentina's Foreign Trade")

2680   "Opadanje Brojnog Stanja Goveda u Argentini. " Belgrade, Nedeljni
        komentari Instituta za spoljnu trgovinu (III: 105), 1958, pp. 597-598.
        ("Decrease of the Number of Cattle in Argentina")

2681   Paligorić, Ljubomir. "Argentinski Politički Mozaik. " Sarajevo,
        Pregled (X: II, 4), 1958, pp. 383-387.
                        ("Argentine Political Mosaic")

2682   Paligorić, Ljubomir. "Zbivanja na Političkoj Sceni Argentine. "
        Belgrade, Naša stvarnost (XIV: 5), 1960, pp. 620-626.
                        ("Events on the Political Scene of Argentina")

2683   "Porast Dohotka u Argentinskoj Poljoprivredi. " Belgrade, Nedeljni
        komentari Instituta za spoljnu trgovinu (I: 5), 1956, p. 5.
        ("Increase of Income in Argentina's Agriculture")

2684 "Porast Industriske Proizvodnje u Argentini. " Belgrade, Nedeljni komentari Instituta za spoljnu trgovinu (V: 190), 1960, p. 329. ("Increase of Industrial Production in Argentina")

2685 "Porast Jugoslovensko-Argentinske Trgovinske Razmene. " Belgrade, Nedeljni komentari Instituta za spoljnu trgovinu (V: 187), 1960, pp. 264-265. ("Increase of Yugoslav-Argentine Trade")

2686 "Privreda Argentine u 1950-1951 Godini. " Belgrade, Bilten narodne banke Jugoslavije (VI: 277), 1951, pp. 14-15. ("Argentina's Economy in 1950-1951")

2687 R. T. (pseud.) "Pred Izbore u Argentini. " Belgrade, Trideset dana (IX: 68-69), 1951, pp. 109-113.
      ("In the Face of the Elections in Argentina")

2688 Redžepagić, Sulejman. "Rascep u Socijalistickoj Pratiji Argentine. " Belgrade, Dokumentacioni bilten (II: 5), 1958, p. 82.
      ("Split in the Socialist Party of Argentina")

2689 Redžepagić, Sulejman. "Sindikalni Pokret u Argentini i Peronizam. " Sarajevo, Pregled (XV, II: 7-8), 1963, pp. 61-75.
      ("Trade Union Movement in Argentina and Peronism")

2690 Redžepagić, Sulejman. "Socijalistička Partija Argentine." Belgrade, Dokumentacioni bilten (IV: 3-4), 1960, pp. 4-6.
      ("The Socialist Party of Argentina")

2691 "Reforma Bankarskog Sistema u Argentini. " Belgrade, Nedeljni komentari Instituta za spoljnu trgovinu (I: 15), 1956, p. 15. ("Reform of the Banking System in Argentina")

2692   Tošić, D. "Naša Robna Razmena sa Argentinom i Spoljnotrgovinske
        Teškoće te Zemlje. " Belgrade, Ekonomski dnevnik trgovinske
        komore FNRJ (II: 162), 1952, p. 3.
                ("Our Trade with Argentina and Foreign Trade Difficulties
        of that Country")

2693   Živančević, Miloš. "Argentina Još Uvek Suočena sa Ekonomskim
        Teškoćama. " Belgrade, Nedeljni komentari Instituta za spoljnu
        trgovinu (VII: 307), 1962, pp. 1051-1052.
                ("Argentina is Still Confronted with Economic
        Difficulties")

2694   Živančević, Miloš. "Argentina Nastavlja Program Stabilizacije. "
        Belgrade, Nedeljni komentari Instituta za spoljnu trgovinu (VII: 283),
        1962, pp. 376-378.
                ("Argentina is Continuing the Stabilization
        Program")

2695   Živančević, Miloš. "Oživljavanje rivredne Aktivnosti u Argentini. "
        Belgrade, Nedeljni komentari Instituta za spoljnu trgovinu (IX: 402),
        1964, pp. 941-943.
                ("Revival of Argentina's Economic Activity")

2696   Živančević, Miloš. "Perspektive Razvoja Argentinske Industrije. "
        Belgrade, Nedeljni komentari Instituta za spoljnu trgovinu (IX: 368),
        1964, pp. 98-100.
                ("Prospects for Developing Industry in Argentina")

2697   Živančević, Miloš. "Petogodišnji Plan Privrednog Razboja Argentine. "
        Belgrade, Nedeljni komentari Instituta za spoljnu trgovinu (IX: 413),
        1964, pp. 1220-1221.
                ("Five Years Plan for Argentina's Economic
        Development")

BOLIVIA

2698   Almuli, Jaša. "Preokret u Boliviji. " Belgrade, Socijalizam
(VIII: 2), 1965, pp. 257-264.
("Total Change in Bolivia")

2699   Južnič, Stane. "Bolivija. " Belgrade, Medunarodni radnički i
progresivni pokreti. Godišnji pregled 1964. 1965, pp. 458-463.
("Bolivia")

2700   Južnič, Stane. "Bolivija. " Belgrade, Medunarodni radnički i
drugi progresivni pokreti. Godišnji pregled 1965. 1966, pp. 108-114.
("Bolivia")

2701   Južnič, Stane. "Bolivijska Drama. " Belgrade, Medunarodna
politika (XVI: 364), 1965, pp. 10-11.
("The Bolivian Drama")

2702   Košta, Vjekoslav. "Bolivija. " Belgrade, Medjunarodni radnički
pokret. Godišnji pregled 1960. 1961, pp. 506-612.
("Bolivia")

2703   Košta, Vjekoslav. "Bolivija. " Belgrade, Medunarodni radnički
pokret. Godišnji pregled 1961. 1962, pp. 49-53.
("Bolivia")

2704   Lilić, Lazar. "Problemi Suvremene Bolivije. " Belgrade, Naša
stvarnost (VIII: 7-8), 1954, pp. 108-116.
("Problems of Contemporary Bolivia")

2705   Lupis-Vukić, Ivan. "Bračani u Boliviji. " Split, Brački zbornik
(22), 1954, pp. 176-185.
                ("The Immigrants from the Island of Brač to
Bolivia")

2706   "Odluka o Ratifikaciji Protokola Izmedju Jugoslavije i Čehoslovačke
        o Zastupanju Interesa Cehoslovačke u Republici Bolivija. " Belgrade,
        Službeni list SFRJ dodatak: Medjunarodni ugovori i drugi sporazumi
        (XIII: 7), 1965, pp. 593-594.
        ("Decree of Ratification of the Protocol Between Yugoslavia and
        Czechoslovakia on Representing Czechoslovakia's Interests in the
        Republic of Bolivia")

2707   "Odluka o Ratifikaciji Protokola o Ekonomskoj Saradnji sa Bolivijom. "
        Belgrade, Službeni list SFRJ-dodatak: Medjunarodni ugovori u
        drugi sporazumi (XII: 5), 1964, pp. 439-440.
        ("Decree of Ratification of the Protocol on Economic Cooperation
        with Bolivia")

2708   Opačić, Nine. "Prevrat u Boliviji. " Belgrade, Medjunarodna
        politika (XV: 351), 1964, pp. 17-18.
                    ("Coup d'État in Bolivia")

2709   Redžepagić, Sulejman. "Dve Taktike u Dve Faze Radničke Borbe
        u Boliviji. " Belgrade, Dokumentacioni bilten (IV: 3-4), 1960,
        pp. 7-13.
                        ("Two Tactics and Two Stages in the
        Struggle of the Working Class in Bolivia")

2710   "Stupila na Snagu Konvencija o Saradnji na Polju Prosvete, Nauke
        i Kulture Izmedju Vlade Jugoslavije i Vlade Bolivije. " Belgrade,
        Službeni list SFRJ-dodatak: Medjunarodni ugovori i drugi sporazumi
        (XI: 13), 1963, p. 822.
        ("Enforcement of the Convention for Cooperation in the Field of
        Education, Science and Culture Between the Government of
        Yugoslavia and the Government of Bolivia")

2711   "Trgovinski Sporazum Izmedju Republike Bolivije i Federativne
        Narodne Republike Jugoslavije. La Paz, 8 oktobra 1954. "
        Belgrade, Medjunarodni ugovori Federativna Narodne Republike
        Jugoslavije (80), 1956, pp. 1-7.
        ("Trade Agreement Between the Federated People's Republic of
        Yugoslavia and the Republic of Bolivia")

2712   "Uredba o Ratifikaciji Konvencije o Saradnji na Polju Prosvete,
        Nauke i Kulture Izmedju Jugoslavije i Bolivije. " Belgrade,
        Sluzbeni list FNRJ -dodatak: Medjunarodni ugovori i drugi
        sporazumi (X: 10), 1962, pp. 41-42.
        ("Act of Ratification of the Convention on Cooperation in the Field
        of Education, Science and Culture Between Yugoslavia and Bolivia")

2713   "Uredba o Ratifikaciji Sporazuma o Finansijskoj i Tehničkoj
        Saradnji sa Bolivijom. " Belgrade, Službeni list SFRJ-dodatak:
        Medjunarodni ugovori i drugi sporazumi (XII: 5), 1964, pp. 395-397.
        ("Act of Ratification: Agreement on Financial and Technical
        Cooperation with Bolivia")

2714   "Uredba o Ratifikaciji Trgovinskog Sporazuma Izmedu Jugoslavije
        i Bolivije. " Belgrade, Službeni list SFRJ - dodatak: Medunarodni
        ugovori i drugi sporazumi (XIII: 2), 1965, pp. 31-32.
        ("Act of Ratification of the Commercial Agreement Between Yugoslavia
        and Bolivia")

2715   Živančević, Miloš. "Bolivija Privrema Monetarnu Reformu. "
        Belgrade, Nedeljni komentari Instituta za spoljnu trgovinu
        (VI: 261), 1961, p. 870.
                        ("Bolivia is Preparing a Monetary Reform")

2716   Živančević, Milos. "Privredni Razvoj Bolivije i Trgovinski
        Odnosi sa Jugoslavijom. " Belgrade, Nedeljni komentari
        Instituta za spoljnu trgovinu (VIII: 355), 1963, pp. 947-951.
                        ("Economic Development of Bolivia and its
        Commercial Relations with Yugoslavia")

2717   Živančević, Miloš. "Privredni Razvoj Bolivije u 1963. "
        Belgrade, Nedeljni komentari Instituta za spoljnu trgovinu (IX:
        381), 1964, pp. 418-419.
                        ("Bolivia's Economic Development in
        1963")

BRAZIL

2718   A. B. (pseud.) "Brazil. " Belgrade, <u>Medunarodni radnički i drugi progresivni pokreti. Godišnji pregled 1965.</u> 1966, pp. 115-126.
        ("Brazil")

2719   Adamović, Ljubiša. "Brazilija: Aktuelni Ekonomski Problemi. " Belgrade, <u>Ekonomska politika</u> (III: 115), 1954, pp. 1-11.
        (Brazil: Current Economic Problems")

2720   Almuli, Jaša. "Brazil. " Belgrade, <u>Medunarodni radnički i progresivni pokreti. Godišnji pregled 1964.</u> 1965, pp. 464-477.
        ("Brazil")

2721   Almuli, Jaša. "Brazil u Odlučujucoj Fazi. " Belgrade, <u>Medunarodna politika</u> (XV: 330), 1964, pp. 22-24.
        ("Brazil in the Determinative Phase")

2722   Almuli, Jaša. "Brazil Ide Udesno. " Belgrade, <u>Medunarodna politika</u> (XVI: 375), 1965, pp. 11-13.
        ("Brazil is Shifting to the Right")

2723   Almuli, Jaša. "Interes za Braziliju Sve Više Raste. " Belgrade, <u>Ekonomska politika</u> (I: 25), 1952, pp. 496-497.
        ("The Increasing Interest in Brazil")

2724   Almuli, Jaša. "Preokret u Brazilu. " Belgrade, <u>Socijalizam</u> (VII: 6), 1964, pp. 800-809.
        ("Total Change in Brazil")

2725   Bjelinski, Bruno. "Moji Susreti sa Brazilijanskom Djecom. " Zagreb, <u>Radio Zagreb</u> (VIII: 49), 1952, pp. 3-11.
        ("My Meetings with Brazilian Children")

2726   "Brazil Ratifikovao Konvenciju o Statusu Izbeglica. " Belgrade,
        Službeni list FNRJ- dodatak: Medjunarodni ugovori i drugi
        sporazumi (IX: 9), 1961, p. 94.
        ("Brazil Ratified the Convention on the Status of Refugees")

2727   "Brazilija. " Belgrade, Zemlje i problemi (IV: 5), 1956, pp. 1-55.
        ("Brazil")

2728   "Brazilija Prihvatila Protokol Kojim se Stavljaju Droge Pod
           Medjunarodnu Kontrolu. " Belgrade, Službeni list FNRJ-dodatak:
        Medjunarodni ugovori i drugi sporazumi (VIII: 6), 1960, p. 104.
        ("Brazil Accepted the Protocol by which Drugs are to be put Under
        International Control")

2729   "Brazilija Pristupila Medunarodnoj Konvenciji Koja se Odnosi na
           Medunarodni Institut za Hladjenje. " Belgrade, Službeni list
        FNRJ- dodatak: Medunarodni ugovori i drugi sporazumi (VIII: 12),
        1960, p. 103.
        ("Brazil Joined the International Convention Concerning the
        International Institute for Refrigeration")

2730   "Brazilijanski Divlji Zapad. " Belgrade, Duga (XVI: 774), 1960,
           pp. 12-13.
        ("The Brazilian Wild West")

2731   "Britanski Izvoz u Braziliji se Poboljšava. " Belgrade, Nedeljni
           komentari Instituta za spoljnu trgovinu (I: 4), 1956, p. 15.
        ("British Exports to Brazil are Increasing")

2732   Butorac, Milan. "Carica Voda - Amazonka. " Zagreb, Priroda
           (XXXVI: 1), 1949, pp. 1-7.
        ("The Empress Water- The Amazon River")

2733   Dragomanović, Vladimir. "Privredni Problemi Brazilije. " Belgrade,
        Medunarodni problemi (V: 4), 1953, pp. 150-155.
        ("Economic Problems of Brazil")

2734   "Industriski Razvoj u Braziliji. " Belgrade, Nedeljni komentari
        Instituta za spoljnu trgovinu (II: 75), 1957,   p. 1046.
        ("Industrial Development in Brazil")

2735   "Iza jva Brazila u Vezi sa Kovnencijom o Statusu Izbeglica. "
        Belgrade, Službeni list FNRJ- dodatak: Medjunarodni ugovori
        i drugi sporazumi (IX: 8), 1961,   p. 79.
        ("Brazil's Declaration Concerning the Convention on the Status
        of Refugees")

2736   "Izvozne Premije u Braziliji. " Belgrade, Nedeljni komentari
        Instituta za spoljnu trgovinu (I: 19), 1956, pp. 15-16.
        ("Export Rewards in Brazil")

2737   "Jugoslovensko-Brazilijanska Spoljnotrgovinska Razmena."
        Belgrade, Nedeljni komentari Instituta za spoljnu trgovinu
        (IV: 172), 1959, pp. 1033-1034.
        ("Yugoslav - Brazilian Foreign Trade")

2738   Južnič, Stane. "Društveno-Političke Komponente Savremenog
        Brazila. " Belgrade, Naša stvarnost (XV: 5), 1961, pp. 536-555.
                    ("Socio-Political Components of Contemporary
        Brazil")

2739   Južnič, Stane. "Novo ob Starem u Braziliji. " Ljubljana,
        Vprašanja naših dni (II: 11), 1961, pp. 364-367.
                    ("New and Old in Brazil")

2740   M. O. (pseud.) "Brazilija in Združene Drzave. " Ljubljana,
        Naši razgledi (I: 9), 1952, p. 9.
                    ("Brazil and the United States")

2741 Marjanović, Milan. "Smrt Našeg Istraživača u Džunglama Ama Zonke." Zagreb, Otkrica (II: 1), 1955, pp. 33-40.
("Our Explorer's Death in the Amazon Jungles")

2742 Milojević, Borivoje Z. "Geografske Oblasti i Glavni Gradovi Brazilije." Belgrade, Nauka i priroda (IX: 10), 1956, pp. 394-404.
("Geographic Regions and Capitals of Brazil")

2743 Mužić, Vladimir. "Školstvo u Braziliji." Zagreb, Pedagoški rad (XI: 8), 1956, pp. 475-477.
("Education in Brazil")

2744 "Nasa Spoljnotrgovinska Razmena sa Brazilijom." Belgrade, Nedeljni komentari Instituta za spoljnu trgovinu (III: 118), 1958, pp. 900-901.
("Our Foreign Trade with Brazil")

2745 "Nepovoljan Razvoj Brazilijanske Spoljne Trgovine." Belgrade, Nedeljni komentari Instituta za spoljnu trgovinu (IV: 170), 1959, pp. 978-979.
("Unfavourable Development of Brazil's Foreign Trade")

2746 "Odluka o Odobrenju Protokola o Radu Mešovite Jugoslovensko- Brazilske Komisije za Robnu Razmenu." Belgrade, Službeni list FNRJ - dodatak: Medjunarodni ugovori i drugi sporazumi (X: 8), 1962, pp. 37-39.
("Decree on the Approval of the Protocol on the Work of the Yugoslav-Brazilian Mixed Committee for Exchange of Commodities")

2747 Opačić, Nine. "Brazil Pred Novim Vidicima." Belgrade, Medjunarodna politika (XII: 263), 1961, pp. 8-9.
("Brazil in the Face of New Prospects")

2748   "Privatne Inostrane Investicije u Braziliji. " Belgrade, <u>Nedeljni</u>
        <u>komentari Instituta za Spoljnu trgovinu</u> (II: 40), 1957,   p. 214.
        ("Private Foreign Investments in Brazil")

2749   "Privredna Situacija Brazilije. " Belgrade, <u>Bilten Narodne banke</u>
        <u>Jugoslavije</u> (VI: 268), 1951, pp. 14-15.
        ("The Economic Situation in Brazil")

2750   "Prva Dejstva Multilateralizma u Braziliji. " Belgrade, <u>Nedeljni</u>
        <u>komentari Instituta za spoljnu trgovinu</u> (I: 4), 1956, pp. 14-15.
        ("The First Effects of Multilateralism in Brazil")

2751   Rakicević, Tomislav L. "Brazilija- Zemlja Kafe. " Belgrade,
        <u>Nauka i priroda</u> (IX: 5), 1956, pp. 213-218.
                            ("Brazil - the Land of Coffee")

2752   "Razvoj Industrije Cementa u Braziliji. " Belgrade, <u>Nedeljni</u>
        <u>komentari Instituta za spoljnu trgovinu</u> (IV: 145), 1959,   p. 387.
        ("Development of Brazil's Cement Industry")

2753   Redžepagić, Sulejman. "Brazil. Opšti Pregled Situacije u Zemlji. "
        Belgrade, <u>Medunarodni radnički pokret. Godišnji pregled 1961,</u>
        1962, pp. 54-62.
                        ("Brazil: General Survey of the Situation
        in the Country")

2754   Redžepagić, Sulejman. "Komunistička Partija Brazila. " Belgrade,
        <u>Dokumentacioni bilten</u> (IV: 3-4), 1960, pp. 14-16.
                        ("The Communist Party of Brazil")

2755   Sekelj, Tibor. "Samanizam (Vračanje) Kod Indijanaca za Rio
        Branco u Braziliji. " Zagreb, <u>Priroda</u> (LX: 1), 1953, pp. 7-12.
                        ("Shamanism (Divination) of the Indians at
        Rio Branco in Brazil")

2756   "Socijalistička Partija Brazilije. (Program i Neposredni Zahtevi). "
        Belgrade, Dokumentacioni bilten (I: 6), 1957, pp. 67-68.
        ("Socialist Party of Brazil: Program and Immediate Requests")

2757   "Ulaganja u Brazilijansku Privredu. " Belgrade, Nedeljni komentari
        Instituta za spoljnu trgovinu (V: 203), 1960, pp. 642-644.
        ("Investments in Brazil's Economy")

2758   "Uredba o Ratifikaciji Kulturne Konvencije Izmedju Jugoslavije i
        Brazila. " Belgrade, Sluzbeni list SFRJ- dodatak: Medjunarodni
        ugovori i drugi sporazumi (XI: 13), 1963, pp. 776-777.
        ("Ratification of the Cultural Convention Between Yugoslavia and
        Brazil")

2759   "Veliki Brazilijanski Uvoz Transportnih Sredstava." Belgrade,
        Nedeljni komentari Instituta za spoljnu trgovinu (III: 120),
        1958, pp. 938-939.
        ("Great Importance of the Means of Transport to Brazil")

2760   Vitez, Milan. "Brazilski Izvoz Gvozdene Rude. " Belgrade,
        Nedeljni komentari Instituta za spoljnu trgovinu (VIII: 353), 1963,
        pp. 902-903.
                    ("Brazilian Exports of Ore")

2761   Vitez, Milan. "Buduće Potrebe Brazila u Mašinama Alatljikama. "
        Belgrade, Nedeljni komentari Instituta za spoljnu trgovinu
        (VIII: 344), 1963, pp. 686-688.
                    ("Brazil's Further Needs for Machine Tools")

2762   Vitez, Milan. "Nepovoljan Razvoj Automobilske Industrije Brazila. "
        Belgrad, Nedeljni komentari Instituta za spoljnu trgovinu
        (VIII: 342), 1963, pp. 631-632.
                    ("Unfavorable Development of Brazil's Automobile
        Industry")

2763   Živančević, Miloš. "Privreda Brazila u 1962." Belgrade,
        Nedeljni komentari Instituta za spoljnu trgovinu (VIII: 319),
        1963, pp. 43-45.
                        ("Brazil's Economy in 1962")

2764   Živančević, Miloš. "Privredna Situacija Brazila i Trgovinski
        Odnosi sa Jugoslavijom." Belgrade, Nedeljni komentari
        Instituta za spoljnu trgovinu (VIII: 352), 1963, pp. 865-869.
                        ("Economic Situation of Brazil and its
        Commercial Relations with Yugoslavia."

2765   Živančević, Miloš. "Razvoj Brazilske Privrede." Belgrade,
        Nedeljni komentari Instituta za spoljnu trgovinu (IX: 380),
        1964, pp. 395-397.
                        ("Development of Brazil's Economy")

2766   Živančević, Miloš. "Reforme u Brazilu i Borba Protiv
        Inflacije." Belgrade, Nedeljni komentari Instituta za
        spoljnu trgovinu (VII: 286), 1962, pp. 457-458.
                        ("Reforms in Brazil and the Struggle Against
        Inflation")

2767   Živančević, Miloš. "Trogodišnji Plan Privrednog Razvoja
        Brazila." Belgrade, Nedeljni komentari Instituta za spoljnu
        trgovinu (IX: 410), 1964, pp. 1150-1151.
                        ("Three Year Plan for Brazil's Economic
        Development")

CENTRAL AMERICA

2768   "Centralna Amerika - Karipsko Područje. " Belgrade, Radio
Belgrade (III: 17), 1955, pp. 1-53.
("Central America: The Caribbean Area")

2769   Južnič, Stane. "Centralna Amerika. " Belgrade, Medunarodni
radnički i drugi progresivni pokreti. Godišnji pregled 1965.
1966, pp. 150-156.
("Central America")

2770   Kos, Francek. "Pisma iz Centralne Amerike. " Ljubljana,
Nasi razgledi (IV: 5), 1955, pp. 103-104.
("Letters from Central America")

2771   M. M. (pseud.) "Centralna Amerika. " Belgrade, Medunarodni
radnički i progresivni pokreti. Godišnji pregled 1964. 1965,
pp. 478-486.
("Central America")

2772   M. O. (pseud.) "Centralna Amerika. " Ljubljana, Obzornik,
(1), 1955, pp. 22-25.
("Central America")

2773   M. R. (pseud.) "Privredna Integracija Centralne Amerike. "
Belgrade, Naše teme (X: 1-2), 1966, pp. 285-295.
("Economic Integration in Central America")

2774   Živančević, Miloš. "Osnivanje Centralnoameričke Konpenzacione
Komore. " Belgrade, Nedeljni komentari Instituta za spoljnu
trgovinu (VI: 253), 1961, p. 714.
         ("Establishing the Central American Customs
Union")

CHILE

2775   Almuli, Jaša. "Smisao Cileanskih Izbora." Belgrade, Socijalizam
(VII: 10), 1964, pp. 1341-1348.
("Sense of the Chilean Elections")

2776   Almuli, Jaša. "Pobeda Ibanjeza na Izborima u Cileu." Belgrade,
Trideset dana (X: 82), 1952, pp. 908-914.
("Ibañez's Victory in the Elections in Chile."

2777   "Čile i Kolumbija Ratifikovale, Gana Prihvatila Statut Medjunarodne
Agencije za Atomsku Energiju." Belgrade, Službni list FNRJ-
dodatak: Medjunarodni Ugovori i drugi sporazumi (IX: 4), 1961,
p. 90.
("Chile and Colombia Ratified, and Ghana Accepted the Statute
of the International Agency for Atomic Energy")

2778   "Čile Pristupio Konvenciji o Drumskom Saobraćaju." Belgrade,
Službeni list FNRJ-dodatak: Medjunarodni ugovori i drugi sporazumi
(IX: 3), 1961, p. 130.
("Chile Joined the Highway Traffic Convention")

2779   "Čile Paimenjuje Konvenciju o Privilegijama i Imunitetu Specijalizovanih
Ustanova na Organizaciju Ujedinjenih Nacija za Prosvrtu, Nauku
i Kulturu." Belgrade, Službeni list FNRJ-dodatak: Medjunarodni
ugovori i drugi sporazumi (X: 2), 1962, p. 79.
("Chile Adopts the Convention on Privileges and Immunity of Specialized
Institutions of UNESCO")

2780   "Inflatorne Tendencije u Čileu." Belgrade, Nedeljni komentari
Instituta za spoljnu trgovinu (IV: 164), 1959, p. 836.
("Inflationary Tendencies in Chile")

2781   "Izgledi na Smanjenje Čileanskog Izvoza Pasulja. " Belgrade,
Nedeljni komentari Instituta za spoljnu trgovinu (II: 52), 1957,
p. 491.
("Lowered Prospects for Chile's Bean Exports")

2782   "Jačanje Naše Spoljnotrgovinske Razmene sa Čileom. " Belgrade,
Nedeljni komentari Instituta za spoljnu trgovinu (III: 122), 1958,
pp. 988-989.
("Increase of our Foreign Trade with Chile")

2783   Južnič, Stane. "Čile Izmedju Dva Narodna Fronta. " Belgrade,
Medjunarodni problemi (X: 2), 1958, pp. 98-106.
("Chile Between two Popular Fronts")

2784   M. A. (pseud.) "Čile. Društveno-Politička Kretanja. " Belgrade,
Medunarodni radnički pokret. Godišnji pregled 1962. 1963, pp.
91-96.
("Chile: Socio-Political Activities")

2785   M. K. (pseud.) "Čile. " Belgrade, Medunarodni r adnički i
drugi progresivni p okreti. Godišnji pregled 1965. 1966, pp.
170-184.
("Chile")

2786   M. R. (pseud.) "Čile. " Belgrade, Medunarodni radnički pokret.
Godišnji pregled 1960. 1961, pp. 480-487.
("Chile")

2787   "Nepovoljan Ekonomski Razvoj Čilea. " Belgrade, Nedeljni komentari
Instituta za spoljnu trgovinu (IV: 141), 1959, pp. 304-305.
("Unfavorable Economic Development of Chile")

2788   "Operavljanje Spoljne Trgovine Čilea. " Belgrade, Nedeljni
        komentari Instituta za spoljnu trgovinu (IV: 173), 1959, pp. 1050-
        1051.
        ("Recovery of Chile's Foreign Trade")

2789   Paligorić, Ljubomir. "Čile. Društveno-Ekonomska Situacija u
        Zemlji. " Belgrade, Medunarodni radnički pokret. Godišnji
        pregled 1959 (II). 1960, pp. 287-308.
                            ("Chile: Socio-Economic Situation in
        the Country")

2790   Paligorić, Ljubomir. "Čile. " Belgrade, Medunarodni radnički
        pokret. Godišnji pregled 1961, 1962, pp. 86-96.
                            ("Chile")

2791   Paligorić, Ljubomir. "Čile Uoči Izbora. " Belgrade, Naša stvarnost
        (XII: 2), 1958, pp. 284-289.
                            ("Chile on the Eve of Elections")

2792   Paligorić, Ljubomir. "Dve Administracije Generala Ibanjeza. "
        i Parlamentarni Izbori u Čileu. " Sarajevo, Pregled (IV, I: 4),
        1957, pp. 271-279.
                            ("Two Administrations of General Ibañez")

2793   Paligorić, Ljubomir. "Jedan Pogled na Čile. " Sarajevo, Pregled
        (XI: 1, 6), 1959, pp. 514-516.
                            ("A Look at Chile")

2794   Paligorić, Ljubomir. "Neki Problemi Čileanskog Radničkog Pokreta.
        Sarajevo, Pregled (XI, II: 10), 1959, pp. 323-329.
                            ("Some Problems of the Chilean Working
        Class Movement")

2795   Paligoric, Ljubomir. "Socijalistička Partija Čilea. " Belgrade,
        Dokumentacioni bilten (IV: 3-4), 1960, pp. 28-30.
                        ("The Socialist Party of Chile")

2796   Paligorić, Ljubomir. "Ujedinjenje Socijalistickih Partija Čilea. "
        Belgrade, Naša stvarnost (XII: 6), 1958, pp. 720-724.
                        ("Fusion of the Socialist Parties of
        Chile")

2797   Papić, Stjepan. "Iz Života Jugoslavenskih Iseljenika u Republici
        Čileu. " Zagreb, Matica (IV: 7-8), 1954, pp. 156-167.
                        ("From the Lives of Yugoslav Immigrants in the
        Republic of Chile")

2798   Papić, Stjepan. "Naši Iseljenici u Chile. " Zagreb, Matičin
        iseljenički kalendar za, 1955, pp. 107-110.
                        ("Our Immigrants in Chile")

2799   Papić, Stjepan. "U Republici Chile. " Zagreb, Matica (IV: 4),
        1954, pp. 80-81; 6, 130-131.
                        ("In the Republic of Chile")

2800   "Politički i Privredni Život u Čileu. " Belgrade, Spoljnopolitička
        Dokumentacija (V: 5), 1953, pp. 168-174.
        ("The Political and Economic Life of Chile")

2801   "Pribicevic, Natalija. "Predsednički Izbori i Društveno-Politička
        Kretanja u Danšanjem Čileu. " Belgrade, Medjunarodni problemi
        (XVI: 4), 1964, pp. 85-97.
        ("Presidential Elections and Socio-Political Movements in Modern
        Chile")

2802   "Promene Deviznog Sistema u Čileu." Belgrade, Nedeljni komentari
        Instituta za spoljnu trgovinu (I: 3), 1956, pp. 14-15.
        ("Modification of the Currency System in Chile")

COLOMBIA

2803   B. J. (pseud.) "Kolombija." Belgrade, Medunarodni radnički
        i drugi progresivni pokreti. Godišnji pregled 1965, 1966, pp.
        350-356.
                ("Colombia")

2804   Košta, Vjekoslav. "Kolumbija." Belgrade, Medunarodni radnički
        pokret. Godišnji pregled 1962. 1963, pp. 203-209.
                ("Colombia")

2805   "Postepena Stabilizacija Privrede u Kolumbiji." Belgrade,
        Nedeljni komentari Instituta za spoljnu trgovinu (V: 178),
        1960, pp. 51-52.
        ("Successive Stabilization of Colombia's Economy")

2806   Redžepagić, Sulejman. "Komunistička Partija Kolumbije." Belgrade,
        Dokumentacioni bilten (IV: 3-4), 1960, pp. 43-44.
                ("The Communist Party of Colombia")

2807   Redžepagić, Sulejman. "Osmi Kongres Komunistička Partije Kolumbij
        Belgrade, Dokumentacioni bilten (III: 3), 1959, pp. 66-67.
                ("The VIIIth Congress of the Communist Party
        of Colombia")

2808   Umljenović, Dejan. "Bolivar i Njegovog Djelo." Zagreb, Hrvatsko
        kolo (V: 9-10), 1952, pp. 584-591.
                ("Bolivar and his Program")

2809   Živančević, Miloš. "Privredna Situacija Kolumbije." Belgrade,
        Nedeljni komentari Instituta za spoljnu trgovinu (VII: 302),
        1962, pp. 920-922.
                ("Colombia's Economic Situation")

2810   Caratan, Branko. "Neke Osobitosti Društvenopolitičkog Razvoja
       Kube. " Zagreb, Naše teme (VIII: 10), 1964, pp. 1626- 1667.
                    ("Some Characteristics of Cuba's Socio-
       Political Development")

2811   Indjić, Trivo. "Kubanska Revolucija i Njeni Tumači. " Belgrade,
       Gledišta (II: 4), 1961, pp. 96-110.
                    ("The Cuban Revolution and its Interpretors")

2812   Južnič, Stane. "Kubanska Revolucija. " Ljubljana, Vprašanja
       naših dni (I: 10), 1960, pp. 300-304.
                    ("The Cuban Revolution")

2813   Košta, Vjekoslav. "Karakteristike drustveno-Ekonomskog
       Razvitka Kube. " Belgrade, Medunarodni problemi (XV: 3),
       1963, pp. 79-102.
                    ("Characteristics of the Socio-Economic
       Development of Cuba")

2814   Košta, Vjekoslav. "Kuba. " Belgrade, Medunarodni radnički pokret.
       Godišnji pregled 1962. 1963, pp. 210-220.
                    ("Cuba")

2815   Košta, Vjekoslav. "Kubanskaja Revoljucija i ee Posledstvija v
       Meždunarodnom Plane. " Belgrade, Meždunarodnaja politika
       (XIII: 301), 1962, pp. 8-10.
                    ("The Cuban Revolution and its International
       Repercussions")

2816 Krall, Jože. "Bila Sam na Kubi." Ljubljana, <u>Borec</u> (XV: 4), 1964, pp. 282-288.
("I Was in Cuba")

2817 M. S. (pseud.) "Grenki Sladkor s Kube." Ljubljana, <u>Naši</u> <u>razgledi</u> (IX: 21), 1960, pp. 483-484.
("Bitter Sugar from Cuba")

2818 Mičković, Radun. "Odnosi SAD - Kuba i Sadašnja Kriza u Karipskom Području." Sarajevo, <u>Pregled</u> (XIV, II: 10), 1962, pp. 330-335.
("Relations Between the United States and Cuba and the Present Crisis in the Caribbean Area."

2819 Mimica, Blaženka. "Kuba." Belgrade, <u>Medunarodni radnički</u> <u>pokret. Godišnji pregled 1961.</u> 1962, pp. 230-241.
("Cuba")

2820 Mitrović, Tomislav. "Intervencija SAD u Karibima i Povelja UN." Belgrade, <u>Medunarodna politika</u> (XVI: 365), 1965, pp. 19-21.
("Intervention of the United States in the Caribbean Area and the Charter of the United Nations")

2821 "Naša Razmena sa Kubom." Belgrade, <u>Nedeljni komentari</u> <u>Instituta za spoljnu trgovinu</u> (V: 183), 1960, pp. 171-172.
("Our Exchange with Cuba")

2822 Nikolić, Radivoj. "Kuba." Belgrade, <u>Medunarodni radnički</u> <u>pokret. Godišnji pregled 1959</u> (II), 1960, pp. 275-285.
("Cuba")

2823 "Odluka o Odobrenju Protokola o razmeni Robe Izmedju Jugoslavije i Kube za 1962 Godinu." Belgrade, <u>Službeni list FNRJ- dodatak:</u> <u>Medjunarodni ugovori i drugi sporazumi</u> (X: 9), 1962, pp. 70-72.
("Decree on the Approval of the Protocol Concluded Between Yugoslavia and Cuba on the Exchange of Commodities for 1962")

2824 Opačić, Nine. "Afirmacija Nove Kube." Belgrade, Medunarodna
politika (XI: 245), 1960, pp. 6-7.
("Affirmation of the New Cuba")

2825 Opačić, Nine. "Nova Kampanja SAD Protiv Kube." Belgrade,
Medjunarodna politika (XII: 265), 1961, pp. 11-12.
("The New U.S. Campaign vs. Cuba")

2826 Opačić, Nine. "Novoe Davlenie na Kubu." Belgrade, Meždunarodnaja
politika (XIV: 320), 1963, pp. 7-8.
("New Pressure on Cuba")

2827 Opačić, Nine. "Obostrenie Amerikano Kubanskih Otnošenii."
Belgrade, Meždunarodnaja politika (XII: 260), 1961, pp. 12-13.
("Sharpening of American-Cuban Relations")

2828 Paligorić, Ljubomir. "Kuba." Belgrade, Medunarodni radnički
i drugi progresivni pokreti. Godišnji pregled 1965. 1966, pp. 366-378.
("Cuba")

2829 "Planska Izgradnja Kube." Belgrade, Nedeljni komentari
Instituta za spoljnu trgovinu (V: 183), 1960, pp. 165-166.
("Planned Development of Cuba")

2830 R. N. (pseud.) "Dva Dokumenta o Ulozi Radničke Klase Kube."
Belgrade, Dokumentacioni bilten (IV: 3-4), 1960, pp. 51-52.
("Two Documents on the Role of the Working
Class in Cuba")

2831 R. S. (pseud.) "Kuba." Belgrade, Medunarodni radnički pokret.
Godišnji pregled 1963. 1964, pp. 415-423.
("Cuba")

2832   Radovanović, Ljubomir. "Sovjetska Podrška Kubi. " Belgrade,
Medunarodna politika (XV: 332), 1964, pp. 7-8.
("The Soviet Union in Support of Cuba")

2833   Redzepagić, Sulejman . "Kubanska Revolucija i Kriterijumi za
Odredjuvanje Karaktera Političkog Sistema. Društveno-političi
Sistemi Socijalistickih Zemalja. " (Materijali sa Savetovanja
Održanog 10. i 11. aprila 1964. u Beogradu). Belgrade, Institut za
Izučavanje radničkog pokreta, 1964, pp. 158-162.
("The Cuban Revolution and Criteria for
Defining the Character of Political Systems")

2834   Redžepagić, Sulejman . "Kubanski Zakon o Agrarnoj Reformi
Revolucionarna Mera. " Belgrade, Dokumentacioni bilten
(III: 4), 1959, pp. 56-57.
("Cuban Law on Agrarian Reform- A
Revolutionary Measure")

2835   Savnik, Dusan. "Kmecka Revolucija na Kubi. " Ljubljana,
Nasi razgledi (VI: 11), 1957, pp. 256-257.
("Peasant Rebellion in Cuba")

2836   "Uredba o Ratifikacji Trgovinskig Sporazuma sa Kubom. " Belgrade,
Službeni list SFRJ-dodatak: Medjunarodni ugovori i drugi
spotazumi (XII: 5), 1964, pp. 392-395.
("Ratification Act of the Commercial Agreement with Cuba")

2837   Vuković, Branislav. "Kuba. " Belgrade, Medunarodni radnički
i progresivni pokreti. Godišnji pregled 1964. 1965, pp. 505-520.
("Cuba")

DOMINICAN REPUBLIC

2838   Almuli, Jaša. "Intervencija u Dominikanskoj Republici." Belgrade,
Socijalizam (VIII: 5), 1965, pp. 656-666.
("Intervention in the Dominican Republic")

2839   Opačić, Nine. "Rasplet Dominikanske Krize?" Belgrade,
Medjunarodna politika (XVI: 371), 1965, pp. 7-8.
("Solution of the Dominican Crisis?")

ECUADOR

2840   "Ekvador Ratifikovao Svetsku Poštansku Konvenciju." Belgrade,
Službeni list FNRJ-dodatak: Medjunarodni ugovori i drugi
sporazumi (XI: 1), 1963, p. 130.
("Ecuador Ratified the World Postal Convention")

2841   Opačić, Nine. "Prevrat u Ekvadoru." Belgrade, Medunarodna
politika (XIV: 320-321), 1963, pp. 7-8.
("Coup d'Etat in Ecuador")

2842   "Razvoj Spoljne Trgovine Ekvadora." Belgrade, Nedeljni
komentari Instituta za spoljnu trgovinu (V: 178), 1960, pp. 52-54.
("Development of Ecuador's Foreign Trade")

2843   Zivančević, Miloš. "Razvoj Privrede Ekvadora u 1964." Belgrade,
Nedeljni komentari Instituta za spoljnu trgovinu (X:420), 1965,
pp. 157-159.
("Ecuador's Economy in 1964")

GUATEMALA

2844   Blum, Rudolf. "Kontrarevolucija u Gvatemali. " Belgrade,
Medunarodna politika (V: 103), 1954, pp. 22-23.
("Counter-Revolution in Guatemala")

2845   Dedijer, Vladimir. "Povelja OUN i Gvatemala. " Belgrade,
Medunarodna politika V: 104-105), 1954, pp. 7-8.
("The United Nations Charter and Guatemala")

2846   "Investicione Teškoće u Gvatemali. " Belgrade, Nedeljni komentari
Instituta za spoljnu trgovinu (IV: 169), 1959, pp. 956-957.
("Investment Difficulties in Guatemala")

2847   Mehinagić, Rizo. "SAD, Gvatemal i Latinska Amerika. " Sarajevo,
Pregled (VI: 1, 6), 1954, pp. 502-506.
("USA, Guatemala and Latin America")

2848   Opačić, Nine. "Prevrat u Gvatemali. " Belgrade, Medunarodna
politika (XIV: 313), 1963, pp. 8-9.
("Coup d'État in Guatemala")

GUYANA

2849   " Opacić, Nine. "Dogadjaji u Britanskoj Gijani. " Belgrade,
Medjunarodna politika (XIV: 316), 1963, pp. 7-8.
("Events in British Guiana")

HAITI

2850 "Haiti. Crnačka Republika u Kojoj su Skoro Svi Stanovnici Slikari
i Igrači. " Belgrade, Duga (XIV: 676), 1958, pp. 19-20.
("Haiti: Black Republic Where Almost all the Inhabitants are
Painters or Dancers")

2851 "Republika Haiti Pristupila Medjunarodnoj Konvenciji o Teretnim
Linijama. " Belgrade, Službeni list FNRJ-dodatak: Medjunarodni
ugovori i drugi sporazumi (IX: 10), 1961, p. 73.
("Republic of Haiti Joined the International Convention on Freight Lines")

MEXICO

2852   Andelković, Lj. "Sjedinjene Države Meksika." Belgrade,
Spoljnopolitička dokumentacija (XVI: 2), 1963, pp. 53-66.
("The United States of Mexico")

2853   Avramović, Miodrag. "Meksiko, Najvažnije Promene u Unutrašnjoj
i Spoljnoj Politici Meksika u Toku 1960, Godine. " Medjunarodni
radnički pokret. Godišnji pregled 1960, 1961. pp. 513-519.
("Mexico: The Most Important Changes in
Mexico's Internal and Foreign Policy During 1960")

2854   Butorac, Milan. "Novi Vulkan u Meksiku." Zagreb, Priroda
(XXXVIII: 2), 1951, pp. 65-67.
("The New Volcano in Mexico")

2855   Dragomanović, Vladimir. "Privreda Savremenog Meksika. "
Belgrade, Medjunarodni problemi (X: 3), 1958, pp. 162-166.
("Economy of Modern Mexico")

2856   "Ekonomska Situacija Meksika u 1959. " Belgrade, Nedeljni
Komentari Instituta za spoljnu trgovinu (V: 198), 1960, pp.
522-523.
("Economic Situation in Mexico in 1959")

2857   "Finansiranje Privrede u Meksiku. " Belgrade, Finansije (XVIII: 11-12),
1963, pp. 614-619.
("Financing the Economy in Mexico")

2858   J. K. (pseud.) "Meksiko." Belgrade, <u>Naša stvarnost</u> (IX: 10), 1955, pp. 484-494.
         ("Mexico")

2859   Janković, Vasilije. "Tržiste Vestačkih Dubriva u Meksiku." Belgrade, <u>Nedeljni komentari Instituta za spoljnu trgovinu</u> (IX: 379), 1964, pp. 357-358.
         ("Artificial Manure Market in Mexico")

2860   Južnić, Stane. "Specifičnosti Društvenoekonomskog Razvoja Meksika." Belgrade, <u>Medunarodni problemi</u> (XVI: 1), 1964, pp. 35-54.
         ("Summary: Specifics of Social and Economic Development of Mexico")

2861   Krunić, Luka. "Meksiko." Belgrade, <u>Medunarodni radnički pokret. Godišnji pregled 1961</u>, 1962, pp. 270-279.
         ("Mexico")

2862   M. M. (pseud.) "Meksiko." Belgrade, <u>Medunarodni radnički pokret. Godišnji pregled 1963</u>, 1964, pp. 424-433.
         ("Mexico")

2863   M. R. (pseud.) "Meksiko." Belgrade, <u>Medunarodni radnički i drugi progresivni pokreti. Godišnji pregled 1965</u>. 1966, pp. 423-433.
         ("Mexico")

2864   Maksimović, Borivoj. "U Području Maja Naroda." Belgrade, <u>Priroda</u> (XLI: 8), 1954, pp. 310-314.
         ("In the Region of Mayas")

2865   "Meksiko. " Belgrade, Zemlje i problemi (VI: 8), 1958, pp. 33-52.
        ("Mexico")

2866   Miles, Konstantin. "Kako je Propalo Carstvo Inka. " Zagreb,
        Otkrica (II: 8), 1955, pp. 580-583.
                        ("The Fall of the Inca Empire")

2867   Oven, Joško. "Slovenski Naseljenici v Mehiki. " Ljubljana
        Ameriški družinski kalendar (XXXI), 1945, pp. 65-70.
        ("Slovenian Immigrants in Mexico")

2868   "Poslednji Inke Još Žive. " Belgrade, Duga (XII: 561), 1956,
        pp. 14-15.
        ("The Last Incas are Still Alive")

2869   Rajh, Zdenko. "Agrarna Reforma u Meksiku. " Belgrade,
        Medunarodni problemi (V: 5-6), 1952, pp. 59-73.
                        ("The Agrarian Reform in Mexico")

2870   Vitez, Milan. "Tržište Mašina Alatljika u Meksiku. "
        Belgrade, Nedeljni komentari Instituta za spoljnu trgovinu
        (IX: 370), 1964, pp. 144-145.
                        ("Machine Tool Market in Mexico")

2871   Vukušić, Branko. "Meksikanska Revolucija iz Današnje
        Perspektive. " Sarajevo, Pregled (VII, II: 9), 1955, pp. 137-141.
                        ("The Mexican Revolution in the Light of
        Current Conditions")

2872   Zvekić, Miroslav. "Razvoj Elektroprivrede u Meksiku. " Belgrade,
        Nedeljni komentari Instituta za spoljnu trgovinu (IX: 402), 1964,
        pp. 933-934.
                        ("Development of Mexico's Electrical Industry")

2873   Živančević, Miloš. "Privredni Razvoj Meksika i Trgovinski
        Odnosi sa Jugoslavijo." Belgrade, Nedeljni komentari Instituta
        za spoljnu trgovinu (VIII: 358), 1963, pp. 1025-1029.
                        ("Economic Development of Mexico and Commercial
        Relations with Yugoslavia")

2874   Živančević, Miloš. "Razvoj Rudarstva i Industrije u Meksiku."
        Belgrade, Nedeljni komentari Instituta za spoljnu trgovinu (VII: 281),
        1962, pp. 308-309.
                        ("Development of Mining and Industry in Mexico")

PANAMA

2875   J. R. (pseud.) "Sueski i Panamski Kanal." Zagreb, Geografski
        glasnik (II: 12), 1949-1950, pp. 233-236.
                        ("The Suez and the Panama Canals")

2876   Krunić, Luka. "Panama." Belgrade, Medunarodni radnički pokret.
        Godišnji pregled 1961. 1962, pp. 302-306.
                        ("Panama")

2877   Mardešić, Petar. "Panamski Kanal." Rijeka, Pomorstvo (V: 10),
        1950, pp. 390-394.
                        ("The Panama Canal")

2878   Radinja, Darko. "Panamski Kanal u Godini 1956." Zagreb,
        Geografski horizont (IV: 3), 1958, pp. 20-22.
                        ("The Panama Canal in 1956")

PARAGUAY

2879 "Opadanje Spoljnotrgovinske Razmene Paragvaja. " Belgrade,
Nedeljni komentari Instituta za spoljnu trgovinu (III: 126),
1958, p. 1079.
("Decrease of Paraguay's Foreign Trade Exchange")

2880 "Spoljna Trgovina Paragvaja u 1959. " Belgrade, Nedeljni komentari
Instituta za spoljnu trgovinu (V: 194), 1960, pp. 419-420.
("Paraguay's Foreign Policy")

2881 "Ugovor o Ratifikaciji Trgovinskog i Platnog Sporazuma Izmedju
Jugoslavije i Paragvaja. " Belgrade, Medjunarodni ugovori
Federativne Narodne Republike Jugoslavije (1), 1959, pp. 57-60.
("Contract on Ratification of the Commercial and Payments
Agreement Between Yugoslavia and Paraguay")

2882 Živančević, Miloš. "Razvoj Privrede Paragvaja. " Belgrade,
Nedeljni komentari Instituta za spoljnu trgovinu (VIII: 320),
1963, pp. 69-71.
("Paraguay's Economic Development")

PERU

2883   Cvetković, Vladimir. "Dalje Povećanje Peruanskog Izvoza
        Ribljeg Brašna. " Belgrade, Nedeljni komentari Instituta
        za spoljnu trgovinu (VI: 252), 1961, pp. 685.
                    ("Peru's Increasing Export of Fish-Meal")

2884   Cvetković, Vladimir. "Ribarstvo u Peruu. " Belgrade, Nedeljni
        komentari Instituta za spoljnu trgovinu (VI: 228), 1961, pp. 131-133.
                    ("Fishing in Peru")

2885   Južnič, Stane. "Peru. " Belgrade, Medunarodni radnički i drugi
        progresivni pokreti. Godišnji pregled 1965. 1966, pp. 509-516.
                    ("Peru")

2886   Košta, Vjekoslav. "Peru. " Belgrade, Medunarodni radnički i
        progresivni pokreti. Godišnji pregled 1964. 1965, pp. 535-541.
                    ("Peru")

2887   "Maske i Nosnje Peruanaca. " Belgrade, Duga (XIII: 608), 1957, pp.
        11-12.
        ("Peruvian Masks and Costumes")

2888   "Narodnorevolucionarni Američki Savez Perua (APRA). " Belgrade,
        Dokumentacioni bilten (I: 1), 1957, pp. 72-73.
        ("The American People's Revolutionary Alliance (APRA) of Peru")

2889   Paligorić, Ljubomir. "Program Peruanske APRA. " Sarajevo,
        Pregled (IX, II: 10), 1957, pp. 251-254.
                    ("Programme of the Peruvian APRA")

URUGUAY

2890   Jakšić, Aleksandar. "Urugvaj." Belgrade, Medunarodni
       radnički pokret. Godišnji pregled 1959 (II). 1960, pp. 309- 322.
                ("Uruguay")

2891   "Programska Deklaracija i Statut Komunističke Partije Urugvaja."
       Belgrade, Dokumentacion bilten (I: 6), 1957, pp. 42-49.
       ("Program Statement and the Statute of the Communist Party of
       Uruguay")

2892   Raos, Jurica. "Urugvaj." Belgrade, Medunarodni radnički i
       drugi progresivni pokreti. Godišnji pregled 1965. 1966, pp. 629-635.
                ("Uruguay")

2893   Redžepagić, Sulejman. "Socijalistička Partija Urugvaja." Belgrade,
       Dokumentacioni bilten (II: 6), 1958, pp. 89-90.
                ("Socialist Party of Uruguay")

2894   "Spoljna Trgovina Urugvaja." Belgrade, Nedeljni komentari Instituta
       za spoljnu trgovinu (V: 205), 1960, pp. 692-694.
       ("Uruguay's Foreign Policy")

2895   Živančević, Miloš. "Mere za Poboljšanje Ekonomsko-Finansijske
       Situacije u Urugvaju." Belgrade, Nedeljni komentari Instituta
       za spoljnu trgovinu (VIII: 341), 1963, pp. 611-612.
                        ("Measures for Improving the Economic-
       Financial Situation in Uruguay")

2896   Živančevic, Miloš. "Privredni Razvoj Urugvaja." Belgrade,
       Nedeljni komentari Instituta za spoljnu trgovinu (VII: 277), 1962,
       pp. 204- 205.
                        ("Uruguay's Economic Progress")

2897   J. B. (pseud.) "Venecuela." Belgrade, Medunarodni radnički pokret. Godišnji pregled 1963, 1964, pp. 434-438.
("Venezuela")

2898   Južnič, Stane. "Venecuela." Belgrade, Medunarodni radnički pokret. Godišnji pregled 1961, 1962, pp. 414-418.
("Venezuela")

2899   Južnič, Stane. "Venecuela Nov Subjekt v Mednarodni Politik." Ljubljana, Vrpašnja naših dni (I: 4), 1960, pp. 119-122.
("Venezuela: a New Subject in International Politics")

2900   Kovačević, Stojan. "Karakas." Belgrade, Naša stvarnost (VIII: 4), 1954, pp. 94-99.
("Caracas")

2901   Redžepagić, Sulejman. "Demokratska Akcija Venecuele." Belgrade, Dokumentacioni bilten (IV: 3-4), 1960, pp. 70-71.
("The Democratic Action Party of Venezuela")

2902   Redžepagić, Sulejman. "Konfederacija Radnika Venecuele." Belgrade, Dokumentacioni bilten (IV: 3-4), 1960, pp. 74-75.
("Worker's Confederation of Venezuela")

2903   Redžepagić, Sulejman. "Venecuela." Belgrade, Medunarodni radnički pokret. Godišnji pregled 1960, 1961, pp. 488-496.
("Venezuela")

2904   Šerbela, Tone. "Nafta u Venecueli." Zagreb, <u>Nafta</u> (VI: 11), 1955, pp. 367—374.

                ("Naphtha in Venezuela")

WEST INDIES AND THE CARIBBEAN

2905   Opačić, Nine. "Intervencija u Karibina." Belgrade, <u>Medunarodna politika</u> (XVI: 363), 1965, pp. 6-7.

                ("Intervention in the Caribbean Area")

ICELAND

The English translation of the title of each bibliographic item is to be found directly under the title
in the original language, and immediately following
the entire bibliographic description.

(La traducción inglesa del título de cada asiento se
encuentra directamente bajo el título de la lengua
original, seguida de la ficha entera).

I. Books

LATIN AMERICA

2906   Árnason, Magnús, _Mexíkó,_ by Magnús Árnason,
Vífill Magnússon og Barbara Árnason. Reykjavík,
Vífill, 1966, 214p.
(Mexico)

2907   Benediktsson, Bjarni. _Rómanska Ameríka._ Samið Hefir
Bjarni Benediktsson. Reykjavík, Menningarsjóður, 1966,
287p.
(Latin America)

2908   Brunborg, Erling. _Um Ísland Til Andesþjóða._ Hersteinn
Pálsson Bjó Til Prentunar. Reykjavík, Guðrún Brunborg,
1957, 334p.
(Via Iceland to the Peoples of the Andes)

2909   _Eldórado. Ferðasaga._ Reykjavík, Setberg, 1958, 202p.
(Eldorado. A Travelogue)

2910   Falk Rønne, Arne. _Frumskógar Ogdemantar._ Þyðandi:
Ólafur þ. Kristjánsson. Hafnarfirði, Snæfell, 1963, 172p.
(The Devil's Diamonds)

2911   Falk Rønne, Arne. _Heljarfljót,_ Þýðendur: Kristján Bersi
Ólafsson, Ólafur þ. Kristjánsson. Myndir, Jørgen Bitsch,
Hafnarfirði, Snæfell, 1960, 188p.
(The River of Fate)

2912   Ólafsson, Kjartan. _Sól í Fullu Suðri._ Ferðasaga Frá
Suður-Ameríku. [Vestmannaeyjum], Hrímfell, 1954,
269p.
(Sun in Due South]

2913   Tómasdóttir, Rannveig. Fjarlæg Lönd og Framandi Þjóðir.
        Bahamaeyjar, Bermudaeyjar, Mexíkó. Reykjavík, Ísafoldarprent-
        smiðja, 1954, 122p.
                                (Faraway Countries and Foreign Nations:
        The Bahamas, The Bermudas, Mexico)

                            ARGENTINA

2914   Laxness, Halldór Kiljan. Rithöfundaþing í Buenos Aires.
        Dagleið á Fjöllum, Greinar. Reykjavík, Heimskringla,
        1937, pp. 279-296.
                                (Writers' Congress in Buenos
        Aires)

BRAZIL

2915   Bjarnason, Jóhann Magnús. <u>Brazilíufararnir.</u> Skáldsaga Eftir
        J. Magnús Bjarnason. 2v. Reykjavík, 1905-1908, 240p.

                    (The Emigrants to Brazil)

2916   <u>Brasilíu-Farar. Saga Íslendinga í Vesturheimi.</u> v. 2.
        Winnipeg, Þjóðræknisfélag Íslendinga í Vesturheimi,
        1943, pp. 67-107.
        (The Emigrants to Brazil. The Story of Icelanders in the
        Western World)

2917   Freuchen, Peter. <u>Frá Thule Til Ríó.</u> Jon Helgason Íslenzkaði.
        Hafnarfirði, Skuggsjá, 1960, 256p.
                    (From Thule to Rio)

2918   Kolbeinsson, Gísli. <u>Rauði Kötturinn.</u> Skáldsaga. Reykjavík,
        Ísafoldarprentsmiðja, 1961, 179p.
                    (The Red Cat)

2919   Þorsteinsson, Þorsteinn þ. <u>Æfintýrið Frá Íslandi Til</u>
        <u>Brasilíu. Fyrstu Fólksflutningarnir Frá Norðurlandi.</u>
        Reykjavík, Sigurgeir Friðriksson, 1937-1938, 399p.
        (The Adventure from Iceland to Brazil. The First Emigration
        from the North of Iceland)

2920   Porsteinson, Porsteinn P. <u>Saga Islendinga i Vesturheimi.</u>
        5v. Reykjavík, Pjódræknisfélag Islendinga i Vesturheimi,
        1940-1953.
                    (The Story of Icelanders in the
        Western World)

CUBA

2921   Kjartansson, Magnús. Byltingin á Kúbu. Reykjavík, Heimskringla,
       1962, 189p.
                    (The Cuban Revolution)

MEXICO

2922   Það Glóir a Gimsteina. Reykjavík, Hjartaásútgáfan, 1951,
       318p.
       (The Diamond's Glimmer)

2923   Traven, B. Flökkulíf. Saga frá Mexíkó. Asgrímur Albertsson
       Pýddi. Siglufirði, Rún, 1942, 163p.
                    (A Tramp's Life: A Tale from Mexico)

PERU

2924   Einarsson, Sigurgeir. Inkarnir í Perú og Hernám Spánverja
       Par. Reykjavík, Guðjón O. Guðjónsson, 1945, 366p.
                            (The Inca of Peru and the Conquest of
       Spaniards)

II. Periodical Articles

CHILE

2925   Vilhjálmsson, Thor. "Skáld Frá Chile." Reykjavik, <u>Nicanor Parra, Birtingur</u> (1, 2), 1961, pp. 71-72.
("A Poet from Chile")

GUATEMALA

2926   Vilhjálmsson, Thor. "Mikjáll Engill Asturias, Nóbelsverðlaunahafi í Bókmenntum 1967." <u>Lesbók Morgunblaðsins</u> (43), pp. 36-37.
("Miguel Angel Asturias, Prize Winner of Literature 1967").

AUTHOR INDEX

Note: Numbers immediately following names of personal and corporate
authors, as well as titles entered as authors, refer to individual,
numbered bibliographic items, and not to pages. In cases where a
given author has also been editor (or compiler, translator, etc.)
of additional works, his name is re-entered in the index, followed
by the appropriate designation. The names of joint authors (not
exceeding a total of two individuals) have also been included. It
should be noted that periodicals have been identified as such.
Each nation has its own author index, with the exception that
Arab nations are grouped under The Arab World.

AFRICA (general)

Rayner, P. R., 1

Algeria

Bassières, L., 2

Nigeria

Verger, P., 3, 23

Angola

Cascudo, L. da C., 4
Elia, A. d', 5
Fernandes, L., 6

Mesquitela, L., 7
Nogueira, H., 8
Panorama das Literaturas das Américas,
de 1900 á Actualidade, 9

Senegal

Arboleda, J. R., 10
Auteurs Africains, Antilles et Malgaches,
11
Chrysostome, P., 12
Debien, I., 13
Debien, G., 20
Debien, G., & J. Houdaille, 21
Franco, J. L., 14
Garavito, J., 15
Lapointe, J., 16
"Les Afro-Américains", 19
Richard, R., & G. Debien, 22
Senghor, L. S., 17, 18
Verger, P., 23

ASIA

659

EASTERN EUROPE

"Zemlje Južne Amerike", 2632
Živančević, Miloš, 2633-2644,
    2693-2697, 2715-2717, 2763-2767,
    2774, 2809, 2843, 2873-2874,
    2882, 2895, 2896
Živanović, Mihailo, 2645
Zvekić, Miroslav, 2872

ICELAND

Árnason, Magnús, 2906
Benediktsson, Bjarni, 2907
Bjarnason, Jóhann Magnús, 2915
Brasiliú-Farar. Saga Íslendinga
    í Vesturheimi, 2916
Brunborg, Erling, 2908
Einarsson, Sigurgeir, 2924
Eldórado. Ferðasaga, 2909
Falk Rønne, Arne, 2910, 2911
Freuchen, Peter, 2917
Kjartansson, Magnús, 2921
Kolbeinsson, Gísli, 2918
Laxness, Halldór Kiljan, 2914
Ólafsson, Kjartan, 2912
Pað Glóir a Gimsteina, 2922
Porsteinson, Porsteinn P., 2919,
    2920
Tómasdóttir, Rannveig, 2913
Traven, B., 2923
Vilhjálmsson, Thor, 2925, 2926

SUBJECT INDEX

Note: Numbers immediately following topics, sub-topics, places and individuals treated as subjects refer not to pages, but rather to individual, numbered bibliographic items. It should be noted that geographic designations follow topics so as to render the index as nearly geographic in character as is possible, thereby leading the user speedily to his field (and geographic area) of interest. In instances where geographic descriptions do not antecede given topics, it should be assumed that the item pertains to more than two nations and/or all of Latin America in general.

The subject index has been arranged geographically by nation, as has the author index, and covers topics of interest in the nation and language in which the books concerning those topics were published. It is thus a general geographic-language-subject index and is comprised of many small nation-indexes (regional or continent-wide, in the instances of The Arab World and Africa), as per the format of the author indexes.

AFRICA

ASIA

China

Korea

MIDDLE EAST

The Arab World

Persia (Iran)

Israel

EASTERN EUROPE

Bulgaria

Czechoslovakia

Finland

Investment: Latin America, 1366;
  Brazil, 1417
Law: Latin America, 1282
Library collections, Finnish: 1369
Literature: Brazil, 1429
Maya Indians: 1437
Monroe Doctrine: 1377
Music: Mexico, 1453
National characteristics: Colombia,
  1441
Paper: Latin America, 1372, 1373,
  1376; Argentina, 1413
Poetry: Mexico, 1454
Religions, Indian: Latin America,
  1286; Peru, 1353
Revolutions: Latin America, 1385;
  Cuba, 1326
Socio-political-economic conditions:
  Latin America, 1382, 1383, 1384;
  Central America, 1434; Guatemala,
  1451
U.S. foreign policy: Latin America,
  1377
Zoology: Latin America, 1297;
  El Salvador, 1333, 1334, 1335,
  1336

Greece

Anthropology: Mexico, 1488, 1490
Description and travel: Latin
  America, 1477, 1484; Dominican
  Republic, 1482; Mexico, 1489
Economic conditions: Argentina,
  1472; Bolivia, 1475; Brazil, 1479;
  Central America, 1481; Chile,
  1472; Colombia, 1475; Cuba,
  1474; Dominican Republic, 1474;
  Ecuador, 1475; Haiti, 1474;
  Mexico, 1474; Panama, 1481;

  Paraguay, 1473; Peru, 1473;
  Uruguay, 1473; Venezuela, 1475
Economic relations, international:
  U.S.S.R.-Latin America, 1485
Geography: Latin America, 1476,
  1478
Geography, physical: Brazil, 1480
Government structure: Guatemala,
  1487
History: Latin America, 1471
History, pre-Conquest: Latin America
  1486
Indians: Mexico, 1491
Labor and laboring classes: Latin
  America, 1470
Market surveys: Latin America,
  1469
Poetry: Mexico, 1483
Population: Latin America, 1477

Hungary

Agriculture: Argentina, 1604; Cuba,
  1668
Alexis, Jacques Stephan, 1679
Anthropogeography: Brazil, 1613
Archaeology: Chile, 1632
Architecture: Brazil, 1615, 1619;
  Cuba, 1642
Art: Peru, 1716
Astronomy: Peru, 1715
Asturias, Miguel Angel: 1675
Botany: Cuba, 1646, 1647
Boundaries: British Guyana-Venezuela,
  1677
Brewing industry: Cuba, 1648
Castroism: 1513
Catholicism: Latin America, 1505,
  1571, 1601; Paraguay, 1564, 1710
Communism: Guyana, 1678; Uruguay,
  1721

1596; Brazil, 1624, 1627; Cuba,
  1651, 1656, 1657
Machinery: Cuba, 1645
Maps and atlases: Latin America,
  1515, 1592
Maximilian I, Emperor of Mexico:
  1562, 1689
Metereology: Latin America, 1573;
  Brazil, 1537, 1613, 1622
Minerals: Peru, 1566
Mining: Mexico, 1694, 1695
Monroe Doctrine: 1659
Neruda, Pablo: 1550
Novels: 1493, 1541, 1548, 1563
Orozco, José Clemente: 1691
Painting: Latin America, 1595
Panama Canal: 1696-1701, 1703
Paper: Cuba, 1652
Poetry: Latin America, 1494;
  Colombia, 1638; Haiti, 1681
Population, rural: Venezuela,
  1724
Press: see Journalism
Railroads: Argentina, 1605
Revolutions: Latin America, 1506,
  1593, 1597; Chile, 1637; Cuba,
  1644, 1650, 1654, 1655, 1659;
  Mexico, 1684; Peru, 1714, 1718
Rivera, Diego: 1682
Science: Latin America, 1511
Scientists, Hungarian: 1636
Siqueiros, David Alfaro: 1690
Slavery: Argentina, 1608
Social classes: Latin America,
  1574; Argentina, 1607
Socio-political-economic conditions:
  Latin America, 1500, 1512, 1581,
  1582, 1586, 1598; Argentina,
  1532; Bolivia, 1610, 1612; Cuba,
  1653; Guatemala, 1674; Panama,
  1702; Puerto Rico, 1720; Vene-
  zuela, 1725
Sociology: Cuba, 1643, 1666;

Guyana, 1676
Swiss in Brazil: 1626
Tobacco: see Agriculture
Transportation: Latin America, 1577
Tri-Continental Conference, Havana,
  Cuba: 1660
Truman Doctrine: 1570
U.S. foreign policy: Latin America,
  1570, 1598
Wars: Latin America, 1512
Zoology: Latin America, 1578, 1579,
  1583; Argentina, 1609; Chile, 1634;
  Paraguay, 1708, 1709; Peru, 1711, 1712,
  1713

Poland

Agriculture: Latin America, 1986, 1991;
  Argentina, 1791, 1996, 2016; Brazil,
  1799, 1867, 1868, 1870, 1887, 2061;
  Colombia, 2091; Cuba, 1915, 2109;
  Guatemala, 2183; Mexico, 2231
Alliance for Progress: Latin America,
  1767
Amado, Jorge: 1852
Animals: see Zoology
Anthropology: Cuba, 2133
Archaeology: Peru, 2245, 2248
Architecture: Brazil, 1879, 2030, 2035
Armed forces: Cuba, 2117, 2123
Art: Cuba, 2112, 2140; Mexico, 2208,
  2214, 2225
Arciszewski, Christopher: 1772, 1773
Area studies: Mexico, 1928
Art, pre-Columbian: 2066
Bananas: see Agriculture
Borman, Martin: 2001
Carnival: in Mato Grosso, Brazil, 2073;
  in Rio de Janeiro, Brazil, 2068; in
  Mexico, 2204
Casa de las Americas, Havana, Cuba,

Panama Canal: 1952, 1953, 1954, 2234, 2239
Peronism: 2008
Poetry: Latin America, 1757; Brazil, 1801, 1871; Mexico, 1944
Political situation: Venezuela, 2269
Poultry: see Agriculture
Public administration and political regimes: Brazil, 2037, 2071, 2075; Ecuador, 2171, 2172; Guyana, 2186-2188, 2190, 2191, 2193, 2194; Haiti, 2195, 2196
Population: Argentina, 2013; Brazil, 1835, 1846, 1849, 1874; Venezuela, 2266
Quadros, Jânio: 2024, 2033
Religion: Latin America, 1740; Mexico, 1927, 1948
Revolutions: Dominican Republic, 2165; Ecuador, 2166-2168; Paraguay, 2243
St. Bartholomew (Island): 2273
Short stories: Latin America, 1743; Brazil, 1828, 1854, 1855, 1862; French Guiana, 1921
Slums: Brazil, 2025
Social change: Latin America, 1983, 1985
Social conditions: Peru, 1967
Socio-political-economic conditions: Latin America, 1728, 1754, 1770, 1978, 1980, 1992, 1993; Argentina, 1998; Brazil, 1824, 1845, 1848, 2036, 2045, 2049, 2051, 2053, 2062, 2065; Chile, 2078; Colombia, 2089; Cuba, 2135, 2143; Dominican Republic: 2147, 2153, 2155, 2162; Ecuador, 2169, 2170; Haiti, 2195-2197; Mexico, 1935; Uruguay, 2256, 2258, 2261; Venezuela, 2263, 2267; West Indies and the Caribbean, 2274
Sociology: Mexico, 2216

Sugar: Brazil, 2039
Taquara Movement in Argentina: 2002
Taxco, Mexico: 2230
Theatre: Argentina, 1999; Cuba, 2107; Mexico, 2232; Peru, 2251
Tiahuanacu, Bolivia: 2018
Trees: see Agriculture
U.S. foreign policy: Latin America, 1754 1783
U.S.-Guatemalan relations: 2179, 2181
U.S.S.R.-Cuban relations: 2117, 2118
Vargas, Getulio: 2054
"Violencia", Colombia: 2094, 2095
Wars: Dominican Republic, 2159
Women, status of: Latin America, 1755
Youth: Cuba, 2134
Zoology: Latin America, 1774; Argentina 1997

Rumania

Agriculture: Latin America, 2325; Brazil, 2369, 2373; Costa Rica, 2414; Mexico, 2455
Anthropology: Latin America, 2276
Archaeology: Mexico, 2447, 2450
Armed forces: Latin America, 2320, 2355; Argentina, 2341; Bolivia, 2361; Brazil, 2387
Arts and crafts (movement): Argentina, 2346; Cuba, 2415; Uruguay, 2474
Asturias, Miguel Angel: 2437, 2438, 2439
Bolivar, Simón: 2478
Brasilia, Brazil: 2380
Castroism: 2417, 2418, 2424
City planning: Brazil, 2365
Communications: Latin America, 2336
Communism: Latin America, 2332
Conferences and congresses: Latin America, 2313, 2355